MASTER THE
CATHOLIC HIGH
SCHOOL ENTRANCE
EXAMS
2013

PETERSON'S
Publishing

About Peterson's Publishing

To succeed on your lifelong educational journey, you will need accurate, dependable, and practical tools and resources. That is why Peterson's is everywhere education happens. Because whenever and however you need education content delivered, you can rely on Peterson's to provide the information, know-how, and guidance to help you reach your goals. Tools to match the right students with the right school. It's here. Personalized resources and expert guidance. It's here. Comprehensive and dependable education content— delivered whenever and however you need it. It's all here.

For more information, contact Peterson's, 2000 Lenox Drive, Lawrenceville, NJ 08648; 800-338-3282 Ext. 54229; or find us online at www.petersonspublishing.com.

Peterson's makes every reasonable effort to obtain from reliable sources accurate, complete, and timely information about the tests covered in this book. Nevertheless, changes can be made in the tests or the administration of the tests at any time and Peterson's makes no representation or warranty, either expressed or implied as to the accuracy, timeliness, or completeness of the information contained in this book.

Bernadette Webster, Director of Publishing; Mark D. Snider, Editor; Ray Golaszewski, Publishing Operations Manager; Linda M. Williams, Composition Manager

ISBN-13: 978-0-7689-3476-2
ISBN-10: 0-7689-3476-1

Printed in the United States of America

10 9 8 7 6 5 4 3 2 1   14 13 12

Eighteenth Edition

Petersonspublishing.com/publishingupdates

Check out our Web site at www.petersonspublishing.com/publishingupdates to see if there is any new information regarding the tests and any revisions or corrections to the content of this book. You should also carefully read the material you receive from the Archdiocese when you register for the test. We've made sure the information in this book is accurate and up-to-date; however, the test format or content may have changed since the time of publication.

Certified Chain of Custody

60% Certified Fiber Sourcing and
40% Post-Consumer Recycled

www.sfiprogram.org

*This label applies to the text stock.

Sustainability—Its Importance to Peterson's, a Nelnet company

What does sustainability mean to Peterson's? As a leading publisher, we are aware that our business has a direct impact on vital resources—most especially the trees that are used to make our books. Peterson's Publishing is proud that its products are certified by the Sustainable Forestry Initiative (SFI) and that all of its books are printed on paper that is 40% post-consumer waste.

Being a part of the Sustainable Forestry Initiative (SFI) means that all of our vendors—from paper suppliers to printers—have undergone rigorous audits to demonstrate that they are maintaining a sustainable environment.

Peterson's Publishing continuously strives to find new ways to incorporate sustainability throughout all aspects of its business.

Contents

Before You Begin xi
Why You Should Use This Book xi
How This Book is Organized xi
How To Use This Book xii
What to Study: TACHS, COOP, and HSPT xiii
What to Study: SSAT and ISEE xiii
Special Study Features xiii
You're Well on Your Way to Success xiv
Find Us On Facebook® xiv
Give Us Your Feedback xv
Top 10 Ways to Raise Your Score xvi

PART I: TACKLING THE EXAMS

**1   All About the New York City Test for Admission into
     Catholic High Schools (TACHS)** 3
The TACHS Exam Format 4
About the TACHS Questions 4
Summing It Up 9

2   All About the Cooperative Entrance Exam (COOP) 11
The COOP Exam Format 11
How the COOP is Scored 12
About the COOP Questions 13
Summing It Up 22

3   All About the High School Placement Test (HSPT) 23
The HSPT Exam Format 23
How the HSPT is Scored 24
About the HSPT Questions 25
The HSPT Optional Tests 29
Summing It Up 30

**4   All About the Secondary School Admission
     Test (SSAT)** 31
The SSAT Exam Format 31
How the SSAT is Scored 32
What is the Writing Sample? 32
About the SSAT Questions 34
Summing It Up 37

**5   All About the Independent School Entrance
     Examination (ISEE)** 39
The ISEE Exam Format 40
How the ISEE is Scored 41

About the ISEE Questions...42

Summing It Up..49

6 Test-Taking Techniques 51

What to Expect When You Take the Exam 51

Tips for Answering Questions 52

Summing It Up..54

PART II: VERBAL SKILLS

7 Synonyms 57

Tips for Answering Synonym Questions.............................57

Exercises: Synonyms 60

Answer Keys and Explanations..64

Summing It Up..66

8 Antonyms 67

Tips for Answering Antonym Questions 68

Exercises: Antonyms 69

Answer Keys and Explanations..72

Summing It Up..74

9 Analogies 75

Tips for Answering Analogy Questions 76

Exercises: Analogies..79

Answer Keys and Explanations..82

Summing It Up..84

10 Verbal Logic 85

HSPT Logic..85

HSPT Verbal Classification...86

COOP Extraction of Information 86

COOP Logic 87

COOP Artificial Language 88

Exercises: Verbal Logic 89

Answer Keys and Explanations..93

Summing It Up..97

11 Reading 99

How to Improve Your Reading Skills 99

Tips for Answering Reading Comprehension Questions 100

Exercises: Reading 101

Answer Keys and Explanations..118

Summing It Up..123

12 Spelling 125

Tips for Improving Your Spelling Skills 125

Twenty-Four Spelling Rules..126

Exercises: Spelling 128

Answer Key and Explanations 129

Summing It Up..130

Contents

13 Punctuation and Capitalization 131

Punctuation Rules..131

Capitalization Rules 137

Exercises: Punctuation and Capitalization 138

Answer Key and Explanations 140

Summing It Up 141

14 English Usage 143

Principles of Grammar 143

Troublesome Words 146

Exercises: English Usage 149

Answer Keys and Explanations 156

Summing It Up 160

15 Language Composition and Expression 161

Tips for Answering Language Composition and Expression Questions.................161

Exercises: Language Composition and Expression.........163

Answer Key and Explanations 166

Summing It Up 167

PART III: QUANTITATIVE AND NONVERBAL SKILLS

16 Quantitative Reasoning 171

The Best Approach 171

Exercises: Quantitative Reasoning....................................175

Answer Key and Explanations 179

Summing It Up 181

17 Mathematics 183

The Number Line 184

Decimals...186

Fractions...188

Percentages..194

Algebra..197

Equations 201

Geometry...202

Coordinate Geometry 207

Word Problems 211

Test Yourself Answers and Explanations 218

Exercises: Mathematics 228

Answer Keys and Explanations 242

Summing It Up 253

18 Series Reasoning 255

Number Series 256

Letter Series...259

Mixed Series...261

Symbol Series..261

Tips for Answering Series Questions 262

Test Yourself Answer Keys and Explanations.................263

Exercises: Series Reasoning...266
Answer Keys and Explanations..270
Summing It Up...273

19 Comparisons...275
Geometric Comparisons...275
Nongeometric Comparisons...276
Exercises: Comparisons..278
Answer Key and Explanations...282
Summing It Up...283

PART IV: EIGHT PRACTICE TESTS

Practice Test 1: TACHS...289
Reading..289
Language...295
Math...300
Ability..306
Answer Keys and Explanations...309

Practice Test 2: TACHS...317
Reading..317
Language...324
Math...328
Ability..335
Answer Keys and Explanations...338

Practice Test 3: COOP...347
Section 1. Sequences...347
Section 2. Analogies...350
Section 3. Quantitative Reasoning..354
Section 4. Verbal Reasoning—Words..359
Section 5. Verbal Reasoning—Context......................................361
Section 6. Reading and Language Arts.....................................364
Section 7. Mathematics...375
Answer Keys and Explanations...380
Score Sheet..393

Practice Test 4: COOP...397
Section 1. Sequences...397
Section 2. Analogies...400
Section 3. Quantitative Reasoning..403
Section 4. Verbal Reasoning—Words..408
Section 5. Verbal Reasoning—Context......................................410
Section 6. Reading and Language Arts.....................................414
Section 7. Mathematics...424
Answer Keys and Explanations...429
Score Sheet..445

Practice Test 5: HSPT **451**
Verbal Skills 451
Quantitative Skills 456
Reading..462
Mathematics 469
Language 476
Answer Keys and Explanations...482
Score Sheet 501

Practice Test 6: HSPT **505**
Verbal Skills 505
Quantitative Skills 510
Reading..516
Mathematics 523
Language 530
Answer Keys and Explanations...538
Score Sheet 556

Practice Test 7: SSAT (Upper Level) **561**
Part I: Writing Sample...561
Part II: Multiple Choice...562
Answer Keys and Explanations...582
Score Yourself 594

Practice Test 8: ISEE (Upper Level) **597**
Section 1: Verbal Reasoning..597
Section 2: Quantitative Reasoning 601
Section 3: Reading Comprehension 607
Section 4: Mathematics Achievement 614
Section 5: Essay 619
Answer Keys and Explanations...620
Score Yourself 634

Before You Begin

WHY YOU SHOULD USE THIS BOOK

If you're in the eighth grade and are preparing to continue your education at a Catholic high school, then this book is just what you need. An essential part of getting into the school of your choice is taking and passing an entrance exam. This book has been specially designed to assist you with preparing for and taking the two most commonly used Catholic high school entrance exams, the COOP and the HSPT. It will also introduce you to the SSAT and the ISEE, two other widely used tests. If you live within the Archdiocese of New York, or the Diocese of Brooklyn and Rockland County, you probably will have to take the Test for Admissions into Catholic High Schools, commonly known as the TACHS. Exercises are included here to prepare you for that test also. You'll find help with answering questions in every test subject and plenty of practice to get you ready for your exam.

Master the Catholic High School Entrance Exams will not only help you develop your test-taking skills, it also includes descriptions and examples of each type of entrance exam and eight full-length practice exams—two TACHS, two COOPs, two HSPTs, one SSAT, and one ISEE. The TACHS, COOP, HSPT, SSAT, and ISEE practice exams simulate the type of questions you can expect to find on the actual exams. However, the test-makers may have instituted changes after this book was published. To see if new information regarding the tests is available, check Peterson's Web site (www.petersonspublishing.com/publishingupdates). In addition, this book provides skills review and practice questions in each of the subject areas covered by typical entrance exams. Use these sections to help you strengthen your weak areas.

HOW THIS BOOK IS ORGANIZED

Divided into sections, this book provides four main parts that can help you with your preparation. Use Part I to learn more about each exam type and how it's scored. You'll find examples of typical questions from each exam. Use Part II to review the verbal skill sections of the TACHS, COOP, and HSPT exams, such as analogies, verbal logic, reading, and composition. Use Part III to review quantitative and nonverbal skills, such as mathematics. Part IV includes practice exams for the TACHS, the COOP, the HSPT, the SSAT, and the ISEE.

HOW TO USE THIS BOOK

Diagnostic Test Method

One way to use this book is to start with a diagnostic test. A diagnostic test is a test that helps you understand your strengths and weaknesses on the exam. It "diagnoses" the skills that need the most improvement.

In this method, you take a diagnostic test first. Then you use the results of your diagnostic to develop a study plan. Use one of the practice tests in Part IV as your diagnostic test. Take this test under "realistic" testing conditions. Go to a quiet setting, away from distractions. Time yourself as you would be timed on the real test, making sure to complete all test sections at once.

Once you've taken your diagnostic test, score yourself to see your strengths and weaknesses. How did you do? Make a list of your strong and weak areas. If you scored well on Math but poorly on Verbal Skills, then you can count Math as a strength. Your Verbal Skills, on the other hand, will need some work. Rank the different sections in terms of your strongest and weakest skills.

Use your ranking list to develop your study plan. Your plan should prioritize boosting your weaker skills. You don't need to spend as much time brushing up on your strengths. However, you should plan to spend *some* time on "strong skills" exercises—just to stay in shape!

Once you've got a study plan, put it to work. Read the introduction to your test in Part I. Then, focus on improving your weak skills by studying the sections in Parts II and III. After you've reviewed the content sections, take your second practice test. This test should show an improvement in your score!

Front-to-Back Method

Another way to use this book is the front-to-back method. In this method, you work through the book the way it is organized. This method might be quickest if you don't have the time to take two practice tests.

Start at Part I of the book and carefully read through the introductory section on your exam. This will help you understand the exam and how it's scored. Next, study the content sections in Parts II and III. Focus on the sections that relate to your exam. If you know your strong and weak skills, you might devote extra time to sections where you need the most improvement.

After you've reviewed the content, take a practice test or two in Part IV. Even taking one test will help you be more prepared for exam day. Sometimes, the process of taking the test itself can actually help increase your score. This is because you become more familiar with the test, which increases your confidence.

After you complete each test, review your answers with the explanations provided. If you still don't understand how to answer a certain question, you might ask a teacher for help. A review session with a friend might prove helpful, too.

WHAT TO STUDY: TACHS, COOP, AND HSPT

Parts II and III of this book provide TACHS, COOP, and HSPT content for you to review. Use the table below to determine which chapters to study for your test.

No.	Chapter	TACHS	COOP	HSPT
	Part II: Verbal Skills			
7	Synonyms	X		X
8	Antonyms			X
9	Analogies		X	X
10	Verbal Logic		X	X
11	Reading	X	X	X
12	Spelling	X	X	X
13	Punctuation and Capitalization	X	X	X
14	English Usage	X	X	X
15	Language Composition and Expression	X	X	X
	Part III: Quantitative and Nonverbal Skills			
16	Quantitative Reasoning		X	
17	Mathematics	X	X	X
18	Series Reasoning	X	X	X
19	Comparisons			X

WHAT TO STUDY: SSAT AND ISEE

If you are thinking about taking the SSAT and the ISEE, you'll find an entire chapter and practice test for each in this book. Although most Catholic high schools prefer scores from the TACHS, COOP, and HSPT, there are some Catholic high schools that will accept SSAT and ISEE scores as well. While Parts I and III in this guide are not specifically dedicated to the SSAT and ISEE, note that the Synonyms, Analogies, Reading, Mathematics, and Quantitative Reasoning chapters do cover much of the same content that appears on these two exams (although the questions may appear in different formats). For more in-depth preparation for the SSAT and ISEE, check out *Peterson's Master the SSAT & ISEE*, available everywhere books are sold.

SPECIAL STUDY FEATURES

Master the Catholic High School Entrance Exams is designed to be as user-friendly as it is complete. To this end, it includes several features to make your preparation much more efficient.

Overview

Each chapter begins with a bulleted overview listing the topics to be covered in the chapter. This will allow you to quickly target the areas in which you are most interested.

Summing It Up

Each chapter ends with a point-by-point summary that captures the most important points contained in the chapter. They are a convenient way to review key points.

Bonus Information

As you work your way through the book, keep your eye on the margins to find bonus information and advice. Information can be found in the following forms:

NOTE

Notes highlight critical information about each test's format.

TIP

Tips draw your attention to valuable concepts, advice, and shortcuts. By reading the tips, you will learn how to approach different question types, pace yourself, and use process-of-elimination techniques.

ALERT!

Wherever you need to be careful of a common pitfall or test-taker trap, you'll find an *Alert!* This information reveals and eliminates the misperceptions and wrong turns so many students take on the exam.

By taking full advantage of all the features presented in *Master the Catholic High School Entrance Exams*, you will become much more comfortable with the test that you need to take and will be more confident about getting a good score.

YOU'RE WELL ON YOUR WAY TO SUCCESS

Remember that knowledge is power. By using this book you will be studying the most comprehensive guide available.

FIND US ON FACEBOOK®

Join the Catholic high school conversation by liking us on Facebook® at facebook.com/peterson-spublishing. Here you'll find additional test-prep tips and advice. Peterson's resources are available to help you do your best on these important exams—and others in your future.

GIVE US YOUR FEEDBACK

Peterson's publishes a full line of books—test prep, education exploration, financial aid, and career preparation. Peterson's publications can be found at high school guidance offices, college libraries and career centers, and your local bookstore and library. Peterson's books are now also available as eBooks.

We welcome any comments or suggestions you may have about this publication. Your feedback will help us make educational dreams possible for you—and others like you.

TOP 10 WAYS TO RAISE YOUR SCORE

When it comes to taking your entrance exam, some test-taking skills will do you more good than others. There are concepts you can learn, techniques you can follow, and tricks you can use that will help you to do your very best. Here are our picks for the top 10 ways to raise your score:

1. **Regardless of which plan you will follow, get started by reading Part I to familiarize yourself with the test formats.**

2. **Make sure to complete the exercises in each chapter you read.**

3. **When you are one third of the way through your preparation, take a practice test.** Make sure you are applying new test-taking strategies.

4. **It's a good idea to have a dictionary nearby while taking the practice test or studying the review sections of this book.** If you come across a word you don't know, circle it and look it up later.

5. **Revisit problematic chapters and chapter summaries.**

6. **After you have completed all of the study sections, take your second practice test.** You should find the second practice test much easier now, and, after your study and practice, you should be able to answer more questions than you could on the first practice test.

7. **If you have the time, you might find it instructive to take the practice tests for the other exams.** For example, if you're required to take the COOP exam, you might also test yourself with the HSPT exam.

8. **During the last phase of your study, review the practice tests.**

9. **Be sure to read the test-taking techniques in Chapter 6 for additional tips to help you on the day of the exam.**

10. **The night before your exam, RELAX.** You'll be prepared.

PART I
TACKLING THE EXAMS

CHAPTER 1   All About the New York City Test for Admission into Catholic High Schools (TACHS)

CHAPTER 2   All About the Cooperative Entrance Exam (COOP)

CHAPTER 3   All About the High School Placement Test (HSPT)

CHAPTER 4   All About the Secondary School Admission Test (SSAT)

CHAPTER 5   All About the Independent School Entrance Examination (ISEE)

CHAPTER 6   Test-Taking Techniques

All About the New York City Test for Admission into Catholic High Schools (TACHS)

OVERVIEW

- **The TACHS exam format**
- **About the TACHS questions**
- **Summing it up**

The Test for Admission into Catholic High Schools (TACHS) is the entrance examination for eighth-grade students wishing to attend a Catholic high school in New York City beginning in the ninth grade.

If you are currently in the eighth grade or will be in the eighth grade and are planning to attend a Catholic high school in the ninth grade, this is the exam you will take as part of your admissions process. You may take the exam only once. If you are planning to attend a New York City Catholic high school as a tenth-, eleventh- or twelfth-grader, you will not need to take the TACHS. Instead, you will need to apply directly to the high school you wish to attend.

The TACHS tests basic knowledge in the areas of reading, language arts, math, and general reasoning ability. The specific details of each of these sections will be discussed later. The TACHS is an instrument used to help high schools make decisions about admissions and placement of eighth-graders into the high school setting as ninth-graders. Therefore, the exam is not designed to trick applicants or present any extremely difficult challenges for applicants. Rather, the TACHS tests knowledge and skills that have been determined to be standard for eighth-grade students. Knowing this ahead of time should help you relax and do your best on the exam.

Results from the exam will be sent to up to three Catholic high schools of your choice. If you are currently enrolled in a Catholic elementary school, your school will also receive the results of your exam. If you are not currently enrolled in a Catholic school, results of the exam will be sent to your home.

You can register for the exam via the Internet or by phone or paper registration. Be sure to complete and submit the Eligibility Form for Students Needing Extended Testing Time, if applicable. Upon registration, you will receive an Admit Card that will confirm your test site. You must bring this Admit Card with you on the day of the test. Complete registration information, including important dates, registration procedures, registration fees, and testing locations can be found online at www.tachsinfo.com.

chapter 1

THE TACHS EXAM FORMAT

The multiple-choice answer format is used throughout the TACHS exam. Most answer choices are given in sets of four, and the sets are grouped as (A), (B), (C), (D) or as (J), (K), (L), (M). For example, the first question might use (A), (B), (C), (D) as the answer choices, and the next question might use (J), (K), (L), (M). Answer choices in the Spelling section are given in groups of five, and the sets are grouped as (A), (B), (C), (D), (E) or as (J), (K), (L), (M), (N). This design should help you keep your place as you flip back and forth between the test booklet and the answer sheet.

ABOUT THE TACHS QUESTIONS

Let's take a look at each one of the sections of the exam, so you have a good idea about what to expect when you take the exam.

Reading

The Reading section of the TACHS contains two parts. Part 1 of the Reading section deals with vocabulary. Here you will be presented with vocabulary words within the context of short phrases. You will be asked to select from a group of possible answers the word that means the same or nearly the same as the underlined vocabulary word in the short phrase. Vocabulary words that appear on the exam may be nouns, verbs, and modifiers. Approximately the same number of each will appear on the exam.

To roam the plains

(A) follow

(B) wander

(C) disguise

(D) destroy

The correct answer is (B), *wander.* Other synonyms include "stray," "ramble," and "rove."

Part 2 of the Reading section measures ability in reading comprehension, or how well you understand what you read. In Part 2, you will be presented with a number of reading passages of varying length. Some passages may be only a few lines while others may be up to a page in length. Reading passages will vary in content. Some passages may be fiction and may include fables, stories, and excerpts from previously published works. Other passages will be nonfiction and may include such topics as social studies and science. The exam will test your ability to comprehend what you read and will not test your understanding of science and social studies, for example. For the most part, you will be asked to make inferences or generalizations about what you read. You may be asked to identify the meaning of a word or phrase in context, to identify the main idea of the passage, and to determine what might come next in the story or to "read between the lines."

Paul Grisham, as a young boy, sold newspapers on the street corner to help his family. He went to work before sunrise, worked until it was time for school, and then returned home after school. Paul walked everywhere he went, regardless of the weather. The work ethic he developed as a youngster contributed to his eventual financial success as an adult.

Based on the information in the passage above, which of the following can be inferred about Paul's family when he was a child?

(A) Paul's family had very little money.

(B) Paul's family was very wealthy.

(C) Paul's family lived in the country.

(D) Paul's family was very large.

The correct answer is (A). Paul worked before school and "walked everywhere he went." It can be inferred from the passage that he worked, because he needed the money, and walked, because the family had no other means of transportation.

Language

The Language section of the TACHS tests different skills and abilities in the language arts. This section covers spelling, capitalization, punctuation, usage, and expression.

The first portion of the TACHS Language section tests your knowledge of spelling. You will be presented with four words, one of which may be spelled incorrectly. You will also be presented with a fifth choice, *(No mistakes)*, in case all four words are correct. This actually tests your knowledge of four words at a time. Spelling errors you may see on the test include common mistakes in adding unnecessary letters, omitting letters, or reversing letters.

(A) demolition

(B) cordial

(C) ocasional

(D) pleasant

(E) *(No mistakes)*

The correct answer is (C). The correct spelling is *occasional*.

The second portion of the Language section tests your skill and ability in capitalization. You will be given several lines including words that are capitalized and words that are not. You will be asked to find mistakes in capitalization. You will also be presented with a fourth choice, *(No mistakes)*, in the event that there are no capitalization errors. Capitalization errors include capitalizing when unnecessary and not capitalizing when necessary for such things as names, holidays, organizations, and titles.

(A) The services for easter

(B) will be held at St. John's

(C) located at 123 Main Street.

(D) *(No mistakes)*

The correct answer is (A). *Easter* should be capitalized.

The third portion of the Language section tests your skill and ability in punctuation. You will be given several lines of writing in which you are to identify punctuation errors. You will be given a fourth choice, *(No mistakes)*, in the event that there are no punctuation errors. You may find errors in punctuation dealing with commas, semicolons, periods, and apostrophes.

(A) The city council met last night

(B) and decided to lower taxes.

(C) in the Brooksmith neighborhood.

(D) *(No mistakes)*

The correct answer is (B). There should be no period at the end of choice (B).

The fourth portion of the Language section measures your ability in usage. You will be presented with several lines of text. You will need to find errors in the underlined parts of the text. These errors may include misuse of verbs, nouns, pronouns, and modifiers. You will also be given a fourth choice, *(No change)*, in the event that there are no mistakes. You will see examples of these types of questions in Part IV.

The fifth portion of the Language section tests your ability in expression. You will be given several lines of text or a paragraph with questions following it. You will be looking for errors in expression, organization, and clarity.

(1) Jerry and Javon usually don't like to ride roller coasters. (2) <u>Since</u>, they might make an exception if they get to spend spring break at Disney World.

(A) Because

(B) However

(C) On account of

(D) *(No change)*

The correct answer is (B). "However" is the closest in meaning to "since."

Math

The Math section of TACHS measures your ability to solve math problems in a variety of ways. For each math question, you will be given answer choices from which to choose. The first portion tests your knowledge of math concepts such as fractions, factors, multiples, multiplication, division, and decimals.

> The fraction $\frac{9}{10}$ can also be expressed as which of the following decimals?
>
> **(A)** 0.9
>
> **(B)** 0.09
>
> **(C)** 0.009
>
> **(D)** 9.0
>
> **The correct answer is (A).** 9 divided by 10 is 0.9.

The second portion of this section tests your ability to solve word problems using the basic math concepts mentioned above.

> Gail has $\frac{2}{3}$ as many French fries as Mindy. Mindy has 12 French fries. How many French fries does Gail have?
>
> **(A)** 8
>
> **(B)** 9
>
> **(C)** 10
>
> **(D)** Not given
>
> **The correct answer is (A).** $\frac{2}{3} \times 12 = 8$

The third portion of this section measures your ability to estimate, or do the math in your head, without using a pencil and paper.

> The closest estimate of 3.9×4.1 is _____.
>
> **(A)** 9
>
> **(B)** 12
>
> **(C)** 16
>
> **(D)** 20
>
> **The correct answer is (C).** $3.9 \times 4.1 \approx 16$

The fourth portion of this section measures your ability to interpret data, or to work with charts and graphs.

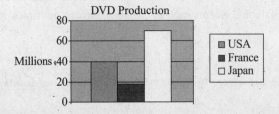

The chart above shows the annual production of DVDs in various countries as measured in millions. Based on the information in the chart, about how many DVDs does Japan produce each year?

(A) 70

(B) 70,000,000

(C) 60

(D) 60,000,000

The correct answer is (B). Japan is represented by the white bar that places yearly DVD production at 70 million.

Ability

The Ability section of the exam tests your abstract reasoning ability. You will be presented with visual tasks that require you to generalize from one item or series of items to another. These are reasoning skills that are going to be tested, not academic abilities, so don't worry if this sounds unlike anything you've been taught in school. Identifying patterns and looking ahead for the logical outcome of series of changes to shapes is all that will be required of you in this section.

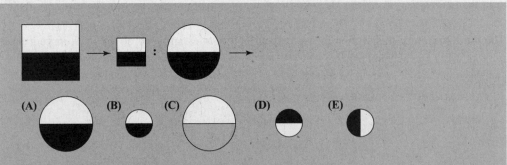

The correct answer is (B). The first pair share a similar item, but with the second rectangle being smaller than the first. The same logic must hold true for the second pair. Choice (B) is a smaller version of the black and white circle in the series above.

SUMMING IT UP

- The Test for Admission into Catholic High Schools (TACHS) is for eighth-grade students wishing to attend a Catholic high school in New York City beginning in the ninth grade.

- The TACHS tests basic knowledge in the areas of reading, language arts, math, and general reasoning ability.

- The TACHS uses a multiple-choice answer format, and the testing time is approximately 2 hours.

- Complete registration information, including important dates, registration procedures, registration fees, and testing locations can be found online at www.tachsinfo.com.

All About the Cooperative Entrance Exam (COOP)

chapter 2

OVERVIEW

- **The COOP exam format**
- **How the COOP is scored**
- **About the COOP questions**
- **Summing it up**

The two most widely used entrance exams for Catholic high schools are the COOP and the HSPT. Trailing these in popularity and acceptance for Catholic high schools are the SSAT and ISEE exams.

What exactly is the COOP exam? The Cooperative Entrance Examination (called COOP, for short) is a multiple-choice-style exam designed to determine the academic aptitude and skills achievement of eighth-graders seeking admission to selective high schools. The COOP tests your understanding of language, reading, and mathematics, among other things.

The COOP is administered only to students planning to enter ninth grade. It is given once each year, during either October or November. If you plan on taking the COOP, you must first preregister for this exam, either through your parochial elementary school, or, if currently enrolled in public school, as directed on the application form obtained from a parochial school.

Once registered, you'll receive a handbook of instructions that includes some sample questions to familiarize you with the exam. Upon registration you will also receive an admission ticket that you must bring with you to the assigned testing location on the assigned testing date.

THE COOP EXAM FORMAT

The multiple-choice answer format is used throughout the COOP exam. Most answer choices are given in sets of four, and the sets are grouped either as (A), (B), (C), (D) or as (F), (G), (H), (J). For example, the first question might use (A), (B), (C), (D) as the answer choices, and the next question might use (F), (G), (H), (J). The test is designed this way to make it easy for you to keep your place as you flip back and forth between the test booklet and the answer sheet.

In the past, various sections of the test have offered five answer choices, so (E) and (K) are added to the answer group range. Note that there is no choice (I). (I) has been omitted to avoid any possible confusion with the number "1." Each year, the publisher of the COOP (CTB/McGraw-Hill) changes 30 percent of the content of the exam. Most of the changes consist of substituting new questions for old ones. Changes also include new question styles, changing numbers of questions or time limits of test sections, or eliminating or combining test sections. The following chart was accurate at the time this book was written. Your own exam might not adhere precisely to these section titles, the number of questions, or the exact timing, but this chart is similar enough for you to use as your guide.

TIMETABLE AND ANALYSIS OF THE COOP

Test Number and Topic	Number of Questions	Time Allotted
1 Sequences	20	15 minutes
2 Analogies	20	7 minutes
3 Quantitative Reasoning	20	15 minutes
4 Verbal Reasoning—Words	20	15 minutes
15-minute break		
5 Verbal Reasoning—Context	20	15 minutes
6 Reading and Language Arts	40	40 minutes
7 Mathematics	40	35 minutes

TIP

On the COOP exam, all questions count the same. You won't get more points for answering a really difficult math question than you get for answering a very simple analogy. Remember that the more time you spend wrestling with the answer to one "stumper," the less time you have to whip through several easier questions.

HOW THE COOP IS SCORED

Raw scores for each test section of the COOP are determined by crediting one point for each question answered correctly. There is no deduction or penalty for any question answered incorrectly. Because each part of the exam contains a different number of questions, your raw score is converted to a scaled score according to a formula devised by the test administrators. The use of scaled scores enables schools to compare your performance on one part of the exam with your performance on other parts of the exam. Your scores are compared to the scores of other students taking the exam and are reported as percentiles. Your percentile rank shows where you stand compared to others who took the test. A percentile rank is reported for each part of the test.

There is no passing grade on the COOP, nor is there a failing grade. All of the high schools to which you have applied receive your scaled scores and your percentile rankings. Each has its own standards, and each makes its own admissions decisions based on test scores, school grades, recommendations, and other factors.

ABOUT THE COOP QUESTIONS

The following questions are examples of what you can expect on the COOP. Each question is preceded by directions like those on the actual exam and is followed by an explanatory answer. Later in this book, you will find two COOP Practice Tests you can take to prepare for the actual exam.

Test 1. Sequences

Directions: There are three forms of questions designed to measure sequential reasoning ability. In each case, you must choose the answer that would best continue the pattern or sequence.

The correct answer is (C). Each frame contains two figures. The second figure within each frame has one more line than the first figure. In the final frame, the first figure has four lines; the second must have five, as in choice (C).

2. 2 4 6 | 3 5 7 | 15 17 ____

   (F) 18

   (G) 16

   (H) 19

   (I) 15

The correct answer is (H). Within each frame, the pattern is simply the number plus 2, plus 2. 17 plus 2 equals 19.

3. Abcde   aBcde   abCde   _____   abcdE

   (A) AbcdE

   (B) abCDe

   (C) aBcDe

   (D) abcDe

The correct answer is (D). In each group of letters, the single capitalized letter moves progressively one space to the right.

The directions ask you to choose the best answer. That's why you should always read all the choices before you make your final decision.

NOTE

Test 2. Analogies

Directions: Analogy questions test your ability to recognize and understand relationships. In these questions, you must choose the picture that would go in the empty box so that the bottom two pictures are related in the same way that the top two are related.

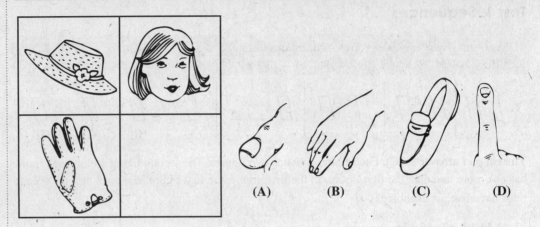

(A)   (B)   (C)   (D)

The correct answer is (B). The relationship of hat to head is that a hat is a head covering; therefore, the best answer is the drawing of a hand, because a glove is a hand covering.

Test 3. Quantitative Reasoning

Three different question styles are used to measure your aptitude for thinking with numbers. The following questions are typical of what you can expect on this test.

Directions: Find the relationship of the numbers in one column to the numbers in the other column. Then find the missing number.

1. $2 \rightarrow \boxed{} \rightarrow 4$

   $3 \rightarrow \boxed{} \rightarrow 9$

   $4 \rightarrow \boxed{} \rightarrow ?$

   (A) 8
   (B) 12
   (C) 13
   (D) 16

The correct answer is (D). If you think of the first pattern as 2 times itself (2) = 4, the second as 3 times itself (3) = 9, then the third would be 4 times itself (4) = 16.

Directions: Find the fraction of the grid that is shaded.

2.

(F) $\frac{1}{2}$

(G) $\frac{1}{4}$

(H) $\frac{1}{6}$

(J) $\frac{1}{8}$

The correct answer is (H). There are six squares. One of them is shaded. We know that 1 over 6 is $\frac{1}{6}$.

Directions: Look at the scale that shows sets of shapes of equal weight. Find an equivalent pair of sets that would also balance the scale.

3.

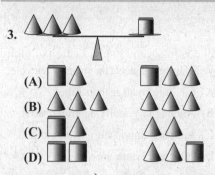

(A)
(B)
(C)
(D)

The correct answer is (B). The scale indicates that 1 cube = 3 cones. The only answer that maintains this relationship is choice (B), since it shows that 3 cones = 3 cones.

Test 4. Verbal Reasoning—Words

Two different question styles are used to measure how well you reason with words. Each question style has its own directions.

Directions: Find the word that names a necessary part of the underlined word.

1. claustrophobia

   (A) closet

   (B) fear

   (C) door

   (D) space

The correct answer is (B). Claustrophobia is the fear of being in small, enclosed places. While the person who suffers from claustrophobia would surely be uncomfortable in a closet or behind a closed door, the *necessary* ingredient of claustrophobia is *fear*.

Directions: The words in the top row are related in some way. The words in the bottom row are related in the same way. Find the word that completes the bottom row of words.

2. best better good
   worst worse _____

   (F) bad

   (G) worser

   (H) okay

   (J) good

The correct answer is (F). The words in the top row are in a comparative series, with the superlative on the left. Likewise, the words in the bottom row must be a similar comparative series. The comparison descends from *worst* to *worse* to *bad*.

Test 5. Verbal Reasoning—Context

1. Julie is in second grade. Laura is in third grade. Julie's sister Anne rides a tricycle.

   (A) Laura is smarter than Julie.

   (B) Anne is physically handicapped.

   (C) Julie is behind Laura in school.

   (D) Julie and Laura are sisters.

The correct answer is (C). The only certainty is that Julie is behind Laura in school. The fact that Laura is ahead in school does not necessarily mean that she is smarter, possibly only older. Anne might be a normal, healthy 2-year-old. Julie and Anne are sisters, but Laura's relationship to them is not given.

2. *ababawayla* means somewhere
   parimoodu means nobody
   pariwayla means somebody
   Which word means *nowhere*?

   (F) waylapari

   (G) pariababa

   (H) mooduababa

   (J) ababamoodu

The correct answer is (J). You will notice that elements of words are repeated among the English words as well as among the artificial words. By noticing the pattern of repetition, you can define and isolate word elements. In this sample, *wayla* means some, *pari* means body, *ababa* means where, and *moodu* means no. The order of the elements of words in this artificial language is the reverse of the order in English but is consistent within the language. Your answer choice must reflect that order, which is the reason that choice (H) is not correct.

Test 6. Reading and Language Arts

Directions: Read the passage and the questions following it. Answer each question based upon what you have read.

NOTE

It's an "open-book" test. In COOP reading comprehension questions, the answers will be directly stated or implied in the passage.

As he threw his head back in the chair, his glance happened to rest upon a bell, a disused bell, that hung in the room and communicated, for some purpose now forgotten, with a chamber in the highest story of the building. It was with great astonishment, and with a strange inexplicable dread, that, as he looked, he saw this bell begin to swing. Soon it rang out loudly, and so did every bell in the house.

This was succeeded by a clanking noise, deep down below as if some person were dragging a heavy chain over the casks in the wine merchant's cellar. Then he heard the noise much louder on the floors below; then coming up the stairs; then coming straight toward his door.

It came in through the heavy door, and a specter passed into the room before his eyes. And upon its coming in, the dying flame leaped up, as though it cried, "I know him! Marley's ghost!"

—from *A Christmas Carol*
by Charles Dickens

1. The bell that began ringing
   (A) was large and heavy.
   (B) did so by itself.
   (C) was attached to every bell in the house.
   (D) rested first on his glance.

The correct answer is (B). The bell began to ring by itself. The bell might have been large and heavy, but we have no way of knowing this from the passage. The ringing of every bell in the house would likely be due to the same supernatural factors that caused the first bell to ring.

2. The man who was listening to the bell
   (F) dragged a chain across the wine casks.
   (G) sat perfectly still.
   (H) was apparently very frightened.
   (J) is Marley's ghost.

The correct answer is (H). Obviously, this was a frightening experience. Also, *inexplicable dread* indicates fear.

3. The man in the story
   (A) first heard noises in his room.
   (B) is probably a wine merchant.
   (C) recognized Marley's ghost.
   (D) set the room on fire.

The correct answer is (C). If the man imagined the flame crying out the identity of the specter, he must have recognized it himself.

4. How would you describe the mood being created by the author?
   (F) Festive
   (G) Depressing
   (H) Exciting
   (J) Spooky

The correct answer is (J). Unexplained bells, creaking, clanking, and ghosts all create a spooky mood. The man in the story might have found the scene depressing, and you, the reader, might find the story exciting, but the overall mood is best described as *spooky*.

Directions: Choose the word that best completes the sentence.

5. I would bring grandma to visit you, _____ I have no car.
   - **(A)** while
   - **(B)** because
   - **(C)** but
   - **(D)** moreover
   - **(E)** therefore

The correct answer is (C). The conjunction *but* is the only choice that makes any sense in the context of the sentence.

Directions: Choose the sentence that is complete and correctly written.

6. **(F)** Cold-blooded reptiles with no mechanism for controlling body temperature.
   - **(G)** Reptiles, which have no mechanism for controlling body temperature, are described as cold-blooded animals.
   - **(H)** Reptiles are described as cold-blooded animals, this means that they have no mechanism for controlling body temperature.
   - **(J)** Reptiles are described as cold-blooded animals and they have no mechanism for controlling body temperature.
   - **(K)** Cold-blooded animals with no mechanism for controlling temperature, a description of reptiles.

The correct answer is (G). Choice (F) is a sentence fragment. Choice (H) is a comma splice of two independent clauses. Choice (J) is a run-on sentence. Choice (K) has no verb, so it is nothing more than a sentence fragment.

Directions: Choose the sentence that uses verbs correctly.

7. **(A)** While we were waiting for the local, the express roared past.
   - **(B)** The sky darkens ominously and rain began to fall.
   - **(C)** The woman will apply for a new job because she wanted to earn more money.
   - **(D)** I wish I knew who will be backing into my car.
   - **(E)** The wind blows, the thunder clapped, lightning will fill the sky, and it rains.

The correct answer is (A). All other choices mix tenses in illogical order.

Directions: Choose the underlined word that is the simple subject of the sentence.

8. The first step in improving your writing
          (F)   (G)   (H)
   is to know what makes a good sentence.
          (J)   (K)

The correct answer is (F). In this sentence, *step* is the simple subject.

Directions: Choose the underlined word or group of words that is the simple predicate (verb) of the sentence.

9. A decrease in the incidence of
      (A)   (B)
   contagious diseases proves that
              (C)
   sanitation is worthwhile.
     (D)   (E)

The correct answer is (C). The subject of the sentence is *decrease*, and the decrease *proves* the value of sanitation.

Directions: Choose the sentence that best combines the two underlined sentences into one.

10. <u>Fish in tropical waters are colorful. They swim among coral reefs.</u>

   (F) In tropical waters there are coral reefs swimming with colorful fish.

   (G) Fish swim among coral reefs in tropical waters, and they are colorful.

   (H) When fish swim among coral reefs, they are colorful in tropical waters.

   (J) Colorful fish swim among coral reefs in tropical waters.

   (K) Colorful tropical waters are home to swimming fish and coral reefs.

The correct answer is (J). Choice (J) is the simplest and most straight forward sentence.

Directions: Choose the topic sentence that best fits the paragraph.

11. _____ However, in reality, they are adaptable, intelligent, and often beautiful. A squid's body appears to be all head and feet. These feet, commonly referred to as arms, have little suction cups on them.

   (A) Because the squid is shy, it is often misunderstood.

   (B) Scientists consider squid the most intelligent mollusks.

   (C) Squid are considered a tasty treat by the other inhabitants of the sea.

   (D) The body of the squid is uniquely adapted for locomotion and for grabbing in its liquid environment.

   (E) Squid are considered by many to be ugly, unpleasant creatures.

The correct answer is (E). The second sentence contradicts the topic statement about the squid's appearance.

Directions: Choose the sentence that does *not* belong in the paragraph.

12. (1) Modern computers are no longer the size of a large room. (2) These contain no wires. (3) Some are so small that they can be held in one hand. (4) The large vacuum tubes of the early computers were replaced by tiny transistors. (5) These, in turn, have given way to infinitesimal microchips.

   (A) Sentence 1

   (B) Sentence 2

   (C) Sentence 3

   (D) Sentence 4

   (E) Sentence 5

The correct answer is (B). The paragraph is about the size of computers, not about computer wiring.

Test 7. Mathematics

The computations in this test are not complicated, but you must have a firm grasp of the meaning of mathematics and a little bit of common sense in order to answer the questions.

1. 350 students are taking this examination in this school today; $\frac{4}{7}$ of these students are girls. How many boys are taking the exam in this school?

   (A) 150
   (B) 200
   (C) 500
   (D) 550

   The correct answer is (A). If $\frac{4}{7}$ are girls, $\frac{3}{7}$ are boys. $\frac{3}{7}$ of $350 = \frac{3}{7} \times \frac{350}{1} = 150$.

2. Which number sentence is true?

   (F) $-12 > 9$
   (G) $-5 > -8$
   (H) $-3 = 3$
   (J) $2 < -6$

   The correct answer is (G). Draw a number line to prove this to yourself, if necessary.

3. Mrs. Breen came home from the store and put two half-gallon containers of milk into the refrigerator. Jim came home from school with a few friends, and they all had milk and cookies.

   When they had finished, only $\frac{1}{2}$ of one container of milk remained. How much milk did the boys drink?

   (A) $1\frac{1}{2}$ pints
   (B) $1\frac{1}{2}$ quarts
   (C) 3 quarts
   (D) $1\frac{1}{2}$ gallons

   The correct answer is (C). There are 4 quarts in a gallon; so there are 2 quarts in each half-gallon container.

4. Look at the figure below. Then choose the statement that is true.

   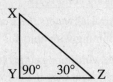

   (F) $m \angle X < m \angle Y < m \angle Z$
   (G) $m \angle X > m \angle Y > m \angle Z$
   (H) $m \angle X = m \angle Z + m \angle Y$
   (J) $m \angle Z < m \angle X < m \angle Y$

   The correct answer is (J). Because the sum of the angles of a triangle is 180°, angle x must be 60°. 60 is greater than 30, and it is smaller than 90.

5. Look at the graph below. Then read the question and choose the correct answer.

   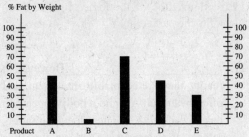

   According to FDA regulations, in order to print the designation "light" on its labels, a product must contain no more than 45% fat by weight. Which of these products may be labeled "light"?

   (A) D only
   (B) B and E only
   (C) B, D, and E only
   (D) A and C only

   The correct answer is (C). The regulations state that a "light" product contains *no more than 45% fat.* Product D, which contains exactly 45% fat, may be labeled "light" along with B and E.

6. The piece of property shown below is to be divided into uniform building lots of 100 × 100 sq. ft. Twenty percent of the property must be left undeveloped. How many houses may be built on this property?

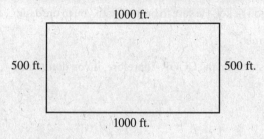

1000 ft.

500 ft.   500 ft.

1000 ft.

(F) 20

(G) 40

(H) 50

(J) 100

The correct answer is (G). The entire property is 1000 ft. × 500 ft., which equals 500,000 sq. ft. Twenty percent must be left undeveloped. 500,000 × 20% = 100,000. 500,000 − 100,000 = 400,000 sq. ft. to be developed. Each building lot is 100 × 100 = 10,000 sq. ft. 400,000 divided by 10,000 = 40 houses.

SUMMING IT UP

- The Cooperative Entrance Examination (COOP) tests eighth-graders' understanding of language, reading, and mathematics.

- When you register, you will receive an admission ticket. Be sure to bring it with you to the exam.

- The COOP uses a multiple-choice answer format.

- There is no deduction or penalty for wrong answers on the COOP. Therefore, if you don't know the answer, guess.

All About the High School Placement Test (HSPT)

OVERVIEW

- **The HSPT exam format**
- **How the HSPT is scored**
- **About the HSPT questions**
- **The HSPT optional tests**
- **Summing it up**

The Scholastic Testing Service High School Placement Test, called HSPT for short, is a five-part, multiple-choice test of verbal, quantitative, reading, mathematics, and language skills. The exam takes approximately 2 hours and 30 minutes. It contains 298 questions that are designed to indicate how well a student performs tasks that can be expected of an eighth-grader.

There are two different kinds of HSPTs: the Closed HSPT and the Open HSPT. The Closed HSPT is administered by the school, but scored by STS. Closed HSPT scores are compared to national standard distribution norms, so nationwide percentiles can be computed. The Open HSPT is administered and scored by the school, so STS does not deal directly with student results. The Open HSPT uses old versions of the Closed HSPT.

Scholastic Testing Service provides, along with the High School Placement Test, a choice of one optional test, in Mechanical Aptitude, Science, or Catholic Religion. Because many schools do not choose any of these tests, and because the results on the optional test are not included as part of the HSPT composite score, this book doesn't cover the optional tests. However, to give you some idea of what you can expect on an optional test, an outline of the Science test is provided at the end of this section. This outline shows you the typical structure and scope of the optional tests. If you are required to take one of the optional tests, be sure to seek study advice from the school to which you are applying.

THE HSPT EXAM FORMAT

Like the COOP exam, the HSPT exam uses a multiple-choice format. Each question offers three or four answer choices, lettered (A), (B), (C), and (D). Take a look at the Timetable and Analysis of the HSPT chart on the next page to see the timing, number of questions, and question types of the basic HSPT exam. Questions on the HSPT exam are numbered consecutively from 1 to 298. This numbering system helps you avoid the pitfall of answering questions in the wrong section of the answer sheet. For example, because there is only one question 25, you aren't able to mark your answer to question 25 in the wrong part of the sheet.

TIMETABLE AND ANALYSIS OF THE HSPT

Test Section	Number of Questions	Time Allotted
Verbal Skills	**60**	**16 minutes**
Verbal Analogies	10	
Synonyms	15	
Logic	10	
Verbal Classifications	16	
Antonyms	9	
Quantitative Skills	**52**	**30 minutes**
Number Series	18	
Geometric Comparison	9	
Nongeometric Comparison	8	
Number Manipulation	17	
Reading	**62**	**25 minutes**
Comprehension	40	
Vocabulary	22	
Mathematics	**64**	**45 minutes**
Concepts	24	
Problem-Solving	40	
Language Skills	**60**	**25 minutes**
Punctuation and Capitalization	12	
Usage	28	
Spelling	10	
Composition	10	

HOW THE HSPT IS SCORED

Your score on the HSPT is based on the number of questions you answer correctly. No points are subtracted for incorrect answers, so it pays to answer as many questions as possible—even if you have to guess.

Scholastic Testing Service converts your raw scores to standard scores that are reported on a scale of 200 to 800. Your HSPT score report includes your standard scores, your national and local percentile rank, your grade equivalent, and your Cognitive Skills Quotient.

Scholastic Testing Service will compare your performance with that of the other 120,000 students taking the exam in some 1,000 schools throughout the United States, many of these among the 1,570 Catholic secondary schools in the country. Scholastic Testing Service will also compare your performance with that of other students in your own area. All of this information is sent to the high schools you have indicated on your answer sheet. It is up to each school to decide what is an acceptable score for admission to the freshman class.

ABOUT THE HSPT QUESTIONS

The following questions are typical of what you can expect on the HSPT exam. Each question is followed by an explanatory answer. In Part IV, you will find two full-length HSPT Practice Tests you can take to prepare for the actual exam.

Part 1. Verbal Skills

VERBAL ANALOGIES

Throw is to ball as shoot is to

(A) policeman.
(B) kill.
(C) arrow.
(D) hunting.

The correct answer is (C). This is an action-to-object relationship. You *throw* a ball, and you *shoot* an arrow.

SYNONYMS

Meager most nearly means

(A) well received.
(B) long overdue.
(C) valuable.
(D) scanty.

The correct answer is (D). *Meager* means lacking in quality or quantity. *Sparse* or *scanty* are synonyms for *meager*.

LOGIC

Bill runs faster than Mike. Jeff runs faster than Bill. Jeff is not as fast as Mike. If the first two statements are true, the third statement is

(A) true.
(B) false.
(C) uncertain.

The correct answer is (B). If the first two statements are true, Jeff runs faster than both Bill and Mike.

VERBAL CLASSIFICATION

Which word does *not* belong with the others?

(A) Car
(B) Plane
(C) Van
(D) Truck

The correct answer is (B). A plane is the only vehicle that flies; all others are modes of ground transportation.

ANTONYMS

Loyal means the *opposite* of

(A) lovely.
(B) unfaithful.
(C) unlucky.
(D) usual.

The correct answer is (B). *Loyal* means faithful. The best antonym is *unfaithful*.

Part 2. Quantitative Skills

NUMBER SERIES

Look at this series: 10, 14, 18, 22, 26, ... What number should come next?

(A) 28
(B) 29
(C) 30
(D) 32

The correct answer is (C). The pattern in this series is to add 4 to each number. 26 + 4 = 30.

NOTE

Don't worry that you don't see directions or instructions about how to answer these question types. In Part II of this book, you'll find in-depth reviews of each question type contained in the entrance exams discussed here.

GEOMETRIC COMPARISONS

Examine hourglasses A, B, and C and find the best answer.

(A)   (B)   (C)

(A) (B) shows the most time passed.

(B) (A) shows the most time passed.

(C) (C) shows the most time passed.

(D) (A), (B), and (C) show the same time passed.

The correct answer is (B). Be especially careful to avoid response errors when answering these questions. The correct answer is hourglass (A), but you must mark the letter of the correct statement, which, of course, is choice (B).

NONGEOMETRIC COMPARISONS

Examine (I), (II), and (III) and find the best answer.

(I) $(4 \times 2) - 3$

(II) $(4 \times 3) - 2$

(III) $(4 + 3) - 2$

(A) (I) is greater than (III).

(B) (I), (II), and (III) are equal.

(C) (III) is greater than (II).

(D) (I) and (III) are equal.

The correct answer is (D). Determine the numerical value of (A), (B), and (C). Then test each answer choice to see which one is true.

(I) $(4 \times 2) - 3 = 8 - 3 = 5$

(II) $(4 \times 3) - 2 = 12 - 2 = 10$

(III) $(4 \times 3) - 2 = 7 - 2 = 5$

NUMBER MANIPULATION

What number is 5 more than $\frac{2}{3}$ of 27?

(A) 14

(B) 32

(C) 9

(D) 23

The correct answer is (D). First find $\frac{2}{3}$ of 27: $\frac{2}{3} \times 27 = 18$. Then add: $18 + 5 = 23$.

Part 3. Reading

COMPREHENSION

The impressions that an individual gets from his environment are greatly influenced by his emotional state. When he is happy, objects and people present themselves to him in a favorable aspect; when he is depressed, he views the same things in an entirely different light. It has been said that a person's moods are the lenses that color life with many different hues. Not only does mood affect impression, but impression also affects mood. The beauty of a spring morning might dissipate the gloom of a great sorrow, the good-natured chuckle of a fat man might turn anger into a smile, or a telegram might transform a house of mirth into a house of mourning.

According to the passage, an individual's perception of his environment

(A) depends on the amount of light available.

(B) is greatly influenced by his emotional state.

(C) is affected by color.

(D) is usually favorable.

The correct answer is (B). The first sentence of the passage makes the point that one's perceptions are influenced by one's emotional state.

VOCABULARY

As used in the passage above, the word dissipate probably means

(A) condense.

(B) draw out.

(C) melt away.

(D) inflate.

The correct answer is (C). *Dissipate* means to "scatter," "dissolve," and "evaporate."

Part 4. Mathematics

CONCEPTS

To the nearest tenth, 52.693 is written

(A) 52.7

(B) 53

(C) 52.69

(D) 52.6

The correct answer is (A). To "round off" to the nearest tenth means to "round off" to one digit to the right of the decimal point. The digit to the right of the decimal point is 6. However, the next digit is 9, which means you must round up to 52.7.

PROBLEM-SOLVING

On a map, 1 inch represents 500 miles. How many miles apart are two cities that are $1\frac{1}{2}$ inches apart on the map?

(A) 750

(B) 1,000

(C) 1,250

(D) 1,500

The correct answer is (A). If 1 inch = 500 miles, then $\frac{1}{2}$ inch = 250 miles. Therefore, $1\frac{1}{2}$ inches = 500 + 250 = 750 miles.

Part 5. Language Skills

PUNCTUATION AND CAPITALIZATION

Find the sentence that has an error in capitalization or punctuation. If you find no mistake, mark choice (D) as your answer.

(A) Sally asked, "What time will you be home?"

(B) Doug hopes to enter John F. Kennedy High School next Fall.

(C) The letter arrived on Saturday, January 15.

(D) No mistakes

The correct answer is (B). This sentence has an error in capitalization. The word *fall* should not be capitalized.

USAGE

Find the sentence that has an error in usage. If you find no mistake, mark (D) as your answer.

(A) Many children adopt the beliefs of their parents.

(B) "Is he always so amusing?" she asked.

(C) All the officers declined except she.

(D) No mistakes

The correct answer is (C). This sentence has an error in usage. The word *she* should be *her* since it acts as the object of the preposition *except*.

TIP

Answer as many questions as possible because points are not subtracted if you choose the wrong answer.

SPELLING

Find the sentence that has an error in spelling. If you find no mistake, mark choice (D) as your answer.

(A) We recieved a letter from the principal.

(B) The library closes at 5 o'clock tomorrow.

(C) I have an appointment with the doctor on Wednesday.

(D) No mistakes

The correct answer is (A). The word *received* is incorrectly spelled.

COMPOSITION

Choose the best word or words to join the thoughts together.

I left my key at school; _____ I had to ring the bell to get in the house.

(A) however

(B) nevertheless

(C) therefore

(D) None of these

The correct answer is (C). *Nevertheless* and *however* are used to express a contrast. *Therefore* is used to express a result. The second half of this sentence is clearly a result of the first half.

THE HSPT OPTIONAL TESTS

Some schools might require that you take one of the three optional tests described at the beginning of this section: Mechanical Aptitude, Science, or Catholic Religion. Not every school to which you apply will require this extra test. However, if you do have to take an optional test, the test is chosen by the school, and like the basic HSPT exam, the test will involve multiple-choice questions and answers.

Your score on the optional test will not be included with your score on the basic HSPT exam. Rather, the school will receive a report on your overall performance on the optional exam and a topic-by-topic evaluation of your performance. The school will use this information to place you in appropriate classes. It might also use the information to determine the background of the student body as a whole in preparing the curriculum for the following year.

The optional science test consists of 40 questions covering a wide variety of topics. The questions are not neatly categorized. For example, a biology question might be followed by a physics question, and then a laboratory methods question might be followed by a chemistry question. The outline below gives you an idea of how many topics are covered and approximately how many questions there are on each topic.

DISTRIBUTION OF TOPICS ON HSPT OPTIONAL SCIENCE TEST

Topic/Content	Number of Items
Biological Sciences:	
Plants	2
Animals	2
Life Processes	2
Health and Safety	1
Ecology	2
Earth Sciences:	
Astronomy	2
Geology	2
Weather	1
Air	2
Water	2
Physical Sciences:	
Matter and Energy	2
Machines and Work	2
Magnetism and Electricity	2
Sound	1
Heat and Light	1
Chemistry	2
Implications of Scientific Technology:	
Societal Benefits	3
Technical Applications	3
Principles of Scientific Research and Experimentation:	
Laboratory Methods	3
Research Practices	3

SUMMING IT UP

- The HSPT is a five-part multiple-choice test of verbal, quantitative, reading, mathematics, and language skills.

- The test takes approximately 2 hours and 30 minutes and contains 298 questions.

- No points are subtracted for incorrect answers, so it pays to answer as many questions as possible, even if you have to guess.

All About the Secondary School Admission Test (SSAT)

OVERVIEW

- **The SSAT exam format**
- **How the SSAT is scored**
- **What is the writing sample?**
- **About the SSAT questions**
- **Summing it up**

The SSAT (which stands for Secondary School Admission Test) is an established independent high school entrance exam that's been around for quite some time. You can take the exam on any one of seven Saturday morning test dates scheduled every year at numerous locations throughout the country. Special arrangements can be made for Sabbath observers, applicants with handicaps, and students who live far from an established test center.

SSAT scores are accepted by more than 600 schools, either exclusively or as an alternative to another exam (most often the Independent School Entrance Examination—ISEE). The schools that accept SSAT scores include independent unaffiliated private schools, non-diocesan Catholic schools or Catholic schools operated by religious orders, and non-Catholic religiously affiliated schools. Many boarding schools also require the SSAT.

The SSAT is offered at two levels. The lower level of the exam is taken by students who are currently in grades 5, 6, and 7; the upper level is taken by students in grade 8 and above. Because each level includes a range of ages and grade levels, scoring takes these factors in mind, and percentile comparisons are made separately within each grade group. Because the emphasis of this book is on Catholic high school entrance exams, it focuses on the upper-level exam. The lower-level exam is similar in structure, but it is geared toward younger students.

THE SSAT EXAM FORMAT

The SSAT is an exam that consists of multiple-choice questions and an essay. The multiple-choice sections test quantitative and verbal reasoning abilities and reading comprehension. The exam is administered in five separately timed sections. The first section is a writing sample. Two sections contain mathematics questions, one includes synonyms and analogies, and one tests reading comprehension. Each question on the SSAT offers five answer choices lettered (A), (B), (C), (D), and (E). The chart below shows a typical SSAT timetable.

ALERT!

On the SSAT exam, you earn one point for each correct answer. One fourth of a point is deducted for every incorrect answer, so random guessing is not a good idea on this exam.

TIMETABLE AND ANALYSIS OF THE SSAT

Part/Section	Number of Questions	Time Allotted
Part I: Writing Sample	1	25 minutes
Part II Section 1: Verbal	60	30 minutes
Synonyms questions	30	
Analogies questions	30	
Part II Section 2: Quantitative (Math)	25	30 minutes
Part II Section 3: Reading Comprehension (questions based on eight or nine reading passages)	40	40 minutes
Part II Section 4: Quantitative (Math)	25	30 minutes

HOW THE SSAT IS SCORED

The SSAT awards you one point for each question you answer correctly. One fourth of a point is deducted for every question that you answer incorrectly. This means that random guessing is not a good idea on this exam. If you have absolutely no idea of the answer to a question, you should leave it blank. On the other hand, if you can eliminate some obviously wrong answer choices, then guessing is a wise move. The more answer choices you can eliminate, the more advisable it is to guess.

Remember: If you will be taking the SSAT for any of the Catholic high schools to which you are applying, we strongly suggest that you purchase *Peterson's Master the SSAT & ISEE*. That book contains two full-length SSAT practice tests with instruction and practice specific to the question types on the SSAT.

WHAT IS THE WRITING SAMPLE?

NOTE

For the writing sample, give specific examples to support your position.

At the beginning of each SSAT testing session, you must write a 25-minute essay on an assigned subject. This essay is not scored. It is duplicated and sent to each school as a sample of your ability to express yourself in writing under the same conditions as all other candidates for admission to the school.

The directions for the SSAT writing sample look like this:

Directions: Read the topic, choose your position, and organize your essay before writing. Write a convincing, legible essay on the paper provided.

Here is a sample SSAT essay topic. Try to organize and write an essay on this topic.

Topic: High schools should require students to maintain a certain grade point level in order to play on competitive sports teams.

Do you agree or disagree? Support your position with examples from your own experience, the experience of others, current events, or your reading.

Example of a well-written essay.

I can understand why some schools require students to maintain their grades if they want to be in sports. Sports are time consuming and cut into study time. But, I think that less competent students should not be deprived of the benefits of sports participation.

The argument that students should keep up their grades if they want to be in sports is worth listening to. After all, the purpose of going to school is to get an education. And sports practice and games do take a lot of time. The grades of a few students might in fact suffer from sports participation, but I think that more students will work harder and will learn to manage time better if they are allowed to play on the team. Learning to organize time is also an important lesson to be gained from school. Happy people tend to reach to meet expectations, and less capable students may even do better in school to prove that being in sports did not do them any harm.

An equally good argument is that everyone must succeed at something. If a poor student can excel at sports, that student will develop self-esteem. Once that student feels good about himself or herself, the student may transfer that confidence to schoolwork and actually get better grades. The old adage that success breeds success applies here.

While the attitude that schoolwork comes first does make a good point, I think that permitting a student to participate in sports and to develop a good self-image is more important. The school should give extra help to the less competent student, especially help in learning time management. Then it should let that student contribute to school spirit on the playing fields as well as in the classroom.

TIP

Educated guessing will boost your score. You should use common sense and the process of elimination to assist you in choosing the best possible answer. If you cannot make an educated guess, leave the answer blank.

ALERT!

Don't spin your wheels. Make sure not to spend too much time on any one question. Give it some thought, take your best shot, and move along.

ABOUT THE SSAT QUESTIONS

The following questions are typical of what you can expect on the SSAT. Each question is followed by an explanatory answer.

Verbal Reasoning

Directions: Each question shows a word in capital letters followed by five words or phrases. Choose the word or phrase whose meaning is most similar to the meaning of the word in CAPITAL letters.

1. NOVICE
   - (A) competitive
   - (B) clumsy
   - (C) aged
   - (D) beginning
   - (E) impulsive

The correct answer is (D). A NOVICE is a *beginner*. A novice might, of course, be competitive, clumsy, aged, or impulsive, but it is his being a beginner that makes him a novice. You might recognize the root of *novel*, meaning *new*, as a clue to the definition.

2. CONVOY
   - (A) hearse
   - (B) thunderstorm
   - (C) group
   - (D) jeep
   - (E) journey

The correct answer is (C). A CONVOY is a group traveling together for protection or convenience. You have probably seen convoys of military vehicles traveling single file up the highway toward summer reserve camp. A jeep might be part of a convoy.

Directions: The following questions ask you to find relationships between words. Read each question, and then choose the answer that best completes the meaning of the sentence.

3. Lid is to box as cork is to
   - (A) float
   - (B) bottle
   - (C) wine
   - (D) blacken
   - (E) stopper

The correct answer is (B). The relationship is one of purpose. The purpose of a *lid* is to close a *box*; the purpose of a *cork* is to close a *bottle*. *Cork* is easily associated with all the choices, so you must recognize the purposeful relationship of the initial pair to choose the correct answer.

4. Poison is to death as
   - (A) book is to pages
   - (B) music is to violin
   - (C) kindness is to cooperation
   - (D) life is to famine
   - (E) nothing is to something

The correct answer is (C). This is a cause-and-effect relationship. *Poison* might cause *death*; *kindness* might lead to *cooperation*. Neither outcome is a foregone conclusion, but both are equally likely, so the parallel is maintained. Choice (B) offers a reversed relationship.

Quantitative (Math)

Directions: Calculate the answers to each of the following questions. Select the answer choice that is best.

5. $\frac{1}{4}\%$ of 1500 =

   (A) 7.50

   (B) 1.50

   (C) 15.00

   (D) 3.75

   (E) 60.00

The correct answer is (D). $\frac{1}{4}\%$ written as a decimal is 0.0025. (1500)(0.0025) = 3.75. You could have done this problem in your head by thinking: 1% of 1500 is 15; $\frac{1}{4}$ of 1% = 15 ÷ 4 = 3.75.

6. If psychological studies of juvenile delinquents show K percent to be emotionally unstable, what is the number of juvenile delinquents not emotionally unstable per one hundred juvenile delinquents?

   (A) 100 minus K

   (B) 1 minus K

   (C) K minus 100

   (D) 100 ÷ K

   (E) K ÷ 100

The correct answer is (A). "Percent" means out of 100. If K percent are emotionally unstable, then K out of 100 are emotionally unstable. The remainder, 100 – K, are stable.

7. A piece of wood 35 feet, 6 inches long was used to make four shelves of equal length. The length of each shelf was

   (A) 9 feet, $1\frac{1}{2}$ inches.

   (B) 8 feet, $10\frac{1}{2}$ inches.

   (C) 7 feet, $10\frac{1}{2}$ inches.

   (D) 7 feet, $1\frac{1}{2}$ inches.

   (E) 8 feet, $1\frac{1}{2}$ inches.

The correct answer is (B). First convert the feet to inches. 35 feet = 420 inches. Add the 6 inches to get 426 inches. 426 ÷ 4 = 106.5 inches per shelf, which makes the answer 8 feet, $10\frac{1}{2}$ inches per shelf.

8. ∠ABD is a(n)

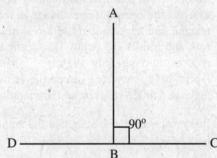

   (A) straight angle and contains 180°.

   (B) acute angle and contains 35°.

   (C) obtuse angle and contains 360°.

   (D) right angle and contains 45°.

   (E) right angle and contains 90°.

The correct answer is (E). ∠ABC and ∠ABD are supplementary angles. Because ∠ABC = 90°, ∠ABD must also equal 90° (180° – 90° = 90°). A right angle contains 90°.

Reading Comprehension

Line Cotton fabrics treated with the XYZ Process have features that make them far superior to any previously known flame-retardant-treated cotton fabrics. XYZ Process-treated
5 fabrics are durable to repeated laundering and dry cleaning and are glow resistant as well as flame resistant; when exposed to flames or intense heat they form tough, pliable, and protective barriers; are inert
10 physiologically to persons handling or exposed to the fabric; are only slightly heavier than untreated fabrics; and are susceptible to further wet and dry finishing treatments. In addition, the treated fabrics
15 exhibit little or no adverse change in feel, texture, and appearance, and are shrink-, rot-, and mildew-resistant. The treatment reduces strength only slightly. Finished fabrics have "easy care" properties in that
20 they are wrinkle-resistant and dry rapidly.

9. It is most accurate to state that the author in the preceding selection presents

   (A) facts, but reaches no conclusion concerning the value of the process.

   (B) a conclusion concerning the value of the process and facts to support that conclusion.

   (C) a conclusion concerning the value of the process, unsupported by facts.

   (D) neither facts nor conclusions, but merely describes the process.

   (E) the case for making all fabrics flame-retardant.

The correct answer is (B). This is a combination main idea and interpretation question. If you cannot answer this question readily, reread the selection. The author clearly thinks that the XYZ Process is terrific and says so in the first sentence. The rest of the selection presents a wealth of facts to support the initial claim.

10. Which of the following articles would be most suitable for the XYZ Process?

    (A) Nylon stockings

    (B) Woolen shirt

    (C) Silk tie

    (D) Cotton bedsheet

    (E) Polyester slacks

The correct answer is (D). At first glance, you might think that this is an inference question requiring you to make a judgment based upon the few drawbacks of the process. Closer reading, however, shows you that there is no contest for the correct answer here. This is a simple question of fact. The XYZ Process is a treatment for cotton fabrics.

11. The main reason for treating a fabric with the XYZ Process is to

    (A) prepare the fabric for other wet and dry finishing treatments.

    (B) render it shrink-, rot- and mildew-resistant.

    (C) increase its weight and strength.

    (D) reduce the chance that it will catch fire.

    (E) justify a price increase.

The correct answer is (D). This is a main idea question. You must distinguish between the main idea and the supporting and incidental facts.

12. Which of the following would be considered a minor drawback of the XYZ Process?

    (A) It forms barriers when exposed to flame.

    (B) It makes fabrics mildew-resistant.

    (C) It adds to the weight of fabrics.

    (D) It is compatible with other finishing treatments.

    (E) It does not wash out of the fabric.

The correct answer is (C). Obviously, a drawback is a negative feature. The selection mentions only two negative features. The treatment reduces strength slightly, and it makes fabrics slightly heavier than untreated fabrics. Only one of these negative features is offered among the answer choices.

SUMMING IT UP

- The SSAT is a multiple-choice exam testing quantitative and verbal abilities and reading comprehension. In addition, there is a 25-minute essay that schools use to measure your ability to express yourself in a timed-writing situation.

- It is important to understand the scoring procedures. On this exam, ¼ of a point is subtracted for an incorrect answer, so try to eliminate one or more answer choices before guessing.

- There are five separately timed sections: one is the writing sample, two cover mathematics, one contains synonyms and analogies, and one tests reading comprehension.

All About the
Independent School
Entrance Examination
(ISEE)

OVERVIEW

- **The ISEE exam format**
- **How the ISEE is scored**
- **About the ISEE questions**
- **Summing it up**

The Independent School Entrance Examination (ISEE) is a newer independent high school admission test that is gaining rapid acceptance around the country. The exam is administered by the Educational Records Bureau. Scheduled exam dates vary from region to region and are centered around major cities, but small group and even individual testing can be arranged for students who don't live near a major city. For specific information on registering for the exam in your area, go online to http://erblearn.org/parents/admission/isee, call 800-446-0320 (toll-free), or write to:

ISEE Operations Office
423 Morris Street
Durham, NC 27701
E-mail: isee@measinc.com

You may also find an *ISEE Student Guide* at http://erblearn.org/uploads/media_items/isee-student-guide.original.pdf.

The ISEE is accepted by more than 1,000 independent schools around the country, most often by day schools. Many boarding schools now accept ISEE scores as an alternative to the SSAT, though few mandate the ISEE. The ISEE is accepted by all member schools of the Independent Schools Association of New York City and is the exam of choice at most of the independent schools in Philadelphia, San Diego, and Nashville. The ISEE has especially good acceptance at non-Catholic religiously affiliated day schools and is gaining acceptance at independent Catholic high schools.

The ISEE is offered at three levels: lower, middle, and upper. The Lower Level of the exam is given to candidates for grades 5 and 6, the Middle Level of the exam is given to candidates for grades 7 and 8, and the Upper Level is given to candidates for grades 9 through 12. Because each level includes a range of ages and grade levels, scoring and percentile ranking are done separately for members of each grade group. The upper and middle levels of the exam differ chiefly in the difficulty of the questions and in the mathematical subjects covered.

chapter 5

THE ISEE EXAM FORMAT

The ISEE is a multiple-choice exam testing verbal reasoning, quantitative reasoning, reading comprehension, and mathematics achievement. The ISEE also requires each applicant to write an essay. The ISEE is administered in five separately timed test sections. The time limit for each section is different, so all applicants take the tests in the same order. The ISEE does not include an experimental section; so every test section and question counts.

Each question on the ISEE offers four answer choices, lettered (A), (B), (C), and (D). The following Timetable and Analysis chart gives you an example of the order of subjects and time limits you can expect on the Middle and Upper Level exams.

TIMETABLE AND ANALYSIS OF THE ISEE

Test Number And Content	Number Of Questions	Time Allotted
1: Verbal Reasoning Synonyms Sentence completions	40	20 minutes
2: Quantitative Reasoning Concepts and understanding and application measured by problem solving and quantitative comparisons	35	35 minutes
3: Reading Comprehension Based on approximately 9 reading passages (science passages, social studies passages)	40	40 minutes
4: Mathematics Achievement Arithmetic concepts Algebraic concepts Geometric concepts	45	40 minutes
5: Essay	1 Prompt	30 minutes

Each section of the ISEE (except the essay) contains several questions that will not be scored but may be used on future ISEE exams.

HOW THE ISEE IS SCORED

Scoring of the ISEE is very straightforward. You receive one point for every question that you answer correctly. There is no penalty for a wrong answer. This means that even a wild guess cannot hurt you. Obviously, you want to mark correct answers to as many questions as possible, but when you're in a pinch, a guess will do.

The number of questions your answer correctly adds up to your raw score. Your raw score is then converted into a scaled score, which you will receive along with a percentile rank. The percentile rank allows allow you to see how your score compares with those of other students.

Some Test-taking Tips for the ISEE

Because you don't lose points for wrong answers on the ISEE, you have nothing to lose by guessing. If you can eliminate one or more answers, you can make an educated guess. If you've made an educated guess, write "EG" (for educated guess) next to it on the answer sheet. If you don't have a clue which answer choice is correct, just mark one choice, then write "WG" (for wild guess) next to it on the answer sheet. If you have time left after you finish the remaining exam questions, go back to these "guesses" to see if you can make a better choice. One big benefit of choosing an answer for every question on the exam is that you don't run the risk of losing your place on the answer sheet, as you do if you just skip a question. Be sure to go back and erase all of the "EGs" and "WGs" that you wrote. If they are not erased, the computer might mark the question wrong.

Because you have a 25 percent chance of making a correct "wild guess," we have one more recommendation: Don't leave any answers blank at the end of a test. A couple of minutes before the test time ends, mark an answer for each of the remaining questions. The odds are that you'll pick up extra points.

Remember: If you learn that you will be taking the ISEE as part of the application process for any of your Catholic high schools, purchase and study *Peterson's Master the SSAT & ISEE*. That book includes instructions for answering questions unique to the ISEE and gives special advice and assistance with writing the ISEE essay. It also contains two full-length practice ISEE exams.

TIP

If you guessed on any answers, mark EG (educated guess) or WG (wild guess) next to the number on your answer sheet. If you have time left after you finish the section, go back and see if you can make a better choice; you don't lose points for incorrect answers. Remember to erase your "EG" and "WG" notes.

ABOUT THE ISEE QUESTIONS

Verbal Reasoning

> **Directions:** Each question is made up of a word in CAPITAL letters followed by four choices. Choose the word that is most nearly the same in meaning as the word in CAPITAL letters.

1. TENANT
   - **(A)** occupant
   - **(B)** landlord
   - **(C)** owner
   - **(D)** farmer

The correct answer is (A). The most common sense synonym of the word TENANT is *occcupant*. As such, the tenant is never the landlord. The owner might be an occupant, but unless he occupies on a very temporary basis he is not considered a tenant. A tenant farmer lives on and cultivates the land of another.

2. CALCULATED
   - **(A)** multiplying
   - **(B)** comparing
   - **(C)** answering
   - **(D)** figuring out

The correct answer is (D). CALCULATING might include multiplying or adding to arrive at the answer, but not all calculations need be mathematical. It is the *figuring out* that is the *calculating*.

> **Directions:** Each of the following questions is made up of a sentence containing one or two blanks. The sentences with one blank indicate that one word is missing. Sentences with two blanks have two missing words. Each sentence is followed by four choices.

3. Utility is not _____, for the usefulness of an object changes with time and place.
   - **(A)** planned
   - **(B)** practical
   - **(C)** permanent
   - **(D)** understandable

The correct answer is (C). If the usefulness of an object changes, then that usefulness is by definition *not* PERMANENT.

4. A string of lies had landed her in such a hopeless _____ that she didn't know how to _____ herself.
   - **(A)** status . . clear
   - **(B)** pinnacle . . explain
   - **(C)** confusion . . help
   - **(D)** predicament . . extricate

The correct answer is (D). Hopeless PREDICAMENT is an idiomatic expression meaning *impossible situation*. This is a reasonable position for one to be in after a string of lies. The second blank is correctly filled with a term that implies that she couldn't get out of the mess she had created.

Quantitative Reasoning

Directions: Work out each problem in your head or in the margins of the test booklet.

5. If $a^2 + b^2 = a^2 + x^2$, then b equals

   (A) $\pm x$

   (B) $x^2 - 2a^2$

   (C) $\pm a$

   (D) $a^2 + x^2$

The correct answer is (A). Subtract a^2 from both sides of the equation: $b^2 = x^2$; therefore, $b = \pm x$.

6. How much time is there between 8:30 a.m. today and 3:15 a.m. tomorrow?

   (A) $17\frac{3}{4}$ hrs.

   (B) $18\frac{2}{3}$ hrs.

   (C) $18\frac{1}{2}$ hrs.

   (D) $18\frac{3}{4}$ hrs.

The correct answer is (D).

$$
\begin{array}{r}
\text{From 8:30 a.m.} \qquad 12:00 = 11:60 \\
\text{until noon today:} \quad \underline{-8:30 = 8:30} \\
\text{3 hrs. 30 min.} \\
\text{From noon until midnight: } +12 \text{ hrs.} \\
\text{From midnight until 3:15 a.m.: } \underline{+3 \text{ hrs. 15 min.}} \\
18 \text{ hrs. 45 min.} \\
= 18\frac{3}{4} \text{ hrs.}
\end{array}
$$

Directions: For each of the following questions, two quantities are given—one in Column A and the other in Column B. Compare the quantities in the two columns and choose:

(A) if the quantity in Column A is greater

(B) if the quantity in Column B is greater

(C) if the quantities are equal

(D) if the relationship cannot be determined from the information given

7.   Column A   Column B

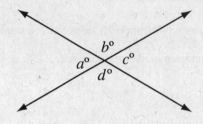

Note: Figure not drawn to scale

$180 - a$ $d + c - b$

The correct answer is (D).

$180 - a$ versus $d + c - b = 180 - b$

Because we do not know if a is greater than, less than, or equal to b, we cannot determine which column is greater.

8.   Column A   Column B

$$\dfrac{\frac{2}{3}}{4}$$ $$\dfrac{\frac{2}{3}}{4}$$

The correct answer is (A).

$\dfrac{\frac{2}{3}}{4} = \dfrac{2}{1} \bullet \dfrac{4}{3} = \dfrac{8}{3}$ versus $\dfrac{\frac{2}{3}}{4} = \dfrac{2}{3} \bullet \dfrac{1}{4} = \dfrac{2}{12}$ Column A > Column B

Reading Comprehension

Directions: Each reading passage is followed by questions based on its content. Answer the questions on the basis of what is stated or implied in the passage.

Line A large proportion of the people who are behind bars are not convicted criminals, but people who have been arrested and are being held until their trial in court. Experts
5 have often pointed out that this detention system does not operate fairly. For instance, a person who can afford to pay bail usually will not get locked up. The theory of the bail system is that the person will make sure to
10 show up in court when he is supposed to since he knows that otherwise he will forfeit his bail—he will lose the money he put up. Sometimes a person who can show that he is a stable citizen with a job and a family
15 will be released on "personal recognizance" (without bail). The result is that the well-to-do, the employed, and the family men can often avoid the detention system. The people who do wind up in detention tend
20 to be the poor, the unemployed, the single, and the young.

9. According to the preceding passage, people who are put behind bars

    (A) are almost always dangerous criminals.

    (B) include many innocent people who have been arrested by mistake.

    (C) are often people who have been arrested but have not yet come to trial.

    (D) are all poor people who tend to be young and single.

The correct answer is (C). The answer to this question is directly stated in the first sentence. Choice (B) might be possible, but it is neither stated nor implied by the passage. The word *all* in choice (D) makes it an incorrect statement.

10. Suppose that two men were booked on the same charge at the same time and that the same bail was set for both of them. One man was able to put up bail, and he was released. The second man was not able to put up bail, and he was held in detention. The writer of the passage would most likely feel that this result is

    (A) unfair, because it does not have any relation to guilt or innocence.

    (B) unfair, because the first man deserves severe punishment.

    (C) fair, because the first man is obviously innocent.

    (D) fair, because the law should be tougher on poor people than on the rich.

The correct answer is (A). You should have no difficulty inferring this attitude from the tone of the passage.

Line Fire often travels inside the partitions of a burning building. Many partitions contain wooden studs that support the partitions, and the studs leave a space through which the
5 fire can travel. Flames might spread from the bottom to the upper floors through the partitions. Sparks from a fire in the upper part of a partition might fall and start a fire at the bottom. Some signs that a fire is spreading
10 inside a partition are: (1) blistering paint, (2) discolored paint or wallpaper, or (3) partitions that feel hot to the touch. If any of these signs is present, the partition must be opened up to look for the fire. Finding
15 cobwebs inside the partition is one sign that fire has not spread through the partition.

11. Fires can spread inside partitions because

    (A) there are spaces between studs inside of partitions.

    (B) fires can burn anywhere.

    (C) partitions are made out of materials that burn easily.

    (D) partitions are usually painted or wallpapered.

The correct answer is (A). This statement of fact is made in the second sentence.

12. If a firefighter sees the paint on a partition beginning to blister, he should first
    - **(A)** wet down the partition.
    - **(B)** check the partitions in other rooms.
    - **(C)** chop a hole in the partition.
    - **(D)** close windows and doors and leave the room.

The correct answer is (C). Blistering paint is a sign that fire is spreading inside a partition. If this sign is present, the firefighter must open the partition to look for the fire. The way to open the partition is to chop a hole in it.

Mathematics Achievement

Directions: Each question is followed by four answer choices. Choose the correct answer to each question.

13. If $\frac{3}{4}$ of a class is absent and $\frac{2}{3}$ of those present leave the room, what fraction of the original class remains in the room?

(A) $\frac{1}{24}$

(B) $\frac{1}{4}$

(C) $\frac{1}{12}$

(D) $\frac{1}{8}$

The correct answer is (C). If $\frac{3}{4}$ are absent, $\frac{1}{4}$ are present. If $\frac{2}{3}$ of the $\frac{1}{4}$ present leave, $\frac{1}{3}$ of the $\frac{1}{4}$ remain. $\frac{1}{3} \times \frac{1}{4} = \frac{1}{12}$ remain in the room.

14. A cog wheel having 8 cogs plays into another cog wheel having 24 cogs. When the small wheel has made 42 revolutions, how many has the larger wheel made?

(A) 14

(B) 16

(C) 20

(D) 10

The correct answer is (A). The larger wheel is 3 times the size of the smaller wheel, so it makes $\frac{1}{3}$ the revolutions. $42 \div 3 = 14$.

15. 75% of 4 is the same as what percent of 9?

(A) 36

(B) 25

(C) 40

(D) $33\frac{1}{3}$

The correct answer is (D). 75% of 4 = 3; $3 = 33\frac{1}{3}\%$ of 9.

16. If $\frac{1}{2}$ cup of spinach contains 80 calories and the same amount of peas contains 300 calories, how many cups of spinach have the same caloric content as $\frac{2}{3}$ cup of peas?

(A) $\frac{2}{5}$

(B) $1\frac{1}{3}$

(C) 2

(D) $2\frac{1}{2}$

The correct answer is (D).

$\frac{1}{2}$ cup spinach = 80 calories

$\frac{1}{2}$ cup peas = 300 calories

1 cup peas = 600 calories

$\frac{2}{3}$ cup peas = 400 calories

$400 \div 80 = 5$ half-cups of spinach

$= 2\frac{1}{2}$ cups of spinach

Essay

Below is a typical essay topic. You are allowed 30 minutes to organize your thoughts, prepare an outline, and write, proofread, and edit a legible essay. Only the final copy will be scored.

Topic: If you could spend an afternoon with any author living or dead, with whom would you spend it? What would you talk about?

Example of a well-written essay.

If I could spend an afternoon with any author, I would have a wonderful conversation with Jules Verne. I think of Jules Verne as the father of science fiction. We would talk about his books and why they make such good reading. I would tell him how much of his fiction has become fact. Then we would probably talk about recent science fiction and about the latest scientific and technological advances. Perhaps we would predict future developments.

The first book I would mention is my favorite, *Twenty Thousand Leagues Under the Sea*. I would ask Mr. Verne how he thought up the book and would tell him how much I admire his works and how I respect his imagination. Then I would tell him about submarines and submarine warfare and would describe all the deep sea explorations that I know about. It is hard to predict a conversation in advance, but *Around the World in Eighty Days* would certainly be a good next topic, and we might well consume the remainder of the afternoon with discussion of modern travel and of all the countries and cultures that can be visited today.

No conversation with Jules Verne could conclude without mention of modern science fiction and of how predictive it might be. I wonder what Jules Verne would think of *Star Trek*. Finally I would tell him about space exploration, moon landings, satellites, and all the exciting space work that is unfolding.

The prospect of a conversation with Jules Verne is very appealing. Even though I know it cannot happen, I am thinking of more and more things I would like to discuss with him. What a stimulating afternoon it would be.

SUMMING IT UP

- The ISEE is a multiple-choice exam testing verbal reasoning, quantitative reasoning, reading comprehension, and mathematics achievement. The ISEE also requires you to write an essay.

- There is no penalty for a wrong answer; you should guess if you are not sure.

- The ISEE is offered at two levels: a middle-level exam is given to candidates for grades 7 and 8, and an upper-level exam is given to students applying for grades 9 through 12.

Test-Taking Techniques

OVERVIEW

- **What to expect when you take the exam**
- **Tips for answering questions**
- **Summing it up**

No test preparation book would be complete without a rundown of surefire test-taking techniques. Some of the techniques and tips listed here are common sense, but it never hurts to be reminded. For example, you should always assemble your materials the night before the exam, get a good night's sleep, get up early enough so that you don't need to rush, and eat breakfast. Here are some more tips:

- The only materials you need to bring to your exam are a few sharpened #2 pencils with clean erasers, positive identification, and your admission ticket (if you were issued one).

- Unless you were expressly instructed to bring a calculator, do not bring one to your exam. Calculators are not permitted on most high school entrance exams.

- It is important to wear a watch even though the room will most likely have a clock. The clock might not be conveniently located to keep track of time. If calculators are not allowed, be sure that your watch is not a calculator watch, because all calculator watches will be confiscated for the duration of the exam. If your watch has an alarm, be sure to turn it off.

- Enter the room early enough to choose a comfortable seat. After you're settled, relax. You'll concentrate more and perform better on the test if you're relaxed and comfortable. Besides, you studied hard for the exam, so what do you have to worry about, right?

WHAT TO EXPECT WHEN YOU TAKE THE EXAM

The first thing you will do in the exam room is fill out forms. You will be given detailed instructions for this procedure. Listen, read, and follow the directions; filling out forms is not timed, so don't rush. The exam will not begin until everyone has finished.

Next, the administrator will give you general instructions for taking the exam. You will be told how to recognize the stop and start signals. You will also find out what to do if you have a problem, such as all your pencils breaking or you find a page missing from your test booklet. Pay attention to the instructions. If you have any questions, ask them before the test begins.

chapter 6

When the signal is given, open your test booklet and read:

- **Read** all directions carefully. The directions will probably be very similar to those in this book, but don't take anything for granted. Test-makers do periodically change the exams.

- **Read** every word of every question. Be alert for little words that might have a big effect on your answer—words such as *not, most, all, every,* and *except.*

- **Read** all of the choices before you select an answer. It is statistically true that the most errors are made when the correct answer is the last choice given. Too many people mark the first answer that seems correct without reading through all of the choices to find out which answer is best.

TIPS FOR ANSWERING QUESTIONS

One of the best test tips we can offer is this: Try to answer every question on the exam, especially if you're running out of time. If you answer every question—even if you guess wildly—you are more likely to earn a high score. (The TACHS and the SSAT are exceptions to this rule. Remember that there is a penalty for wrong answers on these tests, so an educated guess can help, while a wild guess might not.) There is no penalty for wrong answers on the COOP, HSPT, or ISEE, so even a wild guess gives you a 20 or 25 percent chance for credit! Here are some basic tips for making an educated guess.

- If you're uncertain as to the answer to a question, guess—you can always mark the question and return to it for another try later if you have the time.

- An educated guess is worth more than a random guess. To make an educated guess, look carefully at the question and eliminate any answers that you are sure are wrong. Chances are that you can spot some obviously wrong answers among the choices to vocabulary, reading, and language questions. You will probably find some of the choices to math questions to be so far off as to make you chuckle. When it boils right down to it, you have a better chance of guessing correctly when you have three options instead of four or five. Your odds improve even more if you can guess between two choices.

- Keep alert for the moment during the exam when time is about to run out. In those last few seconds, pick one response—preferably not the first, because the first answer tends to be the correct one less often than the others—and mark all remaining blanks on your answer sheet with that same answer. By the law of averages, you should pick up a free point or two.

Another way to make sure you do as well as you can on the exam is to make sure that you don't lose any points through carelessness. Here's a list of eleven suggestions that apply to any entrance exam, including the practice exams you'll take later in Part IV.

1 Mark your answers by completely blackening the answer space of your choice. Be sure not to make any marks outside the lines.

2 Mark only **one** answer for each question, even if you think that more than one answer is correct. If you mark more than one answer, you lose all credit for that question.

3 If you change your mind, erase the answer completely. Leave no doubt as to which answer you mean.

4 Answer every question in the right place on the answer sheet. Make sure that the number of the answer blank matches the number of the question you are answering. You could lose a lot of time if you have to go back and change a lot of answers.

5 Don't spend too much time on any question, even if it poses an interesting challenge. Pick an answer and move on. You can always mark the question in your test booklet and go back to it later if time permits.

6 You are not required to answer every question; however, if you do skip one, **be sure to skip its answer space.** Otherwise, you might throw off your entire answer sheet. For that reason, it's safer to guess than to skip. Just mark the guesses in your test booklet so that you can go back and deliberate some more if you have time.

7 If you use scratch paper (you may on the HSPT but not on the COOP), be sure to mark the answer on the answer sheet. Only the answer sheet is scored; the test booklet and the scratch paper are not.

8 Stay alert. Getting a good night's sleep the night before and eating breakfast on the morning of the test will help you to be alert.

9 If you don't finish a section before the time is up, don't worry. Few people can actually answer every question. If you are accurate, you might earn a high score even without finishing every test section.

10 Don't let your performance on a section affect your performance on any other part of the exam. For example, if you don't think you did very well on mathematics, forget about that section after you are finished and start on the next section. Worrying about a previous section will cause you a lot of stress.

11 Check and recheck. If you finish any part before the time is up, go back and check to be sure that each question is answered in the right space and that there is only one answer for each question. Return to the difficult questions and rethink them.

SUMMING IT UP

- Always assemble everything you will need the night before the exam. You will need a few #2 pencils and a watch (calculator watches are not permitted). Don't bring a calculator unless you have been instructed to do so.

- Get a good night's sleep and get up early enough so you don't have to rush, you can eat breakfast, and you will be sure to arrive at the testing center early. Enter the room early enough to find a comfortable seat and relax.

- **READ.** Read all of the directions carefully, read every word of every question, and read all of the choices before selecting an answer.

- **PRACTICE.** Practice all of the question-answering tips in this chapter when you study and when you take the practice exams. This way, they will come as second nature when you take the exam.

PART II
VERBAL SKILLS

CHAPTER 7   Synonyms

CHAPTER 8   Antonyms

CHAPTER 9   Analogies

CHAPTER 10   Verbal Logic

CHAPTER 11   Reading

CHAPTER 12   Spelling

CHAPTER 13   Punctuation and
             Capitalization

CHAPTER 14   English Usage

CHAPTER 15   Language Composition
             and Expression

Synonyms

OVERVIEW

- **Tips for answering synonym questions**
- **Summing it up**

Synonym questions test your understanding of words. You are asked to choose another word that has the same, or nearly the same, meaning as the given word. On the HSPT, synonyms are tested in the Verbal Skills section and the Reading section under Vocabulary. On the TACHS, synonyms are tested in the Reading section under Vocabulary. Each exam may indicate the synonym in a different fashion. For example, some exams will identify the word they want you to match by italicizing or capitalizing the word, then ask you to choose a synonym from the answer choices. Other exams will use the word in a sentence, usually identifying the synonym in question by italicizing, underlining, or capitalizing the word, and then you must select a matching synonym from the answer choices. For example:

> The surface of the *placid* lake was smooth as glass.
>
> **(A)** cold
>
> **(B)** muddy
>
> **(C)** deep
>
> **(D)** calm
>
> **The correct answer is (D).** In this example, the word *calm* is the correct choice. As you can see, the nice thing about a sentence example is that it might give you contextual clues that make it easier to figure out the synonym's meaning. In the example, when you read that the lake was "smooth as glass," you could infer that, although the lake might have been muddy, deep, or cold, it definitely must have been calm. That made choice (D) the best choice for this question.

TIPS FOR ANSWERING SYNONYM QUESTIONS

Here's a tip to use when choosing the answer for a synonym question: If the given word is in sentence, you should always try substituting the choices in the place of the indicated word. This process can help you find and check your answer.

chapter 7

Sometimes the italicized or underlined word has multiple meanings, which can make the contextual clues of the sentence even more important. Consider the following question:

The camel is sometimes called the ship of the *desert*.

(A) abandon

(B) ice cream

(C) sandy wasteland

(D) leave

The correct answer is (C). Here, the sentence is absolutely necessary to the definition of the word. Without the sentence, you would not know whether the word *desert* is to be pronounced *de-sert'*, which means to leave or to abandon, or *des'-ert*, which means a sandy wasteland. If you are not sure of your spelling, the sentence can also spare you the confusion of *desert* with *dessert*, which is the last course of a meal.

On the other hand, the phrase or sentence might be of little or no use at all in helping you to choose the synonym. The sentence might help you to determine the part of speech of the indicated word, but not its meaning, as in:

The robbery suspect had a *sallow* complexion.

(A) ruddy

(B) pale

(C) pock-marked

(D) freckled

The correct answer is (B). The sentence shows you the proper use of the word *sallow*. It is an adjective used to describe a complexion, but the sentence gives no clue that *sallow* means *pale*. You either know the meaning of the word or you must guess. When the given word isn't part of a sentence, or if the sentence doesn't help define the word, you might have to guess. But before you guess blindly, you need to make sure there are no other clues that could lead you to the correct answer.

Perhaps you have seen the word used but were never sure what it meant. Look carefully. Do you know the meaning of any part of the word? If you can associate the word with something else you've read or you know, you might be able to find the answer. An example:

Remedial most nearly means

(A) reading.

(B) slow.

(C) corrective.

(D) special.

The correct answer is (C). Your association is probably "remedial reading." That association can help you, but be careful! *Remedial* does not mean *reading*. *Remedial* is an adjective, and *reading* is the noun it modifies. Slow readers might receive remedial reading instruction in special classes that are intended to correct bad reading skills. Do you see the word *remedy* in *remedial?* You know that a *remedy* is a *cure* or a *correction* for an ailment. If you combine all the information you now have, you can choose *corrective* as the word that most nearly means *remedial*.

Sometimes you can find the correct answer to a synonym question by eliminating the answers that you know are wrong. If you can eliminate even one of the answers, you have a 33 percent chance of choosing the correct answer. Eliminate two incorrect answers, and you have a 50/50 chance of choosing the right answer from the two remaining choices. For example:

Infamous most nearly means

(A) well known.

(B) poor.

(C) disgraceful.

(D) young.

The correct answer is (C). The first word you see when you look at *infamous* is *famous*. *Famous*, of course, means well known. Because *in*, meaning *not*, is a negative prefix, you should be looking for a negative word as the meaning of *infamous*. With that in mind, you can eliminate choice (A). There is no choice meaning *not famous*, so you must look for negative fame. A person who is not well known might or might not be poor. You should carefully consider the other choices before choosing *poor*, choice (B). Choice (D), *young*, probably can be eliminated for the same reasons. Though many young people are not famous, the terms aren't necessarily synonymous. *Disgrace* is a negative kind of *fame*. A person who behaves *disgracefully* is well known for his bad behavior; he is *infamous*. Therefore, choice (C) becomes the best answer for this question.

All of the previous suggestions can help you use clues to determine the meaning of words and find their synonyms. But many synonym questions might give you no clues at all. The best way to minimize the number of synonym questions that you simply cannot answer is to learn as many vocabulary words as you can. One way to increase your vocabulary is to work with a dictionary when preparing for your exam. Try to read as much as you can during the time before your exam. When you run into a word that's totally unfamiliar to you, look it up. If you run across a word you don't know while doing the practice exams, circle the word and look it up later. Look up words you find in the reading passages, new words from among answer choices, words you find in the explanations, and words you meet in the study chapters. Looking up words for yourself is the best way to learn them.

If you understand every word in this book, you are well on your way toward a broad-based vocabulary and should be able to handle not only the synonym questions, but the other verbal questions as well.

Now try the following exercises. Answer keys and explanations follow Exercise 2.

EXERCISES: SYNONYMS

Exercise 1

Directions: In the following questions, choose the word that means the same as or about the same as the underlined word.

1. a display of affluence
   (A) power
   (B) wealth
   (C) glibness
   (D) junction

2. the gloss of her lips
   (A) goblet
   (B) shadow
   (C) brightness
   (D) blush

3. a devout monk
   (A) reverent
   (B) lacking
   (C) growing
   (D) lonely

4. a thrilling encounter
   (A) meeting
   (B) bar
   (C) ledge
   (D) spaceship

5. to concede one's guilt
   (A) hide
   (B) invent
   (C) admit
   (D) contradict

6. to emerge from hiding
   (A) bury
   (B) come out
   (C) join
   (D) show anger

7. to teem with humanity
   (A) abound
   (B) play
   (C) group
   (D) adolescent

8. to permit to attend
   (A) discourage
   (B) allow
   (C) drive
   (D) card

9. to abate the fury
   (A) minnow
   (B) grow
   (C) formula
   (D) ebb

10. a recurrent theme
    (A) refined
    (B) resultant
    (C) electrifying
    (D) returning

11. on the <u>verge</u> of disaster
    - (A) boat
    - (B) force
    - (C) brink
    - (D) violence

12. to <u>ponder</u> deeply
    - (A) peruse
    - (B) think
    - (C) delay
    - (D) reveal

13. to <u>aspire</u> for success
    - (A) hope
    - (B) breathe
    - (C) exhaust
    - (D) plot

14. an <u>era</u> of apathy
    - (A) mistake
    - (B) war
    - (C) place
    - (D) age

15. <u>temerity</u> to speak out
    - (A) fear
    - (B) nerve
    - (C) flutter
    - (D) cowardice

16. a <u>feat</u> of skill
    - (A) body part
    - (B) celebration
    - (C) big meal
    - (D) achievement

17. <u>zest</u> for adventure
    - (A) relish
    - (B) fluency
    - (C) garment
    - (D) haste

18. a <u>plaintive</u> sound
    - (A) musical
    - (B) famous
    - (C) mournful
    - (D) patient

19. to view with <u>consternation</u>
    - (A) dismay
    - (B) telescope
    - (C) relief
    - (D) pretense

20. <u>flagrant</u> disobedience
    - (A) disguised
    - (B) glaring
    - (C) repeated
    - (D) perfumed

exercises

Exercise 2

Directions: Choose the word or phrase that has the same or nearly the same meaning as the underlined word or group of words.

1. The <u>veracity</u> of her story is without doubt.
   (A) persistence
   (B) truthfulness
   (C) poetry
   (D) horror

2. The drawings were completely <u>identical</u>.
   (A) twin
   (B) unclear
   (C) breathtaking
   (D) same

3. In our cellar, we <u>accumulate</u> old clothes.
   (A) affirm
   (B) donate
   (C) refurbish
   (D) collect

4. This legislation will <u>transform</u> the railroad system.
   (A) improve
   (B) electrify
   (C) change
   (D) sell

5. Candy will <u>gratify</u> the baby.
   (A) satisfy
   (B) fatten
   (C) excite
   (D) teach

6. The arena was <u>girded</u> with ribbons.
   (A) gay
   (B) established
   (C) decorated
   (D) encircled

7. How shall we <u>quell</u> the rebellion?
   (A) begin
   (B) cushion
   (C) crush
   (D) fire

8. His face looked <u>pale and sickly</u>.
   (A) wan
   (B) gabled
   (C) paltry
   (D) ponderous

9. The father was <u>stern and impersonal</u> with his children.
   (A) morose
   (B) gruff
   (C) opinionated
   (D) endeared

10. He was regarded as an <u>outcast</u> by his community.
    (A) paragon
    (B) parasite
    (C) pariah
    (D) pagan

11. Let us <u>hoist</u> the banner now.
    (A) raise
    (B) lower
    (C) wave
    (D) fold

12. The town took <u>drastic</u> measures to ensure its security.
    (A) well-informed
    (B) ill-advised
    (C) haphazard
    (D) extreme

13. The newscaster <u>alluded to</u> the weather forecast.
    - (A) changed
    - (B) complained about
    - (C) praised
    - (D) referred to

14. The strength of the cord <u>exceeds</u> government standards.
    - (A) surpasses
    - (B) equals
    - (C) challenges
    - (D) falls short of

15. The confused old gentleman was an <u>affable</u> soul.
    - (A) appetizing
    - (B) unappetizing
    - (C) foolish
    - (D) amiable

16. I wish that you would stop <u>beating around the bush</u>.
    - (A) running in circles
    - (B) avoiding the subject
    - (C) sweeping the driveway
    - (D) repeating the same thing over and over

17. I generally accept Jim's pronouncements with <u>a grain of salt</u>.
    - (A) some question
    - (B) criticism
    - (C) pleasure
    - (D) relief

18. That explanation is little more than <u>an old wives' tale</u>.
    - (A) a deliberate falsehood
    - (B) a half-truth
    - (C) feminist propaganda
    - (D) folklore

19. The medicine man shared his <u>tried and true</u> remedy with me.
    - (A) new and unusual
    - (B) tested and proven
    - (C) experimental
    - (D) unorthodox but effective

20. You should not <u>look a gift horse in the mouth</u>.
    - (A) question authority
    - (B) quibble over details
    - (C) expose yourself to danger
    - (D) be suspicious of good fortune

ANSWER KEYS AND EXPLANATIONS

Exercise 1

1. B	5. C	9. D	13. A	17. A
2. C	6. B	10. D	14. D	18. C
3. A	7. A	11. C	15. B	19. A
4. A	8. B	12. B	16. D	20. B

1. **The correct answer is (B).** *Affluence* is wealth. *Influence* is power; *confluence* is junction.

2. **The correct answer is (C).** *Gloss* is brightness, polish, or shine.

3. **The correct answer is (A).** *Devout* means reverent, religious, or pious.

4. **The correct answer is (A).** An *encounter* is a face-to-face meeting.

5. **The correct answer is (C).** To *concede* is to admit or to acknowledge.

6. **The correct answer is (B).** To *emerge* is to come out. The word *emerge* is almost opposite to the word *merge*, which means join.

7. **The correct answer is (A).** To *teem* is to abound or to overflow.

8. **The correct answer is (B).** The word *permit*, pronounced *per-mit'*, means allow. If the word were pronounced *per'-mit*, it would mean license (which is not offered as a choice), but in no event would it mean drive or card.

9. **The correct answer is (D).** *Abate* means to subside, diminish, or ebb.

10. **The correct answer is (D).** That which is *recurrent* returns from time to time.

11. **The correct answer is (C).** *Verge* means brink or threshold.

12. **The correct answer is (B).** To *ponder* is to think or to consider. *Peruse* means read.

13. **The correct answer is (A).** To *aspire* is to hope or to desire. To *breathe* is to respire.

14. **The correct answer is (D).** An *era* is an age or period. Read carefully to avoid careless mistakes such as reading *err* or *area*.

15. **The correct answer is (B).** *Temerity* is audacity or nerve. *Timorousness* is timidity, fear, or cowardice.

16. **The correct answer is (D).** A *feat* is an achievement. Beware of homonyms when choosing synonyms.

17. **The correct answer is (A).** *Zest* means relish or gusto.

18. **The correct answer is (C).** *Plaintive* means mournful or melancholy.

19. **The correct answer is (A).** *Consternation* is amazement or dismay that throws one into confusion.

20. **The correct answer is (B).** *Flagrant* means glaring or conspicuously objectionable. The word meaning *perfumed* is *fragrant*.

Exercise 2

1. B	5. A	9. B	13. D	17. A
2. D	6. D	10. C	14. A	18. D
3. D	7. C	11. A	15. D	19. B
4. C	8. A	12. D	16. B	20. D

1. **The correct answer is (B).** *Veracity* is truthfulness or accuracy.

2. **The correct answer is (D).** *Identical* means same. Identical twins are genetically the same.

3. **The correct answer is (D).** To *accumulate* is to collect or to amass.

4. **The correct answer is (C).** To *transform* means to change. A *transformer* converts variations of current in a primary circuit into variations of voltage and current in a secondary circuit. The word *transform* in itself has nothing to do with electricity. One might hope that when the railroad system is *transformed,* it will be improved, but the change in itself is no guarantee.

5. **The correct answer is (A).** To *gratify* is to indulge, to please, or to satisfy.

6. **The correct answer is (D).** *Girded* means encircled.

7. **The correct answer is (C).** To *quell* is to put down, to suppress, or to crush.

8. **The correct answer is (A).** *Wan* means pale, sickly, or feeble.

9. **The correct answer is (B).** *Gruff* means rough or stern.

10. **The correct answer is (C).** A *pariah* is an outcast. A *paragon* is a model of perfection. A *parasite* lives off others and might well become an outcast, but the words are not synonymous. A *pagan* is a heathen. The *pagan* might be cast out by the religious community, but again, the words are not synonyms.

11. **The correct answer is (A).** To *hoist* is to raise or to lift.

12. **The correct answer is (D).** *Drastic* means extreme or severe.

13. **The correct answer is (D).** To *allude* is to make indirect reference or to refer.

14. **The correct answer is (A).** To *exceed* is to surpass.

15. **The correct answer is (D).** *Affable* means pleasant, gracious, sociable, and amiable.

16. **The correct answer is (B).** *Beating around the bush* is talking about irrelevant topics and raising side issues to avoid talking about or committing oneself on a particular subject.

17. **The correct answer is (A).** When one takes something with *a grain of salt,* one does not accept it at face value but questions details, motives, or conclusions.

18. **The correct answer is (D).** *An old wives' tale* is a story or explanation that has been handed "from woman to woman" as an oral tradition until it becomes folklore.

19. **The correct answer is (B).** *Tried and true* means tested and proven.

20. **The correct answer is (D).** Quite literally, the expression means that because one does not know the disposition of a gift horse, one should not risk sticking one's head in its mouth; furthermore, accept a gift as a gift without questioning its value (checking the quality of its teeth). In other words, be happy with what you get and don't be suspicious of good fortune.

answers exercises

SUMMING IT UP

- If the given word is in a sentence, you should try substituting the answer choices in the place of the indicated word.

- When the given word is in a sentence, there are several ways to select the best answer. Look for contextual clues to determine which meaning of the word is being used. Determine which part of speech the word is and look for an answer choice of the same part of speech.

- When you don't know the meaning, try to take apart the word. Look for prefixes, suffixes, and the root word.

- Eliminate answers that you know are wrong and concentrate on the others.

Antonyms

chapter 8

OVERVIEW

- **Tips for answering antonym questions**
- **Summing it up**

Antonym questions are similar to synonym questions in that they test your understanding of words. However, antonym questions are a bit trickier because they challenge you to demonstrate your mental flexibility as well as your verbal skills. On the HSPT, antonym questions appear on the Verbal Skills portion of the exam.

The task in an antonym question is to define the indicated word and pick its opposite. That sounds simple enough, right? Here's why it gets tricky. Where there is no true opposite, you must choose the word or phrase that is most nearly opposite. Where there appears to be two or more opposites, you must choose the best opposite. You must guard against choosing an associated word or phrase that is different in meaning but is not a true opposite. After struggling to define a word, you must then take care to choose its *antonym,* not its *synonym* (the word or phrase that is most similar in meaning).

Let's try an example. Suppose the test question looks like this:

Inaudible means the *opposite* of
- **(A)** invisible.
- **(B)** bright.
- **(C)** loud.
- **(D)** clear.

You do not know the meaning of the word *inaudible*, but you might recognize some of the word's parts. You might know that the prefix *in-* typically means *not*. You also might recognize a part of audio in the word, and you know that the *audio* of your TV is the sound. You might also see *-able* in *-ible* and thereby reconstruct not soundable or not heard.

BEWARE! This is the point at which your reasoning can easily lead you astray. If you associate the word with your TV, you might think, "The opposite of not heard is not seen or invisible, choice (A)." Wrong. These are not true opposites. Or you might associate not heard with not seen and choose choice (B), *bright,* as the opposite of not seen. Wrong again. Or you might think of inaudible as hard to hear and choose choice (D), *clear.* Clear would not be a bad answer, but choice (C), *loud*, is better and is indeed the best answer. The best opposite of inaudible is loud. You can now see how tricky finding the answer can be! To find the right answer to an antonym question, you need to be certain that you remember exactly what you're looking for as you reject or choose an answer choice.

TIPS FOR ANSWERING ANTONYM QUESTIONS

Thankfully, there is a sound approach to handling antonym questions if you're not sure of the correct answer. After reading the word and its four possible answers very carefully, run through the following possibilities.

Possibility #1

You know the meaning of the word, but no answer choice seems correct.

- Perhaps you misread the word. Are there other words that look similar to the word in the question? For example, did you read *revelation* for *revaluation* or *compliment* for *complement*?

- Perhaps you read the word correctly but accented the wrong syllable. Some words have alternative pronunciations with vastly different meanings. Remember *de-sert'* and *des'-ert?*

- Perhaps you are dealing with a single word that can be used as two different parts of speech and therefore has two entirely unrelated meanings. A *moor* (noun) is a boggy wasteland. To *moor* (verb) is to secure a ship or a boat in place. The proper noun *Moor* refers to the Moslem conquerors of Spain.

- Perhaps the word can appear as a number of parts of speech with numerous meanings and shades of meaning within each of these. *Fancy* (noun) can mean inclination, love, notion, whim, taste, judgment, or imagination. *Fancy* (verb) can mean to like, to imagine, and to think. *Fancy* (adjective) can mean whimsical, ornamental, and extravagant. Your task is to choose from among the four choices one word or phrase that is opposite to *one* of these meanings of the word *fancy*.

Possibility #2

You do not know the meaning of the word, but it appears to contain prefix, suffix, or root clues. Examine those clues. For example, the word *inaudible* uses the prefix *in-*, which means *not*, so look for the best opposite of "not audible."

Possibility #3

You do not know the meaning of the word and can see no clues, but you have a feeling that the word has some specific connotation, be it sinister, gloomy, or positive. Play your hunch. Choose a word with the opposite connotation.

Possibility #4

You are stumped. There is no penalty for guessing on the HSPT exam, so when all else fails, guess. If you can eliminate one or more of the choices, you improve the odds of guessing correctly. Eliminate choices as you can, choose from the remaining options, and move on. There's no need to waste time on a question for which you cannot figure out the answer.

Now try the following exercises using the tactics outlined. Answer keys and explanations follow Exercise 2.

EXERCISES: ANTONYMS

Exercise 1

Directions: Choose the best answer.

1. Accelerate means the *opposite* of
   (A) stop.
   (B) slow.
   (C) quicken.
   (D) hasten.

2. Docile means the *opposite* of
   (A) active.
   (B) health.
   (C) probable.
   (D) teachable.

3. Candor means the *opposite* of
   (A) frankness.
   (B) doubt.
   (C) deception.
   (D) enthusiasm.

4. Nomadic means the *opposite* of
   (A) secret.
   (B) anonymous.
   (C) stationary.
   (D) famous.

5. Humble means the *opposite* of
   (A) simple.
   (B) just.
   (C) hurt.
   (D) proud.

6. Defy means the *opposite* of
   (A) desire.
   (B) embrace.
   (C) fight.
   (D) abscond.

7. Gorge means the *opposite* of
   (A) duck.
   (B) diet.
   (C) stuff.
   (D) valley.

8. Curtail means the *opposite* of
   (A) curry.
   (B) open.
   (C) shorten.
   (D) extend.

9. Initiate means the *opposite* of
   (A) instruct.
   (B) begin.
   (C) terminate.
   (D) invade.

10. Grant means the *opposite* of
    (A) confiscate.
    (B) money.
    (C) land.
    (D) swamp.

11. Clamor means the *opposite* of
    (A) ugliness.
    (B) beauty.
    (C) silence.
    (D) dishonor.

12. Rouse means the *opposite* of
    (A) lull.
    (B) alarm.
    (C) complain.
    (D) weep.

13. Credible means the *opposite* of
    (A) believable.
    (B) unbelievable.
    (C) honorable.
    (D) dishonorable.

14. Thorough means the *opposite* of
    (A) around.
    (B) circumvented.
    (C) sloppy.
    (D) slovenly.

15. Wooden means the *opposite* of
    (A) iron.
    (B) slippery.
    (C) rubbery.
    (D) green.

Exercise 2

Directions: Choose the best answer.

1. Succumb means the *opposite* of
   (A) arrive.
   (B) yield.
   (C) eat.
   (D) conquer.

2. Divert means the *opposite* of
   (A) instruct.
   (B) include.
   (C) bore.
   (D) amuse.

3. Assent means the *opposite* of
   (A) agree.
   (B) disagree.
   (C) climb.
   (D) fall.

4. Diminish means the *opposite* of
   (A) lessen.
   (B) begin.
   (C) complete.
   (D) expand.

5. Brazen means the *opposite* of
   (A) frozen.
   (B) humble.
   (C) rustproof.
   (D) leaky.

6. Intent means the *opposite* of
   (A) alfresco.
   (B) busy.
   (C) uninterested.
   (D) shy.

7. Smother means the *opposite* of
   (A) cuddle.
   (B) expel.
   (C) aerate.
   (D) rescue.

8. Lavish means the *opposite* of
   (A) filthy.
   (B) elegant.
   (C) squander.
   (D) conserve.

9. Aloof means the *opposite* of
   (A) sociable.
   (B) humble.
   (C) public.
   (D) ignorant.

10. Elated means the *opposite* of
    (A) on time.
    (B) tardy.
    (C) ideal.
    (D) depressed.

11. Furnish means the *opposite* of
    (A) dress.
    (B) decorate.
    (C) remove.
    (D) polish.

12. Ostracize means the *opposite* of
    (A) include.
    (B) shun.
    (C) hide.
    (D) delight.

13. Exorbitant means the *opposite* of
    (A) priceless.
    (B) worthless.
    (C) reasonable.
    (D) straight.

14. Chastise means the *opposite* of
    (A) dirty.
    (B) cleanse.
    (C) praise.
    (D) straighten.

15. Profit means the *opposite* of
    (A) gain.
    (B) money.
    (C) suffer.
    (D) disgust.

exercises

ANSWER KEYS AND EXPLANATIONS

Exercise 1

1. B	4. C	7. B	10. A	13. B
2. A	5. D	8. D	11. C	14. C
3. C	6. B	9. C	12. A	15. C

1. **The correct answer is (B).** To *accelerate* is to quicken or to hasten. Its best opposite is to *slow*. *Accelerate* implies that the object was already in motion. *Stop* would be the opposite if the original word had meant *to put into motion*.

2. **The correct answer is (A).** *Docile* means calm and easily led. Of the choices offered, its best opposite is *active*.

3. **The correct answer is (C).** *Candor* is frankness; its opposite is *deception*.

4. **The correct answer is (C).** *Nomadic* means wandering; its opposite is *stationary*, staying in one place. The word *nomadic* has nothing to do with names.

5. **The correct answer is (D).** *Humble* means meek and modest. Its best opposite is *proud*.

6. **The correct answer is (B).** To *defy* is to challenge; its opposite is *embrace*.

7. **The correct answer is (B).** To *gorge* oneself is to overeat; the opposite is to *diet*.

8. **The correct answer is (D).** To *curtail* is to shorten; the opposite is to *extend*.

9. **The correct answer is (C).** To *initiate* is to begin; its opposite is to *terminate* or to *end*.

10. **The correct answer is (A).** To *grant* is to give; its opposite is to *confiscate*.

11. **The correct answer is (C).** *Clamor* is noise; its opposite is *silence*. You must read carefully. *Clamor* is not *glamour*.

12. **The correct answer is (A).** To *rouse* is to awaken; to *lull* is to soothe and to cause to sleep.

13. **The correct answer is (B).** *Credible* means believable; its opposite is *unbelievable*.

14. **The correct answer is (C).** *Thorough* means careful and complete; its opposite is *sloppy*, which means careless and inattentive to detail. *Slovenly* also means careless, but it also implies dirty, so sloppy is the better opposite.

15. **The correct answer is (C).** *Wooden* means stiff and unbending; its opposite, *rubbery*, means flexible.

Exercise 2

1. D	4. D	7. C	10. D	13. C
2. C	5. B	8. D	11. C	14. C
3. B	6. C	9. A	12. A	15. C

1. **The correct answer is (D).** To *succumb* is to yield or to give in; its opposite is to *conquer.*

2. **The correct answer is (C).** To *divert* is to amuse (think of *diversion*); its opposite is to *bore*. To divert also means *to change the direction of,* but no opposite to this meaning is offered.

3. **The correct answer is (B).** To *assent* is to agree; its opposite is to *disagree. Assent* is in no way related to *ascend* or *ascent.*

4. **The correct answer is (D).** To *diminish* is to lessen. Therefore, its opposite is *expand.*

5. **The correct answer is (B).** *Brazen* means bold or impudent; its opposite is *humble.*

6. **The correct answer is (C).** To be *intent* is to be engrossed or determined; the opposite is to be *uninterested.*

7. **The correct answer is (C).** To *smother* is to shut out all air; to *aerate* is to supply with air. Although the act of *smothering* might be reversed by rescuing, *aerate* is the more direct antonym.

8. **The correct answer is (D).** To *lavish* is to spend profusely or to squander; its opposite is to *conserve.*

9. **The correct answer is (A).** One who is *aloof* is distant or reserved; an opposite type of person is *sociable.*

10. **The correct answer is (D).** One who is *elated* is bursting with pride; its opposite is *depressed.*

11. **The correct answer is (C).** To *furnish* is to provide; its opposite is to *remove.*

12. **The correct answer is (A).** To *ostracize* is to shut out or to exclude; its opposite is to *include.*

13. **The correct answer is (C).** *Exorbitant* means excessive; its opposite is *reasonable.*

14. **The correct answer is (C).** To *chastise* is to scold; its opposite is to *praise.*

15. **The correct answer is (C).** To *profit* is to benefit; its opposite is to *suffer.*

answers exercises

SUMMING IT UP

- Antonym questions are trickier than synonym questions because they ask you to define the indicated word and choose its opposite—or the word or phrase that is most nearly opposite.

- When you think you know the meaning of the given word but can't find the answer, go back and check the following: Did you misread the word? Did you accent the wrong syllable? Can the word be used as two different parts of speech? Does the word have multiple meanings?

- If you don't know the meaning of the word, look for prefixes, suffixes, and root words. Be sure you are clear on the context and look for the opposite meaning.

- When you have to guess, try to eliminate some answer choices. Consider connotation and the part of speech.

Analogies

OVERVIEW

- **Tips for answering analogy questions**
- **Summing it up**

Verbal analogy questions test your ability to see a relationship between words and to apply that relationship to other words. It is a test of your ability to think things out clearly and logically. Analogies are tested on the COOP and on the HSPT.

Depending on the exam, verbal analogy questions might be presented in a number of different forms. In the HSPT exam, you are given two example words that are related to each other in a certain way. Then you are given a third word and four answer choices. The correct answer choice will have the same relationship to the third word as that shared by the example words. For example:

Man is to boy as woman is to

(A) child.

(B) sister.

(C) girl.

(D) offspring.

The correct answer is (C). Thus, the completed analogy reads "man is to boy as woman is to girl." A woman is an adult girl, just as a man is an adult boy.

The Analogies section on the COOP exam takes a different form, using pictures instead of words. After you have named the object in each picture, you must proceed as with a verbal analogy question, defining and completing the relationships. The Verbal Reasoning—Words section of the COOP exam uses yet another form for analogy questions. Here, you must define the relationship among three words and then complete a second group of three words, this time choosing the third word for the second group. Regardless of which form an analogy question might take, the task is always the same: Define relationships and then apply the relationships to different words.

TIPS FOR ANSWERING ANALOGY QUESTIONS

The first step in tackling an analogy question is to define the first set of words and determine their relationship. Most often you will know the meanings of both words (if you're not sure, make a guess and move on to the next step). Your next step will be to determine how those words are related. Define a specific relationship between the words. Here's an example: Suppose you are confronted with an analogy question that begins *brim* is to *hat*. *Brim* and *hat* are immediately associated in your mind; a *brim* is a part of a *hat*, so the relationship between the two is that of a part to the whole.

Now take a look at the third word in the analogy question and the four choices available. By process of elimination, you must find among the choices a word that bears the same relationship to the third word that the second word bears to the first. The analogy question would look like this:

Brim is to hat as hand is to

(A) glove.

(B) finger.

(C) foot.

(D) arm.

The correct answer is (D). To figure out the answer, consider each answer choice in turn. *Hand* is certainly associated with choice (A), *glove*, but in no way is a hand part of a glove. *Hand* and choice (B), *finger*, are certainly associated and, indeed, a *finger* is part of a *hand*. But BEWARE! Reexamine the relationship of the first two words: *Brim* is a part of *hat*, or in other words, *hat* is the whole of which *brim* is a part. The relationship in choice (B) is the reverse of the relationship of the first two words. *Hand* is the whole and *finger* is the part. Your answer must maintain the same relationship in the same sequence as the original pair.

The relationship of *hand* and choice (C), *foot*, is only one of association, not of part to whole. This answer is no more likely to be correct than choice (A). In fact, because you have found two answers that have equal chances of being incorrect, you now know that neither of them is the answer you are looking for. There must be a best answer.

A *hand* is part of an *arm* in the same way that a *brim* is part of a *hat*, or the *arm* is the whole of which a *hand* is a part in the same way that *hat* is the whole of which a *brim* is the part. When you've determined this, you know that choice (D) is the *best* answer.

So the process is the following five steps:

1 Define the initial terms.

2 Describe the initial relationship.

3 Eliminate incorrect answers.

4 Refine the initial relationship, if necessary.

5 Choose the best of the remaining answer choices.

Usually your biggest problem in solving an analogy question will be that of narrowing your choices down to the *best* answer. Sometimes, however, your difficulty will be in finding even one correct answer. If this happens, you might have to shift gears and completely redefine your initial relationship. Let's look at another analogy example.

Consider an analogy that begins *letter* is to *word*. Initially, you will probably think, "A letter is part of a word; therefore, the relationship is that of part to whole." If the relationship of the third word to any of the choices is also part to whole, then all is well. However, suppose the question looks like this:

> Letter is to word as song is to
>
> **(A)** story.
>
> **(B)** music.
>
> **(C)** note.
>
> **(D)** orchestra.
>
> **The correct answer is (C).** Three of the choices offer an association relationship, so, clearly, you must go along with a more refined definition of the relationship. None of the choices offers a whole of which a song might be a part (such as an opera). Therefore, you must return to the original pair of words and consider other relationships between letter and word. If letter is not "letter of the alphabet," but rather "written communication," then a word is part of a letter and the relationship of the first to the second is whole to part. Then the answer becomes clear: A song is the whole of which *note*, choice (C), is the part. The relationship of *song* and *note* is the same as that of *letter* and *word*.

Analogy questions are a real challenge and can even be fun. Following is a list of a few of the most common, very general relationships.

- Part to whole, e.g., *branch* to *tree*
- whole to part, e.g., *ocean* to *water*
- cause and effect, e.g., *germ* to *disease*
- effect and cause, e.g., *honors* to *study*
- association, e.g., *bat* to *ball*
- degree, e.g., *hut* to *mansion*
- sequence, e.g., *elementary* to *secondary*
- function, e.g., *teacher* to *student*
- characteristic, e.g., *wise* to *owl*
- antonym, e.g., *bad* to *good*
- synonym, e.g., *spring* to *jump*
- purpose, e.g., *mask* to *protection*

Analogy questions also offer many opportunities for errors if every answer is not given careful consideration. A few of the most common pitfalls to avoid are listed below.

- Reversal of sequence of the relationship:

TIP

Know the six most common analogy connections:
1. Characteristic
2. Purpose
3. Antonym
4. Part to whole
5. Whole to part
6. Degree

TIP

Turn the analogy pairs into sentences to help you see the connection. Then fit the answer pairs into the same sentence until you find the one that works best.

o   Part to whole is *not* the same as whole to part.

o   Cause to effect is *not* the same as effect to its cause.

o   Smaller to larger is *not* the same as larger to smaller.

o   Action to object is *not* the same as object to action.

- Confusion of relationship:

  o   Part to part (*geometry* to *calculus*) with part to whole (*algebra* to *mathematics*)

  o   Cause and effect (*fire* to *smoke*) with association (*man* to *woman*)

  o   Degree (*drizzle* to *downpour*) with antonyms (*dry* to *wet*)

  o   Association (*walk* to *limp*) with synonyms (*eat* to *consume*)

- Grammatical inconsistency: The grammatical relationship of the first two words must be retained throughout the analogy. A wrong analogy would be *imprisoned* is to *convict* as *cage* is to *parrot*. While the meaningful relationship exists, the analogy is not parallel in construction. A correct analogy of this sort would have to read *prison* is to *convict* as *cage* is to *parrot,* or *imprisoned* is to *convict* as *caged* is to *parrot.* In analogy questions, you have to create a pair that is grammatically consistent with the first pair, as well as meaningfully correct.

- Concentration on the meanings of words instead of on their relationships: In this type of error, you see *feathers* to *beak,* and you think *bird* instead of part-to-part relationship. Then, you choose as your answer *wing* to *bird* instead of *wing* to *foot*.

Remember: The key to answering verbal analogy questions lies in the relationship between the first two words!

If you are having trouble determining the relationship between the words of the initial pair, you might find it useful to mentally reverse their order. If this works, just remember to mentally reverse the order of the third and fourth terms as well, to maintain parallelism in your answer.

Now try the following verbal analogies exercises and study the answer key and explanations that follow the exercises.

EXERCISES: ANALOGIES

Exercise 1

Directions: In the following questions, the first two words are related to each other in a certain way. The third and fourth words must be related to each other in the same way. Choose from among the four choices the word that is related to the third word in the same way that the second word is related to the first. The answers and explanations appear following Exercise 2.

1. Gasoline is to petroleum as sugar is to
   (A) sweet.
   (B) oil.
   (C) plant.
   (D) cane.

2. Fly is to spider as mouse is to
   (A) cat.
   (B) rat.
   (C) rodent.
   (D) trap.

3. Volcano is to crater as chimney is to
   (A) smoke.
   (B) fire.
   (C) flue.
   (D) stack.

4. Petal is to flower as fur is to
   (A) coat.
   (B) rabbit.
   (C) warm.
   (D) woman.

5. Retreat is to advance as timid is to
   (A) bold.
   (B) cowardly.
   (C) fearful.
   (D) shy.

6. Attorney is to trial as surgeon is to
   (A) doctor.
   (B) operation.
   (C) patient.
   (D) anesthesia.

7. Picture is to see as speech is to
   (A) view.
   (B) enunciate.
   (C) hear.
   (D) soliloquize.

8. Soprano is to high as bass is to
   (A) guitar.
   (B) bad.
   (C) low.
   (D) fish.

9. Addition is to addend as subtraction is to
   (A) difference.
   (B) sum.
   (C) subtrahend.
   (D) minus.

10. Obese is to eat as elected is to
    (A) advertise.
    (B) run.
    (C) count.
    (D) fraud.

11. Acute is to chronic as temporary is to
    - (A) persistent.
    - (B) sick.
    - (C) pretty.
    - (D) narrow.

12. Prostrate is to flat as vertical is to
    - (A) circular.
    - (B) horizontal.
    - (C) geometric.
    - (D) erect.

13. Chariot is to charioteer as automobile is to
    - (A) passenger.
    - (B) engine.
    - (C) motor.
    - (D) driver.

14. Team is to league as player is to
    - (A) piano.
    - (B) team.
    - (C) tournament.
    - (D) football.

15. Honor is to citation as speeding is to
    - (A) citation.
    - (B) hurry.
    - (C) race.
    - (D) stop.

Exercise 2

Directions: In the following questions, the first two words are related to each other in a certain way. The third and fourth words must be related to each other in the same way. Choose from among the four choices the word that is related to the third word in the same way that the second word is related to the first. The answers and explanations follow the answers for Exercise 1.

1. Net is to fisherman as gun is to
   - (A) bullet.
   - (B) policeman.
   - (C) deer.
   - (D) hunter.

2. Educated is to know as rich is to
   - (A) poor.
   - (B) wise.
   - (C) own.
   - (D) money.

3. Distracting is to noise as soothing is to
   - (A) medicine.
   - (B) music.
   - (C) volume.
   - (D) bleeding.

4. Year is to calendar as hour is to
   - (A) decade.
   - (B) minute.
   - (C) clock.
   - (D) month.

5. Father is to brother as mother is to
   - (A) daughter.
   - (B) sister.
   - (C) aunt.
   - (D) niece.

6. Words are to books as notes are to
   - (A) songs.
   - (B) letters.
   - (C) pianos.
   - (D) fragrances.

7. Pungent is to odor as shrill is to
   - (A) whisper.
   - (B) sound.
   - (C) piercing.
   - (D) shriek.

8. Present is to birthday as reward is to
   - (A) accomplishment.
   - (B) medal.
   - (C) punishment.
   - (D) money.

9. Mouse is to rodent as whale is to
   - (A) fish.
   - (B) gigantic.
   - (C) aquatic.
   - (D) mammal.

10. Sky is to ground as ceiling is to
    - (A) floor.
    - (B) roof.
    - (C) top.
    - (D) plaster.

11. Food is to nutrition as light is to
    - (A) watt.
    - (B) bulb.
    - (C) electricity.
    - (D) vision.

12. France is to America as meter is to
    - (A) gallon.
    - (B) degree.
    - (C) yard.
    - (D) pound.

13. Square is to triangle as cube is to
    - (A) circle.
    - (B) line.
    - (C) ball.
    - (D) pyramid.

14. Abacus is to calculator as propeller is to
    - (A) jet.
    - (B) airplane.
    - (C) mathematics.
    - (D) flight.

15. Dizziness is to vertigo as fate is to
    - (A) adversity.
    - (B) order.
    - (C) destiny.
    - (D) pride.

exercises

ANSWER KEYS AND EXPLANATIONS

Exercise 1

1. D	4. B	7. C	10. B	13. D
2. A	5. A	8. C	11. A	14. B
3. C	6. B	9. C	12. D	15. A

1. **The correct answer is (D).** The relationship is that of the product to its source. *Gasoline* comes from *petroleum*; *sugar* comes from *cane*.

2. **The correct answer is (A).** The relationship is that of the eaten to the eater. The fly is eaten by the *spider*; the *mouse* is eaten by the *cat*. You have to refine this analogy to eating in order to solve it. If you were to consider only catching, then you would not be able to distinguish between the *cat* and the *trap*.

3. **The correct answer is (C).** The relationship is functional. The *crater* is the vent for a *volcano*; the *flue* is the vent for a *chimney*.

4. **The correct answer is (B).** The relationship is that of part to whole. A *petal* is part of a *flower; fur* is part of a *rabbit*. Fur might be part of a coat, but it is not a necessary part, so *rabbit* makes a better analogy.

5. **The correct answer is (A).** The relationship is that of antonyms. *Retreat* is the opposite of *advance; timid* is the opposite of *bold*.

6. **The correct answer is (B).** This is an object-to-action relationship. An *attorney* performs at a *trial*; the *surgeon* performs at an *operation*.

7. **The correct answer is (C).** This is another variety of object-to-action relationship. You *see* a *picture*; you *hear* a *speech*.

8. **The correct answer is (C).** The relationship is that of synonyms or definition. A *soprano* voice is *high*; a *bass* voice is *low*. Bass has a number of possible meanings. You must define the word in light of the relationship of the first two words.

9. **The correct answer is (C).** The relationship is that of the whole to a part. The *addend* is one term of an *addition* problem; the *subtrahend* is one term of a *subtraction* problem.

10. **The correct answer is (B).** This is an essential cause-and-effect relationship. You cannot become *obese* if you do not *eat*; you cannot be *elected* if you do not run.

11. **The correct answer is (A).** The relationship is that of antonyms. *Acute* means sudden and short; *chronic* means always present. *Temporary* is the opposite of *persistent*.

12. **The correct answer is (D).** The relationship is that of synonyms. *Prostrate* means *flat*; *vertical* means *erect*.

13. **The correct answer is (D).** The relationship is that of object and actor. The *charioteer* drives the *chariot*; the *driver* drives the *automobile*. You must consider the action in this analogy in order to differentiate between *driver* and *passenger*.

14. **The correct answer is (B).** The relationship is that of the part to the whole. The *team* is part of the *league*; the *player* is part of the *team*.

15. **The correct answer is (A).** This analogy is probably more difficult than any you will get. The trick lies in the fact that citation has two distinct meanings. The relationship is that of cause to effect. When you are to be *honored*, you receive a *citation*, which is a formal document describing your achievements. When you are stopped for *speeding*, you receive a *citation*, which is an official summons to appear in court.

Exercise 2

1. D	4. C	7. B	10. A	13. D
2. C	5. B	8. A	11. D	14. A
3. B	6. A	9. D	12. C	15. C

1. **The correct answer is (D).** The relationship does not fall into a category with a precise name. The *fisherman* uses a *net* for his sport; the *hunter* uses a *gun* for his sport. The policeman also uses a gun but not for sport. You must refine your relationship so as to eliminate all but one choice.

2. **The correct answer is (C).** The relationship is that of cause and effect. When you are *educated*, you *know*; when you are *rich*, you *own*. When you are rich, you also have money. An analogy must maintain parallelism in parts of speech. For *money* to have been the correct answer, the second term would have had to have been a noun such as *knowledge*.

3. **The correct answer is (B).** The relationship is that of effect to its cause. *Noise* is *distracting*; *music* is *soothing*.

4. **The correct answer is (C).** This is a functional relationship. *Years* are measured on a *calendar*; *hours* are measured on a *clock*.

5. **The correct answer is (B).** The relationship of *father* to his same-sex sibling, *brother*, is analogous to the relationship of *mother* to her same-sex sibling, *sister*.

6. **The correct answer is (A).** The relationship is of parts to wholes. *Words* are parts of *books*; *notes* are parts of *songs*.

7. **The correct answer is (B).** The relationship is that of adjective to the noun it modifies. An odor may be described as *pungent*, though there are many other adjectives that may also be used. A *sound* may be described as *shrill*, though certainly not all sounds are shrill. *Shriek* is not the best answer because a shriek is always shrill.

8. **The correct answer is (A).** This is a purpose relationship. The purpose of a *present* is to celebrate a *birthday*; the purpose of a *reward* is to celebrate an *accomplishment*.

9. **The correct answer is (D).** The relationship is one of definition. A *mouse* is a *rodent*; a *whale* is a *mammal*.

10. **The correct answer is (A).** The relationship is one of antonyms. *Sky* is the opposite of *ground*; *ceiling* is the opposite of *floor*.

11. **The correct answer is (D).** The relationship is that of cause and effect. *Food* promotes *nutrition*; *light* promotes *vision*.

12. **The correct answer is (C).** The relationship cannot be defined by looking at the first two words alone. After you look at the third word and see that it is a European measure of length (metric), you might then look for another measure of length. Because the only choice offered is *yard*, you might state the relationship as *European* is to *American* as it applies to countries and measures of length.

13. **The correct answer is (D).** You might loosely state the relationship as *four* is to *three*. A *square* is a four-sided plane figure in relation to a *triangle*, which is a three-sided plane figure. A *cube* is a solid figure based on a square; a *pyramid* is a solid figure based on a triangle.

14. **The correct answer is (A).** The relationship is sequential. An *abacus* is an earlier, more primitive *calculator*; a *propeller* is an earlier, less sophisticated means of propulsion than a *jet*.

15. **The correct answer is (C).** The relationship is that of synonyms. *Vertigo* is *dizziness*; *destiny* is *fate*. One's fate may well be to suffer adversity, but fate is not necessarily negative.

SUMMING IT UP

- Analogies are tested on the COOP and on the HSPT.

- Questions in the Analogy section of the COOP use pictures instead of words. Once you have named the object in each picture, proceed the same way you would with a verbal analogy.

- Follow the steps: define the initial terms, describe the initial relationship, eliminate incorrect answers, refine the initial relationship, and choose the best answer.

- Study and learn the twelve types of analogy questions: part to whole, whole to part, cause and effect, effect and cause, association, degree, sequence, function, characteristic, antonym, synonym, and purpose.

Verbal Logic

OVERVIEW

- **HSPT Logic**
- **HSPT Verbal Classification**
- **COOP Extraction of Information**
- **COOP Logic**
- **COOP Artificial Language**
- **Summing it up**

You'll definitely be tested on your logical thinking on both the COOP and HSPT exams. A test of your reasoning skills will show how you think through a problem or scenario. The HSPT exam tests several types of verbal logic, one under the Logic test section and the other under the Verbal Classifications section, both of which appear under Verbal Skills. In the COOP exam, verbal logic questions are found in the Verbal Reasoning sections.

One measure of verbal logic requires you to extract indisputable information from a series of short sentences. Another asks you to consider a single word and to decide which of four choices is an absolutely necessary component of that word. The third measure of logical thinking is an exercise in translating an artificial language. Let's look at how each exam handles a typical test question for each of these areas of measurement.

HSPT LOGIC

HSPT Logic questions take a slightly different form than other questions on the exam. In these questions, you're given a series of sentences. You are asked to determine if, based on the truth of the other sentences, the final sentence is (A) true, (B) false, or (C) uncertain. If it is not possible to determine if the final sentence is true or false, then the correct answer is choice (C).

chapter 10

Let's look at an example of an HSPT Logic question:

> The black horse jumped over more hurdles than the spotted horse. The white horse jumped over more hurdles than the spotted horse. The white horse jumped over more hurdles than the black horse. If the first two statements are true, the third statement is
>
> **(A)** true.
>
> **(B)** false.
>
> **(C)** uncertain.
>
> **The correct answer is (C).** From the first two statements, we know that both the black horse and the white horse jumped over more hurdles than the spotted horse. This is all that we know. The first two statements do not give us any information about the comparative achievements of the black horse and the white horse. The answer, therefore, is choice (C). The third statement can be neither affirmed nor denied on the basis of the first two statements.

HSPT VERBAL CLASSIFICATION

Here's another type of Verbal Logic question you'll find on the HSPT. In Verbal Classification questions, you are presented with four words and asked to determine which of the words doesn't fit with the other three. Here's an example:

> Which word does *not* belong with the others?
>
> **(A)** crack
>
> **(B)** cleave
>
> **(C)** split
>
> **(D)** pare
>
> **The correct answer is (D).** The first three words are synonyms. All refer to dividing something by opening it into two or more pieces. Choice (D), on the other hand, refers to opening by peeling off the outer layer (to pare is to peel). The key to answering this kind of question lies in figuring the relationship among three of the words. The relationships might be of synonyms, degrees, parts of speech, functions, or along any of a myriad of dimensions.

COOP EXTRACTION OF INFORMATION

The COOP Extraction of Information questions present you with a series of related statements and four answer choices. You must choose the answer statement that is supported by the series of statements that precede the choices. That process probably sounds a lot more complicated than it really is, so let's look at an example:

The little red house on our block is very old. It was once used as a church, and Abraham Lincoln might have worshipped there. It also served as a schoolhouse.

(A) At one time, schools were used for worship.

(B) Abraham Lincoln prayed in school.

(C) The house has an interesting history.

(D) Red is a popular color for schools.

The correct answer is (C). Take one statement at a time. Choice (A) cannot be supported by the paragraph. The paragraph states that the house was once used as a church, not that it was used as a church and a school at the same time. Choice (B) also cannot be supported by the paragraph. If Abraham Lincoln worshipped in the house, he did so when it was a church. Although Abraham Lincoln might have prayed in school as a child, such information is extraneous to the paragraph. Choice (C) is clearly correct. The house does have a long and interesting history dating back to or before the Civil War and having been at various times a church, a school, and a house. Chances are that choice (C) is the correct answer, but check out choice (D) before choosing your answer. Choice (D) makes a statement of fact that is true in its own right, but it is not supported by the information in the passage. You must therefore select choice (C).

COOP LOGIC

The COOP Logic questions ask that you choose a word that names a necessary part or component of an italicized or underlined word. Here's an example:

Which word names a *necessary* part of the underlined word?

colander

(A) water

(B) holes

(C) food

(D) dirt

The correct answer is (B). A *colander* is a perforated dish or bowl for draining off liquids, as in rinsing pasta, fruit, or vegetables. The *holes,* choice (B), are absolutely necessary; all other choices are related, but none is necessary to the existence of the colander.

COOP ARTIFICIAL LANGUAGE

The COOP Artificial Language questions test your ability to transfer information that you have about one word to help define another, related word. The trick here is that all the words you deal with in these questions are nonsense-words, so you have to carefully read the definitions you're given and use those clues to help find the right answer choice. Here's an example:

Here are some words translated from an artificial language.

> *lobobatoba* means insult
>
> *lomonatoba* means inspect
>
> *lobobatabo* means result

Which word means *respect?*

(A) tabolomona

(B) tobatabo

(C) lomonatabo

(D) lobobalomona

The correct answer is (C). Look first at the English words. Notice that each word consists of a prefix and a stem and that among the four words there are only two prefixes and two stems. Now look at the three artificial-language words. Notice that each appears to have two parts, one beginning with *l* and ending with *a* and the other beginning with *t*.

Now return to the first pair of words and separate each into its two halves.

> loboba toba = in sult
>
> lomona toba = in spect

You now have gathered useful information. In the artificial language, the stem comes first and is followed by the prefix. Furthermore, you now know that

> *toba* means *in*
>
> *loboba* means *sult*
>
> *lomona* means *spect*

Confirm this information by looking at the third pair of words:

> loboba tabo = re sult

You already knew that *loboba* means *sult*; now you also know that *tabo* means *re*. At this point, you can figure the answer. Look at the four choices. Immediately eliminate choices (A) and (B) because you know that the stem must be followed by the prefix, and in these two choices the order of the parts of the words is reversed. If you look quickly ahead, you will see that in choice (D) you are offered joined stems with no prefix. You can confidently pick choice (C) as the answer to this question. Confirm: *tabo* means *re*; *lomona* means *spect*.

At first glance, the artificial-language type of a Verbal Logic question seems rather weird, even intimidating. Actually, with concentration and practice, the procedure can become mechanical and not at all difficult.

Try your hand at using the reasoning processes we have just taught you as you tackle the following exercises. Answer keys and explanations follow Exercise 3.

EXERCISES: VERBAL LOGIC

Exercise 1

Directions: Choose the correct answer.

1. George is older than Bob. Fred is younger than George. Bob is older than Fred. If the first two statements are true, the third statement is
   - (A) true.
   - (B) false.
   - (C) uncertain.

2. Group A sings higher than Group C. Group B sings lower than Group C. Group A sings higher than Group B. If the first two statements are true, the third statement is
   - (A) true.
   - (B) false.
   - (C) uncertain.

3. Percolator coffee is weaker than electric-drip coffee. Extractor coffee is stronger than electric-drip coffee. Electric-drip coffee is stronger than extractor coffee. If the first two statements are true, the third statement is
   - (A) true.
   - (B) false.
   - (C) uncertain.

4. Red kites fly higher than yellow kites. Yellow balloons fly higher than red kites. Yellow kites fly higher than yellow balloons. If the first two statements are true, the third statement is
   - (A) true.
   - (B) false.
   - (C) uncertain.

5. The New York team lost fewer games than the Boston team. The Boston team won more games than the Baltimore team, but not as many games as the New York team. The Baltimore team lost the fewest games. If the first two statements are true, the third statement is
   - (A) true.
   - (B) false.
   - (C) uncertain.

6. The history book has more pages than the poetry book, but fewer pages than the math book. The math book has more pages than the science book but fewer pages than the English book. The poetry book has the fewest pages. If the first two statements are true, the third statement is
   - (A) true.
   - (B) false.
   - (C) uncertain.

7. Which word does *not* belong with the others?
   - (A) true.
   - (B) false.
   - (C) uncertain.

8. Which word does *not* belong with the others?
   - (A) orange
   - (B) apple
   - (C) tomato
   - (D) carrot

9. Which word does *not* belong with the others?

   (A) emotion
   (B) love
   (C) anger
   (D) disappointment

10. Which word does *not* belong with the others?

   (A) hurricane
   (B) tornado
   (C) typhoon
   (D) earthquake

11. Which word does *not* belong with the others?

   (A) medicine
   (B) healing
   (C) therapy
   (D) surgery

12. Which word does *not* belong with the others?

   (A) orange
   (B) brown
   (C) red
   (D) purple

Exercise 2

Directions: Choose the statement that is true according to the given information.

1. Mr. Stonehill worked in the corporate headquarters of a large corporation. Another company acquired Mr. Stonehill's company and sold off the operating divisions one by one. There can be no corporate headquarters without any operating divisions. Mr. Stonehill is

   (A) unemployed.
   (B) working for one of the operating divisions.
   (C) no longer working in corporate headquarters.
   (D) working for the new company.

2. Mr. Moffitt is a high school chemistry teacher. As a young man, Mr. Moffitt worked in the textile dyes division of a chemical company. Besides teaching chemistry, Mr. Moffitt operates a business cleaning Oriental carpets.

   (A) Mr. Moffitt changes jobs often.
   (B) Mr. Moffitt teaches students how to clean carpets.
   (C) Mr. Moffitt is a wealthy man.
   (D) Mr. Moffitt is well-qualified for the work he does.

3. Sally and Susie are twins. Sally lives near her parents in a Chicago suburb with her husband and children. Susie lives in a remote area of Alaska and raises dogs.

   (A) Susie does not get along with her parents.
   (B) Twins may have different interests and tastes.
   (C) Sally does not like dogs.
   (D) There are special bonds between twins.

4. The baby woke and cried in the middle of the night. Molly Davis changed the baby's diaper, gave him a warm bottle, and put him back to bed.

   (A) The baby woke because it was time for his bottle.
   (B) The baby's mother's name is Molly Davis.
   (C) The baby woke with a wet diaper.
   (D) After his bottle, the baby went back to sleep.

5. Eight children went trick-or-treating together on Halloween. Each child carried a lighted flashlight and a big bag. Jill and Mary did not wear masks.

   (A) The children went trick-or-treating at night.

   (B) Six children wore masks.

   (C) The bags were heavy.

   (D) The youngest children were Jill and Mary.

Directions: For questions 6–10, find the correct answer.

6. Here are some words translated from an artificial language.

   pritibondo means construct
   kwalaropipiwi means diverge
   kwalarobondo means converge

   Which word means *destruct?*

   (A) pritipepewe

   (B) kwalaropepewe

   (C) bondopriti

   (D) pipiwipriti

7. Here are some words translated from an artificial language.

   hohoysiri means larger
   hohosiriyi means smaller
   hohohoysiri means largest

   Which word means *smallest?*

   (A) ysirisiriyi

   (B) siriyihoho

   (C) ysirihoho

   (D) hohohosiriyi

8. Here are some words translated from an artificial language.

   biblithrop means import
   thropganum means portable
   libibnadgrul means express

   Which word means *impress?*

   (A) bibliganum

   (B) biblinadgrul

   (C) nadgulthrop

   (D) thropganum

9. Here are some words translated from an artificial language.

   eselklup means black dog
   eselrifoulof means white puppy
   finiklupulof means gray cat

   Which word means *gray kitten?*

   (A) finikluprifo

   (B) finirifoklupulof

   (C) finiulofklup

   (D) klupulofrifofini

10. Here are some words translated from an artificial language.

    nipilazokople means base hit
    frixzokople means home run
    nipilazokoptaha means first down

    Which word means *touchdown?*

    (A) nipilazokoptaha

    (B) zokopfrixtaha

    (C) frixlezokop

    (D) frixzokoptaha

Exercise 3

Directions: Choose the word that names a necessary part of the underlined word.

1. mother
   - (A) nurturing
   - (B) home
   - (C) responsibility
   - (D) child

2. essay
   - (A) words
   - (B) organization
   - (C) paper
   - (D) outline

3. fantasy
   - (A) entertainment
   - (B) dream
   - (C) imagination
   - (D) music

4. carpenter
   - (A) house
   - (B) wood
   - (C) saw
   - (D) repair

5. history
   - (A) past
   - (B) social studies
   - (C) documents
   - (D) culture

6. editorial
   - (A) newspaper
   - (B) rebuttal
   - (C) publisher
   - (D) opinion

7. skeleton
   - (A) anatomy
   - (B) death
   - (C) bones
   - (D) skull

8. geometry
   - (A) lines
   - (B) forms
   - (C) numbers
   - (D) mathematics

9. disappointment
   - (A) loss
   - (B) discouragement
   - (C) failure
   - (D) expectation

10. heirloom
    - (A) antique
    - (B) nostalgia
    - (C) ancestor
    - (D) jewelry

ANSWER KEYS AND EXPLANATIONS

Exercise 1

1. C	4. B	7. B	9. A	11. B
2. A	5. C	8. D	10. D	12. C
3. B	6. C			

1. **The correct answer is (C).** We know only that George is the oldest. There is no way to tell whether Bob is older than Fred, or Fred is older than Bob.

2. **The correct answer is (A).** Group A sings the highest of the three.

3. **The correct answer is (B).** Extractor coffee is the strongest, electric-drip comes next, and percolator coffee is the weakest.

4. **The correct answer is (B).** Balloons appear to fly higher than kites.

5. **The correct answer is (C).** We know for certain that Baltimore *won* the fewest games, but without information about how many games were played, we have no knowledge of how many games Baltimore *lost*.

6. **The correct answer is (C).** The English book has the most pages, followed by the math book. The history book has more pages than the poetry book. However, we do not have enough information to rank the science book; it might have more or fewer pages than the poetry book.

7. **The correct answer is (B).** The window is transparent or, at the very least, translucent and probably is movable as well. All of the other choices are solid, opaque, and fixed.

8. **The correct answer is (D).** The carrot is a root vegetable. All of the other choices are seed-bearing fruits.

9. **The correct answer is (A).** The other three choices are all actual emotions.

10. **The correct answer is (D).** All other choices are wind-based natural disasters.

11. **The correct answer is (B).** Medicine, therapy, and surgery are all procedures leading to healing.

12. **The correct answer is (C).** Red is a primary color; all of the others are red-based mixtures.

answers exercises

Exercise 2

1. C	3. B	5. A	7. D	9. B
2. D	4. C	6. A	8. B	10. D

1. **The correct answer is (C).** There is no information as to whether or not Mr. Stonehill is now working, nor for whom. However, if the operating divisions have been sold, there is no corporate headquarters. If there is no corporate headquarters, most certainly Mr. Stonehill does not work there.

2. **The correct answer is (D).** With the credentials required of all schoolteachers and with his specialized experience in a chemical company, Mr. Moffitt is clearly qualified to teach high school chemistry. The training that Mr. Moffitt received working in the textile dyes division applies beautifully to his sideline occupation, cleaning Oriental carpets. The other choices, while all possible, are in no way supported by the paragraph.

3. **The correct answer is (B).** The only statement definitely supported by the paragraph is that twins may have different interests and tastes.

4. **The correct answer is (C).** Nobody changes a dry diaper in the middle of the night. The other choices are possibilities but not certainties. The baby might have woken up for any number of reasons; Molly Davis might be a babysitter; the baby might have played happily in his crib after he was dry and fed.

5. **The correct answer is (A).** If all eight children carried *lighted* flashlights, we might be pretty sure that it was dark. The information that Jill and Mary did not wear masks implies that the other children did but does not prove it. Some of the others might also have not worn masks or might have worn sheets over their heads. Sometimes the youngest children wear masks while older youngsters apply complicated makeup. Jill and Mary were not necessarily the youngest.

6. **The correct answer is (A).** In this language, prefix and stem appear in reverse order. Among these words, the stems are *priti* meaning *struct* and *kwalaro* meaning *verge*. Within the three given words, *bondo* means *con*, and *pipiwi* means *di*. Because the word you must translate includes the stem *struct*, it must begin with *priti*. Only one choice begins with *priti*, so you need look no further. With no further information, you might conclude that because *pipiwi* means *di*, *pepewe* could reasonably stand for *de*.

7. **The correct answer is (D).** In this language, stem and suffix appear in reverse order. *Hoho* is the comparative suffix (*er*) and *hohoho* the superlative suffix (*est*). *Ysiri* means *large* and *siriyi* means *small*. The choice of answer is easy because only one choice begins with *hohoho*.

8. **The correct answer is (B).** In this language, the words are formed in the same order as words in the English language. You learn this fact by studying the first two words. Because *port* appears at the end of *import* but at the beginning of *portable*, and *throp* appears at the end of the first word and at the beginning of the second, you know that *throp* means *port*. If *throp* means *port*, then *bibli* must mean *im*. You can already narrow to choices (A) and (B). Looking back at the original words, if *throp* means *port*, then *ganum* means *able*. You can thus eliminate choice (A). With time pressure, select choice (B) and go on to the next question. If you have time to confirm, note that *nadgrul* is the second half of *express*, so *nadgrul* undoubtedly means *press*.

9. **The correct answer is (B).** Because *esel* is the only word segment appearing in both the first and second words, *esel* must mean

dog. The noun appears before its modifier. *Klup* means *black.* For the moment, we cannot tell within the second word which segment means *white* and which signifies that the dog is young. Moving on to the third word, we find *klup* in the middle. Because the noun comes first, we know that *fini* means *cat.* Black cat *ulof*? But we want gray cat. *Ulof* also appears in the second word that defines a white puppy. *Ulof* must mean *white,* and the juxtaposition of *blackwhite* (*klupulof*) means gray. The remaining segment of the second word, *rifo,* must indicate that the dog is young. Now put together the answer. It must begin with *cat, fini.* The second segment, *rifo,* makes it young, hence a kitten. Finally, *klupulof* (blackwhite) makes it *gray.*

10. **The correct answer is (D).** This question takes even more logical thinking than most others. Because the English words do not have common elements, you must first figure out the basis on which the artificial-language words are formed. The first two words are both related to baseball and both end in *le,* which does not appear in the word related to football. The first and third words begin with *nipila,* and both refer to an initial advance toward scoring in a sport, though not the same sport. Appearing in all three words is *zokop.* Evidently, *zokop* has something to do with either sports or balls. The meaning of *zokop* is unimportant, but because the word you must translate relates to football, *zokop* must appear in the word. If *nipila* refers to the initial advance toward a score and *frix* appears only in the word meaning home run, chances are that *frix* is a scoring word portion. Now, remembering that *taha* appeared only in the word relating to football and was not otherwise accounted for, you can construct the word for *touchdown.* The degree of scoring comes first. A touchdown is a scoring play, so our word must begin with *frix. Zokop* must come into the middle of all words having to do with scoring activities in football or baseball. A touchdown is a scoring play in football, so our word ends in *taha.*

Exercise 3

1. D	3. C	5. A	7. C	9. D
2. A	4. B	6. D	8. A	10. C

1. **The correct answer is (D).** One cannot be a mother without having or having had a child. All the other choices are usual and desirable adjuncts of motherhood, but they are not necessary to its existence.

2. **The correct answer is (A).** An essay is created of words. The most commonly seen essays are well organized and appear on paper, but a poor essay might be disorganized and an essay might appear on electronic media rather than paper.

3. **The correct answer is (C).** Fantasy is based on imagination. Fantasy might be dreamlike, might entertain, and might be musical or embellished by music, but imagination is what is crucial to fantasy.

4. **The correct answer is (B).** A carpenter works with wood. What the carpenter does with wood or how the carpenter accomplishes a goal is immaterial to the existence of the carpenter.

5. **The correct answer is (A).** History is that which is past.

6. **The correct answer is (D).** An editorial is an expression of opinion. We tend to first think of editorials as being essays that are published in newspapers; but editorials—that is, statements of opinion—may also be

broadcast on radio or television. Although an editorial might lead to a rebuttal or might be a rebuttal of a previously expressed opinion, the rebuttal is not necessary to the editorial.

7. **The correct answer is (C).** The skeleton is the bony structure of the body. After death and decomposition, the skeleton might become visible, but death is not necessary to the existence of the skeleton. The skull is a part of the skeleton, necessary in a living person, but not necessary to the existence of any skeleton. The bones themselves, however, are the necessary component.

8. **The correct answer is (A).** There is no geometry without lines. The lines might be straight or curved and might be shaped into forms. Numbers might be assigned and mathematics computed, but there must be lines in geometry.

9. **The correct answer is (D).** Disappointment is what occurs when expectations are not fulfilled. This is the necessary connection.

10. **The correct answer is (C).** An heirloom is an object handed down from an ancestor. Without an ancestor to hand down the object, the object might be an antique, but it is not an heirloom.

SUMMING IT UP

- The HSPT exam tests several measures of verbal logic in its Verbal Skills section, one under the Logic test section and the other under the Verbal Classifications section.

- In the COOP, the verbal logic test is found in the Verbal Reasoning sections.

- On the HSPT Logic questions, you only have three answer choices. NEVER mistakenly choose (D).

Reading

chapter 11

OVERVIEW

- **How to improve your reading skills**
- **Tips for answering reading comprehension questions**
- **Summing it up**

Both the COOP and the HSPT include sections on reading comprehension. They are called Reading and Language Arts on the COOP and Reading on the HSPT (under the Comprehension section). The TACHS tests reading comprehension in the Reading section. The format for reading questions on all three exams differs from the other question types you've learned about so far. The exams present reading passages followed by a series of questions based on the passages. The questions test not only how well you understand what you read, but also how well you can interpret the meaning of the passage and the author's intent. These questions also test how well you draw conclusions based on what you have read.

To do well on the reading comprehension sections of an exam, reading quickly is crucial. You won't be able to answer questions based on a passage if you have not had time to read it. Even if you are able to read the passage through once, you must have enough time left over to reread the selection for detail questions.

HOW TO IMPROVE YOUR READING SKILLS

One of the best techniques for increasing your reading speed and comprehension is also one of the techniques that will help you improve your vocabulary—**reading.** The best way to increase your reading speed between now and the actual exam is to read as much as possible. Read everything in sight—newspapers, magazines, novels, billboards, and so on. Newspaper reading is an especially good way to improve your reading skills. Don't stop with just the opening paragraph of each article. Push yourself to read the whole story and give it your full attention as you read. If your mind wanders, you will not comprehend what you read.

To read with understanding, your eyes must occasionally stop on the page. Most people stop on each word because that is the way reading is taught in the early grades. But once you know how to read well, this method wastes a great deal of time. The key to increasing your reading speed is to take in more words each time your eyes stop. If a line had ten words in it and you were able to read the line by stopping only twice instead of ten times, you would be reading five times as fast as you do now. Try to train yourself.

If you have a habit of softly speaking words as you read, *break that habit now*! This habit is called *subvocalizing*, and no matter how fast you can talk, you can read faster if you stop subvocalizing. Some people chew gum to stop subvocalizing. For others, just being aware of the habit is enough to help them correct it. Not only will it slow you down, but if you're reading aloud during your exam, the administrator will ask you to stop, so you don't disturb other test-takers.

In building your reading speed, try moving your index finger or pencil underneath the line you are reading. Because your eyes tend to move as quickly as your pencil, you will not stop on every word. You will not regress (look back), and you probably will not subvocalize. However, what you might do is concentrate on your pencil and not on the reading passage. This is why you must practice this technique before using it on your test. Start your finger or your pencil at the second or third word in the line and stop it before the last word in the line. Your peripheral vision (what you see at the edges) will pick up the first and last words in the lines, and you will save time by not having to focus on them.

Become more aware of words. Earlier in this part, you were advised to use a dictionary while you read to help increase your vocabulary. That exercise can help you with reading comprehension questions as well. Vocabulary and reading comprehension are very closely interrelated. You cannot have a large vocabulary without reading. You cannot understand what you read without an understanding of the words. When you look up words, study the roots, prefixes, and suffixes so that you can apply all that you know whenever you meet unfamiliar words.

TIPS FOR ANSWERING READING COMPREHENSION QUESTIONS

- Begin by reading over the questions—not the answer choices, just the questions themselves. With an idea of what the questions will be asking, you will be able to focus your reading.

- Skim the passage to get a general idea of the subject matter and of the point that is being made. Pay special attention to the first and last sentences in each paragraph. Those sentences often state the main idea of the passage.

- Reread the passage, giving attention to details and the point of view. Be alert for the author's hints as to what he or she thinks is important. Phrases such as *Note that . . .*, *Of importance is . . .*, and *Do not overlook . . .* give clues to what the writer is stressing.

- If the author has quoted material from another source, be sure that you understand the purpose of the quote. Does the author agree or disagree?

- Carefully read each question or incomplete statement. Determine exactly what is being asked. Watch for negatives or all-inclusive words such as *always, never, all, only, every, absolutely, completely, none, entirely,* and *no*. These words can affect your choice of answer.

- Read all four answer choices. Do not rush to choose the first answer that might be correct. Eliminate those choices that are obviously incorrect. Reread the remaining choices and refer to the passage, if necessary, to determine the *best* answer.

- Don't confuse a *true* answer with the *correct* answer. You can do this best if you avoid inserting your own judgments into your answers. Even if you disagree with the author, or spot a factual error in the passage, you must answer on the basis of what is stated or implied in the passage.

- Don't spend too much time on any one question. If looking back at the passage does not help you to find or figure out the answer, choose from among the answers remaining after you eliminate the obviously wrong ones, and go on to the next question or passage.

Now try these exercises. Correct answers and explanations follow Exercise 2.

EXERCISES: READING

Exercise 1

Directions: The following questions are based on a number of reading passages. Each passage is followed by a series of questions. Read each passage carefully, then answer the questions based on it. You may reread the passage as often as you wish. When you have finished answering the questions based on one passage, go right on to the next passage.

QUESTIONS 1–4 REFER TO THE FOLLOWING PASSAGE.

Like the United States today, Athens had courts where a wrong might be righted. Since any citizen might accuse another of a crime, the Athenian courts of law were very busy. In fact, unless a citizen was unusually peaceful or very unimportant, he would be sure to find himself in the courts at least once every few years.

At a trial, both the accuser and the person accused were allowed a certain time to speak. The length of time was marked by a water clock. Free men testified under oath as they do today, but the oath of a slave was counted as worthless.

To judge a trial, a jury was chosen from the members of the assembly who had reached 30 years of age. The Athenian juries were very large, often consisting of 201, 401, 501, 1,001, or more men, depending upon the importance of the case being tried. The juryman swore by the gods to listen carefully to both sides of the question and to give his honest opinion of the case. Each juryman gave his decision by depositing a white or black stone in a box. To keep citizens from being too careless in accusing each other, there was a rule that if the person accused did not receive a certain number of negative votes, the accuser was condemned instead.

1. The title that best expresses the main idea of this selection is
   (A) "Athens and the United States."
   (B) "Justice in Ancient Athens."
   (C) "Testifying Under Oath."
   (D) "The Duties of Juries."

2. People in Athens were frequently on trial in a court of law because
   (A) they liked to serve on juries.
   (B) a juryman agreed to listen to both sides.
   (C) any person might accuse another of a crime.
   (D) the slaves were troublesome.

3. An Athenian was likely to avoid accusing another without a good reason because
   (A) the jury might condemn the accuser instead of the accused.
   (B) the jury might be very large.
   (C) cases were judged by men over 30 years old.
   (D) there was a limit on the time a trial could take.

4. Which statement is *true* according to the selection?
   (A) An accused person was denied the privilege of telling his side of the case.
   (B) The importance of the case determined the number of jurors.
   (C) A jury's decision was handed down in writing.
   (D) A citizen had to appear in court every few years.

QUESTIONS 5–13 REFER TO THE FOLLOWING PASSAGE.

When a luxury liner or a cargo ship nudges into her slip after an ocean crossing, her first physical contact with land is a heaving line. These streamers with a weight at the end, called a "monkey fist," arch gracefully from deck to pier. On board the ship, the heaving lines are tied to heavy, golden yellow manila mooring lines. Longshoremen quickly pull in the heaving lines until they can fasten the mooring lines to iron bollards (posts). Soon the ship is strung to her pier by four, eight, or as many as twenty-one 9-inch or 10-inch manila lines with perhaps a few wire ropes to stay motion fore and aft. The ship is secure against even the wrath of the storm or hurricane. A ship could dock without the aid of tugboats—and might have in New York in maritime strikes—but not without the lines to moor her to her berth.

The maritime and the related fishing industry find perhaps 250 applications for rope and cordage. There are hundreds of different sizes, constructions, tensile strengths, and weights in rope and twine. Rope is sold by the pound but ordered by length and is measured by circumference rather than by diameter. The maritime variety is made chiefly from fiber of the abaca, or manila plant, which is imported from the Philippines and Central America. Henequen from Mexico and Cuba and sisal from Africa, the Netherlands East Indies, and other areas are also used, but chiefly for twine. Nylon is coming into increasing use, particularly by towing companies. But it is six times more expensive than manila. However, nylon is much stronger, lighter in weight, and longer-wearing than manila. It is also more elastic and particularly adaptable for ocean towing.

5. In docking a ship, rope is
   (A) only a little less important than a tugboat.
   (B) absolutely essential.
   (C) helpful but not necessary.
   (D) seldom used.

6. A monkey fist is a
   (A) device for weaving a rope.
   (B) slang term for a longshoreman.
   (C) rope streamer.
   (D) weight at the end of a rope.

7. Heaving lines are
   (A) tied around iron posts.
   (B) ocean currents.
   (C) used as a means of getting mooring lines to shore.
   (D) used to prevent motion in the bow.

8. A ship is held to her berth by
   (A) wire ropes only.
   (B) wire and fiber ropes.
   (C) heaving ropes.
   (D) hundreds of ropes.

9. Mooring ropes are
   (A) 10 inches in diameter.
   (B) 21 inches in circumference.
   (C) six times thicker than heaving ropes.
   (D) 9 inches in circumference.

10. There are
    (A) more than 200 uses for rope in fishing and shipping.
    (B) few differences in rope construction.
    (C) equal tensile strengths in all ropes.
    (D) no differences in the materials preferred for the making of ropes and twines.

11. Rope is
    (A) ordered by length.
    (B) ordered by the pound.
    (C) paid for by length.
    (D) paid for by tensile.

12. Which of the following are *not* correctly paired?
    (A) Sisal from the Philippines
    (B) Henequen from Cuba
    (C) Abaca from Central America
    (D) Sisal from the Netherlands East Indies

13. As compared with manila rope, nylon rope is
    (A) stronger and cheaper.
    (B) more elastic and more expensive.
    (C) more elastic and heavier.
    (D) longer wearing and six times cheaper.

QUESTIONS 14–20 REFER TO THE FOLLOWING PASSAGE.

A phase of my life which has lost something through <u>refinement</u> is the game of croquet. We used to have an old croquet set whose wooden balls, having been chewed by dogs, were no rounder than eggs. Paint had faded; wickets were askew. The course had been laid out haphazardly and eagerly by a child, and we all used to go out there on summer nights and play good-naturedly, with the dogs romping on the lawn in the beautiful light, and the mosquitoes sniping at us, and everyone in good spirits, racing after balls and making split shots for the sheer love of battle. Last spring, we decided the croquet set was beyond use and invested in a rather fancy new one with hoops set in small wooden sockets, and mallets with rubber faces. The course is now exactly seventy-two feet long and we lined the wickets up with a string, but the little boy is less fond of it now, for we make him keep still while we are shooting. A dog isn't even allowed to cast his shadow across the line of play. There are frequent quarrels of a minor nature, and it seems to me we return from the field of honor tense and out of sorts.

14. The word *refinement* in this context means
    (A) politeness.
    (B) distinction.
    (C) improvement.
    (D) his own dignity.

15. The author of the paragraph is
    (A) very angry.
    (B) deeply grieved.
    (C) indifferent.
    (D) mildly regretful.

16. The mood of the paragraph is
    (A) dogmatic.
    (B) very earnest.
    (C) wistful.
    (D) belligerent.

17. In comparing the earlier and later ways in which they played croquet, the author considers the new way more
    (A) exact and less attractive.
    (B) beneficial for children.
    (C) conducive to family life.
    (D) fun for the dogs.

18. The "quarrels of a minor nature" occur because
    (A) the dog chases the croquet balls.
    (B) the balls do not roll well.
    (C) efficiency has become more important than sociability.
    (D) the little boy interrupts the game with his shouts.

19. The author
    (A) is opposed to all progress.
    (B) is very exact in everything he does.
    (C) dislikes games.
    (D) feels that undue attention to detail can lessen enjoyment.

20. The author thinks that
    (A) children should be seen and not heard.
    (B) dogs are pleasant companions.
    (C) dogs are a nuisance.
    (D) children should not be trusted to arrange croquet wickets.

QUESTIONS 21–25 REFER TO THE FOLLOWING PASSAGE.

On entering the amphitheater, new objects of wonder presented themselves. On a level spot in the center was a company of odd-looking personages playing at nine-pins. They were dressed in a quaint, outlandish fashion, some wore short doublets, others jerkins, with long knives in their belts, and most of them had enormous breeches, of a type similar to that of the guide's. Their visages, too, were peculiar, one had a large beard, broad face, and small piggish eyes. The face of another seemed to consist entirely of nose and was surmounted by a white sugar-loaf hat set off with a little red cock's tail. They all had beards of various shapes and colors. There was one who seemed to be the commander. He was a stout old gentleman, with a weather-beaten countenance; he wore a lace doublet, broad belt and hangar, high crowned hat and feather, red stockings, and high-heeled shoes with roses in them. The whole group reminded Rip of the figures in an old <u>Flemish</u> painting, in the parlor of the village parson, which had been brought over from Holland at the time of the settlement.

What seemed particularly odd to Rip was that though these folks were evidently amusing themselves, yet they maintained the gravest faces, the most mysterious silence, and were the most melancholy party of pleasure he had ever witnessed. Nothing interrupted the stillness of the scene but the noise of the balls, which, whenever they were rolled, echoed along the mountains like rumbling peals of thunder.

—from *Rip Van Winkle*
by Washington Irving

21. Looking at this scene, the observer is apparently
    (A) fascinated.
    (B) frightened.
    (C) repulsed.
    (D) bored.

22. The word *Flemish* possibly refers to
    (A) something from the area near Holland.
    (B) the village parson.
    (C) a certain painter.
    (D) an old-fashioned parlor.

23. The characters were probably playing
    (A) a game like bowling.
    (B) soccer.
    (C) a type of baseball.
    (D) golf.

24. The person observing all of this is
    (A) Flemish.
    (B) a parson.
    (C) melancholic.
    (D) Rip.

25. The observer was surprised that the
    (A) men's beards were of so many shapes and colors.
    (B) men appeared to be so serious while they were playing a game.
    (C) leader was so stout.
    (D) rolling balls sounded like thunder.

exercises

QUESTIONS 26–31 REFER TO THE FOLLOWING PASSAGE.

Powdered zirconium is more fiery and violent than the magnesium powder that went into wartime incendiary bombs. Under some conditions, it can be ignited with a kitchen match, and it cannot be extinguished with water. Munitions makers once tried to incorporate it into explosives, but turned it down as too dangerous even for them to handle.

But when this strange metal is transformed into a solid bar or sheet or tube as lustrous as burnished silver, its temper changes. It is so <u>docile</u> that it can be used by surgeons as a safe covering plate for sensitive brain tissues. It is almost as strong as steel, and it can be exposed to hydrochloric acid or nitric acid without corroding.

Zirconium is also safe and stable when it is bound up with other elements to form mineral compounds, which occur in abundant deposits in North and South America, India, and Australia. Although it is classified as a rare metal, it is more abundant in the earth's crust than nickel, copper, tungsten, tin, or lead. Until a few years ago, scarcely a dozen men had ever seen zirconium in pure form, but today it is the wonder metal of a fantastic new industry, a vital component of television, radar, and radio sets, an exciting structural material for chemical equipment and for superrockets and jet engines, and a key metal for atomic piles.

26. The title that best expresses the main idea of this selection is
    (A) "A Vital Substance."
    (B) "A Safe, Stable Substance."
    (C) "Zirconium's Uses in Surgery."
    (D) "Characteristics of Zirconium."

27. The word *docile* in the second paragraph means
    (A) stable.
    (B) pliable.
    (C) strong.
    (D) profuse.

28. The selection emphasizes that
    (A) zirconium rusts easily.
    (B) chemists are finding uses for zirconium.
    (C) nowadays keys are often made of zirconium.
    (D) zirconium is less abundant in the earth's crust than lead.

29. Zirconium is *not* safe to handle when it is
    (A) lustrous.
    (B) powdered.
    (C) in tubes.
    (D) in bar form.

30. The selection tells us that zirconium
    (A) is a metal.
    (B) is fireproof.
    (C) dissolves in water.
    (D) is stronger than steel.

31. Zirconium is likely to be useful in all of these fields *except*
    (A) surgery.
    (B) television.
    (C) atomic research.
    (D) the manufacture of fireworks.

QUESTIONS 32–36 REFER TO THE FOLLOWING PASSAGE.

In August of 1814, when news came that the British were advancing on Washington, three State Department clerks stuffed all records and valuable papers—including the Articles of Confederation, the Declaration of Independence, and the Constitution—into coarse linen sacks and smuggled them in carts to an unoccupied gristmill on the Virginia side of the Potomac. Later, fearing that a cannon factory nearby might attract a raiding party of the enemy, the clerks procured wagons from neighboring farmers, took the papers 35 miles away to Leesburg, and locked them in an empty house. It was not until the British fleet had left the waters of the Chesapeake that it was considered safe to return the papers to Washington.

On December 26, 1941, the five pages of the Constitution together with the single leaf of the Declaration of Independence were taken from the Library of Congress, where they had been kept for many years, and were stored in the vaults of the United States Bullion Depository at Fort Knox, Kentucky. Here they "rode out the war" safely.

Since 1952, visitors to Washington may view these historic documents at the Exhibition Hall of the National Archives. Sealed in bronze and glass cases filled with helium, the documents are protected from touch, light, heat, dust, and moisture. At a moment's notice, they can be lowered into a large safe that is bombproof, shockproof, and fireproof.

32. The title that best expresses the main idea of this selection is
(A) "Three Courageous Clerks."
(B) "The Constitution and Other Documents."
(C) "How to Exhibit Valuables."
(D) "Preserving America's Documents of Freedom."

33. Before the War of 1812, the Constitution and the Declaration of Independence were apparently kept in
(A) Independence Hall.
(B) Fort Knox, Kentucky.
(C) the office of the State Department.
(D) a gristmill in Virginia.

34. Nowadays, these documents are on view in the
(A) National Archives' Exhibition Hall.
(B) Library of Congress.
(C) United States Bullion Depository.
(D) United States Treasury Building.

35. An important reason for the installation of an apparatus for quick removal of the documents is the
(A) possibility of a sudden disaster.
(B) increasing number of tourists.
(C) need for more storage space.
(D) lack of respect for the documents.

36. The documents have been removed from Washington at least twice in order to preserve them from
(A) dust, heat, and moisture.
(B) careless handling.
(C) possible war damage.
(D) sale to foreign governments.

QUESTIONS 37–41 REFER TO THE FOLLOWING PASSAGE.

Few animals are as descriptively named as the varying hare (*Lepus americanus*), also commonly known as the snowshoe hare, white rabbit, or snowshoe rabbit. The species derives its various names from its interesting adaptations to the seasonal changes affecting its habitat.

The color changes are affected by means of a molt, and are timed (although the hares have no voluntary control over them) to coincide with the changing appearances of the background. The periods of transition—from white to brown in the spring, and from brown to white in the fall—require more than two months from start to completion, during which time the hares are a mottled brown and white. In addition to the changes in color, in the fall the soles of the feet develop a very heavy growth of hair that functions as snowshoes.

In New York State, hares are most abundant in and around the Adirondack and Catskill Mountains. Thriving populations with less extensive ranges are found in Allegany, Cattaraugus, Rensselaer, and Chenango counties. Smaller colonies of limited range are found in scattered islands.

37. The title that best expresses the main idea of this selection is
   (A) "Seasonal Changes in Birds."
   (B) "The Varying Hare."
   (C) "An American Animal."
   (D) "The Abundance of Hares."

38. Terms used to name these rabbits are related to their
   (A) abundance in many parts of New York State.
   (B) sensitivity to weather conditions throughout the state.
   (C) ability to adapt to the change of seasons.
   (D) thick white coats.

39. These rabbits have both brown and white markings in
   (A) summer and winter.
   (B) spring and fall.
   (C) spring and summer.
   (D) fall and winter.

40. The parts of New York State where rabbit populations are most plentiful are
   (A) Allegany, Cattaraugus, Rensselaer, and Chenango counties.
   (B) Adirondack and Catskill Mountain regions.
   (C) islands within the state.
   (D) snowy areas in the hills.

41. Which statement about these rabbits is *true* according to the selection?
   (A) They are becoming fewer in number.
   (B) They are capable of leaping great distances.
   (C) They are more plentiful in winter.
   (D) They have no control over their color changes.

QUESTIONS 42–45 REFER TO THE FOLLOWING PASSAGE.

Between 1780 and 1790, in piecemeal fashion, a trail was established between Catskill on the Hudson and the frontier outpost, Ithaca, in the Finger Lakes country. This path, by grace of following the valleys, managed to thread its way through the mountains by what are on the whole surprisingly easy grades. Ultimately, this route became the Susquehanna Turnpike, but in popular speech it was just the Ithaca Road. It was, along with the Mohawk Turnpike and the Great Western Turnpike, one of the three great east-west highways of the state. Eventually it was the route taken by thousands of Yankee farmers, more especially Connecticut Yankees, seeking new fortunes in southwestern New York. Along it, the tide of pioneer immigration flowed at flood crest for a full generation.

As the road left Catskill, there was no stream that might not be either forded or crossed on a crude bridge until the traveler reached the Susquehanna, which was a considerable river and a real obstacle to his progress. The road came down out of the Catskills via the valley of the Ouleout Creek and struck the Susquehanna just above the present village of Unadilla. Hither about the year 1784 came a Connecticut man, Nathaniel Wattles. He provided both a skiff and a large flat-bottomed scow so that the homeseeker, his family, team, and household baggage, and oftentimes a little caravan of livestock, might be set across the river dry-shod and in safety. Wattles here established an inn where one might find lodging and entertainment, and a general store where might be purchased such staples as were essential for the journey. So it was that Wattles' Ferry became the best known landmark on the Ithaca Road.

42. The author indicates that the Susquehanna Turnpike

- **(A)** began as a narrow trail.
- **(B)** was the most important north-south highway in the state.
- **(C)** furnished travelers with surprising obstacles.
- **(D)** went out of use after a generation.

43. The western end of the Susquehanna Turnpike was located at

- **(A)** the Hudson River.
- **(B)** the Connecticut border.
- **(C)** Ithaca.
- **(D)** Catskill.

44. The Susquehanna Turnpike was also known as

- **(A)** the Ithaca Road.
- **(B)** Wattles' Ferry.
- **(C)** the Catskill Trail.
- **(D)** the Mohawk Turnpike.

45. According to this selection, Nathaniel Wattles was prepared to offer travelers all of the following *except*

- **(A)** guides.
- **(B)** a place to sleep.
- **(C)** entertainment.
- **(D)** groceries.

QUESTIONS 46–50 REFER TO THE FOLLOWING PASSAGE.

About the year 1812, two steam ferryboats were built under the direction of Robert Fulton for crossing the Hudson River, and one of the same description was built for service on the East River. These boats were what are known as twin boats, each of them having two complete hulls united by a deck or bridge. Because these boats were pointed at both ends and moved equally well with either end foremost, they crossed and recrossed the river without losing any time in turning about. Fulton also contrived, with great ingenuity, floating docks for the reception of the ferryboats and a means by which they were brought to the docks without a <u>shock</u>. These boats were the first of a fleet that has since carried hundreds of millions of passengers to and from New York.

46. The title that best expresses the main idea of this selection is

(A) "Crossing the Hudson River by Boat."

(B) "Transportation of Passengers."

(C) "The Invention of Floating Docks."

(D) "The Beginning of Steam Ferryboat Service."

47. The steam ferryboats were known as twin boats because

(A) they had two complete hulls united by a bridge.

(B) they could move as easily forward as backward.

(C) each ferryboat had two captains.

(D) two boats were put into service at the same time.

48. Which statement is *true* according to the selection?

(A) Boats built under Fulton's direction are still in use.

(B) Fulton planned a reception to celebrate the first ferryboat.

(C) Fulton piloted the first steam ferryboats across the Hudson.

(D) Fulton developed a satisfactory way of docking the ferryboats.

49. Robert Fulton worked in the

(A) seventeenth century.

(B) eighteenth century.

(C) nineteenth century.

(D) twentieth century.

50. In this paragraph, the word *shock* is used to mean an

(A) unpleasant surprise.

(B) impact.

(C) illness following an accident.

(D) electrical impulse.

Exercise 2

Directions: Read each selection, then answer the questions that follow it. Indicate your answer by circling its letter.

QUESTIONS 1–5 REFER TO THE FOLLOWING PASSAGE.

If you are asked the color of the sky on a fair day in summer, your answer will most probably be, "Blue." This answer is only partially correct. Blue sky near the horizon is not the same kind of blue as it is straight overhead. Look at the sky some fine day and you will find that the blue sky near the horizon is slightly greenish. As your eye moves upward toward the zenith, you will find that the blue changes into pure blue, and finally shades into a violet-blue overhead.

Have you heard the story of a farmer who objected to the color of the distant hills in the artist's picture? He said to the artist, "Why do you make those hills blue? They are green; I've been over there and I know!"

The artist asked him to do a little experiment. "Bend over and look at the hills between your legs." As the farmer did this, the artist asked, "Now what color are the hills?"

The farmer looked again, then he stood up and looked. "By gosh, they turned blue!" he said.

It is quite possible that you have looked at many colors which you did not really recognize. Sky is not just blue; it is many kinds of blue. Grass is not plain green; it might be one of several varieties of green. A red brick wall frequently is not pure red. It might vary from yellow-orange to violet-red in color, but to the unseeing eye it is just red brick.

1. The title that best expresses the ideas of this passage is
   (A) "The Summer Sky."
   (B) "Artists vs. Farmers."
   (C) "Recognizing Colors."
   (D) "Blue Hills."

2. At the zenith, the sky is usually
   (A) violet-blue.
   (B) violet-red.
   (C) greenish-blue.
   (D) yellow-orange.

3. The author suggests that
   (A) farmers are color-blind.
   (B) ability to see color varies.
   (C) brick walls should be painted pure red.
   (D) some artists use poor color combinations.

4. The farmer might be best described as being
   - (A) opinionated.
   - (B) stubborn.
   - (C) uninterested.
   - (D) open-minded.

5. The author would probably be pleased if
   - (A) more days were sunny.
   - (B) more people became farmers.
   - (C) more people became artists.
   - (D) people looked more carefully at the world around them.

QUESTIONS 6–11 REFER TO THE FOLLOWING PASSAGE.

The Alaska Highway, which runs 1,523 miles from Dawson Creek, British Columbia, to Fairbanks, Alaska, was built by U.S. Army Engineers to counter a threatened Japanese invasion of Alaska. It was rushed through in an incredibly short period of nine months and was therefore never properly surveyed. Some of the territory it passes through has not even been explored.

Although the story that the builders followed the trail of a wandering moose is probably not true, the effect is much the same. The leading bulldozer simply crashed through the brush wherever the going was easiest, avoiding the big trees, swampy hollows, and rocks. The project was made more complicated by the necessity of following not the shortest or easiest route, but one that would serve the string of United States-Canadian airfields that stretch from Montana to Alaska. Even on flat land, the road twists into hairpin curves. In rough terrain it goes up and down like a roller coaster. In the mountains, sometimes clinging to the sides of cliffs 400 feet high, it turns sharply, without warning, and gives rear seat passengers the stomach-gripping sensation of taking off into space. There is not a guardrail in its entire 1,500-mile length. Dust kicks up in giant plumes behind every car and on windless days hovers in the air like a thick fog.

Both the Canadian Army and the Alaskan Road Commission, which took over from the Army Engineers in 1946, do a commendable but nearly impossible job of maintaining the road. Where it was built on eternally frozen ground, it buckles and heaves; on the jellylike muskeg it is continually sinking, and must be graveled afresh every month. Bridges thrown across rivers are swept away in flash floods. Torrential thaws wash out miles of highway every spring. On mountainsides, you can tell the age of the road by counting the remains of earlier roads that have slipped down the slope.

6. The title that best expresses the main idea of this selection is

   (A) "The Alaskan Road Commission."

   (B) "Building and Maintaining the Alaska Highway."

   (C) "Exploring Alaska."

   (D) "Driving Conditions in the Far North."

7. The Alaska Highway was built to

   (A) make the route between Alaska and the United States shorter.

   (B) promote trade with Canada.

   (C) meet a wartime emergency.

   (D) aid exploration and surveying efforts.

8. The job of maintaining the road is complicated by the

   (A) threat of invasion.

   (B) forces of nature.

   (C) lack of surveying.

   (D) age of the road.

9. The route followed by the Alaska Highway

   (A) was determined by a moose.

   (B) follows the shortest route from Dawson Creek, British Columbia, to Fairbanks, Alaska.

   (C) connects a number of airfields.

   (D) connects a number of oil fields.

10. The road twists into many hairpin curves because

    (A) bulldozers are hard to steer.

    (B) the road goes around trees, swamps, and rocks.

    (C) the ground is eternally frozen.

    (D) flash floods wash it down the mountainside.

11. A trip on the Alaska Highway is dangerous because

    (A) some of the territory was never explored.

    (B) there are no guardrails.

    (C) snow cuts down on visibility.

    (D) wild animals abound in the area.

exercises

QUESTIONS 12–18 REFER TO THE FOLLOWING PASSAGE.

The seasonal comings and goings of birds have excited the attention and wonder of all sorts of people in all ages and places. The oracles of Greece and the augurs of Rome wove them into ancient mythology. They are spoken of in the Books of Job and Jeremiah.

Nevertheless, it has been difficult for many to believe that small birds, especially, are capable of migratory journeys. Aristotle was convinced that the birds that wintered in Greece were not new arrivals, but merely Greece's summer birds in winter dress. According to a belief persisting in some parts of the world to this day, swallows and swifts do not migrate, but spend the winter in hibernation. (Swifts and swallows *do* migrate, just as most other northern hemisphere birds do.) Another old and charming, but untrue, legend enlists the aid of the stork in getting small birds to and from winter quarters: Small birds are said to hitch rides on the European stork's back.

It is clear why northern hemisphere birds fly south in the fall; they go to assure themselves of food and a more favorable climate for the winter months. It is also clear where most of the migrants come from and where they go. Years of bird-banding have disclosed the routes of the main migratory species.

But there are other aspects of migration that remain, for all our powers of scientific investigation, as puzzling and mysterious to modern man as to the ancients. Why do migrant birds come north each spring? Why don't they simply stay in the warm tropics the whole twelve months of the year? What determines the moment of departure for north or south? Above all, how do birds—especially species like the remarkable golden plover, which flies huge distances directly across trackless ocean wastes—find their way?

12. The best title for this selection would be
    (A) "The Solution of an Ancient Problem."
    (B) "Mysterious Migrations."
    (C) "The Secret of the Plover."
    (D) "Aristotle's Theory."

13. Bird banding has revealed
    (A) the kind of food birds eat.
    (B) why the birds prefer the tropics in the summer.
    (C) why birds leave at a certain time.
    (D) the route taken by different types of birds.

14. Swallows and swifts

    (A) remain in Greece all year.

    (B) change their plumage in winter.

    (C) hibernate during the winter.

    (D) fly south for the winter.

15. The article proves that

    (A) nature still has secrets that man has not fathomed.

    (B) the solutions of Aristotle are accepted by modern science.

    (C) we live in an age that has lost all interest in bird lore.

    (D) man has no means of solving the problem of bird migration.

16. Aristotle, the famous Greek philosopher,

    (A) explained the function of storks during migration.

    (B) deciphered the explanations of the oracles.

    (C) traveled south to watch the birds.

    (D) was wrong in his disbelief in migration.

17. Birds fly south in the winter

    (A) for breeding purposes.

    (B) to avoid bad weather.

    (C) for travel and adventure.

    (D) out of habit.

18. The mysteries about birds include

    (A) the routes they follow, the dates they leave, and the food they eat.

    (B) where they hibernate, how they find their way, and who put on their bands.

    (C) why they return north, how they find their way, and what triggers migration dates.

    (D) where storks winter, why birds fly over oceans, and why there are so many birds in Greece.

exercises

QUESTIONS 19–23 REFER TO THE FOLLOWING PASSAGE.

The proud, noble American eagle appears on one side of the Great Seal of the United States, which is printed on every dollar bill. The same majestic bird can be seen on state seals, half dollars, and even in some commercial advertising. In fact, though we often encounter artistic representations of our national symbol, it is rarely seen alive in its native habitat. It is now all but extinct.

In the days of the founding fathers, the American eagle resided in nearly every corner of the territory now known as the continental United States. Today the eagle survives in what ornithologists call significant numbers only in two regions. An estimated 350 pairs inhabit Florida, and perhaps another 150 live in the Chesapeake Bay area of Delaware, Maryland, and Virginia. A few stragglers remain in other states, but in most, eagles have not been sighted for some time.

A federal law passed in 1940 protects these birds and their nesting areas, but it came too late to save more than a pitiful remnant of the species' original population.

19. An ornithologist is a person who studies
    (A) geographic regions.
    (B) the history of extinct species.
    (C) the populations of certain areas.
    (D) the habits and habitats of birds.

20. Today, eagles are found in the greatest numbers in
    (A) Florida.
    (B) Delaware.
    (C) the Chesapeake Bay region.
    (D) Virginia.

21. The selection implies that
    (A) the number of eagles is likely to increase.
    (B) the eagle population decreased because of a lack of protective game laws.
    (C) there were only two localities where eagles could survive.
    (D) the government knows very little about eagles.

22. A 1940 federal law
    (A) established wildlife sanctuaries for eagles.
    (B) declared the American eagle to be our national bird.
    (C) banned the use of the eagle in commercial advertising.
    (D) protects American eagles and their nesting areas.

23. The American eagle is able to live
    (A) only east of the Mississippi.
    (B) only in bird sanctuaries.
    (C) almost anywhere in the United States.
    (D) only in warm climates.

QUESTIONS 24–28 REFER TO THE FOLLOWING PASSAGE.

The Rhodora

In May, when sea-winds pierced our solitudes,

I found the fresh Rhodora in the woods,

Spreading its leafless blooms in a damp nook,

To please the desert and the sluggish brook.

The purple petals, fallen in the pool,

Made the black water with their beauty gay;

Here might the red-bird come his plumes to cool,

And court the flower that cheapens his array.

Rhodora! if the sages ask thee why

This charm is wasted on the earth and sky,

Tell them, dear, that if eyes were made for seeing,

Then Beauty is its own excuse for being:

Why thou wert there, O rival of the rose!

I never thought to ask, I never knew:

But, in my simple ignorance suppose

The self-same Power that brought me there brought you.

—*Ralph Waldo Emerson*

24. The poet is impressed with the beauty of
    (A) the sea.
    (B) the woods.
    (C) a bird.
    (D) a flower.

25. When the poet says that the flower cheapens the array of the red-bird, he means that the
    (A) bird gets nothing from the flower.
    (B) flower gets nothing from the bird.
    (C) color of the flower is brighter than that of the bird.
    (D) bird ruins the flower.

26. In saying "This charm is wasted on the earth and sky," the poet means that
    (A) the earth and sky do not appreciate beauty.
    (B) no one sees a flower that blooms deep in the woods.

    (C) wise men sometimes ask foolish questions.
    (D) the bird does not even notice the beauty of the flower.

27. The poet believes that
    (A) flower petals pollute the water.
    (B) red birds are garish.
    (C) beauty exists for its own sake.
    (D) sea-wind is refreshing.

28. The poet probably
    (A) is an insensitive person.
    (B) dislikes solitude.
    (C) is a religious person.
    (D) is ignorant.

ANSWER KEYS AND EXPLANATIONS

Exercise 1

1. B	11. A	21. A	31. D	41. D
2. C	12. A	22. A	32. D	42. A
3. A	13. B	23. A	33. C	43. C
4. B	14. C	24. D	34. A	44. A
5. B	15. D	25. B	35. A	45. A
6. D	16. C	26. D	36. C	46. D
7. C	17. A	27. A	37. B	47. A
8. B	18. C	28. B	38. C	48. D
9. D	19. D	29. B	39. B	49. C
10. A	20. B	30. A	40. B	50. B

1. **The correct answer is (B).** The entire selection is about court practices in ancient Athens.

2. **The correct answer is (C).** The answer is in the second sentence.

3. **The correct answer is (A).** See the last sentence.

4. **The correct answer is (B).** You will find the correct answer in the third paragraph.

5. **The correct answer is (B).** The last sentence of the first paragraph states unequivocally that a ship cannot dock without rope.

6. **The correct answer is (D).** See the second sentence.

7. **The correct answer is (C).** The heaving lines are tied to mooring lines. The mooring lines are the heavy ropes that secure the boat to the pier.

8. **The correct answer is (B).** The ship is held to her pier by up to 21 manila-fiber mooring lines and a few wire lines.

9. **The correct answer is (D).** You need to incorporate information from both paragraphs to answer this question. The second paragraph tells us that rope is measured by circumference. The first paragraph tells us that mooring lines are 9- or 10-inch manila lines.

10. **The correct answer is (A).** The first sentence of the second paragraph answers this question. All the other choices are contradicted by the selection.

11. **The correct answer is (A).** The third sentence of the second paragraph states that rope is sold by the pound but ordered by length.

12. **The correct answer is (A).** Sisal comes from Africa and the Netherlands East Indies, not from the Philippines. Abaca, also known as the manila plant, comes from the Philippines, as well as from Central America.

13. **The correct answer is (B).** Reread the last three sentences for the answer.

14. **The correct answer is (C).** Find this answer by substituting the choices for the word

refinement. Then continue reading the passage following the substituted word, and the correct contextual meaning should be clear.

15. **The correct answer is (D).** The author is not terribly upset but does seem to regret the changes that have been made.

16. **The correct answer is (C).** This answer ties in with the answer to question 15.

17. **The correct answer is (A).** The author's description of the new set and new croquet course as compared with the old makes it clear that the new arrangement is far more exact. On the other hand, all concerned seem to have less fun.

18. **The correct answer is (C).** The narrator has explained the tense environment during the games.

19. **The correct answer is (D).** This answer is also to be inferred from the selection.

20. **The correct answer is (B).** The author appears to be a genial sort who enjoys children, animals, sunsets, and sport for sport's sake. All of the other choices imply negativism on the part of the author.

21. **The correct answer is (A).** If necessary, reread the selection. Clearly, the observer is fascinated by the scene before him. He gives no indication of being frightened or repulsed and is far too interested to be bored.

22. **The correct answer is (A).** The Flemish painting was brought over from Holland.

23. **The correct answer is (A).** At the beginning of the selection, the game is being played on a level spot with nine pins. At the end of the passage, balls are rolled, presumably at the pins. This is a variety of bowling.

24. **The correct answer is (D).** The second paragraph begins "What seemed particularly odd to Rip . . . ." Rip must be the observer. All of the other choices *could* be true, but we have no confirming evidence in the

selection, whereas the selection does tell us that the man's name is Rip.

25. **The correct answer is (B).** In the first sentence of the last paragraph, Rip found it "particularly odd" that the men maintained such grave faces while evidently amusing themselves.

26. **The correct answer is (D).** The selection describes the properties of zirconium in its various forms.

27. **The correct answer is (A).** Consider the use of the word *docile* as applied to solid zirconium, in contrast to the use of the word *violent* as applied to powdered zirconium.

28. **The correct answer is (B).** An emphasis of the selection is that increasing uses are being found for zirconium.

29. **The correct answer is (B).** The first paragraph makes this point.

30. **The correct answer is (A).** In both the second and third paragraphs, zirconium is described as a metal.

31. **The correct answer is (D).** If zirconium is too dangerous to be used in ammunition, it is most certainly too dangerous to be used in fireworks.

32. **The correct answer is (D).** The selection traces the history of protection of our documents of freedom during times of war.

33. **The correct answer is (C).** If State Department clerks in Washington scooped up the documents and stuffed them into linen sacks, the documents must have been lying around the office.

34. **The correct answer is (A).** See the last paragraph.

35. **The correct answer is (A).** Bombs, shock, and fire are sudden disasters.

36. **The correct answer is (C).** The British advanced on and burned Washington in

1814 during the War of 1812; December 26, 1941, occurred during the opening days of World War II. The Japanese attacked Pearl Harbor on December 7, 1941.

37. **The correct answer is (B).** The selection describes the varying hare.

38. **The correct answer is (C).** As the names imply, the rabbits vary with the seasons.

39. **The correct answer is (B).** The rabbits are mottled brown and white while in the middle of the molting process in spring and fall.

40. **The correct answer is (B).** This is stated in the first sentence of the last paragraph.

41. **The correct answer is (D).** The second paragraph states that the hares have no voluntary control over the changes in their appearance.

42. **The correct answer is (A).** The first paragraph describes the original trail as a path. The road is also described as an east-west route. It presented travelers with surprisingly few obstacles.

43. **The correct answer is (C).** The frontier outpost, Ithaca, was at the western end of the highway.

44. **The correct answer is (A).** Reread the first paragraph.

45. **The correct answer is (A).** Guides are not mentioned.

46. **The correct answer is (D).** The selection describes the construction and use of ferryboats.

47. **The correct answer is (A).** See the second sentence.

48. **The correct answer is (D).** The next-to-last sentence describes Fulton's ingenious docking method.

49. **The correct answer is (C).** 1812 was in the nineteenth century.

50. **The correct answer is (B).** In the context of the paragraph, *shock* must refer to the *impact* of the boat running into the dock.

Exercise 2

1. C	7. C	13. D	19. D	24. D
2. A	8. B	14. D	20. A	25. C
3. B	9. C	15. A	21. B	26. B
4. D	10. B	16. D	22. D	27. C
5. D	11. B	17. B	23. C	28. C
6. B	12. B	18. C		

1. **The correct answer is (C).** The subject of the passage is variations in the composition and appearance of color. The story of the farmer and the artist is included only by way of illustration; it is not the subject of the selection.

2. **The correct answer is (A).** The zenith is straight overhead. The last sentence of the first paragraph answers this question.

3. **The correct answer is (B).** The author makes this point in the last paragraph.

4. **The correct answer is (D).** The farmer was willing to do the artist's bidding and look at the hills through his legs. A highly opinionated or stubborn person would not have submitted to the experiment. An uninterested person would not have noticed the difference between the artist's colors and his own observations.

5. **The correct answer is (D).** The author finds variations of color fascinating; he certainly would be pleased if others could have their lives enriched by appreciating this variety.

6. **The correct answer is (B).** The article is all about the building and maintaining of the Alaska Highway.

7. **The correct answer is (C).** The Alaska Highway does provide an overland route from Alaska to the 48 contiguous states, and it might promote some trade with Canada, but the reason for its original construction is stated in the first sentence.

8. **The correct answer is (B).** The last paragraph describes in detail the interference of nature with maintenance of the road. The poor layout of the road itself might be blamed on the threat of invasion and the lack of proper surveying. While a poorly built road is more difficult to maintain, the chief culprit in the maintenance situation is nature.

9. **The correct answer is (C).** The answer to this question is buried in the middle of the second paragraph. If you missed it, reread.

10. **The correct answer is (B).** This question is answered near the beginning of the second paragraph.

11. **The correct answer is (B).** The second paragraph is full of details. The answer to this question is near the end of the paragraph.

12. **The correct answer is (B).** The selection is about the migration of birds and raises a number of questions about migration that are not yet understood.

13. **The correct answer is (D).** See the last sentence of the third paragraph.

14. **The correct answer is (D).** A parenthetical remark in the second paragraph specifically makes this statement.

15. **The correct answer is (A).** The last paragraph poses a number of questions about migration that still puzzle scientists.

answers exercises

Although we might not understand much about bird migration, it does not pose any problem that must be solved, so (D) is not the correct answer.

16. **The correct answer is (D).** Aristotle was a very clever man, but he erred in thinking that all birds change their plumage and remain in the same region despite the change of seasons.

17. **The correct answer is (B).** Birds fly south so that they might enjoy warmer weather and avoid problems of finding food in snow-covered or frozen areas.

18. **The correct answer is (C).** The last paragraph details the major puzzles regarding bird migration.

19. **The correct answer is (D).** An ornithologist studies birds.

20. **The correct answer is (A).** Approximately 350 pairs live in Florida, 150 pairs in the Chesapeake region, and only a few elsewhere.

21. **The correct answer is (B).** In stating that the 1940 protective law came too late to save the eagles, the last sentence implies that the eagle population decreased because of the lack of such a law. (You might be aware that the eagle population has indeed rebounded, but you must answer this question, and all questions, on the basis of what is stated or implied by the passage.)

22. **The correct answer is (D).** The 1940 law protects American eagles and their nesting areas everywhere in the United States, not just in bird sanctuaries.

23. **The correct answer is (C).** If in the 1700s the American eagle resided in nearly every corner of the territory that became the 48 states, its habitat is not limited to any particular climatic or geographic region.

24. **The correct answer is (D).** The poem really is an ode to the flower.

25. **The correct answer is (C).** The poet is saying that while the bird is splendid, the flower is even more beautiful.

26. **The correct answer is (B).** The flower blooms deep in the woods where, except for the occasional wanderer like himself, no one sees it.

27. **The correct answer is (C).** "Then beauty is its own excuse for being."

28. **The correct answer is (C).** In saying "The self-same Power that brought me there brought you," the poet is expressing his faith in a Supreme Being that created man and nature.

SUMMING IT UP

- This section is called Reading and Language Arts on the COOP and Reading on the HSPT (under the Comprehension section). It's called "Reading" on the TACHS. Each test presents reading passages followed by a series of questions.

- To do well on this section, you will need to be able to read quickly. If you do not read quickly, study the section "How to Improve Your Reading Skills" in this chapter.

- Study and remember all of the steps for answering reading comprehension questions: read over the question, skim the passage for the main idea, reread the passage with attention to details and point of view, carefully read each question or incomplete statement, read all four answer choices, and don't spend too much time on any one question.

Spelling

OVERVIEW

- **Tips for improving your spelling skills**
- **Twenty-four spelling rules**
- **Summing it up**

The COOP, HSPT, and TACHS exams all include several test questions that check spelling skills. In these questions, you are presented with a series of answer choices. Some of the choices contain sentences; the last choice is "No Mistakes." You are asked to read the sentences and check for errors in capitalization, punctuation, usage, or spelling. If you believe that none of the sentences contains an error, you choose "No Mistakes."

Spelling is a weakness for many students. The ability to spell well does not seem to be directly related to any measurable factor. A few fortunate individuals are just natural spellers—they can hear a word and instinctively spell it correctly. Most people, however, must memorize rules, memorize spellings, and rely on a dictionary.

To help you excel on the spelling questions found on the COOP, the HSPT, and the TACHS exams, this section includes tips for improving your spelling and a list of spelling rules.

TIPS FOR IMPROVING YOUR SPELLING SKILLS

You can improve your spelling by keeping a list of words that you spell incorrectly or that you must often look up. Add to your list whenever you find a word you cannot spell. When you have a few minutes to study spelling, write each word correctly ten times. If you know how to type, type each word ten times, too. Let your hand get used to the feel of the correct spelling, and let your eye become accustomed to seeing the word spelled correctly. Periodically, ask someone to read your list aloud to you, and try writing them correctly. Frequent self-testing of problem spelling words should help you learn the correct spellings. On the day before the test, read over your list carefully.

Another way to improve your spelling is by developing mnemonic devices. A mnemonic device is a private clue that you develop to help you remember something. For example, if you have trouble spelling the word *friend*, you might find it helpful to remember the sentence, "A friend is true to the *end*." This little sentence will help you remember to place the "i" before the "e." If you have trouble distinguishing between *here* and *hear* try a sentence like "To listen is to hear with an ear." If you confuse the spellings *principle* and *principal*, remember (whether you believe it or not) "The princiPAL is your PAL."

When you have trouble spelling a word, try to invent your own mnemonic device, and you will have a built-in "prompter" when you encounter spelling questions on the exam. Much of spelling must simply be learned. However, there are some rules that apply to the spelling of root words and more rules that apply to the adding of suffixes. The following list presents some of the most useful spelling rules and some of the most common exceptions to those rules. Try to learn them all! The explanations that accompany the spelling exercises, as well as the exam questions that test spelling, refer to these rules by number when they apply.

TWENTY-FOUR SPELLING RULES

1 *i* before *e*
Except after *c*
Or when sounded like *ay*
As in *neighbor* or *weigh*.
Exceptions: Neither, leisure, foreigner, seized, weird, heights.

2 If a word ends in *y* preceded by a vowel, keep the *y* when adding a suffix.
Examples: day, days; attorney, attorneys

3 If a word ends in *y* preceded by a consonant, change the *y* to *i* before adding a suffix.
Examples: try, tries, tried; lady, ladies
Exceptions: To avoid double *i*, retain the *y* before -*ing* and -*ish*.
Examples: fly, flying; baby, babyish

4 Silent *e* at the end of a word is usually dropped before a suffix beginning with a vowel.
Examples: dine + ing = dining
locate + ion = location
use + able = usable
offense + ive = offensive

Exceptions: Words ending in *ce* and *ge* retain *e* before -*able* and -*ous* in order to retain the soft sounds of *c* and *g*.
Examples: peace + able = peaceable
courage + ous = courageous

5 Silent *e* is usually kept before a suffix beginning with a consonant.
Examples: care + less = careless
late + ly = lately
one + ness = oneness
game + ster = gamester

6 Some exceptions must simply be memorized. Some exceptions to the last two rules are *truly, duly, awful, argument, wholly, ninth, mileage, dyeing, acreage, canoeing.*

7 A word of one syllable that ends in a single consonant preceded by a single vowel doubles the final consonant before a suffix beginning with a vowel or before the suffix -*y*.
Examples: hit, hitting; drop, dropped; big, biggest; mud, muddy; **but:** *help, helping* because *help* ends in two consonants; *need, needing, needy* because the final consonant is preceded by two vowels.

8 A word of more than one syllable that accents the last syllable and that ends in a single consonant preceded by a single vowel doubles the final consonant when adding a suffix beginning with a vowel.

Examples: begin, beginner; admit, admitted; **but:** *enter*, *entered* because the accent is not on the last syllable.

9 A word ending in *er* or *ur* doubles the *r* in the past tense if the word is accented on the last syllable.

Examples: occur, occurred; prefer, preferred; transfer, transferred

10 A word ending in *er* does not double the *r* in the past tense if the accent falls before the last syllable.

Examples: answer, answered; offer, offered; differ, differed

11 When -*full* is added to the end of a noun, the final *l* is dropped.

Examples: cheerful, cupful, hopeful

12 All words beginning with *over* are one word.

Examples: overcast, overcharge, overhear

13 All words with the prefix *self* are hyphenated.

Examples: self-control, self-defense, self-evident

14 The letter *q* is always followed by *u*.

Examples: quiz, bouquet, acquire

15 Numbers from twenty-one to ninety-nine are hyphenated.

16 *Per cent* is *never* hyphenated. It may be written as one word (*percent*) or as two words (*per cent*).

17 *Welcome* is one word with one *l*.

18 *All right* is always two words. *Alright* is a nonstandard form of English and should not be used.

19 *Already* means prior to some specified time. *All ready* means *completely ready*.

Example: By the time I was *all ready* to go to the play, the tickets were *already* sold out.

20 *Altogether* means entirely. *All together* means *in sum* or *collectively*.

Example: There are *altogether* too many people to seat in this room when we are *all together*.

21 *Their* is the possessive of *they*.
They're is the contraction for *they are*.
There means *at that place*.

Example: *They're* going to put *their* books over *there*.

22 *Your* is the possessive of *you*.
You're is the contraction for *you are*.

Example: *You're* certainly planning to leave *your* muddy boots outside.

23 *Whose* is the possessive of *who*.
Who's is the contraction for *who is*.

Example: Do you know *who's* ringing the doorbell or *whose* car is in the street?

24 *Its* is the possessive of *it*. *It's* is the contraction for it is.

Example: *It's* I who lost the letter and *its* envelope.

EXERCISES: SPELLING

Directions: Look for errors in spelling. Choose the letter of the sentence that contains the error. No question contains more than one sentence with a spelling error. If you find no error, choose (D) as your answer.

1. (A) In the teacher's absence, the pupils had an eraser fight.
   (B) The laws of apartheid prohibited marriage between blacks and whites.
   (C) We may be haveing a fire drill this afternoon.
   (D) No mistakes

2. (A) The Indian squaw carried her papoose strapped to a board on her back.
   (B) Christopher Columbus is credited with the discovary of America.
   (C) Innocent victims should not have to stand trial.
   (D) No mistakes

3. (A) The sailor shouted, "All ashore that are going ashore."
   (B) The turtle crawled accross the street.
   (C) For lunch, I ate a turkey sandwich.
   (D) No mistakes

4. (A) Meet me at the bus depot promptly at four.
   (B) On Saturday, we will have dinner at a restaurant.
   (C) The whipping post was in use as punishment in Delaware until recent times.
   (D) No mistakes

5. (A) The shepherd would be lonely without his dog.
   (B) The experiment served to confirm the hypothesis.
   (C) The divinity fudge was truly deliscious.
   (D) No mistakes

6. (A) The golfer took a break after the nineth hole.
   (B) Let me acquaint you with the new rules.
   (C) The slugger wields a heavy bat.
   (D) No mistakes

7. (A) Biology is always a laboratory science.
   (B) The short story is really a memoir.
   (C) My neice will enter college in the fall.
   (D) No mistakes

8. (A) The currency of Mexico is the peso.
   (B) The detective traveled incognito.
   (C) Is there anything one can buy for a nickel?
   (D) No mistakes

9. (A) Our senator is a staunch supporter of the president.
   (B) I heard a rumer that our principal is about to retire.
   (C) A surgeon must have steady hands.
   (D) No mistakes

10. (A) To grow crops in the desert, we must irrigate daily.
    (B) Most convenience stores have very long hours.
    (C) There was a lovly centerpiece on the table.
    (D) No mistakes

ANSWER KEY AND EXPLANATIONS

1. C	3. B	5. C	7. C	9. B
2. B	4. D	6. A	8. D	10. C

1. **The correct answer is (C).** The correct spelling is having (rule 4)

2. **The correct answer is (B).** The correct spelling is discovery (The base word is *discover*. There is no reason to change the *e* to *a*.)

3. **The correct answer is (B).** The correct spelling is across (No special rule applies. Learn to spell *across*.)

4. **The correct answer is (D).** *(No mistakes)*

5. **The correct answer is (C).** The correct spelling is delicious (There is no *s* in the middle of this word.)

6. **The correct answer is (A).** The correct spelling is ninth (rule 6)

7. **The correct answer is (C).** The correct spelling is niece (rule 1)

8. **The correct answer is (D).** *(No mistakes)*

9. **The correct answer is (B).** The correct spelling is rumor (No rule; just learn the spelling.)

10. **The correct answer is (C).** The correct spelling is lovely (rule 5)

answers exercises

SUMMING IT UP

- The HSPT, the COOP, and the TACHS exams have several questions specifically testing spelling.

- You are given some choices containing sentences; the last choice says "No mistakes." You must find the spelling error and choose that sentence, or choose "No mistakes" if all sentences are correct.

- Keep a list of words that you spell incorrectly or that you have to look up. Periodically write the words and have someone test you on them.

- Read the "Twenty-Four Spelling Rules" section, and write some examples for yourself.

Punctuation and Capitalization

OVERVIEW

- **Punctuation rules**
- **Capitalization rules**
- **Summing it up**

Along with spelling, the HSPT, the TACHS, and the COOP exams also test your knowledge of punctuation and capitalization. To help you review, check out the following list of punctuation and capitalization rules. Because rules can be boring and very difficult to study, we've broken the rules into categories to help you study them in "chunks." Most will be familiar to you, but if you find anything surprising, or if you have trouble understanding any of the rules, be sure to talk to your teacher.

PUNCTUATION RULES

The Period

- Use a period at the end of a sentence that makes a statement, gives a command, or makes a "polite request" in the form of a question that does not require an answer.
  Examples: I am brushing up on my verbal skills.
  Study the chapter on verbs for tomorrow.
  Would you please read this list of words so that I may practice my spelling lesson.

- Use a period after an abbreviation and after an initial in a person's name.
  Examples: Gen. Robert E. Lee led the Confederate forces.
  Minneapolis and St. Paul are known as the "twin cities."
  Exception: Do not use a period after postal service state name abbreviations.
  Example: St. Louis, MO

- Use a period as a decimal point in numbers.
  Example: A sales tax of 5.5% amounts to $7.47 on a $135.80 purchase.

The Question Mark

- Use a question mark at the end of a direct and genuine question.
  Example: Why do you want to borrow that book?

chapter 13

- Do not use a question mark after an indirect question; use a period.
  Example: He asked if they wanted to accompany him.

- A direct and genuine question must end with a question mark even if the question is only part of the sentence.
  Example: "Daddy, are we there yet?" the child asked.

- Use a question mark (within parentheses) to indicate uncertainty as to the correctness of a piece of information.
  Example: John Carver, (first governor of Plymouth colony?) was born in 1575 and died in 1621.

The Exclamation Mark

- The only reason to use an exclamation mark is to express strong feeling, emotion, or extreme importance.
  Examples: Congratulations! You broke the record.
  Rush! Perishable contents.

The Comma

- The salutation of a personal letter is followed by a comma.
  Example: Dear Mary,

- The complimentary close of a letter is ordinarily followed by a comma, though this use is optional.
  Example: Cordially yours,

- An appositive must be set off by commas.
  Example: Jim Rodgers, my next-door neighbor, is an excellent baby-sitter.

- A noun of address is set apart by commas.
  Example: When you finish your homework, Jeff, please take out the garbage.

- Use commas to set off parenthetical words.
  Example: I think, however, that a move might not be wise at this time.

- When two or more adjectives all modify a noun equally, all but the last must be followed by commas. If you can add the word *and* between the adjectives without changing the sense of the sentence, then use commas.
  Example: The refined, tall, stern-looking man stood at the top of the stairs.

- An introductory phrase of five or more words must be separated by a comma.
  Example: Because the prisoner had a history of attempted jailbreaks, he was put under heavy guard.

- After a short introductory phrase, the comma is optional. The comma should be used where needed for clarity.
  Examples: As a child she was a tomboy. (comma unnecessary)
  To Dan, Phil was friend as well as brother. (comma clarifies)
  In 1978, 300 people lost their lives in one air disaster. (comma clarifies)

- A comma is not generally used before a subordinate clause that ends a sentence, though in long, unwieldy sentences like this one, use of such a comma is optional.

- A comma precedes the coordinating conjunction unless the two clauses are very short.
  Examples: Kevin wanted to borrow a book from the library, but the librarian would not allow him to take it until he had paid his fines.
  Roy washed the dishes and Helen dried.

- Words, phrases, or clauses in a series are separated by commas. The use of a comma before *and* is optional. If the series ends in *etc.*, use a comma before *etc.* Do not use a comma after *etc.* in a series, even if the sentence continues.
  Examples: Coats, umbrellas, and boots should be placed in the closet at the end of the hall.
  Pencils, scissors, paper clips, etc. belong in your top desk drawer.

- A comma separates a short direct quotation from the speaker.
  Examples: She said, "I must be home by six."
  "Tomorrow I begin my new job," he told us.

- Use a comma to indicate that you have omitted a word or words, such as *of* or *of the*.
  Example: President, XYZ Corporation

- Use a comma to separate a name from a title or personal-name suffix.
  Examples: Paul Feiner, Chairman
  Carl Andrew Pforzheimer, Jr.

- Use a comma when first and last names are reversed.
  Example: Bernbach, Linda

- Use a comma to separate parts of dates or addresses.
  Example: Please come to a party on Sunday, May 9, at the Pine Tavern on Drake Road, Cheswold, Delaware.
  Exception: Do not use a comma between the postal service state abbreviation and the zip code.
  Example: Scarsdale, NY 10583

- A comma ordinarily separates thousands, millions, and trillions.
  Example: 75,281,646

- A nonrestrictive adjective phrase or clause must be set off by commas. A nonrestrictive phrase or clause is one that can be omitted without essentially changing the meaning of the sentence.
  Example: Our new sailboat, which has bright orange sails, is very seaworthy.

- A restrictive phrase or clause is vital to the meaning of a sentence and cannot be omitted. Do not set it off with commas.
  Example: A sailboat without sails is useless.

- A comma must be used if the sentence might be subject to different interpretation without it.
  Example: He saw the woman who had rejected him, and blushed.

- If a pause would make the sentence clearer and easier to read, insert a comma.

  Examples: Inside the people were dancing. (confusing)

  Inside, the people were dancing. (clearer)

  After all crime must be punished. (confusing)

  After all, crime must be punished. (clearer)

  The pause rule is not infallible, but it is your best resort when all other rules governing use of the comma fail you.

The Hyphen

- Use a hyphen to divide a word at the end of a line.

- Hyphenate numbers from twenty-one through ninety-nine, except for multiples of ten: twenty, thirty, forty, etc.

- Use a hyphen to join two words serving together as a single adjective before a noun.

  Examples: We left the highway and proceeded on a well-paved road.

  That baby-faced man is considerably older than he appears to be.

- Use a hyphen with the prefixes *ex-*, *self-*, *all-*, and the suffix *-elect*.

  Examples: ex-Senator, self-appointed, all-State, Governor-elect

- Use a hyphen to avoid ambiguity.

  Example: After the custodian recovered the use of his right arm, he re-covered the office chairs.

- Use a hyphen to avoid an awkward union of letters.

  Examples: semi-independent; shell-like

- Refer to a dictionary whenever you are uncertain as to whether you should write two words, a hyphenated word, or one word.

The Dash

- You may use a dash (—) or parentheses ( ) for emphasis or to set off an explanatory group of words.

  Example: The tools of his trade—probe, mirror, cotton swabs—were neatly arranged on the dentist's tray.

  Unless the set-off expression ends a sentence, dashes must be used in pairs.

- Use a dash to mark a sudden break in thought that leaves a sentence unfinished.

  Example: He opened the door a crack and saw—

The Colon

- Use a colon after the salutation in a business letter.

  Example: Dear Board Member:

- Use a colon to separate hours from minutes.

  Example: The eclipse occurred at 10:36 a.m.

- A colon may, but need not always, be used to introduce a list, introduce a long quotation, or introduce a question.

  Example: My question is this: Are you willing to punch a time clock?

The Semicolon

- A semicolon may be used to join two short, related independent clauses.

  Example: Anne is working at the front desk on Monday; Ernie will take over on Tuesday.

  Two main clauses must be separated by a conjunction or by a semicolon or must be written as two sentences. A semicolon never precedes a coordinating conjunction. The same two clauses may be written as follows:

  > Autumn had come and the trees were almost bare.
  > Autumn had come; the trees were almost bare.
  > Autumn had come. The trees were almost bare.

- A semicolon may be used to separate two independent clauses that are joined by an adverb such as *however*, *therefore*, *otherwise*, or *nevertheless*. The adverb must be followed by a comma.

  Example: You may use a semicolon to separate this clause from the next; however, you will not be incorrect if you choose to write two separate sentences.

  If you are uncertain about how to use the semicolon to connect independent clauses, write two sentences instead.

- A semicolon should be used to separate a series of phrases or clauses when each of them contains commas.

  Example: The old gentleman's heirs were Margaret Whitlock, his half-sister; James Bagley, the butler; William Frame, his late cousin; Robert Bone; and his favorite charity, the Salvation Army.

The Apostrophe

- In a contraction, insert an apostrophe in place of the omitted letter or letters.

  Examples: have + not = haven't
  we + are = we're
  let + us = let's
  of the clock = o'clock
  class of 1985 = class of '85

- The apostrophe, when used to indicate possession, means *belonging to everything to the left of the apostrophe*.

  Examples: lady's = belonging to the lady
  ladies' = belonging to the ladies
  children's = belonging to the children

  To test for correct placement of the apostrophe, read *of the*.

  Examples: childrens' = of the childrens (therefore incorrect)
  girls' = of the girls (correct if it is the meaning intended)

NOTE

Never begin a paragraph with a contraction.

Quotation Marks

- All directly quoted material must be enclosed by quotation marks. Words not quoted must remain outside the quotation marks.
  Example: "If it is hot on Sunday," she said, "we will go to the beach."

- An indirect quote must not be enclosed by quotation marks.
  Example: She said that we might go to the beach on Sunday.

- When a multiple-paragraph passage is quoted, each paragraph of the quotation must begin with quotation marks, but ending quotation marks are used only at the end of the last quoted paragraph.

- A period always goes inside the quotation marks, whether the quotation marks are used to denote quoted material, to set off titles—such as chapters in a book or titles of short stories—or to isolate words used in a special sense.
  Examples: Jane explained: "The house is just around the corner."

  The first chapter of *The Andromeda Strain* is entitled "The Country of Lost Borders."

- A comma always goes inside the quotation marks.
  Examples: "We really must go home," said the dinner guests.

  If your skills have become "rusty," you must study before you take the test.

  Three stories in Kurt Vonnegut's *Welcome to the Monkey House* are "Harrison Bergeron," "Next Door," and "EPICAC."

- A question mark goes inside the quotation marks if it is part of the quotation. If the whole sentence containing the quotation is a question, the question mark goes outside the quotation marks.
  Examples: He asked, "Was the airplane on time?"

  What did you really mean when you said "I do"?

- An exclamation mark goes inside the quotation marks if the quoted words are an exclamation, outside if the entire sentence including the quotation is an exclamation.
  Examples: The sentry shouted, "Drop your gun!"

  Save us from our "friends"!

- A colon and a semicolon always go *outside* the quotation marks.
  Example: He said, "War is destructive"; she added, "Peace is constructive."

- Words used in an unusual way may be placed inside quotation marks.
  Example: A surfer who "hangs ten" is performing a tricky maneuver on a surfboard, not staging a mass execution.

- A quotation within a quotation may be set apart by single quotes.
  Example: George said, "The philosophy 'I think, therefore I am' may be attributed to Descartes."

CAPITALIZATION RULES

- Capitalize the first word of a complete sentence.
  Example: Your desk top should appear neat and orderly.

- Capitalize the first word of a quoted sentence.
  Example: The teacher said, "Please write your name at the top of the paper."
  Do *not* capitalize the first word within quotation marks if it does not begin a complete sentence.
  Examples: "I was late," she explained, "because of the snow."
  Some groups would like to restrict certain liberties in the interest of "patriotism."

- Capitalize the letter *I* when it stands alone.

- Capitalize the first letter of the first, last, and each important word in the title of a book, play, article, etc.
  Examples: "The Mystery of the Green Ghost"
  A Night at the Opera

- Capitalize a title when it applies to a specific person, group, or document.
  Examples: The President will give a press conference this afternoon.
  Senators Goldwater and Tower are leading figures in the Conservative Party.
  Our Constitution should be strictly interpreted.
  Do *not* capitalize the same type of title when it does not make a specific reference.
  Examples: Some congressmen are liberal; others are more conservative.
  It would be useful for our club to write a constitution.

- Capitalize days of the week, months of the year, and holidays, but do *not* capitalize the seasons.
  Example: Labor Day, the last holiday of the summer, falls on the first Monday in September.

- Capitalize all proper names, including but not limited to: names of people, *John F. Smith;* buildings, *Empire State Building;* events, *Armistice Day;* places, *Panama*, and words formed using those places, *Panamanian;* organizations, *The United Fund;* and words referring to a sole God, *Allah*.

- Capitalize the points of the compass only when referring to a specific place or area.
  Example: Many retired persons spend the winter in the South.

- Do *not* capitalize the points of the compass when they refer to a direction.
  Example: Many birds fly south in the winter.

- The only school subjects that are regularly capitalized are languages and specific place names used as modifiers.
  Example: Next year I will study French, biology, English literature, mathematics, European history, and ancient philosophy.

- A noun not regularly capitalized should be capitalized when it is used as part of a proper name.
  Example: Yesterday I visited Uncle Charles, my favorite uncle.

- In a letter:
  a. Capitalize all titles in the address and closing.
  Examples: Mr. John Jones, President Mary Smith, Chairman of the Board
  b. Capitalize the first and last words, titles, and proper names in the salutation.
  Examples: Dear Dr. Williams, My dear Sir:
  c. Capitalize only the first word in a complimentary closing.
  Example: Very truly yours,

EXERCISES: PUNCTUATION AND CAPITALIZATION

Directions: Among the following sentences, look for errors in capitalization or punctuation. If you find no mistake, mark (D).

1. **(A)** He was not informed, that he would have to work overtime.
   (B) The wind blew several papers off his desk.
   (C) This is the man whom you interviewed last week.
   (D) No mistakes

2. **(A)** If an employee wishes to attend the conference, she should fill out the necessary forms.
   (B) Mr. Wright's request cannot be granted under any conditions.
   (C) Charles Dole, who is a member of the committee, was asked to confer with commissioner Wilson.
   (D) No mistakes

3. **(A)** He is the kind of person who is always willing to undertake difficult assignments.
   (B) The teacher entered the room and said, "the work must be completed today."
   (C) The special project was assigned to Mary Green and me.
   (D) No mistakes

4. **(A)** Mr. Barnes, the bus dispatcher, has many important duties.
   (B) We checked the addresses once more and sent the letters to the mailroom.
   (C) Do you agree that this year's class is the best yet?
   (D) No mistakes

5. **(A)** The new teacher aides were given their assignments and, they were asked to begin work immediately.
   (B) Jim's sister, Carol, will begin college in the fall.
   (C) My favorite subjects are English, science, and American history.
   (D) No mistakes

6. **(A)** Although I am willing to work on most holidays, I refuse to work on Labor Day.
   (B) Every Tuesday afternoon, Joan volunteers at Children's Hospital.
   (C) If you wish to be considered for the scholarship, you must file your application promptly.
   (D) No mistakes

7. **(A)** The new student asked the gym teacher if he could join the baseball team?

   (B) Girl Scout Troop 71 will march in the parade.

   (C) Mrs. Garcia asked Louisa and Henry to help bake cookies for the party.

   (D) No mistakes

8. **(A)** I find his study of the birds of North America to be fascinating.

   (B) The doctor suggested that my grandfather go South for the winter to avoid frequent colds.

   (C) Under the new rules, when do we revert to Eastern Standard Time?

   (D) No mistakes

9. **(A)** If you would like to spend the night, you may sleep in Tom's room.

   (B) The attack on Pearl Harbor, on December 7, 1941, came as a complete surprise.

   (C) "May I use the computer this afternoon," the boy asked?

   (D) No mistakes

10. **(A)** "If it rains on Friday," the boy mused, "the game may be played on Saturday instead."

    (B) The child's new bicycle lay on its side near the curb.

    (C) Whenever I drive on a New York street, I watch for potholes.

    (D) No mistakes

exercises

ANSWER KEY AND EXPLANATIONS

1. A	3. B	5. A	7. A	9. C
2. C	4. D	6. D	8. B	10. D

1. **The correct answer is (A).** There is no reason for a comma between the verb and its object.

2. **The correct answer is (C).** Commissioner Wilson is a specific commissioner, and so the *C* must be capitalized.

3. **The correct answer is (B).** The direct quote must begin with a capital *T*.

4. **The correct answer is (D).** No mistakes.

5. **The correct answer is (A).** The comma is misplaced. The comma must be placed before the conjunction (in this case *and*) that joins two independent clauses.

6. **The correct answer is (D).** No mistakes.

7. **The correct answer is (A).** This is a declaratory statement, not a direct question; it must end with a period.

8. **The correct answer is (B).** Do not capitalize directions, only place names.

9. **The correct answer is (C).** The boy's question is: "May I use the computer this afternoon?" The question must end with a question mark. The entire sentence is a simple statement that should end with a period.

10. **The correct answer is (D).** No mistakes.

SUMMING IT UP

- The HSPT, the COOP, and the TACHS exams test your writing skills regarding punctuation and capitalization.

- To prepare for this section, you must PRACTICE. Read the rules listed in this chapter and practice them.

English Usage

OVERVIEW

- **Principles of grammar**
- **Troublesome words**
- **Summing it up**

The HSPT, the TACHS, and the COOP exams will quiz you on your expertise in language usage. The COOP exam does this in the Reading and Language Arts section. The HSPT lumps this subject with spelling, punctuation and capitalization, and composition in the Language Skills section. The TACHS tests this subject in the Language section.

Language usage includes a student's grasp of correct English and how it's used. Your expertise in this area is based on years of reading and hundreds of hours of classroom instruction on grammar. In answering language usage questions, you may have to consider problems of agreement, double negatives, and dangling modifiers. Word choice, punctuation, tense, and case may also enter into your decision on which answer is best.

The "Principles of Grammar" that follow may prove useful to you as you prepare for English usage questions. Just remember, a simple, direct statement is more effective than a wordy one.

PRINCIPLES OF GRAMMAR

Subject-Verb Agreement

- A verb must agree with its subject in number.
  Single subjects require singular verbs.
  Example: *She walks* to school every day.
  Plural subjects need plural verbs.
  Example: *They walk* home together.

- The number of the subject is not affected by a prepositional phrase that follows it.
  Examples: The *girl together with* her friends *walks* to school every day.
  One of the apples *is* rotten.

- In sentences beginning with *there* or *here*, the verb must agree with the noun that follows it.
  Examples: There *are* six *boys* in the class.
  Here *is* the *book* you wanted.

chapter 14

- *Each, every, everyone, everybody, someone, somebody, anyone, anybody, no one, nobody, either* and *neither* are singular and require singular verbs and pronouns.
  Example: *Everyone* on the team *thinks he can* win the prize.

- Singular subjects joined by *and* take a plural verb.
  Example: *John and Ted are* good friends.

- Two singular subjects joined by *or* or *nor* take a singular verb.
  Example: Meg or Mary is always first to answer.

- A singular and a plural subject joined by *or* or *nor* take a singular or plural verb, depending on which subject is nearer the verb.
  Examples: Neither Kim nor her *sisters are* ready yet.
  Neither her sisters nor *Kim is* ready yet.

- *Don't* is a contraction for *do not*. It is correct for first- and second-person singular and plural (*I don't, you don't, we don't*) and for third-person plural (*they don't*). Use *doesn't* with third-person singular pronouns or nouns.
  Examples: *It doesn't* matter to me.
  Bill doesn't know that song.

Pronoun Agreement

- A pronoun agrees with the words to which it refers in person (first, second, or third), number (singular or plural), and gender (masculine, feminine, or neuter).
  Examples: When the *boys* left, *they* took *their* books with *them*.
  Each *girl* must have *her* ticket.

- A pronoun following a linking verb must be in the subject form (*I, you, he, she, it, we, they*).
  Example: The woman in the photo *was she*.

- If a pronoun is the object of a preposition or an action verb, the pronoun must be in the object form (*me, you, him, her, it, us, them*).
  Examples: Would you like to go to the movies *with* John and *me*?
  The teacher *selected* Joan and *me* to lead the class.

- When a pronoun is used as an appositive, it must be in the same form as the word to which it refers. An appositive is a noun or pronoun that follows another noun or pronoun to identify or explain it.
  Example: Ms. Ross, *my adviser*, suggested that I apply to this school.
  If the appositive refers to a subject, use the subject form.
  Example: The two pilots, *Captain Miller* and *he*, sat in the cockpit.
  (*Captain Miller* and *he* are appositives referring to the subject. Therefore, the subject form, *he*, is required.)
  If the appositive refers to an object, use the object form.
  Example: The class chose two representatives—*Jeff* and *him*—to attend the meeting. (*Jeff* and *him* are appositives referring to *representatives*, the object of the verb *chose*. Therefore, the object form, *him*, is required.)

- A noun ending in *-ing* (a gerund) takes a possessive pronoun.
  Example: My mother objected to *my getting* home so late.

- Use the pronouns *who* and *whom* the same way you would use *he/she* and *him/her*. Use *who* wherever you could substitute *he*, and *whom* where you could substitute *him*.
  Examples: The prize was won by a man *who* everyone agreed was deserving of it.
  (Think: Everyone agreed *he* was deserving of it.)
  The woman *whom* they elected to be chairperson accepted with pleasure. (Think: They elected *her* to be chairperson.)

- *This* and *that* are singular and refer to singular words: *this kind* of book, *that sort* of book. *These* and *those* are plural and refer to plural words: *these kinds* of books, *those sorts of books*.

Adjective and Adverb Usage

- Use adverbs to modify action verbs.
  Example: The car drove *slowly* and *carefully* (not *slow* and *careful*) on the icy road.

- Use an adjective after a linking verb.
  Example: The flower smelled *sweet* (not *sweetly*).

- Use the comparative form of an adjective or adverb (the form that ends in *-er* or uses the word *more*) when comparing two things.
  Examples: Jim runs *faster* than Joe.
  Beth is *taller* than Amy.

- Use the superlative form of an adjective or adverb (the form that ends in *-est* or uses the word *most*) when comparing more than two things.
  Examples: Of all the boys on the team, Jim runs *fastest*.
  Beth is the *tallest* girl in the class.

- Avoid double negatives.
  Examples: The rain was so heavy we *could hardly* see.
  (*not*: The rain was so heavy we couldn't hardly see.)
  They *don't have any* homework tonight.
  (*not*: They don't have no homework tonight.)

TIP

One way to decide between *who* and *whom* in a sentence is to remember two things:
1. *Who* is followed by a verb
2. *Whom* is followed by a noun (which can also be a subject or a pronoun).

TROUBLESOME WORDS

There are a few groups of words that span the realms of spelling, punctuation, and usage. You probably have many of these under control. Others might consistently give you trouble. Your choice of the best version of a sentence might hinge upon your understanding the correct uses of the words in these troublesome groups.

- **their, they're, there**
  Their is the possessive of *they*.
  Example: The Martins claimed *their* dog from the pound because it belonged to them.
  They're is the contraction for *they are*.
  Example: Tom and Marie said that *they're* going skiing in February.
  There means at that place.
  Example: You may park your car over *there*.
  This last form is also used in sentences or clauses where the subject comes after the verb.
  Example: *There* is no one here by that name.

- **your, you're**
  Your is the possessive of *you*.
  Example: Didn't we just drive past *your* house?
  You're is the contraction for *you are*.
  Example: When we finish caroling, *you're* all invited inside for hot chocolate.

- **whose, who's**
  Whose is the possessive of *who*.
  Example: The handwriting is very distinctive, but I cannot remember *whose* it is.
  Who's is the contraction for *who is*.
  Example: *Who's* calling at this hour of night?

- **its, it's**
  Its is the possessive of *it*.
  Example: The injured cat is licking *its* wounds.
  It's is the contraction for *it is*.
  Example: *It's* much too early to leave for the airport.

- **which, who, that**
  Which as a relative pronoun refers only to objects.
  Example: This is the vase *which* the cat knocked over.
  Who and *whom* refer only to people.
  Example: The boy *who* won the prize is over there.
  That may refer to either objects or people. *That* is used only in restrictive clauses.
  Example: This is the vase *that* the cat knocked over. The boy *that* won the prize is over there.

- **learn, teach**
  To *learn* is to *acquire* knowledge. To *teach* is to *impart* knowledge.
  Example: My mother *taught* me all that I have *learned*.

- **between, among**

  Between commonly applies to only two people or things.

  Example: Let us keep this secret *between you and me*.

  Among always implies that there are more than two.

  Example: The knowledge is secure *among the members* of our club.

  Exception: Between may be used with more than two objects to show the relationship of each object to each of the others, as in "The teacher explained the difference *between* adjective, adverb, and noun clauses."

- **beside, besides**

  Beside is a preposition meaning *by the side of*.

  Example: He sat *beside* his sick father.

  Besides, an adverb, means *in addition to*.

  Example: *Besides* his father, his mother also was ill.

- **lay, lie**

  The verb to *lay*, except when referring to hens, may be used only if you could replace it with the verb to *put*. At all other times, use a form of the verb to *lie*.

  Examples: You may *lay* the books upon the table.

  Let sleeping dogs *lie*.

- **many/much, fewer/less, number/amount**

  The use of *many/much, fewer/less, number/amount* is governed by a simple rule of thumb. If the object can be counted, use *many, fewer, number*. If the object is thought of as a single mass or unit, use *much, less, amount*.

  Examples: *Many* raindrops make *much* water.

  If you have *fewer* dollars, you have *less* money.

  The *amount* of property you own depends upon the *number* of acres in your lot.

- **I, me**

  The choice of *I* or *me* when the first-person pronoun is used with one or more proper names may be tested by eliminating the proper names and reading the sentence with the pronoun alone.

  Examples: John, George, Marylou, and (me *or* I) went to the movies last night. (By eliminating the names, you can readily choose *I went to the movies*.)

  It would be very difficult for Mae and (I *or* me) to attend the wedding. (Without *Mae*, it is clear that *difficult for me* is correct.)

- **as, like**

  As is a conjunction introducing a subordinate clause, while *like*, in cases where the two words are confused, is a preposition. The object of a preposition is a noun or phrase.

  Examples: Speeding is a traffic violation, *as* you should know. (*You* is the subject of the clause; *should* is its verb.)

  He behaves *like* a fool.

  She prefers green vegetables *like* spinach.

NOTE

The English language has many irregularities; therefore, items like the troublesome words must be memorized in order to use them correctly in a sentence.

- **already, all ready**

  Already means *prior to some specified time.*

  Example: It is *already* too late to submit your application.

  All ready means *completely ready.*

  Example: The cornfield is *all ready* for the seed to be sown.

- **altogether, all together**

  Altogether means *entirely.*

  Example: It is *altogether* too foggy to drive safely.

  All together means *in sum* or *collectively.*

  Example: The family will be *all together* at the Thanksgiving dinner table.

- **two, to, too**

  Two is the numeral 2.

  Example: There are *two* sides to every story.

  To means *in the direction of.*

  Example: We shall go *to* school.

  Too means *more than* or *also.*

  Examples: It's *too* cold to go swimming today.

  　　　　　 We shall go, *too*.

EXERCISES: ENGLISH USAGE

Exercise 1

Directions: In the following questions, choose which of the four sentences is constructed best. The answer keys and explanations follow Exercise 3.

1. **(A)** It is the opinion of the commissioners that programs that include the construction of cut-rate municipal garages in the central business district is inadvisable.

   (B) Having reviewed the material submitted, the program for putting up cut-rate garages in the central business district seemed likely to cause traffic congestion.

   (C) The commissioners believe that putting up cut-rate municipal garages in the central business district is inadvisable.

   (D) Making an effort to facilitate the cleaning of streets in the central business district, the building of cut-rate municipal garages presents the problem that it would encourage more motorists to come into the central city.

2. **(A)** Since the report lacked the needed information, it was of no use to him.

   (B) This report was useless to him because there were no needed information in it.

   (C) Since the report did not contain the needed information, it was not real useful to him.

   (D) Being that the report lacked the needed information, he could not use it.

3. **(A)** In reviewing the typists' work reports, the job analyst found records of unusual typing speeds.

   (B) It says in the job analyst's report that some employees type with great speed.

   (C) The job analyst found that, in reviewing the typists' work reports, that some unusual typing speeds had been made.

   (D) In the reports of typists' speeds, the job analyst found some records that are kind of unusual.

4. **(A)** They do not ordinarily present these kind of reports in detail like this.

   (B) A report of this kind is not hardly ever given in such detail as this one.

   (C) This report is more detailed than what such reports ordinarily are.

   (D) A report of this kind is not ordinarily presented in as much detail as this one is.

5. **(A)** Nobody but you and your brother know the reason for my coming.

   (B) The reason for my coming is only known to you and your brother.

   (C) My reason for coming is known by nobody except you and your brother.

   (D) My reason for coming is known only by you and your brother.

6. (A) If properly addressed, the letter will reach my mother and I.

   (B) The letter had been addressed to myself and my mother.

   (C) I believe the letter was addressed to either my mother or I.

   (D) My mother's name, as well as mine, was on the letter.

7. (A) The paper we use for this purpose must be light, glossy, and stand hard usage as well.

   (B) Only a light and a glossy, but durable, paper must be used for this purpose.

   (C) For this purpose, we want a paper that is light, glossy, but that will stand hard wear.

   (D) For this purpose, paper that is light, glossy, and durable is essential.

8. (A) This kind of worker achieves success through patience.

   (B) Success does not often come to men of this type except they who are patient.

   (C) Because they are patient, these sort of workers usually achieve success.

   (D) This worker has more patience than any man in his office.

9. (A) You have got to get rid of some of these people if you expect to have the quality of the work improve.

   (B) The quality of the work would improve if they would leave fewer people do it.

   (C) I believe it would be desirable to have fewer persons doing this work.

   (D) If you had planned on employing fewer people than this to do the work, this situation would not have arose.

10. (A) It is quite possible that we shall reemploy anyone whose training fits them to do the work.

    (B) It is probable that we shall reemploy those who have been trained to do the work.

    (C) Such of our personnel that have been trained to do the work will be again employed.

    (D) We expect to reemploy the ones who have had training enough that they can do the work.

Exercise 2

Directions: Choose the word or group of words that should go into the blank to make a correct sentence.

1. All of the boys and Joyce took _____ baseball gloves to the ball game.
   - (A) her
   - (B) their
   - (C) his
   - (D) our

2. Dana was the _____ person who dared go into the haunted house.
   - (A) most only
   - (B) onliest
   - (C) sole only
   - (D) only

3. My father will drive Althea and _____ to the airport.
   - (A) me
   - (B) I
   - (C) myself
   - (D) we

4. If Duncan had joined the soccer team, he _____ been the star.
   - (A) should have
   - (B) could of
   - (C) would of
   - (D) might have

5. Even before the wind had stopped, the rain _____ down.
   - (A) was slowed
   - (B) has been slowing
   - (C) had been slowing
   - (D) had been slowed

6. Last week, I had lunch with the girl _____ won the English prize.
   - (A) who
   - (B) whom
   - (C) which
   - (D) what

7. In choosing between chocolate and vanilla ice cream, I like chocolate ice cream _____.
   - (A) most
   - (B) best
   - (C) better
   - (D) more better

8. The jury is depending _____ the witness' statements.
   - (A) about
   - (B) of
   - (C) upon
   - (D) from

9. I would bring Grandma to visit you, _____ I have no car.
   - (A) except
   - (B) while
   - (C) because
   - (D) moreover

10. The little girl next door _____ on her swings all day.
    - (A) swinged
    - (B) swang
    - (C) swung
    - (D) has swinged

11. Neither Kenneth nor Larry _____ book report.

    (A) has completed their

    (B) have completed their

    (C) have completed his

    (D) has completed his

12. We had just finished shoveling the driveway _____ the plow came through again.

    (A) if

    (B) until

    (C) when

    (D) than

13. You must wait for the election results until we _____ the ballots.

    (A) had counted

    (B) have counted

    (C) are counting

    (D) have had counted

Directions: Make a complete sentence by choosing the words that should go into the blank.

14. After completing the lifesaving course _____.

    (A) and taking both the written and practical exams

    (B) gaining months of practical experience as an apprentice

    (C) you will be eligible to take the examination

    (D) at the YMCA under the auspices of the Red Cross

15. _____, when the telephone rang.

    (A) Returning from a frustrating day at the office

    (B) No sooner said than done

    (C) In the middle of dinner

    (D) We had just turned off the lights

Directions: Select the sentence that means the same or most nearly the same as the underlined sentences.

16. The hiker was lost. A St. Bernard rescued him. It happened in the Alps.

    (A) The hiker was rescued by a St. Bernard lost in the Alps.

    (B) The lost Alpine hiker was rescued by a St. Bernard.

    (C) The hiker in the lost Alps was rescued by a St. Bernard.

    (D) In the Alps, the hiker was rescued by a lost St. Bernard.

17. Taxes are deducted from all wages. Workers who must work at night are paid overtime. The rate of tax to be withheld is fixed by law.

    (A) The law requires that people who are paid overtime must pay taxes.

    (B) According to the law, people who work at night must be paid overtime and deduct taxes.

    (C) The tax rate on overtime pay is deducted from wages by law and is paid at night.

    (D) By law, a fixed rate of taxes is deducted from all wages, including those paid as overtime for night work.

Directions: Choose the word or group of words that makes the second sentence have the same meaning as the underlined sentence.

18. The accident victim was not only frightened but also in pain.

    The accident victim was _____.

    (A) neither frightened nor in pain

    (B) both frightened and in pain

    (C) either frightened or in pain

    (D) only frightened, not in pain

19. I may go to the movies tomorrow if I baby-sit today.

_____ baby-sitting today, I may go to the movies tomorrow.

(A) By

(B) While

(C) Until

(D) Once

20. The criminal received consecutive sentences for his three crimes.

The criminal has to serve his sentences _____.

(A) all at once

(B) after a period of delay

(C) one at a time

(D) with no opportunity for parole

21. We bought the house; moreover, we bought the adjacent lot.

We bought _____.

(A) the house because we bought the lot next door

(B) the lot because we bought the house next door

(C) the house but not the lot next door

(D) the house and the lot next door

Exercise 3

Directions: For questions 1–8, look for errors in grammar, usage, or composition. If you find no mistakes, mark (D).

1. (A) He got off of the horse.

(B) Your umbrella is better than mine.

(C) How could I be other than glad?

(D) No mistakes

2. (A) No one was there except Charles.

(B) Your sample is the most satisfactory of all that I have seen.

(C) I couldn't hardly do it.

(D) No mistakes

3. (A) There should be no secrets between you and me.

(B) I knew him to be the ringleader.

(C) Everyone has studied his lesson.

(D) No mistakes

4. (A) There are a piano and a phonograph in the room.

(B) This is the man whom you interviewed last week.

(C) He is reported to be killed.

(D) No mistakes

5. (A) I have met but one person.

(B) She is the tallest of the two girls.

(C) The child is able to shape the clay easily.

(D) No mistakes

6. **(A)** I wish I were going to Mexico with you.

   (B) Please loan me five dollars until payday.

   (C) The audience was enthusiastic.

   (D) No mistakes

7. **(A)** Because of the downpour, the carnival was postponed.

   (B) He walks up and said "Hello."

   (C) I already anticipate the good time I shall have at camp.

   (D) No mistakes

8. **(A)** The student gave the most unique excuse for being late.

   (B) We watched the kite soar high in the sky.

   (C) Whom did you ask to go to the dance?

   (D) No mistakes

Directions: For questions 9–14, choose the answer that best describes the group of words.

9. The worst feature of my summer camp was the food next was the latrine.

   (A) Run-on sentence

   (B) Complete sentence

   (C) *Not* a complete sentence

10. The man with the wart on the end of his nose gave his seat to the old woman.

    (A) Run-on sentence

    (B) Complete sentence

    (C) *Not* a complete sentence

11. Tom, Jerry, Brad, and Genevieve, all wearing jeans and riding bicycles.

    (A) Run-on sentence

    (B) Complete sentence

    (C) *Not* a complete sentence

12. Once upon a time in a corner of the kitchen lived a small black cricket and the cricket made a lot of noise which annoyed the woman who lived in the house and so the woman swept the cricket out the door.

    (A) Run-on sentence

    (B) Complete sentence

    (C) *Not* a complete sentence

13. Bob and his brother Ted, who is a Civil War buff, went to Gettysburg during summer vacation and studied the battlefield together.

    (A) Run-on sentence

    (B) Complete sentence

    (C) *Not* a complete sentence

14. The strong wind suddenly increased to gale force and the sailboat to capsize.

    (A) Run-on sentence

    (B) Complete sentence

    (C) *Not* a complete sentence

Directions: For questions 15–20, choose the sentence that is correctly written.

15. **(A)** She had done much the people began to realize.

    (B) When the people began to realize how much she had done.

    (C) Soon the people began to realize how much she had done.

    (D) The people began to realize and how much she had done.

16. **(A)** Mounting the curb, the empty car crossed the sidewalk and came to rest against a building.

    (B) The empty car mounts the curb, crossed the sidewalk, and will come to rest against a building.

    (C) Mounting the curb when the empty car crosses the sidewalk and comes to rest against a building.

    (D) The curb was mounted by the empty car and crossed the sidewalk and came to rest against a building.

17. **(A)** I had forgotten my gloves realizing and returning to the theater.

    (B) Because I will realize that I forgot my gloves, I returned to the theater.

    (C) My gloves forgotten, realized, and returned to the theater.

    (D) Realizing I had forgotten my gloves, I returned to the theater.

18. **(A)** She learned that further practice will have had a good effect on her swimming ability.

    (B) She learned that further practice would have a good effect on her swimming ability.

    (C) Having learned and practiced had a good effect on her swimming ability.

    (D) Learning and practicing to have a good effect on her swimming ability.

19. **(A)** Assisting him his friend who lives in the next house.

    (B) Assisting him and living in the next house his friend.

    (C) His friend who lives in the next house assisting.

    (D) He was assisted by his friend, who lives in the next house.

20. **(A)** The driver does all that it will be possible to do.

    (B) The driver, having done all that was possible.

    (C) The driver did all that was possible to do.

    (D) Doing all that is possible to do and driving.

ANSWER KEYS AND EXPLANATIONS

Exercise 1

1. C	3. A	5. D	7. D	9. C
2. A	4. D	6. D	8. A	10. B

1. **The correct answer is (C).** Choice (A) has an agreement error (*programs . . . are*). Choice (B) is incorrect because the program did not review the material. Choice (D) is totally garbled.

2. **The correct answer is (A).** In choice (B), the subject of the second clause is *information*, which is singular. In choice (C), the adverb should be *really*. *Being that*, in choice (D), is not an acceptable form.

3. **The correct answer is (A).** The indefinite pronoun *it* in choice (B) refers to nothing at all, so it means nothing. In choice (C), the *that* after *found* should be omitted. Choice (D) uses colloquial language, which is unacceptable in Standard Written English.

4. **The correct answer is (D).** Choice (A) contains an error of agreement (*these kind*). Choice (B) contains a double negative, *not hardly*. *What* is an extra word in choice (C).

5. **The correct answer is (D).** In choice (A), the subject is *nobody*, which is singular and requires the singular verb *knows*. Choices (B) and (C) are awkward and poorly written.

6. **The correct answer is (D).** Choices (A) and (C) use the subject-form pronoun, *I*, where the object-form, *me*, is required. In choice (B), the object of the preposition *to* should be *me*, not *myself*.

7. **The correct answer is (D).** The first three sentences are not parallel in construction. All the words that modify *paper* should be in the same form.

8. **The correct answer is (A).** In choice (B), *men* is the implied subject of the verb *are*. Inserting the subject into the phrase, you can see that it must read *. . . except to those (men) who are patient*. Choice (C) contains an error of number; to be correct, the phrase must read either *this sort of worker* or *these sorts of workers*. In choice (D), the comparison is incomplete. It must read *than any other man*.

9. **The correct answer is (C).** Choice (A) is wordy. In choice (B), the correct verb should be *have* in place of *leave*. In choice (D), *arose* is incorrect; the correct form is *arisen*.

10. **The correct answer is (B).** In choice (A), *them* should be *him* because it refers to *anyone*, which is singular. Choices (C) and (D) are wordy and awkward.

Exercise 2

1. B	6. A	10. C	14. C	18. B
2. D	7. C	11. D	15. D	19. A
3. A	8. C	12. C	16. B	20. C
4. D	9. A	13. B	17. D	21. D
5. C				

1. **The correct answer is (B).** The subject is plural and the object is plural; therefore, the possessive pronoun must be plural. The subject is in the third person, not the first.

2. **The correct answer is (D).** *Only* is an exclusive term. It cannot be modified in any way.

3. **The correct answer is (A).** The objects of the verb *drive* are *Althea and me*.

4. **The correct answer is (D).** *Of* is not an auxiliary verb, so choices (B) and (C) are automatically incorrect. Choice (D) is more in tune with the nature of the sentence than is choice (A).

5. **The correct answer is (C).** To show that one past activity (the *slowing*) occurred before another past activity (the *stopping*) requires the *had been* construction (past perfect). *Had been slowed*, choice (D), implies that an external force was working on the rain. *Had been slowing* more accurately describes the end of a storm.

6. **The correct answer is (A).** *Who* is the subject of the verb *won*. *Which* may only be used to apply to things. *What* is not a pronoun.

7. **The correct answer is (C).** The comparison between two objects requires *more* or *better*. *More better* is redundant and incorrect. *Most* and *best* refer to comparison among three or more objects.

8. **The correct answer is (C).** The proper idiomatic use is *depend on* or *depend upon*.

9. **The correct answer is (A).** In this sentence, *except* serves as a conjunction. *But* would fit into the blank in the same way. All of the other choices make no sense in the context of the sentence.

10. **The correct answer is (C).** The past tense of *swing* is *swung*.

11. **The correct answer is (D).** The construction *neither/nor* creates a singular subject (or object). Because the subject is singular, both the verb and the possessive pronoun must be singular as well.

12. **The correct answer is (C).** The sentence describes two activities in terms of their relationship in time. Only choice (C) makes sense.

13. **The correct answer is (B).** A present activity that is dependent on a future activity requires that the future activity be stated in the present perfect, *have counted*.

14. **The correct answer is (C).** The sentence fragment is nothing more than an introductory prepositional phrase. The completion must supply both subject and verb.

15. **The correct answer is (D).** The fragment is a subordinate clause. The sentence needs an independent clause.

16. **The correct answer is (B).** The correct answer must give correct information as to who was lost, where he was lost, and how he was rescued.

17. **The correct answer is (D).** The tax rate and the fact of withholding are established by law. Overtime pay is not established by law, but it does constitute wages subject to withholding.

18. **The correct answer is (B).** The term *not only . . . but also* is inclusive.

19. **The correct answer is (A).** The sentence is conditional and in reverse sequence: "I may do something tomorrow *if* I do something today." Reverse the sentence: "By doing something today, I may do something else tomorrow."

20. **The correct answer is (C).** *Consecutive* means *one after the other*. The word that means *all at the same time* is concurrent.

21. **The correct answer is (D).** The word *moreover* simply means *in addition to* or *also*. It does not imply any causality.

Exercise 3

1. A	5. B	9. A	13. B	17. D
2. C	6. B	10. B	14. C	18. B
3. D	7. B	11. C	15. C	19. D
4. C	8. A	12. A	16. A	20. C

1. **The correct answer is (A).** *Off of* is an unacceptable construction: He got off the horse.

2. **The correct answer is (C).** *Hardly* is a negative word, and so *couldn't hardly* is an unacceptable double negative: I could hardly do it.

3. **The correct answer is (D).** No mistakes.

4. **The correct answer is (C).** The activity began in the past (he *was* killed) and is completed in the present (is reported *now*). Therefore, the present perfect tense should be used. The sentence should read: "He is reported to *have been killed*."

5. **The correct answer is (B).** The comparison is between two girls; therefore, *taller* is correct.

6. **The correct answer is (B).** *Loan* is a noun. The sentence requires the verb *lend*.

7. **The correct answer is (B).** The two verbs should be in the same tense. He *walked* up and *said* "Hello."

8. **The correct answer is (A).** *Unique* means that there is only one like it. Because there is only one, there can be no comparison. The construction *most unique* is meaningless and impossible.

9. **The correct answer is (A).** The two complete, independent clauses must either be separated into two sentences or be joined by a semicolon.

10. **The correct answer is (B).** This sentence is complete.

11. **The correct answer is (C).** This sentence fragment consists of subject and modifying clause. *Wearing* and *riding* are *verbals* (gerunds), not verbs. They cannot make a statement, ask a question, nor give a command, so they cannot act alone as verbs.

12. **The correct answer is (A).** There are actually three independent clauses here. The best correction would be to eliminate the first *and* and to begin a second sentence with "The cricket." The second *and* should be eliminated and be replaced by a comma.

13. **The correct answer is (B).** This sentence is complete.

14. **The correct answer is (C).** The sentence fragment, as organized, calls for a compound verb: *increased* to gale force and (try inserting) *caused* the sailboat to capsize.

15. **The correct answer is (C).** Choice (A) is a run-on sentence. Choice (B) is a sentence fragment. In choice (D), the *and* is superfluous.

16. **The correct answer is (A).** Choice (B) mixes tenses illogically. Choice (C) is a sentence fragment. In choice (D), the curb crosses the street and comes to rest against the building.

17. **The correct answer is (D).** No other choice makes sense.

18. **The correct answer is (B).** Choice (A) confuses tenses; choices (C) and (D) are sentence fragments.

19. **The correct answer is (D).** No other choice is a complete sentence.

20. **The correct answer is (C).** Choice (A) confuses tenses; choices (B) and (D) are sentence fragments.

answers exercises

SUMMING IT UP

- The COOP exam tests English usage in the Reading and Language Arts section. The HSPT includes it in the Language Skills section with spelling, punctuation, and capitalization. The TACHS includes it in the Language section.

- Study, learn, and practice the "Principles of Grammar" given in this chapter. They will help you not only on the test, but also throughout school and life.

Language Composition and Expression

chapter 15

OVERVIEW

- **Tips for answering language composition and expression questions**
- **Summing it up**

Your studies of spelling, punctuation, capitalization, and grammar all contribute to your skills in language expression, another crucial part of any entrance exam. Language expression, also called language composition, is a skill that you'll use in all kinds of high school course work and exams and in your college applications, as well.

The Catholic high school entrance examinations' multiple-choice format does not lend itself to testing your ability to write a well-organized paragraph. Essay-writing is the best measure of your skills in composition, but of the exams covered in this book, only the ISEE and the SSAT include essay questions.

But never fear! The COOP, TACHS, and HSPT exams have found a few ways to test your language expression skills. These exams have tucked questions into test sections of English usage and language expression that are designed to tap your potential for composition. Among these are questions that ask you to move a sentence to another location in the paragraph or to remove a sentence that does not belong. Other composition questions require you to identify topic sentences or choose the best development of topic sentences that are given.

The area of language expression is one in which all test-makers are experimenting at this time. New measures might crop up on the next edition of many of the high school exams administered over the next few years.

TIPS FOR ANSWERING LANGUAGE COMPOSITION AND EXPRESSION QUESTIONS

Composition questions make up only a small portion of the exam, but those few questions might be among the most difficult and time-consuming on the test. Though you can't become an expert essayist in just a few weeks, you can familiarize yourself with some of the basic guidelines of composition, and you can learn how to focus your concentration to address these questions on your exam. Language expression questions typically test topic development and appropriateness. The following sections give you some common-sense tips and guidelines to use when you encounter questions dealing with these areas of language expression.

Tackling Topic Development Questions

What do we mean by "development"? The concept is relatively simple, though the task can be a bit more difficult. Topic development requires that you be able to clearly understand the main point or idea of information, and then recognize additional information that logically expands upon or further clarifies that main point or idea. Topic development is much like finishing a story that someone else has started.

Topic development questions come in a number of forms. Here are four tips that will help you tackle these questions on the exams:

1. If the question gives you a topic sentence and asks you to develop that sentence, your task is to choose a second and third sentence that best develop the idea presented in the first sentence. You aren't just choosing some sentences that refer to the same subject presented in the topic sentence. You have to choose the sentences that best expand upon or clarify the topic.

2. The question might give you an essay title and then ask that you choose a topic sentence that would best express the idea of that essay. You have to choose a sentence that relates well to the subject presented by the title and that is broad enough to allow for further development of a paragraph.

3. If the question gives you a title and asks you simply to choose a sentence that belongs under that title, you must weed out the sentences that are related to but not entirely relevant to the topic.

4. The occasional answer choice "None of these" complicates your task and makes the question much more difficult. On the other questions, you know that one of the answers is the best solution to topic development, and you can use the process of elimination to improve your odds of landing on the correct response. When you're faced with a "None of these" response, you might not be able to use your guessing skills to find the right answer. If you can't find the answer to one of these questions, just move on. Don't let it hold you up too long.

Tackling Appropriateness Questions

Questions that ask whether a particular sentence is appropriate to a specific paragraph are, in a way, asking you to perform the same skills you use in topic development, but in reverse! With these questions, rather than choosing the best way to add to the information about a topic, you're asked to choose which information definitely does or does not belong, or to determine where the best placement of that information might be.

If you can write a well-organized composition, you'll know how to allocate ideas into paragraphs. Unfortunately, these are not skills that you can develop right this minute. Take time to go over your returned written class work and learn from your teachers' comments. If you do not understand some comments or the reasons for some low grades, ask your teachers for explanations and help.

EXERCISES: LANGUAGE COMPOSITION AND EXPRESSION

Directions: Choose the pair of sentences that best develops the topic sentence.

1. Salting highways in winter is undoubtedly helpful to the motorist, yet this practice may actually cause a great deal of harm.

   (A) Salt works more quickly than chemical ice melters because it does not require heat to go into action. Salt mixed with sand offers especially good traction.

   (B) While melting the ice and eliminating slippery conditions, the same salt eats into the road surface itself, creating dangerous potholes. Further, the salty runoff leaches into the soil and kills surrounding vegetation.

   (C) A small amount of salt is a dietary necessity, especially in hot, dry climates. Large amounts of dietary salt, however, lead to water retention and high blood pressure.

   (D) Salt is inexpensive because it occurs abundantly in nature. Highways in the Rocky Mountains should have good safety records because they are so close to Utah, a great source of salt.

2. Mesa Verde is a great flat-topped mountain that rises dramatically above the surrounding Colorado desert.

   (A) In contrast to this desert, Mesa Verde is fertile and well-watered, a green oasis to which men have been drawn since ancient times. Within the sheer cliff walls of these canyons, nature has carved out vast caverns in soft sandstone rock.

   (B) In 1275, a severe 24-year drought hit the Mesa Verde area. The Cliff Dwellers, hounded by their relentless enemies and forces they could not comprehend, abandoned their cities and fields and fled from Mesa Verde.

   (C) At Mesa Verde, the *Anasazi* found favorable growing conditions. The legends call them the *Anasazi*, the Ancient Ones.

   (D) Villages, towns, and ultimately great cities appeared on the mesa tops. Tools and implements became more diverse and elaborate.

3. They set fires for many different reasons. Sometimes a shopkeeper sees no way out of losing his business and sets fire to it to collect the insurance. Another type of arsonist wants revenge and sets fire to the home or shop of someone he feels has treated him unfairly.

   (A) They don't look like criminals, but they cost the nation millions of dollars in property loss and sometimes loss of life.

   (B) Arsonists of this type have even been known to help fight the fire.

   (C) Arsonists are persons who set fires deliberately.

   (D) Some arsonists just like the excitement of seeing the fire burn and watching the firefighters at work.

4. But you ought not to despise it, for it can help you and your family obtain many of the good things of life. It can buy an adequate diet, one of the basics of good health. It can make it easier for your children to secure an education. When necessary, it can provide medicine and medical care.

   (A) Money can offer a great opportunity for you to help others.

   (B) Money can be the means for a comfortable house, for travel, for good books, and for hobbies and recreation.

   (C) Mainly people consider that amassing great wealth is a goal in itself.

   (D) Certainly money should not be your chief aim in life.

5. (1) The geologist studies the earth as it is today and as it has been throughout its long history. (2) He is interested in every aspect of the history of the earth, its changing geography, its life, its climate, the way the frost breaks away the tops of the highest mountains, and the way mud accumulates in the deepest parts of the sea. (3) Being mere man, the geologist can only study the surface of this planet. (4) Of course, geology is not necessarily a man's science; it is open to women as well. (5) By using the methods of modern physics, the geologist can make some inspired guesses as to what lies below, but his first concern is with rocks at the surface and with the natural processes that affect them.

   (A) Sentence 2

   (B) Sentence 3

   (C) Sentence 4

   (D) Sentence 5

6. (1) If something becomes suddenly popular, it is called a fad. (2) Parents are often dismayed by teenage fads. (3) If something's popularity endures, it is called a trend. (4) If something's popularity affects other things, it is called a style.

   (A) Sentence 1

   (B) Sentence 2

   (C) Sentence 3

   (D) Sentence 4

Directions: Choose the best answer.

7. Where should the sentence, "Prior to the Civil War, the steamboat was the center of life in the thriving Mississippi towns," be placed in the paragraph below?

(1) With the war came the railroads. (2) River traffic dwindled, and the white-painted vessels rotted at the wharves. (3) During World War I, the government decided to relieve rail congestion by reviving the long-forgotten waterways. (4) Today, steamers, diesels, and barges ply the Mississippi.

(A) Before sentence 1

(B) Between sentences 2 and 3

(C) Between sentences 3 and 4

(D) The sentence does not fit in this paragraph.

8. Where should the sentence, "Drivers who use alcohol tend to disregard their usual safety practices," be placed in the paragraph below?

(1) Many experiments on the effects of alcohol consumption show that alcohol decreases alertness and efficiency. (2) It decreases self-consciousness and at the same time increases confidence and feelings of ease and relaxation. (3) It impairs attention and judgment. (4) It destroys fear of consequences. (5) Usual cautions are thrown to the wind. (6) Their reaction time slows down; normally quick reactions are not possible for them.

(A) Between sentences 1 and 2

(B) Between sentences 2 and 3

(C) Between sentences 4 and 5

(D) Between sentences 5 and 6

9. Which of the following sentences best fits under the topic, "The Symbolic Use of Bears"?

(A) Dancing bears provide a comical form of entertainment at street fairs.

(B) Small children love to hug teddy bears because they are soft and warm.

(C) The bear has long been the symbol of Russia.

(D) None of these

10. Which topic is best for a one-paragraph theme?

(A) Development and Decline of the Whaling Industry

(B) The Effects of Automation upon the Farming Industry

(C) The Advantage of Using a Heavier Baseball Bat

(D) None of these

ANSWER KEY AND EXPLANATIONS

1. B	3. C	5. C	7. A	9. C
2. A	4. D	6. B	8. D	10. C

1. **The correct answer is (B).** Choice (B) picks up where the topic sentence leaves off. It explains how the salt is helpful and then gives examples of the harm caused by salt. Choice (A) is also not a bad one. This choice amplifies the action of salt on ice and tells of its beneficial effects. Choices (C) and (D) do not develop the topic sentence at all. If you were not offered choice (B), you could choose choice (A) over choices and (D) and have an acceptable answer. However, because you must choose the *best* from among all of the choices, choice (B) is the answer.

2. **The correct answer is (A).** The topic sentence introduces both Mesa Verde and the Colorado desert, and choice (A) flows naturally by contrasting Mesa Verde to the desert and then further describing Mesa Verde. A clear second-best choice is (C). However, a transitional sentence would be desirable to introduce the *Anasazi*. Choices (B) and (D) do nothing to develop the topic sentence.

3. **The correct answer is (C).** Most often, a definition makes a good topic sentence. This definition sets a good reference point for the pronoun, "they," which begins the next sentence. Choices (A) and (B) cannot be first sentences since they refer to antecedents that aren't there. Choice (D) might serve as a topic sentence but not as the topic sentence for this particular paragraph. Choice (D) would lead to a very different paragraph development.

4. **The correct answer is (D).** Choice (D) as topic sentence sets up a nice contrast with the "but" that follows it. Choices (A) and (B) set up meaningless contrasts. Choice (C) makes a weak topic sentence, creating confusion of person (people . . . you) and leaving an unclear reference for the "it" that is not to be despised.

5. **The correct answer is (C).** Use of "man" and "he" may be politically incorrect, but clarification of the possibility of the term's being gender-inclusive has no place in the middle of the paragraph.

6. **The correct answer is (B).** This paragraph serves to define the terms *fad*, *trend*, and *style*. While the reaction of parents to teenage fads is certainly a related topic, it belongs in another paragraph.

7. **The correct answer is (A).** The organization of this paragraph is chronological. Because the third sentence discusses relief of rail congestion during World War I, it is clear that the war of the first sentence is the Civil War. Events prior to the Civil War should be mentioned before events that happened during the Civil War.

8. **The correct answer is (D).** The topic sentence introduces the subject of the deleterious effects of alcohol. The second, third, and fourth sentences clearly follow with their use of "it" to refer to alcohol. The sentence being placed might logically follow the fourth sentence, but that would leave the "their" of the sixth sentence without a reference noun. Sentence (6) obviously refers to "drivers," so the sentence about the drivers must appear between sentences (5) and (6).

9. **The correct answer is (C).** Choices (A) and (B) tell of actual uses of bears.

10. **The correct answer is (C).** This is a limited topic that could be dealt with in one paragraph. The topic also lends itself to being one paragraph in a longer, more comprehensive essay.

SUMMING IT UP

- Only the ISEE and the SSAT include essay questions.

- The COOP, the HSPT, and the TACHS use multiple-choice questions that ask you to move a sentence to another location in the paragraph, remove a sentence that does not belong, identify topic sentences, or choose the best development of topic sentences.

- Topic development requires that you be able to clearly understand the main point or idea of information, and then recognize additional information that logically expands upon or further clarifies that main point or idea.

- Appropriateness questions ask you to choose which information definitely does or does not belong, or to determine where the best placement of that information might be.

PART III
QUANTITATIVE AND NONVERBAL SKILLS

CHAPTER 16   Quantitative Reasoning

CHAPTER 17   Mathematics

CHAPTER 18   Series Reasoning

CHAPTER 19   Comparisons

Quantitative Reasoning

OVERVIEW

- **The best approach**
- **Summing it up**

The COOP includes a Quantitative Reasoning section. Unlike the other test components, the Quantitative Reasoning section does not test your knowledge of formulas or facts. Instead, it tests your ability to determine the relationship between elements and the process of deducing these relationships.

This chapter gives you some in-depth instruction for working with reasoning questions by focusing on number relationships, visual problems, and symbol relationships. These are the most common types of quantitative reasoning questions you'll see on the COOP. The information and practice you'll get in this chapter will give you all the help you need to solve any quantitative reasoning questions you may encounter on other standardized tests.

The Quantitative Reasoning section is similar to the Series Reasoning section of the test because you need to use the same skills to work through the questions—concentration, logical thinking, and the ability to be flexible in how you approach the questions. When you begin to work through the quantitative reasoning questions to try to figure out the relationship between the elements, you may find that the answer you come up with is not one of the answer choices! Don't be discouraged. All you need to do is to try another approach to find out what other relationship is reasonable. We're going to show you how.

THE BEST APPROACH

On the COOP, the quantitative reasoning questions will appear as groups of similar questions. In other words, each type of question will be presented in a group. Before each group of questions, there will be instructions telling you how to answer the questions. While it is important that you read the instructions and make sure that you understand them, it is equally important to know that all the questions are really asking you the same thing: "What is the relationship between the elements in each expression?"

Number Relationships

Before each group of number relationship questions, the instructions will say that you must find the relationship between the two numbers in an expression. Each question will consist of three expressions, one on each line. Each of the first two will have a number with an arrow pointing to an empty box, then an arrow pointing to another number. The last line, the "question expression," will have the number on the left with an arrow pointing to an empty box, then an arrow pointing to a question mark. The entire question looks like the following:

$2 \rightarrow \boxed{} \rightarrow 4$
$6 \rightarrow \boxed{} \rightarrow 8$ 6   8   10   12
$8 \rightarrow \boxed{} \rightarrow ?$ **(A)**   **(B)**   **(C)**   **(D)**

To solve this question, approach each expression separately and calculate which operation and number should go into the box.

For instance, to get from 2 to 4, you could stick in the relationship

+2 (or plus 2)

so that

2 + 2 = 4.

Now look at the next expression. To get from 6 to 8, you would also put in the relationship

+2

so that

6 + 2 = 8.

This means that the relationship between the numbers in each expression is + 2. So just stick that same relationship into the question expression.

8 + 2 = 10.

So, choice (C) is correct.

Now remember that it is sometimes possible for more than one relationship to fit into the box. You'll know if you've chosen the wrong relationship because you won't get the same relationship for the first two expressions.

Let's look at our sample question again:

$2 \rightarrow \boxed{} \rightarrow 4$
$6 \rightarrow \boxed{} \rightarrow 8$ 6   8   10   12
$8 \rightarrow \boxed{} \rightarrow ?$ **(A)**   **(B)**   **(C)**   **(D)**

Let's say that for the first expression you thought the relationship was

×2 (or times 2)

so that

2 × 2 = 4.

This doesn't work for the second expression.

6 × 2 = 12, not 8.

So you know that ×2 (or times 2) is not the correct relationship, and you should go back to the first expression and look for another relationship that fits.

If you use this method of finding the relationship that applies to each expression, you will be able to work through any number question in the Quantitative Reasoning section.

Visual Problems

Visual problems ask you to assess a drawing visually. Essentially, these questions are asking you to express the relationship of the parts of the drawing in the same terms in which the answer choices are written. Let's take a look at a question:

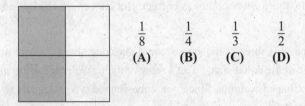

$$\frac{1}{8} \quad \frac{1}{4} \quad \frac{1}{3} \quad \frac{1}{2}$$
$$\text{(A)} \quad \text{(B)} \quad \text{(C)} \quad \text{(D)}$$

In this drawing, the square is separated into four smaller squares. Two of them are shaded and two are white.

The directions for this question type say, "Find the fraction of the grid that is shaded." There are four squares total. Two of the four squares are shaded. You know that $\frac{2}{4}$ is equal to $\frac{1}{2}$. Therefore, the correct answer is (D).

Symbol Relationships

Symbol relationship questions are questions that use symbols or drawings of objects to represent numbers. There are two steps to answering a symbol question. The first is to figure out how the symbols relate to each other. The second is to answer the question in the instructions.

Each question will consist of a drawing with two symbols. Then there will be four answer choices, also containing drawings of the symbols. Look at the symbols and anything else in the drawing to figure out the relationship between the symbols. Take a look at this question:

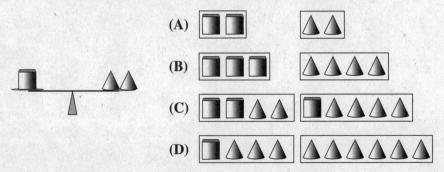

In this question, the symbols are cube and cone shapes.

The instructions say, "Look at the scale that shows sets of shapes of equal weight. Find an equivalent pair of sets that could also balance the scale." In other words, figure out what the relationships are between the answer choice expressions, and choose the one that equals the relationship on the scale.

Choice (A) shows that two cube shapes equal two cone shapes, or 2 cubes = 2 cones. We know that one cube shape equals two cone shapes, or 1 cube = 2 cones.

Choice (B) shows that three cube shapes equal four cone shapes, or 3 cubes = 4 cones. We already know that two cube shapes equal four cone shapes, so this can't be correct.

Choice (C) shows that two cube shapes and two cone shapes equal one cube shape and four cone shapes, or (2 cubes + 2 cones) = (1 cube + 4 cones). This one's a little tricky. There's a cube shape on each side of the equal sign, so let's remove it. We're left with one cube shape and two cone shapes equal four cones, or (1 cube + 2 cones) = 4 cones. Now we've got two cone shapes on each side of the equal sign, so let's remove those. We're left with one cube shape equals two cone shapes. Since one cube equals two cones on our scale, this answer choice is correct. But let's check the last one, choice (D), just to be sure.

Choice (D) shows that one cube shape plus three cone shapes equal six cone shapes. There are three cone-shaped weights on each side of the equal sign, so let's remove them. We're left with one cube-shaped weight equals three cone-shaped weights. Since one cube-shaped weight equals two cone-shaped weights, this can't be correct.

If you use this same method of finding the relationship that applies to each set of symbols, you will be able to work through any symbol question in the Quantitative Reasoning section.

EXERCISES: QUANTITATIVE REASONING

Directions: For numbers 1–7, find the relationship of the numbers in one column to the numbers in the other column. Then find the missing number.

1. $1 \rightarrow \boxed{} \rightarrow 5$
   $5 \rightarrow \boxed{} \rightarrow 9$
   $9 \rightarrow \boxed{} \rightarrow ?$

1	5	13	19
(A)	(B)	(C)	(D)

2. $8 \rightarrow \boxed{} \rightarrow 10$
   $16 \rightarrow \boxed{} \rightarrow 18$
   $12 \rightarrow \boxed{} \rightarrow ?$

12	14	16	18
(A)	(B)	(C)	(D)

3. $10 \rightarrow \boxed{} \rightarrow 7$
   $9 \rightarrow \boxed{} \rightarrow 6$
   $7 \rightarrow \boxed{} \rightarrow ?$

4	5	6	7
(A)	(B)	(C)	(D)

4. $\frac{1}{4} \rightarrow \boxed{} \rightarrow \frac{1}{2}$
   $\frac{1}{2} \rightarrow \boxed{} \rightarrow 1$
   $3 \rightarrow \boxed{} \rightarrow ?$

2	3	5	6
(A)	(B)	(C)	(D)

5. $2 \rightarrow \boxed{} \rightarrow 4$
   $3 \rightarrow \boxed{} \rightarrow 9$
   $4 \rightarrow \boxed{} \rightarrow ?$

8	12	13	16
(A)	(B)	(C)	(D)

6. $10 \rightarrow \boxed{} \rightarrow 2$
   $2 \rightarrow \boxed{} \rightarrow \frac{2}{5}$
   $15 \rightarrow \boxed{} \rightarrow ?$

$\frac{3}{5}$	1	3	5
(A)	(B)	(C)	(D)

7. $5 \rightarrow \boxed{} \rightarrow 1$
   $4 \rightarrow \boxed{} \rightarrow 1$
   $3 \rightarrow \boxed{} \rightarrow ?$

1	2	3	4
(A)	(B)	(C)	(D)

Directions: For numbers 8–13, find the fraction of the grid that is shaded.

8.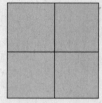

$\frac{1}{4}$ $\frac{1}{3}$ $\frac{1}{2}$ 1
(A)   (B)   (C)   (D)

9.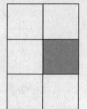

$\frac{1}{3}$ $\frac{1}{4}$ $\frac{1}{5}$ $\frac{1}{6}$
(A)   (B)   (C)   (D)

10.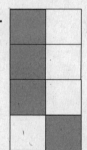

$\frac{1}{2}$ $\frac{1}{3}$ $\frac{1}{5}$ $\frac{1}{8}$
(A)   (B)   (C)   (D)

11.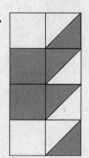

$\frac{1}{2}$ $\frac{1}{4}$ $\frac{1}{8}$ $\frac{1}{16}$
(A)   (B)   (C)   (D)

12.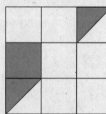

$\frac{1}{2}$ $\frac{1}{3}$ $\frac{2}{7}$ $\frac{2}{9}$
(A)   (B)   (C)   (D)

13.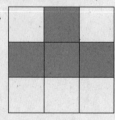

$\frac{1}{2}$ $\frac{4}{9}$ $\frac{5}{9}$ $\frac{8}{9}$
(A)   (B)   (C)   (D)

4

Directions: For questions 14–20, look at the scale that shows sets of shapes of equal weight. Find an equivalent pair of sets that would also balance the scale.

14.

(A)

(B)

(C)

(D)

15.

(A)

(B)

(C)

(D)

16.

(A)

(B)

(C)

(D)

17.

(A)

(B)

(C)

(D)

exercises

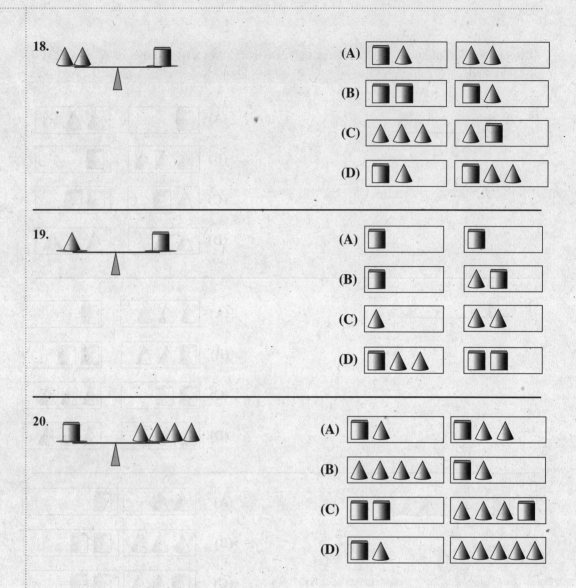

18.

(A)

(B)

(C)

(D)

19.

(A)

(B)

(C)

(D)

20.

(A)

(B)

(C)

(D)

ANSWER KEY AND EXPLANATIONS

1. C	5. D	9. D	13. B	17. B
2. B	6. C	10. A	14. A	18. C
3. A	7. A	11. A	15. B	19. A
4. D	8. D	12. D	16. D	20. D

1. **The correct answer is (C).**
$1 + 4 = 5$
$5 + 4 = 9$
$9 + 4 = 13$

2. **The correct answer is (B).**
$8 + 2 = 10$
$16 + 2 = 18$
$12 + 2 = 14$

3. **The correct answer is (A).**
$10 - 3 = 7$
$9 - 3 = 6$
$7 - 3 = 4$

4. **The correct answer is (D).**
$\frac{1}{4}$ plus itself $\left(\frac{1}{4}\right) = \frac{1}{2}$
$\frac{1}{2}$ plus itself $\left(\frac{1}{2}\right) = 1$
3 plus itself (3) = 6

5. **The correct answer is (D).**
2 times itself (2) = 4
3 times itself (3) = 9
4 times itself (4) = 16

6. **The correct answer is (C).**
10 divided by 5 = 2
2 divided by 5 = $\frac{2}{5}$
15 divided by 5 = 3

7. **The correct answer is (A).**
5 divided by itself (5) = 1
4 divided by itself (4) = 1
3 divided by itself (3) = 1

8. **The correct answer is (D).** There are four squares, all of which are shaded. 4 over 4 is $\frac{4}{4}$, or 1.

9. **The correct answer is (D).** There are six squares. One of them is shaded. 1 over 6 is $\frac{1}{6}$.

10. **The correct answer is (A).** There are eight squares. Four of them are shaded. 4 over 8 is $\frac{4}{8}$, or $\frac{1}{2}$.

11. **The correct answer is (A).** There are eight squares. Two complete squares and four half-squares are shaded. $2 + \frac{1}{2} + \frac{1}{2} + \frac{1}{2} + \frac{1}{2}$ equals 4. Four squares are shaded. 4 over 8 is $\frac{4}{8}$, or $\frac{1}{2}$.

12. **The correct answer is (D).** There are nine squares. One complete square and two half-squares are shaded. $1 + \frac{1}{2} + \frac{1}{2}$ is 2. So, 2 over 9 is $\frac{2}{9}$.

13. **The correct answer is (B).** There are nine squares. Four of them are shaded. So, 4 over 9 is $\frac{4}{9}$.

14. **The correct answer is (A).** The scale indicates that 2 cones = 1 cube. The only answer that maintains this relationship is choice (A), since it has 1 cube = 2 cones.

15. **The correct answer is (B).** The scale indicates that 1 cube = 2 cones. The only answer that maintains this relationship is choice (B), since it has 1 cube + 2 cones = 2 cubes.

16. **The correct answer is (D).** The scale indicates that 1 cube = 3 cones. The only answer that maintains this relationship is choice (D), since it has 2 cubes = 1 cube + 3 cones.

17. **The correct answer is (B).** The scale indicates that 1 cube = 3 cones. The only answer that maintains this relationship is choice (B), since it has 1 cube + 1 cone = 4 cones.

18. **The correct answer is (C).** The scale indicates that 1 cube = 2 cones. The only answer that maintains this relationship is choice (C), since it has 3 cones = 1 cone + 1 cube.

19. **The correct answer is (A).** The scale indicates that 1 cube = 1 cone. The only answer that maintains this relationship is choice (A), since it has 1 cube = 1 cube.

20. **The correct answer is (D).** The scale indicates that 1 cube = 4 cones. The only answer that maintains this relationship is choice (D), since it has 1 cube + 1 cone = 5 cones.

SUMMING IT UP

- The Quantitative Reasoning section of the COOP contains approximately 20 questions.

- It does not test your knowledge of formulas or specific facts.

- To answer a quantitative reasoning question, find the relationship between the elements, and then use that relationship to find the answer to the question.

Mathematics

OVERVIEW

- **The number line**
- **Decimals**
- **Fractions**
- **Percentages**
- **Algebra**
- **Equations**
- **Geometry**
- **Coordinate geometry**
- **Word problems**
- **Summing it up**

Whether you love math or hate it, it's always a part of your life. Mathematics questions are found on all scholastic aptitude and achievement tests, including Catholic high school entrance exams. On the COOP exam, these questions are called Mathematics. On the HSPT, math questions include the categories of Mathematics and Quantitative Skills. On the TACHS, the questions are called Math.

In the pages that follow, we have tried to condense eight years of mathematics instruction into a comprehensive review that touches on most of the topics covered on the exams. This is only a review, not a course. If you find that you're having difficulties with any mathematics topic, talk with a teacher or refer to any of your mathematics textbooks. This chapter really helps you most by letting you know what you *don't* know, so you can focus some of your test-prep time on brushing up your skills in problem areas. The explanations that accompany the mathematics exercises are very complete. These explanations will be a big help to you, because they help you understand the processes involved in finding the right answers to mathematics questions. For extra practice with math questions, do the math sections of all the practice exams that follow.

The following sections in this part outline some of the basic mathematics rules, procedures, and formulas that you've learned over the past eight years in school. You also have an opportunity to practice your skills with some exercises, and you can judge your progress by checking your work against the answer explanations that follow the exercises. Work through these sections and the exercises carefully, and be honest with yourself about the accuracy and speed with which you solve these problems. Note which problems are difficult for you as well as those that are easy. After you've completed this section, you'll know exactly which areas you need to strengthen.

THE NUMBER LINE

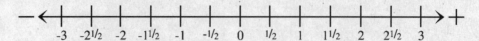

A *number line* is a convenient concept to keep as a mental picture. The number line above shows whole numbers and fractions greater than zero and less than zero. Numbers increase in size as you move to the right and decrease in size as you move to the left. The number line above has an arrow at each end, meaning that the number line goes on infinitely in both positive and negative directions.

Number lines can be drawn up to aid in basic mathematical calculations. Either fractions, whole numbers, or decimals can be used to name the intervals on the line. We suggest that you use number lines when dealing with signed (+, −) numbers and inequalities.

Here is a list of a few basic rules that must be mastered for speed and accuracy in mathematical computation. You should memorize these rules:

Any number multiplied by 0 = 0.

$5 \times 0 = 0$

If 0 is divided by any number, the answer is 0.

$0 \div 2 = 0$

If 0 is added to any number, that number does not change.

$7 + 0 = 7$

If 0 is subtracted from any number, that number does not change.

$4 - 0 = 4$

If a number is multiplied by 1, that number does not change.

$3 \times 1 = 3$

If a number is divided by 1, that number does not change.

$6 \div 1 = 6$

A number added to itself is doubled.

$4 + 4 = 8$

If a number is subtracted from itself, the answer is 0.

$9 - 9 = 0$

If a number is divided by itself, the answer is 1.

$8 \div 8 = 1$

If you have memorized these rules, you should be able to write the answers to the questions in the following exercise as fast as you can read the questions.

Test Yourself 1

Answers follow Test Yourself 19.

1. $1 - 1 =$
2. $3 \div 1 =$
3. $6 \times 0 =$
4. $6 - 0 =$
5. $0 \div 8 =$
6. $9 \times 1 =$
7. $5 + 0 =$
8. $4 - 0 =$
9. $2 \div 1 =$
10. $7 - 7 =$
11. $8 \times 0 =$
12. $0 \div 4 =$
13. $1 + 0 =$
14. $3 - 0 =$
15. $5 \times 1 =$
16. $9 \div 1 =$
17. $6 + 6 =$
18. $4 - 4 =$
19. $5 \div 5 =$
20. $6 \times 1 =$

The more rules, procedures, and formulas you are able to memorize, the easier it will be to solve mathematical problems on your exam and throughout life. Become thoroughly familiar with the rules in this section, and try to commit to memory as many as possible.

When multiplying a number by 10, 100, 1000, etc., move the decimal point to the right a number of spaces equal to the number of zeros in the multiplier. If the number being multiplied is a whole number, push the decimal point to the right by inserting the appropriate number of zeros.

$$0.36 \times 100 = 36$$
$$1.2 \times 10 = 12$$
$$5. \times 10 = 50$$
$$60.423 \times 100 = 6,042.3$$

When dividing a number by 10, 100, 1000, etc., again count the zeros, but this time move the decimal point to the left.

$$123. \div 100 = 1.23$$
$$352.8 \div 10 = 35.28$$
$$16. \div 100 = 0.16$$
$$7. \div 1000 = 0.007$$

Test Yourself 2

1. $18 \times 10 =$
2. $5 \div 100 =$
3. $1.3 \times 1000 =$
4. $3.62 \times 10 =$
5. $9.86 \div 10 =$
6. $0.12 \div 100 =$
7. $4.5 \times 10 =$
8. $83.28 \div 1000 =$
9. $761 \times 100 =$
10. $68.86 \div 10 =$

TIP

Remember, decimals are a way of writing fractions using tenths, hundredths, thousandths, etc.

DECIMALS

Decimals are a way of writing fractions using tenths, hundredths, thousandths, and so forth. If you can count money, make change, or understand a batting average, decimals should present no problem.

When writing decimals, the most important step is placing the decimal point. The whole system is based on its location. Remember the decimal places?

1, 2 3 6, 5 4 0 . 1 3 2 4 5 6

MILLIONS | HUNDRED THOUSANDS | TEN THOUSANDS | THOUSANDS | HUNDREDS | TENS | ONES | DECIMAL POINT | TENTHS | HUNDREDTHS | THOUSANDTHS | TEN THOUSANDTHS | HUNDRED THOUSANDTHS | MILLIONTHS

When adding or subtracting decimals, it is most important to keep the decimal points in line. After the decimal points are aligned, proceed with the problem in exactly the same way as with whole numbers, simply maintaining the location of the decimal point.

Example: Add 36.08 + 745 + 4.362 + 58.6 + 0.0061.

Solution:
```
   36.08
  745.
    4.362
   58.6
+   0.0061
  844.0481
```

If you find it easier, you may fill in the spaces with zeroes. The answer will be unchanged.
```
  036.0800
  745.0000
  004.3620
  058.6000
+ 000.0061
  844.0481
```

Example: Subtract 7.928 from 82.1.

Solution:
```
  82.1        82.100
-  7.928      - 7.928
  74.172       74.172
```

Test Yourself 3

1. $1.52 + 0.389 + 42.9 =$
2. $0.6831 + 0.01 + 4.26 + 98 =$
3. $84 - 1.9 =$
4. $3.25 + 5.66 + 9.1 =$
5. $17 - 12.81 =$

6. $46.33 - 12.1 =$
7. $51 + 7.86 + 42.003 =$
8. $35.4 - 18.21 =$
9. $0.85 - 0.16 =$
10. $7.6 + 0.32 + 830 =$

When multiplying decimals, you can ignore the decimal points until you reach the product. Then the placement of the decimal point is dependent on the sum of the places to the right of the decimal point in both the multiplier and number being multiplied.

$$
\begin{array}{r}
1.482 \quad \text{(3 places to the right of decimal point)} \\
\times\ 0.16 \quad \text{(2 places to the right of decimal point)} \\
\hline
8892 \\
14820 \\
\hline
0.23712 \quad \text{(5 places to the right of decimal point)}
\end{array}
$$

You cannot divide by a decimal. If the divisor is a decimal, you must move the decimal point to the right until the divisor becomes a whole number, an integer. Count the number of spaces by which you moved the decimal point to the right and move the decimal point in the dividend (the number being divided) the same number of spaces to the right. The decimal point in the answer should be directly above the decimal point in the dividend.

$$0.06 \overline{)4.212} \quad 70.2$$

Decimal point moves two spaces to the right.

Test Yourself 4

Solve the following problems.

1. $3.62 \times 5.6 =$
2. $92 \times 0.11 =$
3. $18 \div 0.3 =$
4. $1.5 \times 0.9 =$
5. $7.55 \div 5 =$

6. $6.42 \div 2.14 =$
7. $12.01 \times 3 =$
8. $24.82 \div 7.3 =$
9. $0.486 \div 0.2 =$
10. $0.21 \times 12 =$

FRACTIONS

Fractions are used when we wish to indicate parts of things. A fraction consists of a numerator and a denominator.

$$\frac{3}{4}\begin{matrix}\leftarrow \text{ numerator}\\ \leftarrow \text{denominator}\end{matrix}\begin{matrix}\rightarrow\\ \rightarrow\end{matrix}\frac{7}{8}$$

The denominator tells you how many equal parts the object or number has been divided into, and the numerator tells how many of those parts we are concerned with.

Example: Divide a baseball game, a football game, and a hockey game into convenient numbers of parts. Write a fraction to answer each equation.

   1. If a pitcher played two innings, how much of the whole baseball game did he play?

   2. If a quarterback played three quarters of a football game, how much of the whole game did he play?

   3. If a goalie played two periods of a hockey game, how much of the whole game did he play?

Solution 1:   A baseball game is conveniently divided into nine parts (each an inning). The pitcher pitched two innings. Therefore, he played $\frac{2}{9}$ of the game. The denominator represents the nine parts the game is divided into; the numerator, the two parts we are concerned with.

Solution 2:   Similarly, there are four quarters in a football game, and a quarterback playing three of those quarters plays in $\frac{3}{4}$ of the game.

Solution 3:   There are three periods in hockey, and the goalie played in two of them. Therefore, he played in $\frac{2}{3}$ of the game.

Equivalent Fractions

Fractions having different denominators and numerators might actually represent the same amount. Such fractions are equivalent fractions.

For example, the following circle is divided into two equal parts. Write a fraction to indicate how much of the circle is shaded.

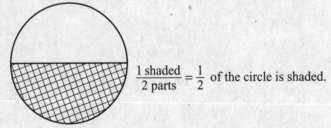

$\dfrac{1 \text{ shaded}}{2 \text{ parts}} = \dfrac{1}{2}$ of the circle is shaded.

The circle below is divided into four equal parts. Write a fraction to indicate how much of the circle is shaded.

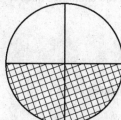 $\dfrac{2 \text{ shaded}}{4 \text{ parts}} = \dfrac{2}{4}$ of the circle are shaded.

This circle is divided into eight equal parts. Write a fraction to indicate how much of the circle is shaded.

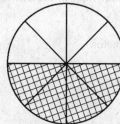 $\dfrac{4 \text{ shaded}}{8 \text{ parts}} = \dfrac{4}{8}$ of the circle are shaded.

In each circle, the same amount was shaded. This should show you that there is more than one way to indicate one half of something.

The fractions $\dfrac{1}{2}$, $\dfrac{2}{4}$, and $\dfrac{4}{8}$ that you wrote are *equivalent fractions* because they all represent the same amount. Notice that the denominator is twice as large as the numerator in every case. Any fraction you write that has a denominator that is exactly twice as large as the numerator will be equivalent to $\dfrac{1}{2}$.

Example: Write other fractions equivalent to $\dfrac{1}{2}$.

Solution: Any fraction that has a denominator that is twice as large as the numerator: $\dfrac{3}{6}$, $\dfrac{5}{10}$, $\dfrac{6}{12}$, $\dfrac{32}{64}$, etc.

Example: Write other fractions equivalent to $\dfrac{1}{4}$.

Solution: Any fraction that has a denominator that is four times as large as the numerator: $\dfrac{2}{8}$, $\dfrac{4}{16}$, $\dfrac{5}{20}$, $\dfrac{15}{60}$, etc.

Example: Write other fractions equivalent to $\dfrac{2}{3}$.

Solution: Any fraction that has a denominator that is one and one-half times as large as the numerator: $\dfrac{4}{6}$, $\dfrac{10}{15}$, $\dfrac{14}{21}$, $\dfrac{16}{24}$, etc.

When the numerator and denominator of a fraction cannot be divided evenly by the same whole number (other than 1), the fraction is said to be in simplest forms. In the examples above, $\frac{1}{2}$, $\frac{1}{4}$, and $\frac{2}{3}$ are in simplest form.

To write equivalent fractions where the numerator is not 1 requires one more step.

Example: What is the equivalent fraction for $\frac{4}{5}$ using 10 as a denominator?

Solution: Each $\frac{1}{5}$ is equivalent to $\frac{2}{10}$; therefore, $\frac{4}{5}$ is equivalent to $\frac{8}{10}$.

The quickest way to find an equivalent fraction is to divide the denominator of the fraction you want by the denominator you know. Take the result and multiply it by the numerator of the fraction you know. This becomes the numerator of the equivalent fraction.

Example: Rename $\frac{3}{8}$ as an equivalent fraction having 16 as a denominator.

Solution: $16 \div 8 = 2; 2 \times 3 = 6$

Answer: $\frac{6}{16}$

Example: Rename $\frac{3}{4}$ as equivalent fractions having 8, 12, 24, and 32 as denominators.

Solution: $\frac{3}{4} = \frac{6}{8}$ $(8 \div 4 = 2; 2 \times 3 = 6)$

$\frac{3}{4} = \frac{9}{12}$ $(12 \div 4 = 3; 3 \times 3 = 9)$

$\frac{3}{4} = \frac{18}{24}$ $(24 \div 4 = 6; 6 \times 3 = 18)$

$\frac{3}{4} = \frac{24}{32}$ $(32 \div 4 = 8; 8 \times 3 = 24)$

A fraction that has a numerator greater than the denominator is called an *improper fraction*. A number expressed as an integer together with a proper fraction is called a *mixed number*.

Examples of improper fractions include $\frac{3}{2}$, $\frac{12}{7}$, and $\frac{9}{5}$. Note that each is in simplest form because the numerator and denominator cannot be divided evenly by a number other than 1.

Examples of mixed numbers include $1\frac{1}{2}$, $1\frac{5}{7}$, and $1\frac{4}{5}$. These are called mixed numbers because they have a whole number part and a fractional part. These mixed numbers are equivalent to the improper fractions given previously. To rename a mixed number as an improper fraction is easy.

Example: Rename $2\frac{1}{4}$ as an improper fraction.

Solution: The whole number 2 contains 8 fourths. Add to it the $\frac{1}{4}$ to write the equivalent fraction $\frac{9}{4}$.

An alternative way of figuring this is to multiply the denominator of the fraction by the whole number and add the numerator.

Example: Rename $2\frac{1}{4}$ as an improper fraction.

Solution: $4 \times 2 = 8 + 1 = 9; \frac{9}{4}$

To rename an improper fraction as a mixed number, just proceed backward.

Example: Rename $\frac{9}{4}$ as a mixed number.

Solution: Divide the numerator by the denominator and use the remainder (R) as the fraction numerator:

$$9 \div 4 = 2 \text{ R1 or } 9 \div 4 = 2\frac{1}{4}$$

Adding and Subtracting Fractions

To add fractions having the same denominators, simply add the numerators and keep the common denominator.

Example: Add $\frac{1}{4} + \frac{3}{4} + \frac{3}{4}$.

Solution: The denominators are the same, so just add the numerators to arrive at the answer, $\frac{7}{4}$ or $1\frac{3}{4}$.

To find the difference between two fractions having the same denominators, simply subtract the numerators, leaving the denominators alone.

Example: Find the difference between $\frac{7}{8}$ and $\frac{3}{8}$.

Solution: $\frac{7}{8} - \frac{3}{8} = \frac{4}{8}$. Simplified to simplest form $\frac{4}{8} = \frac{1}{2}$.

To add or subtract fractions having different denominators, you will have to find a *common denominator*. A common denominator is a number that can be divided by the denominators of all the fractions in the problem without a remainder.

Example: Find a common denominator for $\frac{1}{4}$ and $\frac{1}{3}$.

Solution: 12 can be divided by both 4 and 3:

$\frac{1}{4}$ is equivalent to $\frac{3}{12}$

$\frac{1}{3}$ is equivalent to $\frac{4}{12}$

We can now add the fractions because we have written equivalent fractions with a common denominator.

$$\frac{3}{12} + \frac{4}{12} = \frac{7}{12}$$

Therefore:

$$\frac{1}{4} + \frac{1}{3} = \frac{7}{12}$$

Seven twelfths is in simplest form because 7 and 12 do not have a whole number (other than 1) by which they are both divisible.

Example: Add $\frac{3}{8}$, $\frac{5}{6}$, $\frac{1}{4}$, and $\frac{2}{3}$.

Solution: Find a number into which all denominators will divide evenly. For 8, 6, 4, and 3, the best choice is 24. Now convert each fraction to an equivalent fraction having a denominator of 24:

$$\frac{3}{8} = \frac{9}{24} \quad (24 \div 8 = 3; 3 \times 3 = 9)$$

$$\frac{5}{6} = \frac{20}{24} \quad (24 \div 6 = 4; 4 \times 5 = 20)$$

$$\frac{1}{4} = \frac{6}{24} \quad (24 \div 4 = 6; 6 \times 1 = 6)$$

$$\frac{2}{3} = \frac{16}{24} \quad (24 \div 3 = 8; 8 \times 2 = 16)$$

Now add the fractions:

$$\frac{9}{24} + \frac{20}{24} + \frac{6}{24} + \frac{16}{24} = \frac{51}{24}$$

The answer, $\frac{51}{24}$, is an improper fraction; that is, the numerator is greater than the denominator. To rename the answer to a mixed number, divide the numerator by the denominator and express the remainder as a fraction.

$$\frac{51}{24} = 51 \div 24 = 2\frac{3}{24} = 2\frac{1}{8}$$

Test Yourself 5

Express your answers as simple mixed numbers.

1. $\frac{2}{4} + \frac{3}{5} + \frac{1}{2} =$

2. $\frac{6}{8} - \frac{2}{4} =$

3. $\frac{1}{3} + \frac{1}{2} =$

4. $\frac{4}{5} - \frac{3}{5} =$

5. $\frac{7}{8} + \frac{3}{4} + \frac{1}{3} =$

6. $\frac{1}{2} + \frac{1}{4} + \frac{2}{3} =$

7. $\frac{5}{6} - \frac{1}{2} =$

8. $\frac{5}{8} - \frac{1}{3} =$

9. $\frac{5}{12} + \frac{3}{4} =$

10. $\frac{8}{9} - \frac{2}{3} =$

Multiplying and Dividing Fractions

When multiplying fractions, multiply numerators by numerators and denominators by denominators.

$$\frac{3}{5} \times \frac{4}{7} \times \frac{1}{5} = \frac{3 \times 4 \times 1}{5 \times 7 \times 5} = \frac{12}{175}$$

When multiplying fractions, try to work with numbers that are as small as possible. You can make numbers smaller by dividing out common factors. Do this by dividing the numerator of any one fraction and the denominator of any one fraction by the same number.

$$\frac{^1 3}{4_2} \times \frac{^1 2}{9_3} = \frac{1 \times 1}{2 \times 3} = \frac{1}{6}$$

In this case, the numerator of the first fraction and the denominator of the other fraction were divided by 3, while the denominator of the first fraction and the numerator of the other fraction were divided by 2.

To divide by a fraction, multiply by the reciprocal of the divisor.

$$\frac{3}{16} \div \frac{1}{8} = \frac{3}{16_2} \times \frac{8^1}{1} = \frac{3}{2} = 1\frac{1}{2}$$

Test Yourself 6

Divide out common factor wherever possible and express your answers in simplest form.

1. $\frac{4}{5} \times \frac{3}{6} =$

2. $\frac{2}{4} \times \frac{8}{12} \times \frac{7}{1} =$

3. $\frac{3}{4} \div \frac{3}{8} =$

4. $\frac{5}{2} \div \frac{3}{6} =$

5. $\frac{8}{9} \times \frac{3}{4} \times \frac{1}{2} =$

6. $\frac{7}{8} \div \frac{2}{3} =$

7. $\frac{4}{16} \times \frac{8}{12} \times \frac{10}{13} =$

8. $\frac{1}{6} \times \frac{7}{6} \times \frac{12}{3} =$

9. $\frac{3}{7} \div \frac{9}{4} =$

10. $\frac{2}{3} \div \frac{2}{3} =$

The fraction bar in a fraction means "divided by." To rename a fraction as a decimal, follow through on the division.

$$\frac{4}{5} = 4 \div 5 = 0.8$$

To rename a decimal as a percent, multiply by 100, move the decimal point two places to the right, and attach a percent sign.

$$0.8 = 80\%$$

Test Yourself 7

Rename each fraction, first as a decimal to three places, and then as a percent.

1. $\dfrac{2}{4}$ 6. $\dfrac{2}{3}$

2. $\dfrac{7}{8}$ 7. $\dfrac{3}{5}$

3. $\dfrac{5}{6}$ 8. $\dfrac{4}{10}$

4. $\dfrac{6}{8}$ 9. $\dfrac{1}{4}$

5. $\dfrac{3}{4}$ 10. $\dfrac{2}{5}$

PERCENTAGES

One percent is one hundredth of something. The last syllable of the word *percent*, *-cent*, is the name we give to one hundredth of a dollar.

One percent of $1.00, then, is one cent. Using decimal notation, we can write one cent as $0.01, five cents as $0.05, twenty-five cents as $0.25, and so forth.

Twenty-five cents represents twenty-five hundredths of a dollar. Rather than say that something is so many hundredths of something else, we use the word percent. Twenty-five cents, then, is twenty-five percent of a dollar. We use the symbol % to stand for percent.

Percentage ("hundredths of") is a convenient and widely used way of measuring all sorts of things. By measuring in hundredths, we can be very precise and notice very small changes.

Percentage is not limited to comparing other numbers to 100. You can divide any number into hundredths and talk about percentage.

Example: Find 1% of 200.

Solution: 1% of 200 is one hundredth of 200.

    $200 \div 100 = 2$

Using decimal notation, we can calculate one percent of 200 by:

$$200 \times 0.01 = 2$$

Similarly, we can find a percentage of any number we choose by multiplying it by the correct decimal notation. For example:

Five percent of 50: $0.05 \times 50 = 2.5$

Three percent of 150: $0.03 \times 150 = 4.5$

Ten percent of 60: $0.10 \times 60 = 6.0$

All percentage measurements are not between one percent and 100 percent. We may wish to consider less than one percent of something, especially if it is very large.

For example, if you were handed a book 1,000 pages long and were told to read one percent of it in 5 minutes, how much would you have to read?

$$1000 \times 0.01 = 10 \text{ pages}$$

Quite an assignment! You might bargain to read one half of one percent, or one-tenth of one percent in the 5 minutes allotted to you.

Using decimal notation, we write one-tenth of one percent as 0.001, the decimal number for one thousandth. If you remember that a percent is one hundredth of something, you can see that one tenth of that percent is equivalent to one thousandth of the whole.

In percent notation, one tenth of one percent is written as 0.1%. On high school entrance exams, students often mistakenly think that 0.1% is equal to 0.1. As you know, 0.1% is really equal to 0.001.

Sometimes we are concerned with more than 100% of something. But, you may ask, since 100% constitutes all of something, how can we speak of *more* than all of it?

Where things are growing, or increasing in size or amount, we may want to compare their new size to the size they once were. For example, suppose we measured the heights of three plants to be 6 inches, 9 inches, and 12 inches one week and discover a week later that the first plant is still 6 inches tall but the second and third ones are now 18 inches tall.

The 6-inch plant grew *zero percent* because it didn't grow at all.
The second plant *added 100%* to its size. It doubled in height.
The third plant *added 50%* to its height.

We can also say:

The first plant is 100% of its original height.
The second plant grew to 200% of its original height.
The third plant grew to 150% of its original height.

Here are some common percentage and fractional equivalents you should remember:

- Ten percent (10%) is one tenth $\left(\frac{1}{10}\right)$, or 0.10.

- Twelve and one-half percent (12.5%) is one eighth $\left(\frac{1}{8}\right)$, or 0.125.

- Twenty percent (20%) is one fifth $\left(\frac{1}{5}\right)$, or 0.20.

- Twenty-five percent (25%) is one quarter $\left(\frac{1}{4}\right)$, or 0.25.

- Thirty-three and one-third percent $\left(33\frac{1}{3}\%\right)$ is one third $\left(\frac{1}{3}\right)$, or $0.33\overline{3}$.

- Fifty percent (50%) is one half $\left(\frac{1}{2}\right)$, or 0.50.

- Sixty-six and two-thirds percent $\left(66\frac{2}{3}\%\right)$ is two thirds $\frac{2}{3}$, or $0.66\overline{6}$.

- Seventy-five percent (75%) is three quarters $\left(\frac{3}{4}\right)$, or 0.75.

Caution: When solving problems involving percentages, be careful of common errors:

- **Read the notation carefully.** 0.50% is *not* fifty percent, but one half of one percent.

- When solving problems for percentage increases or decreases in size, **read the problems carefully.**

- **Use common sense.** If you wish to find less than 100% of a number, your result will be smaller than the number you started with. For example, 43% of 50 is less than 50. Using common sense works in the other direction as well. For example, 70 is 40% of what number? The number you are looking for must be larger than 70, since 70 is only $\frac{40}{100}$ of it. Moreover, you can estimate that the number you are looking for will be a little more than twice as large as 70, since 70 is almost half (50%) of that number.

To find a percent of a number, rename the percent as a decimal and multiply the number by it.

Example: What is 5% of 80?

Solution: 5% of 80 = 80 × 0.05 = 4

To find out what a number is when a percent of it is given, rename the percent as a decimal and divide the given number by it.

Example: 5 is 10% of what number?

Solution: 5 ÷ 0.10 = 50

To find what percent one number is of another number, create a fraction by placing the part over the whole. Simplify the fraction if possible, then rename it as a decimal (remember the fraction bar means *divided by,* so divide the numerator by the denominator) and rename the answer as a percent by multiplying by 100, moving the decimal point two places to the right.

Example: 4 is what percent of 80?

Solution: $\frac{4}{80} = \frac{1}{20} = 0.05 = 5\%$

Test Yourself 8

1. 10% of 32 =

2. 8 is 25% of what number?

3. 12 is what percent of 24?

4. 20% of 360 =

5. 5 is what percent of 60?

6. 12 is 8% of what number?

7. 6% of 36 =

8. 25 is 5% of what number?

9. 70 is what percent of 140?

10. What percent of 100 is 19?

ALGEBRA

If you are finishing the eighth grade this year, you might not yet have had a formal algebra class. Nevertheless, you have probably used algebraic terms and expressions, and you have probably solved simple equations. This section will review the skills you have acquired so far and will show you the kinds of questions you can expect to find on a high school entrance examination.

Signed Numbers

The number line exists to both sides of zero. Each positive number on the right of zero has a negative counterpart to the left of zero. The number line below shows the location of some pairs of numbers ($+4$, -4; $+2$, -2; $+1$, -1).

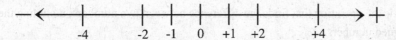

Because each number of a pair is located the same distance from zero (though in different directions), each has the same absolute value. Two vertical bars symbolize absolute value:

$$|+4| = |-4| = 4$$

The absolute value of $+4$ equals the absolute value of -4. Both are equivalent to 4. If you think of absolute value as the distance from zero, regardless of direction, you will understand it easily. The absolute value of any number, positive or negative, is always expressed as a positive number.

Addition of Signed Numbers

When two oppositely signed numbers having the same absolute value are added, the sum is zero.

$$(+10) + (-10) = 0$$

$$(-1.5) + (+1.5) = 0$$

$$(-0.010) + (+0.010) = 0$$

$$\left(+\frac{3}{4}\right) + \left(-\frac{3}{4}\right) = 0$$

If one of the two oppositely signed numbers is greater in absolute value, the sum is equal to the amount of that excess and carries the same sign as the number having the greater absolute value.

$$(+2) + (-1) = +1$$

$$(+8) + (-9) = -1$$

$$(-2.5) + (+2.0) = -0.5$$

$$\left(-\frac{3}{4}\right) + \left(+\frac{1}{2}\right) = -\frac{1}{4}$$

TIP

To add signed numbers with the same sign, add the magnitudes of the numbers and keep the same sign. To add signed numbers with different signs, subtract the magnitudes of the numbers and use the sign of the number with the greater magnitude.

Test Yourself 9

1. $(+5) + (+8) =$
2. $(+6) + (-3) =$
3. $(+4) + (-12) =$
4. $(-7) + (+2) =$
5. $(-21) + (-17) =$

6. $(-9) + (-36) =$
7. $(+31) + (-14) =$
8. $(-16.3) + (-12.5) =$
9. $\left(-8\frac{1}{2}\right) + \left(+4\frac{1}{4}\right) =$
10. $(+66) + (-66) =$

NOTE

Change the sign of the number being sub-tracted and follow the rules for addition.

Subtraction of Signed Numbers

Subtraction is the operation that finds the difference between two numbers, including the difference between signed numbers.

When subtracting signed numbers, it is helpful to refer to the number line.

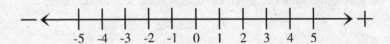

For example, if we wish to subtract +2 from +5, we can use the number line to see that the difference is +3. We give the sign to the difference that represents the direction we are moving along the number line from the number being subtracted to the number from which you are subtracting. In this case, because we are subtracting +2 from +5, we count three units in a positive direction from +2 to +5 on the number line.

When subtracting signed numbers:

- The distance between the two numbers gives you the absolute value of the difference.

- The direction you have to move from the number being subtracted to get to the number from which you are subtracting gives you the sign of the difference.

Example: Subtract –3 from +5.

Solution: Distance on the number line between –3 and +5 is 8 units.
Direction is from negative to positive—a positive direction.
Answer is +8.

Example: Subtract –6 from –8.

Solution: Distance on number line between 6 and 8 is 2 units. Direction is from –6 to –8—a negative direction. Answer is –2.

Example: Subtract +1.30 from –2.70.

Solution: Distance between them on the number line is 4.0. Direction is from +1.30 to –2.70 —a negative direction. Answer is –4.0.

A quick way to subtract signed numbers accurately involves placing the numbers in columns, reversing the sign of the number being subtracted and then adding the two.

Example: Subtract +26 from +15.

Solution:

$$+15 = +15$$
$$\underline{-+26 = -26}$$
$$ = -11$$

Example: Subtract −35 from +10.

Solution:

$$+10 = +10$$
$$\underline{--35 = +35}$$
$$ = +45$$

Notice that in each of the examples, the correct answer was found by reversing the sign of the number being subtracted and then adding.

Test Yourself 10

1. $(-6) - (-12) =$
2. $(+17) - (-8) =$
3. $(+45) - (+62) =$
4. $(-34) - (+21) =$
5. $(+4) - (-58) =$

6. $(+75) - (+27) =$
7. $(-12.6) - (-5.3) =$
8. $\left(-15\frac{1}{4}\right) - \left(+26\frac{1}{2}\right) =$
9. $(-35) - (+35) =$
10. $(+56.1) - (+56.7) =$

Multiplication of Signed Numbers

Signed numbers are multiplied as any other numbers would be, with the following exceptions:

The product of two negative numbers is positive.

$$(-3) \times (-6) = +18$$

The product of two positive numbers is positive.

$$(+3.05) \times (+6) = +18.30$$

The product of a negative and positive number is negative.

$$\left(+4\frac{1}{2}\right) \times (-3) = -13\frac{1}{2}$$

$$(+1) \times (-1) \times (+1) = -1$$

NOTE

If the signs are the same, the product is positive. If the signs are different, the product is negative.

Test Yourself 11

1. $(+5) \times (+8) =$

2. $(+12) \times (-3) =$

3. $(-6) \times (-21) =$

4. $(-4) \times (-10) =$

5. $(+3.3) \times (-5.8) =$

6. $(-7.5) \times (+4.2) =$

7. $\left(-6\frac{1}{2}\right) \times \left(-7\frac{1}{4}\right) =$

8. $(+9) \times (-1) =$

9. $(0) \times (-5.7) =$

10. $(-12) \times (-12) =$

Division of Signed Numbers

As with multiplication, the division of signed numbers requires you to observe three simple rules:

❶ When dividing a positive number by a negative number, the result is negative.

$$(+6) \div (-3) = -2$$

❷ When dividing a negative number by a positive number, the result is negative.

$$(-6) \div (+3) = -2$$

❸ When dividing a negative number by a negative number or a positive number by a positive number, the result is positive.

$$(-6) \div (-3) = +2$$
$$(+6) \div (+3) = +2$$

Test Yourself 12

1. $(+3) \div (-1) =$

2. $(+36) \div (+12) =$

3. $(-45) \div (-9) =$

4. $(-75) \div (+3) =$

5. $(+5.6) \div (-0.7) =$

6. $(-3.5) \div (-5) =$

7. $\left(+6\frac{1}{2}\right) \div \left(+3\frac{1}{4}\right) =$

8. $(-8.2) \div (-1) =$

9. $\left(+12\frac{1}{2}\right) \div \left(-12\frac{1}{2}\right) =$

10. $(0) \div (-19.6) =$

EQUATIONS

An equation is an equality. The values on either side of the equal sign in an equation must be equal. In order to learn the value of an unknown in an equation, do the same thing to both sides of the equation so as to leave the unknown on one side of the equal sign and its value on the other side.

Example: $x - 2 = 8$

Solution: Add 2 to both sides of the equation:

$$x - 2 + 2 = 8 + 2$$
$$x = 10$$

Example: $5x = 25$

Solution: Divide both sides of the equation by 5:

$$\frac{{}^{1}\cancel{5}x}{\cancel{5}_{1}} = \frac{25}{5}$$
$$x = 5$$

Example: $y + 9 = 15$

Solution: Subtract 9 from both sides of the equation:

$$y + 9 - 9 = 15 - 9$$
$$y = 6$$

Example: $a \div 4 = 48$

Solution: Multiply both sides of the equation by 4:

$${}^{1}\cancel{4}\left(\frac{a}{\cancel{4}_{1}}\right) = 48 \times 4$$
$$a = 192$$

Sometimes more than one step is required to solve an equation.

Example: $6a \div 4 = 48$

Solution: First, multiply both sides of the equation by 4:

$$\frac{6a}{4} \times \frac{4}{1} = 48 \times 4$$
$$6a = 192$$

Then divide both sides of the equation by 6:

$$\frac{{}^{1}\cancel{6}a}{\cancel{6}_{1}} = \frac{192}{6}$$
$$a = 32$$

Test Yourself 13

Solve for x.

1. $x + 13 = 25$

2. $4x = 84$

3. $x - 5 = 28$

4. $x \div 9 = 4$

5. $3x + 2 = 14$

6. $\dfrac{x}{4} - 2 = 4$

7. $10x - 27 = 73$

8. $2x \div 4 = 13$

9. $8x + 9 = 81$

10. $2x \div 11 = 6$

GEOMETRY

Area of Plane Figures

Area is the space enclosed by a plane (flat) figure. A rectangle is a plane figure with four right angles. Opposite sides of a rectangle are of equal length and are parallel to each other. To find the area of a rectangle, multiply the length of the base of the rectangle by the length of its height. Area is always expressed in square units.

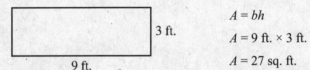

$A = bh$

$A = 9 \text{ ft.} \times 3 \text{ ft.}$

$A = 27 \text{ sq. ft.}$

A square is a rectangle in which all four sides are the same length. The area of a square is found by squaring the length of one side, which is exactly the same as multiplying the square's length by its width.

$A = s^2$

$A = 4 \text{ in.} \times 4 \text{ in.}$

$A = 16 \text{ sq. in.}$

A triangle is a three-sided plane figure. The area of a triangle is found by multiplying the base by the altitude (height) and dividing by two.

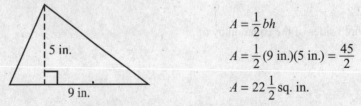

$A = \dfrac{1}{2}bh$

$A = \dfrac{1}{2}(9 \text{ in.})(5 \text{ in.}) = \dfrac{45}{2}$

$A = 22\dfrac{1}{2} \text{ sq. in.}$

A circle is a perfectly round plane figure. The distance from the center of a circle to its rim is its radius. The distance from one edge to the other through the center is its diameter. The diameter is twice the length of the radius.

Like us at facebook.com/petersonspublishing

Pi (π) is a mathematical value equal to approximately 3.14, or $\frac{22}{7}$. Pi(π) is frequently used in calculations involving circles. The area of a circle is found by squaring the radius and multiplying it by π. You may leave the area in terms of pi unless you are told what value to assign π.

$A = \pi r^2$

$A = \pi(4 \text{ cm.})^2$

$A = 16\pi$ sq. cm.

Test Yourself 14

Find the area of each figure. Assume that any angle which appears to be a right angle is a right angle.

1.
4 ft.
8 ft.

7.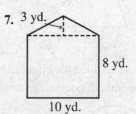
3 yd.
8 yd.
10 yd.

2.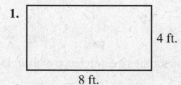
8 in.
7 in.

8.
6 ft.

3.
1 mile

9.
2 ft.
26 ft.

4.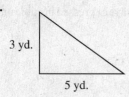
3 yd.
5 yd.

10.
6 meters
5 meters
17 meters
20 meters

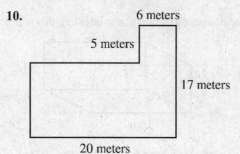

5.
2 cm.

6.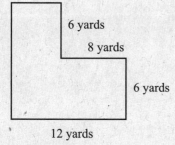
6 yards
8 yards
6 yards
12 yards

Perimeter of Plane Figures

The *perimeter* of a plane figure is the distance around the outside. To find the perimeter of a polygon (a plane figure bounded by line segments), just add the lengths of the sides.

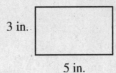

$P = 3 \text{ in.} + 5 \text{ in.} + 3 \text{ in.} + 5 \text{ in.}$
$= 16 \text{ in.}$

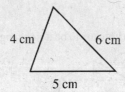

$P = 4 \text{ cm} + 6 \text{ cm} + 5 \text{ cm}$
$= 15 \text{ cm}$

The perimeter of a circle is called the circumference. The formula for the circumference of a circle is πd or $2\pi r$, which are both, of course, the same thing.

$C = 2 \times 3 \times \pi = 6\pi$

Volume of Solid Figures

The volume of a solid figure is the measure of the space within. To find the volume of a solid figure, multiply the area of the base by the height or depth.

The volume of a rectangular solid is length × width × height. Volume is always expressed in cubic units.

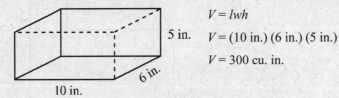

$V = lwh$
$V = (10 \text{ in.})(6 \text{ in.})(5 \text{ in.})$
$V = 300 \text{ cu. in.}$

The volume of a cube is the cube of one side.

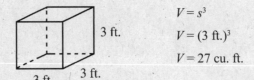

$V = s^3$
$V = (3 \text{ ft.})^3$
$V = 27 \text{ cu. ft.}$

The volume of a cylinder is the area of the circular base (πr^2) times the height.

$V = \pi r^2 h$

$V = \pi (4 \text{ in.})^2 (5 \text{ in.})$

$V = \pi (16)(5) = 80\pi$ cu. in.

Test Yourself 15

1. Find the perimeter.

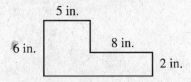

2. Find the volume.

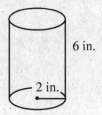

3. Find the circumference.

4. Find the volume.

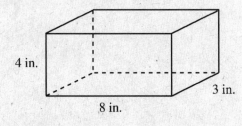

5. Find the volume.

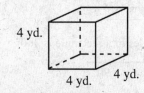

6. Find the perimeter.

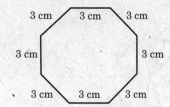

7. Find the perimeter.

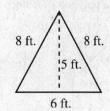

8. Find the perimeter.

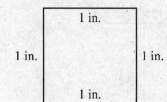

Angles

The sum of the angles of a straight line is 180°.

The sum of the angles of a triangle is 180°.

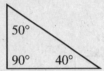

The sum of the angles of a rectangle is 360°.

The sum of the angles of a circle is 360°.

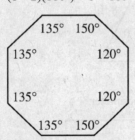

The sum of the angles of a polygon of *n* sides is $(n-2)180°$.

$$(8-2)(180°) = 6 \times 180° = 1080°$$

Test Yourself 16

What is the size of the unlabeled angle?

1.

2.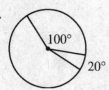

3.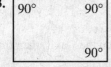

4.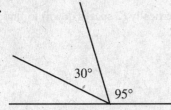

5.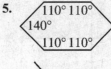

6.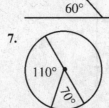

7.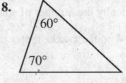

8.

COORDINATE GEOMETRY

Coordinate geometry is used to locate and graph points and lines on a plane.

The coordinate system is made up of two perpendicular number lines that intersect at 0. Any point on the plane has two numbers, or coordinates, that indicate its location relative to the number lines.

The x-coordinate (abscissa) is found by drawing a vertical line from the point to the horizontal number line (the x-axis). The number found on the x-axis is the abscissa.

The y-coordinate (ordinate) is found by drawing a horizontal line from the point to the vertical number line (the y-axis). The number found on the y-axis is the ordinate.

The two coordinates are always written in the order (x,y).

The x-coordinate of point A is 3. The y-coordinate of point A is 2. The coordinates of point A are given by the ordered pair (3,2). Point B has coordinates (–1,4). Point C has coordinates (–4,–3). Point D has coordinates (2,–3).

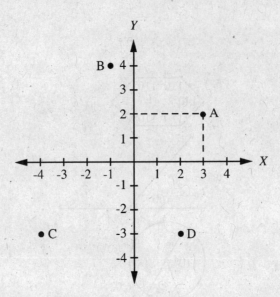

To graph a point whose coordinates are given, first locate the *x*-coordinate on the *x*-axis, then from that position move vertically the number of spaces indicated by the *y*-coordinate.

To graph (4,–2), locate 4 on the *x*-axis, then move –2 spaces vertically (2 spaces down) to find the given point.

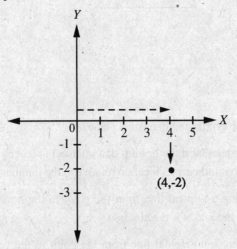

The point at which the *x*-axis and the *y*-axis meet has coordinates (0,0) and is called the origin. Any point on the *y*-axis has 0 as its *x*-coordinate. Any point on the *x*-axis has 0 as its *y*-coordinate.

Test Yourself 17

1. In the graph below, the coordinates of point A are

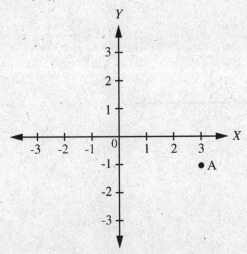

2. The coordinates of point P on the graph are

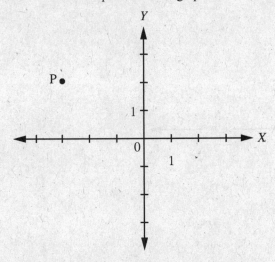

3. Which point is named by the ordered pair (5,1)?

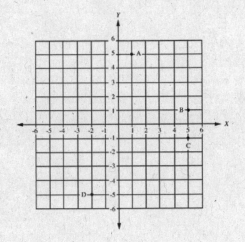

4. Which point might possibly have the coordinates (2,–3)?

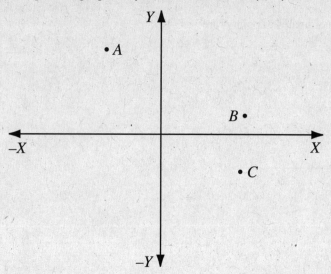

5. The point with the coordinate (3,0) is

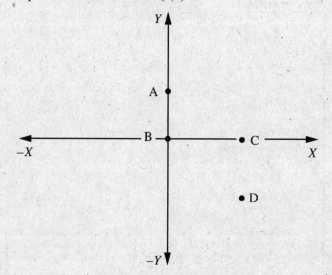

WORD PROBLEMS

Two very common kinds of word problems that you might encounter on high school entrance examinations are *rate, time, and distance problems* and *work problems*.

Rate, Time, and Distance Problems

The basic formula used in solving problems for distance is: $D = RT$ (Distance = Rate × Time)

Use this formula when you know rate (speed) and time.

To find rate, use: $R = \frac{D}{T}$ (Rate = Distance ÷ Time)

To find time, use: $T = \frac{D}{R}$ (Time = Distance ÷ Rate)

Study the following problems:

Example: Two hikers start walking from the city line at different times. The second hiker, whose speed is 4 miles per hour, starts 2 hours after the first hiker, whose speed is 3 miles per hour. Determine the amount of time and distance that will be consumed before the second hiker catches up with the first.

Solution 1: Since the first hiker has a 2-hour head start and is walking at the rate of 3 miles per hour, he is 6 miles from the city line when the second hiker starts.

$$\text{Rate} \times \text{Time} = \text{Distance}$$

Subtracting 3 miles per hour from 4 miles per hour gives us 1 mile per hour, or the difference in the rates of speed of the two hikers. In other words, the second hiker gains 1 mile on the first hiker in every hour.

Because there is a 6-mile difference to cut down and it is cut down 1 mile every hour, it is clear that the second hiker will need 6 hours to overtake his companion. In this time, he will have traveled 4 × 6 = 24 miles. The first hiker will have been walking 8 hours, since he had a 2-hour head start, 8 × 3 = 24 miles.

Solution 2: One excellent way to solve distance (or mixture) problems is to organize all of the data in a chart. For distance problems, make columns for Rate, Time, and Distance and separate lines for each moving object. In the problem about the two hikers, the chart technique works like this:

STEP 1: Draw the chart.

	Rate	× Time	= Distance
Hiker 1			
Hiker 2			

TIP

When solving word problems, remember to read the question carefully. The information given to you is important, but also examine the problem for information that is not given to you. The unknown information can be represented in the problem as x.

STEP 2: Since the problem states that Hiker 1 is traveling at 3 miles per hour and Hiker 2 is traveling at 4 miles per hour, enter these two figures in the Rate column.

	Rate	× Time	= Distance
Hiker 1	3 mph		
Hiker 2	4 mph		

STEP 3: The problem does not tell us how long each hiker traveled, but it does say that Hiker 1 started 2 hours before Hiker 2. Therefore, if we use the unknown x to represent the number of hours Hiker 2 traveled, we can set Hiker 1's time as $x + 2$. Enter these two figures in the Time column.

	Rate	× Time	= Distance
Hiker 1	3 mph	$x + 2$	
Hiker 2	4 mph	x	

STEP 4: Using the formula $D = R \times T$, we can easily find each hiker's distance by multiplying the figures for rate and time already in the chart.

For Hiker 1: $3(x + 2) = 3x + 6$

For Hiker 2: $4(x) = 4x$

	Rate	× Time	= Distance
Hiker 1	3 mph	$x + 2$	$3x + 6$
Hiker 2	4 mph	x	$4x$

STEP 5: When the two hikers meet, each will have covered the same distance. Using this information, we can set up an equation:

Distance covered by Hiker 1		Distance covered by Hiker 2
$3x + 6$	=	$4x$

Solving this equation for x, we find that $x = 6$. This means that Hiker 1 has walked for $6 + 2 = 8$ hours when Hiker 2 catches up to him.

STEP 6: Because Hiker 1 started 2 hours earlier than Hiker 2, Hiker 2 will have walked for 6 hours to catch up to Hiker 1.

STEP 7: Using this information, we can determine that Hiker 1 walked 8 hours at 3 miles per hour to cover 24 miles. Hiker 2 walked for 6 hours at 4 miles per hour to cover the same 24 miles.

Let's try another example:

Example: The same two hikers start walking toward each other along a road connecting two cities that are 60 miles apart. Their speeds are the same as in the preceding example, 3 and 4 miles per hour, respectively. How much time will elapse before they meet?

Solution 1: In each hour of travel toward each other, the hikers will cut down a distance equal to the sum of their speeds, $3 + 4 = 7$ miles per hour. To meet, they must cut down 60 miles, and at 7 miles per hour this would be:

$$\frac{D}{R} = T \text{ OR } \frac{60}{7} = 8\frac{4}{7} \text{ hours}$$

Solution 2: In this problem, we know that the distance traveled by Hiker 1 plus the distance traveled by Hiker 2 equals 60 miles and that the two hikers will have been traveling for the same length of time when they meet. Therefore, we set up an equation to represent this information and solve for x to find the time that will have elapsed before the two hikers meet:

$$3x + 4x = 60$$
$$7x = 60$$
$$x = 8\frac{4}{7}$$

The problem might also have asked: "How much distance must the slower hiker cover before the two hikers meet?" In such a case, we should have gone through the same steps plus one additional step:

The time consumed before meeting was $8\frac{4}{7}$ hours. To find the distance covered by the slower hiker, we merely multiply his rate by the time elapsed:

$$R \times T = D \qquad 3 \times 8\frac{4}{7} = 25\frac{5}{7}$$

Test Yourself 18

1. A sailor on leave drove to Yosemite Park from his home at 60 miles per hour. On his trip home, his rate was 10 miles per hour less, and the trip took 1 hour longer. How far is his home from the park?

2. Two cars leave a restaurant at the same time and travel along a straight highway in opposite directions. At the end of 3 hours, they are 300 miles apart. Find the rate of the slower car if one car travels at a rate 20 miles per hour faster than the other.

3. At 10:30 a.m., a passenger train and a freight train left from stations that were 405 miles apart and traveled toward each other. The rate of the passenger train was 45 miles per hour faster than that of the freight train. If they passed each other at 1:30 p.m., how fast was the passenger train traveling?

4. Susie left her home at 11 a.m. traveling along Route 1 at 30 miles per hour. At 1 p.m., her brother Richard left home and started after her on the same road at 45 miles per hour. At what time did Richard catch up to Susie?

5. How far can a man drive into the country if he drives out at 40 miles per hour, returns over the same road at 30 miles per hour, and spends 8 hours away from home, including a 1-hour stop for lunch?

6. At 10 a.m., two cars started traveling toward each other from towns 287 miles apart. They passed each other at 1:30 p.m. If the rate of the faster car exceeded the rate of the slower car by 6 miles per hour, find the rate in miles per hour of the faster car.

7. A driver covered 350 miles in 8 hours. Before noon he averaged 50 miles per hour, but after noon he averaged only 40 miles per hour. At what time did he leave?

8. At 3 p.m., a plane left New York City for Los Angeles traveling at 600 mph. At 3:30 p.m., another plane left the same airport on the same route traveling at 650 mph. At what time did the second plane overtake the first?

9. A soldier with a 24-hour pass and no special plans left the base at 10 a.m. and walked out into the country at 4 miles per hour. He returned on the same road at 2 miles per hour. If he arrived back at the base at 4 p.m., how many miles into the country did he walk?

10. Two cars leave the gas station at the same time and proceed in the same direction along the same route. One car averages 36 miles per hour and the other 31 miles per hour. In how many hours will the faster car be 30 miles ahead of the slower car?

Work Problems

Work problems generally involve two or more workers doing a job at different rates. The aim of work problems is to predict how long it will take to complete a job if the number of workers is increased or decreased. Work problems may also involve determining how fast pipes can fill or empty tanks. In solving pipe and tank problems, you must think of the pipes as workers.

In most work problems, a job is broken up into several parts, each representing a fractional portion of the entire job. For each part represented, the numerator should represent the time actually spent working, while the denominator should represent the total time needed for the worker to do the job alone. The sum of all the individual fractions must be 1 if the job is completed. The easiest way to understand this procedure is to carefully study the examples that follow. By following the step-by-step solutions, you will learn how to make your own fractions to solve the practice problems that follow and the problems you may find on your exam.

Example: If A does a job in 6 days, and B does the same job in 3 days, how long will it take the two of them, working together, to do the job?

Solution:

STEP 1: Write the fractions as follows.

$$\frac{\text{Time actually spent}}{\text{Time needed to do entire job alone}} \quad \overset{A}{\frac{x}{6 \text{ days}}} + \overset{B}{\frac{x}{3 \text{ days}}} = 1$$

The variable x represents the amount of time each worker will work when both work together. 1 represents the completed job.

STEP 2: Multiply all the terms by the same number (in this case, 6) in order to clear the fractions so as to work with whole numbers.

$$x + 2x = 6$$

STEP 3: Solve for x.

$$3x = 6$$
$$x = 2 \text{ days}$$

Working together, A and B will get the job done in 2 days.

Example: A and B, working together, do a job in $4\frac{1}{2}$ days. B, working alone, is able to do the job in 10 days. How long would it take A to do the job working alone?

Solution:

STEP 1: Write the fractions as follows.

$$\frac{\text{Time actually spent}}{\text{Time needed to do entire job alone}} \quad \overset{A}{\frac{4.5 \text{ days}}{x \text{ days}}} + \overset{B}{\frac{4.5 \text{ days}}{10 \text{ days}}} = 1$$

STEP 2: Multiply all the terms by $10x$ to clear the fractions.

$$45 + 4.5x = 10x$$

STEP 3: Solve for x.

$$45 = 5.5x$$
$$x = 8\frac{2}{11} \text{ or } 8.18 \text{ days}$$

It would take A nearly $8\frac{2}{11}$ days to do the job alone.

Example: If A can do a job in 6 days that B can do in $5\frac{1}{2}$ days, and C can do in $2\frac{1}{5}$ days, how long would the job take if A, B, and C were working together?

Solution:

STEP 1: This example is very similar to the first one. The number of workers is greater, but the procedure is the same. First write the fractions as follows.

$$\frac{\text{Time actually spent}}{\text{Time needed to do entire job alone}} \quad \overset{A}{\frac{x}{6 \text{ days}}} + \overset{B}{\frac{x}{5.5 \text{ days}}} + \overset{C}{\frac{x}{2.2 \text{ days}}} = 1$$

Convert all the decimals to fractions:

$$\frac{x}{6} + \frac{2x}{11} + \frac{5x}{11} = 1$$

Remember that 1 represents the completed job regardless of the number of days involved.

STEP 2: Multiply all terms by 66 to clear the fractions.

$$11x + 12x + 30x = 66$$

STEP 3: Solve for x.

$$53x = 66$$
$$x = 1.245 \text{ days}$$

A, B, and C all working together at their usual rates would get the job done in about $1\frac{1}{4}$ days.

Example: One pipe can fill a pool in 20 minutes, a second pipe can fill the pool in 30 minutes, and a third pipe can fill it in 10 minutes. How long would it take the three pipes together to fill the pool?

Solution:

STEP 1: Treat the pipes as workers and write the fractions as follows.

$$\frac{\text{Time actually spent}}{\text{Time needed to do entire job alone}} \quad \overset{A}{\frac{x}{20 \text{ mins.}}} + \overset{B}{\frac{x}{30 \text{ mins.}}} + \overset{C}{\frac{x}{10 \text{ mins.}}} = 1$$

STEP 2: Multiply all terms by 60 to clear the fractions.

$$3x + 2x + 6x = 60$$

STEP 3: Solve for x.

$$11x = 60$$
$$x = 5\frac{5}{11} \text{ minutes}$$

If the water flows from all three pipes at once, the pool will be filled in $5\frac{5}{11}$ minutes.

Test Yourself 19

1. John can complete a paper route in 20 minutes. Steve can complete the same route in 30 minutes. How long will it take them to complete the route if they work together?

2. Mr. Powell can mow his lawn twice as fast as his son Rick can. Together they do the job in 20 minutes. How many minutes would it take Mr. Powell to do the job alone?

3. Mr. White can paint his barn in 5 days. What part of the barn is still unpainted after he has worked for x days?

4. Mary can clean the house in 6 hours. Her younger sister Ruth can do the same job in 9 hours. In how many hours can they do the job if they work together?

5. A swimming pool can be filled by an inlet pipe in 3 hours. It can be drained by a drainpipe in 6 hours. By mistake, both pipes are opened at the same time. If the pool is empty, in how many hours will it be filled?

6. Mr. Jones can plow his field with his tractor in 4 hours. If he uses his manual plow, it takes three times as long to plow the same field. One day, after working with the tractor for 2 hours, he ran out of gas and had to finish with the manual plow. How long did it take to complete this job after the tractor ran out of gas?

7. Michael and Barry can complete a job in 2 hours when working together. If Michael requires 6 hours to do the job alone, how many hours does Barry need to do the job alone?

8. A girl can sweep the garage in 20 minutes, while her brother needs 30 minutes to do the same job. How many minutes will it take them to sweep the garage if they work together?

9. One printing press can print the school newspaper in 12 hours, while another press can print it in 18 hours. How long will the job take if both presses work simultaneously?

10. If John can do $\frac{1}{4}$ of a job in $\frac{3}{4}$ of a day, how many days will it take him to do the entire job?

TEST YOURSELF ANSWERS AND EXPLANATIONS

Test Yourself 1

1. 0	5. 0	9. 2	13. 1	17. 12
2. 3	6. 9	10. 0	14. 3	18. 0
3. 0	7. 5	11. 0	15. 5	19. 1
4. 6	8. 4	12. 0	16. 9	20. 6

Test Yourself 2

1. 180	3. 1,300	5. 0.986	7. 45	9. 76,100
2. 0.05	4. 36.2	6. 0.0012	8. 0.08328	10. 6.886

Test Yourself 3

1. 44.809	3. 82.1	5. 4.19	7. 100.863	9. 0.69
2. 102.9531	4. 18.01	6. 34.23	8. 17.19	10. 837.92

Test Yourself 4

1. 20.272	3. 60	5. 1.51	7. 36.03	9. 2.43
2. 10.12	4. 1.35	6. 3	8. 3.4	10. 2.52

Test Yourself 5

1. $\frac{32}{20} = 1\frac{12}{20} = 1\frac{3}{5}$ 5. $\frac{47}{24} = 1\frac{23}{24}$ 8. $\frac{7}{24}$

2. $\frac{2}{8} = \frac{1}{4}$ 6. $\frac{17}{12} = 1\frac{5}{12}$ 9. $\frac{14}{12} = 1\frac{2}{12} = 1\frac{1}{6}$

3. $\frac{5}{6}$ 7. $\frac{2}{6} = \frac{1}{3}$ 10. $\frac{2}{9}$

4. $\frac{1}{5}$

Test Yourself 6

1. $\frac{2}{5}$ 5. $\frac{1}{3}$ 8. $\frac{7}{9}$

2. $2\frac{1}{3}$ 6. $\frac{21}{16} = 1\frac{5}{16}$ 9. $\frac{4}{21}$

3. 2   7. $\frac{5}{39}$ 10. 1

4. $\frac{15}{3} = 5$

Test Yourself 7

1. $0.5 = 50\%$ **4.** $0.75 = 75\%$ **7.** $0.60 = 60\%$ **9.** $0.25 = 25\%$

2. $0.875 = 87\frac{1}{2}\%$ **5.** $0.75 = 75\%$ **8.** $0.40 = 40\%$ **10.** $0.40 = 40\%$

3. $0.833 = 83\frac{1}{3}\%$ **6.** $0.666 = 66\frac{2}{3}\%$

Test Yourself 8

1. $32 \times 0.10 = 3.2$

2. $8 \div 0.25 = 32$

3. $\frac{12}{24} = \frac{1}{2} = 0.5 = 50\%$

4. $360 \times 0.20 = 72$

5. $\frac{5}{60} = \frac{1}{12} = 0.08\overline{33} = 8\frac{1}{3}\%$

6. $12 \div 0.08 = 150$

7. $36 \times 0.06 = 2.16$

8. $25 \div 0.05 = 500$

9. $\frac{70}{140} = \frac{1}{2} = 0.5 = 50\%$

10. $\frac{19}{100} = 0.19 = 19\%$

Test Yourself 9

1. $+13$ **3.** -8 **5.** -38 **7.** $+17$ **9.** $-4\frac{1}{4}$

2. $+3$ **4.** -5 **6.** -45 **8.** -28.8 **10.** 0

Test Yourself 10

1. $+6$ **3.** -17 **5.** $+62$ **7.** -7.3 **9.** -70

2. $+25$ **4.** -55 **6.** $+48$ **8.** $-41\frac{3}{4}$ **10.** -0.6

Test Yourself 11

1. $+40$ **3.** $+126$ **5.** -19.14 **7.** $+47\frac{1}{8}$ **9.** 0

2. -36 **4.** $+40$ **6.** -31.5 **8.** -9 **10.** $+144$

Test Yourself 12

1. -3 **3.** $+5$ **5.** -8 **7.** $+2$ **9.** -1

2. $+3$ **4.** -25 **6.** $+0.7$ **8.** $+8.2$ **10.** 0

Test Yourself 13

1. $x = 12$ **4.** $x = 36$ **7.** $x = 10$ **10.** $x = 33$

2. $x = 21$ **5.** $x = 4$ **8.** $x = 26$

3. $x = 33$ **6.** $x = 24$ **9.** $x = 9$

Test Yourself 14

1. $A = bh$
$A = 8 \times 4 = 32$ sq. ft.

2. $A = \frac{1}{2}bh$

$A = \frac{1}{2}(7 \times 8)$

$A = \frac{1}{2}(56) = 28$ sq. in.

3. $A = s^2$
$A = 1^2 = 1$ sq. mile

4. $A = \frac{1}{2}bh$

$A = \frac{1}{2}(5 \times 3)$

$A = \frac{1}{2}(15) = 7\frac{1}{2}$ sq. yds.

5. $A = \pi r^2$
$A = \pi 2^2$
$A = 4\pi$ sq. cm

6. $A = bh$
$A = 12 \times 6 + (12 - 8) \times 6$
$A = 12 \times 6 + 4 \times 6$
$A = 72 \times 24 = 96$ sq. yds.

7. $A = bh$
$A = 10 \times 8 = 80$ sq. yds.

$A = \frac{1}{2}bh$

$A = \frac{1}{2}(10 \times 3) = \frac{1}{2}(30)$

$A = 15$ sq. yds.
$80 + 15 = 95$ sq. yds.

8. $A = \pi r^2$
$A = \pi 6^2$
$A = 36\pi$ sq. ft.

9. $A = \frac{1}{2}bh$

$A = \frac{1}{2}(26 \times 2) = \frac{1}{2}(52)$

$A = 26$ sq. ft.

10. $A = bh$
$A = 6 \times 5 + 20 \times (17 - 5)$
$A = 6 \times 5 + 20 \times 12$
$A = 30 + 240 = 270$ sq. meters

Test Yourself 15

1. $P = 6 + 5 + (6 - 2) + 8 + 2 + (8 + 5)$
$P = 38$ in.

2. $V = \pi r^2 h$
$V = \pi \times 2^2 \times 6$
$V = \pi \times 4 \times 6$
$V = 24\pi$ cu. in.

3. $C = 2\pi r$
$C = 2 \times \pi \times 7$
$C = 14\pi$ cm

4. $V = lwh$
$V = 8 \times 3 \times 4$
$V = 96$ cu. in.

5. $V = s^3$
$V = 4^3 = 4 \times 4 \times 4$
$V = 64$ cu.yd.

6. $P = 3 + 3 + 3 + 3 + 3 + 3 + 3 + 3$
$P = 24$ cm

7. $P = 8 + 8 + 6 = 22$ ft.

8. $P = 1 + 1 + 1 + 1 = 4$ in.

Test Yourself 16

1. 80°	**3.** 90°	**5.** 140°	**7.** 180°
2. 240°	**4.** 55°	**6.** 120°	**8.** 50°

Test Yourself 17

1. (3,–1) A vertical line through A meets the x-axis at 3; therefore, the x-coordinate is 3. A horizontal line through A meets the y-axis at –1; therefore, the y-coordinate is –1. The coordinates of point A are (3,–1).

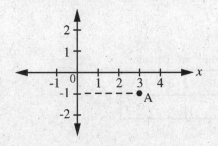

2. Point P has coordinates $x = -3$ and $y = 2$.

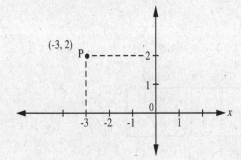

3. Because both coordinates are positive numbers, the point must be located in the upper-right quadrant of the graph. Location along the x-axis is always stated first, so the correct answer is point B.

4. Start by moving in a positive direction along the x-axis. Then you must move along the y-axis in a negative direction. The actual number of spaces you move is irrelevant, since point C is the only possible answer.

5. Again, make your moves in order. First move in the positive direction along the x-axis. Because the second coordinate is 0, make no move on the y-axis. Point C is your answer.

Test Yourself 18

To solve any type of motion problem, it is helpful to organize the information in a chart with columns for Rate, Time, and Distance. A separate line should be used for each moving object. Be very careful of units used. If the rate is given in *miles per hour*, the time must be in hours and the distance will be in *miles*.

1. 300 miles

	Rate ×	Time =	Distance
Going	60 mph	x	$60x$
Return	50 mph	$x + 1$	$50x + 50$

Let x = time of trip at 60 mph
The distances are, of course, equal.

$$60x = 50x + 50$$
$$10x = 50$$
$$x = 5$$

$R \times T = D$; 60 mph × 5 hours = 300 miles

2. 40 mph

	Rate ×	Time =	Distance
Slow Car	x	3	$3x$
Fast Car	$x + 20$	3	$3x + 60$

Let x = rate of slower car

$$\xleftarrow{} \frac{3x+60+3x}{300 \text{ miles}} \xrightarrow{}$$

$$3x + 3x + 60 = 300$$
$$6x = 240 \text{ mph}$$
$$x = 40 \text{ mph}$$

3. 90 mph

	Rate ×	Time =	Distance
Passenger	$x + 45$	3	$3x + 135$
Freight	x	3	$3x$

Let x = rate of freight train
$$3x + 135 + 3x = 405$$
$$6x = 270$$
$$x = 45$$
$$x + 45 = 45 + 45 = 90 \text{ mph}$$

4. 5 p.m.

	Rate ×	Time =	Distance
Susie	30	x	$30x$
Richard	45	$x - 2$	$45x - 90$

Let x = time Susie traveled

Richard left 2 hours later than Susie, so he traveled for $x - 2$ hours. Since Richard caught up to Susie, the distances are equal.

$$30x = 45x - 90$$
$$90 = 15x$$
$$x = 6 \text{ hours}$$

Susie traveled for 6 hours. 11 a.m. + 6 hours = 5 p.m. when Richard caught up to her.

5. 120 miles

	Rate	×	Time	=	Distance
Going	40		x		$40x$
Return	30		$7 - x$		$210 - 30x$

Let x = time for trip out
Total driving time = $8 - 1 = 7$ hours
Therefore, time for return trip = $7 - x$ hours

$$40x = 210 - 30x$$
$$70x = 210$$
$$x = 3 \text{ hours}$$

$R \times T = D$; 40 mph × 3 hours = 120 miles

6. 44 mph

	Rate	×	Time	=	Distance
Slow Car	x		3.5		$3.5x$
Fast Car	$x + 6$		3.5		$3.5(x + 6)$

Let x = rate of slow car

The cars traveled from 10 a.m. to 1:30 p.m., which is 3.5 hours.

$$3.5x + 3.5(x + 6) = 287$$
$$3.5x + 3.5x + 21 = 287$$
$$7x + 21 = 287$$
$$7x = 266$$
$$x = 38 \text{ mph}$$
$$x + 6 = 44 \text{ mph}$$

7. 9 a.m.

	Rate	×	Time	=	Distance
Before Noon	50		x		$50x$
After Noon	40		$8 - x$		$40(8 - x)$

Let x = hours traveled before noon

Note that the 8 hours must be divided into two parts.

$$50x + 40(8 - x) = 350$$
$$50x + 320 - 40x = 350$$
$$10x = 30$$
$$x = 3 \text{ hours}$$

If he traveled 3 hours before noon, he left at 9 a.m.

8. 9:30 p.m.

	Rate	×	Time	=	Distance
3 p.m. Plane	600		x		$600x$
3:30 p.m. Plane	650		$x - \frac{1}{2}$		$650(x - \frac{1}{2})$

Let x = travel time of 3 p.m. plane.

The later plane traveled $\frac{1}{2}$ hour less.

$$600x = 650\left(x - \frac{1}{2}\right)$$
$$600x = 650x - 325$$
$$325 = 50x$$
$$x = 6\frac{1}{2} \text{ hours}$$

The plane that left at 3 p.m. traveled for $6\frac{1}{2}$ hours. The time then was 9:30 p.m.

9. 8 miles

	Rate	×	Time	=	Distance
Going	4		x		$4x$
Return	2		$6 - x$		$2(6 - x)$

Let x = time for walk out into country

The soldier was gone for 6 hours. Therefore, time of trip back = $6 - x$.

$$4x = 2(6 - x)$$
$$4x = 12 - 2x$$
$$6x = 12$$
$$x = 2 \text{ hours}$$
$$R \times T = D; \ 2 \text{ hours at 4 mph} = 8 \text{ miles}$$

10. 6 hours

	Rate	×	Time	=	Distance
Faster Car	36		x		$36x$
Slower Car	31		x		$31x$

Let x = travel time

$$36x - 31x = 30$$
$$5x = 30$$
$$x = 6 \text{ hours}$$

Test Yourself 19

1. 12 minutes

$$\frac{\text{Time actually spent}}{\text{Time needed to do entire job alone}} \quad \overset{\text{John}}{\frac{x}{20}} + \overset{\text{Steve}}{\frac{x}{30}} = 1$$

Multiply all terms by 60 to clear the fractions.

$$3x + 2x = 60$$
$$5x = 60$$
$$x = 12$$

2. 30 minutes

It takes Mr. Powell x minutes to mow the lawn. Rick alone will take twice as long, or $2x$ minutes.

$$\frac{\text{Time actually spent}}{\text{Time needed to do entire job alone}} \quad \overset{\text{Mr. Powell}}{\frac{20}{x}} + \overset{\text{Rick}}{\frac{20}{2x}} = 1$$

Multiply all terms by $2x$ to clear the fractions.

$$40 + 20 = 2x$$
$$60 = 2x$$
$$x = 30 \text{ minutes}$$

3. $\dfrac{5-x}{5}$

In x days, he has painted $\dfrac{x}{5}$ of the barn. To find what part is still unpainted, subtract the part completed from $1\left(\dfrac{5}{5}\right)$.

$$\frac{5}{5} - \frac{x}{5} = \frac{5-x}{5}$$

4. $3\dfrac{3}{5}$ hours

$$\frac{\text{Time actually spent}}{\text{Time needed to do entire job alone}} \quad \overset{\text{Mary}}{\frac{x}{6}} + \overset{\text{Ruth}}{\frac{x}{9}} = 1$$

Multiply all terms by 18 to clear the fractions.

$$3x + 2x = 18$$
$$5x = 18$$
$$x = 3\frac{3}{5}$$

5. 6 hours

$$\frac{\text{Time actually spent}}{\text{Time needed to do entire job alone}} \quad \overset{\text{Inlet}}{\frac{x}{3}} - \overset{\text{Drain}}{\frac{x}{6}} = 1$$

Multiply all terms by 6 to clear the fractions.

$2x - x = 6$

$x = 6$

Note that the two fractions are subtracted because the drainpipe does not help the inlet pipe but rather works against it.

6. 6 hours

$$\frac{\text{Time actually spent}}{\text{Time needed to do entire job alone}} \quad \overset{\text{Tractor}}{\frac{2}{4}} + \overset{\text{Plow}}{\frac{x}{12}} = 1$$

You do not need to calculate the answer. Because half the job $\left(\frac{2}{4}\right)$ was completed by the tractor, the other half $\left(\frac{6}{12}\right)$ was done by the plow, and x, therefore, must equal 6.

7. 3 hours

$$\frac{\text{Time actually spent}}{\text{Time needed to do entire job alone}} \quad \overset{\text{Michael}}{\frac{2}{6}} + \overset{\text{Barry}}{\frac{2}{x}} = 1$$

Multiple all the terms by $6x$ to clear the fractions.

$2x + 12 = 6x$

$12 = 4x$

$3 = x$

8. 12 minutes

$$\frac{\text{Time actually spent}}{\text{Time needed to do entire job alone}} \quad \overset{\text{Girl}}{\frac{x}{20}} + \overset{\text{Brother}}{\frac{x}{30}} = 1$$

Multiply all the terms by 60 to clear the fractions.

$3x + 2x = 60$

$5x = 60$

$x = 12$

9. 7 hours 12 minutes

	Fast Press	Slower Press

$$\frac{\text{Time actually spent}}{\text{Time needed to do entire job alone}} \qquad \frac{x}{12} \quad + \quad \frac{x}{18} \quad = 1$$

Multiply all the terms by 36 to clear the fractions.

$$3x + 2x = 36$$
$$5x = 36$$
$$x = 7.2 \text{ hours} = 7 \text{ hours } 12 \text{ minutes}$$

10. 3 days

If John completes $\frac{1}{4}$ of the job in $\frac{3}{4}$ day, it will take him 4 times as long to do the entire job.

$$\frac{4}{1} \times \frac{3}{4} = 3$$

EXERCISES: MATHEMATICS

Exercise 1

Directions: In the following questions, work out each problem and mark the letter that corresponds to the correct answer. If the correct answer does not appear among the choices, mark (E) for ''Not given.'' Answers are found following Exercise 4.

1. $\begin{array}{r} 896 \\ \times 708 \end{array}$

    (A) 643,386

    (B) 634,386

    (C) 634,368

    (D) 643,368

    (E) Not given

2. $9 \overline{)4266}$

    (A) 447

    (B) 477

    (C) 474

    (D) 475

    (E) Not given

3. $\begin{array}{r} \$125.25 \\ 0.50 \\ 70.86 \\ + \quad 6.07 \\ \hline \end{array}$

    (A) $201.68

    (B) $202.69

    (C) $200.68

    (D) $202.68

    (E) Not given

4. $\begin{array}{r} \$1250.37 \\ - \quad 48.98 \\ \hline \end{array}$

    (A) $1201.39

    (B) $1201.49

    (C) $1200.39

    (D) $1201.38

    (E) Not given

5. $29 \overline{)476.92}$

    (A) 16.4445

    (B) 17.4445

    (C) 16.4555

    (D) 17.4455

    (E) Not given

6. $\begin{array}{r} 28 \\ 19 \\ 17 \\ + \quad 24 \\ \hline \end{array}$

    (A) 87

    (B) 88

    (C) 90

    (D) 89

    (E) Not given

7. $3.7 \overline{)2339.86}$

    (A) 632.4

    (B) 62.34

    (C) 642.3

    (D) 63.24

    (E) Not given

8. $\begin{array}{r} 45286 \\ \times \quad 4\frac{1}{5} \\ \hline \end{array}$

    (A) $190,021\frac{1}{5}$

    (B) 190,234

    (C) $190,201\frac{1}{5}$

    (D) $190,202\frac{2}{5}$

    (E) Not given

9. $8\frac{1}{6}$

$- \ 5\frac{2}{3}$

(A) $3\frac{2}{3}$

(B) $2\frac{1}{3}$

(C) $3\frac{1}{6}$

(D) $2\frac{1}{2}$

(E) Not given

10. $\frac{1}{9} \times \frac{2}{3} \times \frac{7}{8} =$

(A) $\frac{6}{108}$

(B) $\frac{7}{108}$

(C) $\frac{14}{27}$

(D) $\frac{12}{52}$

(E) Not given

11. $4\frac{1}{3} \overline{)\frac{1}{4}}$

(A) $\frac{3}{52}$

(B) $\frac{5}{52}$

(C) $17\frac{1}{3}$

(D) $\frac{12}{52}$

(E) Not given

12.   78523
        21457
         3256
    $+$ 1478

(A) 104,715

(B) 105,714

(C) 104,814

(D) 105,814

(E) Not given

13.   12689
    $\times$ 37

(A) 569,493

(B) 468,493

(C) 469,493

(D) 568,493

(E) Not given

14. Find $6\frac{2}{3}\%$ of $13.50

(A) $0.89

(B) $0.91

(C) $0.88

(D) $0.95

(E) Not given

15. Rename $\frac{11}{16}$ as a decimal.

(A) 0.8675

(B) 0.6875

(C) 0.6785

(D) 0.6578

(E) Not given

exercises

Exercise 2

Directions: Work each problem on scratch paper or in the margins, then look at the answer choices. If your answer is among those choices, circle the letter before your answer. If your answer is not among the choices, mark (E) for "None of these." Answers are found following Exercise 4.

1.   5239
   $\times$ 706

     (A) 3,698,734
     (B) 3,708,734
     (C) 398,164
     (D) 68,107
     (E) None of these

2.   48207
   $\times$ 926

     (A) 44,639,682
     (B) 45,739,682
     (C) 45,638,682
     (D) 46,739,682
     (E) None of these

3. $4628 \div 7 =$
     (A) 662 R1
     (B) 661
     (C) 661 R1
     (D) 660 R6
     (E) None of these

4. $419\overline{)5063}$
     (A) 11 R408
     (B) 12 R9
     (C) 12 R37
     (D) 14 R81
     (E) None of these

5. $\$59.60 \div \$0.40 =$
     (A) 0.149
     (B) 1.49
     (C) 14.9
     (D) 149
     (E) None of these

6. $3.41 + 5.6 + 0.873 =$
     (A) 4.843
     (B) 9.883
     (C) 15.264
     (D) 17.743
     (E) None of these

7.   58769
   $-$ 4028

     (A) 54,641
     (B) 44,741
     (C) 54,741
     (D) 53,741
     (E) None of these

8. $0.3 \times 0.08 =$
     (A) 0.0024
     (B) 0.024
     (C) 0.240
     (D) 2.40
     (E) None of these

9. $0.33\overline{)9.9}$
     (A) 0.3
     (B) 3
     (C) 30
     (D) 33
     (E) None of these

10. 16% of $570 =$
     (A) 85.3
     (B) 89.41
     (C) 90.68
     (D) 92
     (E) None of these

11. 135 is what percent of 900?

(A) 12%

(B) 15%

(C) 17.5%

(D) 19%

(E) None of these

> **Directions:** Express all fractions in lowest terms.

12. $\dfrac{3}{4} + \dfrac{3}{8} =$

(A) $\dfrac{7}{8}$

(B) $\dfrac{8}{9}$

(C) $1\dfrac{1}{8}$

(D) $1\dfrac{3}{8}$

(E) None of these

13.
$$3\dfrac{1}{4}$$
$$4\dfrac{1}{8}$$
$$+\quad 4\dfrac{1}{2}$$

(A) $11\dfrac{5}{8}$

(B) $11\dfrac{3}{4}$

(C) $11\dfrac{7}{8}$

(D) 12

(E) None of these

14.
$$10\dfrac{2}{3}$$
$$-\quad 9\dfrac{1}{2}$$

(A) $1\dfrac{1}{3}$

(B) $1\dfrac{1}{2}$

(C) $1\dfrac{1}{6}$

(D) $\dfrac{13}{32}$

(E) None of these

15.
$$14\dfrac{7}{24}$$
$$-\quad 5\dfrac{2}{3}$$

(A) $8\dfrac{11}{12}$

(B) $8\dfrac{5}{6}$

(C) $9\dfrac{1}{3}$

(D) $9\dfrac{15}{24}$

(E) None of these

16. $\dfrac{8}{15} \times \dfrac{3}{4} =$

(A) $\dfrac{1}{5}$

(B) $\dfrac{2}{5}$

(C) $\dfrac{3}{5}$

(D) $\dfrac{3}{10}$

(E) None of these

17. $5\frac{1}{4} \times 2\frac{2}{7} =$

   (A) 12

   (B) $11\frac{3}{28}$

   (C) $11\frac{4}{7}$

   (D) $10\frac{3}{28}$

   (E) None of these

18. $\frac{3}{4} \overline{\smash{\big)}\frac{9}{16}}$

   (A) $\frac{27}{64}$

   (B) $\frac{3}{4}$

   (C) $\frac{5}{8}$

   (D) $\frac{7}{16}$

   (E) None of these

19. $(-12) + (+4) =$

   (A) +16

   (B) −8

   (C) +8

   (D) −16

   (E) None of these

20. $(-22) - (-18) =$

   (A) +13

   (B) +6

   (C) −6

   (D) −30

   (E) None of these

21. $(+7) \times (-7) =$

   (A) +49

   (B) 0

   (C) +1

   (D) −14

   (E) None of these

22. $(+56) \div (-7) =$

   (A) −6

   (B) −8

   (C) +8

   (D) +6

   (E) None of these

Exercise 3

Directions: Choose the correct answer to each problem and circle its letter. Answers are found following Exercise 4.

1. Six girls sold the following numbers of boxes of cookies: 42, 35, 28, 30, 24, 27. What was the average number of boxes sold?

   (A) 26
   (B) 29
   (C) 30
   (D) 31

2. The cost of sending a telegram is 52 cents for the first ten words and $2\frac{1}{2}$ cents for each additional word. The cost of sending a 14-word telegram is

   (A) 62 cents.
   (B) 63 cents.
   (C) 69 cents.
   (D) 87 cents.

3. A stock clerk has on hand the following items:

   500 pads worth 4 cents each
   130 pencils worth 3 cents each
   50 dozen rubber bands worth 2 cents per dozen

   If, from this stock, he issues 125 pads, 45 pencils, and 48 rubber bands, what would be the value of the remaining stock?

   (A) $6.43
   (B) $8.95
   (C) $17.63
   (D) $18.47

4. As an employee at a clothing store, you are entitled to a 10% discount on all purchases. When the store has a sale, employees are also entitled to the 20% discount offered to all customers. What would you have to pay for a $60 jacket bought on a sale day?

   (A) $6.00
   (B) $10.80
   (C) $36.00
   (D) $43.20

5. How many square yards of linoleum are needed to cover a floor having an area of 270 square feet?

   (A) 24
   (B) 28
   (C) 30
   (D) 33

6. If a pie is divided into 40 parts, what percent is one part of the whole pie?

   (A) 0.4
   (B) 2.5
   (C) 4.0
   (D) 25

7. A recipe for 6 quarts of punch calls for $\frac{3}{4}$ cups of sugar. How much sugar is needed for 9 quarts of punch?

   (A) $\frac{5}{8}$ of a cup
   (B) $\frac{7}{8}$ of a cup
   (C) $1\frac{1}{8}$ cups
   (D) $2\frac{1}{4}$ cups

8. How many yards of ribbon will it take to make 45 badges if each badge uses 4 inches of ribbon?

   (A) 5
   (B) 9
   (C) 11
   (D) 15

9. Oil once sold at $42\frac{1}{2}$ cents a quart. What was the cost of 4 gallons of oil?

(A) $6.50

(B) $6.60

(C) $6.70

(D) $6.80

10. A clerk can add 40 columns of figures an hour by using an adding machine. He can add 20 columns of figures an hour without using an adding machine. What is the total number of hours it will take the clerk to add 200 columns of figures if $\frac{3}{5}$ of the work is done by machine and the rest without the machine?

(A) 6 hours

(B) 7 hours

(C) 8 hours

(D) 9 hours

11. Two rectangular boards, each measuring 5 feet by 3 feet, are placed together to make one large board. How much shorter will the perimeter be if the two long sides are placed together than if the two short sides are placed together?

(A) 2 feet

(B) 4 feet

(C) 6 feet

(D) 8 feet

12. 1% of 8 =

(A) 8

(B) 0.8

(C) 0.08

(D) 0.008

13. When 81.3 is divided by 10, the quotient is

(A) 0.0813

(B) 0.813

(C) 8.13

(D) 813

14. +1 −1 +1 −1 +1 . . . and so on, where the last number is +1 has a sum of

(A) 0

(B) −1

(C) +1

(D) 2

15. If a plane travels 1000 miles in 5 hours 30 minutes, what is its average speed in miles per hour?

(A) $181\frac{9}{11}$

(B) 200

(C) 215

(D) $191\frac{1}{5}$

16. A jacket that normally sells for $35 can be purchased on sale for 2,975 pennies. What is the rate of discount represented by the sale price?

(A) 5%

(B) 10%

(C) 15%

(D) 20%

17. Perform the indicated operations and express your answer in inches: 12 feet minus 7 inches, plus 2 feet 1 inch, minus 7 feet, minus 1 yard, plus 2 yards 1 foot 3 inches.

(A) 130 inches

(B) 128 inches

(C) 129 inches

(D) 131 inches

18. What is the value of x when $5x = 5 \times 4 \times 2 \times 0$?

(A) 6

(B) 8

(C) 0

(D) 1

19. A square has an area of 49 sq. in. The number of inches in its perimeter is

(A) 7

(B) 28

(C) 14

(D) 98

20. $(3 + 4)^3 =$
- **(A)** 21
- **(B)** 91
- **(C)** 343
- **(D)** 490

21. A roll of carpeting will cover 224 square feet of floor space. How many rolls will be needed to carpet a room 36' × 8' and another 24' × 9'?
- **(A)** 2.25
- **(B)** 4.50
- **(C)** 2.50
- **(D)** 4.25

22. A library contains 60 books on arts and crafts. If this is 0.05% of the total number of books on the shelves, how many books does the library own?
- **(A)** 120,000
- **(B)** 12,000
- **(C)** 1,200,000
- **(D)** 1,200

23. A court clerk estimates that the untried cases on the docket will occupy the court for 150 trial days. If new cases are accumulating at the rate of 1.6 trial days per day (Saturday and Sunday excluded) and the court sits 5 days a week, how many days' business will remain to be heard at the end of 60 trial days?
- **(A)** 168 trial days
- **(B)** 188 trial days
- **(C)** 185 trial days
- **(D)** 186 trial days

24. A house plan uses the scale $\frac{1}{4}$ inch = 1 foot, and in the drawing the living room is 7 inches long. If the scale is changed to 1 inch = 1 foot, what will the length of the living room be in the new drawing?
- **(A)** 18 in.
- **(B)** 28 in.
- **(C)** 30 in.
- **(D)** 36 in.

25. A store sold suits for $65 each. The suits cost the store $50 each. The percentage of increase of selling price over cost is
- **(A)** 40%
- **(B)** $33\frac{1}{2}$%
- **(C)** $33\frac{1}{3}$%
- **(D)** 30%

26. A man borrowed $5000 and agreed to pay $11\frac{1}{2}$% annual interest. If he repaid the loan in 6 months, how much interest would he pay?
- **(A)** $2875.00
- **(B)** $5750.00
- **(C)** $287.50
- **(D)** $575.00

27. After deducting a discount of 30%, the price of a coat was $35.00. What was the regular price of the coat?
- **(A)** $116.67
- **(B)** $24.50
- **(C)** $50.00
- **(D)** $42.00

28. Two cars start from the same point at the same time. One drives north at 20 miles an hour, and the other drives south on the same straight road at 36 miles an hour. How many miles apart are they after 30 minutes?
- **(A)** Fewer than 10
- **(B)** Between 10 and 20
- **(C)** Between 20 and 30
- **(D)** Between 30 and 40

29. During his summer vacation, a boy earned $14.50 per day and saved 60% of his earnings. If he worked 45 days, how much did he save?
- **(A)** $391.50
- **(B)** $287.93
- **(C)** $402.75
- **(D)** $543.50

30. The number of cubic feet of soil needed for a flower box 3 feet long, 8 inches wide, and 1 foot deep is
   (A) 24
   (B) 12
   (C) $4\frac{2}{3}$
   (D) 2

31. The scale of a certain map is 4 inches = 32 miles. The number of inches that would represent 80 miles is
   (A) 8
   (B) 12
   (C) 10
   (D) 16

32. The daily almanac report for one day during the summer stated that the sun rose at 6:14 a.m. and set at 6:06 p.m. Find the number of hours and minutes in the time between the rising and setting of the sun on that day.
   (A) 11 hr. 52 min
   (B) 12 hr. 8 min.
   (C) 11 hr. 2 min.
   (D) 12 hr. 48 min.

33. One piece of wire is 25 feet 8 inches long and another is 18 feet 10 inches long. What is the difference in length?
   (A) 6 ft. 10 in.
   (B) 6 ft. 11 in.
   (C) 7 ft. 2 in.
   (D) 7 ft. 4 in.

34. If a vehicle is to complete a 20-mile trip at an average rate of 30 miles per hour, it must complete the trip in
   (A) 20 min.
   (B) 30 min.
   (C) 40 min.
   (D) 50 min.

35. A snapshot measures $2\frac{1}{2}$ inches by $1\frac{7}{8}$ inches. It is to be enlarged so that the longer dimension will be 4 inches. The length of the enlarged shorter dimension will be
   (A) $2\frac{1}{2}$ inches.
   (B) 3 inches.
   (C) $3\frac{3}{8}$ inches.
   (D) $2\frac{5}{8}$ inches.

36. An adult's ski lift ticket costs twice as much as a child's. If a family of three children and two adults can ski for $49, what is the cost of an adult ticket?
   (A) $7
   (B) $10
   (C) $12
   (D) $14

37. A recipe calls for $1\frac{1}{2}$ cups of sugar. It is necessary to make eight times the recipe for a church supper. If 2 cups of sugar equal 1 pound, how many pounds of sugar will be needed to make the recipe for the supper?
   (A) 4
   (B) 6
   (C) 8
   (D) 10

38. In the fraction $\frac{1}{\Delta - 2}$, Δ can be replaced by all of the following except
   (A) 0
   (B) +3
   (C) +2
   (D) −2

39. If one pipe can fill a tank in $1\frac{1}{2}$ hours and another can fill the same tank in 45 minutes, how long will it take for the two pipes to fill the tank together?

(A) 1 hour

(B) $\frac{1}{2}$ hour

(C) $1\frac{1}{2}$ hours

(D) $\frac{1}{3}$ hour

40. Two cars are 550 miles apart and traveling toward each other on the same road. If one travels at 50 miles per hour, the other at 60 miles per hour, and they both leave at 1:00 p.m., what time will they meet?

(A) 4:00 p.m.

(B) 4:30 p.m.

(C) 5:45 p.m.

(D) 6:00 p.m.

Exercise 4

Directions: Choose the correct answer to each problem and circle its letter. Answers are found at the end of this chapter.

1. Any number that is divisible by both 5 and 6 is also divisible by

(A) 11

(B) 9

(C) 7

(D) 3

2. 3,482,613 rounded to the nearest million is

(A) 2,000,000

(B) 3,500,000

(C) 3,000,000

(D) 4,000,000

3. The number that is *not* a factor of 120 is

(A) 5

(B) 6

(C) 7

(D) 8

4. What is the place value of 3 in 4.9236?

(A) Hundredths

(B) Thousandths

(C) Ten thousandths

(D) Hundred thousandths

5. Which symbol belong in the circle 0.0983 ○ 0.124

(A) <

(B) >

(C) =

(D) ≅

6. The greatest common factor of 24 and 12 is

(A) 2

(B) 4

(C) 6

(D) 12

7. 1000% is equal to

(A) 0.0001

(B) 0.1

(C) 10

(D) 100

8. In the simplest form, $\frac{12}{16}$ is

(A) $\frac{3}{4}$

(B) $\frac{2}{3}$

(C) $\frac{2}{6}$

(D) $\frac{4}{8}$

9. $\frac{9}{25}$ is equal to

(A) 0.036

(B) 0.04

(C) 0.36

(D) 0.45

10. What number belongs in the box?

$-5 + \square = 0$

(A) -5

(B) 0

(C) -1

(D) $+5$

11. $\sqrt{81}$ is equal to

(A) 8

(B) 9

(C) 18

(D) 40.5

12. Solve for x: $\frac{x}{2} + 3 = 15$

(A) 18

(B) 20

(C) 22

(D) 24

13. If $y + 2 > 10$, then y must be

(A) smaller than 10.

(B) smaller than 8.

(C) greater than 8.

(D) equal to 0.

14. If $a + b = 200°$, and $c + d + e + f = 140°$, what is the number of degrees in angle g?

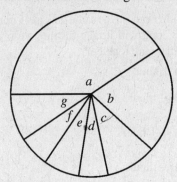

(A) 10°

(B) 20°

(C) 30°

(D) 45°

15. The area of the shaded portion of the rectangle below is

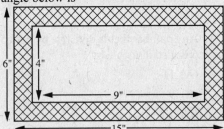

(A) 54 sq. in.

(B) 90 sq. in.

(C) 45 sq. in.

(D) 36 sq. in.

16. Which point shown below corresponds to (8,3)?

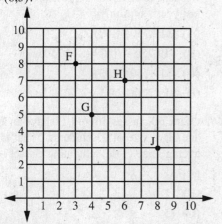

(A) Point F
(B) Point G
(C) Point H
(D) Point J

QUESTIONS 17–23 ARE BASED ON THE FOLLOWING PASSAGE.

Mr. Shea, a shop teacher at the junior high school, owns a ski lodge in Vermont. The lodge is open to guests on weekends and during school vacations. Mr. Shea's regular rates, which include breakfast and dinner, are $25 per night for dormitory-style accommodations. He gives a 30 percent discount to all members of organized student groups from his community.

17. Sixteen members of Boy Scout Troop 60 and two of their leaders went on a ski weekend and stayed at Mr. Shea's lodge. The two-night cost of room and board for each boy was

(A) $25
(B) $35
(C) $50
(D) $60

18. The leaders shared a room instead of sleeping in the dormitory. The total bill for the two of them was $84 for the two nights. The surcharge per person for the semi-private room was

(A) 7%
(B) 20%
(C) 32%
(D) 42%

19. Lift tickets cost $20 per day for adults and $14 per day for juniors (persons under 13 years of age). Five of the boys were 12 years old, while the others were older. What was the total cost of lift tickets for a day of skiing?

(A) $220
(B) $290
(C) $330
(D) $390

20. Among the boys, $\frac{1}{4}$ considered themselves to be expert skiers. Of those who were less experienced, $\frac{3}{4}$ took ski lessons. Of those who took ski lessons, $\frac{1}{3}$ rented ski equipment. How many boys rented ski equipment?

(A) 9
(B) 6
(C) 4
(D) 3

21. The mountain on which the troop skied had 27 trails served by a T-bar lift, two J-bars lifts, and three chair lifts. The proportion of trails to lifts was

(A) 5:1
(B) 7:2
(C) 9:3
(D) 9:2

22. One boy skied the length of a 4.6-mile trail in just under 14 minutes. His average speed was approximately

    (A) 15 mph.
    (B) 20 mph.
    (C) 25 mph.
    (D) 30 mph.

23. The bus chartered for the trip cost $250. The rooms and lift tickets totaled $1,304. The troop contributed $400 from its treasury to help defray expenses of the trip. If the rest was divided equally among the 16 boys and 2 leaders, how much did each individual pay?

    (A) $64.11
    (B) $71.13
    (C) $75.28
    (D) $83.07

QUESTIONS 24–28 REFER TO THE FOLLOWING PASSAGE.

Applesville High School, an accredited 4-year institution (grades 9 to 12), is located on a picturesque 128-acre campus. At Applesville, the student-teacher ratio is 7:1, average class size is 15, and current annual tuition is $19,750. The historic library is located at the center of campus and has a collection of 30,000 volumes.

24. If $\frac{7}{8}$ of the campus is devoted to woods and gardens and the rest is developed for academic use, how many acres are used for academics?

    (A) 16
    (B) 32
    (C) 48
    (D) 96

25. This year, annual tuition is 7% higher than it was last year. Which expression represents last year's tuition?

    (A) ($19,750)(1.07)
    (B) $19,750 – (0.07)($19,750)
    (C) ($19,750)(0.93)
    (D) $19,750/1.07

26. Of the 60 classes offered, 20 have an average class size of 21 students. What is the average size of the remaining classes?

    (A) 9
    (B) 12
    (C) 15
    (D) 21

27. Next year, Applesville will loan its rare book collection (2% of its volumes) to the local university. How many volumes will Applesville's library have on campus next year?

    (A) 29,000
    (B) 29,400
    (C) 29,600
    (D) 29,800

28. Excluding maintenance and administrative personnel, if there are 304 persons (teachers and students) at school, how many teachers work at Applesville High School?

    (A) 7
    (B) 14
    (C) 38
    (D) 152

QUESTIONS 29–32 REFER TO THE FOLLOWING PASSAGE.

On an icy day, the Bergs' car skidded into a telephone pole and suffered two smashed doors and a broken drive shaft. After four weeks in a body shop, the car was fully repaired. The Bergs' insurance company paid the body shop's bill, less the $200 deductible, which the Bergs paid.

29. For what portion of the year were the Bergs unable to use their car?

    (A) $\frac{1}{4}$

    (B) $\frac{1}{10}$

    (C) $\frac{1}{12}$

    (D) $\frac{1}{13}$

30. In the year before the accident, the Bergs' insurance premium was $1100. The year following the accident, their premium rose to $1500. The new premium was about what percent of the old premium?

    (A) $26\frac{2}{3}\%$

    (B) $36\frac{1}{3}\%$

    (C) $136\frac{1}{3}\%$

    (D) 140%

31. To match the blue paint of the car, the man in the body shop had to add $1\frac{1}{2}$ ounces of black paint for each pint of blue paint. He used three gallons of blue paint on the car. What was the total amount of paint he used?

    (A) $2\frac{1}{4}$ pints

    (B) $21\frac{3}{4}$ pints

    (C) 24 pints

    (D) $26\frac{1}{4}$ pints

32. Three men of about equal efficiency were assigned to work on the Bergs' car. One man worked on the car full-time. He was always assisted by one of the other men. If the full-time man needed to complete the job alone, the car would have been in the shop for

    (A) 2 weeks.

    (B) 4 weeks.

    (C) 6 weeks.

    (D) 8 weeks.

exercises

ANSWER KEYS AND EXPLANATIONS

Exercise 1

1. C	4. A	7. A	10. B	13. C
2. C	5. E	8. C	11. A	14. E
3. D	6. B	9. D	12. E	15. B

1. The correct answer is (C).

```
      896
  ×   708
     7168
    62720
   634368
```

2. The correct answer is (C).

```
      474
  9)4266
     36
     66
     63
     36
     36
```

3. The correct answer is (D). $202.68

4. The correct answer is (A). $1201.39

5. The correct answer is (E).

```
        16.44551 ≈ 16.4455
   29)476.9200
      29
      186
      174
      129
      116
      132
      116
      160
      145
      150
      145
       50
```

6. The correct answer is (B). 88

7. The correct answer is (A).

```
          63 2.39 ≈ 632.4
   3.7)2339.8 60
       222
       119
       111
        88
        74
       146
       111
       350
       333
        17
```

8. The correct answer is (C).

$$\frac{1}{5} = 0.20$$

$$\begin{array}{r} 45286 \\ \times \quad 4.20 \\ \hline 905720 \\ 181144 \quad \\ \hline 190201.20 = 190,201\frac{1}{5} \end{array}$$

9. The correct answer is (D).

$$\begin{array}{r} 8\frac{1}{6} = 7\frac{7}{6} \\ -5\frac{2}{3} = 5\frac{4}{6} \\ \hline 2\frac{3}{6} = 2\frac{1}{2} \end{array}$$

10. The correct answer is (B).

$$\frac{1}{9} \times \frac{\cancel{2}^{1}}{3} \times \frac{7}{\cancel{8}_{4}} = \frac{7}{108}$$

11. The correct answer is (A).

$$\frac{1}{4} \div 4\frac{1}{3} = \frac{1}{4} \div \frac{13}{3} = \frac{1}{4} \times \frac{3}{13} = \frac{3}{52}$$

12. The correct answer is (E). 104,714

13. The correct answer is (C).

$$\begin{array}{r} 12689 \\ \times \quad 37 \\ \hline 88823 \\ 38067 \quad \\ \hline 469493 \end{array}$$

14. The correct answer is (E).

$$\$13.50 \times 6\frac{2}{3}\% = \$13.50 \times 0.06\frac{2}{3}$$
$$= \frac{\$13.50}{1} \times \frac{0.20}{3}$$
$$= \frac{\$2.70}{3} = \$0.90$$

15. The correct answer is (B).

$$\frac{11}{16} = 16 \overline{)11.0000} \quad \begin{array}{r} 0.6875 \end{array}$$

$$\begin{array}{r} 9\ 6 \\ \hline 1\ 40 \\ 1\ 28 \\ \hline 120 \\ 112 \\ \hline 80 \\ 80 \end{array}$$

Exercise 2

1. A	6. B	11. B	15. E	19. B
2. A	7. C	12. C	16. B	20. E
3. C	8. B	13. C	17. A	21. E
4. E	9. C	14. C	18. B	22. B
5. D	10. E			

1. The correct answer is (A).

$$
\begin{array}{r}
5239 \\
\times\ 706 \\
\hline
31434 \\
366730 \\
\hline
3698734
\end{array}
$$

2. The correct answer is (A).

$$
\begin{array}{r}
48207 \\
\times\ \ 926 \\
\hline
289242 \\
96414 \\
433863 \\
\hline
44639682
\end{array}
$$

3. The correct answer is (C).

$$
\begin{array}{r}
661\ R\ 1 \\
7\overline{)4628} \\
42 \\
\hline
42 \\
42 \\
\hline
08 \\
7 \\
\hline
1
\end{array}
$$

4. The correct answer is (E).

$$
\begin{array}{r}
12\ R\ 35 \\
419\overline{)5063} \\
419 \\
\hline
873 \\
838 \\
\hline
35
\end{array}
$$

5. The correct answer is (D).

$$
\begin{array}{r}
1\ 49 \\
\$0.40\overline{)\$59.60} \\
40 \\
\hline
19\ 6 \\
16\ 0 \\
\hline
3\ 60 \\
3\ 60
\end{array}
$$

6. The correct answer is (B).

$$
\begin{array}{r}
3.410 \\
5.600 \\
+0.873 \\
\hline
9.883
\end{array}
$$

7. The correct answer is (C). 54,741

8. The correct answer is (B). 0.024
Add up the places to the right of the decimal point.

9. The correct answer is (C).

$$
\begin{array}{r}
30. \\
.33\overline{)9.90}
\end{array}
$$

10. The correct answer is (E).

$$
\begin{array}{r}
570 \\
\times\ 0.16 \\
\hline
34\ 20 \\
570 \\
\hline
91.20
\end{array}
$$

11. **The correct answer is (B).**

$135 \div 900 = 0.15 = 15\%$

12. **The correct answer is (C).**

$$\begin{aligned} \frac{3}{4} &= \frac{6}{8} \\ + \frac{3}{8} &= \frac{3}{8} \\ \hline \frac{9}{8} &= 1\frac{1}{8} \end{aligned}$$

13. **The correct answer is (C).**

$$\begin{aligned} 3\frac{1}{4} &= 3\frac{2}{8} \\ 4\frac{1}{8} &= 4\frac{1}{8} \\ + 4\frac{1}{2} &= 4\frac{4}{8} \\ \hline &\; 11\frac{7}{8} \end{aligned}$$

14. **The correct answer is (C).**

$$\begin{aligned} 10\frac{2}{3} &= 10\frac{4}{6} \\ - 9\frac{1}{2} &= 9\frac{3}{6} \\ \hline &\; 1\frac{1}{6} \end{aligned}$$

15. **The correct answer is (E).**

$$\begin{aligned} 14\frac{7}{24} &= 14\frac{7}{24} = 13\frac{31}{24} \\ - 5\frac{2}{3} &= 5\frac{16}{24} = 5\frac{16}{24} \\ \hline & \qquad\qquad\;\; 8\frac{15}{24} = 8\frac{5}{8} \end{aligned}$$

16. **The correct answer is (B).**

$$\frac{{}^2\cancel{8}}{\cancel{15}_5} \times \frac{{}^1\cancel{3}}{\cancel{4}_1} = \frac{2}{5}$$

17. **The correct answer is (A).**

$$5\frac{1}{4} \times 2\frac{2}{7} = \frac{{}^3\cancel{21}}{\cancel{4}_1} \times \frac{{}^4\cancel{16}}{\cancel{7}_1} = \frac{12}{1} = 12$$

18. **The correct answer is (B).**

$$\frac{9}{16} \div \frac{3}{4} = \frac{{}^3\cancel{9}}{\cancel{16}_4} \times \frac{{}^1\cancel{4}}{\cancel{3}_1} = \frac{3}{4}$$

19. **The correct answer is (B).** When adding two numbers of unlike sign, subtract and assign the sign of the larger number.

20. **The correct answer is (E).** Minus negative becomes plus positive. The problem then reads: $(-22) + (+18) = -4$

21. **The correct answer is (E).** When multiplying two numbers of unlike sign, the product is always negative. $(7) \times (-7) = -49$

22. **The correct answer is (B).** When you divide two numbers of unlike sign, the quotient is always negative. $(+56) \div (-7) = -8$

Exercise 3

1. D	9. D	17. C	25. D	33. A
2. A	10. B	18. C	26. C	34. C
3. D	11. B	19. B	27. C	35. B
4. D	12. C	20. C	28. C	36. D
5. C	13. C	21. A	29. A	37. B
6. B	14. C	22. A	30. D	38. C
7. C	15. A	23. D	31. C	39. B
8. A	16. C	24. B	32. A	40. D

1. **The correct answer is (D).** To find the average, add all the numbers and divide the sum by the number of terms.

$$42 + 35 + 28 + 30 + 24 + 27 = 186$$
$$186 \div 6 = 31$$

2. **The correct answer is (A).**

14 words = 10 words + 4 words

10 words cost 52 cents

4 words @ 2.5 cents = $4 \times 2.5 = 10$ cents

52 cents + 10 cents = 62 cents

3. **The correct answer is (D).**

500 − 125 = 375 pads @ $0.04 = \$15.00$

130 − 45 = 85 pencils @ $0.03 = \$2.55$

50 dozen − 4 dozen = 46 dozen rubber bands @ $0.02 = \$0.92$

$15 + \$2.55 + \$0.92 = \$18.47$

4. **The correct answer is (D).**

$60 \times 0.10 = \$6$ (employee discount)

$60 − \$6 = \$54$

$54 \times 0.20 = \$10.80$ (sale discount)

$54 − \$10.80 = \$43.20$

5. **The correct answer is (C).**

9 square feet = 1 square yard
270 sq. ft. ÷ 9 = 30 sq. yds.

6. **The correct answer is (B).**

The whole pie is 100%.

Each part is $\frac{1}{40}$.

$100 \div 40 = 2.5\%$

7. **The correct answer is (C).** First find out how much sugar is needed for one quart of punch.

$$\frac{3}{4} \text{ cups} \div 6 = \frac{3}{4} \div \frac{6}{1} = \frac{\cancel{3}^1}{4} \times \frac{1}{\cancel{6}_2} = \frac{1}{8}$$

For 9 quarts of punch:

$$9 \times \frac{1}{8} = \frac{9}{8} = 1\frac{1}{8}$$

8. **The correct answer is (A).** 45 badges × 4 inches each = 180 inches needed. There are 36 inches in one yard. 180 inches ÷ 36 = 5 yards of ribbon needed.

9. **The correct answer is (D).**

1 gallon = 4 quarts

4 gals. = 16 qts.

$16 \text{ qts.} \times 42\frac{1}{2} \text{ cents} = 16 \times \$0.425 = \$6.80$

10. The correct answer is (B).

$\frac{3}{5}$ of 200 = 120 columns by machine

@ 40 columns per hour = 3 hours

200 − 120 = 80 columns without machine @ 20 columns per hour = 4 hours

3 hours + 4 hours = 7 hours to complete the job

11. The correct answer is (B). Perimeter = $2l + 2w$. If the two long sides are together, the perimeter will be 5 + 3 + 3 + 5 + 3 + 3 = 22.

If the two short sides are together, the perimeter will be 3 + 5 + 5 + 3 + 5 + 5 = 26.

26 − 22 = 4 feet shorter

12. The correct answer is (C). To remove a % sign, divide the number by 100.

Thus, 1% = $\frac{1}{100}$ = 0.01 . 1% of 8 is the same as 1% times 8 = 0.01 × 8 = 0.08.

13. The correct answer is (C).

$$
\begin{array}{r}
8.13 \\
10\overline{)81.30} \\
\underline{80} \\
1\ 3 \\
\underline{1\ 0} \\
30 \\
\underline{30} \\
0
\end{array}
$$

14. The correct answer is (C).

Each −1 cancels out the +1 before it.

Because the final term is +1, which is not canceled out by a −1, the sum is + 1.

15. The correct answer is (A).

5 hours 30 minutes = $5\frac{1}{2}$ hours

1000 miles ÷ $5\frac{1}{2}$ hours = 1000 ÷ $\frac{11}{2}$ =

$1000 \times \frac{2}{11} = 181\frac{9}{11}$ mph

16. The correct answer is (C).

2975 pennies = $29.75

$35.00 − $29.75 = $5.25 amount of discount

Rate of discount = $\frac{5.25}{35} \times 100$

= 0.15 × 100

= 15%

17. The correct answer is (C). First convert all the yards and feet into inches so that all addition and subtraction can be done using the same units.

$$
\begin{array}{rl}
12\ \text{feet} = & 144\ \text{inches} \\
-7\ \text{inches} = & -7\ \text{inches} \\
+2\ \text{feet, 1 inch} = & +25\ \text{inches} \\
-7\ \text{feet} = & -84\ \text{inches} \\
-1\ \text{yard} = & -36\ \text{inches} \\
+2\ \text{yards, 1 foot,} & \\
3\ \text{inches} = & \underline{+87\ \text{inches}} \\
= & 129\ \text{inches}
\end{array}
$$

18. The correct answer is (C). Any number multiplied by 0 equals 0. Since one multiplier on one side of the equals sign is 0, the product on that side of the sign must be 0.

$5x = 5 \times 4 \times 2 \times 0$

$5x = 40 \times 0$

$5x = 0$

$x = 0$

19. The correct answer is (B).

Area of a square = s^2

$49 = 7^2$

One side = 7 inches

$P = 4s$

$P = 4 \times 7" = 28$ inches

20. The correct answer is (C). First perform the operation within the parentheses. To cube a number, multiply it by itself, two times.

$(3 + 4)^3 = (7)^3 = 7 \times 7 \times 7 = 343$

21. The correct answer is (A).

First room:

    36 ft. × 8 ft. = 288 sq. ft.

Second room:

    24 ft × 9 ft. = $\dfrac{216 \text{ sq. ft.}}{504 \text{ sq. ft.}}$

504 ÷ 224 = 2.25 rolls needed

22. The correct answer is (A).

0.05% of the total (x) = 60

$0.0005x = 60$

$x = 60 \div 0.0005 = 120{,}000$

23. The correct answer is (D). If the court does a day's work every day, it will dispense with 60 days' worth of new cases. The excess work is $0.6 \times 60 = 36$ days of work. Add the 36 newly accumulated hours of excess work to the backlog of 150 days of work to learn that the court will be 186 trial days behind.

24. The correct answer is (B). $\dfrac{1}{4}$ in. = 1 ft., so 1 in. = 4 ft. and the living room is $7 \times 4 = 28$ ft. long. When the scale is changed to 1 in. = 1 ft., the 28-ft. living room will be 28 in. on the new drawing.

25. The correct answer is (D). To find percent of change, subtract the original figure from the new figure to determine amount of change; then divide the amount of change by the original figure to determine percent of change.

$\$65 - \$50 = \$15 \div 50 = 0.3 = 30\%$

26. The correct answer is (C). $11\dfrac{1}{2}\%$ of \$5000 is \$575. Because he repaid the loan in one-half of a year, his interest payment is \$575 ÷ 2 = \$287.50.

27. The correct answer is (C). If 30% has been deducted, \$35 is 70% of the original price. To find out what a number is when a percent of it is given, rename the percent as a decimal and divide the given number by it.

$\$35 \div 0.70 = \$50$

28. The correct answer is (C). One car went 20 mph for $\dfrac{1}{2}$ hour = 10 miles. The other went 36 mph for $\dfrac{1}{2}$ hour = 18 miles. Because they went in opposite directions, add the two distances to find the total number of miles apart: $10 + 18 = 28$.

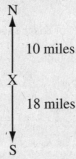

29. The correct answer is (A). The boy worked 45 days × \$14.50 per day, so he earned \$652.50. He saved 60% of \$652.50 = \$391.50.

30. The correct answer is (D). Rename 8 in. as $\dfrac{2}{3}$ ft. so that all measurements are in the same unit. Then multiply $l \times w \times h$.

$3 \text{ ft.} \times \dfrac{2}{3} \text{ ft.} \times 1 \text{ ft.} = 2$ cu. ft.

31. **The correct answer is (C).** 4 in. = 32 miles; therefore, 1 in. = 32 ÷ 4 = 8 miles. 80 miles would be represented by 10 in.

32. **The correct answer is (A).** You do not need to do complicated calculations to answer this question: $14 - 6 = 8$. The sun was above the horizon for 8 minutes less than 12 hours, which is 11 hours 52 minutes ($60 - 8 = 52$).

33. **The correct answer is (A).**

$$
\begin{array}{r}
25 \text{ ft. } 8 \text{ in.} = 24 \text{ ft. } 20 \text{ in.} \\
18 \text{ ft. } 10 \text{ in.} = \underline{18 \text{ ft. } 10 \text{ in.}} \\
6 \text{ ft. } 10 \text{ in.}
\end{array}
$$

34. **The correct answer is (C).** No calculations are needed here. Note that a 20-mile trip at 60 mph (which is 1 mile per minute) would take 20 minutes. Because the vehicle is traveling half as fast (30 mph), the 20-mile trip should take twice as long, or 40 minutes.

35. **The correct answer is (B).** This is a proportion problem. Set up the proportion as follows:

$$\frac{2\frac{1}{2}}{4} = \frac{1\frac{7}{8}}{?}$$

Substitute x for ?:

$$\frac{2\frac{1}{2}}{4} = \frac{1\frac{7}{8}}{x}$$

Cross-multiply:

$$2\frac{1}{2}x = 4 \times 1\frac{7}{8}$$

$$\frac{5}{2}x = \frac{60}{8}$$

Divide both sides by the coefficient of x and calculate:

$$x = \frac{60}{8} \div \frac{5}{2}$$

$$x = \frac{60}{8} \times \frac{2}{5}$$

$$x = 3$$

36. **The correct answer is (D).** A child's ticket costs x dollars. Each adult ticket costs twice as much, or $2x$ dollars. $2(2x) = 2$ adult tickets; $3x = 3$ children tickets. Write a simple equation and solve for x.

$$2(2x) + 3x = \$49$$
$$4x + 3x = \$49$$
$$7x = \$49$$
$$x = \$7$$

$7 is the cost of a child's ticket; $14 is the cost of an adult's ticket.

37. **The correct answer is (B).**

$$1\frac{1}{2} \text{ c. sugar } \times 8 = 12 \text{ c. sugar}$$

$$12 \text{ c. } \div 2 \text{ c. per lb.} = 6 \text{ lb. of sugar}$$

38. **The correct answer is (C).** By substituting +2 for the triangle, the denominator of the fraction becomes zero. A denominator of zero is undefined in mathematics.

39. **The correct answer is (B).** The first pipe can fill the tank in $1\frac{1}{2}$ hours, or $\frac{3}{2}$ hours; that is, it can do $\frac{2}{3}$ of the job in 1 hour. The second pipe can fill the tank in 45 minutes, or $\frac{3}{4}$ of an hour, or it can do $\frac{4}{3}$ of the job in 1 hour. Together the pipes can complete $\frac{4}{3} + \frac{2}{3} = \frac{6}{3}$ of the job in 1 hour. $\frac{6}{3} = 2$, or twice the job in 1 hour. Therefore, together the two pipes could fill the tank in $\frac{1}{2}$ hour.

40. **The correct answer is (D).** The cars are traveling toward each other, so the distance between them is being reduced at 60 + 50 or 110 miles per hour. At a rate of 110 mph, 550 miles will be covered in 5 hours. If both cars left at 1:00 p.m., they should meet at 6:00 p.m.

answers exercises

Exercise 4

1. D	8. A	15. A	21. D	27. B
2. C	9. C	16. D	22. B	28. C
3. C	10. D	17. B	23. A	29. D
4. B	11. B	18. B	24. A	30. C
5. A	12. D	19. C	25. D	31. D
6. D	13. C	20. D	26. B	32. D
7. C	14. B			

1. **The correct answer is (D).** Not many numbers are divisible by both 5 and 6. Only multiples of 5 × 6 are divisible by both. Multiples of 5 × 6 are multiples of 30, which are all divisible by 3.

2. **The correct answer is (C).** The seventh digit to the left of the decimal point is in the millions place. Because 482 is less than 500, round down.

3. **The correct answer is (C).** 120 is not divisible by 7.

4. **The correct answer is (B).** The place values are: four ones, nine tenths, two hundredths, three thousandths, six ten thousandths.

5. **The correct answer is (A).** Look immediately to the right of the decimal point. 0 is less than 1.

6. **The correct answer is (D).** The greatest number by which both 12 and 24 can be divided is 12.

7. **The correct answer is (C).** To rename a percent as a decimal, move the decimal point two places to the left.

   $$1000\% = 10.00$$

8. **The correct answer is (A).** To simplify $\frac{12}{16}$ to simplest form, divide both numerator and denominator by 4.

9. **The correct answer is (C).** The fraction bar in a fraction means "divided by."
   $$9 \div 25 = 0.36$$

10. **The correct answer is (D).** The positive and negative cancel each other out. Addition may be done in any order. To check this problem, reverse the order of the addends.

    $$5 - 5 = 0$$

11. **The correct answer is (B).** The square root of 81 is 9.

12. **The correct answer is (D).**

    $$\frac{x}{2} + 3 = 15$$
    $$\frac{x}{2} = 15 - 3$$
    $$\frac{x}{2} = 12$$
    $$x = 12 \times 2$$
    $$x = 24$$

13. **The correct answer is (C).**

    $$y + 2 > 10$$
    $$y > 10 - 2$$
    $$y > 8$$

14. **The correct answer is (B).** The sum of the angles of a circle = 360°. Angles a through f total 340°. Angle g must be 20°.

15. **The correct answer is (A).** The area of the entire rectangle is 6 in. × 15 in. = 90 sq. in. The area of the unshaded portion is 4 in. × 9 in. = 36 sq. in. 90 sq. in. − 36 sq. in. = 54 sq. in. in the shaded portion.

16. **The correct answer is (D).** In reading a graph, always read along the horizontal axis first.

17. **The correct answer is (B).** The charge for one night is $25; for two nights, $50. The Boy Scouts receive a 30% discount, so they pay 70%. 70% of $50 = $35.

18. **The correct answer is (B).** As part of the group, the leaders received the same 30% discount as the boys. If they had slept in the dormitory, they would have paid $35 each for the two nights. Their total bill (2 men, 2 nights) would have been $70. However, they paid extra for a semi-private room. To find the percent of increase, subtract the original number from the new number and divide the difference by the original number.

    $84 − $70 = $14 ÷ $70 = 20%

19. **The correct answer is (C).** Of the 18 people, there are 13 adults and 5 juniors. The adult tickets cost $20 × 13 = $260. The junior tickets cost $14 × 5 = $70. The total cost of lift tickets for one day is $260 + $70 = $330.

20. **The correct answer is (D).** $\frac{1}{4}$ of 16 = 4 expert skiers. That leaves 16 − 4 = 12 less experienced skiers. $\frac{3}{4}$ of 12 = 9 who took ski lessons. $\frac{1}{3}$ of 9 = 3 who rented equipment.

21. **The correct answer is (D).** There were 27 trails and 6 lifts, which simplifies to 9:2.

22. **The correct answer is (B).** The formula for determining rate is $\frac{D}{T}$. The distance skied is 4.6 miles. The time, just under 14 minutes, is approximately 0.25 hour.

    $4.6 ÷ 0.25 = 18.4$ mph

    Because he skied the distance in slightly less than 0.25 hour, his average speed was very close to 20 mph.

23. **The correct answer is (A).** First add up the expenses:

    Rooms and lift tickets = $1304
    Bus = $250
    $1554

    Subtract the troop contribution − 400
    $1154

    Now divide by the 18 people:
    $2254 ÷ 18 = $64.11 each

24. **The correct answer is (A).** If $\frac{7}{8}$ of the campus is devoted to woods and gardens, then $\frac{1}{8}$ is used for academics.

    $\frac{1}{8}$ of 128 acres = $\frac{1}{8} × 128 = 16$

25. **The correct answer is (D).** Let x = tuition last year. This year's tuition is 7% greater:

    $1.07x = $19,750

    $x = $19,750/1.07

26. **The correct answer is (B).** Average class size = (sum of the class sizes) ÷ (total number of classes). If 20 classes have an average size of 21 students, that's 20 × 21 students. Let x = average class size of the other 40 classes. Then:

    $\frac{(20)(21)+40x}{60}=15$

    Multiplying both sides by 60:

    $420 + 40x = 900$
    $40x = 480$
    $x = 12$

    Or, since we know that $\frac{1}{3}$ of the classes have an average size of 21, which is 6 above the given average size of 15, then the remaining $\frac{2}{3}$ of the classes (twice as many as $\frac{1}{3}$) must have an average size of 3 below 15.

    $15 − 3 = 12$

27. **The correct answer is (B).** The library has 30,000 volumes. Ten percent of 30,000 = 3,000. So, 2% = 3,000/5 = 600. The number of volumes left on campus next year will be:

$$30,000 - 600 = 29,400$$

28. **The correct answer is (C).** Based on the information given, the student-teacher ratio is 7:1. This means that for every 7 students, there is 1 teacher. So, we can let $7x$ = number of students and $1x$ = number of teachers. Then:

$$7x + 1x = 304$$
$$8x = 304$$
$$x = 38$$

29. **The correct answer is (D).** 4 weeks is $\frac{4}{52} = \frac{1}{13}$.

30. **The correct answer is (C).** Again find what percent one number is of another by creating a fraction. This time, the part that you want to know about happens to be larger than the whole.

$$\$1500 \div 1100 = 1.3636 \approx 136\frac{1}{3}\%$$

31. **The correct answer is (D).** 3 gallon = 24 pints. $1\frac{1}{2}$ ounces of black paint $\times$ 24 = 36 ounce of black paint. 36 ounces = $2\frac{1}{4}$ pints. 24 pints of blue + $2\frac{1}{4}$ pints of black = $26\frac{1}{4}$ pints of paint.

32. **The correct answer is (D).** You do not have to calculate this problem. If you read carefully, you will see that 2 men worked full-time and the work took 4 weeks. If only one man (half the number) had worked, the job would have taken twice the time, or 8 weeks.

SUMMING IT UP

- If you are having special difficulties with any mathematics topic, talk with a teacher or refer to any of your math textbooks.

- Use the exercises in this chapter to determine what you DON'T know well, and concentrate your study on those areas.

- When adding or subtracting decimals, it is important to keep the decimal points in line.

- The fastest way to find an equivalent fraction is to divide the denominator of the fraction you know by the denominator you want. Take the result and multiply it by the numerator.

- When solving a percentage problem, be sure to read the notation carefully, read the problem carefully, and use common sense.

- Remember the number line when subtracting signed numbers.

- Memorizing some simple rules will help you to move through the test more quickly and with less anxiety. An example of some of those rules is the following: The product of two negative numbers is positive; the product of two positive numbers is positive; and the product of a negative number and a positive number is negative.

- Memorize the basic equations of geometry. These may not be given to you on the test. For example, to find the area of a rectangle, you must multiply the length times the width, $A = lw$.

Series Reasoning

OVERVIEW

- **Number series**
- **Letter series**
- **Mixed series**
- **Symbol series**
- **Tips for answering series questions**
- **Summing it up**

Series reasoning questions crop up on the TACHS, COOP, and HSPT exams. On the COOP, these questions are called Sequences. On the TACHS, these questions are dealt with in the Ability section. On the HSPT, you find these questions in the Number Series section under Quantitative Skills. Series reasoning questions—symbol series, number series, letter series, or mixed—are designed to test your ability to reason without words. These questions can be challenging, fun, and sometimes very frustrating.

In some ways, series questions are a lot like analogy questions—you remember, the questions that ask you to find the relationships between words. In series questions, you have to determine the relationship between a series of symbols, numbers, or letters, then choose the next item for the series.

This chapter gives you some in-depth instruction in working with series, by showing you how to complete number and letter series. These are the most common kinds of series questions that you'll encounter on the TACHS, COOP, and the HSPT exams. The information and practice you get in this chapter will help you develop your own methods and strategies for solving these series questions. And you can use those same strategies to solve mixed series and even symbol series.

All series reasoning questions require the same concentration, the same logical thinking, and the same flexibility of approach. With all series reasoning questions, you run the risk of working out a sequence and then finding that the answer you would choose to complete the sequence is not among the choices. Don't be discouraged! Just start over and try to determine what other relationship is reasonable.

chapter 18

NUMBER SERIES

Number series questions measure your ability to think with numbers and to see the relationship between elements of a series. Even though this type of task might be new and unfamiliar to you, the actual mathematics of number series questions is not complicated. The problems involve nothing more than simple arithmetic and a few other mathematical concepts. What the questions do require of you is concentration; you must be able to see how the numbers in a series are related so that you can supply the next number in that series. You must be flexible enough in your thinking so that if the first pattern you consider for a series turns out to be invalid, you can try a different pattern.

There is a system with which to approach number series questions. Look hard at the series. The pattern might be obvious to you on inspection. A series such as 1, 2, 3, 1, 2, 3, 1 . . . should not require any deep thought. Clearly, the sequence 1, 2, 3 is repeating itself over and over. The next number in the series must be 2. You might also instantly recognize the pattern of a simple series into which one number periodically intrudes. An example of such a series is 1, 2, 15, 3, 4, 15, 5 . . . . The number 15 appears after each set of two numbers in a simple +1 series. The next number in this series is 6, which is followed by 15. Can you see why?

Test Yourself 1

Here are five series questions, which you should be able to answer by inspection. Choose the number that should come next in the series.

The answer keys and explanations appear after Test Yourself 8 and Tips for Answering Series Questions.

1. 12, 10, 13, 10, 14 . . .
   (A) 15
   (B) 14
   (C) 10
   (D) 9

2. 20, 40, 60, 20, 40 . . .
   (A) 60
   (B) 20
   (C) 40
   (D) 80

3. 9, 1, 9, 3, 9 . . .
   (A) 5
   (B) 6
   (C) 8
   (D) 4

4. 5, 8, 5, 8, 5 . . .
   (A) 5
   (B) 8
   (C) 6
   (D) 9

5. 10, 9, 8, 7, 6 . . .
   (A) 7
   (B) 4
   (C) 5
   (D) 6

Sometimes you might find that your ear is more adept than your eye. You might be able to "hear" a pattern or "feel" a rhythm more easily than you can "see" it. If you cannot immediately spot a pattern, try saying the series softly to yourself. First read the series through. If that does not help, try accenting the printed numbers and speaking the missing intervening numbers even more softly. Try grouping the numbers within the series into twos or threes. After grouping, try accenting the last number, or the first. If you read aloud 2, 4, 6, 8, 10, you will hear that the next number is 12. Likewise, if you see the series 31, 32, 33, 32, 33, 34, 33, and you group that series this way: 31, 32, 33/ 32, 33, 34/ 33 . . ., you will feel the rhythm. The series consists of three-number mini-series. Each mini-series begins with a number one higher than the first number of the previous mini-series. The next number of the above series is 34, then 35, and then the next step will be 34, 35, 36.

Test Yourself 2

You might be able to answer the next five series questions by inspection. If you cannot, try sounding them out.

1. 1, 2, 5, 6, 9, 10, 13 . . .
   (A) 14
   (B) 15
   (C) 16
   (D) 17

2. 2, 3, 4, 3, 4, 5, 4 . . .
   (A) 3
   (B) 4
   (C) 5
   (D) 6

3. 10, 10, 12, 14, 14, 16 . . .
   (A) 16
   (B) 18
   (C) 20
   (D) 22

4. 1, 2, 3, 2, 2, 3, 3, 2, 3 . . .
   (A) 1
   (B) 2
   (C) 3
   (D) 4

5. 10, 9, 8, 9, 8, 7, 8 . . .
   (A) 6
   (B) 7
   (C) 8
   (D) 9

If you cannot hear the pattern of a series, the next step is to mark the degree and direction of change between the numbers. Most series progress by either + (plus) or − (minus) or a combination of both directions, so first try marking your changes in terms of + and −. If you cannot make sense of a series in terms of + and −, try x (times) and ÷ (divided by). You may mark the changes between numbers right on your exam paper, but be sure to mark the letter of the answer on your answer sheet when you figure it out. Only your answer sheet will be scored. The exam booklet will be collected, but it will not be scored.

Test Yourself 3

Try this next set of practice questions. If you cannot "see" or "hear" the pattern, mark the differences between the numbers to establish the pattern. Then continue the pattern to determine the next number of the series.

1. 9, 10, 12, 15, 19, 24 . . .
   - (A) 25
   - (B) 29
   - (C) 30
   - (D) 31

2. 35, 34, 31, 30, 27, 26 . . .
   - (A) 22
   - (B) 23
   - (C) 24
   - (D) 25

3. 16, 21, 19, 24, 22, 27 . . .
   - (A) 20
   - (B) 25
   - (C) 29
   - (D) 32

4. 48, 44, 40, 36, 32, 28 . . .
   - (A) 27
   - (B) 26
   - (C) 25
   - (D) 24

5. 20, 30, 39, 47, 54, 60 . . .
   - (A) 65
   - (B) 66
   - (C) 68
   - (D) 70

Arithmetical series such as those above might be interrupted by a particular number that appears periodically or by repetition of numbers according to a pattern. For example: 3, 6, 25, 9, 12, 25, 15, 18, 25 . . . and 50, 50, 35, 40, 40, 35, 30, 30, 35 . . . . In these cases, you must search a bit harder to spot both the arithmetic pattern and the pattern of repetition. When choosing your answer, you must be alert to the point at which the pattern was interrupted.

Test Yourself 4

Choose the number that should come next in the series. Do not repeat a number that has already been repeated, but do not forget to repeat before continuing the arithmetical pattern if repetition is called for at this point in the series.

1. 10, 13, 13, 16, 16, 19 . . .
   (A) 16
   (B) 19
   (C) 21
   (D) 22

2. 2, 4, 25, 8, 16, 25, 32 . . .
   (A) 25
   (B) 32
   (C) 48
   (D) 64

3. 80, 80, 75, 75, 70, 70 . . .
   (A) 60
   (B) 65
   (C) 70
   (D) 75

4. 35, 35, 32, 30, 30, 27 . . .
   (A) 25
   (B) 26
   (C) 27
   (D) 28

5. 76, 70, 12, 65, 61, 12 . . .
   (A) 12
   (B) 54
   (C) 55
   (D) 58

LETTER SERIES

In letter series, each question consists of letters that are arranged according to a definite pattern. You must discover what that pattern is and then use that knowledge to determine which of the four alternatives offered is the missing letter or group of letters in the series. Series might be simple alphabetical progressions or intricate combinations that alternate between forward and backward steps.

Because each question is based on the twenty-six letters of the alphabet, it is a good idea to keep a copy of the alphabet in front of you as you work. In addition, it is well worth your time to assign a number to each letter, jotting down the numbers from one to twenty-six directly under the letters to which they correspond. The seconds spent doing this might save you precious minutes as you work through the letter series.

There is more than one method of attack for letter series questions. You may solve these problems by inspection whenever possible. If that fails, try numerical analysis.

Inspection

The first line of attack should always be inspection, for this is the quickest and easiest approach. Look at the letters. Are they progressing in normal or reverse alphabetical order? Are the letters consecutive, or do they skip one or more letters between terms? Are certain letters repeated?

Test Yourself 5

Here are some simple series that you should be able to solve by inspection only.

1. c a d a e a f a g a
   - (A) a
   - (B) g
   - (C) h
   - (D) b

2. a b c c d e f f g h i
   - (A) f
   - (B) j
   - (C) k
   - (D) i

3. gij jlm mop
   - (A) prq
   - (B) prs
   - (C) rst
   - (D) qur

Numerical Analysis

If inspection does not make the answer apparent, switch to a numerical analysis of the series. Assign each letter in the series a numerical value according to its position in the alphabet. Write the direction and degree of difference between letters. Once you have done this, you will find yourself with a pattern of pluses and minuses similar to those you utilized in number series.

Test Yourself 6

Choose the letter or group of letters that will continue the pattern or sequence.

1. c d b e f d g h f i j
   - (A) h
   - (B) k
   - (C) f
   - (D) l

2. a b d g k p
   - (A) q
   - (B) u
   - (C) w
   - (D) v

3. mpt jmq gjn dgk
   - (A) cfj
   - (B) bei
   - (C) kos
   - (D) adh

MIXED SERIES

With mixed series, you must once again ask yourself, "What's happening?" In what direction and in what manner are the numbers progressing? What about the letters? Are changes occurring in the relationships of numbers to letters? According to what pattern?

Test Yourself 7

Choose the answer that will continue the pattern or sequence or that should fill in the blank in the series.

1. $RA_1T_2 \ RA_3T_4 \ RA_1T_2 \ RA_4T_5$ _____
   - **(A)** RA_5T_6
   - **(B)** RA_5T_4
   - **(C)** RA_1T_2
   - **(D)** R_1AT_2

2. $L^2M_2N^2 \ O_3P^3Q_3 \ R^2S_2T^2$ _____ $X^2Y_2Z^2$
   - **(A)** $U_4V^4W_4$
   - **(B)** $T_3U^3V_3$
   - **(C)** $U^3V_3W^3$
   - **(D)** $V^4W_3X^4$

SYMBOL SERIES

In symbol series, the figures might be unfamiliar and thus intimidating, but the task is the same. You must study the relationships of the individual members within a group and then determine what changes occur in that relationship as you move from one group to the next. While this activity is classified as nonverbal reasoning, you must verbalize to yourself exactly what is happening in the creation of the series.

Test Yourself 8

Choose the answer that will continue the pattern or sequence or that should fill in the blank in the series.

1.
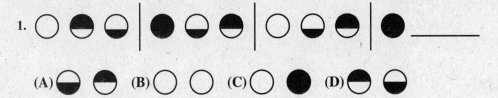

2.
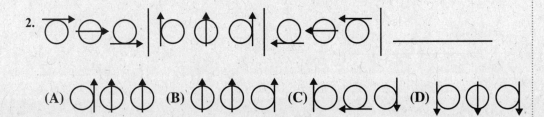

TIPS FOR ANSWERING SERIES QUESTIONS

- Tackle first the questions that seem easiest for you. Questions generally tend to be arranged in order of difficulty, with the easiest questions first, but problems that might seem easy to some people might be more difficult to others, and vice versa. Answer quickly the questions that require little of your time and leave yourself extra time for the more difficult questions.

- When you skip a question, put a mark before the question number in the test booklet and leave its answer space blank. When you return to a question that you have skipped, be sure to mark its answer in the correct space. The time you spend checking to make sure that question and answer number are alike is time well spent.

- Follow the procedures outlined in this chapter. First, look for an obvious pattern. Second, sound out the series; if necessary, group the numbers or letters and sound out again. Third, write the direction and amount of change between the numbers or letters.

- If you do any figuring in the test booklet, be sure to mark the letter of the correct answer on your answer sheet. All answers must be marked on the answer sheet.

- If none of the answers given fits the rule you have figured out, try again. Try to figure out a rule that makes one of the four answers a correct one.

- Do not spend too much time on any one question. If a question seems impossible, skip it and come back to it later. A fresh look will sometimes help you find the answer. If you still cannot figure out the answer, guess. Remember that there is no penalty for a wrong answer.

- Keep track of time. Because there is no penalty for a wrong answer, you will want to answer every question. Leave yourself time to go back to the questions you skipped to give them a second look. If you are not finished as the time limit approaches, mark random answers for the remaining questions.

TEST YOURSELF ANSWER KEYS AND EXPLANATIONS

Test Yourself 1

1. C	2. A	3. A	4. B	5. C

1. **The correct answer is (C).** The series is a simple +1 series with the number 10 inserted after each step of the series.

2. **The correct answer is (A).** The sequence 20, 40, 60 repeats itself over and over again.

3. **The correct answer is (A).** This is a simple +2 series with the number 9 appearing before each member of the series.

4. **The correct answer is (B).** In this series, the sequence 5, 8 repeats.

5. **The correct answer is (C).** You should be able to see that this is a descending series; each number is one less than the one before it. You can call this a −1 series.

Test Yourself 2

1. A	2. C	3. B	4. D	5. B

1. **The correct answer is (A).** If you group the numbers in pairs, you can whisper the bracketed "missing numbers" to determine the pattern: 1, 2, [3, 4,] 5, 6, [7, 8,] 9, 10, [11, 12,] 13

   The next number to read aloud is 14, to be followed by a whispered 15, 16, and then aloud again, 17.

2. **The correct answer is (C).** If you group the numbers into threes and read them aloud, accenting either the first or last number of each group, you should feel that each group of three begins and ends with a number one higher than the previous group.
   Read 2, 3, 4/ 3, 4, 5/ 4, 5, 6;
   or 2, 3, 4/ 3, 4, 5/ 4, 5, 6.

3. **The correct answer is (B).** Once more, group the numbers into threes. This time, be certain to accent the third number in each group in order to sense the rhythm, and thereby the pattern, of the series: 10, 10, 12/ 14, 14, 16/ 18 . . .

4. **The correct answer is (D).** In this series, the rhythm emerges when you accent the first number in each group: 1, 2, 3/ 2, 2, 3/ 3, 2, 3/ 4, 2, 3.

5. **The correct answer is (B).** After you have seen a number of series of this type, you might be able to spot the pattern by inspection alone. If not, read aloud, group, and read again.

PART III: Quantitative and Nonverbal Skills

Test Yourself 3

1. C	2. B	3. B	4. D	5. A

1. **The correct answer is (C).** $9^{+1}\ 10^{+2}\ 12^{+3}$ $15^{+4}\ 19^{+5}\ 24^{+6}\ 30$

2. **The correct answer is (B).** $35^{-1}\ 34^{-3}\ 31^{-1}$ $30^{-3}\ 27^{-1}\ 26^{-3}\ 23$

3. **The correct answer is (B).** $16^{+5}\ 21^{-2}\ 19^{+5}$ $24^{-2}\ 22^{+5}\ 27^{-2}\ 25$

4. **The correct answer is (D).** $48^{-4}\ 44^{-4}\ 40^{-4}$ $36^{-4}\ 32^{-4}\ 28^{-4}\ 24$

5. **The correct answer is (A).** $20^{+10}\ 30^{+9}\ 39^{+8}$ $47^{+7}\ 54^{+6}\ 60^{+5}\ 65$

Test Yourself 4

1. B	2. D	3. B	4. A	5. D

(r = repeat; ○ = extraneous number repeated periodically)

1. **The correct answer is (B).** $10^{+3}\ 13^{r}\ 13^{+3}\ 16^{r}$ $16^{+3}\ 19^{r}\ 19$

2. **The correct answer is (D).** $2^{\times2}\ 4^{\times2}\ ㉕\ 8^{\times2}$ $16^{\times2}\ ㉕\ 32^{\times2}\ 64$

3. **The correct answer is (B).** $80^{r}\ 80^{-5}\ 75^{r}\ 75^{-5}$ $70^{r}\ 70^{-5}\ 65$

4. **The correct answer is (A).** $35^{r}\ 35^{-3}\ 32^{-2}\ 30^{r}$ $30^{-3}\ 27^{-2}\ 25$

5. **The correct answer is (D).** $76^{-6}\ 70^{-5}\ ⑫$ $65^{-4}\ 61^{-3}\ ⑫\ 58$

Test Yourself 5

1. C	2. D	3. B

1. **The correct answer is (C).** The letters progress in consecutive alphabetical order, with the letter *a* inserted between each step. The next letter in this series must, therefore, be *h*.

2. **The correct answer is (D).** This is also a consecutive alphabetical progression, but here the third letter of each set is repeated. Thus, we have abcc deff ghii. Because only one *i* is given in the original series, the next letter must be the second *i* needed to complete the third set.

3. **The correct answer is (B).** This is a bit more difficult, but with the grouping already done for you, you should be able to solve it by inspection. The pattern is as follows: From the first letter, skip one, then let the next letter in sequence follow immediately. Start each new three-letter sequence with the last letter of the previous sequence. The missing sequence begins with the *p* of the previous sequence, skips one letter to *r*, then continues immediately with *s*.

Like us at facebook.com/petersonspublishing

Test Yourself 6

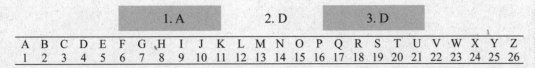

A	B	C	D	E	F	G	H	I	J	K	L	M	N	O	P	Q	R	S	T	U	V	W	X	Y	Z
1	2	3	4	5	6	7	8	9	10	11	12	13	14	15	16	17	18	19	20	21	22	23	24	25	26

1. The correct answer is (A).

c		d		b		e		f		d		g		h		f		i		j		h
3		4		2		5		6		4		7		8		6		9		10		8

$$+1 \quad -2 \quad +3 \quad +1 \quad -2 \quad +3 \quad +1 \quad -2 \quad +3 \quad +1 \quad -2$$

Now it is obvious that the series progresses by the formula +1 –2 +3. According to this pattern, the next letter must be 10 –2, or 8, which corresponds to the letter *h*.

2. The correct answer is (D).

a		b		d		g		k		p		v
1		2		4		7		11		16		22

$$+1 \quad +2 \quad +3 \quad +4 \quad +5 \quad +6$$

The progression is obvious.

3. The correct answer is (D).

m	p	t	j	m	q	g	j	n	d	g	k	a	d	h
13	16	20	10	13	17	7	10	14	4	7	11	1	4	8

$$+3 \quad +4 \quad -10 \quad +3 \quad +4 \quad -10 \quad +3 \quad +4 \quad -10 \quad +3 \quad +4 \quad -10 \quad +3 \quad +4$$

Within each group of three, the pattern is +3, +4. Between groups of three, subtract 10.

Test Yourself 7

1. C   2. A

1. The correct answer is (C). A good solid look at the groupings within the series shows that the unit RA_1T_2 intervenes between the other units of the series. With no further information on which to base any other features of the series, you must select choice (C).

2. The correct answer is (A). The first thing that becomes clear in this mixed series is that the letters form a simple alphabetical progression. You can immediately narrow your choices to (A) and (C). On the basis of the information given, there is no way to know whether the numbers in the missing unit should be 3s or 4s, but we do have information about their position with relation to the letters. The pattern of the groups in which the numbers are 2s is superscript, subscript, superscript. In the only given group in which the numbers are not 2s, the pattern is subscript, superscript, subscript. Because, in addition, there is evidence of possible alternation of patterns, the proper choice is (A), in which the pattern of the numbers is subscript, superscript, subscript.

Test Yourself 8

| 1. D | 2. D |

1. **The correct answer is (D).** If you look from the first group to the second, you will see that the second group is precisely the reverse of the first. Where the first is empty, upper half full, lower half full, the second is full, lower half full, upper half full. In the third group, the empty first circle of the first group is repeated, but the other two circles are reversed. Because the final group begins with a full circle (in both instances, the group with its first circle full follows a group with its first circle empty), the missing two circles should be the reverse of the second and third circles in the preceding group.

2. **The correct answer is (D).** In each group, all of the arrows go in the same direction, and in each group, the arrows go in a direction different from those in any other group. The arrows in the last group should point down. In all three groups, the middle arrow goes through the middle circle and the outer arrows go along the outer edges of the circles. This is clearest in the second group. Choice (D) fulfills all requirements best.

EXERCISES: SERIES REASONING

Exercise 1

Directions: Choose the number that should come next or that should fill the blank in the series. The answer keys and explanations appear after Exercise 3.

1. 75, 75, 72, 72, 69, 69,
   (A) 63
   (B) 66
   (C) 68
   (D) 69

2. 12, 16, 21, 27, 31,
   (A) 33
   (B) 35
   (C) 36
   (D) 37

3. 22, 24, 12, 26, 28, 12,
   (A) 12
   (B) 30
   (C) 34
   (D) 36

4. 13, 22, 32, 43, _____, 68
   (A) 53
   (B) 54
   (C) 55
   (D) 56

5. 4, 2, 1, $\frac{1}{2}$, $\frac{1}{4}$,
   (A) 0
   (B) $\frac{1}{8}$
   (C) $\frac{3}{8}$
   (D) $\frac{1}{16}$

6. 100, 81, _____, 49, 36
   (A) 60
   (B) 64
   (C) 65
   (D) 75

7. 32, 25, 86, 32, 25,
   (A) 5

   (B) 32
   (C) 68
   (D) 86

8. 51, 51, 30, 47, 47, 30, 43,
   (A) 30
   (B) 41
   (C) 43
   (D) 45

9. 3 3 9 | 15 15 21 | 27 27 _____
   (A) 1
   (B) 27
   (C) 30
   (D) 33

10. 95 90 86 | 83 78 74 | 51 _____ 42
    (A) 45
    (B) 46
    (C) 47
    (D) 50

11. 1 5 1 | 2 6 2 | 3 _____ 3
    (A) 0
    (B) 3
    (C) 4
    (D) 7

12. 50 52 48 | 35 37 33 | _____ 14 10
    (A) 9
    (B) 11
    (C) 12
    (D) 15

13. 39 40 80 | 10 11 22 | 17 18 _____
    (A) 9
    (B) 33
    (C) 36
    (D) 38

14. 36 12 4 | 63 21 7 | _____ 36 12
    (A) 72
    (B) 85
    (C) 97
    (D) 108

Exercise 2

Directions: Choose the letter or group of letters that should come next or that should fill the blank in the series.

1. n n o p p q r r s t
   (A) t
   (B) u
   (C) v
   (D) r

2. a j e b u q i y e p a
   (A) k
   (B) d
   (C) f
   (D) w

3. d e f d g h i g j k l j m n o
   (A) j
   (B) m
   (C) n
   (D) o

4. a c d a a c d b a c d c a c
   (A) a
   (B) b
   (C) c
   (D) d

5. a d h l b e i m c f j
   (A) l
   (B) m
   (C) n
   (D) o

6. z a z c z f z j z
   (A) g
   (B) o
   (C) z
   (D) s

7. hat | mat | rat | bat | _____
   (A) jat
   (B) qat
   (C) pat
   (D) uat

8. mnp | hik | bce | _____ | kln
   (A) uvx
   (B) gij
   (C) rqp
   (D) xyz

9. ZWT WTQ TQN _____ NKH
   (A) PNL
   (B) NLJ
   (C) MJG
   (D) QNK

10. ABC IRS GNO DHI
    (A) BDG
    (B) FKL
    (C) EJK
    (D) NYZ

Exercise 3

Directions: Choose the answer that will continue the pattern or sequence or that should fill the blank in the series.

1. $STPR_1$ STP_1R_2 $STPR_3$ _____ $STPR_5$
   - (A) $STPR_4$
   - (B) STP_4R_5
   - (C) $ST_1P_2R_3$
   - (D) STP_2R_3

2. $F^1G_2H^3I_4G_6H^7I_8J^9H_4I^5J_6K^7I^3J_4K^5L_6$ _____
   - (A) $J^7K_8L^9M_{10}$
   - (B) $M^5N_6O^7P_8$
   - (C) $J^8K_9L^{10}M_{11}$
   - (D) $K^1L_3M^5N_9$

3. $D_4F_6H_8E_5G_7I_9$ _____ $K_{11}M_{13}O_{15}P_{16}R_{18}T_{20}$
   - (A) $J_{10}K_{11}L_{12}$
   - (B) $J_{10}L_{12}N_{14}$
   - (C) $J_{10}L_{11}N_{12}$
   - (D) $J_{10}K_{12}L_{14}$

4. $R^2D^2R^2D_{12}R_2D_2R_2D^2D^2R^2$ _____
   - (A) D_2R_2
   - (B) R^2D_2
   - (C) D^2R_2
   - (D) D_2R^2

5.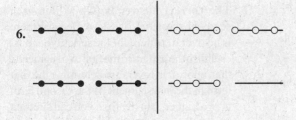

6.

7.

8.

ANSWER KEYS AND EXPLANATIONS

Exercise 1

1. B	4. C	7. D	10. B	13. C
2. C	5. B	8. C	11. D	14. D
3. B	6. B	9. D	12. C	

1. **The correct answer is (B).** The pattern is: repeat the number, –3; repeat the number, –3; repeat the number, –3.

2. **The correct answer is (C).** The pattern is +4, +5, +6; +4, +5, +6. The next number must be 31 + 5, which is 36.

3. **The correct answer is (B).** The basic pattern is a simple +2. The number 12 is inserted after each two terms of the series.

4. **The correct answer is (C).** The numbers are large, but the progression is simple. If you mark the differences between numbers, you will recognize: +9, +10, +11, supply the +12 term, then continue with +13.

5. **The correct answer is (B).** This is a simple ÷2 series.

6. **The correct answer is (B).** This series consists of the squares of the whole numbers in descending order.

7. **The correct answer is (D).** This series follows no mathematical rule. You must solve it by inspection. The sequence 32, 25, 86 simply repeats.

8. **The correct answer is (C).** The basic pattern is: repeat the number, –4; repeat the number, –4. The number 30 appears each time after the repeat and before the –4.

9. **The correct answer is (D).** The entire series pattern is repeat, +6, +6; repeat, +6, +6. To answer the question, it is enough to recognize that the pattern within each segment of the series is: repeat, +6.

10. **The correct answer is (B).** Within each segment of the series, the pattern is – 5, – 4. In the final segment, 51 – 5 = 46 – 4 = 42.

11. **The correct answer is (D).** You might see the pattern within each segment as +4, –4, or you might recognize by inspection or vocalization that each segment is simply a step up from the previous one.

12. **The correct answer is (C).** Within each segment, the pattern is +2, –4. Because there is no overall pattern for the series, you must establish the pattern in the first two segments, then apply it in reverse to determine the first term in the last segment. If the second term is two higher than the first, you can subtract 2 from the second term to determine the first.

13. **The correct answer is (C).** The pattern is +1, ×2.

14. **The correct answer is (D).** In the first two segments, you can establish that the pattern is ÷3. When you reach the third segment, multiply the second term by 3 to achieve the number that when divided by 3 equals 36.

Exercise 2

1. A	3. B	5. C	7. C	9. D
2. A	4. D	6. B	8. A	10. C

1. **The correct answer is (A).** This pattern alternates double and single letters in alphabetical order: nn o pp q rr s t. The next letter must be the second *t* needed to maintain the pattern.

2. **The correct answer is (A).** In this series, each set of two letters is a vowel followed by a consonant that contains the sound of the vowel with which it is paired: aj eb uq iy ep a. The only consonant offered that contains the sound of *a* is *k*.

3. **The correct answer is (B).** This series is an alphabetical progression of four-letter sequences where each fourth letter repeats the first letter of each sequence: defd ghig jklj mno. The missing letter is therefore the *m* needed to complete the fourth set.

4. **The correct answer is (D).** This pattern consists of the letters *acd* followed by consecutive letters of the alphabet. Thus: acda acdb acdc acd. The next letter must be *d*.

5. **The correct answer is (C).** The best way to visualize this pattern is to assign the letters of the alphabet numbers from 1 to 26. This series then becomes:

```
a  d  h  l   b  e  i  m   c  f  j  n
1  4  8  12  2  5  9  13  3  6  10 14
 +3 +4 +4 -10 +3 +4 +4 -10 +3 +4 +4
```

The last number must be 10 + 4, which is 14, corresponding to the letter *n*.

6. **The correct answer is (B).** Starting at the beginning of the alphabet, the space between letters increases by one with each new letter:

```
a     c     f     j      o
  +2    +3    +4    +5
```

The letter *z* is a constant between each term. The next step in this series must be five letters after *j*, which is *o*.

7. **The correct answer is (C).** In this series, each set of three letters makes a word composed of a consonant plus *at*: hat, mat, rat, bat. The next segment, therefore, must consist of a consonant plus *at* that may be combined to form an English word.

8. **The correct answer is (A).** The easiest way to solve this series is to verify the numerical relationship within segments. In each instance, the sequence is +1, +2. The only option that satisfies this sequence is u + 1 = v + 2 = x.

9. **The correct answer is (D).** Look at the alphabet written out before you. From *Z*, skip over two letters back to *W*, and from *W* skip two more to *T*. In the next group, the procedure is exactly the same, and in each of the following groups as well. In addition, note that each succeeding group begins with the middle letter of the group before it. Thus, the missing group begins with the *Q* in the middle of the preceding group, continues with the skip of two back to *N*, and concludes with the further skip back to *K*.

10. **The correct answer is (C).** It is very important to have written the entire alphabet and to have assigned each letter its numerical equivalent in order to choose the answer to this question.

```
ABC  I R S  G N O  D H I   E J K
1 2 3  9 18 19  7 14 15  4 8 9  5 10 11
×2 +1  ×2 +1  ×2 +1  ×2 +1  ×2 +1
```

Obviously, you must figure out the relationship on groups other than the first one, then confirm that the relationship of the first three letters is not simple alphabetical succession. It is also clear that no group of three bears any external relationship to any other group of three letters. Only the relationship within a group of three will determine the correct answer. Only choice (C) satisfies the ×2, +1 formula.

Exercise 3

1. D	3. B	5. B	7. C	8. B
2. A	4. C	6. D		

1. **The correct answer is (D).** In all groupings, the letters are the same. You might assume that the answer choice will contain those same letters. When there is only one subscript number, it is at the end. When there are two, they follow the last and the next-to-last letter. Your best guess, if you can find reasonable choices to fit, is that the number pattern appears to alternate: one number, two numbers, one number, two numbers. Choices (B) and (D) might fit into this pattern. Then look for the rationale for the numbers themselves. The numbers of the second group add to make the number of the third. Because the numbers of choice (D) add to make the number in the final group, this is the most logical choice.

2. **The correct answer is (A).** By inspection, you can find the pattern of the letters. Each succeeding group picks up with the second letter of the preceding group and proceeds in alphabetical order. This narrows your answer choices to (A) or (C). Now look at the numbers. Within each set of four, the numbers go in order, but there seems to be no rule by which numbers are assigned to succeeding groups. So you must look for a pattern of some sort. Note that even numbers always appear as subscripts and odd numbers are always superscripts. Now you know why choice (A) is the correct answer.

3. **The correct answer is (B).** Some series questions are easier than others. The numbers that follow the letters are the numbers assigned to the letters according to their position in the alphabet. Immediately, you may narrow to choices (A) and (B). Now look at the pattern of the letters. In each group, there is a skip-one pattern. Because choice (A) gives letters in sequence, the correct answer must be (B).

4. **The correct answer is (C).** In the first four groupings, the 2s position themselves in all possible combinations around the R and the D. The fifth group reverses the positions of R

and D and appears to begin anew the circuit of 2s around the letters. The final group, then, should continue the rotation of the 2s, following in the same manner as when the letters were in their original position. Thus, the second D R should have the 2s placed in the same manner as the second R D.

5. **The correct answer is (B).** As the pattern progresses, in each succeeding frame an additional circle is darkened. Thus, in the first, none; in the second, one; in the third, two; and in the fourth, three. Because three circles have already been darkened in the fourth frame, the frame must be completed with undarkened circles, horizontal as in all frames.

6. **The correct answer is (D).** Because frames one and three are identical, you must assume that the pattern is of alternating identities and that frames two and four must also be identical.

7. **The correct answer is (C).** In the first three frames, the farthest-right figure is always a U shape. In the first frame, the next-to-last figure is upended; in the second frame, an additional figure is upended, reading from right to left; in the third frame, three figures are upended. Logically, as the series progresses, the fourth frame should include the four left-hand figures upended, with only the farthest right maintaining its position as a U.

8. **The correct answer is (B).** The darkened figures seem to be following no particular pattern within themselves, but they do seem to be alternating frames with the undarkened figures. The positions of the undarkened arrows in the first and third frames are identical. There is no reason to expect their positions to change the next time they appear in the series. With the alternating dark, light pattern, the undarkened arrows are due to appear in the next frame, and choice (B) maintains their same position as in the two previous appearances.

SUMMING IT UP

- On the COOP, these questions are called Sequences.

- On the TACHS, these questions are in the Ability section.

- On the HSPT, these questions are in the Number Series section under Quantitative Skills.

- In series questions, you have to determine the relationship between a series of symbols, numbers, or letters, then choose the next item for the series.

- First read the series through. If that does not help, try accenting the printed numbers and speaking the missing intervening numbers even more softly. Try grouping the numbers within the series into twos or threes. After grouping, try accenting the last number, or the first.

- It is a good idea to keep a copy of the alphabet in front of you as you work. In addition, it is well worth your time to assign a number to each letter, jotting down the numbers from 1 to 26 directly under the letters to which they correspond.

- Study and practice the series reasoning question tactics in this chapter. Remember: Answer the easy ones first; if you skip a question, make a mark on your answer sheet so you don't mark your answer sheet incorrectly; follow the system—look, sound, and group; don't spend too much time on any one question; and keep track of time.

Comparisons

OVERVIEW

- **Geometric comparisons**
- **Nongeometric comparisons**
- **Summing it up**

The comparison questions in the Quantitative Skills section of the HSPT require a little bit of mathematical skill and a lot of patience and logical thinking. You can't rush through any of these questions! To get the maximum number of right answers, you have to study and count when you're answering geometric comparison questions. You begin by performing all of the operations of nongeometric comparison questions. Then you work through the answer choices one by one, eliminating each statement that proves to be false, based on the facts of the problem. When you find what you think is the correct choice, you still need to continue trying all of the other answers, as a check on your own reasoning. To give you a feel for these questions, let's work through a few together.

GEOMETRIC COMPARISONS

1. Examine (A), (B), and (C) and find the best answer.

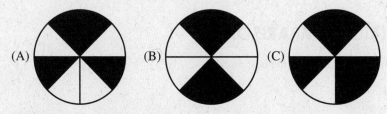

- **(A)** (A) is more shaded than (B).
- **(B)** (B) is more shaded than (A) and less shaded than (C).
- **(C)** (A) and (B) are equally shaded and less shaded than (C).
- **(D)** (A), (B), and (C) are equally shaded.

Begin by studying the three circles. Note that each circle is divided into eight segments. Now count the number of shaded segments in each circle, and write that number next to the letter of the circle. If you have counted accurately, you have written: (A) 4, (B) 4, (C) 5. Read the statements one by one, and mark true or false next to the letter of each statement. The statement in choice (A) is false because both (A) and (B) have four shaded segments. The statement in choice

(B) must be marked false because it is not entirely true. (B) is indeed less shaded than (C), but it is not more shaded than (A). To be true, a statement must be 100 percent true. The statement in choice (C) is true. (A) and (B) are equally shaded (4) and both are less shaded than (C) with its five shaded segments. Check out choice (D) just to be certain that you have not made an error. No problem here. The statement in choice (D) is clearly false.

2. The pie is divided into sixteen equal portions. Study the pie and find the best answer.

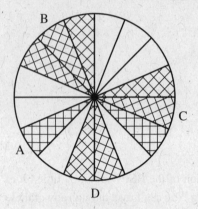

   (A) A plus D equals B plus C.

   (B) D minus A equals B minus C.

   (C) C minus D equals A.

   (D) B equals A plus C.

Begin by counting the pie wedges in each portion; write the number of wedges next to the letter—A (1), B (3), C (3), D (2). Now perform the very simple arithmetic for each statement.

   (A) 1 + 2 = 3 + 3; 3 = 6—false

   (B) 2 – 1 = 3 – 3; 1 = 0—false

   (C) 3 – 2 = 1—true

   (D) 3 = 1 + 3; 3 = 4—false

NONGEOMETRIC COMPARISONS

1. Examine (A), (B), and (C) and find the best answer.
   (A) (5 × 4) – 10
   (B) (3 × 6) + 4
   (C) (8 × 3) – 6

   (A) (B) is equal to (C) and greater than (A).

   (B) (C) is greater than (A) but less than (B).

   (C) (A) is greater than (C).

   (D) (A) is less than (C) but more than (B).

Obviously, you must begin by performing the indicated operations.

(A) $20 - 10 = 10$

(B) $18 + 4 = 22$

(C) $24 - 6 = 18$

Now you can substitute these numbers for the letters in the four statements and choose the correct one.

(A) 22 is equal to 18 and greater than 10—false

(B) 18 is greater than 10 but less than 22—true

(C) 10 is greater than 18—false

(D) 10 is less than 18 but more than 22—false

2. Examine (A), (B), and (C) and find the best answer.

(A) 4^3

(B) 3^4

(C) $(3 \times 4)(4)$

(A) $A > B > C$

(B) $A = B > C$

(C) $B > A > C$

(D) $A = C < B$

First, perform the operations.

(A) $4^3 = 64$

(B) $3^4 = 81$

(C) $(3 \times 4)(4) = 12 \times 4 = 48$

Substitute the numbers in the statements.

(A) 64 is greater than 81, which is greater than 48—false

(B) 64 equals 81, which is greater than 48—false

(C) 48 is smaller than 81, which is greater than 64—true

(D) 64 is equal to 48, which is smaller than 81—false

EXERCISES: COMPARISONS

Directions: Examine (A), (B), and (C) and find the best answer. The answer key and explanations follow this exercise.

1.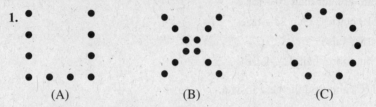
   (A)   (B)   (C)

   (A) (B) and (C) have the same number of dots.

   (B) (A) has fewer dots than (B) but more dots than (C).

   (C) (C) has more dots than (A).

   (D) (B) has more dots than (A) and (C), which have the same number of dots.

2. The distance from X to Y is one inch.

   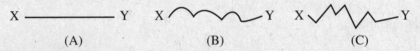
   (A)   (B)   (C)

   (A) Lines (A), (B), and (C) are of equal length.

   (B) Line (A) is longer than lines (B) and (C), which are of equal length.

   (C) Line (B) is shorter than line (A) but longer than line (C).

   (D) Line (A) is shorter than line (C).

3.
   (A)   (B)   (C)

   (A) (C) has more rings than (A).

   (B) (A) has the same number of rings as (B).

   (C) (B) and (C) have the same number of rings, which are more rings than (A).

   (D) (B) has fewer rings than either (A) or (C).

4.

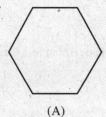  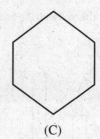

   (A)   (B)   (C)

(A) (C) has more corners than (A).

(B) (B) has the same number of corners as (C) and more corners than (A).

(C) (A) has fewer corners than (B).

(D) (A), (B), and (C) all have the same number of corners.

5.

   (A)   (B)   (C)

(A) (C) is more shaded than (B), which is more shaded than (A).

(B) (C) is more shaded than (A), which is not less shaded than (B).

(C) (B) and (C) are equally shaded.

(D) (A) and (B) are equally shaded.

6. Examine the rectangle and find the best answer.

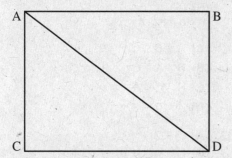

(A) AB is equal to CD, which is longer than AD.

(B) BD is shorter than AC.

(C) CD is longer than AD.

(D) AC is equal to BD.

7. Examine the graph and find the best answer.

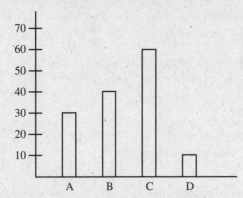

(A) C plus D minus A equals B.

(B) B plus D equals C.

(C) A plus B equals C.

(D) C minus D equals A plus B.

Directions: Examine (A), (B), and (C) and find the best answer.

8. (A) 30% of 30

(B) 25% of 40

(C) 20% of 50

(A) (A), (B), and (C) are equal.

(B) (A) and (C) are equal and are greater than (B).

(C) (A) and (B) are equal and are less than (C).

(D) (B) and (C) are equal and are greater than (A).

9. (A) $(4 + 8) \times 10$

(B) $(8 + 10) \times 4$

(C) $(4 + 10) \times 8$

(A) (A) is greater than (B), which is smaller than (C).

(B) (A) and (C) are equal and are greater than (B).

(C) (C) is greater than (A), which is less than (B).

(D) (A), (B), and (C) are equal.

10. (A) $(12 - 4) - 6$

(B) $(12 - 6) - 4$

(C) $12 - (6 - 4)$

(A) (A) is greater than (B) but less than (C).

(B) (C) is equal to (A) and greater than (B).

(C) (A), (B), and (C) are equal.

(D) (A) and (B) are equal but are less than (C).

11. (A) $\frac{2}{3}$ of 27

(B) $\frac{2}{5}$ of 10

(C) $\frac{3}{7}$ of 28

(A) (A) is greater than (C) but less than (B).

(B) (C) is smaller than (A) and (B).

(C) (B) is smaller than (C), which is greater than (A).

(D) (A) is greater than (C), which is greater than (B).

12. (A) 8%

(B) 0.8

(C) 0.08%

(A) $A = B < C$

(B) $B > A > C$

(C) $B - C < A$

(D) $A < C < B$

13. (A) $(8 \div 2) \times 12$

(B) $(15 \div 3) \times 10$

(C) $(22 \div 1) \times 4$

(A) (A) is greater than (B), which is less than (C).

(B) (C) is greater than (A), which is greater than (B).

(C) (A) is equal to (B), which is less than (C).

(D) (C) is greater than (A), which is less than (B).

14. (A) $\sqrt{144}$
    (B) 3.5^2
    (C) $\dfrac{27}{2}$

    (A) $A = B = C$
    (B) $A = B < C$
    (C) $B = C > A$
    (D) $A < B < C$

15. (A) $7(x + 2y)$
    (B) $7x + 2y$
    (C) $7(x + 2y) + 2x$
    x and y are positive integers.

    (A) (C) is greater than (B), which is smaller than (A).

    (B) (B) is smaller than (C), which is smaller than (A).

    (C) (A) is equal to (B), which is smaller than (C).

    (D) (C) is greater than (A), which is smaller than (B).

exercises

ANSWER KEY AND EXPLANATIONS

1. C	4. C	7. A	10. D	13. D
2. D	5. A	8. D	11. D	14. D
3. B	6. D	9. A	12. B	15. A

1. **The correct answer is (C).** (A) has 10 dots; (B) has 12 dots; (C) has 11 dots. 11 is greater than 10, so (C) has more dots than (A). Test the other statements, and you will find them all false.

2. **The correct answer is (D).** A straight line is the shortest distance between two points, so line (A) is the shortest line. The statement that declares that line (A) is shorter than either of the other two is the correct one.

3. **The correct answer is (B).** Each of the three figures has five rings, so any statement that speaks of more or fewer rings must be incorrect.

4. **The correct answer is (C).** (A) and (C) are hexagons with six sides and six corners; (B) is an octagon with eight sides and eight corners. Try this information out on the statements to find the true one.

5. **The correct answer is (A).** (C) is exactly half shaded; (B) is somewhat less than half shaded; (A) is very sparsely shaded. That is exactly the statement made in choice (A).

6. **The correct answer is (D).** In a rectangle, parallel sides are equal in length. Therefore, AB is equal to CD, and AC is equal to BD. AD is a hypotenuse. The hypotenuse is always the longest leg of a right triangle. AD cannot be shorter than any other line segment.

7. **The correct answer is (A).** Do the arithmetic. $60 + 10 - 30 = 40$. In other words, 40 equals 40, which is true. The other choices are all false. 40 plus 10 does not equal 60; 30 plus 40 does not equal 60; 60 minus 10 does not equal 30 plus 40.

8. **The correct answer is (D).** Do the arithmetic. 30% of 30 = 9; 25% of 40 = 10; 20% of 50 = 10. Therefore, (B) and (C) are equal and are both greater than (A).

9. **The correct answer is (A).** Do the arithmetic. $12 \times 10 = 120$; $18 \times 4 = 72$; $14 \times 8 = 112$. 120 is greater than 72, which is smaller than 112.

10. **The correct answer is (D).** Do the arithmetic. $8 - 6 = 2$; $6 - 4 = 2$; $12 - 2 = 10$. (A) and (B), both equaling 2, are equal but are far less than the 10 of (C).

11. **The correct answer is (D).** Do the arithmetic. $\frac{2}{3}$ of 27 = 18; $\frac{2}{5}$ of 10 = 4; $\frac{3}{7}$ of 28 = 12. 18 is greater than 12, which is greater than 4.

12. **The correct answer is (B).** Convert the percents to decimals so that the three numbers will be comparable. 8% = 0.08; 0.8 = 0.8; 0.08% = 0.0008. 0.8 is greater than 0.08, which is greater than 0.0008.

13. **The correct answer is (D).** Do the arithmetic. $4 \times 12 = 48$; $5 \times 10 = 50$; $22 \times 4 = 88$. 88 is greater than 48, which is less than 50.

14. **The correct answer is (D).** Do the arithmetic. $\sqrt{144} = 12$; $3.5^2 = 12.25$; $27 \div 2 = 13.5$. 12 is smaller than 12.25, which is smaller than 13.5.

15. **The correct answer is (A).** You could substitute numerical values for x and y and arrive at the correct answer, but it is unnecessary to work with numbers. Simply perform the algebraic multiplications to make your comparisons. $7(x + 2y) = 7x + 14y$; $7x + 2y = 7x + 2y$; $7(x + 2y) + 2x = 7x + 14y + 2x = 9x + 14y$. $9x + 14y$ is greater than $7x + 2y$, which is smaller than $7x + 14y$.

SUMMING IT UP

- First, perform all of the operations for nongeometric comparison questions.

- Next, work through all of the answer choices one by one and eliminate each statement that is false.

- Then, when you think you have found the correct answer, continue until you have tried each answer choice.

PART IV

EIGHT PRACTICE TESTS

Practice Test 1: TACHS

Practice Test 2: TACHS

Practice Test 3: COOP

Practice Test 4: COOP

Practice Test 5: HSPT

Practice Test 6: HSPT

Practice Test 7: SSAT (Upper Level)

Practice Test 8: ISEE (Upper Level)

ANSWER SHEET PRACTICE TEST 1: TACHS

Reading

PART 1

1. Ⓐ Ⓑ Ⓒ Ⓓ   3. Ⓐ Ⓑ Ⓒ Ⓓ   5. Ⓐ Ⓑ Ⓒ Ⓓ   7. Ⓐ Ⓑ Ⓒ Ⓓ   9. Ⓐ Ⓑ Ⓒ Ⓓ
2. Ⓙ Ⓚ Ⓛ Ⓜ   4. Ⓙ Ⓚ Ⓛ Ⓜ   6. Ⓙ Ⓚ Ⓛ Ⓜ   8. Ⓙ Ⓚ Ⓛ Ⓜ   10. Ⓙ Ⓚ Ⓛ Ⓜ

PART 2

11. Ⓐ Ⓑ Ⓒ Ⓓ   13. Ⓐ Ⓑ Ⓒ Ⓓ   15. Ⓐ Ⓑ Ⓒ Ⓓ   17. Ⓐ Ⓑ Ⓒ Ⓓ   19. Ⓐ Ⓑ Ⓒ Ⓓ
12. Ⓙ Ⓚ Ⓛ Ⓜ   14. Ⓙ Ⓚ Ⓛ Ⓜ   16. Ⓙ Ⓚ Ⓛ Ⓜ   18. Ⓙ Ⓚ Ⓛ Ⓜ   20. Ⓙ Ⓚ Ⓛ Ⓜ

Language

PART 1

1. Ⓐ Ⓑ Ⓒ Ⓓ Ⓔ   6. Ⓙ Ⓚ Ⓛ Ⓜ Ⓝ   11. Ⓐ Ⓑ Ⓒ Ⓓ   16. Ⓙ Ⓚ Ⓛ Ⓜ
2. Ⓙ Ⓚ Ⓛ Ⓜ Ⓝ   7. Ⓐ Ⓑ Ⓒ Ⓓ Ⓔ   12. Ⓙ Ⓚ Ⓛ Ⓜ   17. Ⓐ Ⓑ Ⓒ Ⓓ
3. Ⓐ Ⓑ Ⓒ Ⓓ Ⓔ   8. Ⓙ Ⓚ Ⓛ Ⓜ Ⓝ   13. Ⓐ Ⓑ Ⓒ Ⓓ   18. Ⓙ Ⓚ Ⓛ Ⓜ
4. Ⓙ Ⓚ Ⓛ Ⓜ Ⓝ   9. Ⓐ Ⓑ Ⓒ Ⓓ Ⓔ   14. Ⓙ Ⓚ Ⓛ Ⓜ   19. Ⓐ Ⓑ Ⓒ Ⓓ
5. Ⓐ Ⓑ Ⓒ Ⓓ Ⓔ   10. Ⓙ Ⓚ Ⓛ Ⓜ Ⓝ   15. Ⓐ Ⓑ Ⓒ Ⓓ   20. Ⓙ Ⓚ Ⓛ Ⓜ

PART 2

21. Ⓐ Ⓑ Ⓒ Ⓓ   23. Ⓐ Ⓑ Ⓒ Ⓓ   25. Ⓐ Ⓑ Ⓒ Ⓓ   27. Ⓐ Ⓑ Ⓒ Ⓓ   29. Ⓐ Ⓑ Ⓒ Ⓓ
22. Ⓙ Ⓚ Ⓛ Ⓜ   24. Ⓙ Ⓚ Ⓛ Ⓜ   26. Ⓙ Ⓚ Ⓛ Ⓜ   28. Ⓙ Ⓚ Ⓛ Ⓜ   30. Ⓙ Ⓚ Ⓛ Ⓜ

Math

PART 1

1. Ⓐ Ⓑ Ⓒ Ⓓ   7. Ⓐ Ⓑ Ⓒ Ⓓ   13. Ⓐ Ⓑ Ⓒ Ⓓ   19. Ⓐ Ⓑ Ⓒ Ⓓ   25. Ⓐ Ⓑ Ⓒ Ⓓ
2. Ⓙ Ⓚ Ⓛ Ⓜ   8. Ⓙ Ⓚ Ⓛ Ⓜ   14. Ⓙ Ⓚ Ⓛ Ⓜ   20. Ⓙ Ⓚ Ⓛ Ⓜ   26. Ⓙ Ⓚ Ⓛ Ⓜ
3. Ⓐ Ⓑ Ⓒ Ⓓ   9. Ⓐ Ⓑ Ⓒ Ⓓ   15. Ⓐ Ⓑ Ⓒ Ⓓ   21. Ⓐ Ⓑ Ⓒ Ⓓ   27. Ⓐ Ⓑ Ⓒ Ⓓ
4. Ⓙ Ⓚ Ⓛ Ⓜ   10. Ⓙ Ⓚ Ⓛ Ⓜ   16. Ⓙ Ⓚ Ⓛ Ⓜ   22. Ⓙ Ⓚ Ⓛ Ⓜ   28. Ⓙ Ⓚ Ⓛ Ⓜ
5. Ⓐ Ⓑ Ⓒ Ⓓ   11. Ⓐ Ⓑ Ⓒ Ⓓ   17. Ⓐ Ⓑ Ⓒ Ⓓ   23. Ⓐ Ⓑ Ⓒ Ⓓ   29. Ⓐ Ⓑ Ⓒ Ⓓ
6. Ⓙ Ⓚ Ⓛ Ⓜ   12. Ⓙ Ⓚ Ⓛ Ⓜ   18. Ⓙ Ⓚ Ⓛ Ⓜ   24. Ⓙ Ⓚ Ⓛ Ⓜ   30. Ⓙ Ⓚ Ⓛ Ⓜ

PART 2

31. Ⓐ Ⓑ Ⓒ Ⓓ   33. Ⓐ Ⓑ Ⓒ Ⓓ   35. Ⓐ Ⓑ Ⓒ Ⓓ   37. Ⓐ Ⓑ Ⓒ Ⓓ   39. Ⓐ Ⓑ Ⓒ Ⓓ
32. Ⓙ Ⓚ Ⓛ Ⓜ   34. Ⓙ Ⓚ Ⓛ Ⓜ   36. Ⓙ Ⓚ Ⓛ Ⓜ   38. Ⓙ Ⓚ Ⓛ Ⓜ   40. Ⓙ Ⓚ Ⓛ Ⓜ

Ability

1. Ⓐ Ⓑ Ⓒ Ⓓ Ⓔ   4. Ⓙ Ⓚ Ⓛ Ⓜ Ⓝ   7. Ⓐ Ⓑ Ⓒ Ⓓ Ⓔ   9. Ⓐ Ⓑ Ⓒ Ⓓ Ⓔ
2. Ⓙ Ⓚ Ⓛ Ⓜ Ⓝ   5. Ⓐ Ⓑ Ⓒ Ⓓ Ⓔ   8. Ⓙ Ⓚ Ⓛ Ⓜ Ⓝ   10. Ⓙ Ⓚ Ⓛ Ⓜ Ⓝ
3. Ⓐ Ⓑ Ⓒ Ⓓ Ⓔ   6. Ⓙ Ⓚ Ⓛ Ⓜ Ⓝ

answer sheet

Practice Test 1: TACHS

READING

Part 1

5 MINUTES

Directions: For each question, decide which one of the four possible answers has most nearly the same meaning as the underlined word above it. Then, on your answer sheet, find the row of answer spaces numbered the same as the question. Fill in the answer space that has the same letter as the answer you chose.

1. Lofty goals
   - (A) elevated
   - (B) unworthy
   - (C) apparent
   - (D) confusing

2. Pleasing demeanor
   - (J) smell
   - (K) sight
   - (L) mood
   - (M) understanding

3. Mangled wreckage
   - (A) intact
   - (B) disfigured and torn
   - (C) lost
   - (D) faded

4. Move hastily
   - (J) slowly
   - (K) deliberately
   - (L) steadily
   - (M) quickly

5. To achieve recognition
   - (A) attain
   - (B) deserve
   - (C) seek
   - (D) squander

6. Placid waters
   - (J) stormy
   - (K) churning
   - (L) muddied
   - (M) peaceful

7. Many diverse cultures
   - (A) identical
   - (B) unknown
   - (C) varied
   - (D) ancient

8. Much rejoicing
   - (J) celebrating
   - (K) mourning
   - (L) relaxing
   - (M) studying

9. A large <u>segment</u>
   - **(A)** hole
   - **(B)** section
   - **(C)** discussion
   - **(D)** mystery

10. <u>Fascinating</u> new development
   - **(J)** boring
   - **(K)** important
   - **(L)** confusing
   - **(M)** interesting

STOP If you finish before time is up, check over your work on this part only. Do not go on until the signal is given.

Part 2

15 MINUTES

Directions: Read the passages below and then answer the questions. Four possible answers are given for each question. You are to choose the answer that you think is better than the others. Then, on your answer sheet, find the row of answer spaces numbered the same as the question. Fill in the best answer in the ovals on your answer sheet.

PASSAGE 1

When Abe was just four years old, he discovered books for the first time. Although he could not read at the age of four, he could follow the story of particular books by studying the pictures. The books he discovered once belonged to his grandparents. His parents, however, did not see the value in books because they were simple farmers. Abe's parents did not understand why anyone would need to be able to read if they were going to be farmers for a living.

Abe didn't want to upset his parents but he also didn't want to give up his books. After he finished his daily chores, Abe sneaked away to a neighbor's house where the teenaged neighbor girl taught him the alphabet and simple words. Before long, Abe was reading like a schoolboy. At night, before he went to sleep, Abe lay in his bed and read a book by the light of his lantern. He always read quietly, and he always kept the lantern light soft and low.

When Abe became old enough to leave the farm, he went away to college. His parents didn't understand but they let him go anyway. Abe finished college with honors and went on to become a successful doctor. In the end, Abe's parents were proud of Abe's accomplishments.

11. Why did Abe's parents believe that reading was unimportant?

    (A) They thought books were bad.

    (B) They thought reading was too hard.

    (C) They didn't think that reading was necessary for people who worked all day in the fields.

    (D) They had never seen books.

12. Why did Abe only read at night just before he slept?

    (J) He didn't want his parents to see him reading.

    (K) He wanted to dream about what he read.

    (L) He could only read with a lantern.

    (M) He was too busy working all day in the fields.

PASSAGE 2

Barrett had always dreamed of opening a photography studio. As soon as he finished photography school, he rented a small space in a strip mall just off the highway. For the first few years, he barely made ends meet. He took just enough photos to pay for rent and materials.

Barrett knew his business was not going to be successful if he continued to do business the way he had since he opened his studio. He researched a number of business strategies before he made his decision. Barrett advertised a month-long special in the newspaper. He decided to reduce his standard pricing by one third for the entire month. He knew this was a calculated risk, but it was one he felt he had to take.

13. The phrase "made ends meet" is another way of saying which of the following?
    - (A) Opened the doors
    - (B) Took nice pictures
    - (C) Took care of customers
    - (D) Balanced the budget

14. If Barrett was struggling financially, why did he reduce his prices?
    - (J) He hoped to increase the number of customers.
    - (K) He was giving up.
    - (L) He was paying too many taxes.
    - (M) His research was faulty.

PASSAGE 3

In ancient Egypt, there once was a pharaoh who turned the entire kingdom upside down. The ancient Egyptians believed that many deities existed and these deities controlled all of nature and human activity. For example, there were deities who controlled the flood stages of the Nile, the stars in the sky, and the weather. Others had responsibilities in the afterlife. Egyptians never questioned this system until Amenhotep IV took the throne.

Amenhotep IV, who changed his name to Akhenaton, did away with the system of worshipping many deities and replaced it with the worship of a single deity, Aton, who was the sun god. Historians debate Akhenaton's motives. Some argue that he was mentally disturbed and obsessed with the sun. Others argue that he made a brilliant political move by taking power away from the kingdom's many priests who were loyal to various deities. Regardless of his motives, Akhenaton's bold decision temporarily altered life for everyone in Egypt.

15. Which of the following, based on the information in the paragraphs, is most likely true?
    - (A) Egyptians never worshipped the sun until Akhenaton changed the religion.
    - (B) There may have been a power struggle between kings and priests before Akhenaton ruled.
    - (C) Akhenaton hoped to make Egypt's climate warmer by worshipping the sun.
    - (D) Akhenaton hoped to confuse historians.

16. Using context clues, the word "pharaoh" is most closely defined as which of the following?
    - (J) Governor
    - (K) King
    - (L) Mayor
    - (M) Priest

PASSAGE 4

In recent years, experts have not been able to make any substantial conclusions regarding the effect of e-mail and instant messaging on the social skills of computer users. Some experts in fields such as communications argue that e-mail and instant messaging have increased the social skills of computer users because people now communicate with each other more frequently than ever before. Others, however, maintain that computer users are able to hide behind their anonymity, thus allowing them to take on false personality traits and characteristics. Such experts further contend that the more communication takes place via e-mail and instant messaging, the less effective communication becomes in face-to-face settings. Experts on both sides of the debate do, however, agree that the frequency of communications has increased since the advent of electronic correspondence and that this alone should have some positive effect on the communication skills of computer users. After all, the adage says that practice makes perfect.

17. Which of the following would be the best title for the passage above?

(A) "The Problems with E-mail and Instant Messaging"

(B) "The Electronic Communications Revolution"

(C) "The Possible Effects of Electronic Communication on Communication Skills of Computer Users"

(D) "The Debate over Instant Communications and Its Effects on E-mail"

18. The phrase "practice makes perfect" in the last sentence refers to which of the following?

(J) The increased frequency of electronic communication

(K) Public speaking engagements

(L) Practice with computer software

(M) Research conducted by experts in the field

PASSAGE 5

The reality TV craze that began in the United States several years ago apparently is here to stay, at least for several more years. Strangely, though, people who watch reality TV still have not caught on to the fact that there is little or no reality at all in reality television shows. Producers and directors often coerce reality show stars to say particular things or act in a particular manner. Filming stops frequently to re-shoot certain scenes or pieces of dialogue between cast members. Those who are chosen to be part of the reality show casts must sign contracts that require them to follow scores of rules. Furthermore, cast members are forbidden from revealing any secrets of the show. The public, though, is still being bombarded by staged, contrived shows that are being advertised as reality.

19. Which of the following is the main idea of the passage above?

   (A) Reality shows are the most popular shows on TV.

   (B) Reality shows lure watchers through fancy advertising slogans and cute stars.

   (C) Reality TV actually consists of very little reality.

   (D) Reality show cast members usually become big stars and famous celebrities.

20. The author of the passage above is most likely which of the following?

   (J) A reality show winner

   (K) A reality show producer

   (L) A critic of reality TV

   (M) An executive from a TV network

STOP If you finish before time is up, check over your work on this part only. Do not go on until the signal is given.

LANGUAGE

Part 1

25 MINUTES FOR PARTS 1 AND 2

Directions: This is a test of how well you can find mistakes in writing. For the questions with mistakes in spelling, capitalization, and punctuation, choose the answer with the same letter as the **line** containing the mistake. For the questions with mistakes in usage and expression, choose the answer with the same letter as the **line** containing the mistake, or choose the word, phrase, or sentence that is better than the others. When there is no mistake or no change needed, choose the last answer choice.

1. (A) dictionery
   (B) tragic
   (C) vintage
   (D) surprise
   (E) *(No mistakes)*

2. (J) vacation
   (K) discovery
   (L) collide
   (M) patience
   (N) *(No mistakes)*

3. (A) fortress
   (B) obtane
   (C) complete
   (D) interview
   (E) *(No mistakes)*

4. (J) invention
   (K) coffee
   (L) perswade
   (M) employer
   (N) *(No mistakes)*

5. (A) disscuss
   (B) manager
   (C) exam
   (D) advisory
   (E) *(No mistakes)*

6. (J) fortune
   (K) traffic
   (L) intrude
   (M) messinger
   (N) *(No mistakes)*

7. (A) peasant
   (B) ancient
   (C) marriage
   (D) problematic
   (E) *(No mistakes)*

8. (J) cancellashun
   (K) invest
   (L) remark
   (M) mall
   (N) *(No mistakes)*

9. (A) wander
   (B) mygrate
   (C) functional
   (D) disappear
   (E) *(No mistakes)*

10. (J) mountain
    (K) progress
    (L) batter
    (M) profit
    (N) *(No mistakes)*

11. **(A)** Jamey is going to College
    (B) at Outback University, which
    (C) is located in Australia.
    (D) *(No mistakes)*

12. **(J)** The Mississippi river travels south-ward
    (K) toward the Gulf of Mexico
    (L) and passes many states along the way.
    (M) *(No mistakes)*

13. **(A)** My family lives so far out in the country
    (B) that aunt Janice has to walk three miles
    (C) just to visit Mr. McDonald, her closest neighbor.
    (D) *(No mistakes)*

14. **(J)** We're planning a nice dinner at the steak restaurant
    (K) to celebrate valentine's day; we're planning to see
    (L) the movie *Shrek* after dinner.
    (M) *(No mistakes)*

15. **(A)** You just can't beat a cold drink
    (B) or a few scoops of Ben and Jerry's
    (C) on a scorching-hot Summer day.
    (D) *(No mistakes)*

16. **(J)** Mrs. Samson said that Archie,
    (K) her sister's third cousin, used to
    (L) live across the street from Usher.
    (M) *(No mistakes)*

17. **(A)** The astronauts aboard the Apollo rocket
    (B) said that the moon looked much different in Space
    (C) than it did from the earth.
    (D) *(No mistakes)*

18. **(J)** He's so smart because he reads *Newsweek*
    (K) and the Newspaper in the morning
    (L) before he even gets to school.
    (M) *(No mistakes)*

19. **(A)** She accompanied her mother
    (B) on a visit to father O'Reilly to
    (C) thank him for visiting her brother in the hospital.
    (D) *(No mistakes)*

20. **(J)** The Dirt Road that wound through the woods
    (K) was just a few miles from Interstate 95,
    (L) which led to many major eastern cities.
    (M) *(No mistakes)*

Part 2

Directions: For questions 21–30, choose the best answer based on the following paragraphs.

(1) Archie Zambroski was one of America's premier inventors. (2) <u>Additionally</u>, few Americans have ever heard of Archie. (3) Archie's earliest invention was the piece of metal that attaches the eraser to the pencil. (4) Archie then developed the plastic tip that keeps the ends of shoelaces bound up tight. (5) Archie went on to invent other gizmos and gadgets found in most households in <u>America: including</u> the under-the-cabinet paper towel roll holder and the lint catcher for dryers. (6) Unfortunately, Zambroski never made the fortune of which he dreamed.

21. What is the best way to write the underlined part of sentence 2?

    (A) However,

    (B) In spite of,

    (C) Once,

    (D) *(No change)*

22. What is the best way to write the underlined part of sentence 5?

    (J) America; including

    (K) America: For example

    (L) America including

    (M) *(No change)*

---

(1) Researchers have done numerous studies in recent years to determine the effects of video games on the motor skills of preschoolers. (2) In other <u>words. Scientists</u> want to see if video games have an effect on preschoolers' coordination. (3) Researchers once thought that video games slowed the development of physical abilities of preschoolers. (4) Now, <u>however</u>, researchers tend to agree that preschoolers can develop hand-eye coordination by playing video games. (5) Researchers add that video games can be played on computers or on televisions.

23. What is the best way to write the underlined part of sentence 2?

    (A) words: scientists

    (B) words, scientists

    (C) words—Scientists

    (D) *(No change)*

24. What is the best way to write the underlined part of sentence 4?

    (J) miraculously

    (K) simultaneously

    (L) but

    (M) *(No change)*

(1) The Office of the Director of Transportation, the administration that oversees the subway and bus systems, logged in more than 24,000 items in the city's Lost and Found warehouse last year. (2) The records indicate that of the items logged in, only about 5,000 were claimed by the owners. (3) This means that approximately 19,000 became property of the city at the end of the year. (4) The office is required by law to catalog the unclaimed items and then donate them to Charitable Organizations. (5) According to the catalog of items, the most frequently unclaimed items are shoes mittens lunchboxes and purses.

25. What is the best way to write the underlined part of sentence 4?

    (A) to: charitable organizations

    (B) to, Charitable Organizations

    (C) to charitable organizations

    (D) *(No change)*

26. What is the best way to write the underlined part of sentence 5?

    (J) are shoes, mittens, lunchboxes, and purses

    (K) are shoes; mittens; lunchboxes; purses

    (L) are: shoes and mittens and lunchboxes and purses

    (M) *(No change)*

---

(1) Photographers and poets are more alike than most people might believe. (2) For example, when an average person looks at a mailbox or a dead tree, he or she sees just a mailbox or a dead tree. (3) Likewise, a photographer can look at the same items and envision beautiful and interesting photographs. (4) By the same token, a poet can find in those items inspiration for beautiful lines of poetry. (5) The World might be a more delightful place if everyone viewed the world around them through the eyes of a photographer or a poet.

27. What is the best way to write the underlined part of sentence 3?

    (A) Furthermore,

    (B) Additionally,

    (C) On the other hand,

    (D) *(No change)*

28. What is the best way to write the underlined part of sentence 5?

    (J) world

    (K) planet

    (L) worldwide

    (M) *(No change)*

(1) Professor Johnson and dr. Tannebaum spent years working together on a novel. (2) Johnson contributed his knowledge of science, and Tannebaum contributed his knowledge of medicine. (3) The novel that they was writing slowly took shape and finally reached completion ten years after they typed the first words. (4) Only two weeks after the release of the novel, *The Mad Doctor*, their work had sold nearly a million copies. (5) After they received their royalty checks from the publisher, they retired to Jamaica where they began work on the sequel, *The Mad Professor*.

29. What is the best way to write the underlined part of sentence 1?

    (A) doctor Tannebaum

    (B) Dr. Tannebaum

    (C) doc Tannebaaum

    (D) *(No change)*

30. What is the best way to write the underlined part of sentence 3?

    (J) wrote

    (K) had wrote

    (L) had been written

    (M) *(No change)*

STOP If you finish before time is up, check over your work on this part only. Do not go on until the signal is given.

MATH

Part 1

30 MINUTES

Directions: Four answers are given for each problem. Choose the best answer.

1. Which of the following is *not* a factor of 20?
   - (A) 10
   - (B) 5
   - (C) 4
   - (D) 3

2. The fraction $\frac{2}{3}$ is approximately which of the following?
   - (J) $\frac{3}{2}$
   - (K) 0.23
   - (L) 0.67
   - (M) 23.67

3. Which of the following is *not* a prime number?
   - (A) 3
   - (B) 9
   - (C) 13
   - (D) 19

4. Which of the following is a multiple of 3?
   - (J) 29
   - (K) 49
   - (L) 69
   - (M) 89

5. What is the difference between 97 and 10?
   - (A) 87
   - (B) 107
   - (C) 970
   - (D) 9.7

6. The number 0.003 can also be represented by which of the following?
   - (J) $\frac{3}{10}$
   - (K) $\frac{3}{100}$
   - (L) $\frac{3}{1,000}$
   - (M) $\frac{3}{10,000}$

7. Which of the following is the equivalent of 3^3?
   - (A) 3×3
   - (B) $3 \times 3 \div 3$
   - (C) 27
   - (D) 30

8. What is the sum of $\frac{1}{2} + \frac{2}{4} + \frac{3}{3}$?
   - (J) 1
   - (K) 2
   - (L) $2\frac{1}{2}$
   - (M) 3

9. What is the sum of $(3 \times 3) + (4 \times 4) + (5 \times 5)$?
   - (A) 24
   - (B) 50
   - (C) 60
   - (D) 345

10. Which of the following represents the reduced form for 1.6?
   - (J) $1\frac{6}{10}$
   - (K) $1\frac{3}{5}$
   - (L) $\frac{16}{10}$
   - (M) $\frac{32}{20}$

Directions: Four answer choices are given for each problem. Choose the best answer.

11. Jeff has 6 notebooks in his locker. Maggie has in her locker twice as many notebooks as Jeff. Darnell has in his locker twice as many notebooks as Maggie and Jeff combined. How many notebooks does Darnell have stuffed into his locker?

    (A) 12
    (B) 18
    (C) 24
    (D) 36

12. Baxter needed to replenish his supply of bottled water. The water dispenser in his kitchen holds 14 gallons of water. Baxter buys his water one half-gallon at a time at his local grocery store. How many half-gallon water purchases will Baxter need to make to fill his water dispenser?

    (J) 7
    (K) 14
    (L) 21
    (M) 28

13. Jared has $5 in his savings account now. He just took a job earning $20 per week. How many weeks will it take Jared to have enough money to buy a bicycle that costs $65?

    (A) 2 weeks
    (B) 3 weeks
    (C) 4 weeks
    (D) Not given

14. Sam's scooter gets 50 miles per gallon, and the scooter's gas tank holds 3 gallons of gasoline. If the gas tank in Sam's scooter is $\frac{2}{3}$ full, how many miles can Sam expect to travel before the tank is empty?

    (J) 75
    (K) 100
    (L) 150
    (M) 175

15. The rim on a basketball goal is 10 feet from the floor. If a player made 6 baskets, what is the sum of the distances that the ball would travel between the rim and the floor below?

    (A) 60 feet
    (B) 70 feet
    (C) 160 feet
    (D) Not given

16. If every car that travels along Highway 27 has four wheels and there are 72 cars driving on Highway 27, how many wheels are touching the road on Highway 27?

    (J) 54
    (K) 144
    (L) 108
    (M) 288

17. Maxine types 70 words per minute. Dorian types 10 percent faster than Maxine. How many words can Dorian type in 15 minutes?

    (A) 1,045
    (B) 1,155
    (C) 1,375
    (D) Not given

18. Aunt Ethel has 7 dozen antique ornaments for her Christmas tree. She anticipates needing a total of 200 ornaments to finish decorating her tree. How many ornaments should Aunt Ethel purchase at the antique fair to reach her goal of 200 antique ornaments for her tree?

    (J) 84
    (K) 96
    (L) 116
    (M) 124

19. Mandie and Mary Beth are planning to paint the concession stand at school. They have four walls to paint. Each wall is exactly the same size. The walls are each 12 feet long and 10 feet high. How many square feet of walls should they plan to paint if they are going to paint all four walls?

(A) 120 square feet

(B) 240 square feet

(C) 480 square feet

(D) 1,200 square feet

20. The penguins at the zoo eat 36,500 pounds of fish each year. How many pounds of fish do the penguins eat each day?

(J) 100

(K) 365

(L) 1,000

(M) Not given

Directions: Four answer choices are given for each problem. Choose the best answer.

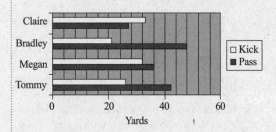

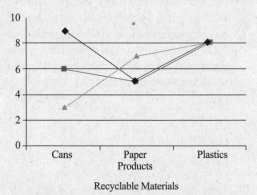

Recyclable Materials

◆— Ford HS   ■— Holmes HS   ▲— King HS

21. The city recently held a football skills competition at Barton Park. Based on the information in the chart above, which competitor passed the football the shortest distance?

(A) Claire

(B) Bradley

(C) Megan

(D) Tommy

22. Based on the information in the chart above, which competitor passed 4 more yards than he/she kicked the football?

(J) Claire

(K) Bradley

(L) Megan

(M) Tommy

23. The City School District sponsored a week-long recycling campaign in which the three city high schools collected items to be recycled. The chart indicates the results of the campaign as measured in hundreds of pounds. Based on the information in the chart above, which of the high schools collected the most cans and paper products combined?

(A) Ford HS

(B) Holmes HS

(C) King HS

(D) Holmes HS and King HS

24. Based on the information in the chart above, what was the total weight of all plastics collected in the campaign?

(J) 800 pounds

(K) 1,600 pounds

(L) 2,400 pounds

(M) 6,900 pounds

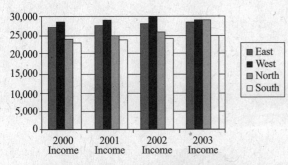

2000 Income   2001 Income   2002 Income   2003 Income

East   West   North   South

25. According to the bar graph above that illustrates per capita income by region in thousands of dollars, which region experienced the most income growth from 2000 to 2003?

(A) East

(B) West

(C) North

(D) South

26. According to the bar graph above, what was the approximate income of Southerners in 2003?

(J) $25,000

(K) $26,000

(L) $27,000

(M) $28,000

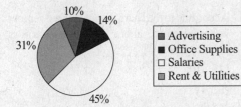

10%   14%
31%
45%

- Advertising
- Office Supplies
- Salaries
- Rent & Utilities

27. The pie chart above illustrates the proposed budget for a new company opening soon around the corner. Based on the information in the chart, what will be the most expensive part of running the new company?

(A) Advertising

(B) Office Supplies

(C) Salaries

(D) Rent & Utilities

28. Which two items in the proposed budget when added together equal the amount spent on salaries?

(J) Advertising and Office Supplies

(K) Rent & Utilities and Office Supplies

(L) Advertising and Salaries

(M) Advertising and Rent & Utilities

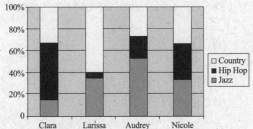

Clara   Larissa   Audrey   Nicole

- Country
- Hip Hop
- Jazz

29. The chart above represents the CD collections of four high school seniors. Based on the information in the chart, which of the girls has a CD collection composed of approximately 60 percent country music?

(A) Clara

(B) Larissa

(C) Audrey

(D) Nicole

30. Based on the information in the chart, if all four collections are the same size, which girl seems to prefer jazz to both hip hop and country music?

(J) Clara

(K) Larissa

(L) Audrey

(M) Nicole

STOP   If you finish before time is up, check over your work on this part only. Do not go on until the signal is given.

practice test

Part 2

10 MINUTES

Directions: For the following questions, <u>estimate</u> the answer in your head. No scratch work is allowed. Do NOT try to compute exact answers.

31. The closest estimate of 6544 − 3466 is
_____.

    (A) 1000
    (B) 2000
    (C) 3000
    (D) 4000

32. The closest estimate of 45,174 ÷ 9022 is
_____.

    (J) 5000
    (K) 500
    (L) 50
    (M) 5

33. The average class size at Kennedy High School is 31 students. There are 30 classes in session at any one time. About how many Kennedy High students are in class at any given time?

    (A) 800
    (B) 900
    (C) 1000
    (D) Not given

34. The closest estimate of 3988 + 2177 is
_____.

    (J) 5000
    (K) 5500
    (L) 6000
    (M) 6500

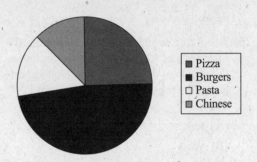

FAVORITE FOODS OF NEW YORK HIGH SCHOOL SENIORS

35. According to the chart above, about what percent of New York high school seniors prefers burgers?

    (A) 15%
    (B) 25%
    (C) 33%
    (D) 50%

36. According to the chart, if one hundred seniors were surveyed, about how many seniors prefer pizza?

    (J) 10
    (K) 15
    (L) 25
    (M) Not given

37. Most half-hour television shows are actually 23 minutes long once commercial time is deducted. If this is true, approximately how many seconds of commercials do viewers see in one half-hour show?

    (A) 300
    (B) 400
    (C) 500
    (D) 600

38. The closest estimate of $43 + 71 + 19 + 68 + 11 + 29$ is _____.

    (J) 200
    (K) 210
    (L) 240
    (M) 300

39. The closest estimate of $63,977 \div 7,991$ is _____.

    (A) 8
    (B) 80
    (C) 256
    (D) Not given

40. The closest estimate of $207 - 109 + 99 - 111 + 202 - 104$ is _____.

    (J) 0
    (K) 100
    (L) 200
    (M) 300

STOP If you finish before time is up, check over your work on this part only. Do not go on until the signal is given.

ABILITY

5 MINUTES

Directions: In questions 1–3, the first three figures are alike in certain ways. Choose the answer choice that corresponds to the first three figures.

1.

(A)   (B)   (C)   (D)   (E)

2.

(J)   (K)   (L)   (M)   (N)

3.

(A)   (B)   (C)   (D)   (E)

Directions: In questions 4–7, the first figure is related to the second figure. Determine that relationship. The third figure is changed in the same way to make one of the answer choices. Choose the answer choice that relates to the third figure.

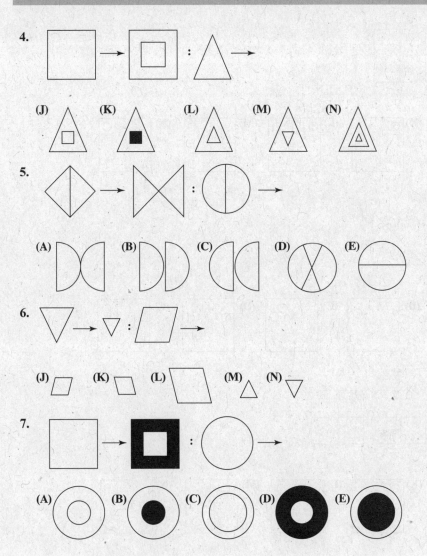

Directions: In questions 8–10, look at the top row to see how a square piece of paper is folded and where holes are punched into it. Then look at the bottom row to decide which answer choice shows how the paper will look when it is completely unfolded.

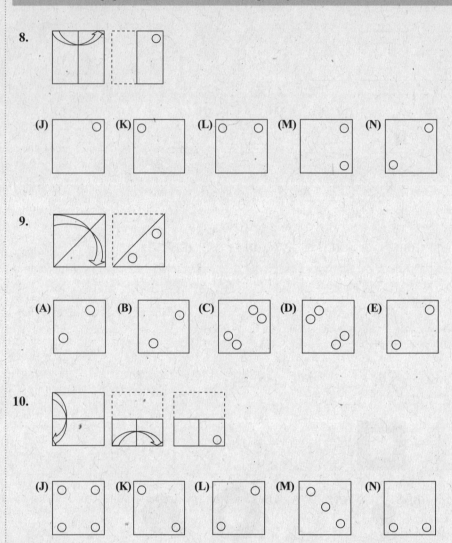

STOP — If you finish before time is up, check over your work on this section only. Do not go back to any previous parts.

Like us at facebook.com/petersonspublishing

ANSWER KEYS AND EXPLANATIONS

Reading

PART 1

1. A	3. B	5. A	7. C	9. B
2. L	4. M	6. M	8. J	10. M

1. **The correct answer is (A),** *elevated.* Other synonyms include "raised," "towering," and "high."

2. **The correct answer is (L),** *mood.* Other synonyms include "manner" and "deportment."

3. **The correct answer is (B),** *disfigured and torn.* Other synonyms include "distorted" and "corrupted."

4. **The correct answer is (M),** *quickly.* Other synonyms include "swiftly" and "hurriedly."

5. **The correct answer is (A),** *attain.* Other synonyms include "accomplish," "gain," and "reach."

6. **The correct answer is (M),** *peaceful.* Other synonyms include "calm" and "serene."

7. **The correct answer is (C),** *varied.* Other synonyms include "assorted" and "dissimilar."

8. **The correct answer is (J),** *celebrating.* Other synonyms include "reveling" and "exulting."

9. **The correct answer is (B),** *section.* Other synonyms include "fragment" and "division."

10. **The correct answer is (M),** *interesting.* Other synonyms include "intriguing," "captivating," and "enticing."

PART 2

11. C	13. D	15. B	17. C	19. C
12. J	14. J	16. K	18. J	20. L

11. **The correct answer is (C).** They didn't think that reading was necessary for people who worked all day in the fields. The passage implies that Abe's parents, who worked with their hands for a living, didn't believe reading was an essential skill for those whose livelihoods depended on other skills such as plowing, planting, and harvesting.

12. **The correct answer is (J).** He didn't want his parents to see him reading. Other than the times that Abe was able to go the neighbor's for reading instruction, bedtime was the one time that Abe could read quietly and by himself. In addition, Abe didn't want his parents to see him reading because he understood their lack of interest. He didn't want a confrontation with them about his reading.

13. **The correct answer is (D).** "Making ends meet" is a common way of saying that a budget is balanced. In other words, when one makes ends meet, he or she makes his money last long enough to pay all expenses. The last sentence of the first paragraph gives the context clue about the phrase.

14. **The correct answer is (J).** He hoped to increase the number of customers. Barrett

knew he needed more customers, and the first paragraph indicates that he had just enough customers to balance his budget; it is implied that he was not making much, if any, profit. In order to increase his profit, he needed more paying customers.

15. **The correct answer is (B).** There may have been a power struggle between kings and priests before Akhenaton ruled. The second paragraph indicates that he took power away from the priests and that this may have been a politically motivated move. This is the clue that there may have been political competition between priests and other kings like Akhenaton.

16. **The correct answer is (K).** The context clues that point to a pharaoh being a king are the references to the kingdom, the throne, and the idea that Akhenaton's decision affected everyone in Egypt.

17. **The correct answer is (C).** This is the best title because the passage directly addresses the social skills of computer users and the ways that those skills are affected by communicating electronically, via e-mail and instant messaging.

18. **The correct answer is (J).** The phrase implies that the more something is practiced by someone, the better he or she becomes at whatever is practiced. The next-to-last sentence mentions increased communications, so it is implied that "practice makes perfect" refers to that increase in communications.

19. **The correct answer is (C).** Reality TV actually consists of very little reality. The author of the passage contends that there is little reality in reality TV because the producers and directors still have a huge influence on the things that are filmed and televised, and this prevents reality TV from being real, which theoretically is the defining characteristic of reality.

20. **The correct answer is (L).** An author who criticizes and points out flaws or weaknesses is most likely a person who is a critic or opponent of that about which he or she writes.

Language

PART 1

1. A	5. A	9. B	13. B	17. B
2. N	6. M	10. N	14. K	18. K
3. B	7. E	11. A	15. C	19. B
4. L	8. J	12. J	16. M	20. J

1. **The correct answer is (A).** The correct spelling is dictionary.

2. **The correct answer is (N).** *(No mistakes)*

3. **The correct answer is (B).** The correct spelling is obtain.

4. **The correct answer is (L).** The correct spelling is persuade.

5. **The correct answer is (A).** The correct spelling is discuss.

6. **The correct answer is (M).** The correct spelling is messenger.

7. **The correct answer is (E).** *(No mistakes)*

8. **The correct answer is (J).** The correct spelling is cancellation.

9. **The correct answer is (B).** The correct spelling is migrate.

10. **The correct answer is (N).** *(No mistakes)*

11. **The correct answer is (A).** The word "college" is only capitalized when included in a proper noun such as Boston College or Ithaca College.

12. **The correct answer is (J).** The word "river" is capitalized when included as part of a proper noun such as Mississippi River.

13. **The correct answer is (B).** Words such as "aunt" and "uncle" should be capitalized when they are part of a person's name such as "Aunt Bee" or "Uncle Buck."

14. **The correct answer is (K).** Holidays, because they are proper nouns, should be capitalized.

15. **The correct answer is (C).** Names of seasons are not proper nouns and do not need capitalization.

16. **The correct answer is (M).** *(No mistakes)*

17. **The correct answer is (B).** "Space" needs no capitalization because it is a common noun, but related terms such as "Haley's Comet" or "Jupiter" should be capitalized because they are proper nouns.

18. **The correct answer is (K).** The word "newspaper" is a common noun and would only be capitalized as part of a proper noun such as the "Baltimore Newspaper Publishing Company."

19. **The correct answer is (B).** Words like "father" or "sister" require capitalization when used as part of a person's name, as in the cases of "Father Dowling" or "Sister Wendy."

20. **The correct answer is (J).** Names of streets, roads, or avenues are to be capitalized, as in "Abbey Road" or "Penny Lane," but not when used as common nouns like "the dirt road" or "the winding country lane."

PART 2

21. A	23. B	25. C	27. C	29. B
22. L	24. M	26. J	28. J	30. J

21. **The correct answer is (A).** The word "however" generally means "nevertheless," "yet," or "even though." It is correct in this instance because the sentences indicate Zambroski was one of America's premier inventors even though few have heard of him.

22. **The correct answer is (L).** A colon is only necessary before a long list of items.

23. **The correct answer is (B).** The phrase "in other words" would be a sentence fragment and should have been used as an introductory phrase for the rest of the sentence that follows. The only punctuation needed after the phrase is a comma, and "Scientists" would be rewritten as "scientists."

24. **The correct answer is (M).** *(No change)*

25. **The correct answer is (C).** The words "charitable organizations" are not the name of a specific organization that needs to be capitalized the way that "Red Cross" or "Catholic Youth Organization" would be.

26. **The correct answer is (J).** Commas are needed to separate the listed items in this sentence. It should be noted that there is some debate as to whether or not a comma should be included just prior to the word "and" (in this sentence, after the word "lunchboxes"). Both options are acceptable.

27. **The correct answer is (C).** The phrase "on the other hand" means "conversely" and is used to link two ideas that are dissimilar or opposite.

28. The correct answer is (J). The word "world" is a common noun and would need capitalization only if used as part of a name like "World Health Organization."

29. The correct answer is (B). The word "doctor" by itself is a common name but both "Doctor" and its abbreviation, "Dr.," require capitalization when used as part of a title or a name.

30. The correct answer is (J). The passage is written in past tense and the past tense form of the verb "write" is "wrote."

Math

PART 1

1. D	7. C	13. B	19. C	25. C
2. L	8. K	14. K	20. J	26. J
3. B	9. B	15. A	21. A	27. C
4. L	10. K	16. M	22. L	28. K
5. A	11. D	17. B	23. A	29. B
6. L	12. M	18. L	24. L	30. L

1. The correct answer is (D). 20 cannot be divided evenly by 3.

2. The correct answer is (L). $\frac{2}{3}$ is the same as 0.67, rounded to the nearest hundredth.

3. The correct answer is (B). 9 is divisible by three numbers—1, 3, and 9.

4. The correct answer is (L). 3 multiplied by 23 is 69.

5. The correct answer is (A). The term "difference" is a clue to subtract.

6. The correct answer is (L). The third place to the right of the decimal is thousandths.

7. The correct answer is (C). $3 \times 3 \times 3 = 3 \times 9 = 27$

8. The correct answer is (K). $\frac{1}{2} + \frac{2}{4} + \frac{3}{3} = \frac{1}{2} + \frac{1}{2} + 1 = 1 + 1 = 2$

9. The correct answer is (B). $(3 \times 3) + (4 \times 4) + (5 \times 5) = 9 + 16 + 25 = 50$

10. The correct answer is (K). $1.6 = 1\frac{6}{10}$, which must be reduced to $1\frac{3}{5}$.

11. The correct answer is (D). Jeff has 6 notebooks. Maggie has 2×6 notebooks. Jeff and Maggie combined have 18 notebooks. Darnell has 2×18, or 36, notebooks.

12. The correct answer is (M). Baxter needs two half-gallons for each gallon, or $2 \times 14 = 28$.

13. The correct answer is (B). $3 \times \$20 = \$60$. \$60 earned, plus \$5 in savings = \$65.

14. The correct answer is (K). A full tank would go 3×50, or 150 miles. $\frac{2}{3} \times 150 = 100$.

15. The correct answer is (A). 6 trips from rim to floor, or $6 \times 10 = 60$.

16. **The correct answer is (M).** 72 cars with 4 wheels each, or 72 × 4 = 288.

17. **The correct answer is (B).** Dorian types 110 percent of Maxine's speed, or 1.10 × 70 = 77. In 15 minutes, Dorian types 77 × 15 = 1155.

18. **The correct answer is (L).** Seven dozen is 7 × 12 = 84. 200 − 84 = 116.

19. **The correct answer is (C).** Each wall is 12 × 10, or 120 square feet. Four walls of 120 square feet is 4 × 120 = 480.

20. **The correct answer is (J).** 36,500 ÷ 365 days in a year is 100.

21. **The correct answer is (A).** Claire passed for only 27 yards.

22. **The correct answer is (L).** Megan passed for 36 yards and kicked 32 yards.

23. **The correct answer is (A).** Ford HS collected 900 pounds of cans and 500 pounds of paper products.

24. **The correct answer is (L).** Each school collected 800 pounds. 800 × 3 = 2400.

25. **The correct answer is (C).** The income in the North grew from about $24,000 to nearly $29,000.

26. **The correct answer is (J).** $25,000

27. **The correct answer is (C).** The money that will be spent on salaries is more than any other single expenditure.

28. **The correct answer is (K).** When added together, Rent & Utilities and Office Supplies (31% + 14% = 45%) equal Salaries (45%).

29. **The correct answer is (B).** Larissa's collection consists of approximately 35% jazz, 5% hip hop, and 60% country.

30. **The correct answer is (L).** Audrey's collection consists of approximately 50% jazz, 20% hip hop, and 30% country.

PART 2

31. C	33. B	35. D	37. B	39. A
32. M	34. L	36. L	38. L	40. L

31. **The correct answer is (C).** 6544 − 3466 is approximately 6500 − 3500.

32. **The correct answer is (M).** 45,174 ÷ 9022 is approximately 45,000 ÷ 9000.

33. **The correct answer is (B).** 31 × 30 is approximately 30 × 30.

34. **The correct answer is (L).** 3988 + 2177 is approximately 4000 + 2000.

35. **The correct answer is (D).** About half, or 50 percent, chose burgers.

36. **The correct answer is (L).** About one fourth, or 25 percent, chose pizza. 100 × 25% = 25.

37. **The correct answer is (B).** Seven minutes is 7 × 60 seconds = 420 seconds, which is about 400.

38. **The correct answer is (L).** 43 + 71 + 19 + 68 + 11 + 29 can be approximated to 40 + 70 + 20 + 70 + 10 + 30, which is 240.

39. **The correct answer is (A).** 63,977 ÷ 7,991 is about 64,000 ÷ 8000, which is 8.

40. **The correct answer is (L).** 207 − 109 + 99 − 111 + 202 − 104 can be approximated to 200 − 100 + 100 − 100 + 200 − 100, which equals 200.

Ability

1. C	3. C	5. A	7. D	9. C
2. K	4. L	6. J	8. L	10. J

1. **The correct answer is (C).** The three given figures are all triangles.

2. **The correct answer is (K).** The three given figures are all ovals.

3. **The correct answer is (C).** Each of the three given figures has one line segment in its interior.

4. **The correct answer is (L).** For the first pair, the second figure has a smaller version of the first figure inside it. Thus, for the second figure of the second pair, we need a triangle drawn inside the given triangle and appearing in the same way. Answer choice (M) is incorrect because the triangle is upside down.

5. **The correct answer is (A).** For the first pair, the second figure results from pulling apart the two triangles where they are connected, then flipping over each triangle, and reconnecting them at a common point. Answer choices (B) and (C) are incorrect because one of the half-circles has not been flipped over.

6. **The correct answer is (J).** For the first pair, the second figure is simply a smaller version of the first figure. Answer choice (K) is incorrect because it appears different from the original first figure of the second pair.

7. **The correct answer is (D).** For the first pair, the second figure is one in which a smaller circle is drawn and the area between the two circles is shaded.

8. **The correct answer is (L).** After the figure is folded over the center vertical line, a hole is punched in the upper right-hand corner. When this figure is unfolded, a hole will appear in both the upper right and upper left portions of the original figure.

9. **The correct answer is (C).** This figure is folded over its diagonal, and then two holes are punched next to the diagonal. When unfolded, there will appear four holes next to the diagonal. Answer choice (D) is incorrect because the holes are too far away from the diagonal.

10. **The correct answer is (J).** This figure is folded first over a horizontal line and than folded again over a vertical line. After a hole is punched, when unfolded, there will be a hole in each corner.

ANSWER SHEET PRACTICE TEST 2: TACHS

Reading

PART 1

1. Ⓐ Ⓑ Ⓒ Ⓓ   3. Ⓐ Ⓑ Ⓒ Ⓓ   5. Ⓐ Ⓑ Ⓒ Ⓓ   7. Ⓐ Ⓑ Ⓒ Ⓓ   9. Ⓐ Ⓑ Ⓒ Ⓓ
2. Ⓙ Ⓚ Ⓛ Ⓜ   4. Ⓙ Ⓚ Ⓛ Ⓜ   6. Ⓙ Ⓚ Ⓛ Ⓜ   8. Ⓙ Ⓚ Ⓛ Ⓜ   10. Ⓙ Ⓚ Ⓛ Ⓜ

PART 2

11. Ⓐ Ⓑ Ⓒ Ⓓ   13. Ⓐ Ⓑ Ⓒ Ⓓ   15. Ⓐ Ⓑ Ⓒ Ⓓ   17. Ⓐ Ⓑ Ⓒ Ⓓ   19. Ⓐ Ⓑ Ⓒ Ⓓ
12. Ⓙ Ⓚ Ⓛ Ⓜ   14. Ⓙ Ⓚ Ⓛ Ⓜ   16. Ⓙ Ⓚ Ⓛ Ⓜ   18. Ⓙ Ⓚ Ⓛ Ⓜ   20. Ⓙ Ⓚ Ⓛ Ⓜ

Language

PART 1

1. Ⓐ Ⓑ Ⓒ Ⓓ Ⓔ   6. Ⓙ Ⓚ Ⓛ Ⓜ Ⓝ   11. Ⓐ Ⓑ Ⓒ Ⓓ   16. Ⓙ Ⓚ Ⓛ Ⓜ
2. Ⓙ Ⓚ Ⓛ Ⓜ Ⓝ   7. Ⓐ Ⓑ Ⓒ Ⓓ Ⓔ   12. Ⓙ Ⓚ Ⓛ Ⓜ   17. Ⓙ Ⓚ Ⓛ Ⓜ
3. Ⓐ Ⓑ Ⓒ Ⓓ Ⓔ   8. Ⓙ Ⓚ Ⓛ Ⓜ Ⓝ   13. Ⓐ Ⓑ Ⓒ Ⓓ   18. Ⓙ Ⓚ Ⓛ Ⓜ
4. Ⓙ Ⓚ Ⓛ Ⓜ Ⓝ   9. Ⓐ Ⓑ Ⓒ Ⓓ Ⓔ   14. Ⓙ Ⓚ Ⓛ Ⓜ   19. Ⓐ Ⓑ Ⓒ Ⓓ
5. Ⓐ Ⓑ Ⓒ Ⓓ Ⓔ   10. Ⓙ Ⓚ Ⓛ Ⓜ Ⓝ   15. Ⓐ Ⓑ Ⓒ Ⓓ   20. Ⓙ Ⓚ Ⓛ Ⓜ

PART 2

21. Ⓐ Ⓑ Ⓒ Ⓓ   23. Ⓐ Ⓑ Ⓒ Ⓓ   25. Ⓐ Ⓑ Ⓒ Ⓓ   27. Ⓐ Ⓑ Ⓒ Ⓓ   29. Ⓐ Ⓑ Ⓒ Ⓓ
22. Ⓙ Ⓚ Ⓛ Ⓜ   24. Ⓙ Ⓚ Ⓛ Ⓜ   26. Ⓙ Ⓚ Ⓛ Ⓜ   28. Ⓙ Ⓚ Ⓛ Ⓜ   30. Ⓙ Ⓚ Ⓛ Ⓜ

Math

PART 1

1. Ⓐ Ⓑ Ⓒ Ⓓ   7. Ⓐ Ⓑ Ⓒ Ⓓ   13. Ⓐ Ⓑ Ⓒ Ⓓ   19. Ⓐ Ⓑ Ⓒ Ⓓ   25. Ⓐ Ⓑ Ⓒ Ⓓ
2. Ⓙ Ⓚ Ⓛ Ⓜ   8. Ⓙ Ⓚ Ⓛ Ⓜ   14. Ⓙ Ⓚ Ⓛ Ⓜ   20. Ⓙ Ⓚ Ⓛ Ⓜ   26. Ⓙ Ⓚ Ⓛ Ⓜ
3. Ⓐ Ⓑ Ⓒ Ⓓ   9. Ⓐ Ⓑ Ⓒ Ⓓ   15. Ⓐ Ⓑ Ⓒ Ⓓ   21. Ⓐ Ⓑ Ⓒ Ⓓ   27. Ⓐ Ⓑ Ⓒ Ⓓ
4. Ⓙ Ⓚ Ⓛ Ⓜ   10. Ⓙ Ⓚ Ⓛ Ⓜ   16. Ⓙ Ⓚ Ⓛ Ⓜ   22. Ⓙ Ⓚ Ⓛ Ⓜ   28. Ⓙ Ⓚ Ⓛ Ⓜ
5. Ⓐ Ⓑ Ⓒ Ⓓ   11. Ⓐ Ⓑ Ⓒ Ⓓ   17. Ⓐ Ⓑ Ⓒ Ⓓ   23. Ⓐ Ⓑ Ⓒ Ⓓ   29. Ⓐ Ⓑ Ⓒ Ⓓ
6. Ⓙ Ⓚ Ⓛ Ⓜ   12. Ⓙ Ⓚ Ⓛ Ⓜ   18. Ⓙ Ⓚ Ⓛ Ⓜ   24. Ⓙ Ⓚ Ⓛ Ⓜ   30. Ⓙ Ⓚ Ⓛ Ⓜ

PART 2

31. Ⓐ Ⓑ Ⓒ Ⓓ   33. Ⓐ Ⓑ Ⓒ Ⓓ   35. Ⓐ Ⓑ Ⓒ Ⓓ   37. Ⓐ Ⓑ Ⓒ Ⓓ   39. Ⓐ Ⓑ Ⓒ Ⓓ
32. Ⓙ Ⓚ Ⓛ Ⓜ   34. Ⓙ Ⓚ Ⓛ Ⓜ   36. Ⓙ Ⓚ Ⓛ Ⓜ   38. Ⓙ Ⓚ Ⓛ Ⓜ   40. Ⓙ Ⓚ Ⓛ Ⓜ

Ability

1. Ⓐ Ⓑ Ⓒ Ⓓ Ⓔ   4. Ⓙ Ⓚ Ⓛ Ⓜ Ⓝ   7. Ⓐ Ⓑ Ⓒ Ⓓ Ⓔ   9. Ⓐ Ⓑ Ⓒ Ⓓ Ⓔ
2. Ⓙ Ⓚ Ⓛ Ⓜ Ⓝ   5. Ⓐ Ⓑ Ⓒ Ⓓ Ⓔ   8. Ⓙ Ⓚ Ⓛ Ⓜ Ⓝ   10. Ⓙ Ⓚ Ⓛ Ⓜ Ⓝ
3. Ⓐ Ⓑ Ⓒ Ⓓ Ⓔ   6. Ⓙ Ⓚ Ⓛ Ⓜ Ⓝ

answer sheet

Practice Test 2: TACHS

READING

Part 1

5 MINUTES

Directions: For each question, decide which one of the four possible answers has most nearly the same meaning as the underlined word above it. Then, on your answer sheet, find the row of answer spaces numbered the same as the question. Fill in the answer space that has the same letter as the answer you chose.

1. Highly anticipated arrival
   (A) expected
   (B) late
   (C) departed
   (D) unclear

2. Decaying leaves
   (J) growing
   (K) falling
   (L) rotting
   (M) colorful

3. An alternate plan
   (A) replacement
   (B) ineffective
   (C) ambitious
   (D) inferior

4. To estimate the cost
   (J) calculate approximately
   (K) approve of
   (L) discount
   (M) pay for

5. Weary runner
   (A) energetic
   (B) lost
   (C) tired
   (D) winning

6. Vibrant colors
   (J) drab and dull
   (K) bold and bright
   (L) transparent
   (M) black and white

7. A puzzling dilemma
   (A) game
   (B) answer
   (C) appearance
   (D) problem

8. Driving recklessly
   (J) easily
   (K) carelessly
   (L) carefully
   (M) for the first time

9. A <u>rambling</u> speaker
   (A) interesting
   (B) motivational
   (C) long-winded and wordy
   (D) loud

10. <u>Enormous</u> buildings
   (J) intricate
   (K) close together
   (L) huge
   (M) stone

STOP If you finish before time is up, check over your work on this part only. Do not go on until the signal is given..

Part 2

15 MINUTES

Directions: Read the passages below and then answer the questions. Four answers are given for each question. You are to choose the answer that you think is better than the others. Then, on your answer sheet, find the row of answer spaces numbered the same as the question. Fill in the best answer in the ovals on your answer sheet.

PASSAGE 1

Charlie finally decided that he had had enough of city life. He made up his mind that he was tired of riding the subway an hour to work every day, tired of living in a tiny apartment, and tired of not seeing the sunrise and sunset. Charlie gathered his family around the dinner table and informed them of his desire to escape the concrete jungle permanently. After a few hours, Charlie persuaded his wife and two kids to give the country life a try.

Two weeks after Charlie made his decision, the family moved into a ranch house in rural Texas. On the day the family moved in, Charlie's youngest, Laurie, got stung by a small scorpion. Only a few hours later, Charlie's wife began sneezing uncontrollably and developed red, watery eyes. Charlie's son found a rattlesnake in the shed shortly thereafter. Before the movers unloaded half the furniture from the truck, Charlie was on the phone with a Realtor back in New York City.

11. In sentence 1 of paragraph 2, what does the word "rural" mean?

(A) Western

(B) In the country

(C) Primitive

(D) Scenic

12. Why did Charlie call his Realtor before he was even unpacked in Texas?

(J) He was upset with the view from his porch.

(K) He wanted to double-check the price of his new house.

(L) The country life wasn't what he hoped for, and he was ready to move back to the city.

(M) He was disappointed in the movers.

PASSAGE 2

In the nineteenth century, a wave of liberalism swept across Europe. Liberals—those who advocated liberalism—heavily favored liberty, equality, and natural rights for citizens of European nations. Specifically, liberals hoped to win for citizens such things as voting rights and equal protection under the law. Ironically, the vast majority of liberals sought these rights for men only and not for women.

Standing in the way of liberal reform were the wealthy nobles, aristocrats, and the monarchs seated precariously on the thrones of Europe. The nobility felt threatened by liberalism because nobles held nearly all political power in early nineteenth-century Europe. Because they held all the power, the common man was left with virtually no say in the government. The nobles knew that their political positions would be in jeopardy if the common citizens were allowed to choose government officials. Ultimately, liberalism proved too strong a force for the aristocracy to defeat.

13. What was the nobles' greatest fear about common citizens winning the right to vote?

(A) Citizens didn't know how to vote.

(B) Citizens might not exercise their right to vote.

(C) Nobles may not get the right to vote.

(D) Citizens probably would elect people who had not been the power-holding nobles prior to elections, thus leaving the nobles with little or no power.

14. Based on context clues in the second paragraph, the word "monarchs" probably means which of the following?

(J) Commoners

(K) Kings and queens

(L) Jesters

(M) Judges

PASSAGE 3

"Lefty" Gordon was an obscure outfielder who had a brief major league career with the Cleveland Indians in the 1960s. He never hit dozens of home runs in a single season, he never stole many bases, he didn't have blazing speed, and he didn't have the flashy style that many modern players have. What Lefty did have, though, was a connection with the fans, particularly the ones in the cheap seats behind the centerfield wall. For one fan in particular, Lefty Gordon was the greatest baseball player ever.

Mitchell Haskins was just a kid in the 1960s. Mitchell's family had very little money, but he was fortunate enough to be able to attend a few Indians games, in the cheap seats, as a kid. One warm June afternoon in the final inning of a lopsided game, Lefty Gordon made his first appearance of the game in centerfield. On the final out of the game, Gordon chased down a fly ball and made a nice catch. Mitchell, just a kid then, applauded wildly. Gordon saw Mitchell cheering, climbed the fence, and tossed Mitchell the ball. As he climbed down from the fence, he said to Mitchell, "If every fan cheered as hard as you, we'd win every game. Thanks, kid!"

15. Why didn't Lefty Gordon get into the game until the final innings?

   (A) He was left-handed.

   (B) The game was lopsided so the Indians didn't want to run up the score on the visiting team.

   (C) The coaches didn't like Lefty.

   (D) Lefty was not good enough to start the game and probably played only as a reserve player.

16. Why did Mitchell think Lefty was one of the greatest players?

   (J) Lefty had amazing skills.

   (K) Lefty wasn't being treated fairly.

   (L) Mitchell saw talent in Lefty that the coaches didn't see.

   (M) Lefty made a personal connection with Mitchell and the fans that other players didn't make.

PASSAGE 4

As Margie strolled through the mall, a muscular young man handed her a pamphlet advertising a brand new workout facility across town. Margie took the pamphlet; she had been pondering a new fitness routine. She read as she walked past store after store. On her way through the department store at the end of the mall, she stopped and browsed the fitness equipment in the store. Margie was convinced that she needed to do something to help herself feel better, have more energy, and generally lead a healthier life.

After much thought, Margie decided that an expensive exercise apparatus eventually would turn into an expensive clothes rack in her bedroom. Margie also decided that the new workout facility would be better than the exercise equipment. However, she wondered if a facility on the other side of town would actually deter her from working out regularly. Margie ultimately decided to spend a fraction of the money she would have spent otherwise, and she purchased small set of weights and some workout videos.

17. What was Margie's true feeling about purchasing the expensive exercise equipment?

(A) She was afraid she wouldn't know how to use the equipment.

(B) She wanted to hang clothes somewhere other than in her closet.

(C) She feared that she wouldn't use the equipment enough to justify the price.

(D) She didn't think the equipment would fit anywhere except in her bedroom.

18. Based on context clues, what does the word "deter" mean in the passage?

(J) allow

(K) include

(L) encourage

(M) discourage

PASSAGE 5

The camp director stood in front of the staff late Friday evening to address her camp counselors. The counselors had been working for two weeks without a break and faced another two weeks of the same routine before camp was to be dismissed for the summer. The counselors directed or participated in activities with the campers for 12 or 14 hours every day. In addition, the counselors made themselves available to the campers for one-on-one attention, including giving advice and just listening. The counselors poured themselves into their jobs.

The director looked at the face of each counselor and smiled. She knew how much of themselves they invested in making the camp a success. She said, "When my elbows get rough, dry, and cracked from work and exposure, I rub lotion on them. It's amazing how that can relax and refresh. I want to give each of you some proverbial lotion to soothe your souls. You get tomorrow off!"

19. Which of the following most likely describes the counselors?

    (A) Unruly
    (B) Disinterested
    (C) Exhausted
    (D) Confused

20. Why did the director tell the counselors that she wanted to give them "some proverbial lotion"?

    (J) She wanted to give them real lotion, but she didn't have enough for everyone.
    (K) She wanted to help them be relaxed and refreshed by giving them a day off.
    (L) She wanted to give the counselors the hint that some of them had dry skin.
    (M) She wanted to encourage them to use suntan lotion when working with the campers.

STOP If you finish before time is up, check over your work on this part only. Do not go on until the signal is given.

LANGUAGE

Part 1

25 MINUTES FOR PARTS 1 AND 2

Directions: This is a test of how well you can find mistakes in writing. For the questions with mistakes in spelling, capitalization, and punctuation, choose the answer with the same letter as the **line** containing the mistake. For the questions with mistakes in usage and expression, choose the answer with the same letter as the **line** containing the mistake, or choose the word, phrase, or sentence that is better than the others. When there is no mistake or no change needed, choose the last answer choice.

1. **(A)** ocean
   (B) calculater
   (C) trench
   (D) minute
   (E) *(No mistakes)*

2. **(J)** transport
   (K) attitude
   (L) sinse
   (M) evaluate
   (N) *(No mistakes)*

3. **(A)** receive
   (B) fault
   (C) liquid
   (D) lable
   (E) *(No mistakes)*

4. **(J)** notebook
   (K) famine
   (L) zebra
   (M) knolledge
   (N) *(No mistakes)*

5. **(A)** destination
   (B) declare
   (C) mischief
   (D) concquer
   (E) *(No mistakes)*

6. **(J)** forfit
   (K) vital
   (L) avalanche
   (M) comfortable
   (N) *(No mistakes)*

7. **(A)** finished
   (B) relyable
   (C) chrome
   (D) disappoint
   (E) *(No mistakes)*

8. **(J)** credible
   (K) starlight
   (L) venom
   (M) accelerate
   (N) *(No mistakes)*

9. **(A)** initiate
   (B) simply
   (C) govenor
   (D) decline
   (E) *(No mistakes)*

10. **(J)** monstrous
    (K) protection
    (L) fields
    (M) decieve
    (N) *(No mistakes)*

11. **(A)** To find my dog, rover, I
    (B) sailed across the ocean
    (C) to the Johnson's farm.
    (D) *(No mistakes)*

12. **(J)** The king's jet flew
    (K) over the Andes Mountains
    (L) and beyond the river.
    (M) *(No mistakes)*

13. **(A)** The New York Jets' kicker and
    (B) the Dallas cowboys' punter
    (C) are actually Atlanta Falcons' fans.
    (D) *(No mistakes)*

14. **(J)** President Jefferson once lived
    (K) in the famous Virginia Home
    (L) known as Monticello.
    (M) *(No mistakes)*

15. **(A)** For christmas last year,
    (B) mom and dad gave me
    (C) a coat just like Jamie's.
    (D) *(No mistakes)*

16. **(J)** The Basketball Coach sent
    (K) the injured basketball player
    (L) to see Dr. Moore.
    (M) *(No mistakes)*

17. **(A)** Queen Mary ordered her daughter,
    (B) the Princess, to marry the son of
    (C) one of the country's richest dukes.
    (D) *(No mistakes)*

18. **(J)** How many times did j.j.
    (K) take a bite of Buddy's ice cream
    (L) when Buddy was talking to Sally?
    (M) *(No mistakes)*

19. **(A)** The leading candy company,
    (B) Sweet Tooth, inc., just announced
    (C) a new candy bar called O Yum.
    (D) *(No mistakes)*

20. **(J)** I can't remember if California
    (K) is the biggest State
    (L) or if Texas is the biggest.
    (M) *(No mistakes)*

practice test

Part 2

Directions: For questions 21–30, choose the best answer based on the following paragraphs.

(1) Many people believe that cooks and chefs learn their craft in their home kitchens or from their mothers and grandmothers. (2) In fact, most of the very successful chefs, especially in expensive restaurants, actually attend College to learn to cook. (3) Many of the world's greatest cities boast a number of culinary schools, or schools for aspiring chefs. (4) Athens, Paris, New York, San Francisco, Tokyo. Are home to such culinary institutes. (5) Such institutes are to cooking what Harvard and Yale are to the study of law. (6) Coincidentally, such culinary educations are similar in costs to Ivy League educations.

21. What is the best way to write the underlined part of sentence 2?
    (A) a College
    (B) college
    (C) College,
    (D) *(No change)*

22. What is the best way to write the underlined part of sentence 4?
    (J) San Francisco, and Tokyo are home
    (K) San Francisco, Tokyo—Are home
    (L) San Francisco and Tokyo is home
    (M) *(No change)*

---

(1) One of the fastest growing industries of the last twenty-five years is the baby food manufacturing industry. (2) Millions of Americans each year use canned or jarred baby food as a regular part of the diet of their children. (3) Because each baby food company wants to outsell the other baby food companies, new flavors and food combinations are created each month. (4) Unfortunately for some who work at the baby food companies, someone has to taste the baby food before it hits the shelves. (5) These ''tasters'' have to try such new flavors as peas, potatoes, and meatloaf or squash, prunes, and beef. (6) Without the taste buds of these loyal employees—millions of American babies would be forced to eat old-fashioned baby foods like green beans or strained carrots.

23. What is the best way to write the underlined part of sentence 1?
    (A) twenty five
    (B) Twenty Five
    (C) twentyfive
    (D) *(No change)*

24. What is the best way to write the underlined part of sentence 6?
    (J) employees: millions
    (K) employees and millions
    (L) employees, millions
    (M) *(No change)*

(1) Although small schools usually have good teacher-to-student ratios and small classes, large schools have advantages, two. (2) For example, large schools often have more course offerings than small schools. (3) Large schools can offer advanced courses instead of just History, Science, and Math. (4) Also, large schools frequently have more extra-curricular activities, such as volleyball, choir, and football. (5) There simply is no black-and-white answer as to which school size is preferable.

25. What is the best way to write the underlined part of sentence 1?

(A) in addition to

(B) too

(C) besides

(D) *(No change)*

26. What is the best way to write the underlined part of sentence 3?

(J) history, science, and math

(K) History; Science; Math

(L) history, and science, and math

(M) *(No change)*

---

(1) Valerie knows more about fashion than anyone else in her class. (2) She watched all the fashion shows on television, reads all the fashion magazines, and attends all the city's fashion premiers. (3) Valerie has said many times that she wants to be a fashion designer when she gets out of school. (4) Her plan is to stockpile as much vintage clothing as she can afford. (5) She's going to save it for about fifteen or twenty years. (6) Than, when the time is right, she'll design new, cutting-edge fashion lines using her stockpile of vintage things. (7) Someone fifteen years from now will probably pay a high price for Valerie's crazy idea.

27. What is the best way to write the underlined part of sentence 2?

(A) had watched

(B) had been watching

(C) watches

(D) *(No change)*

28. What is the best way to write the underlined part of sentence 6?

(J) Then

(K) Regardless

(L) Before

(M) *(No change)*

---

(1) Mr. and Mrs. Johannson were a retired couple from Wisconsin. (2) They had lived in Wisconsin all their lives. (3) For sixty years, they had put up with the bitterly cold Winter in Wisconsin and they had had enough. (4) The Johannsons sold their house and their cars and bought a recreational vehicle, or RV, and hit the road. (5) They headed directly for Florida where they were sure they would not have to cope with blizzard-like conditions. (6) Ironically, the week they arrived, hurricane Emma struck the Florida coast. (7) Hoping for a compromise of some kind, the Johannsons decided to spend the rest of their days exploring Kansas.

29. What is the best way to write the underlined part of sentence 3?

(A) winter

(B) Weather

(C) Winter Weather

(D) *(No change)*

30. What is the best way to write the underlined part of sentence 7?

(J) there

(K) they're

(L) Their

(M) *(No change)*

STOP If you finish before time is up, check over your work on this part only. Do not go on until the signal is given.

MATH

Part 1

30 MINUTES

Directions: Four answers are given for each problem. Choose the best answer.

1. Which of the following is a prime number?
   - **(A)** 27
   - **(B)** 28
   - **(C)** 29
   - **(D)** 30

2. The fraction $\frac{8}{4}$ can be reduced to which of the following?
   - **(J)** 84
   - **(K)** $\frac{1}{2}$
   - **(L)** $\frac{4}{8}$
   - **(M)** 2

3. Which of the following is the product of 16 and 4?
   - **(A)** 4
   - **(B)** 12
   - **(C)** 20
   - **(D)** 64

4. Which of the following is the equivalent of 6^7?
   - **(J)** 6×7
   - **(K)** $7 \times 6 \times 6 \times 6 \times 6 \times 6 \times 6$
   - **(L)** $6 \times 6 \times 6 \times 6 \times 6 \times 6 \times 6$
   - **(M)** $(6 + 6) \times 7$

5. The fraction $2\frac{6}{1000}$ can be expressed as a decimal by which of the following?
   - **(A)** 2.006
   - **(B)** 0.0026
   - **(C)** 26,000.000
   - **(D)** 26.1000

6. What is the difference between $\frac{7}{8}$ and $\frac{1}{2}$?
   - **(J)** $\frac{3}{8}$
   - **(K)** $\frac{6}{8}$
   - **(L)** $\frac{6}{2}$
   - **(M)** $\frac{3}{4}$

7. What is the sum of $(6 - 1) + (1 \times 5) + (10 \div 2) + (2.5 + 2.5)$?
   - **(A)** 25
   - **(B)** 20
   - **(C)** 15
   - **(D)** 125

8. Which of the following is *not* a multiple of 4?
   - **(J)** 24
   - **(K)** 34
   - **(L)** 44
   - **(M)** 64

9. Which of the following is the equivalent of $3 - (-6)$?
   - **(A)** –9
   - **(B)** –3
   - **(C)** 9 **(D)**   3

10. What is the least common multiple of 6, 12, and 72?
    - **(J)** 6
    - **(K)** 12
    - **(L)** 36
    - **(M)** 72

Directions: Four answer choices are given for each problem. Choose the best answer.

11. A new restaurant, The Pizza Parlor, boasts the widest variety of toppings in the city. The owners claim that their 72 topping choices are 50 percent more than the next closest competitor, Patty's Pizzas. If The Pizza Parlor's claim is true, how many topping choices does Patty's Pizzas offer?

   (A) 24
   (B) 36
   (C) 48
   (D) Not given

12. Carl has collected 27 of the 32 available Captain Cosmos comic books, 19 of the 24 available Galactic General comic books, and 21 of the 23 available Larry the Laser comic books. If Carl wanted to acquire the missing comics from each series he collects, how many comic books would he need to buy?

   (J) 7
   (K) 67
   (L) 79
   (M) Not given

13. The school library recently relocated to a new building on campus. In the new library are many new bookshelves. Each bookshelf holds 245 books. The library has 12 bookshelves that are 100 percent full and one bookshelf that is $\frac{4}{5}$ full. How many books are in the new library?

   (A) 2,940
   (B) 3,136
   (C) 2,989
   (D) 294,000

14. Paul's digital camera normally holds 200 images. If Paul sets his camera to take extra-high-quality pictures, his camera holds only 40 pictures. Paul has already saved 100 normal images on his camera, but he wants to take as many pictures as possible of the sunset over the bay. How many extra-high-quality pictures can Paul hold on his camera

in addition to the 100 normal images he's already saved?

   (J) 40
   (K) 30
   (L) 20
   (M) 10

15. If Paige spends $3\frac{1}{4}$ hours per day practicing piano and she practices 4 days per week, how many hours does Paige practice piano each week?

   (A) $12\frac{1}{4}$
   (B) $12\frac{3}{4}$
   (C) 13
   (D) 14

16. Audrey and Ginnie volunteer each month to drive meals to elderly people. The first month they volunteered, they delivered a total of 60 meals. The next month they delivered $33\frac{1}{3}$ percent more than they did the first month. The third month they delivered twice as many meals as the first two months combined. How many meals did the two girls deliver in the third month?

   (J) 80
   (K) 90
   (L) 160
   (M) 280

17. If Taylor earns $7.50 per hour, how many 40-hour weeks will he need to work to earn enough to buy a new computer system that costs $1350?

   (A) 3
   (B) 4
   (C) $4\frac{1}{2}$
   (D) $12\frac{1}{2}$

18. Wallie wants to wallpaper her bedroom. Each roll of wallpaper covers 75 square feet of wall space. Her room has four walls that are 10 feet high and 15 feet wide. How many rolls of wallpaper will Wallie need to cover all four walls?

(J) 2

(K) 8

(L) 16

(M) 20

19. While trying to achieve a new high score at Blastomatic, the hottest video game on the market, Eric recorded scores of 6776, 6892, 6990, 7010, and 7012. What was his average score for those five games?

(A) 6890

(B) 6936

(C) 6990

(D) Not given

20. Gee-Whiz electronics company exports 400,000 electronic devices each year. Gee-Whiz wants to merge with Go Electro, a new electronics company that exports 1,900 electronic devices each month. After the merger, how many electronic devices will the new company export per year?

(J) 35,233

(K) 401,900

(L) 422,800

(M) 6,333,333

Directions: Four answer choices are given for each problem. Choose the best answer.

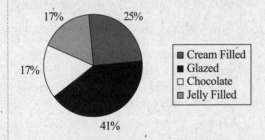

21. At Doodle's Donuts, the most popular item on the menu is Doodle's Dozen. The chart shows the typical distribution of donuts in each Doodle's Dozen that is sold. According to the chart, the single most widely consumed donuts in Doodle's Dozen is which of the following?

(A) Cream Filled

(B) Glazed

(C) Chocolate

(D) Jelly Filled

22. Based on the information in the chart, Doodle's Dozen includes three of which type of donut?

(J) Cream Filled

(K) Glazed

(L) Chocolate

(M) Jelly Filled

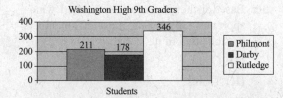

Washington High 9th Graders

23. The chart above shows the feeder schools from which current ninth-graders at Washington High School came. If these are the only feeder schools that sent students to the ninth grade at Washington High School, which school sent the largest percentage of current Washington ninth-graders?

(A) Philmont

(B) Darby

(C) Rutledge

(D) Not given

24. Based on the information in the chart above, Washington High School currently has how many ninth-graders?

(J) 211

(K) 178

(L) 346

(M) 735

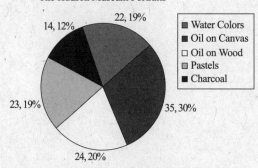

The Hudson Museum Portraits

25. The pie chart above illustrates the number and types of portraits at the Hudson Museum. Based on the information in the chart, which of the following is true of the number of portraits in the museum?

(A) There are fewer than 100 portraits.

(B) There are 100 portraits.

(C) There are more than 100 portraits.

(D) Not given

26. The combination of which portrait types make up half of the entire collection?

(J) Oils

(K) Water Colors and Oil on Canvas

(L) Charcoal and Pastels

(M) Pastels and Water Colors

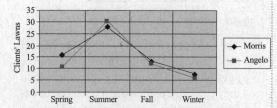

27. The chart above shows the amount of yards serviced by Morris and Angelo, each of whom runs a small lawn-care business. Based on the information in the chart, what is the busiest season for lawn care?

(A) Spring

(B) Summer

(C) Fall

(D) Winter

28. Based on the information in the chart, which of the following statements is true?

(J) Morris experienced a bigger decline in business from the summer to the winter than did Angelo.

(K) Angelo experienced a bigger decline in business from the summer to the winter than did Morris.

(L) Angelo and Morris experienced the same decline in business from the summer to the winter.

(M) Neither Morris nor Angelo experienced a decline in business from the summer to the winter.

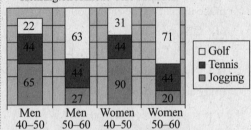

Kensington Athletic Club Members

30. Based on the information in the chart, which sport currently has the most total members participating in it?

(J) Golf

(K) Tennis

(L) Jogging

(M) Not enough information available

29. The chart above illustrates the members of the Kensington Athletic Club between the ages of 40 and 60 and the sports in which they currently participate. Based on the information in the chart, which sport becomes the most popular as both men and women grow older?

(A) Golf

(B) Tennis

(C) Jogging

(D) Not enough information available

STOP If you finish before time is up, check over your work on this part only. Do not go on until the signal is given.

Part 2

10 MINUTES

Directions: For the following questions, <u>estimate</u> the answer in your head. No scratch work is allowed. Do NOT try to compute exact answers.

31. The closest estimate of 46,922 + 32,090 is _____.

    (A) 70,000
    (B) 75,000
    (C) 80,000
    (D) 85,000

32. The closest estimate of 7988 ÷ 397 is _____.

    (J) 20
    (K) 25
    (L) 200
    (M) 220

33. On a trip to his grandmother's house, Skippy averaged 15 miles per hour on his bicycle. If his grandmother's house is 78 miles away, about how long did it take Skippy to get to his grandmother's house?

    (A) $3\frac{1}{2}$ hours
    (B) 5 hours
    (C) 6 hours
    (D) $13\frac{1}{2}$ hours

34. Coach Hollingsworth has a total of 653 wins in her career, and she has coached for 40 years. About how many wins has she averaged per year?

    (J) 13
    (K) 16
    (L) 19
    (M) 24

35. The closest estimate of 148 + 153.5 + 146 + 154.1 + 151 + 145.9 + 149 + 153 + 152.5 + 147.75 is _____.

    (A) 1375
    (B) 1400
    (C) 1500
    (D) 1575

36. A typical plain bagel has about 250 calories, and a typical glass of orange juice has about 160 calories. A jelly donut with chocolate icing and sprinkles has about 740 calories, and a large soda has about 255 calories. About how many bagel–juice combos would it take to equal the amount of calories in the jelly donut and a large soda?

    (J) $1\frac{1}{2}$
    (K) 2
    (L) $2\frac{1}{2}$
    (M) 3

37. The closest estimate of $(4.9 \times 10.9) + 44.9$ is _____.

    (A) 534
    (B) 44.9^2
    (C) 900
    (D) 100

38. George earns $10 per week. How many weeks will it take him to earn about $255?

    (J) 25
    (K) 52
    (L) 144
    (M) Not given

39. The closest estimate of 7.1×7.9 is _____.

(A) 49

(B) 56

(C) 63

(D) 70

40. The closest estimate of $221.8 \div 9.989$ is _____.

(J) 22

(K) 20

(L) 12

(M) 11

STOP   If you finish before time is up, check over your work on this part only. Do not go on until the signal is given.

ABILITY

5 MINUTES

Directions: In questions 1–2, the first three figures are alike in certain ways. Choose the answer choice that corresponds to the first three figures.

1.
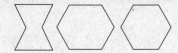

 (A)   (B)   (C)   (D)   (E)

2.

 (J)   (K)   (L)   (M)   (N)

Directions: In questions 3–7, the first figure is related to the second figure. Determine that relationship. The third figure is changed in the same way to make one of the answer choices. Choose the answer choice that relates to the third figure.

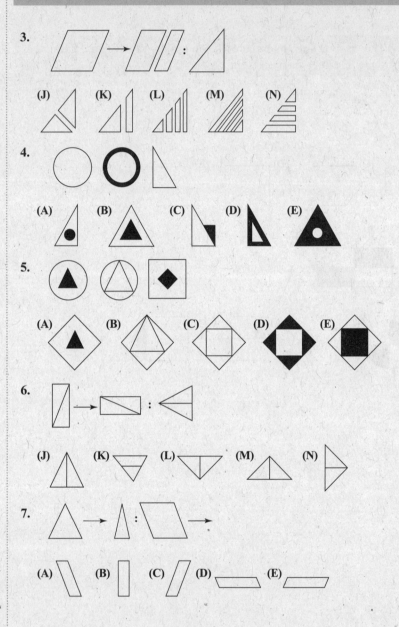

Directions: In questions 8–10, look at the top row to see how a square piece of paper is folded and where holes are punched in it. Then look at the bottom row to decide which answer choice shows how the paper will look when it is completely unfolded.

8.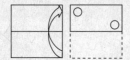

(J)   (K)   (L)   (M)   (N)

9.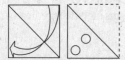

(A)   (B)   (C)   (D)   (E)

10.

(J)   (K)   (L)   (M)   (N)

STOP   If you finish before time is up, check over your work on this section only. Do not go back to any previous parts.

ANSWER KEYS AND EXPLANATIONS

Reading

PART 1

1. A	3. A	5. C	7. D	9. C
2. L	4. J	6. K	8. K	10. L

1. **The correct answer is (A),** *expected*. Other synonyms include "hoped for" and "awaited."

2. **The correct answer is (L),** *rotting*. Other synonyms include "decomposing" and "disintegrating."

3. **The correct answer is (A),** *replacement*. Other synonyms include "substitute" and "stand-in."

4. **The correct answer is (J),** *calculate approximately*. Other synonyms include "approximate" and "reckon."

5. **The correct answer is (C),** *tired*. Other synonyms include "fatigued" and "exhausted."

6. **The correct answer is (K),** *bold and bright*. Other synonyms include "vivid" and "dazzling."

7. **The correct answer is (D),** *problem*. Other synonyms include "predicament" and "quandary."

8. **The correct answer is (K),** *carelessly*. Other synonyms include "thoughtlessly" and "wildly."

9. **The correct answer is (C),** *long-winded and wordy*. Other synonyms include "verbose" and "garrulous."

10. **The correct answer is (L),** *huge*. Other synonyms include "gigantic," "immense," and "monstrous."

PART 2

11. B	13. D	15. D	17. C	19. C
12. L	14. K	16. M	18. M	20. K

11. **The correct answer is (B).** The last sentence of the first paragraph gives the context clue when it mentions "the country life."

12. **The correct answer is (L).** The country life wasn't what he hoped for, and he was ready to move back to the city. Charlie made a hurried and rash decision to move from the city to the country. Therefore, it was characteristic of Charlie to call his Realtor quickly and make another rushed decision, the decision that he didn't like life in the country.

13. **The correct answer is (D).** Citizens probably would elect people who had not been the power-holding nobles prior to elections, thus leaving the nobles with little or no power. The nobles were people whose power didn't depend on the favor of those they controlled and exploited. The nobles knew that common citizens would most likely elect candidates with whom they had something in common.

14. **The correct answer is (K).** The reference to thrones in the first sentence of the second paragraph is the context clue that

"monarchs" is synonymous with "kings and queens."

15. **The correct answer is (D).** Lefty was not good enough to start the game and probably played only as a reserve player. The passage points out that Lefty wasn't a standout player, so it is reasonable that the weakest players are the last to play on a professional team.

16. **The correct answer is (M).** Lefty made a personal connection with Mitchell and the fans that other players didn't make. Lefty was outgoing and friendly toward Mitchell and that allowed Mitchell to connect to and identify with Lefty. It was Lefty's personality, not his physical ability, that made him likable to Mitchell.

17. **The correct answer is (C).** She feared that she wouldn't use the equipment enough to justify the price. Margie had a feeling that after a while, she would stop using the equipment for exercise. The line about the expensive clothes rack is a metaphor for exercise equipment that is not used for exercising.

18. **The correct answer is (M).** The use of the word "however" at the beginning of the sentence indicates a shift in thought. In other words, using "however" at the beginning of a sentence means that the information in the second sentence is contrary to that in the first sentence. Margie initially considered the new workout facility in the sentence before, so a sentence beginning with "however" would mean that she wasn't considering it or was deciding against the workout facility.

19. **The correct answer is (C).** The entire first paragraph describes the grueling and demanding schedule of the counselors. It is reasonable to expect people to be tired after a schedule like the one described in the first paragraph.

20. **The correct answer is (K).** She wanted to help them be relaxed and refreshed by giving them a day off. The director was using "proverbial lotion" as a metaphor for something that would relax and refresh, i.e., a day off. A metaphor is symbolic and representative and, therefore, shouldn't be interpreted literally.

Language

PART 1

1. B	5. D	9. C	13. B	17. B
2. L	6. J	10. M	14. K	18. J
3. D	7. B	11. A	15. A	19. B
4. M	8. N	12. M	16. J	20. K

1. **The correct answer is (B).** The correct spelling is calculator.

2. **The correct answer is (L).** The correct spelling is either sense or since.

3. **The correct answer is (D).** The correct spelling is label.

4. **The correct answer is (M).** The correct spelling is knowledge.

5. **The correct answer is (D).** The correct spelling is conquer.

6. **The correct answer is (J).** The correct spelling is forfeit.

7. **The correct answer is (B).** The correct spelling is reliable.

8. **The correct answer is (N).** *(No mistakes)*

9. **The correct answer is (C).** The correct spelling is governor.

answers practice test 2

10. The correct answer is (M). The correct spelling is deceive.

11. The correct answer is (A). The name "Rover" should be capitalized because a name is a proper noun.

12. The correct answer is (M). *(No mistakes)*

13. The correct answer is (B). The Dallas Cowboys are a professional team and, as with names of other professional organizations including teams, should be capitalized because it is a proper noun.

14. The correct answer is (K). In this sentence, "home" simply means a house and is not part of a title. Therefore, "home" is a common noun and needs no capitalization.

15. The correct answer is (A). Holidays are proper nouns and should be capitalized.

16. The correct answer is (J). As used in this sentence, "basketball coach" is a common noun. If "coach" were included in a title like "Coach Van Gundy" or "Coach Parcells," then it would be capitalized.

17. The correct answer is (B). The words "prince," "princess," "king," and the like are common nouns unless included in someone's title. Therefore, a proper noun such as "Prince William" would be capitalized.

18. The correct answer is (J). Even though these initials are abbreviated, they are to be capitalized because they are a person's name, a proper noun.

19. The correct answer is (B). The abbreviation "Inc." is short for "Incorporated," which is part of the official name of a business organization and must be capitalized because it is a proper noun.

20. The correct answer is (K). The word "state" is a common noun; the names of states, Texas or New York, for example, are proper nouns and should be capitalized.

PART 2

21. B	23. D	25. B	27. C	29. A
22. J	24. L	26. J	28. J	30. M

21. The correct answer is (B). The word "college" is only capitalized when included in a proper noun, such as Austin College or Mississippi College.

22. The correct answer is (J). A list of cities by itself would be a sentence fragment as would a sentence beginning with a verb and having no subject.

23. The correct answer is (D). *(No change)*

24. The correct answer is (L). A phrase such as "without the taste buds of these loyal employees" should be set apart from the rest of the sentence by a comma.

25. The correct answer is (B). Meaning "also," the word "too" is often mistakenly replaced by the homonym "two."

26. The correct answer is (J). These subjects are common nouns and would only need capitalization if they were included in a proper noun, such as the name of a college course like "The History of Science and Math in Western Civilization."

27. The correct answer is (C). The passage is written in present tense and the verb "watch" must be in agreement with the rest of the passage, hence the use of the word "watches."

28. The correct answer is (J). The word "then" indicates sequence of events. Many people mistakenly use the word "than" in its place.

29. The correct answer is (A). The names of the four seasons are common nouns and do not need capitalization unless they are included in a title like "the Winter Olympics."

30. The correct answer is (M). *(No change)*

Math

PART 1

1. C	7. B	13. B	19. B	25. C
2. M	8. K	14. L	20. L	26. J
3. D	9. C	15. C	21. B	27. B
4. L	10. M	16. M	22. J	28. K
5. A	11. C	17. C	23. C	29. A
6. J	12. M	18. K	24. M	30. L

1. **The correct answer is (C).** 29 is divisible only by 1 and 29.

2. **The correct answer is (M).** $\frac{8}{4}$ can be reduced to $\frac{2}{1}$, or 2.

3. **The correct answer is (D).** The term "product" is a clue to multiply.

4. **The correct answer is (L).** $6 \times 6 \times 6 \times 6 \times 6 \times 6 \times 6$; 6^7 means that 6 is multiplied by itself 7 times.

5. **The correct answer is (A).** The number 2.006 is the same as $2\frac{6}{1000}$.

6. **The correct answer is (J).** $\frac{7}{8} - \frac{1}{2}$ is the same as $\frac{7}{8} - \frac{4}{8}$, which equals $\frac{3}{8}$.

7. **The correct answer is (B).** $(6 - 1 = 5) + (1 \times 5 = 5) + (10 \div 2 = 5) + (2.5 + 2.5 = 5) = 20$

8. **The correct answer is (K).** No whole number multiplied by 4 equals 34.

9. **The correct answer is (C).** Subtracting a negative is the same as adding a positive.

10. **The correct answer is (M).** 72 is the lowest number of which 6, 12, and 72 are all factors.

11. **The correct answer is (C).** If the Pizza Parlor's 72 toppings are 50% more, then they are 150% of Patty's Pizzas' toppings. So, if Patty's Pizzas' toppings = x:

$$150\% \text{ of } x = 72$$
$$1.50x = 72$$
$$x = \frac{72}{1.5}$$
$$x = 48$$

12. **The correct answer is (M).** $32 - 27 = 5$, $24 - 19 = 5$, and $23 - 21 = 2$. $5 + 5 + 2 = 12$ comics that Carl needs to buy. 12 is not an answer choice.

13. **The correct answer is (B).** $12 \times 245 = 2940$ books on the 100 percent full book shelves. $\frac{4}{5}$ of 245 is the same as 80% of 245, or 0.8×245, which equals 196. $2940 + 196 = 3136$.

14. **The correct answer is (L).** 100 normal images is the same as $\frac{1}{2}$, or 50 percent, of the 200 high-quality images. If $\frac{1}{2}$ of the memory is already used, then only $\frac{1}{2}$ the camera's memory is still available. $\frac{1}{2}$ of 40 high-quality images the camera normally would hold is 20.

15. **The correct answer is (C).** $4 \times 3\frac{1}{4} = 13$ hours each week.

16. **The correct answer is (M).** 60 meals in the first month plus $33\frac{1}{3}$ percent more meals in the second month $(60 + 20 = 80)$ equals 140 meals. In third month, they delivered 2×140, or 280 meals.

17. **The correct answer is (C).** $\$7.50 \times 40 = \$300$. $\$1350 \div \$300 = 4.5$, or $4\frac{1}{2}$.

18. **The correct answer is (K).** There are $4 \times (10 \times 15 = 150)$ square feet of wall space, or 600 square feet. $600 \div 75 = 8$ rolls.

19. **The correct answer is (B).** $6776 + 6892 + 6990 + 7010 + 7012 = 34,680$. $34,680 \div 5 = 6936$.

20. **The correct answer is (L).** 1,900 devices $\times 12 = 22,800$ devices per year. $400,000 + 22,800 = 422,800$.

21. **The correct answer is (B).** Forty-one percent of the donuts consumed are glazed.

22. **The correct answer is (J).** Twenty-five percent of a dozen, or 12, equals 3.

23. **The correct answer is (C).** Because Rutledge sent more students to Washington High than the other two schools, it represents the largest percentage.

24. **The correct answer is (M).** $211 + 178 + 346 = 735$.

25. **The correct answer is (C).** There are more than 100 portraits. By adding the values, not the percentages, of each section it can be determined that there are 118 portraits.

26. **The correct answer is (J).** Oil on Wood and Oil on Canvas comprise 59 of 118 portraits, or 50 percent of the portraits.

27. **The correct answer is (B).** Morris had 28 lawns in the summer and Angelo had 30 lawns in the summer.

28. **The correct answer is (K).** Angelo experienced a bigger decline in business from the summer to the winter than Morris did; Angelo's business went from 30 lawns in the summer to 6 lawns in the winter, whereas Morris' business went from 28 to 7 in that period.

29. **The correct answer is (A).** The number of members who play golf in the older-age category is much more than the number of members who play golf in the younger-age category.

30. **The correct answer is (L).** A total of 202 members currently participate in jogging, whereas 187 members participate in golf and 176 members participate in tennis.

PART 2

31. C	33. B	35. C	37. D	39. B
32. J	34. K	36. L	38. J	40. J

31. **The correct answer is (C).** $46,922 + 32,090$ is approximately $47,000 + 32,000$, which equals 79,000. 79,000 is approximately 80,000.

32. **The correct answer is (J).** $7988 \div 397$ is approximately $8000 \div 400 = 20$.

33. **The correct answer is (B).** $78 \div 15 = 5.2$, which is approximately 5.

34. **The correct answer is (K).** $40 \times 16 = 640$, which is an approximation of 653.

35. **The correct answer is (C).** $148 + 153.5 + 146 + 154.1 + 151 + 145.9 + 149 + 153 + 152.5 + 147.75$ is approximately 150 added 10 times.

36. **The correct answer is (L).** It would take $2\frac{1}{2}$ combos of about 400 calories to equal the approximately 1,000 calories of the donut-soda combo.

37. The correct answer is (D). 4.9 × 10.9 is approximately 5 × 11, or 55. 55 + approximately 45 is 100.

38. The correct answer is (J). $10 per week is about $500 per year, so it would take about 25 weeks to earn $255.

39. The correct answer is (B). 7.1 × 7.9 is approximately 7 × 8, which is 56.

40. The correct answer is (J). 221.8 ÷ 9.989 is approximately 222 ÷ 10. 222 ÷ 10 is 22.2, or about 22.

Ability

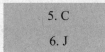

| 1. C | 3. K | 5. C | 7. A | 9. C |
| 2. K | 4. D | 6. J | 8. K | 10. M |

1. **The correct answer is (C).** The first three figures each have six sides, as does choice (C).

2. **The correct answer is (K).** Each of the given figures has half its area shaded in black, as does choice (K).

3. **The correct answer is (K).** For the first pair, a segment parallel to one side is drawn in the interior, and then the figure is split into two parts.

4. **The correct answer is (D).** For the first pair, the second figure is one in which a smaller circle is drawn and the area between the two circles is shaded. Thus, the fourth figure would be a triangle inside the given triangle, and the area between them must be shaded. Choice (D) represents this description.

5. **The correct answer is (C).** For the first pair, the inside figure changes from black to white and the inside figure is enlarged so that its vertices touch the outside figure. Choice (C) shows the same changes, including the color change.

6. **The correct answer is (J).** For the first pair, the figure is simply rotated 90° clockwise.

Choice (J) also shows a 90° clockwise rotation, without any other changes.

7. **The correct answer is (A).** For the first pair, the figure undergoes a dilation, which means it is kept similar, but changes in size. (In this case, it gets smaller.)

8. **The correct answer is (K).** After the figure is folded over a horizontal line, a hole is punched in the upper left and lower right corners. When unfolded, there will be four holes. The additional two holes will be, respectively, the same distance from the horizontal line as the original two holes.

9. **The correct answer is (C).** After the figure is folded over a diagonal, two holes are punched along the other diagonal (not drawn). When unfolded, there are four holes, all places on the other diagonal.

10. **The correct answer is (M).** This figure is folded over twice before three holes are punched. After unfolding, there are (3)(2)(2) = 12 holes positioned in the northern, eastern, southern, and western parts of the square, as shown by choice (M).

ANSWER SHEET PRACTICE TEST 3: COOP

Section 1. Sequences

1. Ⓐ Ⓑ Ⓒ Ⓓ	5. Ⓐ Ⓑ Ⓒ Ⓓ	9. Ⓐ Ⓑ Ⓒ Ⓓ	13. Ⓐ Ⓑ Ⓒ Ⓓ	17. Ⓐ Ⓑ Ⓒ Ⓓ
2. Ⓕ Ⓖ Ⓗ Ⓙ	6. Ⓕ Ⓖ Ⓗ Ⓙ	10. Ⓕ Ⓖ Ⓗ Ⓙ	14. Ⓕ Ⓖ Ⓗ Ⓙ	18. Ⓕ Ⓖ Ⓗ Ⓙ
3. Ⓐ Ⓑ Ⓒ Ⓓ	7. Ⓐ Ⓑ Ⓒ Ⓓ	11. Ⓐ Ⓑ Ⓒ Ⓓ	15. Ⓐ Ⓑ Ⓒ Ⓓ	19. Ⓐ Ⓑ Ⓒ Ⓓ
4. Ⓕ Ⓖ Ⓗ Ⓙ	8. Ⓕ Ⓖ Ⓗ Ⓙ	12. Ⓕ Ⓖ Ⓗ Ⓙ	16. Ⓕ Ⓖ Ⓗ Ⓙ	20. Ⓕ Ⓖ Ⓗ Ⓙ

Section 2. Analogies

1. Ⓐ Ⓑ Ⓒ Ⓓ	5. Ⓐ Ⓑ Ⓒ Ⓓ	9. Ⓐ Ⓑ Ⓒ Ⓓ	13. Ⓐ Ⓑ Ⓒ Ⓓ	17. Ⓐ Ⓑ Ⓒ Ⓓ
2. Ⓕ Ⓖ Ⓗ Ⓙ	6. Ⓕ Ⓖ Ⓗ Ⓙ	10. Ⓕ Ⓖ Ⓗ Ⓙ	14. Ⓕ Ⓖ Ⓗ Ⓙ	18. Ⓕ Ⓖ Ⓗ Ⓙ
3. Ⓐ Ⓑ Ⓒ Ⓓ	7. Ⓐ Ⓑ Ⓒ Ⓓ	11. Ⓐ Ⓑ Ⓒ Ⓓ	15. Ⓐ Ⓑ Ⓒ Ⓓ	19. Ⓐ Ⓑ Ⓒ Ⓓ
4. Ⓕ Ⓖ Ⓗ Ⓙ	8. Ⓕ Ⓖ Ⓗ Ⓙ	12. Ⓕ Ⓖ Ⓗ Ⓙ	16. Ⓕ Ⓖ Ⓗ Ⓙ	20. Ⓕ Ⓖ Ⓗ Ⓙ

Section 3. Quantitative Reasoning

1. Ⓐ Ⓑ Ⓒ Ⓓ	5. Ⓐ Ⓑ Ⓒ Ⓓ	9. Ⓐ Ⓑ Ⓒ Ⓓ	13. Ⓐ Ⓑ Ⓒ Ⓓ	17. Ⓐ Ⓑ Ⓒ Ⓓ
2. Ⓕ Ⓖ Ⓗ Ⓙ	6. Ⓕ Ⓖ Ⓗ Ⓙ	10. Ⓕ Ⓖ Ⓗ Ⓙ	14. Ⓕ Ⓖ Ⓗ Ⓙ	18. Ⓕ Ⓖ Ⓗ Ⓙ
3. Ⓐ Ⓑ Ⓒ Ⓓ	7. Ⓐ Ⓑ Ⓒ Ⓓ	11. Ⓐ Ⓑ Ⓒ Ⓓ	15. Ⓐ Ⓑ Ⓒ Ⓓ	19. Ⓐ Ⓑ Ⓒ Ⓓ
4. Ⓕ Ⓖ Ⓗ Ⓙ	8. Ⓕ Ⓖ Ⓗ Ⓙ	12. Ⓕ Ⓖ Ⓗ Ⓙ	16. Ⓕ Ⓖ Ⓗ Ⓙ	20. Ⓕ Ⓖ Ⓗ Ⓙ

Section 4. Verbal Reasoning—Words

1. Ⓐ Ⓑ Ⓒ Ⓓ	4. Ⓐ Ⓑ Ⓒ Ⓓ	7. Ⓐ Ⓑ Ⓒ Ⓓ	9. Ⓐ Ⓑ Ⓒ Ⓓ	11. Ⓐ Ⓑ Ⓒ Ⓓ
2. Ⓕ Ⓖ Ⓗ Ⓙ	5. Ⓕ Ⓖ Ⓗ Ⓙ	8. Ⓕ Ⓖ Ⓗ Ⓙ	10. Ⓕ Ⓖ Ⓗ Ⓙ	12. Ⓕ Ⓖ Ⓗ Ⓙ
3. Ⓐ Ⓑ Ⓒ Ⓓ	6. Ⓐ Ⓑ Ⓒ Ⓓ			

Section 5. Verbal Reasoning—Context

1. Ⓐ Ⓑ Ⓒ Ⓓ	5. Ⓐ Ⓑ Ⓒ Ⓓ	9. Ⓐ Ⓑ Ⓒ Ⓓ	13. Ⓐ Ⓑ Ⓒ Ⓓ	17. Ⓐ Ⓑ Ⓒ Ⓓ
2. Ⓕ Ⓖ Ⓗ Ⓙ	6. Ⓕ Ⓖ Ⓗ Ⓙ	10. Ⓕ Ⓖ Ⓗ Ⓙ	14. Ⓕ Ⓖ Ⓗ Ⓙ	18. Ⓕ Ⓖ Ⓗ Ⓙ
3. Ⓐ Ⓑ Ⓒ Ⓓ	7. Ⓐ Ⓑ Ⓒ Ⓓ	11. Ⓐ Ⓑ Ⓒ Ⓓ	15. Ⓐ Ⓑ Ⓒ Ⓓ	19. Ⓐ Ⓑ Ⓒ Ⓓ
4. Ⓕ Ⓖ Ⓗ Ⓙ	8. Ⓕ Ⓖ Ⓗ Ⓙ	12. Ⓕ Ⓖ Ⓗ Ⓙ	16. Ⓕ Ⓖ Ⓗ Ⓙ	20. Ⓕ Ⓖ Ⓗ Ⓙ

answer sheet

Section 6. Reading and Language Arts

1. Ⓐ Ⓑ Ⓒ Ⓓ	11. Ⓐ Ⓑ Ⓒ Ⓓ	21. Ⓐ Ⓑ Ⓒ Ⓓ	31. Ⓐ Ⓑ Ⓒ Ⓓ	41. Ⓐ Ⓑ Ⓒ Ⓓ
2. Ⓕ Ⓖ Ⓗ Ⓙ	12. Ⓕ Ⓖ Ⓗ Ⓙ	22. Ⓕ Ⓖ Ⓗ Ⓙ	32. Ⓕ Ⓖ Ⓗ Ⓙ	42. Ⓕ Ⓖ Ⓗ Ⓙ
3. Ⓐ Ⓑ Ⓒ Ⓓ	13. Ⓐ Ⓑ Ⓒ Ⓓ	23. Ⓐ Ⓑ Ⓒ Ⓓ	33. Ⓐ Ⓑ Ⓒ Ⓓ	43. Ⓐ Ⓑ Ⓒ Ⓓ
4. Ⓕ Ⓖ Ⓗ Ⓙ	14. Ⓕ Ⓖ Ⓗ Ⓙ	24. Ⓕ Ⓖ Ⓗ Ⓙ	34. Ⓕ Ⓖ Ⓗ Ⓙ	44. Ⓕ Ⓖ Ⓗ Ⓙ
5. Ⓐ Ⓑ Ⓒ Ⓓ	15. Ⓐ Ⓑ Ⓒ Ⓓ	25. Ⓐ Ⓑ Ⓒ Ⓓ	35. Ⓐ Ⓑ Ⓒ Ⓓ	45. Ⓐ Ⓑ Ⓒ Ⓓ
6. Ⓕ Ⓖ Ⓗ Ⓙ	16. Ⓕ Ⓖ Ⓗ Ⓙ	26. Ⓕ Ⓖ Ⓗ Ⓙ	36. Ⓕ Ⓖ Ⓗ Ⓙ	46. Ⓕ Ⓖ Ⓗ Ⓙ
7. Ⓐ Ⓑ Ⓒ Ⓓ	17. Ⓐ Ⓑ Ⓒ Ⓓ	27. Ⓐ Ⓑ Ⓒ Ⓓ	37. Ⓐ Ⓑ Ⓒ Ⓓ	47. Ⓐ Ⓑ Ⓒ Ⓓ
8. Ⓕ Ⓖ Ⓗ Ⓙ	18. Ⓕ Ⓖ Ⓗ Ⓙ	28. Ⓕ Ⓖ Ⓗ Ⓙ	38. Ⓕ Ⓖ Ⓗ Ⓙ	48. Ⓕ Ⓖ Ⓗ Ⓙ
9. Ⓐ Ⓑ Ⓒ Ⓓ	19. Ⓐ Ⓑ Ⓒ Ⓓ	29. Ⓐ Ⓑ Ⓒ Ⓓ	39. Ⓐ Ⓑ Ⓒ Ⓓ	49. Ⓐ Ⓑ Ⓒ Ⓓ
10. Ⓕ Ⓖ Ⓗ Ⓙ	20. Ⓕ Ⓖ Ⓗ Ⓙ	30. Ⓕ Ⓖ Ⓗ Ⓙ	40. Ⓕ Ⓖ Ⓗ Ⓙ	50. Ⓕ Ⓖ Ⓗ Ⓙ

Section 7. Mathematics

1. Ⓐ Ⓑ Ⓒ Ⓓ	9. Ⓐ Ⓑ Ⓒ Ⓓ	17. Ⓐ Ⓑ Ⓒ Ⓓ	25. Ⓐ Ⓑ Ⓒ Ⓓ	33. Ⓐ Ⓑ Ⓒ Ⓓ
2. Ⓕ Ⓖ Ⓗ Ⓙ	10. Ⓕ Ⓖ Ⓗ Ⓙ	18. Ⓕ Ⓖ Ⓗ Ⓙ	26. Ⓕ Ⓖ Ⓗ Ⓙ	34. Ⓕ Ⓖ Ⓗ Ⓙ
3. Ⓐ Ⓑ Ⓒ Ⓓ	11. Ⓐ Ⓑ Ⓒ Ⓓ	19. Ⓐ Ⓑ Ⓒ Ⓓ	27. Ⓐ Ⓑ Ⓒ Ⓓ	35. Ⓐ Ⓑ Ⓒ Ⓓ
4. Ⓕ Ⓖ Ⓗ Ⓙ	12. Ⓕ Ⓖ Ⓗ Ⓙ	20. Ⓕ Ⓖ Ⓗ Ⓙ	28. Ⓕ Ⓖ Ⓗ Ⓙ	36. Ⓕ Ⓖ Ⓗ Ⓙ
5. Ⓐ Ⓑ Ⓒ Ⓓ	13. Ⓐ Ⓑ Ⓒ Ⓓ	21. Ⓐ Ⓑ Ⓒ Ⓓ	29. Ⓐ Ⓑ Ⓒ Ⓓ	37. Ⓐ Ⓑ Ⓒ Ⓓ
6. Ⓕ Ⓖ Ⓗ Ⓙ	14. Ⓕ Ⓖ Ⓗ Ⓙ	22. Ⓕ Ⓖ Ⓗ Ⓙ	30. Ⓕ Ⓖ Ⓗ Ⓙ	38. Ⓕ Ⓖ Ⓗ Ⓙ
7. Ⓐ Ⓑ Ⓒ Ⓓ	15. Ⓐ Ⓑ Ⓒ Ⓓ	23. Ⓐ Ⓑ Ⓒ Ⓓ	31. Ⓐ Ⓑ Ⓒ Ⓓ	39. Ⓐ Ⓑ Ⓒ Ⓓ
8. Ⓕ Ⓖ Ⓗ Ⓙ	16. Ⓕ Ⓖ Ⓗ Ⓙ	24. Ⓕ Ⓖ Ⓗ Ⓙ	32. Ⓕ Ⓖ Ⓗ Ⓙ	40. Ⓕ Ⓖ Ⓗ Ⓙ

Practice Test 3: COOP

SECTION 1. SEQUENCES

15 MINUTES

Directions: For questions 1–20, choose the part that would continue the pattern or sequence. Mark the letter of your answer on the answer sheet.

1. △ △ ○ | ○ △ △ | △ ○ ○ | ○ ○ ____

    (A) △ (B) ● (C) ○ (D) ▽

2. + ✳ + ✳ | ✳ + ✳ + | + + ✳ + | ✳ ✳ ____

    (F) ✳ + (G) ✳ ✳ (H) + + (J) + ✳

3. (figures) ____

    (A) (B) (C) (D)

4. S S S SS | S S SS SS | S SS SS SS | ____

    (F) S S SS SSS (G) SSS SS SS S (H) S S SS SS (J) S SS SS SSS

347

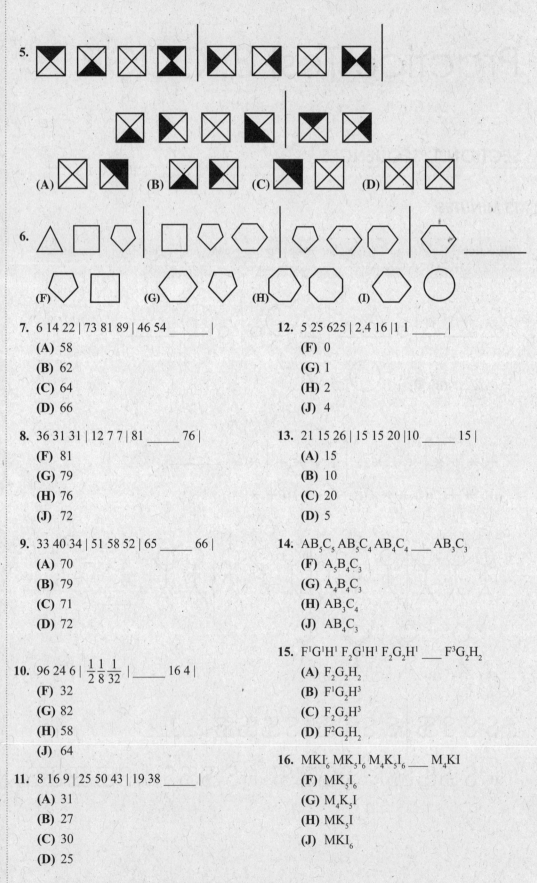

7. 6 14 22 | 73 81 89 | 46 54 _____ |
(A) 58
(B) 62
(C) 64
(D) 66

8. 36 31 31 | 12 7 7 | 81 _____ 76 |
(F) 81
(G) 79
(H) 76
(J) 72

9. 33 40 34 | 51 58 52 | 65 _____ 66 |
(A) 70
(B) 79
(C) 71
(D) 72

10. 96 24 6 | $\frac{1}{2}$ $\frac{1}{8}$ $\frac{1}{32}$ | _____ 16 4 |
(F) 32
(G) 82
(H) 58
(J) 64

11. 8 16 9 | 25 50 43 | 19 38 _____ |
(A) 31
(B) 27
(C) 30
(D) 25

12. 5 25 625 | 2,4 16 | 1 1 _____ |
(F) 0
(G) 1
(H) 2
(J) 4

13. 21 15 26 | 15 15 20 | 10 _____ 15 |
(A) 15
(B) 10
(C) 20
(D) 5

14. AB_5C_5 AB_5C_4 AB_4C_4 ___ AB_3C_3
(F) $A_5B_4C_3$
(G) $A_4B_4C_3$
(H) AB_3C_4
(J) AB_4C_3

15. $F^1G^1H^1$ $F_2G^1H^1$ $F_2G_2H^1$ ___ $F^3G_2H_2$
(A) $F_2G_2H_2$
(B) $F^1G_2H^3$
(C) $F_2G_2H^3$
(D) $F^2G_2H_2$

16. MKI_6 MK_5I_6 $M_4K_5I_6$ ___ M_4KI
(F) MK_5I_6
(G) M_4K_5I
(H) MK_5I
(J) MKI_6

17. BCD FGH JKL MNP _____
    (A) RST
    (B) QUR
    (C) QST
    (D) QRS

18. CADA EAFA GAHA _____ KALA
    (F) HAKA
    (G) AIAJ
    (H) MANA
    (J) IAJA

19. PTL TLP LPT PTL _____
    (A) LTP
    (B) TLP
    (C) LPT
    (D) TPL

20. ZYWV VUSR RQON _____ JIGF
    (F) ONLK
    (G) NMLJ
    (H) MLKJ
    (J) NMKJ

STOP If you finish before time is up, check over your work on Section 1 only. Do not go on until the signal is given.

practice test

SECTION 2. ANALOGIES

7 MINUTES

Directions: For questions 1–20, choose the picture that should go in the empty box so that the bottom two pictures are related in the same way that the top two are related.

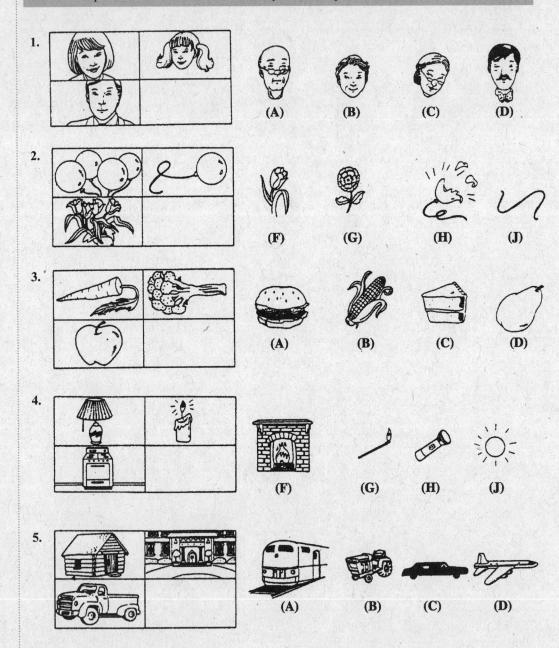

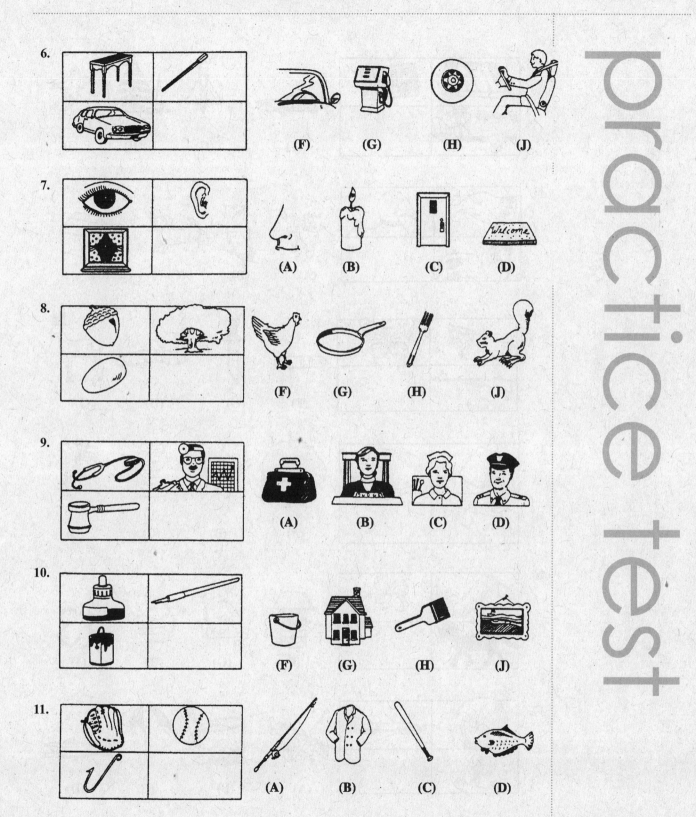

6.
(F)   (G)   (H)   (J)

7.
(A)   (B)   (C)   (D)

8.
(F)   (G)   (H)   (J)

9.
(A)   (B)   (C)   (D)

10.
(F)   (G)   (H)   (J)

11.
(A)   (B)   (C)   (D)

practice test

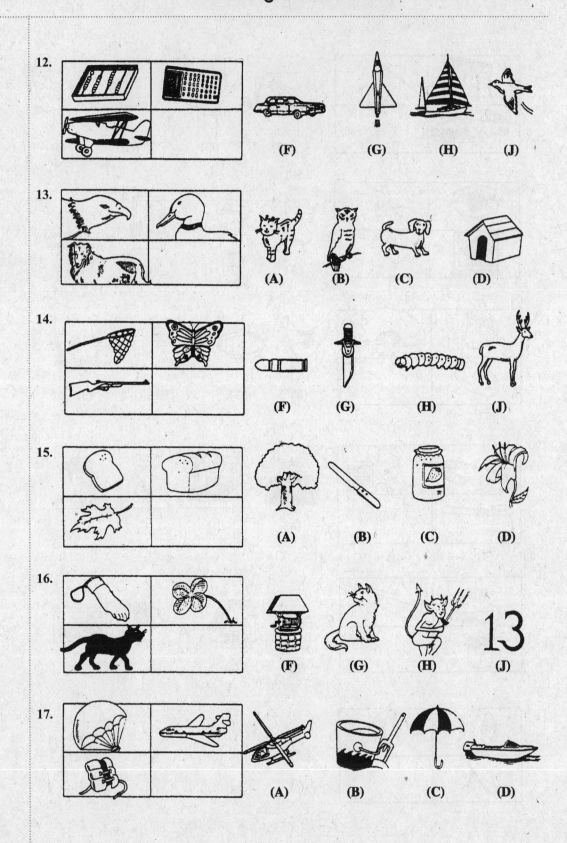

12.

(F)   (G)   (H)   (J)

13.

(A)   (B)   (C)   (D)

14.

(F)   (G)   (H)   (J)

15.

(A)   (B)   (C)   (D)

16.

(F)   (G)   (H)   (J)

17.

(A)   (B)   (C)   (D)

18.

   (F)   (G)   (H)   (J)

19.

   (A)   (B)   (C)   (D)

20.

   (F)   (G)   (H)   (J)

practice test

STOP If you finish before time is up, check over your work on Section 2 only. Do not go back to the previous section. Do not go on until the signal is given.

SECTION 3. QUANTITATIVE REASONING

5 MINUTES

Directions: For questions 1–7, find the relationship of the numbers in one column to the numbers in the other column. Then find the missing number.

1. $2 \rightarrow \square \rightarrow 6$
   $1 \rightarrow \square \rightarrow 3$
   $3 \rightarrow \square \rightarrow ?$

3	7	9	12
(A)	(B)	(C)	(D)

2. $4 \rightarrow \square \rightarrow 8$
   $5 \rightarrow \square \rightarrow 9$
   $7 \rightarrow \square \rightarrow ?$

10	11	12	13
(F)	(G)	(H)	(J)

3. $7 \rightarrow \square \rightarrow 4$
   $4 \rightarrow \square \rightarrow 1$
   $1 \rightarrow \square \rightarrow ?$

–2	0	2	7
(A)	(B)	(C)	(D)

4. $12 \rightarrow \square \rightarrow 3$
   $8 \rightarrow \square \rightarrow 2$
   $16 \rightarrow \square \rightarrow ?$

1	2	3	4
(F)	(G)	(H)	(J)

5. $10 \rightarrow \square \rightarrow 5$
   $8 \rightarrow \square \rightarrow 3$
   $6 \rightarrow \square \rightarrow ?$

1	2	3	4
(A)	(B)	(C)	(D)

6. $\frac{2}{3} \rightarrow \square \rightarrow 2$
   $2 \rightarrow \square \rightarrow 6$
   $3 \rightarrow \square \rightarrow ?$

2	3	9	12
(F)	(G)	(H)	(J)

7. $\frac{1}{2} \rightarrow \square \rightarrow 1$
   $\frac{3}{2} \rightarrow \square \rightarrow 2$
   $3 \rightarrow \square \rightarrow ?$

$\frac{3}{2}$	$\frac{5}{2}$	$\frac{7}{2}$	$\frac{9}{2}$
(A)	(B)	(C)	(D)

Directions: For questions 8–14, find the fraction of the grid that is shaded.

8.

$\frac{1}{2}$ $\frac{1}{3}$ $\frac{1}{4}$ $\frac{1}{8}$

(F)   (G)   (H)   (J)

9.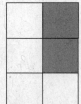

$\frac{1}{2}$ $\frac{1}{3}$ $\frac{1}{6}$ $\frac{1}{8}$

(A)   (B)   (C)   (D)

10.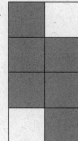

$\frac{1}{2}$ $\frac{3}{4}$ $\frac{2}{3}$ $\frac{1}{4}$

(F)   (G)   (H)   (J)

11.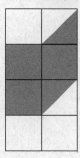

$\frac{1}{2}$ $\frac{1}{3}$ $\frac{1}{4}$ $\frac{1}{6}$

(A)   (B)   (C)   (D)

12.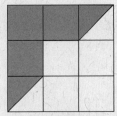

$\dfrac{5}{9}$ $\dfrac{4}{9}$ $\dfrac{2}{9}$ $\dfrac{1}{9}$

(F)   **(G)**   **(H)**   **(J)**

13.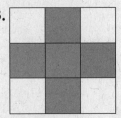

$\dfrac{5}{6}$ $\dfrac{4}{5}$ $\dfrac{3}{4}$ $\dfrac{5}{9}$

(A)   **(B)**   **(C)**   **(D)**

14.

$\dfrac{1}{2}$ $\dfrac{1}{4}$ $\dfrac{1}{8}$ $\dfrac{1}{16}$

(F)   **(G)**   **(H)**   **(J)**

Directions: For questions 15–20, look at the scale that shows sets of shapes of equal weight. Find an equivalent pair of sets that would also balance the scale.

15.

(A)
(B)
(C)
(D)

16.

(F)
(G)
(H)
(J)

17.

(A)
(B)
(C)
(D)

18.

(F)
(G)
(H)
(J)

practice test

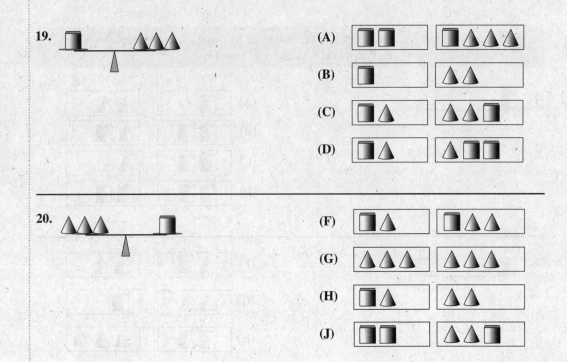

19.

(A)

(B)

(C)

(D)

20.

(F)

(G)

(H)

(J)

SECTION 4. VERBAL REASONING—WORDS

15 MINUTES

Directions: For questions 1–6, find the word that names a necessary part of the underlined word.

1. burning
   - (A) flame
   - (B) smoke
   - (C) ash
   - (D) heat

2. verbalize
   - (F) verb
   - (G) word
   - (H) hearing
   - (J) sound

3. legislation
   - (A) laws
   - (B) lawyers
   - (C) senate
   - (D) debate

4. terrarium
   - (F) darkness
   - (G) animals
   - (H) water
   - (J) earth

5. violin
   - (A) bow
   - (B) notes
   - (C) strings
   - (D) melody

6. chronometer
   - (F) watch
   - (G) standard
   - (H) time
   - (J) ticking

Directions: In questions 7–12, the words in the top row are related in some way. The words in the bottom row are related in the same way. For each item, find the word that completes the bottom row of words.

7. vest   jacket   coat
   sandal   shoe

   - (A) slipper
   - (B) boot
   - (C) ski
   - (D) moccasin

8. gold   mercury   iron
   water   air

   - (F) oxygen
   - (G) helium
   - (H) steel
   - (J) atmosphere

9. color   odor   sound
   feel   see

   - (A) hear
   - (B) soft
   - (C) sound
   - (D) tell

10. forsythia   tulip   crocus
    holly   poinsettia

    - (F) lilac
    - (G) mistletoe
    - (H) wreath
    - (J) tree

11. bird   dog   spider
     man   horse

   (A) crab
   (B) fly
   (C) eel
   (D) unicorn

12. baseball football basketball
     skiing   shotput

   (F) hockey
   (G) soccer
   (H) tennis
   (J) marathon

STOP   If you finish before time is up, check over your work on Section 4 only. Do not go back to the previous sections. Do not go on until the signal is given.

SECTION 5. VERBAL REASONING—CONTEXT

15 MINUTES

Directions: For questions 1–5, find the statement that is true according to the given information.

1. Jeffrey is a law student. On Monday evenings, he plays the violin in an orchestra. On Tuesdays and Thursdays, he goes square dancing. On Friday afternoon, Jeffrey fiddles for a children's folk dancing group.

   (A) Jeffrey plays the violin at least twice a week.

   (B) Jeffrey likes music better than the law.

   (C) Jeffrey dances three times a week.

   (D) Musicians are good dancers.

2. Debbie took the written Foreign Service Officer examination in December. Today, Debbie received an appointment date for her Oral Assessment. Debbie is very happy.

   (F) Debbie failed the written exam.

   (G) Debbie is now a Foreign Service officer.

   (H) Everyone who takes the Foreign Service Officer exam must take an oral exam as well.

   (J) Debbie is still under consideration for appointment as a Foreign Service officer.

3. Bill and Dan were exploring an abandoned house. The windows swung loose, the floorboards creaked, and dust and cobwebs filled the air. Suddenly, the two boys ran from the house.

   (A) The house was haunted.

   (B) Something frightened the boys.

   (C) There were bats flying about.

   (D) Someone told the boys to get out.

4. Mr. and Mrs. Chen drive a blue Chevrolet station wagon that they keep in their driveway. Their son Warren has a red Toyota that he puts in the garage each night.

   (F) Blue cars are less susceptible to ravages of weather than are red cars.

   (G) The Chens have a one-car garage.

   (H) Warren has a new car.

   (J) Warren's car is garaged regularly.

5. Mark was distracted by his dog while jumping on the trampoline; he slipped and broke his right arm. That same afternoon, the dog chased the cat up a tree. Another time Mark was walking his dog, the dog pulled Mark too fast; Mark fell and broke his right arm.

   (A) Mark's dog is dangerous and must be destroyed.

   (B) Mark should let his sister walk the dog.

   (C) Mark is left-handed.

   (D) Mark is accident-prone.

Directions: For questions 6–8, find the correct answer.

6. Here are some words translated from an artificial language.

chekiruala means eating
duangfrit means hidden
duangruala means eaten

Which word means *hiding*?

(F) chekifrit

(G) rualafrit

(H) chekiduang

(J) fritcheki

7. Here are some words translated from an artificial language.

jokiohakaflis means creek
luraohakaflis means river
jokiohakasloo means pond

Which word means *lake*?

(A) slooohakalura

(B) jokilurasloo

(C) ohakasloolura

(D) luraohakasloo

8. Here are some words translated from an artificial language.

frushuwamba means dissolve
uwambakuta means solution
hamauwamba means resolve

Which word means *resolution*?

(F) kutafrush

(G) hamauwambakuta

(H) uwambakutahama

(J) frushkutauwamba

Directions: For questions 9–20, find the statement that is true according to the given information.

9. Lexi's teacher tells her to write an essay of no more than 500 words on the French-Indian War. Lexi's essay is close to 1,000 words.

(A) Lexi is on the honor roll.

(B) Lexi really enjoys researching the French-Indian War.

(C) Lexi exceeds the word limit on her assignment.

(D) Lexi's teacher gives her a poor grade.

10. Bob used to live in Milwaukee, but he moved to Atlanta when he was 16. He lived in several other cities before settling in San Diego.

(F) Bob likes city life.

(G) Bob has moved more than three times.

(H) Bob likes the West coast better than the Midwest or Northeast.

(J) Bob enjoys living near the ocean.

11. Bud is taller than Chase but shorter than Rob. Pete is taller than Rob but shorter than Garrett.

(A) None of the boys are over six feet tall.

(B) Chase is five feet tall.

(C) Chase and Rob pick on Bud.

(D) Garrett is the tallest of the boys.

12. If Patsy does not catch the 7:30 a.m. bus, she will have to walk to school. Patsy arrives at the bus stop at 7:45 a.m.

(F) Unless her bus is late, Patsy must walk to school.

(G) Patsy's bus is running late.

(H) Patsy's bus has broken down.

(J) Patsy arrives to school late.

13. Amber runs a 5K race and finishes in under an hour. Brittany runs the same race in a little over an hour.

    (A) It is raining on race day.
    (B) Amber places ahead of Brittany in the race.
    (C) Brittany places ahead of several other racers.
    (D) Amber's parents are in the crowd.

14. Shelly works at the blood drive but does not donate blood herself. Her shift ends at noon, and Shelly plans to eat lunch then.

    (F) Shelly cannot donate blood.
    (G) Shelly is afraid of needles.
    (H) Shelly is too busy to donate blood.
    (J) Shelly will not work at the blood drive after lunch.

15. Melanie is assigned three books to read over spring break. She reads two books over the break.

    (A) Melanie is a slow reader.
    (B) Melanie fails to complete her assignment of reading all three books.
    (C) Melanie only likes science fiction books.
    (D) Melanie reads two hours a day.

16. Andrew and Chelsea are on their school's Quiz Bowl team, and they attend every Quiz Bowl meet. There is a Quiz Bowl meet Thursday night.

    (F) Andrew and Chelsea both take advanced placement classes.
    (G) Andrew and Chelsea study together before Quiz Bowl meets.
    (H) Andrew and Chelsea will be at a Quiz Bowl meet Thursday night.
    (J) Andrew and Chelsea are co-captains of the Quiz Bowl team.

17. Art and Lee agree to meet at the Burger Palace at 6 p.m. Art brings his little sister Arianna.

    (A) Art, Lee, and Arianna meet at the Burger Palace.
    (B) Lee is upset with Art for bringing an uninvited guest.
    (C) Lee orders for everyone.
    (D) Arianna enjoys having dinner with Lee.

18. My cat always knows when I have been around other cats, and she snubs me when she smells other cats on me. When I returned from my friend Lisa's house, my cat smelled Lisa's cat on me.

    (F) My cat does not like Lisa.
    (G) My cat is very young.
    (H) My cat dislikes strangers.
    (J) My cat snubbed me.

19. Hilary scores higher on the math test than Gina, but lower than Amanda.

    (A) Hilary studies more than the other girls.
    (B) Gina scores lowest on the math test.
    (C) Amanda and Hilary are the best math students in the class.
    (D) Amanda scores lower than Hilary and Gina.

20. Shelly put together a scrapbook for her grandparents' fiftieth anniversary party. Her grandparents do not know about the surprise party.

    (F) Shelly's grandparents hate surprise parties.
    (G) Shelly is an only grandchild.
    (H) Shelly's grandparents love scrapbooks.
    (J) Shelly's grandparents have been married for 50 years.

STOP If you finish before time is up, check over your work on Section 5 only. Do not go back to the previous section. Do not go on until the signal is given.

SECTION 6. READING AND LANGUAGE ARTS

40 MINUTES

QUESTIONS 1–4 REFER TO THE FOLLOWING PASSAGE.

Yesterday morning I saw for the first time an animal that is rarely encountered face to face. It was a wolverine. Though relatively small, rarely weighing more than 40 pounds, he is, above all animals, the one most hated by the Indians and trappers. He is a fine tree climber and a relentless destroyer. Deer, reindeer, and even moose succumb to his attacks. We sat on a rock and watched him come, a bobbing rascal in blackish-brown. Since the male wolverine occupies a very large hunting area and fights to the death any male that intrudes on his domain, wolverines are always scarce, and in order to avoid extinction need all the protection that man can give. As a trapper, Henry wanted me to shoot him, but I refused, for this is the most fascinating and little-known of all our wonderful predators. His hunchback gait was awkward and ungainly, lopsided yet tireless.

1. Wolverines are very scarce because
   (A) they suffer in the survival of the fittest.
   (B) they are afraid of all humankind.
   (C) the males kill each other.
   (D) trappers take their toll of them.

2. Henry is
   (F) the author.
   (G) the author's dog.
   (H) the author's companion.
   (J) a hunchback.

3. The author of this selection is most probably a(n)
   (A) conscious naturalist.
   (B) experienced hunter.
   (C) inexperienced trapper.
   (D) young Indian.

4. Why do you suppose that the wolverine is so hated by Indians and trappers?
   (F) The wolverine climbs trees better than man.
   (G) Hunchback wolverines are incredibly ugly.
   (H) Wolverines are scarce and demand man's protection.
   (J) Wolverines are successful in destroying the same game that the Indians and trappers seek.

QUESTIONS 5–7 REFER TO THE FOLLOWING PASSAGE.

The history of modern pollution problems shows that most have resulted from negligence and ignorance. We have an appalling tendency to interfere with nature before all of the possible consequences of our actions have been studied in depth. We produce and distribute radioactive substances, synthetic chemicals, and many other potent compounds before fully comprehending their effects on living organisms. Our education is dangerously incomplete.

It will be argued that the purpose of science is to move into unknown territory, to explore, and to discover. It can be said that similar risks have been taken before and that these risks are necessary to technological progress.

These arguments overlook an important element. In the past, risks taken in the name of scientific progress were restricted to a small place and a brief period of time. The effects of the processes we now strive to master are neither localized nor brief. Air pollution covers vast urban areas. Ocean pollutants have been discovered in nearly every part of the world. Synthetic chemicals spread over huge stretches of forest and farmland may remain in the soil for decades. Radioactive pollutants will be found in the biosphere for generations. The size and persistence of these problems have grown with the expanding power of modern science.

One might also argue that the hazards of modern pollutants are small compared to the dangers associated with other human activity. No estimate of the actual harm done by smog, fallout, or chemical residues can obscure the reality that the risks are being taken before being fully understood.

The importance of these issues lies in the failure of science to predict and control human intervention into natural processes. The true measure of the danger is represented by the hazards we will encounter we enter the new age of technology without first evaluating our responsibility to the environment.

5. According to the author, the major cause of pollution problems is
   (A) designing synthetic chemicals to kill living organisms.
   (B) a lack of understanding of the history of technology.
   (C) scientists who are too willing to move into unknown territory.
   (D) changing our environment before understanding the effects of these changes.

6. The author believes that the risks taken by modern science are greater than those taken by earlier scientific efforts because
   (F) the effects may be felt by more people for a longer period of time.
   (G) science is progressing faster than ever before.
   (H) technology has produced more dangerous chemicals.
   (J) the materials used are more dangerous to scientists.

7. The author apparently believes that the problem of finding solutions to pollution depends on
   (A) the removal of present hazards to the environment.
   (B) the removal of all potential pollutants from their present uses.
   (C) overcoming technical difficulties.
   (D) the willingness of scientists to understand possible dangers before using new products in the environment.

QUESTIONS 8–12 REFER TO THE FOLLOWING PASSAGE.

Ages ago, when that part of our Earth was cut off from the Asian mainland, this fantastic animal from nature's long-ago was also isolated. There are about two dozen species distributed through Australasia, southward to Tasmania and northward to New Guinea and neighboring islands. Some are no bigger than rabbits; some can climb trees. They are known by a variety of picturesque names: wallabies, wallaroos, potoroos, boongaries, and paddymelons. But the kangaroo—the one that is Australia's national symbol—is the great grey kangaroo of the plains, admiringly known throughout the island continent as the Old Man, and also as Boomer, Forester, and Man of the Woods. His smaller mate, in Australian talk, is called a flyer. Their baby is known as Joey.

A full-grown kangaroo stands taller than a man and commonly weighs 200 pounds. Even when he sits in his favorite position, reposing on his haunches and tilting back on the propping support of his "third leg"—his tail—his head is five feet or more above the ground. His huge hind legs, with steel-spring power, can send him sailing over a ten-foot fence with ease, or in a fight can beat off a dozen dogs. A twitch of his tail can break a man's leg like a matchstick.

Kangaroos provide an endless supply of tall tales to which wide-eyed visitors are treated in the land Down Under. The beauty of the tall tales about the kangaroos is that they can be almost as tall as you please and still be close to fact.

8. Choose the best topic sentence for this passage.
   (F) The kangaroo is found nowhere in the world but in Australia.
   (G) Kangaroos are popular throughout the world.
   (H) "Joeys" are kangaroo babies.
   (J) Kangaroos don't make very good pets.

9. The amazing jumping power of the kangaroo is chiefly due to
   (A) the power of his hind legs.
   (B) the support of his tail.
   (C) his size.
   (D) his weight.

10. Australasia is
   (F) another name for Australia.
   (G) an area that includes Australia and part of the continent of Asia.
   (H) Australia and some surrounding islands to the north and south of it.
   (J) all of the land in the Southern Hemisphere.

11. Which statement is true according to the passage?
   (A) The name "Old Man" shows the people's dislike of kangaroos.
   (B) Visitors to Australia hear very little about kangaroos.
   (C) A kangaroo's tail is a powerful weapon.
   (D) The most widely known species of kangaroo is no larger than a rabbit.

12. The author believes that the stories told about kangaroos are generally
   (F) harmful.
   (G) true.
   (H) suspicious.
   (J) beautiful.

QUESTIONS 13–17 REFER TO THE FOLLOWING PASSAGE.

For generations, historians and boat lovers have been trying to learn more about the brave ship that brought the Pilgrims to America. The task is a difficult one because *Mayflower* was such a common name for ships back in early seventeenth-century England that there were at least twenty of them when the Pilgrims left for the New World.

An exact duplicate of the *Mayflower* has been built in England and given to the people of the United States as a symbol of goodwill and common ancestry linking Britons and Americans. The Pilgrims' *Mayflower* apparently was built originally as a fishing vessel. It seems to have been 90 feet long by 22 feet wide, displacing 180 tons of water. The duplicate measures 90 feet by 26 feet, displaces 183 tons of water, and has a crew of 21, as did the original vessel. The new *Mayflower* has no motor but travels faster than the old boat.

What happened to the historic boat? So far as can be told, the *Mayflower* went back to less colorful jobs and, not too many years later, was scrapped. What happened to the beams, masts, and planking is questionable. In the English city of Abingdon, there is a Congregational church that contains two heavy wooden pillars. Some say these pillars are masts from the *Mayflower*. A barn in the English town of Jordans seemed to be built on old ship timbers. Marine experts said these timbers were impregnated with salt and, if put together, would form a vessel 90 feet by 22 feet. The man who owned the farm when the peculiar barn was built was a relative of the man who appraised the *Mayflower* when it was scrapped.

So the original *Mayflower* may still be doing service ashore while her duplicate sails the seas.

13. A long search was made for the Pilgrims' boat because it
    (A) contained valuable materials.
    (B) might still do sea service.
    (C) has historical importance.
    (D) would link Great Britain and America.

14. It has been difficult to discover what happened to the original *Mayflower* because
    (F) many ships bore the same name.
    (G) it was such a small vessel.
    (H) the search was begun too late.
    (J) it has become impregnated with salt.

15. The British recently had a duplicate of the *Mayflower* built because
    (A) the original could not be located.
    (B) they wanted to make a gesture of friendship.
    (C) parts of the original could be used.
    (D) historians recommended such a step.

16. Compared with the original Mayflower, the modern duplicate
    (F) is longer.
    (G) is identical.
    (H) carries a larger crew.
    (J) is somewhat wider.

17. Choose the sentence that is written correctly.
    (A) The original Mayflower may still be doing service ashore while her duplicate sails the seas.
    (B) The original Mayflower doing service ashore and her duplicate sails the seas.
    (C) The original Mayflower does service ashore while her duplicate sail the seas.
    (D) The original Mayflower may still does service ashore while her duplicate sailing the seas.

QUESTIONS 18–21 REFER TO THE FOLLOWING PASSAGE.

A third of our lives is spent in the mysterious state of sleep. Throughout his history, man has attempted to understand this remarkable experience. Many centuries ago, for example, sleep was regarded as a type of anemia of the brain. Alcmaeon, a Greek scientist, believed that blood retreated into the veins, and the partially starved brain went to sleep. Plato supported the idea that the soul left the body during sleep, wandered through the world, and woke up the body when it returned.

Recently, more scientific explanations of sleep have been proposed. According to one theory, the brain is put to sleep by a chemical agent that accumulates in the body when it is awake. Another theory is that weary branches of certain nerve cells break connections with neighboring cells. The flow of impulses required for staying awake is then disrupted. These more recent theories have to be subjected to laboratory research.

Why do we sleep? Why do we dream? Modern sleep research is said to have begun in the 1950s, when Eugene Aserinsky, a graduate student at the University of Chicago, and Nathaniel Kleitman, his professor, observed periods of rapid eye movements (REMs) in sleeping subjects. When awakened during these REM periods, subjects almost always remembered dreaming. On the other hand, when awakened during non-REM phases of sleep, the subjects rarely could recall their dreams.

Guided by REMs, it became possible for investigators to "spot" dreaming from outside and then awaken the sleeper to collect dream stories. They could also alter the dreamers' experiences with noises, drugs, or other stimuli before or during sleep.

Since the mid-1950s researchers have been drawn into sleep laboratories. There, bedrooms adjoin other rooms that contain recorders known as electroencephalograph (EEG) machines.

The EEG amplifies signals from sensors on the face, head, and other parts of the body, which together yield tracings of respiration, pulse, muscle tension, and changes of electrical potential in the brain that are sometimes called brain waves. These recordings supply clues to the changes of the sleeping person's activities.

18. Sleep has been the subject of awe for many centuries because

(F) it is a form of anemia.

(G) no one knows the destination of the wandering soul.

(H) it is mysterious and remarkable.

(J) dream interpretation is important.

19. According to this article,

(A) sleep is caused by REMs.

(B) we are awake for two thirds of our lives.

(C) modern sleep research began at the turn of the twentieth century.

(D) dreams are caused by REMs.

20. Electroencephalograph recordings made during sleep provide clues about

(F) broken nerve cells.

(G) the content of dreams.

(H) the meaning of dreams.

(J) physical changes during sleep.

21. All of the following were mentioned as possible causes of sleep except

(A) exhausted nerve endings.

(B) a buildup of certain body chemicals.

(C) recurrent periods of rapid eye movement.

(D) the absence of the conscious spirit.

QUESTIONS 22–25 REFER TO THE FOLLOWING PASSAGE.

What is a cord of wood? Some people say the cord is the most elastic unit of measure ever devised by the mind of man. A "standard" cord is a pile of stacked wood 4 × 4 × 8 feet; that's 128 cubic feet. How much of this is wood? That depends on what kind of wood, the size and straightness of the sticks, and who does the piling. Small crooked sticks, cut from hardwood limbs and piled by one of those cordwood artists who know how to make air spaces, may contain less than 30 cubic feet of solid wood per cord. Smooth, round wood such as birch or spruce, in sizes 8 inches and better, will average 100 cubic feet or more per cord. That's with the bark on. Peeled wood will make 10 to 12 percent more cubic volume in the same sized stack.

The heating value of wood varies enormously with the kind of tree. Black locust, white oak, hickory, black birch, and iron-wood are the best. A cord of any of these woods, when seasoned, is worth approximately a ton of coal. Beech, yellow birch, sugar maple, ash, and red oak are next. White birch, cherry, soft maple, sycamore, and elm are comparatively poor fuel woods, with basswood, butternut, poplar, and the softwoods at the bottom of the scale.

22. The title that best expresses the main idea of this selection is

(F) "Fuels."

(G) "The Value of a Cord of Wood."

(H) "Kinds of Trees."

(J) "Standard Measures."

23. A standard cord of wood
    (A) always contains 128 cubic feet of wood.
    (B) will average 100 cubic feet of smooth wood.
    (C) contains less than 30 cubic feet of solid wood.
    (D) is stacked wood in a pile 4 × 4 × 8 feet.

24. Removal of the bark from wood before stacking
    (F) increases the cubic volume of wood in a cord.
    (G) makes the stacking easier.
    (H) allows more air spaces in a cord of wood.
    (J) prevents seasoning of wood.

25. The cord is considered to be an elastic unit of measure because
    (A) if one jumps on a stack of wood, it is bouncy.
    (B) the amount of heat to be derived from a cord of wood varies with the kind of tree from which the wood comes.
    (C) the amount of wood in a cord varies with the wood itself and the method of stacking.
    (D) cord is string and can be stretched.

QUESTIONS 26–29 REFER TO THE FOLLOWING PASSAGE.

As recently as the 1840s, most people believed that the Earth, and humans with it, was created a mere 6,000 to 7,000 years ago. For centuries, beautifully worked flints were regarded as the work of elves, a notion once far more plausible than the idea that man roamed the world's wildernesses in small bands long before the days of Greece and Rome. Even when these stones were accepted as man-made tools, they were attributed to the Romans or early Britons.

Today we think in wider terms. The arliest dated works of man have been found on the floor of Olduvai Gorge, a miniature Grand Canyon in East Africa, and include carefully made stone tools about 2,000,000 years old. Furthermore, fossil evidence suggests that members of the family of man used tools millions of years before that.

Opposition to these ideas began to fade during the late eighteenth and early nineteenth centuries. Excavators, mainly enthusiastic amateurs, pointed to material associated with the tools—fossil remains of men and extinct animals: Most geologists still thought in biblical terms, maintaining that such associations were accidental, that the Flood had mixed the bones of ancient animals and the tools and remains of recent man. But their last-ditch defenses crumbled with the finding of bones and tools together in unflooded and undisturbed deposits, including a number of important sites on the banks of the Somme River. British investigators came to check the French deposits, were convinced, and announced their conclusions in 1859, the year that saw publication of Darwin's *On the Origin of Species*. This date marks the beginning of modern research into human evolution.

26. All of the following types of archeology-cal information were mentioned except
    (F) carbon dating.
    (G) fossils.
    (H) flints.
    (J) extinct animals.

27. According to the article, man has lived on Earth for
    (A) about 7,000 years.
    (B) between 7,000 and 100,000 years.
    (C) about 2,000,000 years.
    (D) far more than 2,000,000 years.

28. The scientific turning point in theories about the age of man's existence was the

- **(F)** publication of *On the Origin of Species*.
- **(G)** discovery in France of the remains of extinct animals and men together.
- **(H)** new theological research of the Bible.
- **(J)** new theories about the Flood and its effects on mankind.

29. In the early nineteenth century,

- **(A)** small bands of Romans roamed the Earth.
- **(B)** geologists dated man's existence back 2,000,000 years.
- **(C)** the stones were accepted as ancient tools.
- **(D)** most people believed that man's existence was 6,000 to 7,000 years old.

QUESTIONS 30–34 REFER TO THE FOLLOWING PASSAGE.

Eight of the city's twelve workers in Venetian glass recently finished one of the most unusual murals ever made for a New York skyscraper. It is an abstract, the creation of Hans Hofman, a 77-year-old German-born painter.

The mural covers 1,200 square feet of the outer wall of the elevator shaft in the William Kaufman Building at 711 Third Avenue. More than a half-million tiles in close to 500 shades of color have gone into it. Blue, red, and yellow are the chief colors. Each tile was made in Venice and is somewhat less than postage-stamp size. Each is beaten into a special everlasting concrete with a kind of flat wooden hand tool used for nothing else.

Mr. Hofman did the original color sketch about one-sixth the final size. This was photographed, and from the negative an enlargement was hand-colored by the artist, cut into sections, and sent in that form to the Vincent Foscato plant in Long Island City, which specializes in Venetian glass tile, or mosaic. There the Venetian specialists, whose trade has been handed down, father to son, through centuries, set each mosaic into place on the cartoon section, with painstaking fidelity to Mr. Hofman's color rendering. Although Mr. Foscato's plant keeps 1,400 shades of the glass mosaic, it had to have twelve additional shades specially made in Venice to match the sketch coloring for perfect blending. When all the sections had been filled and approved, they were carried by truck to the building lobby, the walls were covered with the special cement, and the workmen carefully beat each bit into place.

30. The best title for this selection would be

- **(F)** "Picture by German Artist to Hang in New York."
- **(G)** "New Mosaic Designed by Vincent Foscato."
- **(H)** "Unusual Photograph Decorates New York Building."
- **(J)** "Venetian Glass Mural Installed in Skyscraper."

31. The mosaic work was done by

- **(A)** Hans Hofman.
- **(B)** the 1,400 workers in the Foscato plant.
- **(C)** a dozen men skilled in photography.
- **(D)** two thirds of the New York workers in Venetian glass mosaics.

32. The original design was

- **(F)** painted on the wall of the Kaufman building.
- **(G)** a fraction of the size of the finished mural.
- **(H)** imported from Venice.
- **(J)** larger than the finished mural.

33. In the making of the mural,

- **(A)** the shades of tile that the Foscato plant had in stock were not adequate.
- **(B)** 1,412 shades were needed.
- **(C)** half a million colors were used.
- **(D)** more than 500 shades of color were used.

34. Mr. Hofman
    (F) used only the most unusual shades of red, blue, and green.
    (G) had no further connection with the work after making the original sketch.
    (H) died shortly before the mural was completed.
    (J) colored the enlarged reproduction of the original.

QUESTIONS 35–40 REFER TO THE FOLLOWING PASSAGE.

The dark and the sea are full of dangers to the fishermen of Norway. A whale might come and destroy the floating chain of corks that edges the nets, break it, and carry it off. Or a storm might come suddenly, unexpectedly, out of the night. The sea seems to turn somersaults. It opens and closes immense caverns with terrible clashes, chasing boats and fishermen who must flee from their nets and the expected catch. Then the fishermen might lift their nets as empty as they set them. At other times, the herring might come in such masses that the lines break from the weight when lifted, and the fishermen must return home empty-handed, without line, nets, or herring.

But often the nets are full of herring that shine and glisten like silver. Once in awhile, a couple of fishermen will venture in their boats along the net lines to see whether the herring are coming, and when the corks begin to bob and jerk as if something were hitting the nets to which they are attached, they then know that the herring are there. The nets are being filled, and all the fishermen sit in quiet excitement. They dare only to whisper to each other, afraid to disturb, and quite overcome by the over-helming generosity of the sea. Eyes shine happy anticipation; hands are folded in thanks. Then muscles strain with power. It is as though the strength of the body doubled. They can work day and night without a thought of weariness. They need neither food nor rest; the thought of success keeps their vigor up almost endlessly. They will take food and rest when it is all over.

35. The best title for this passage is
    (A) "Hard Work in Norway."
    (B) "The Perils and Rewards of Fishing."
    (C) "Risky Business."
    (D) "The Generosity of the Sea."

36. The difficulties faced by the Norwegian fishermen include
    (F) the eating of the herring by whales.
    (G) the difficulty of being very calm.
    (H) interference by rough seas.
    (J) the jerking of the corks.

37. At the first indication that herring are entering the nets, the fishermen
    (A) try not to frighten the fish away.
    (B) strain every muscle to haul in the catch.
    (C) collect the nets quickly.
    (D) row quickly along the edge of the nets.

38. When the article says that the sea opens and closes immense caverns, it is referring to
    (F) caves along the shoreline.
    (G) deep holes in the ocean floor.
    (H) dangerous large boulders that get rolled around.
    (J) hollow pockets beneath very high waves.

39. The fishermen are described as
    (A) strong, angry, and excitable.
    (B) skillful, religious, and impatient.
    (C) patient, brave, and grateful.
    (D) surly, hardworking, and cautious.

40. Of the following, the one that is *not* mentioned as posing a problem to the fishermen is
    (F) destruction of the nets.
    (G) theft of the nets by other fishermen.
    (H) too large a catch.
    (J) whales.

Directions: For questions 41–43, choose the topic sentence that best fits the paragraph.

41. _____

First, your ability to secure a position might depend on your English. Your prospective employer will notice how well you write the answers to the questions on your application blank. And when you are interviewed, he will notice how well you speak.

(A) As you move up the success ladder, what you write and what you say will determine in part your rate of climb.

(B) If you wish to enter business, there are three good reasons why you should study English.

(C) You will need to write reports accurately and interestingly.

(D) You will need to talk effectively with your fellow workers, with your superiors, and perhaps with the public.

42. _____

On the one hand, we call history a science since the historian has a method for gathering evidence and evaluating it. On the other hand, it is less accurate in its ability to predict than a science should be. History can be literature because it involves the views and interpretations of the historian.

(F) History is sometimes compared to literature.

(G) The great history that has stirred people's minds has also been the theme of great literature.

(H) Is history a science?

(J) The question of whether history is a science or literature is difficult to answer.

43. _____

There are important areas in our lives in which opinions play a major role. Every time we look into the future, we depend on opinions. Every time we attempt to judge facts, we depend on opinions. And every time we attempt to advance into the "not yet known area," we depend on opinions.

(A) Opinions should not be taken lightly.

(B) Newspaper editorials are based upon opinion rather than upon facts.

(C) In some ways, they actually go beyond facts.

(D) Scientific inquiry leaves no room for opinions.

Directions: For questions 44–46, choose the pair of sentences that best develops the topic sentence.

44. One of the most difficult problems in America today is that of homelessness.

(F) I think that homeless people tend to be dirty, lazy, and shiftless. They are an eyesore for honest, hardworking citizens.

(G) Homelessness was a problem during the Depression. The Salvation Army operated soup kitchens to feed the homeless.

(H) While the bulk of the homeless are single men, many are families with small children. Among the causes of homelessness are fires, poverty, and just plain hard luck.

(J) Some people are homeless by choice. Nomads like to wander from place to place without having to care for a stable residence.

45. Many young people today are choosing to become vegetarians.

(A) A vegetarian diet can be healthful, but it must be carefully planned. Complete proteins can be created by combining rice and beans in proper proportion.

(B) Some religions frown upon vegetarianism. These religions require the eating of meat at certain ritual occasions.

(C) If I were to tell my mother that I wanted to become a vegetarian, she would be very angry. My mother likes everyone at the table to eat the same food.

(D) New vegetarians can be very annoying. Converts to new ideas or new ways often talk of nothing else.

46. One of the most important safety features on your car is the condition of the tires.

(F) The first tires were made of solid rubber and were very uncomfortable to ride on. Later tires had an inflatable inner tube that gave a softer ride.

(G) Studded tires give good traction on icy roads. Some states prohibit tire studs because they destroy the road surface.

(H) Today's steel-belted radial tires give long service. If you use radials, you should put them on all four wheels.

(J) Once the brakes are applied, it is the front tires that determine how quickly the car will stop and whether or not it will skid. Deep, matched treads on the two front tires will ensure a quick, smooth stop.

Directions: For question 47, choose the sentence that does not belong in the paragraph.

47. (1) Human forms of cultural behavior are found among the Japanese monkey. (2) Members of the Japan Monkey Center have found among local monkey groups a wide variety of customs based on social learning. (3) The males of certain groups, for instance, take turns looking after the infants while the mothers are eating. (4) The scientists have also been able to observe the process by which behavioral innovations, such as swimming and sweet potato washing, developed and spread from individual to individual in the monkey group. (5) Japanese scientists found that female tigers swam more than male monkeys.

(A) Sentence 1
(B) Sentence 2
(C) Sentence 3
(D) Sentence 5

Directions: For questions 48–50, read the paragraph and choose the sentence that best fills the blank.

48. A handy all-round wrench that is generally included in every toolbox is the adjustable open-end wrench. This wrench is not intended to take the place of the regular solid open-end wrench. _____ Its usefulness is achieved by its ability to fit.

(F) As the jaw opening increases, the length of the wrench increases.

(G) Adjustable wrenches are available in varying sizes, ranging from 4 to 24 inches in length.

(H) This flexibility is achieved although one jaw of the adjustable open-end wrench is fixed because the other jaw is moved along a slide by a thumbscrew adjustment.

(J) In addition, it is not built for use on extremely hard-to-turn items.

49. Matter may change either by a physical change or by a chemical change. _____ Changing water into ice or steam and dissolving sugar in water are examples of physical change. In a chemical change, molecules of new matter are formed that are different from the original matter.

   (A) The burning of coal or the rusting of iron are examples of chemical change.

   (B) There are four types of chemical reactions: synthesis, decomposition, single displacement, and double displacement.

   (C) The form, size, or shape of matter is altered in a physical change, but the molecules remain unchanged.

   (D) The molecules that enter the reaction are called *reactants*.

50. Along the shores of the Indian Ocean is found a pretty little shellfish that is noted for furnishing what may have been the first money ever used. _____ Millions of people around the ocean were using these cowries for money long before furs or cattle or other kinds of money were used anywhere, as far as is known. Cowries have been found in Assyria, many miles inland.

   (F) Now, after thousands of years, there are still some tribes in Africa, India, and the South Seas that use cowries.

   (G) In China, they were used with several other kinds of shells.

   (H) Its shell, called a cowrie, is white or light yellow and is about one inch long.

   (J) Tortoise shells had the highest value, so it might be said that the tortoise shells were the dollar bills while the cowries were the coins.

STOP   If you finish before time is up, check over your work on Section 6 only. Do not go back to the previous sections. Do not go on until the signal is given.

SECTION 7. MATHEMATICS

35 MINUTES

Directions: For questions 1–40, read each problem and find the answer.

1. Two hundred million, one hundred seventy-three thousand, and sixty-three =
   - (A) 200,173,630
   - (B) 2,173,063
   - (C) 20,173,063
   - (D) 200,173,063

2. Seventeen million sixty thousand thirty-four =
   - (F) 1,760,034
   - (G) 17,634
   - (H) 17,060,034
   - (J) 17,600,034

3. 0.5% is equal to
   - (A) 0.5
   - (B) 0.005
   - (C) 0.05
   - (D) $\frac{1}{2}$

4. A group of 6 people raised $690 for charity. One person raised 35% of the total. What was the amount raised by the other 5 people?
   - (F) $241.50
   - (G) $448.50
   - (H) $449.50
   - (J) $445.50

5. If a pie is divided into 20 parts, what percent is one part of the whole pie?
   - (A) 20%
   - (B) 5%
   - (C) 2.0%
   - (D) 0.5%

6. A millimeter is what part of a meter?
   - (F) $\frac{1}{10}$
   - (G) $\frac{1}{100}$
   - (H) $\frac{1}{1000}$
   - (J) $\frac{1}{10,000}$

7. Find the area of a rectangle with a length of 176 feet and a width of 79 feet.
   - (A) 13,904 sq. ft.
   - (B) 13,854 sq. ft.
   - (C) 13,304 sq. ft.
   - (D) 13,804 sq. ft.

8. Mr. Lawson makes a weekly salary of $250 plus 7% commission on his sales. What will his income be for a week in which he made sales totaling $1250?
   - (F) $337.50
   - (G) $87.50
   - (H) $267.50
   - (J) $327.50

9. Complete the following statement:
   $7(3 \times \underline{}) + 4 = 2104$.
   - (A) $10 + 2$
   - (B) 10
   - (C) 10^2
   - (D) 10^3

10. Find the area of a triangle whose dimensions are: $b = 14$ inches, $h = 20$ inches.
    - (F) 208 sq. inches
    - (G) 280 sq. inches
    - (H) 140 sq. inches
    - (J) 288 sq. inches

11. What is the difference between (4×10^3) + 6 and $(2 \times 10^3) + (3 \times 10) + 8$?
   (A) 168
   (B) 55,968
   (C) 3,765
   (D) 1,968

12. The set of common factors for 30 and 24 is
   (F) {1,2,3,6}
   (G) {1,2,3,4,6}
   (H) {1,2,4,6}
   (J) {1,2,4,6,12}

13. If the scale on a blueprint is $\frac{1}{4}$ inch = 1 foot, give the blueprint dimensions of a room that is actually 29 feet long and 23 feet wide.
   (A) $7\frac{1}{2}" \times 5\frac{1}{4}"$
   (B) $6\frac{3}{4}" \times 6"$
   (C) $7\frac{1}{4}" \times 5\frac{1}{2}"$
   (D) $7\frac{1}{4}" \times 5\frac{3}{4}"$

14. A scalene triangle has
   (F) two equal sides.
   (G) two equal sides and one right angle.
   (H) no equal sides.
   (J) three equal sides.

15. On a recent trip, the Smiths drove at an average speed of 55 miles per hour. If the trip took $5\frac{1}{2}$ hours, how many miles did they drive?
   (A) 320.75
   (B) 312.50
   (C) 320.5
   (D) 302.5

16. $\frac{17}{30}$ is greater than
   (F) $\frac{7}{8}$
   (G) $\frac{9}{20}$
   (H) $\frac{9}{11}$
   (J) $\frac{22}{25}$

17. One centimeter equals what part of a meter?
   (A) $\frac{1}{10}$
   (B) $\frac{1}{100}$
   (C) $\frac{1}{1,000}$
   (D) $\frac{1}{10,000}$

18. A baseball team won 18 games, which was 40% of its season. How many games did the team lose?
   (F) 25
   (G) 45
   (H) 32
   (J) 27

19. If $-2 < q < -1$, which of the following is true?
   (A) $q = \frac{1}{2}$
   (B) $q > -1$
   (C) $q > 0$
   (D) $q > -2$

20. Which pair of values for x and □ will make the following statement true?
   $2x$ □ 8
   (F) $(6, <)$
   (G) $(4, >)$
   (H) $(0, <)$
   (J) $(-3, >)$

21. $(6 \times 2) + (7 \times 3) =$
    (A) $(6 \times 7) + (2 \times 3)$
    (B) $(7 - 6) + (3 - 2)$
    (C) $(7 \times 3) + (6 \times 2)$
    (D) $(7 \times 3) \times (6 \times 2)$

22. Which of the following will substitute for
    x and make the statement below true?
    $56 - (7 - x) = 53$
    (F) 4
    (G) 3
    (H) 2
    (J) 1

23. An angle that is greater than 90° and less
    than 180° is a(n)
    (A) acute angle.
    (B) right angle.
    (C) reflex angle.
    (D) obtuse angle.

24.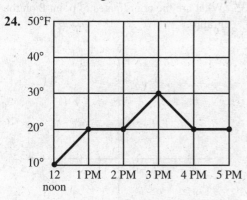

    What was the average temperature on the
    afternoon shown on the above graph?
    (F) 20°
    (G) 24°
    (H) 25°
    (J) 30°

25. Mr. Jones has agreed to borrow $3500 for
    one year at 10% interest. What is the total
    amount he will pay back to the bank?
    (A) $3675
    (B) $350
    (C) $3700
    (D) $3850

26. Which of the following statements is true?
    (F) $7 \times 11 > 78$
    (G) $6 + 4 < 10.5$
    (H) $8 - 3 = 7 + 4$
    (J) $16 \div 2 > 9$

27. If one angle of a triangle measures 115°,
    then the sum of the other two angles is
    (A) 245°
    (B) 75°
    (C) 195°
    (D) 65°

28. At 20 miles per hour, how long does it take
    to travel 1 mile?
    (F) 1 min.
    (G) 2 min.
    (H) 3 min.
    (J) 4 min.

29. Approximate the circumference of a circle
    whose radius is 21 feet. (Use $\pi = \frac{22}{7}$.)
    (A) 153 feet
    (B) 65.94 feet
    (C) 132 feet
    (D) 1769.4 feet

30. If $x > -4$, and $x < 2$, then $\{x\}$ includes
    (F) $-4, 0, 1, 2$
    (G) $-2, -1, 1, 2$
    (H) $1, 2, 3, 4$
    (J) $-3, -2, -1, 0, 1$

31.

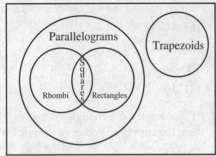

From the diagram above, we know that

(A) all trapezoids are parallelograms.

(B) some rhombi are parallelograms.

(C) some rectangles are rhombi.

(D) all parallelograms are rectangles.

32. How many 2-inch tiles would have to be put around the outside edge of a 4-foot × 12-foot rectangle to completely frame the rectangle?

(F) 32

(G) 36

(H) 192

(J) 196

33. A certain highway intersection has had A accidents over a ten-year period, resulting in B deaths. What is the yearly average death rate for the intersection?

(A) $A + B - 10$

(B) $\dfrac{B}{10}$

(C) $10 - \dfrac{A}{B}$

(D) $\dfrac{AB}{12}$

34. Which point is named by the ordered pair $(-4,4)$?

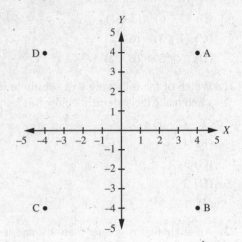

(F) A

(G) B

(H) C

(J) D

35. What are the coordinates of point P on the graph?

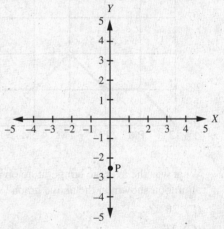

(A) $\left(-2\dfrac{1}{2},0\right)$

(B) $\left(0,-3\dfrac{1}{2}\right)$

(C) $\left(0,-2\dfrac{1}{2}\right)$

(D) $\left(-1,-2\dfrac{1}{2}\right)$

36. On a blueprint, 2 inches represent 24 feet. How long must a line be to represent 72 feet?

(F) 36 inches

(G) 12 inches

(H) 6 inches

(J) 4 inches

37. A store puts a pair of $14 jeans on sale at a 25% discount. What is the new selling price?

(A) $13.75

(B) $10.50

(C) $3.50

(D) $13.65

38.

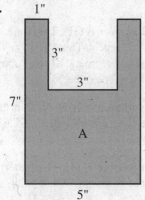

The area of figure A is

(F) 26 sq. in.

(G) 19 sq. in.

(H) 44 sq. in.

(J) 30 sq. in.

39. A boy M years old has a brother six years older and a sister four years younger. The combined age of the three is

(A) $M + 10$

(B) $3M + 2$

(C) $3M - 2$

(D) $2M - 6$

40. Event A occurs every 14 minutes and event B every 12 minutes. If they both occur at 1:00 p.m., when will be the next time that both occur together?

(F) 2:12 p.m.

(G) 1:48 p.m.

(H) 2:24 p.m.

(J) 3:48 p.m.

STOP If you finish before time is up, check over your work on Section 7 only. Do not go back to any previous sections.

ANSWER KEYS AND EXPLANATIONS

Section 1. Sequences

1. A	5. A	9. D	13. A	17. D
2. J	6. H	10. J	14. J	18. J
3. B	7. B	11. A	15. A	19. B
4. G	8. H	12. G	16. G	20. J

1. **The correct answer is (A).** In the first three segments, the pattern is small figure, large figure, small figure. The fourth segment begins: small figure, large figure . . . The final figure should be small. Because none of the figures are filled in, there is no reason for the final figure to be filled in.

2. **The correct answer is (J).** The pattern in the second segment is exactly the opposite of that in the first. The first two figures in the fourth segment give every indication that the fourth segment will be the exact opposite of the third. Choice (J) carries this out.

3. **The correct answer is (B).** The position of the arms governs. In the first segment, down, up/down, up; in the second, down, down/up (a reversal), up; in the third, down, up, up/down; in the fourth, down, up . . . If a reversal is offered, it would be most reasonable. Choice (B) offers this completion.

4. **The correct answer is (G).** In each succeeding segment, the number of double S's (SS) increases by one. The fourth segment should have four double S's.

5. **The correct answer is (A).** The third figure is always blank. This information narrows your choice to (A) or (D). In addition, the fourth figure is always a combination of the first two. This confirms (A) as the correct answer.

6. **The correct answer is (H).** The basis of the sequence is the number of sides of the figures. In the first segment, the number of sides is 3, 4, 5; in the second, 4, 5, 6; in the third, 5, 6, 7; the fourth must be 6, 7, 8.

7. **The correct answer is (B).** This is a +8 series. Within each segment, each number is 8 more than the number before it. $54 + 8 = 62$.

8. **The correct answer is (H).** This time, the pattern is −5 and repeat. Thus, from the first number in the last segment, 81, we subtract 5 to get 76, then repeat the 76.

9. **The correct answer is (D).** Within each segment, the pattern is +7, −6. So, $65 + 7 = 72$; $72 − 6 = 66$.

10. **The correct answer is (J).** The pattern is ÷4. In the first segment, $96 ÷ 4 = 24$, and $24 ÷ 4 = 6$; in the second segment, $\frac{1}{2} ÷ 4 = \frac{1}{8}$ and $\frac{1}{8} ÷ 4 = \frac{1}{32}$. Having established that the second number is the first divided by 4, multiply the second number of the fourth segment by 4 to find the first number.

11. **The correct answer is (A).** The pattern is ×2, −7; $38 − 7 = 31$.

12. **The correct answer is (G).** Within each segment, the series consists of repeated squares. 5 squared is 25; 25 squared is 625. 2 squared is 4; 4 squared is 16. 1 squared is 1; 1 squared is 1.

13. **The correct answer is (A).** Each segment consists of a +5 series with 15 in the middle. $21 + 5 = 26$, 15 intervenes. $15 + 5 = 20$, with 15 intervening to confuse you. $10 + 5 = 15$. The 15 needed to fill the blank is the 15 that appears in each segment.

14. The correct answer is (J). The numbers and letters remain in the same relationship to one another throughout, that is, there is no number between A and B, and the numbers are always subscripts. The letters remain static. The pattern of the numbers appears to be 5 5, 5 4, 4 4, 4 3, 3 3. Isolating the numbers in this way, you can see the manner in which the numbers step down.

15. The correct answer is (A). The letters are static; each letter always has a number attached; odd numbers are superscripts, even numbers subscripts. The numbers are slowly increasing, with the changes occurring from left to right. The numbers in isolation read 111, 211, 221, 222, 322. Remember the superscript/subscript rule in choosing the answer.

16. The correct answer is (G). Because the letters are static and the numbers are all subscripts, concentrate at once on the pattern of the numbers: 6, 56, 456, 45, 4.

17. The correct answer is (D). The series consists of the consonants in alphabetical order.

18. The correct answer is (J). This series consists of the letters of the alphabet in alphabetical order, beginning with the letter *C*. The letter *A* appears after each letter in the series.

19. The correct answer is (B). This series consists of the three letters *P-T-L* in constant rotation. In each succeeding grouping of letters, the first letter of the group before moves to the end of the group, and the other two letters move to the left, so the letter that was second in the previous group becomes the first letter of the next. After *PTL*, the *P* must move to the rear, and the next group must begin with *T* followed by *LP*.

20. The correct answer is (J). This series can be solved mathematically. Starting at the end of the alphabet, –1, –2, –1, repeat the last letter of the first group, then continue: –1, –2, –1, and so on.

Section 2. Analogies

1. B	5. C	9. B	13. C	17. D
2. F	6. H	10. H	14. J	18. H
3. D	7. C	11. D	15. A	19. A
4. F	8. F	12. G	16. J	20. H

1. The correct answer is (B). Mother is to daughter as father is to son. The analogy is one of parallel relationships.

2. The correct answer is (F). The analogy is that of the whole to one of its parts.

3. The correct answer is (D). Vegetable is to vegetable as fruit is to fruit. This is a part-to-part relationship. Carrot and broccoli are both part of the vegetable group. Apple and pear are both part of the fruit group.

4. The correct answer is (F). This is a relationship of new to old. A lamp is a modern version of the candle. A stove is a modern version of a fireplace.

5. The correct answer is (C). This is a relationship of degree. The mansion is a large, elegant version of the cabin. The stretch limousine is larger and more elegant than the pickup truck, though still a car.

6. The correct answer is (H). This is a functional relationship. The table leg holds up the table. The tire holds up the car. This could not be a simple part-to-whole relationship because too many car parts are offered as choices.

7. **The correct answer is (C).** This is a part-to-part relationship. Both eye and ear are parts of the head. Both window and door are parts of the house.

8. **The correct answer is (F).** This is a sequential relationship. From an acorn grows an oak tree; from an egg comes a chicken.

9. **The correct answer is (B).** This is a relationship between people and the tools they use. A stethoscope is used by a doctor; a gavel is used by a judge.

10. **The correct answer is (H).** The relationship is functional. Again, it is easiest read in reverse. A pen is used to apply ink; a brush is used to apply paint.

11. **The correct answer is (D).** Another functional relationship. This time, read forward. The baseball glove catches the ball. The hook catches the fish.

12. **The correct answer is (G).** Sequential relationship. The abacus preceded the calculator as a mathematical aid. The biplane preceded the jet.

13. **The correct answer is (C).** Part-to-part relationship. Both eagle and duck are part of the group of birds. Both collie and dachshund are part of the group of dogs.

14. **The correct answer is (J).** This relationship is between a hunting implement and the animal hunted with it. The butterfly net is used to hunt the butterfly. The rifle is used to hunt the deer.

15. **The correct answer is (A).** This is a part-to-whole relationship. A slice of bread is part of a loaf; a leaf is part of a tree.

16. **The correct answer is (J).** Call this one what you will—association or part-to-part relationship. The rabbit's foot and four leaf clover are considered good luck. The black cat and the number 13 are considered bad luck.

17. **The correct answer is (D).** A parachute is a safety device on planes; a life preserver is a safety device on boats.

18. **The correct answer is (H).** This is a relationship between real animals and mythical ones. A unicorn is a type of mythical horse; a dragon is a type of mythical reptile.

19. **The correct answer is (A).** Cars travel on roads, and trains travel on tracks.

20. **The correct answer is (H).** A necklace and a necktie are both worn around the neck. Socks and shoes are worn on your feet.

Section 3. Quantitative Reasoning

1. C	5. A	9. B	13. D	17. C
2. G	6. H	10. G	14. H	18. F
3. A	7. C	11. A	15. B	19. A
4. J	8. H	12. G	16. F	20. G

1. **The correct answer is (C).**

   $2 \times 3 = 6$

   $1 \times 3 = 3$

   $3 \times 3 = 9$

2. **The correct answer is (G).**

   $4 + 4 = 8$

   $5 + 4 = 9$

   $7 + 4 = 11$

3. **The correct answer is (A).**

   $7 - 3 = 4$

   $4 - 3 = 1$

   $1 - 3 = -2$

4. **The correct answer is (J).**

   $12 \div 4 = 3$

   $8 \div 4 = 2$

   $16 \div 4 = 4$

5. **The correct answer is (A).**

   $10 - 5 = 5$

   $8 - 5 = 3$

   $6 - 5 = 1$

6. **The correct answer is (H).**

   $\frac{2}{3} \times 3 = 2$

   $2 \times 3 = 6$

   $3 \times 3 = 9$

7. **The correct answer is (C).**

   $\frac{1}{2} + \frac{1}{2} = 1$

   $\frac{3}{2} + \frac{1}{2} = 2$

   $3 + \frac{1}{2} = \frac{7}{2}$

8. **The correct answer is (H).** There are four squares. One of them is shaded. We know that 1 over 4 is the same as $\frac{1}{4}$.

9. **The correct answer is (B).** There are six squares. Two of them are shaded. We know that 2 over 6 is $\frac{2}{6}$, or $\frac{1}{3}$.

10. **The correct answer is (G).** There are eight squares. Six of them are shaded. We know that 6 over 8 is $\frac{6}{8}$, or $\frac{3}{4}$.

11. **The correct answer is (A).** There are eight squares. Three complete squares and two half-squares are shaded. If we add $3 + \frac{1}{2} + \frac{1}{2}$, the answer is 4. So, four squares are shaded. We know that 4 over 8 is $\frac{4}{8}$, or $\frac{1}{2}$.

12. **The correct answer is (G).** There are nine squares. Three complete squares and two half-squares are shaded. If we add $3 + \frac{1}{2} + \frac{1}{2}$, the answer is 4. We know that 4 over 9 is $\frac{4}{9}$.

13. **The correct answer is (D).** There are nine squares. Five squares are shaded. We know that 5 over 9 is $\frac{5}{9}$.

14. **The correct answer is (H).** There are eight squares. One of them is shaded. We know that 1 over 8 is the same as $\frac{1}{8}$.

15. **The correct answer is (B).** The scale indicates that 1 cube = 1 cone. The only answer that maintains this relationship is choice (B), since it shows that 2 cubes = 1 cube 1 + 1 cone.

16. **The correct answer is (F).** The scale indicates that 1 cube = 1 cone. The only answer that maintains this relationship is choice (F), since it has 1 cone + 1 cube = 2 cones.

17. **The correct answer is (C).** The scale indicates that 1 cube = 2 cones. The only answer that maintains this relationship is choice (C), since it shows that 2 cubes = 4 cones.

18. **The correct answer is (F).** The scale indicates that 1 cube = 2 cones. The only answer that maintains this relationship is choice (F), since it shows that 2 cubes + 1 cone = 1 cube + 3 cones.

19. **The correct answer is (A).** The scale indicates that 1 cube = 3 cones. The only answer that maintains this relationship is choice (A), since it shows that 2 cubes = 1 cube and 3 cones.

20. **The correct answer is (G).** The scale indicates that 1 cube = 3 cones. The only possible answer choice here is choice (G), since it shows that 3 cones = 3 cones.

Section 4. Verbal Reasoning—Words

1. D	4. J	7. B	9. A	11. A
2. G	5. C	8. H	10. G	12. J
3. A	6. H			

1. **The correct answer is (D).** Flame and smoke often accompany burning, and ash often follows it. However, there can be no burning without heat; heat is the necessary component.

2. **The correct answer is (G).** To verbalize is to put into words; therefore, the essential ingredient of *verbalization* is *words*.

3. **The correct answer is (A).** Legislation is the enactment of laws. Laws may be enacted by any legislative body—city council, Congress, or a student organization. Debate is common but not required.

4. **The correct answer is (J).** A terrarium is an enclosure for growing and observing plants or plants and tiny animals indoors. A terrarium never has standing water, though water may be added for the benefit of the living things. Because there are always plants in a terrarium, there is always earth.

5. **The correct answer is (C).** The bow is an adjunct of a violin. Notes and melody are products. Strings are absolutely necessary to a violin.

6. **The correct answer is (H).** A chronometer is a device for measuring time. There must be time to measure. The chronometer may be a watch, a sundial, or even an hourglass.

7. **The correct answer is (B).** The relationship is progressive: from light covering, to heavier or warmer covering, to heaviest or most protective.

8. **The correct answer is (H).** The items above the line are all elements; those below the line are all compounds. Oxygen and helium are both elements. Atmosphere is a more general term than a simple compound.

9. The correct answer is (A). Color, odor, and sound are all properties of matter. Feeling, seeing, and hearing are all sensory means for being affected by the properties of matter.

10. The correct answer is (G). Above the line are spring flowers. Below the line are winter flowers, particularly flowers associated with Christmas.

11. The correct answer is (A). Count the feet. Above the line: 2, 4, 8. Below the line: 2, 4, and the crab has 8. A fly has 6 legs; an eel, none at all; and a unicorn, 4.

12. The correct answer is (J). Above the line are team sports. Below the line are individual sports.

Section 5. Verbal Reasoning—Context

1. A	5. D	9. C	13. B	17. A
2. J	6. F	10. G	14. J	18. J
3. B	7. D	11. D	15. B	19. B
4. J	8. G	12. F	16. H	20. J

1. The correct answer is (A). Jeffrey definitely plays the violin at least twice a week, on Monday and Friday. Although we know that Jeffrey enjoys both music and dancing, we have no way of knowing if he prefers either of these activities to the study of law. From this paragraph, you cannot tell how often Jeffrey dances.

2. The correct answer is (J). Chances are that Debbie did not fail the written exam because she is about to go for an Oral Assessment. Surely the person who failed the first step would not be called for the second. Likewise, we can assume that only people who pass the written exam take the oral exam. Otherwise, both exams could be scheduled in advance. However, we can't know for sure from the information given. If Debbie were already a Foreign Service officer, she would not need to go for an Oral Assessment. You can assume from this paragraph that Debbie is happy because she passed the exam and is still under consideration for appointment as a Foreign Service officer.

3. The correct answer is (B). The only certainty is that something frightened the boys, and they got out in a hurry.

4. The correct answer is (J). All of the choices could be true, but the only fact of which

you may be certain is that Warren's car is garaged regularly.

5. The correct answer is (D). Clearly Mark is accident-prone and breaks his right arm easily. His dog is not dangerous; we do not even know if Mark has a sister; he may be learning to use his left hand out of necessity, but we do not know if he is left- or right-handed.

6. The correct answer is (F). In this language, the suffix comes before the stem of the word.

cheki means *ing*
ruala means *eat*
duang means *en*
frit means *hide* or *hid*

7. The correct answer is (D). Because the three given English words contain neither common prefixes, suffixes, nor stems, you must determine another basis on which to make your translation. All three words contain the central element *ohaka*. Chances are that this element refers to water and that it must appear in the middle of the word *lake* as well. The two words that refer to moving water end in *flis*. Since a pond and lake are both still, *lake* will probably end with *sloo*, as does pond. Creek and pond are basically small versions of river and lake. *Creek* and *pond* both begin with *joki*, which probably means small. So *lura* probably means large. Choice (D) allows you to form a word based on all these assumptions. Large water still means lake.

8. **The correct answer is (G).** Pull apart each word, then reassemble the pieces to suit.

   frush means *dis*
   uwamba means *solve* or *solute* as a
     combination form
   kuta means *tion*
   hama means *re*

   If you are alert, all you need do is isolate the prefix meaning *re* and put it in front of the given word for *solution*.

9. **The correct answer is (C).** While all the answers could be correct, only choice (C) must be true. It acknowledges the very definite fact that Lexi is over her essay word limit.

10. **The correct answer is (G).** While all of the answers could be correct, only choice (G) is definitely true. Having moved to Atlanta, San Diego, and several other cities, Bob has moved more than three times.

11. **The correct answer is (D).** According to the statements, the boys, from shortest to tallest, are Chase, Bud, Rob, Pete, and Garrett. Therefore, Garrett is the tallest.

12. **The correct answer is (F).** Because Patsy arrives at 7:45 a.m., she misses the 7:30 a.m. pickup. Thus, she must walk to school. There is no reason to conclude that the bus is late or broken down, or that Patsy is necessarily late for school.

13. **The correct answer is (B).** Because Amber runs the race in less time than Brittany, she places ahead of Brittany in the race. While the other answer choices could be true, we can't be sure that they must be true.

14. **The correct answer is (J).** All of the answers could be true, but the only facts we know for certain are that Shelly's shift ends at noon, and that she eats lunch when her shift ends. Thus, she will not be back after lunch to further assist with the blood drive.

15. **The correct answer is (B).** While any of the statements could be true, the only certain fact is that Melanie, by reading only two books, fell short of completing her assignment to read all three books over spring break.

16. **The correct answer is (H).** Any of the four statements could be true, but the only statement that must be true is that Andrew and Chelsea will be at the Thursday night meet. We know this because they are both members of the Quiz Bowl team, and they attend every meet.

17. **The correct answer is (A).** Since Art brings Arianna to the Burger Palace, we know that Art, Lee, and Arianna all meet at the Burger Palace. While the other choices could be true, there is not enough information to conclude that they are indeed true.

18. **The correct answer is (J).** The only fact we know for certain, based on the given statements, is that the narrator's cat snubbed her. The cat always snubs the narrator whenever she smells other cats on the narrator.

19. **The correct answer is (B).** In order of best math test scores to worst, the girls place as follows: Amanda, Hilary, and Gina. Thus, Gina scores lowest on the test.

20. **The correct answer is (J).** Shelly's grandparents must have been married for 50 years, if their family is throwing them a fiftieth anniversary party. The other statements could be true, but we can't be sure that they must be true.

Section 6. Reading and Language Arts

1. C	11. C	21. C	31. D	41. B
2. H	12. J	22. G	32. G	42. J
3. A	13. C	23. D	33. A	43. A
4. J	14. F	24. F	34. J	44. H
5. D	15. B	25. C	35. B	45. A
6. F	16. J	26. F	36. H	46. J
7. D	17. A	27. D	37. A	47. D
8. F	18. H	28. G	38. J	48. J
9. A	19. B	29. D	39. C	49. C
10. H	20. J	30. J	40. G	50. H

1. **The correct answer is (C).** ". . . the male wolverine occupies a very large hunting area and fights to the death any male . . ."

2. **The correct answer is (H).** Because Henry wanted the author to shoot the wolverine, Henry obviously was the author's companion.

3. **The correct answer is (A).** The attitude of the author is clearly that of a naturalist.

4. **The correct answer is (J).** In effect, wolverines are the Indians' and trappers' competition. Because the wolverines are successful, they are the hated competition.

5. **The correct answer is (D).** Both the first and last paragraphs make the point that we have been too quick to put into use chemicals and other technological developments before fully understanding their long-range effects.

6. **The correct answer is (F).** The third paragraph discusses this aspect of the problem.

7. **The correct answer is (D).** The author devotes his whole selection to the need for scientists to evaluate the impact of new products on the environment.

8. **The correct answer is (F).** This sentence best describes what the rest of the passage is about.

9. **The correct answer is (A).** The kangaroo's hind legs are described as having "steel-spring power."

10. **The correct answer is (H).** The first paragraph tells us that kangaroos are found only in Australasia and that this part of the earth was cut off from the Asian mainland. Specifically, kangaroos are found in Australia, Tasmania to the south, and New Guinea to the north.

11. **The correct answer is (C).** The last sentence of the second paragraph makes this very clear. The name "Old Man" is an affectionate one.

12. **The correct answer is (J).** The author obviously enjoys tall tales about kangaroos. The author tells us that the tall tales may be close to fact but not that they are true, so choice (J) is the best answer.

13. **The correct answer is (C).** Clues may be found in the first sentence, which states that historians are trying to learn more about the *Mayflower*, and in the first sentence of the third paragraph, which describes the boat as historic.

14. **The correct answer is (F).** If you have this wrong, reread the first paragraph.

15. **The correct answer is (B).** The first sentence of the second paragraph answers this question.

16. **The correct answer is (J).** The original *Mayflower* was 22 feet wide; the duplicate is 26 feet wide.

17. **The correct answer is (A).** The sentence is written correctly. The other choices contain errors of grammar and usage.

18. **The correct answer is (H).** The first two sentences make it clear that sleep is mysterious and therefore the subject of awe.

19. **The correct answer is (B).** The answer to this question is found in the first sentence. Just subtract. The 1950s, when modern sleep research began, is mid-century, not the turn of the century. Neither sleep nor dreams are caused by REMs.

20. **The correct answer is (J).** Respiration, pulse rate, muscle tension, and electrical changes in the brain are physical factors.

21. **The correct answer is (C).** REMs occur during sleep, but nowhere is it suggested that they cause sleep.

22. **The correct answer is (G).** The selection speaks of the value of a cord of wood in terms of how much wood there is in a cord and how much heat is produced by the wood.

23. **The correct answer is (D).** Read carefully. The third sentence is the definition.

24. **The correct answer is (F).** The last sentence of the first paragraph makes the statement.

25. **The correct answer is (C).** The elasticity of the measure is based on the fact that even though dimensions are standard, the actual amount of wood in a cord varies greatly.

26. **The correct answer is (F).** Carbon dating, the most recently developed method for determining the age of archeological finds and the most scientific, is not mentioned in this article.

27. **The correct answer is (D).** The second paragraph suggests that man used tools for a lot longer than only 2,000,000 years.

28. **The correct answer is (G).** This is stated toward the end of the last paragraph. The Somme River is in France, and it is there that the British investigators went to check the French deposits.

29. **The correct answer is (D).** The 1840s are in the early to mid-nineteenth century.

30. **The correct answer is (J).** The selection is about the mural and how it was installed.

31. **The correct answer is (D).** Eight of the city's twelve workers in Venetian glass constitute two thirds of such artisans.

32. **The correct answer is (G).** The original sketch was one-sixth the final size.

33. **The correct answer is (A).** The plant keeps 1,400 shades of glass in stock but had to send to Venice for 12 additional ones. All 1,400 shades in stock were not necessarily used for this one mural.

34. **The correct answer is (J).** The procedure followed from original sketch to completion of the mural is outlined at the beginning of the third paragraph.

35. **The correct answer is (B).** The first paragraph speaks of the perils of fishing; the second speaks about its rewards.

36. **The correct answer is (H).** The middle of the first paragraph discusses the problems created by rough seas. None of the other choices is mentioned as a difficulty.

37. **The correct answer is (A).** In the middle of the second paragraph, we learn that when fishermen note that herring are entering the nets, they sit in quiet excitement so as not to frighten the fish away. They row along the net earlier in order to find out if the net is filling and haul in the nets later, when they are full.

38. **The correct answer is (J).** This phrase represents a powerful metaphor. Picture huge waves rising over empty space and crashing down upon fishermen and boats.

39. **The correct answer is (C).** All the other choices include at least one trait that is not ascribed to these fishermen.

40. **The correct answer is (G).** One might add honesty to the traits of the fishermen. Theft is not mentioned as a problem. If you had forgotten about the whales, reread the first sentence.

41. **The correct answer is (B).** Consider that this answer is practically a "gift." Because the second sentence begins with the word *first,* it is obvious that the sentence that is about to offer *three good reasons* will be the topic sentence. If choice (B) were not offered, choice (A) might well have served as a topic sentence, but choice (B) is clearly better. Choices (C) and (D) are quite obviously development sentences.

42. **The correct answer is (J).** Because the first development sentence begins with *On the one hand,* you should look for a topic sentence that offers an alternative. As in the previous question, this question offers you a good second choice. If choice (J) were not offered, you would select choice (H) because it raises the question of history's being a science, and the first development sentence speaks of history as a science. Still, the choice that raises the possibility of alternatives is the better of the two. The other choices prematurely introduce the subject of literature.

43. **The correct answer is (A).** The first development sentence is practically a restatement of the topic sentence. If opinions play a major role in important areas in our lives, obviously they should not be taken lightly. Choice (B) is clearly a development sentence; choice (C) could not possibly serve as a topic sentence because its subject is "they," which has no reference; choice (D) contradicts the paragraph; and choice (E) might be a development sentence or might even belong in the next paragraph.

44. **The correct answer is (H).** The first sentence tells us that homelessness presents a difficult problem. Develop the paragraph by describing the extent and causes of the problem. Choice (F) is a statement of opinion that does not really address the problem. Choice (G) digresses into a narrow aspect of homelessness—hunger; it might appear later in the paragraph or in another paragraph of the same article. Choice (J) is totally irrelevant.

45. **The correct answer is (A).** Any one of the choices could possibly develop the paragraph, but the *best* development discusses the vegetarian diet itself.

46. **The correct answer is (J).** Note that the topic sentence speaks of the *condition* of the tires. Only choice (J) follows that theme.

47. **The correct answer is (D).** The paragraph is about Japanese monkeys and their human behaviors. Tigers have no place in this paragraph.

48. **The correct answer is (J).** The second sentence tells of one use for which the open-end wrench is not intended. Choice (J) tells of additional unintended use. Choices (F) and (G) address the length of the wrench rather than the opening of its jaws. Choice (H) logically follows the last sentence of the paragraph.

49. **The correct answer is (C).** The paragraph will discuss two ways in which matter may change. The third sentence gives examples of physical change, and the fourth sentence describes a chemical change. It is reasonable to expect the missing sentence to describe a physical change. Choice (A) would logically follow the description of a chemical change. All other choices might best find their places in another paragraph.

50. **The correct answer is (H).** In a paragraph about the use of cowries as money, an explanation of exactly what a cowrie is should be offered as early as possible.

Section 7. Mathematics

1. D	9. C	17. B	25. D	33. B
2. H	10. H	18. J	26. G	34. J
3. B	11. D	19. D	27. D	35. C
4. G	12. F	20. H	28. H	36. H
5. B	13. D	21. C	29. C	37. B
6. H	14. H	22. F	30. J	38. F
7. A	15. D	23. D	31. C	39. B
8. F	16. G	24. F	32. J	40. H

1. **The correct answer is (D).** Remember, the hundreds place will not be mentioned if its value is zero.

2. **The correct answer is (H).** Notice that the 6 is in the ten-thousands place.

3. **The correct answer is (B).** 1% = 0.01; one-half of 1 percent is written 0.005.

4. **The correct answer is (G).** One person raised 35% of $690. $690 × 0.35 = $241.50. The remainder raised by the others was $690 − $241.50 = $448.50.

5. **The correct answer is (B).** The whole pie is 100%. Each part is $\frac{1}{20}$; 100 ÷ 20 = 5%.

6. **The correct answer is (H).** There are 1,000 millimeters in a meter.

7. **The correct answer is (A).**

   Area = length × width

   = 176 ft. × 79 ft.

   = 13,904 sq. ft.

8. **The correct answer is (F).** His total income is equal to 7% of his sales plus $250. 7% of his sales is $1250 × 0.07 = $87.50 + $250 = $337.50.

9. **The correct answer is (C).** Substitute n for the blank space.

   $$7(3 \times n) + 4 = 2104$$
   $$7(3n) + 4 = 2104$$
   $$21n + 4 = 2104$$
   $$21n = 2100$$
   $$n = 100, \text{ or } 10^2$$

10. **The correct answer is (H).** The area of a triangle is found by using

    $$A = \frac{1}{2}bh$$

    $$A = \frac{1}{2} \times 14 \times 20$$

    $$A = 140 \text{ sq. in.}$$

11. **The correct answer is (D).**

    $$(4 \times 10^3) + 6 = 4006$$
    $$-(2 \times 10^3) + (3 \times 10) + 8 = 2038$$

    The difference is 1.968.

12. **The correct answer is (F).** The set of factors for 24 is:

    {1,2,3,4,6,8,12,24}

    The set of factors for 30 is:

    {1,2,3,5,6,10,15,30}

    The set of common factors is: {1,2,3,6}

13. **The correct answer is (D).** For the length, 29 feet would be represented by 29 units of $\frac{1}{4}$ inch, resulting in $\frac{29}{4}$, or $7\frac{1}{4}$, inches. For the width, 23 feet would be represented by 23 units of $\frac{1}{4}$ inch, resulting in $\frac{23}{4}$, or $5\frac{3}{4}$, inches.

14. **The correct answer is (H).** A scalene triangle has no equal sides.

15. **The correct answer is (D).**

Distance = Rate × Time

$$= 55 \text{ mph} \times 5\frac{1}{2} \text{ hours}$$

$$= 302.5 \text{ miles}$$

16. **The correct answer is (G).** Note that $\frac{17}{30}$ is only slightly larger than $\frac{15}{30}$ or $\frac{1}{2}$. Choices (F), (H), and (J) are much closer in value to 1 than to $\frac{1}{2}$.

17. **The correct answer is (B).** 100 centimeters = 1 meter. Each centimeter is $\frac{1}{100}$ of a meter.

18. **The correct answer is (J).** If 18 games constituted 40% of the season, the season was 18 ÷ 0.40, or 45 games long. If the team won 18 games, it lost 45 − 18, or 27 games.

19. **The correct answer is (D).** The inequality should be conceptualized as "q is between −2 and −1." Because q must be closer to 0 than −2, it is *larger* than −2.

20. **The correct answer is (H).** If $x = 0$, then $2x < 8$ because $2(0) < 8$. None of the other pairs results in a true statement.

21. **The correct answer is (C).** The order in which numbers are added does not affect the sum; changing the signs does.

22. **The correct answer is (F).** We want the amount in the parentheses to be equal to 3. The value of x that will make the amount in parentheses equal to 3 is 4.

23. **The correct answer is (D).** Review your geometry if you got this wrong.

24. **The correct answer is (F).** The temperature over the 6 hours graphed was 10° + 20° + 20° + 30° + 20° + 20°= 120° ÷ 6 = 20°.

25. **The correct answer is (D).** He will pay back $3500 plus 10% interest. Ten percent of $3500 is $350. $3500 + $350 = $3850.

26. **The correct answer is (G).** 6 plus 4 is 10, and 10 is less than 10.5 $\left(10\frac{1}{2}\right)$.

27. **The correct answer is (D).** The sum of the angles of a triangle is 180°. Therefore, 180° − 115° = 65°.

28. **The correct answer is (H).** Because Distance = Rate × Time, Time = Distance ÷ Rate. Therefore, time = $\frac{1}{20}$ of an hour = 3 minutes. Or, because 60 mph is 1 mile per minute, 20 mph is 1 mile every 3 minutes.

29. **The correct answer is (C).**

Diameter = 2 × Radius

$$\pi = \frac{22}{7}$$

Circumference = π × Diameter

$$C = \pi \times 21 \times 2$$
$$C = \pi \times 42$$
$$= \frac{22}{7} \times 42$$
$$= 132 \text{ feet}$$

30. **The correct answer is (J).** The set $\{x\}$ includes all those numbers larger than −4 and smaller than 2. Considering only whole numbers, this set includes −3, −2, −1, 0, and 1.

31. **The correct answer is (C).** Careful study of the Venn diagram shows overlap of the circles enclosing rectangles and rhombi, so some rectangles are rhombi as those same rhombi are rectangles. The other statements should read as follows: No trapezoids are parallelograms; all rhombi are parallelograms; and some parallelograms are rectangles, or all rectangles are parallelograms.

32. The correct answer is (J). There are 72 tiles along each length and 24 tiles along each width. $2 \times 96 = 192$ tiles along the perimeter. But 4 more are needed for the corners of the frame.

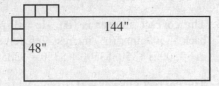

144"

48"

Hence, 196 tiles are needed.

33. The correct answer is (B). The number of accidents is irrelevant to the question. B deaths occurred in 10 years, so each year, an average of one tenth of B deaths occurred.

34. The correct answer is (J). First read to the left along the negative x-axis, then read up on the y-axis.

35. The correct answer is (C). Because point P has not moved along the x-axis, the x-coordinate is 0. Moving down on the y-axis, point P is located at $-2\frac{1}{2}$.

36. The correct answer is (H). If 2 inches equal 24 feet, 1 inch equals 12 feet. A line representing 72 feet, therefore, must be 6 inches long ($72 \div 12 = 6$).

37. The correct answer is (B). Reduce the $14.00 price by 25%.

25% of $14.00 = $14 \times 0.25 = $3.50

$14.00 - $3.50 = $10.50 (new price)

Therefore, (B) is the correct answer. Choice (A) indicates a reduction of only 25 cents. Choice (C) represents a reduction *to* 25% of the original price, or a 75% decrease in price.

38. The correct answer is (F). The area is most easily found by multiplying the length of the figure by its width, and then subtracting the area of the small 3" × 3" square.

$(7" \times 5") - (3" \times 3") = $ area

35 sq. in – 9 sq. in. = 26 sq. in.

Shapes such as this are often used for irregular pieces of carpeting or covering.

39. The correct answer is (B). The boy's age is M years. His older brother is $M + 6$ years old, and his younger sister is $M - 4$ years old. Adding the three ages together:

$M + (M + 6) + (M - 4) = 3M + 2$

40. The correct answer is (H). This problem requires two steps. First, find the smallest number divisible by both 14 and 12 (the least common multiple, or LCM). Secondly, add the number to 1:00 and rename it as time of day. The LCM of 14 and 12 is 84. Both events will occur simultaneously 84 minutes past 1:00, or 2:24 p.m.

SCORE SHEET

CTB/McGraw-Hill will score your actual exam and send your scaled scores and your percentile scores directly to the schools you indicated. Scaled scores are scores converted by a special formula to make comparable your performance on tests of unequal lengths and unequal importance. Percentile scores compare your performance on each test and the whole exam with the performance of other students who took the same exam at the same time. Your scores will not be reported either as raw scores—that is, number correct—nor as percents. Right now, however, you will find it very useful to convert your own scores on the practice exam into simple percentages. In this way you can compare your own performance on each test of the exam with your performance on each other test. You can then focus your study where it will do you the most good.

Subject	No. Correct ÷ No. of Questions	× 100 = ____%
Sequences	____ ÷ 20 =	____ × 100 = ____%
Analogies	____ ÷ 20 =	____ × 100 = ____%
Quantitative Reasoning	____ ÷ 20 =	____ × 100 = ____%
Verbal Reasoning—Words	____ ÷ 12 =	____ × 100 = ____%
Verbal Reasoning—Context	____ ÷ 20 =	____ × 100 = ____%
Reading and Language Arts	____ ÷ 50 =	____ × 100 = ____%
Mathematics	____ ÷ 40 =	____ × 100 = ____%
TOTAL EXAM	____ ÷ 182 =	____ × 100 = ____%

ANSWER SHEET PRACTICE TEST 4: COOP

Section 1. Sequences

1. Ⓐ Ⓑ Ⓒ Ⓓ   5. Ⓐ Ⓑ Ⓒ Ⓓ   9. Ⓐ Ⓑ Ⓒ Ⓓ   13. Ⓐ Ⓑ Ⓒ Ⓓ   17. Ⓐ Ⓑ Ⓒ Ⓓ
2. Ⓕ Ⓖ Ⓗ Ⓙ   6. Ⓕ Ⓖ Ⓗ Ⓙ   10. Ⓕ Ⓖ Ⓗ Ⓙ   14. Ⓕ Ⓖ Ⓗ Ⓙ   18. Ⓕ Ⓖ Ⓗ Ⓙ
3. Ⓐ Ⓑ Ⓒ Ⓓ   7. Ⓐ Ⓑ Ⓒ Ⓓ   11. Ⓐ Ⓑ Ⓒ Ⓓ   15. Ⓐ Ⓑ Ⓒ Ⓓ   19. Ⓐ Ⓑ Ⓒ Ⓓ
4. Ⓕ Ⓖ Ⓗ Ⓙ   8. Ⓕ Ⓖ Ⓗ Ⓙ   12. Ⓕ Ⓖ Ⓗ Ⓙ   16. Ⓕ Ⓖ Ⓗ Ⓙ   20. Ⓕ Ⓖ Ⓗ Ⓙ

Section 2. Analogies

1. Ⓐ Ⓑ Ⓒ Ⓓ   5. Ⓐ Ⓑ Ⓒ Ⓓ   9. Ⓐ Ⓑ Ⓒ Ⓓ   13. Ⓐ Ⓑ Ⓒ Ⓓ   17. Ⓐ Ⓑ Ⓒ Ⓓ
2. Ⓕ Ⓖ Ⓗ Ⓙ   6. Ⓕ Ⓖ Ⓗ Ⓙ   10. Ⓕ Ⓖ Ⓗ Ⓙ   14. Ⓕ Ⓖ Ⓗ Ⓙ   18. Ⓕ Ⓖ Ⓗ Ⓙ
3. Ⓐ Ⓑ Ⓒ Ⓓ   7. Ⓐ Ⓑ Ⓒ Ⓓ   11. Ⓐ Ⓑ Ⓒ Ⓓ   15. Ⓐ Ⓑ Ⓒ Ⓓ   19. Ⓐ Ⓑ Ⓒ Ⓓ
4. Ⓕ Ⓖ Ⓗ Ⓙ   8. Ⓕ Ⓖ Ⓗ Ⓙ   12. Ⓕ Ⓖ Ⓗ Ⓙ   16. Ⓕ Ⓖ Ⓗ Ⓙ   20. Ⓕ Ⓖ Ⓗ Ⓙ

Section 3. Quantitative Reasoning

1. Ⓐ Ⓑ Ⓒ Ⓓ   5. Ⓐ Ⓑ Ⓒ Ⓓ   9. Ⓐ Ⓑ Ⓒ Ⓓ   13. Ⓐ Ⓑ Ⓒ Ⓓ   17. Ⓐ Ⓑ Ⓒ Ⓓ
2. Ⓕ Ⓖ Ⓗ Ⓙ   6. Ⓕ Ⓖ Ⓗ Ⓙ   10. Ⓕ Ⓖ Ⓗ Ⓙ   14. Ⓕ Ⓖ Ⓗ Ⓙ   18. Ⓕ Ⓖ Ⓗ Ⓙ
3. Ⓐ Ⓑ Ⓒ Ⓓ   7. Ⓐ Ⓑ Ⓒ Ⓓ   11. Ⓐ Ⓑ Ⓒ Ⓓ   15. Ⓐ Ⓑ Ⓒ Ⓓ   19. Ⓐ Ⓑ Ⓒ Ⓓ
4. Ⓕ Ⓖ Ⓗ Ⓙ   8. Ⓕ Ⓖ Ⓗ Ⓙ   12. Ⓕ Ⓖ Ⓗ Ⓙ   16. Ⓕ Ⓖ Ⓗ Ⓙ   20. Ⓕ Ⓖ Ⓗ Ⓙ

Section 4. Verbal Reasoning—Words

1. Ⓐ Ⓑ Ⓒ Ⓓ   4. Ⓐ Ⓑ Ⓒ Ⓓ   7. Ⓐ Ⓑ Ⓒ Ⓓ   9. Ⓐ Ⓑ Ⓒ Ⓓ   11. Ⓐ Ⓑ Ⓒ Ⓓ
2. Ⓕ Ⓖ Ⓗ Ⓙ   5. Ⓕ Ⓖ Ⓗ Ⓙ   8. Ⓕ Ⓖ Ⓗ Ⓙ   10. Ⓕ Ⓖ Ⓗ Ⓙ   12. Ⓕ Ⓖ Ⓗ Ⓙ
3. Ⓐ Ⓑ Ⓒ Ⓓ   6. Ⓐ Ⓑ Ⓒ Ⓓ

Section 5. Verbal Reasoning—Context

1. Ⓐ Ⓑ Ⓒ Ⓓ   5. Ⓐ Ⓑ Ⓒ Ⓓ   9. Ⓐ Ⓑ Ⓒ Ⓓ   13. Ⓐ Ⓑ Ⓒ Ⓓ   17. Ⓐ Ⓑ Ⓒ Ⓓ
2. Ⓕ Ⓖ Ⓗ Ⓙ   6. Ⓕ Ⓖ Ⓗ Ⓙ   10. Ⓕ Ⓖ Ⓗ Ⓙ   14. Ⓕ Ⓖ Ⓗ Ⓙ   18. Ⓕ Ⓖ Ⓗ Ⓙ
3. Ⓐ Ⓑ Ⓒ Ⓓ   7. Ⓐ Ⓑ Ⓒ Ⓓ   11. Ⓐ Ⓑ Ⓒ Ⓓ   15. Ⓐ Ⓑ Ⓒ Ⓓ   19. Ⓐ Ⓑ Ⓒ Ⓓ
4. Ⓕ Ⓖ Ⓗ Ⓙ   8. Ⓕ Ⓖ Ⓗ Ⓙ   12. Ⓕ Ⓖ Ⓗ Ⓙ   16. Ⓕ Ⓖ Ⓗ Ⓙ   20. Ⓕ Ⓖ Ⓗ Ⓙ

Section 6. Reading and Language Arts

1. Ⓐ Ⓑ Ⓒ Ⓓ   11. Ⓐ Ⓑ Ⓒ Ⓓ   21. Ⓐ Ⓑ Ⓒ Ⓓ   31. Ⓐ Ⓑ Ⓒ Ⓓ   41. Ⓐ Ⓑ Ⓒ Ⓓ
2. Ⓕ Ⓖ Ⓗ Ⓙ   12. Ⓕ Ⓖ Ⓗ Ⓙ   22. Ⓕ Ⓖ Ⓗ Ⓙ   32. Ⓕ Ⓖ Ⓗ Ⓙ   42. Ⓕ Ⓖ Ⓗ Ⓙ
3. Ⓐ Ⓑ Ⓒ Ⓓ   13. Ⓐ Ⓑ Ⓒ Ⓓ   23. Ⓐ Ⓑ Ⓒ Ⓓ   33. Ⓐ Ⓑ Ⓒ Ⓓ   43. Ⓐ Ⓑ Ⓒ Ⓓ
4. Ⓕ Ⓖ Ⓗ Ⓙ   14. Ⓕ Ⓖ Ⓗ Ⓙ   24. Ⓕ Ⓖ Ⓗ Ⓙ   34. Ⓕ Ⓖ Ⓗ Ⓙ   44. Ⓕ Ⓖ Ⓗ Ⓙ
5. Ⓐ Ⓑ Ⓒ Ⓓ   15. Ⓐ Ⓑ Ⓒ Ⓓ   25. Ⓐ Ⓑ Ⓒ Ⓓ   35. Ⓐ Ⓑ Ⓒ Ⓓ   45. Ⓐ Ⓑ Ⓒ Ⓓ
6. Ⓕ Ⓖ Ⓗ Ⓙ   16. Ⓕ Ⓖ Ⓗ Ⓙ   26. Ⓕ Ⓖ Ⓗ Ⓙ   36. Ⓕ Ⓖ Ⓗ Ⓙ   46. Ⓕ Ⓖ Ⓗ Ⓙ
7. Ⓐ Ⓑ Ⓒ Ⓓ   17. Ⓐ Ⓑ Ⓒ Ⓓ   27. Ⓐ Ⓑ Ⓒ Ⓓ   37. Ⓐ Ⓑ Ⓒ Ⓓ   47. Ⓐ Ⓑ Ⓒ Ⓓ
8. Ⓕ Ⓖ Ⓗ Ⓙ   18. Ⓕ Ⓖ Ⓗ Ⓙ   28. Ⓕ Ⓖ Ⓗ Ⓙ   38. Ⓕ Ⓖ Ⓗ Ⓙ   48. Ⓕ Ⓖ Ⓗ Ⓙ
9. Ⓐ Ⓑ Ⓒ Ⓓ   19. Ⓐ Ⓑ Ⓒ Ⓓ   29. Ⓐ Ⓑ Ⓒ Ⓓ   39. Ⓐ Ⓑ Ⓒ Ⓓ   49. Ⓐ Ⓑ Ⓒ Ⓓ
10. Ⓕ Ⓖ Ⓗ Ⓙ   20. Ⓕ Ⓖ Ⓗ Ⓙ   30. Ⓕ Ⓖ Ⓗ Ⓙ   40. Ⓕ Ⓖ Ⓗ Ⓙ   50. Ⓕ Ⓖ Ⓗ Ⓙ

Section 7. Mathematics

1. Ⓐ Ⓑ Ⓒ Ⓓ   9. Ⓐ Ⓑ Ⓒ Ⓓ   17. Ⓐ Ⓑ Ⓒ Ⓓ   25. Ⓐ Ⓑ Ⓒ Ⓓ   33. Ⓐ Ⓑ Ⓒ Ⓓ
2. Ⓕ Ⓖ Ⓗ Ⓙ   10. Ⓕ Ⓖ Ⓗ Ⓙ   18. Ⓕ Ⓖ Ⓗ Ⓙ   26. Ⓕ Ⓖ Ⓗ Ⓙ   34. Ⓕ Ⓖ Ⓗ Ⓙ
3. Ⓐ Ⓑ Ⓒ Ⓓ   11. Ⓐ Ⓑ Ⓒ Ⓓ   19. Ⓐ Ⓑ Ⓒ Ⓓ   27. Ⓐ Ⓑ Ⓒ Ⓓ   35. Ⓐ Ⓑ Ⓒ Ⓓ
4. Ⓕ Ⓖ Ⓗ Ⓙ   12. Ⓕ Ⓖ Ⓗ Ⓙ   20. Ⓕ Ⓖ Ⓗ Ⓙ   28. Ⓕ Ⓖ Ⓗ Ⓙ   36. Ⓕ Ⓖ Ⓗ Ⓙ
5. Ⓐ Ⓑ Ⓒ Ⓓ   13. Ⓐ Ⓑ Ⓒ Ⓓ   21. Ⓐ Ⓑ Ⓒ Ⓓ   29. Ⓐ Ⓑ Ⓒ Ⓓ   37. Ⓐ Ⓑ Ⓒ Ⓓ
6. Ⓕ Ⓖ Ⓗ Ⓙ   14. Ⓕ Ⓖ Ⓗ Ⓙ   22. Ⓕ Ⓖ Ⓗ Ⓙ   30. Ⓕ Ⓖ Ⓗ Ⓙ   38. Ⓕ Ⓖ Ⓗ Ⓙ
7. Ⓐ Ⓑ Ⓒ Ⓓ   15. Ⓐ Ⓑ Ⓒ Ⓓ   23. Ⓐ Ⓑ Ⓒ Ⓓ   31. Ⓐ Ⓑ Ⓒ Ⓓ   39. Ⓐ Ⓑ Ⓒ Ⓓ
8. Ⓕ Ⓖ Ⓗ Ⓙ   16. Ⓕ Ⓖ Ⓗ Ⓙ   24. Ⓕ Ⓖ Ⓗ Ⓙ   32. Ⓕ Ⓖ Ⓗ Ⓙ   40. Ⓕ Ⓖ Ⓗ Ⓙ

Practice Test 4: COOP

SECTION 1. SEQUENCES

15 MINUTES

Directions: For questions 1–20, choose the part that would continue the pattern or sequence. Mark the letter of your answer on the answer sheet.

1.

(A) (B) (C) (D)

2.

(F) (G) (H) (J)

3.

(A) (B) (C) (D)

4.

(F) (G) (H) (J)

5.

(A) (B) (C) (D)

6.

(F) $\bigvee\!\!\!\bigvee$ (G) $\bigvee\!\!\!\bigvee$ (H) $\bigvee\!\!\!\bigvee$ (J) $\bigcap\!\!\!\bigvee$

7. 44 39 35 | 87 82 78 | 61 56 _____
   - **(A)** 53
   - **(B)** 52
   - **(C)** 50
   - **(D)** 48

8. 3 6 3 | 12 24 12 | 9 _____ 9
   - **(F)** 18
   - **(G)** 3
   - **(H)** 6
   - **(J)** 27

9. 5 10 8 | 7 14 8 | 3 6 _____
   - **(A)** 9
   - **(B)** 7
   - **(C)** 5
   - **(D)** 8

10. 75 25 8.$\overline{3}$ | 90 30 10 | _____ 7 2.3
    - **(F)** 23
    - **(G)** 21
    - **(H)** 30
    - **(J)** 15

11. 23 41 41 | 7 25 25 | 41 _____ 59
    - **(A)** 23
    - **(B)** 25
    - **(C)** 59
    - **(D)** 41

12. 2 4 6 | 3 6 9 | 4 8 _____
    - **(F)** 16
    - **(G)** 10
    - **(H)** 12
    - **(J)** 32

13. 100 80 90 | 60 40 50 | 80 _____ 70
    - **(A)** 60
    - **(B)** 90
    - **(C)** 50
    - **(D)** 100

14. $R_1S_2T^3$ | $R^3S_1T_2$ | $R_2S^3T_1$ | _____ $R^3S_1T_2$
    - **(F)** $R^1S_2T_3$
    - **(G)** $R^3S_2T_1$
    - **(H)** $R_3S_1T^2$
    - **(J)** $R_1S_2T^3$

15. $P^6D^4Q^2$ | $P^6D^4Q_2$ | $P^6D_4Q_2$ | _____ $P_6D_4Q^2$
    - **(A)** $P^6D^4Q^2$
    - **(B)** $P_6D_4Q_2$
    - **(C)** $P_6D^4Q_2$
    - **(D)** $P^6D_4Q^2$

16. $L^5M^5N_4$ | $L^5M_4N_4$ | $L_4M_4N_4$ | _____ $L_4M^3N^3$
    - **(F)** $L_4M_4N^3$
    - **(G)** $L^5M_4N^3$
    - **(H)** $L^5M^5N^5$
    - **(J)** $L_4M^5N_3$

17. ABC FED GHI LKJ _____
    - **(A)** ONM
    - **(B)** NOP
    - **(C)** MNO
    - **(D)** MON

18. ABDB ACEB ADFB _____ AFHB
    - **(F)** ADGB
    - **(G)** AEGB
    - **(H)** AFGB
    - **(J)** ACGB

19. ABC EFG JKL PQR _____
    (A) XYZ
    (B) UVW
    (C) TUV
    (D) WXY

20. ZYWX VUST RQOP _____ JIGH
    (F) MNKL
    (G) LKMN
    (H) NMKL
    (J) NMLK

STOP   If you finish before time is up, check over your work on Section 1 only. Do not go on until the signal is given.

SECTION 2. ANALOGIES

7 MINUTES

Directions: For questions 1–20, choose the picture that should go in the empty box so that the bottom two pictures are related in the same way that the top two are related.

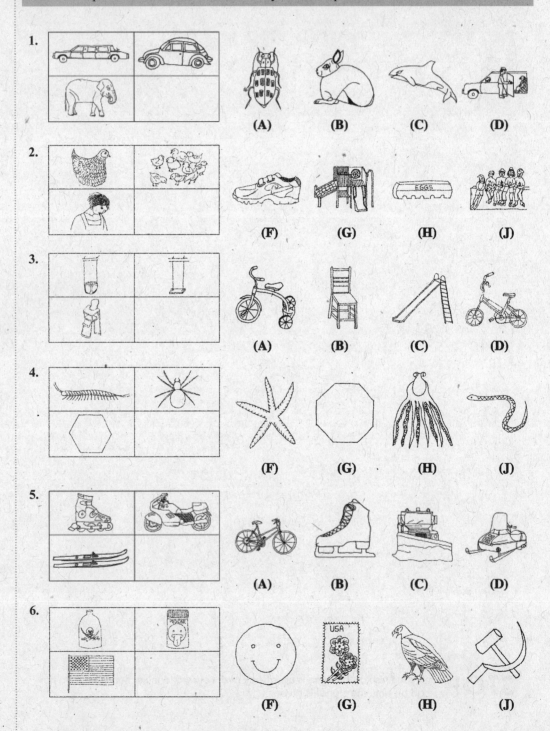

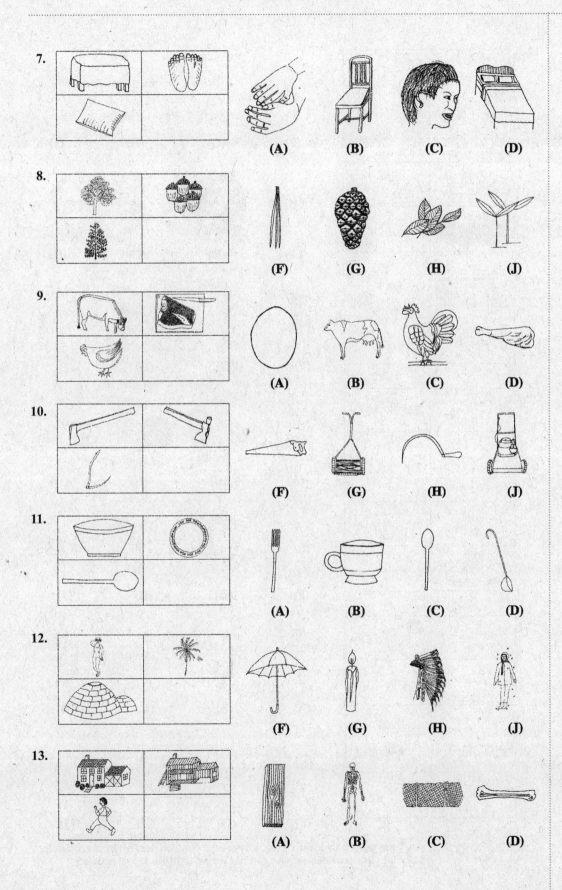

7.

(A) (B) (C) (D)

8.

(F) (G) (H) (J)

9.

(A) (B) (C) (D)

10.

(F) (G) (H) (J)

11.

(A) (B) (C) (D)

12.

(F) (G) (H) (J)

13.

(A) (B) (C) (D)

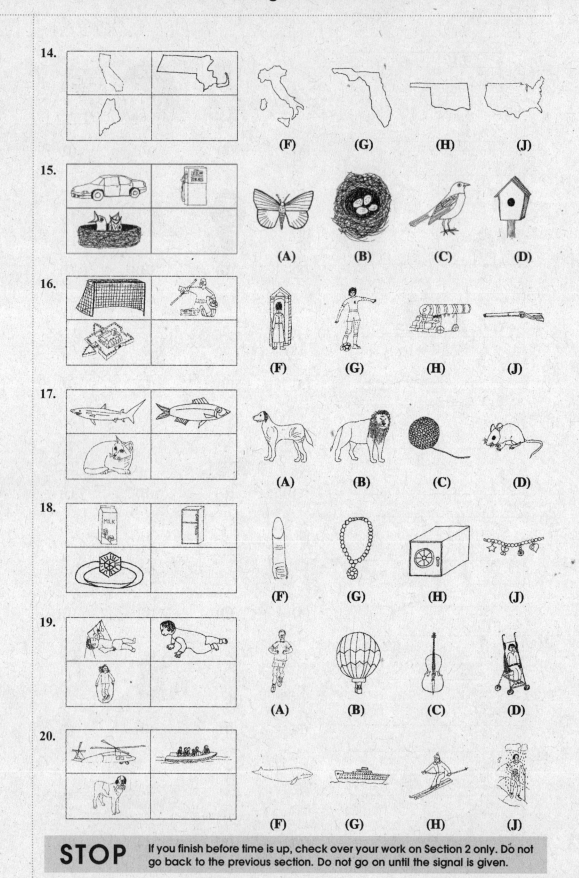

14.   (F)   (G)   (H)   (J)

15.   (A)   (B)   (C)   (D)

16.   (F)   (G)   (H)   (J)

17.   (A)   (B)   (C)   (D)

18.   (F)   (G)   (H)   (J)

19.   (A)   (B)   (C)   (D)

20.   (F)   (G)   (H)   (J)

STOP   If you finish before time is up, check over your work on Section 2 only. Do not go back to the previous section. Do not go on until the signal is given.

SECTION 3. QUANTITATIVE REASONING

5 MINUTES

Directions: For questions 1–6, find the relationship of the numbers in one column to the numbers in the other column. Then find the missing number.

1.
$2 \rightarrow \boxed{} \rightarrow 6$
$3 \rightarrow \boxed{} \rightarrow 7$
$5 \rightarrow \boxed{} \rightarrow ?$

9	11	13	15
(A)	(B)	(C)	(D)

2.
$5 \rightarrow \boxed{} \rightarrow 6$
$2 \rightarrow \boxed{} \rightarrow 3$
$6 \rightarrow \boxed{} \rightarrow ?$

6	7	8	9
(F)	(G)	(H)	(J)

3.
$30 \rightarrow \boxed{} \rightarrow 27$
$20 \rightarrow \boxed{} \rightarrow 17$
$10 \rightarrow \boxed{} \rightarrow ?$

3	7	10	13
(A)	(B)	(C)	(D)

4.
$8 \rightarrow \boxed{} \rightarrow 6$
$5 \rightarrow \boxed{} \rightarrow 3$
$3 \rightarrow \boxed{} \rightarrow ?$

1	2	3	4
(F)	(G)	(H)	(J)

5.
$2 \rightarrow \boxed{} \rightarrow 4$
$5 \rightarrow \boxed{} \rightarrow 10$
$9 \rightarrow \boxed{} \rightarrow ?$

16	17	18	19
(A)	(B)	(C)	(D)

6.
$3 \rightarrow \boxed{} \rightarrow 1$
$6 \rightarrow \boxed{} \rightarrow 2$
$15 \rightarrow \boxed{} \rightarrow ?$

2	3	4	5
(F)	(G)	(H)	(J)

Directions: For questions 7–13, find the fraction of the grid that is shaded.

7.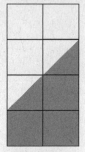

$\frac{1}{2}$ $\frac{1}{3}$ $\frac{1}{4}$ $\frac{1}{5}$
(A)   (B)   (C)   (D)

8.

$\frac{1}{6}$ $\frac{2}{5}$ $\frac{3}{2}$ $\frac{1}{2}$
(F)   (G)   (H)   (J)

9.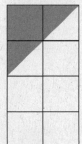

$\frac{1}{2}$ $\frac{1}{3}$ $\frac{1}{4}$ $\frac{1}{5}$
(A)   (B)   (C)   (D)

10.

$\frac{1}{2}$ $\frac{1}{3}$ $\frac{1}{4}$ $\frac{1}{5}$
(F)   (G)   (H)   (J)

11.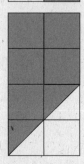

$\frac{4}{5}$ $\frac{3}{4}$ $\frac{2}{3}$ $\frac{1}{2}$
(A)   (B)   (C)   (D)

12.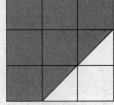

$\frac{7}{9}$ $\frac{5}{6}$ $\frac{1}{3}$ $\frac{2}{9}$
(F)   (G)   (H)   (J)

13.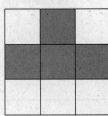

$\frac{1}{2}$ $\frac{1}{3}$ $\frac{1}{4}$ $\frac{4}{9}$
(A)   (B)   (C)   (D)

Directions: For questions 14–20, look at the scale showing sets of shapes of equal weight. Find an equivalent pair of sets that would also balance the scale.

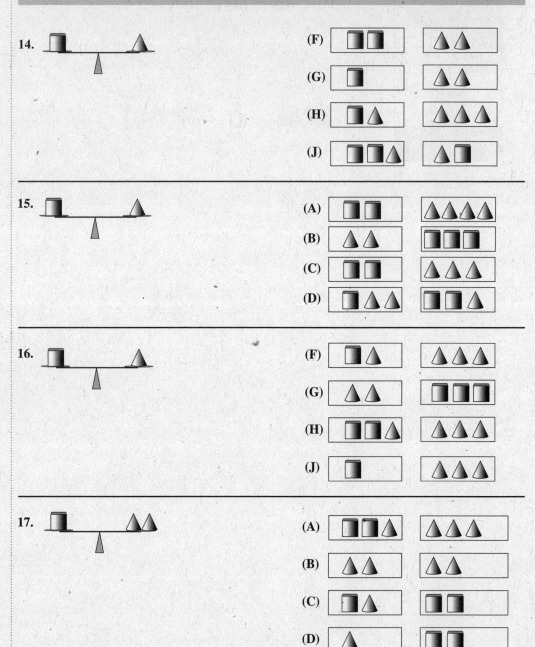

18.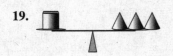

(F) | ▯▯▯ | △△△ |
(G) | ▯ △ | △△△△ |
(H) | ▯ △ | △△△ |
(J) | △△ | ▯△ |

19.

(A) | ▯▯△△△ | ▯▯▯ |
(B) | ▯ △ | △△ |
(C) | ▯ △ | △△△ |
(D) | △△▯ | △△△ |

20.

(F) | ▯△△△△ | ▯▯ |
(G) | ▯ | △△△ |
(H) | ▯ △ | △△△ |
(J) | ▯△△ | ▯▯ |

practice test

SECTION 4. VERBAL REASONING—WORDS

15 MINUTES

Directions: For questions 1–6, find the word that names a necessary part of the underlined word.

1. cartoon
   - (A) humor
   - (B) animation
   - (C) drawing
   - (D) message

2. heroine
   - (F) hero
   - (G) woman
   - (H) crisis
   - (J) victim

3. pump
   - (A) water
   - (B) air
   - (C) handle
   - (D) pressure

4. lantern
   - (F) light
   - (G) glass
   - (H) handle
   - (J) fuel

5. data
   - (A) numbers
   - (B) information
   - (C) charts
   - (D) words

6. biography
   - (F) facts
   - (G) book
   - (H) life
   - (J) fame

Directions: In questions 7–12, the words in the top row are related in some way. The words in the bottom row are related in the same way. For each item, find the word that completes the bottom row of words.

7. red   yellow   blue
   orange   green
   - (A) turquoise
   - (B) aqua
   - (C) violet
   - (D) gray

8. wind   water   sun
   coal   gas
   - (F) uranium
   - (G) fission
   - (H) wood
   - (J) oil

9. flamingo   egret   heron
   finch   chickadee
   - (A) sparrow
   - (B) woodpecker
   - (C) robin
   - (D) crane

10. saturated   wet   damp
    doctor   master
    - (F) nurse
    - (G) bachelor
    - (H) mistress
    - (J) hospital

11.

apple	tomato	watermelon
plum	mango	

(A) pear
(B) cherry
(C) strawberry
(D) papaya

12.

toe	foot	ankle
finger	hand	

(F) leg
(G) nail
(H) arm
(J) wrist

STOP If you finish before time is up, check over your work on Section 4 only. Do not go back to the previous sections. Do not go on until the signal is given.

Like us at facebook.com/petersonspublishing

SECTION 5. VERBAL REASONING—CONTEXT

15 MINUTES

Directions: For questions 1–5, find the statement that is true according to the given information.

1. Bob walked into the convenience store and requested a package of cigarettes. The clerk asked Bob some questions. Bob left the store without cigarettes.

   (A) Bob is too young to purchase cigarettes in this state.

   (B) The store does not carry the brand that Bob prefers.

   (C) Bob did not have enough money with him.

   (D) The clerk did not sell cigarettes to Bob.

2. Tara purchased an airplane ticket for a vacation trip to Bermuda. The airplane crashed at takeoff. Tara's name was not among the list of injured passengers.

   (F) Tara missed the flight and was not on the airplane.

   (G) Tara survived the crash.

   (H) Tara was not injured.

   (J) Tara never got to Bermuda.

3. A lavishly staged new play based on a very successful movie recently opened at a Broadway theater. A popular, but temperamental, aging actress was cast in the leading role. After three weeks, the play closed.

   (A) The star walked out on the show.

   (B) The movie was not suited to be performed as a stage play.

   (C) The play was not a box office success.

   (D) The play had only been scheduled for a three-week run.

4. Before Bernie left Tucson for a two-week vacation trip, he brought his dog, Michelle, to the home of his son Jack. Jack was unexpectedly called out of town on a business trip, so he took Michelle to a kennel. Jack's business kept him away from Tucson for three days.

   (F) Michelle spent some time at a kennel.

   (G) The kennel is in Tucson.

   (H) Jack took Michelle out of the kennel after three days.

   (J) Michelle eagerly awaited Bernie's return.

5. When the weather in Canada gets very cold, the Canadian geese fly south in search of a warmer climate and more plentiful food supply. In each flock, one goose is the leader, and other geese follow in a V-formation. It is January now, and there is a Canadian goose in my backyard in Maine.

   (A) The goose was injured and unable to continue its flight.

   (B) The goose is not where it should be at this time.

   (C) This goose finds Maine to be warm enough for it.

   (D) This is an independent goose that refused to follow the leader.

Directions: For questions 6–8, find the correct answer.

6. Here are some words translated from an artificial language.

   adabamikula means north pole
   bomanitinkipu means south wind
   adabagotono means north star

   Which word means *east wind*?

   (F) adabatinkipu
   (G) manitutinkipu
   (H) mikulamanitu
   (J) manitugotono

7. Here are some words translated from an artificial language.

   pataracolufax means biography
   pataragantropo means biology
   lognosocolufax means cartography

   Which word means *geophysics*?

   (A) damaniposiflo
   (B) lognosodamani
   (C) damanigantropo
   (D) parataposiflo

8. Here are some words translated from an artificial language.

   elemehotuto means red fruit
   zigarunaftama means green vegetable
   zigarubiganinaftama means green leafy vegetable

   Which word means *red flower*?

   (F) hotutotoribuz
   (G) biganieleme
   (H) zigaruhotuto
   (J) toribuzhotuto

Directions: For questions 9–20, find the statement that is true according to the given information.

9. Angela's student advisor tells her that taking advanced biology will help her get into her first choice college. Angela really wants to go to her first choice college, and she always follows her advisor's recommendations.

   (A) Angela signs up for the advanced biology course.
   (B) Duke University is Angela's first choice college.
   (C) Angela wants to go into pre-med studies at college.
   (D) Angela's advisor tells all college-bound students to take advanced biology.

10. Kim always packs lunches for herself and her two brothers to take to school. Kim's brother Kyle is sick and misses school on Monday.

    (F) Kim has to get up early to pack all the lunches.
    (G) Kim makes peanut butter and jelly sandwiches every other day.
    (H) Kim only packs two lunches for school on Monday.
    (J) Kim's brothers are too young to make their own lunches.

11. Sharon, Kelly, Peter, and Alex all run for senior class president. They are the only candidates for the position. Sharon and Alex both get the least number of votes, while Peter only gets five fewer votes than Kelly.

    (A) Sharon and Alex are not very popular.

    (B) Peter thinks the role of class president will look good on his scholarship application.

    (C) Peter has a strong campaign team.

    (D) Kelly is the new senior class president.

12. If Heather does not leave school by 3 p.m., she will miss her dance class at the community center. Heather leaves school at 2:50 p.m. after the last bell.

    (F) Heather leaves school in time to make it to her dance class.

    (G) Heather hates hurrying around on Wednesday afternoons for dance practice.

    (H) Heather wants to win a dance scholarship.

    (J) Heather cannot perform in dance competitions if she misses more than three classes.

13. The Agriculture Club cannot host its annual Farm Day if there is bad weather. On the morning of Farm Day, the sky is dark and thunderstorms are moving through the area.

    (A) The Agriculture Club moves Farm Day activities to the gymnasium.

    (B) The Agricultural Club does not host Farm Day.

    (C) Farm Day is always in the spring.

    (D) Farm Day has been rained out for the past two years.

14. Renee leaves Charleston at 3 p.m. It takes her four hours to get to Charlotte.

    (F) Renee drives for four hours.

    (G) Renee's car gets very good gas mileage.

    (H) Renee arrives in Charlotte at about 7 p.m.

    (J) Renee stops to eat at 5 p.m.

15. All dogs are descended from wolves. Button is a St. Bernard from a breeder in Sweden.

    (A) Button is a very strong guard dog.

    (B) Button's owner takes her to dog shows every weekend.

    (C) Button is afraid of wolves and sleeps inside.

    (D) Button's ancestors are wolves.

16. Abby's parents warn that if she does not get at least a "C" on her history exam, she cannot go out with her friends on Saturday. Abby gets a "B+" on the history test.

    (F) Abby's parents take her out for a celebratory dinner.

    (G) Abby scores high enough to be allowed to go out with her friends on Saturday.

    (H) Abby's history teacher tells her she applied herself well.

    (J) Abby plans to go to the mall with her friends on Saturday.

17. Jack and his friend Tim meet at their friend Rick's house. Rick's parents do not want the boys playing soccer in the house, and the boys uphold this rule.

    (A) Jack, Tim, and Rick play video games inside the house.

    (B) Jack, Tim, and Rick decide to go to Jack's house.

    (C) Jack, Tim, and Rick think Rick's parents are too strict.

    (D) If Jack, Tim, and Rick play soccer at Rick's house, they play outside.

18. Rob places better than Nancy and Georgia in the spelling contest. Rob also does better than Joe and Diego, but Martha places better than Rob.

    (F) Martha places best out of the students mentioned.

    (G) Joe and Diego both miss words ending in consonants.

    (H) Nancy and Georgia both miss difficult words.

    (J) Diego wishes he had placed higher than Rob in the contest.

19. The yearbook staff can only take pictures when the school's camera is not in use by the student newspaper staff. The newspaper staff members never take pictures on the paper's publishing day, which is every Thursday.

   (A) The newspaper staff only uses black and white film.

   (B) The newspaper editor does not like the yearbook editor.

   (C) The school's publication budget is smaller than the sports budget.

   (D) The yearbook staff can use the school's camera on Thursdays.

20. Amber starts a community service group to visit residents at a local nursing home. She can visit nursing home residents on nights when she is not working. Amber works at the Ice Cream Palace every weeknight, but never on weekends.

   (F) Amber can visit with the nursing home residents on weekends.

   (G) Amber's favorite ice cream flavor is peanut butter fudge.

   (H) Amber brings ice cream to the nursing home staff members.

   (J) Amber's great aunt is a resident at the nursing home.

STOP If you finish before time is up, check over your work on Section 5 only. Do not go back to the previous section. Do not go on until the signal is given.

practice test

SECTION 6. READING AND LANGUAGE ARTS

40 MINUTES

QUESTIONS 1–4 REFER TO THE FOLLOWING PASSAGE.

Using new tools and techniques, scientists, almost unnoticed, are remaking the world of plants. They have already remodeled 65 sorts of flowers, fruits, vegetables, and trees, giving us, among other things, tobacco that resists disease, cantaloupes that are immune to the blight, and lettuce with crisper leaves. The chief new tool they are using is colchicine, a poisonous drug that has astounding effects upon growth and upon heredity. It creates new varieties with astonishing frequency, whereas such mutations occur rarely in nature. Colchicine has thrown new light on the fascinating jobs of the plant hunters. The Department of Agriculture sends agents all over the world to find plants native to other lands that can be grown here and that are superior to those already here. Scientists have crossed these foreign plants with those at home, thereby adding to our farm crops many desirable characteristics. The colchicine technique has enormously facilitated their work because hybrids so often can be made fertile and because it takes so few generations of plants now to build a new variety with the qualities desired.

1. The title that best expresses the ideas of the paragraph is
   (A) "Plant Growth and Heredity."
   (B) "New Plants for Old."
   (C) "Remodeling Plant Life."
   (D) "A More Abundant World."

2. Mutation in plant life results in
   (F) diseased plants.
   (G) hybrids.
   (H) new varieties.
   (J) fertility.

3. Colchicine speeds the improvement of plant species because it
   (A) makes possible the use of foreign plants.
   (B) makes use of natural mutations.
   (C) creates new varieties very quickly.
   (D) can be used with 65 different vegetables, fruits, and flowers.

4. According to the passage, colchicine is a
   (F) poisonous drug.
   (G) blight.
   (H) kind of plant hunter.
   (J) hybrid plant.

QUESTIONS 5–8 REFER TO THE FOLLOWING PASSAGE.

The peopling of the Northwest Territory by companies from the eastern states, such as the Ohio Company under the leadership of Reverend Manasseh Cutler of Ipswich, Massachusetts, furnishes us with many interesting historical tales.

The first towns to be established were Marietta, Zanesville, Chillocothe, and Cincinnati. After the Ohio Company came the Connecticut Company, which secured all the territory bordering Lake Erie save a small portion known as fire lands and another portion known as Congress lands. The land taken up by the Connecticut people was called the Western Reserve and was settled almost entirely by New England people. The remainder of the state of Ohio was settled by Virginians and Pennsylvanians. Because the British controlled Lakes Ontario and Erie, the Massachusetts and Connecticut people made their journey into the Western Reserve through the southern part of the state. General Moses Cleaveland, the agent for the Connecticut Land Company, led a body of surveyors to the tract, proceeding by way of Lake Ontario. He quieted the Indian claims to the eastern portion of the reserve by giving them five hundred pounds, two heads of cattle, and one hundred gallons of whiskey. Landing at the mouth of the Conneaut River, General Moses Cleaveland and his party of fifty, including two women, celebrated Independence Day, 1796, with a feast of pork and beans with bread. A little later, a village was established at the mouth of the Cuyahoga River and was given the name of Cleaveland in honor of the agent of the company. It is related that the name was afterward shortened to Cleveland by one of the early editors because he could not get so many letters into the heading of his newspaper.

5. Reverend Manasseh Cutler
   (A) led the Ohio Company.
   (B) owned the Western Reserve.
   (C) led the Connecticut Land Company.
   (D) settled the Congress lands.

6. The title that best expresses the main idea of this selection is
   (F) "Control of the Great Lake Region."
   (G) "The Accomplishments of Reverend Manasseh Cutler."
   (H) "The Naming of Cleveland, Ohio."
   (J) "The Settling of the Northwest Territory."

7. In the last sentence of the selection, the word *related* is used to mean
   (A) associated with.
   (B) rumored.
   (C) reported.
   (D) thought.

8. The selection suggests that General Cleaveland at first found the Indians to be
   (F) extremely noisy people.
   (G) hostile to his party of strangers.
   (H) starving.
   (J) eager to work with him.

QUESTIONS 9–12 REFER TO THE FOLLOWING PASSAGE.

From Gettysburg to the Battle of the Bulge, carrier pigeons have winged their way through skies fair and foul to deliver the vital messages of battle. Today, in spite of electronics and atomic weapons, these feathered heroes are still an important communication link in any army.

No one could be surer of this than the men at Fort Monmouth, New Jersey, the sole Army pigeon breeding and training center in this country. On the roosts at Fort Monmouth perch many genuine battle heroes, among them veteran G. I. Joe.

In 1943, 1,000 British troops moved speedily ahead of the Allied advance in Italy to take the small town of Colvi Vecchia. Since communications could not be established in time to relay the victory to headquarters, the troops were due for a previously planned Allied bombing raid. Then one of the men released carrier pigeon G. I. Joe. With a warning message on his back, he flew 20 miles in 20 minutes, arriving just as the bombers were warming up their engines. For saving the day for the British, the Lord Mayor of London later awarded G. I. Joe the Dickin Medal, England's highest award to an animal.

Even when regular message channels are set up, equipment can break or be overloaded or radio silence must be observed. Then the carrier pigeon comes into his own. Ninety-nine times out of a hundred, he completes his mission. In Korea, Homer the homing pigeon was flying from the front to a rear command post when he developed wing trouble. Undaunted, Homer made a forced landing, hopped the last two miles, and delivered his message. For initiative and loyalty, Homer was promoted to Pfc.—Pigeon First Class!

9. The writer of this selection evidently believes that carrier pigeons
   (A) have no usefulness in modern warfare.
   (B) should be forced to fly only in emergencies.
   (C) are remarkably reliable as message carriers.
   (D) should receive regular promotions.

10. G. I. Joe was rewarded for
    (F) preventing unnecessary loss of life.
    (G) guiding a bomber's flight.
    (H) returning in spite of an injured wing.
    (J) bringing the news of an allied victory.

11. G. I. Joe's reward was a
    (A) promotion.
    (B) reception given by the Lord Mayor.
    (C) chance to retire to Fort Monmouth.
    (D) medal.

12. Choose the sentence that is written correctly.
    (F) For initiative and loyalty, Homer was promoted to Pfc.— Pigeon First Class.
    (G) Homer for initiative and loyalty, was promoted to Pfc.—Pigeon First Class.
    (H) For initiative and loyalty Homer promoted to Pfc.—Pigeon First Class!
    (J) Initiative and loyalty was the reason why Homer was promoting to Pfc.—Pigeon First Class.

QUESTIONS 13–17 REFER TO THE FOLLOWING PASSAGE.

"There are many things from which I might have derived good, by which I have not profited, I dare say, Christmas among the rest. But I am sure I have always thought of Christmastime, when it has come round— apart from the veneration due to its sacred origin, if anything belonging to it *can* be apart from that—as a good time; a kind, forgiving, charitable, pleasant time; the only time I know of, in the long calendar of the year, when men and women seem by one consent to open their shut-up hearts freely and to think of people below them as if they really were fellow travelers to the grave, and not another race of creatures bound on other journeys. And therefore, Uncle, though it has never put a scrap of gold or silver in my pocket, I believe that it *has* done me good, and *will* do me good; and I say, God bless it!" The clerk in the tank involuntarily applauded.

"Let me hear another sound from *you*," said Scrooge, "and you'll keep your Christmas by losing your situation! You're quite a powerful speaker, sir," he added, turning to his nephew. "I wonder you don't go into Parliament."

—From *A Christmas Carol* by Charles Dickens

13. The word *veneration* probably means
    (A) worship.
    (B) disapproval.
    (C) agreement.
    (D) love.

14. The first speaker
    (F) is a very religious person.
    (G) enjoys and celebrates Christmas.
    (H) is defending Christmas.
    (J) has been fired by Scrooge.

15. The first speaker believes that Christmas
(A) is a pleasant nuisance.
(B) brings out the best in people.
(C) has been separated from its religious origin.
(D) could be a profitable time of year.

16. The phrase by *one consent* is synonymous with
(F) affirmatively.
(G) contractually.
(H) partially.
(J) unanimously.

17. Scrooge probably is angry with
(A) the speaker and the clerk.
(B) only the speaker.
(C) only the clerk.
(D) people who celebrate Christmas.

QUESTIONS 18–22 REFER TO THE FOLLOWING PASSAGE.

The police department of New York City has one branch that many do not know about, even though it was established almost a century ago. This is the harbor precinct's 14-boat fleet of police launches, which patrol 578 miles of waters around the city, paying particular attention to the areas containing 500 piers and some 90 boat clubs.

The boats are equipped for various jobs. One boat is an ice breaker; another is equipped to render aid in the event of an airplane crash at La Guardia Airport. All of the boats are equipped with lifeline guns, heavy grappling irons to raise sunken automobiles, and lasso-sticks to rescue animals in the water. They have power pumps to bail out sinking craft, first-aid kits, extra life preservers, signal flags, and searchlights.

The force consists of 183 officers who have all had previous experience with boats. Some of the officers are Navy and Coast Guard veterans. Many members of the harbor police force have oceangoing Master's or Harbor Captain's licenses. All are highly trained in the care and handling of engines and in navigation. All are skilled in giving first aid, and each officer is a qualified radio operator and a trained marksman with a revolver.

The work of the police includes many tasks. One duty of this force is to check the operation of the fleet of 43 junk boats that ply their trade in the harbor, buying scrap, rope, and other items for resale ashore. These boats could just as easily be used to smuggle narcotics, gems, aliens, or spies into the country, so they are watched closely by the city's harbor police force. The officers also arrest those who break navigation laws or who endanger the safety of bathers by approaching too near the shore in speed boats. And during the last summer alone, police launches towed 450 disabled boats and gave some kind of help to thousands of others.

18. The harbor police were
(F) introduced by order of the mayor.
(G) first used in the twentieth century.
(H) in use before the Civil War.
(J) introduced by Naval and Coast Guard veterans.

19. The boats used
(A) are uniform in design.
(B) can all serve as ice breakers.
(C) work at Kennedy Airport.
(D) vary in function.

20. The harbor police
(F) prevent the resale of scrap material.
(G) regulate the admission of spies.
(H) ensure the legal operation of junk boats.
(J) regulate disabled boats.

21. The services of the harbor police include
(A) towing, life saving, and salvage.
(B) customs collection, towing, and the sending of radio messages.
(C) first aid, the rescue of animals, and fire patrol.
(D) ice breaking, the collection of junk, and the transportation of aliens.

22. Police boats
- **(F)** have no responsibility for bathers.
- **(G)** assist boats of all kinds.
- **(H)** warn offenders but do not make arrests.
- **(J)** cannot detain other boats.

QUESTIONS 23–26 REFER TO THE FOLLOWING PASSAGE.

America's national bird, the bald eagle, which has flown high since the Revolutionary War, may soon be grounded. The eagle population of the United States is decreasing at an alarming rate, so the National Audubon Society has launched a full-scale survey to find out how many bald eagles are left and what measures are necessary to protect them from extinction. The survey, a year-long project, focuses attention on the bird chosen to appear on the Great Seal of the United States.

When it gained its official status over 200 years ago, the bald eagle was undisputed king of America's skies. Many thousands of the great birds roamed the country, and both the sight of the bald eagle and its piercing scream were familiar to almost every American. Today, naturalists fear that there are fewer than a thousand of them still in the lower forty-eight.

Nature is partly to blame. Severe hurricanes have destroyed many eggs, fledglings, and aeries, the eagles' mammoth nests. But man is the chief culprit. Despite legislation passed by Congress in 1940 to protect the emblematic birds, thousands of them have been gunned out of the skies by over-eager shooters who perhaps mistook them for large hawks.

The bald eagle was known as the bald-headed eagle when Congress began the search for a seal in 1776. The archaic meaning of bald—white or streaked with white—refers to his head, neck, and tail coloring rather than to any lack of plumage in our fine-feathered friend.

23. The Audubon Society is trying to
- **(A)** rid the country of the bald eagle.
- **(B)** introduce the bald eagle into Alaska and Hawaii.
- **(C)** prevent the extinction of the bald eagle in this country.
- **(D)** have Congress pass a law forbidding the shooting of eagles.

24. There are now
- **(F)** more eagles in this country than there were in 1776.
- **(G)** fewer eagles here than there were more than 200 years ago.
- **(H)** many thousands of bald eagles.
- **(J)** eagles whose scream is familiar to every American.

25. Aeries are
- **(A)** fledglings.
- **(B)** eggs.
- **(C)** mating areas.
- **(D)** nests.

26. The eagle is called an *emblematic bird* because it is
- **(F)** bald.
- **(G)** handsome and powerful.
- **(H)** prized by hunters.
- **(J)** a symbol of a nation.

QUESTIONS 27–30 REFER TO THE FOLLOWING PASSAGE.

You know, of course, that in China the Emperor is a Chinaman, and all the people around him are Chinamen, too. It happened a good many years ago, but that's just why it's worthwhile to hear the story, before it is forgotten. The Emperor's palace was the most splendid in the world; entirely and altogether made of porcelain, so costly, but so brittle, so difficult to handle that one had to be terribly careful. In the garden were to be seen the strangest flowers, and to the most splendid of them silver bells were tied, which tinkled so that nobody should pass by without noticing the flowers. Oh, the Emperor's garden had been laid out very smartly, and it extended so far that the gardener himself didn't know where the end was. If you went on and on, you came into the loveliest forest with high trees and deep lakes. The forest went right down to the sea, which was blue and deep; tall ships could sail right in under the branches of the trees; and in the trees lived a nightingale which sang so sweetly that even the poor fisherman, who had many other things to do, stopped still and listened when he had gone out at night to take up his nets and then heard the nightingale.

—From *The Nightingale*
by Hans Christian Andersen

27. The author wants to tell this story
    (A) before it is forgotten.
    (B) because he is enchanted by China.
    (C) because he is a writer and storyteller.
    (D) in order to describe the garden.

28. The Emperor's palace was made of
    (F) silver bells.
    (G) high trees.
    (H) porcelain.
    (J) large stones and boulders.

29. Silver bells were tied to flowers in the garden to
    (A) further enhance their beauty.
    (B) draw attention to their beauty.
    (C) accompany the singing of the nightingale.
    (D) discourage flower picking.

30. The Emperor's garden
    (F) was too large to care for.
    (G) led into a lovely forest.
    (H) housed a rare nightingale.
    (J) was a source of pleasure for all in the kingdom.

QUESTIONS 31–35 REFER TO THE FOLLOWING PASSAGE.

On a population map of the world, deserts are shown as great blank spaces, but, in fact, these areas contribute many things to our lives.

When you go to the market to buy a box of dates, you are buying a bit of sunshine and dry air from the oases of the Sahara Desert or the Coachella Valley. Fresh peas or a lettuce salad for your winter dinner might be the product of an irrigation farmer in the Salt River Valley or the Imperial Valley. That fine broadcloth shirt you received for your birthday was made from silky, long-fibered cotton grown in Egypt. A half-wool, half-cotton sweater might contain Australian wool and Peruvian cotton, which are steppe and desert products.

These are only a few of the contributions these desert areas make to the quality of our lives. They have also made important cultural contributions.

Our number system is derived from the system used by the ancient civilizations of Arabia. The use of irrigation to make farming of dry areas possible was developed by the inhabitants of desert regions. The necessity of measuring water levels and noting land boundaries following flooding by the Nile River led to the development of mathematics and the practice of surveying and engineering. The desert people were also our early astronomers. They studied the locations of the stars in order to find their way across the limitless expanse of the desert at night.

31. The population of the world's deserts is
    (A) nomadic.
    (B) scientific.
    (C) vegetarian.
    (D) sparse.

32. The Imperial Valley produces
    (F) vegetables.
    (G) winter dinners.
    (H) shirts.
    (J) irrigation.

33. According to this passage, broadcloth is made of

(A) wool.

(B) cotton.

(C) silk.

(D) half wool, half cotton.

34. Culturally, desert civilizations have

(F) far surpassed those of all other regions.

(G) made important contributions.

(H) not influenced western civilizations.

(J) been blank spaces.

35. Surveying was developed because people needed to

(A) study astronomy.

(B) find their way across the deserts.

(C) determine land boundaries after floods.

(D) irrigate their crops.

QUESTIONS 36–40 REFER TO THE FOLLOWING PASSAGE.

Residents of Montana laughingly refer to the small, windblown settlement of Ekalaka in the eastern Badlands as "Skeleton Flats," but as curious as it may sound, the name is appropriate.

So many fossils have been dug up in this otherwise unremarkable town that it has become a paradise for paleontologists, scientists who use fossils to study prehistoric life forms. In fact, dinosaur bones are so plentiful in this area that ranchers have been known to use them as doorstops!

Ekalaka's fame began to grow more than 50 years ago when Walter H. Peck, whose hobby was geology, found the bones of a Stegosaurus, a huge, plant-eating dinosaur. The entire community soon became infected with Peck's enthusiasm for his find, and everyone began digging for dinosaur bones. Led by the local science teacher, groups of people would go out looking for new finds each weekend, and they rarely returned empty-handed.

It would seem there is no end to the fossil riches to be found in Ekalaka.

Among the most prized finds were the remains of a Brontosaurus, an 80-foot-long monster that probably weighed 40 tons. The skeleton of a Triceratops was also found. The head of this prehistoric giant alone weighed more than 1,000 pounds. Careful searching also yielded small fossilized fishes, complete with stony scales, and the remains of a huge sea reptile.

The prize find was a Pachycephalosaurus, a dinosaur whose peculiar skull was several inches thick. When descriptions of it reached scientific circles in the East, there was great excitement because this particular prehistoric animal was then completely unknown to scientists.

36. In the first sentence, the writer places "Skeleton Flats" in quotation marks to show that this phrase is

(F) a nickname given to the town by Montana residents, not the actual name of the town.

(G) spelled incorrectly.

(H) being spoken by someone other than the writer.

(J) a scientific term.

37. This article is primarily about

(A) paleontology.

(B) products in the state of Montana.

(C) fossil finds in Ekalaka.

(D) the Pachycephalosaurus.

38. A paleontologist is

(F) someone whose hobby is geology.

(G) a bone pit.

(H) a plant-eating dinosaur.

(J) someone who studies fossils.

39. In the third paragraph, the writer is describing the

(A) bones of a Stegosaurus.

(B) variety of fossils found in Ekalaka.

(C) town of Ekalaka.

(D) people of Ekalaka.

40. Discovery of a Pachycephalosaurus caused excitement because
- **(F)** its skull was several inches thick.
- **(G)** it was the first evidence of this previously unknown creature.
- **(H)** news of it quickly reached eastern scientific circles.
- **(J)** it received a prize.

Directions: For questions 41–43, choose the topic sentence that best fits the paragraph.

41. _____

These people lose sight of an important fact. Many of the founding fathers of our country were comparatively young men. Today more than ever, our country needs young, idealistic politicians.
- **(A)** Young people don't like politics.
- **(B)** Many people think that only older men and women who have had a great deal of experience should hold public office.
- **(C)** The holding of public office should be restricted to highly idealistic people.
- **(D)** Our Constitution prescribes certain minimum ages for certain elected federal officeholders.

42. _____

Mass and weight are not the same. Mass is the amount of matter any object contains. Weight is the pull of gravity on that mass.
- **(F)** Matter is anything that has mass and occupies space.
- **(G)** The phenomenon of weightlessness in outer space is created by the weak pull of gravity.
- **(H)** Matter is composed of basic substances known as *elements*.
- **(J)** Atomic weight is the weight of one atom of an element expressed in atomic mass units.

43. _____

In some cases, it consists only of ordinances, with little or no attempt at enforcement. In other cases, good control is obtained through wise ordinances and an efficient inspecting force and laboratory. While inspection alone can do much toward controlling the quality and production of milk, there must also be frequent laboratory tests of the milk.
- **(A)** The bacterial count of milk indicates the condition of the dairy and the methods of milk handling.
- **(B)** When the milk-producing animals are free from disease, the milk that they provide registers a low bacterial count.
- **(C)** Inefficient sterilization of equipment and utensils represented a source of milk contamination in dairies at the turn of the century.
- **(D)** Most cities carrying on public health work exercise varying degrees of inspection and control over their milk supplies.

Directions: For questions 44–46, choose the pair of sentences that best develops the topic sentence.

44. A passage leads from the outer ear to a membrane called the eardrum.
- **(F)** Earaches are caused by infection within the ear. Untreated chronic earaches may lead to eventual deafness.
- **(G)** Sound waves striking the eardrum make it vibrate. On the other side of the eardrum lies a space called the middle ear.
- **(H)** This tube ends near the throat opening of the nose, close to the tonsils. Doctors often remove both tonsils and adenoids in the same operation.
- **(J)** The sounds we hear are created by the vibration of air waves. The frequency of the vibrations determines the pitch of the sound.

45. Urban open-air markets originally came into existence spontaneously when groups of pushcart peddlers congregated in spots where business was good.

(A) There was confusion and disorder in these open-air markets because the peddlers paid no licensing fees. The strongest and toughest peddlers secured the best locations.

(B) One problem created by open-air markets is that of garbage in the streets. Another is obstruction of traffic.

(C) In some Asian countries, fixed stores represent a very small percent of all commerce. Nearly all buying and selling is done by merchants in the streets.

(D) Good business induced them to return to these spots daily, and unofficial open-air markets thus arose. These peddlers paid no fees, and cities received no revenue from them.

46. With well over a million different kinds of plants and animals living on Earth, there is a need for a system of classification.

(F) The animal and plant kingdoms are the two principal kingdoms and contain virtually all life. Scientists have struggled to find the best method of grouping organisms for hundreds of years.

(G) Viruses are a type of life that scientists have difficulty in defining. They do not fit easily into any classification scheme because they do not have a true cell structure.

(H) The system currently in use is based principally upon relationships and similarities in structure. The scientific name consists of two terms identifying the genus and the species.

(J) The first letter of the genus is capitalized, whereas the species is written in small letters. The scientific name for man is Homo sapien.

Directions: For question 47, choose the sentence that does not belong in the paragraph.

47. (1) The island countries of the Caribbean area produce large quantities of oil, tropical fruits, and vegetables. (2) They are also rich in minerals. (3) The Caribbean Sea is to the American continent a central sea, just as the Mediterranean is to the European continent. (4) This region is capable of supplying the United States with many goods formerly imported from Africa and Asia. (5) In exchange, the countries of this region need the manufactured goods that can be provided only by an industrial nation.

(A) Sentence 1

(B) Sentence 2

(C) Sentence 3

(D) Sentence 4

Directions: For questions 48–50, read the paragraph and choose the sentence that best fills the blank.

48. Many experiments on the effects of alcohol consumption show that alcohol decreases alertness and efficiency. It decreases self-consciousness and at the same time increases confidence and feelings of ease and relaxation. _____ It destroys the fear of consequences.

(F) They become highway menaces.

(G) The alcohol content of one ounce of whiskey is equal to that in one can of beer and in one glass of wine.

(H) The legal drinking age has been set at 21 so as to save the lives of young drivers.

(J) It impairs attention and judgment.

49. Kindling temperature is the lowest temperature at which a substance catches fire and continues to burn. Different fuels have different kindling temperatures. _____ Coal, because of its high kindling temperature, requires much heat before it will begin to burn. Matches are tipped with phosphorus or some other low kindling material to permit the small amount of heat produced by friction to ignite the match.

   (A) Safety matches are so called because they can be ignited only by striking on a strip on the package in which they are sold.

   (B) Paper catches fire easily because it has a low kindling temperature.

   (C) The United States consumes so much energy that it is rapidly consuming its store of fossil fuels.

   (D) Thin dry twigs are used as kindling wood for open fires.

50. Arsonists are persons who set fires deliberately. They don't look like criminals, but they cost the nation millions of dollars in property loss and sometimes loss of life. _____ Sometimes a shopkeeper sees no way out of losing his business and sets fire to it to collect the insurance. Some arsonists just like the excitement of seeing the fire burn and watching the firefighters at work.

   (F) Arsonists set fires for many different reasons.

   (G) Forest fires usually stem from carelessness or from natural causes rather than from the acts of arsonists.

   (H) Another type of arsonist wants revenge and sets fire to the home or shop of someone he feels has treated him unfairly.

   (J) Arsonists have even been known to help fight the fire.

STOP If you finish before time is up, check over your work on Section 6 only. Do not go back to the previous sections. Do not go on until the signal is given.

SECTION 7. MATHEMATICS

35 MINUTES

Directions: For questions 1–40, read each problem and find the answer.

1. If $x = 1\frac{2}{3}$, the reciprocal of x equals

    (A) $\frac{2}{3}$

    (B) $\frac{5}{3}$

    (C) $\frac{3}{5}$

    (D) $\frac{1}{x}$

2. The product of $\frac{7}{16}$ and a number x is 1. The number is

    (F) $1\frac{7}{16}$

    (G) $\frac{16}{7}$

    (H) $\frac{31}{14}$

    (J) 1

3. $\dfrac{\frac{1}{x} + 1}{1 + \frac{1}{x}}$ is equivalent to

    (A) 1

    (B) $\frac{1}{x}$

    (C) $\frac{1}{x} + 2$

    (D) $1 + x$

4. $\dfrac{\frac{2}{3} + \frac{3}{8}}{\frac{1}{4} - \frac{3}{16}}$ equals

    (F) $15\frac{2}{3}$

    (G) $\frac{25}{16}$

    (H) $\frac{13}{32}$

    (J) $\frac{50}{3}$

5. In the formula $L = \frac{3}{4}bxh$, if $b = 2$, $x = 7$, and $h = \frac{1}{2}$, L equals

    (A) $\frac{21}{2}$

    (B) $\frac{21}{4}$

    (C) $\frac{21}{8}$

    (D) $\frac{7x}{4}$

6. Two angles of a triangle are 45° and 75°. What is the measure of the third angle?

    (F) 60°

    (G) 35°

    (H) 180°

    (J) 45°

7.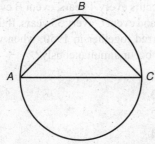

Isosceles $\triangle ABC$ is inscribed in a circle that has a diameter of 10 centimeters. The area of the triangle is

(A) 78.5 sq. cm.

(B) 12.5 sq. cm.

(C) 25 sq. cm.

(D) 50 sq. cm.

8. The volume of a small warehouse measuring 75 feet long, 50 feet wide, and 30 feet high is

(F) 1,112,500 cubic feet.

(G) 112,500 square feet.

(H) 112,500 feet.

(J) 112,500 cubic feet.

9. A department store marks up its clothing 80% over cost. If it sells blue jeans for $14, how much did the store pay for them?

(A) $7.78

(B) $17.50

(C) $11.20

(D) $1.12

10. The monthly finance charge on a charge account is $1\frac{1}{2}$% on the unpaid amount up to $500 and 1% on the unpaid amount over $500. What is the finance charge on an unpaid amount of $750?

(F) $22.50

(G) $1.00

(H) $10.00

(J) $100.00

11.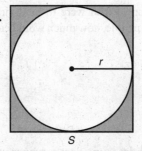

The square above has a side 4" long. The area of the shaded portion is approximately

(A) $\frac{22}{7}$ sq. in.

(B) 16 sq. in.

(C) $3\frac{3}{7}$ sq. in.

(D) $4\frac{3}{7}$ sq. in.

12. The ratio of teachers to students in a certain school is 1:14. If there are fourteen teachers in the school, how many students are there?

(F) 14

(G) 196

(H) 206

(J) 176

13. Evaluate $\frac{100^4}{10^8}$.

(A) 10^4

(B) 1,000

(C) 1

(D) 10^{12}

14. If x is an odd whole number, which of the following also represents an odd number?

(F) $2x + 1$

(G) $x - 2$

(H) $4x - 3$

(J) All of the above

15. Sum of 4 hours 17 minutes, 3 hours 58 minutes, 45 minutes, and 7 hours 12 minutes is

(A) 15 hr. 32 min.

(B) 17 hr. 32 min.

(C) 16 hr. 12 min.

(D) 14 hr. 50 min.

16. If 8 lb. 12 oz. of fruit were to be divided among eight people, how much would each receive?

   (F) 1 lb. 1.5 oz.
   (G) 10.5 oz.
   (H) 2.0 lb.
   (J) 13.5 oz.

17. In how much less time does a runner who finishes a marathon in 2 hours 12 minutes 38 seconds complete the race than a runner who finishes in 3 hours 2 minutes 24 seconds?

   (A) 48 min. 56 sec.
   (B) 49 min. 46 sec.
   (C) 1 hr. 51 min. 22 sec.
   (D) 1 hr. 26 min. 12 sec.

18. The drawing of a wheel in a book is done at $\frac{1}{16}$ scale. If the drawing is 1.8 inches in diameter, what is the wheel's diameter?

   (F) 32"
   (G) 28.8"
   (H) 24"
   (J) 0.1125"

19. If a man runs M miles in T hours, his speed is

   (A) M/T
   (B) $M + T$
   (C) $M - T$
   (D) MT

20. How many square inches are there in R rooms, each having S square feet?

   (F) RS
   (G) $144RS$
   (H) $9/RS$
   (J) $S + R$

21. The ratio of the six inches to six feet is

   (A) 1:6
   (B) 12:1
   (C) 1:12
   (D) 24:1

22. Event A occurs every 4 years, event B every 11 years, and event C every 33 years. If they last occurred together in 1950, when will they next occur simultaneously?

   (F) 3,402
   (G) 1,983
   (H) 2,082
   (J) 6,804

23.

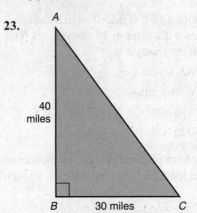

Two drivers begin at point C simultaneously. One drives from C to B to A. The other drives directly to A at 50 mph. How fast must the first person drive to get to A first?

   (A) Less than 50 mph
   (B) Less than 60 mph
   (C) Less than 70 mph
   (D) More than 70 mph

24.

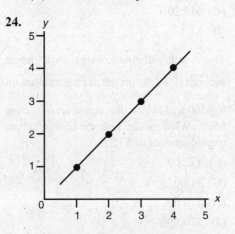

The graph above shows

   (F) x increasing faster than y.
   (G) y increasing faster than x.
   (H) x increasing as fast as y.
   (J) no relationship between x and y.

25. In the number 6,000,600,000, there are
    (A) 6 billions and 6 hundred thousands.
    (B) 6 millions and 6 thousands.
    (C) 6 billions and 6 millions.
    (D) 6 millions and 60 thousands.

26. One of the scales used in drawing topo-
    graphic maps is 1:24,000. On a scale of this
    sort, 1 inch on the map would equal how
    much distance on the ground?
    (F) 1 inch
    (G) 2,000 feet
    (H) 24,000 feet
    (J) 1 mile

27. If A number of people each make L things,
    the total number of things made is
    (A) A/L
    (B) $A + L$
    (C) $A - L$
    (D) AL

28.

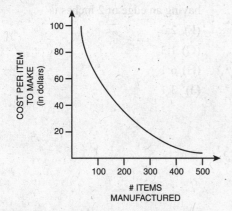

Based upon the graph above, what is the
cost per item if 300 items are manufactured?
    (F) $40
    (G) $28
    (H) $20
    (J) < $20

29.

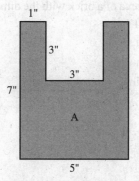

Note: In the figure above, assume that
any angle which appears to be a right
angle is a right angle.

The perimeter of figure A is
    (A) 19 in.
    (B) 30 in.
    (C) 23 sq. in.
    (D) 19 sq. in.

30. Of 27 people in a certain group, 15 are men
    and 12 are women. What is the ratio of men
    to women?
    (F) 15:12
    (G) 12:15
    (H) 5:4
    (J) 27:12

31.

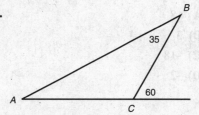

The measure of angle A is
    (A) 15°
    (B) 20°
    (C) 25°
    (D) 35°

32. The difference between 1,001,000 and
    999,999 is
    (F) 101,001
    (G) 1,999
    (H) 10,001
    (J) 1,001

33. The surface area of a brick with the dimensions 6" × 3" × 2" is

    (A) 36 sq. in.

    (B) 72 sq. in.

    (C) 128 sq. in.

    (D) 72 cu. in.

34. Simplify: $-3 - [-2 + (5 - 6) - 3]$

    (F) +3

    (G) −1

    (H) +1

    (J) −3

35. Simplify: $0.6 + 1\frac{1}{2} + \frac{3}{4}$

    (A) 2.31

    (B) 2.52

    (C) 2.85

    (D) $2\frac{13}{20}$

36. Simplify: $-6 - [2 - (3a - b) + b] + a$

    (F) $4 - 3a + 2b$

    (G) $-6 + 3a + b$

    (H) $-8 + 4a - 2b$

    (J) $-8 + 3a - b$

37. Simplify: $-2 [-4 (2 - 1) + (3 + 2)]$

    (A) 18

    (B) 2

    (C) −18

    (D) −2

38.

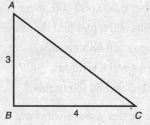

The length of AC in the right triangle above is

    (F) 4.5

    (G) 3.5

    (H) 5

    (J) 4

39. 5:6 as 15:?

    (A) 25

    (B) 16

    (C) 18

    (D) 12

40. The ratio of surface area to volume of a cube having an edge of 2 inches is

    (F) 2:3

    (G) 1:3

    (H) 6:1

    (J) 3:1

STOP If you finish before time is up, check over your work on Section 7 only. Do not go back to any previous sections.

ANSWER KEYS AND EXPLANATIONS

Section 1. Sequences

1. B	5. C	9. D	13. A	17. C
2. H	6. G	10. G	14. J	18. G
3. A	7. B	11. C	15. B	19. D
4. J	8. F	12. H	16. F	20. H

1. **The correct answer is (B).** The little circle is moving around the box in a counter-clockwise direction. In the first frame, the circle is on the outside of the box. After one complete circuit, the little circle straddles the perimeter of the box as it continues its counter-clockwise travel in the second frame. After the straddling circuit, the little circle moves into the box. The correct answer represents continuation of the circle in its counterclockwise travel inside the box.

2. **The correct answer is (H).** Look at the first three frames and note that in each frame, the first and last elements are identical. Eliminate choice (F). Look again at the first three frames and note that in each of the central elements, only one segment is darkened. Eliminate choice (G). Now notice that within each frame, the single darkened elements are positioned opposite each other.

3. **The correct answer is (A).** In each of the first three frames, the two dark-headed arrows are of the same length and point in the same direction on the right. This pattern is carried out only in choice (A). Check to be certain of your choice by looking at the other two arrows. One is long, one short; both heads are clear; they point in opposite directions. This is consistent with the behavior of the left-hand arrows in the first three frames. All other choices break the pattern in more than one way.

4. **The correct answer is (J).** In the first three frames, the first figure stands on both legs. Eliminate choice (G). Looking again at the first figure, in each of the first three frames,

the arms are in a different position. Choice (J) offers the fourth position for this figure's arms. Confirm this by looking at the other two figures. The arm and leg positions are exactly reversed in the first and third frames. The arm and leg positions of the second and third figures in choice (J) are the reverse of those in the second frame.

5. **The correct answer is (C).** Of the four figures in each frame, the first two are always alike while the other two vary. There are only three different figures. The easiest way to derive a pattern is to assign a number to each figure. Thus, in the first frame, we have 1-1-2-3; in the second, 2-2-3-1; and in the third, 3-3-1-2. The progression shows that in each succeeding frame, the figure in the third position in the preceding frame is doubled. Thus, the fourth frame should consist of 1-1-2-3, as found in choice (C).

6. **The correct answer is (G).** Name the patterns. First frame: plain, vee, left up, right down. Second frame: plain, vee, left down, right up. Third frame: plain, vee, right up, left down. Fourth frame must follow the up-down, left-right reversal pattern established: plain, vee, right down, left up.

7. **The correct answer is (B).** In the first frame, $44 - 5 = 39$ and $39 - 4 = 35$. Try this pattern in the second frame, and you will see that the -5, -4 rule holds. In the third frame, $61 - 5 = 56$, so the answer is $56 - 4 = 52$.

8. **The correct answer is (F).** In each frame, the first and last numbers are the same, so you need only figure the relationship of the middle number to each of these. In both the

first and second frames, the central number is 2 × the first, so choose 2 × 9 = 18 for your answer.

9. **The correct answer is (D).** In each frame, the second number is 2 × the first. However, the third number seems to follow no rule at all. Since the third number in each of the first two frames is 8, and 8 is offered as a choice, choose it and state to yourself the rule. "The third number is 8."

10. **The correct answer is (G).** The rule appears most clearly in the second frame: divide by 3, divide by 3. Applied to the first frame, it works. To choose the answer, you must choose the number that yields 7 when divided by 3. Multiply 7 × 3 to find 21.

11. **The correct answer is (C).** In each frame, the second number is repeated, so you really might just guess that the middle number in the last frame will be the same as the last. To double check, you might note that the second number in each frame is 18 more than the first.

12. **The correct answer is (H).** This problem looks simple, but you might have to look twice. In each frame, the first number becomes the addend for the progression. Thus, in the first frame, 2 + 2 = 4; 4 + 2 = 6. In the second frame, 3 + 3 = 6; 6 + 3 = 9. And in the third frame, 4 + 4 = 8, and 8 + 4 = 12.

13. **The correct answer is (A).** In each frame, the first and second numbers set the limits, and the last number is halfway between. So, in the last frame, 70 is halfway between 80 and the correct answer 60.

14. **The correct answer is (J).** Look carefully and you will see that in every case, *1* and *2* are subscripts and *3* is a superscript. The letters remain in the same order, and the numbers simply move one letter to the right and then back to the first letter.

15. **The correct answer is (B).** The numbers and the letters all remain in the same order; only the locations (that is, subscript or superscript) of the numbers change. The logical progression between one superscript and

two subscripts and two subscripts and one superscript is all subscripts.

16. **The correct answer is (F).** Again the letters remain the same and in the same order, but here the numbers both change and change their positions. Looking carefully, you will note that the odd numbers are superscripts while the even numbers are subscripts. Furthermore, the numbers themselves are decreasing in value one at a time. Concentrate on numbers alone: 5-5-4; 5-4-4; 4-4-4; fill in 4-4-3; then 4-3-3.

17. **The correct answer is (C).** This series is basically the alphabet, but every other set presents the letters in reverse order. As we reach the next set, we are back to alphabetical order again. If you quickly write the alphabet across the page in your test booklet, you will find alphabetic series much easier to figure out.

18. **The correct answer is (G).** Each set begins with *A* and ends with *B*. Then we find an alphabetic sequence beginning with *B* at the second position in each set and an alphabetic sequence beginning with *D* in the third position in each set.

19. **The correct answer is (D).** Within each grouping, the letters move in direct alphabetical sequence. Between groups, the space increases each time. Thus, moving from the first group to the second, we skip over one letter, *D*; from the second group to the third, over two letters, *H* and *I*; from the third group to the fourth, *M*, *N*, and *O*. Skip over four letters to choose the answer. The alphabet you have written in your test booklet will prove very helpful.

20. **The correct answer is (H).** This is a difficult question. You can see immediately that we are dealing with the alphabet in reverse and that no letters have been skipped. But what is the rule that governs? Assign a number to each letter in the first group, basing the number on natural sequence. Thus, figure W-X-Y-Z would be 1-2-3-4; here they appear Z-Y-W-X or 4-3-1-2. Follow through with the remaining groupings and you will find that all adhere to the same 4-3-1-2 rule. Now it is easy to choose the answer.

Section 2. Analogies

1. B	5. D	9. D	13. B	17. D
2. J	6. H	10. H	14. G	18. H
3. B	7. C	11. A	15. C	19. A
4. F	8. G	12. J	16. F	20. J

1. **The correct answer is (B).** Large four-footed mammal is to small four-footed mammal as large car is to small car. Large is to small is not an adequate formulation of the relationship because the elephant is also larger than the bug. You must refine your relationship until you find only one answer.

2. **The correct answer is (J).** The mother has lots of children as the hen has lots of chickens.

3. **The correct answer is (B).** The analogy here is sequential. Progress is from high chair to chair as it is from baby swing to swing. If asked to locate another analogous relationship, you would choose that of the tricycle to the bicycle.

4. **The correct answer is (F).** The relationship here is that of more to fewer. The centipede has more legs than the spider. The hexagon has more sides than the starfish has arms. The octagon and the octopus both sport eight sides or arms (more than the hexagon, not fewer), and the snake has none at all.

5. **The correct answer is (D).** In-line skates are wheeled vehicles worn on the feet and propelled by the person wearing them; a motorcycle is a wheeled vehicle ridden by a person and propelled by a motor. Analogously, skis are runnered, worn on the feet, and propelled by the person wearing them; a snowmobile is a runnered vehicle ridden by a person and propelled by a motor.

6. **The correct answer is (H).** The skull and crossbones and the "Mister Yuk" face on containers are both symbols for poisons. They say, "Danger. Don't eat or drink me." The American flag and the American eagle are both symbols for the United States. The hammer and sickle is the symbol for Russia. When faced with two possible choices to fit an analogy, you must refine the relationship. Here you must go beyond *symbol* to *symbol for the same thing*.

7. **The correct answer is (C).** A head goes on a pillow as feet go on a hassock. The relationship is one of purpose. The pillow goes on the bed, but that represents a reversal of the analogy.

8. **The correct answer is (G).** Pine cones are the seed carriers of the pine tree as acorns are the seed of the oak. Pine needles are part of the pine tree but not the seed-carrying part.

9. **The correct answer is (D).** Steak is an edible part of the steer; a drumstick is an edible part of the chicken. The egg is an edible product of the chicken, but it is not part of the meat of the chicken that is eaten.

10. **The correct answer is (H).** The analogy is of large to small of objects with similar functions. Thus, an axe is a long-handled wood-chopping tool, while the hatchet serves the same function but has a short handle. Similarly, the scythe is a long-handled grass-cutting tool, while the sickle serves the same function but has a short handle.

11. **The correct answer is (A).** Sometimes it is easier to explain an analogy by reading down instead of across. Thus, one eats from a soup bowl with a soup spoon and from a plate with a fork. Actually, this analogy is easy enough to solve visually, without words at all.

12. **The correct answer is (J).** This analogy is based on association. The swimsuited woman is associated with the palm tree;

think "hot." The igloo is associated with the parka-clad person; think "cold."

13. **The correct answer is (B).** To solve this analogy, think "outside is to inside." The human body bears the same relationship to its skeleton as the full, finished house bears to its framework.

14. **The correct answer is (G).** California is a coastal state of the far west; Massachusetts is its counterpart on the east coast. Maine is the northernmost state on the east coast, while Florida is southernmost. You could articulate this analogy as: "west is to east as north is to south." Actually, this analogy need not be so carefully refined. It would be adequate to say: "coastal state is to coastal state as coastal state is to coastal state." No other choice makes sense in the analogy.

15. **The correct answer is (C).** The car consumes gasoline; the source of that fuel is the gas pump. The baby birds consume worms, moths, and insects; the source of their fuel is the mother bird. Do not confuse the source of the fuel with the fuel itself.

16. **The correct answer is (F).** The hockey goal is guarded by the goalie; the fort is guarded by the sentry. The goalie and the sentry are both guardians of the gates; they have analogous functions.

17. **The correct answer is (D).** The analogy is that of the eater to the eaten. The shark eats the little fish; the cat eats the mouse.

18. **The correct answer is (H).** Milk, when not being drunk, is preserved in the refrigerator. A diamond ring, when not being worn, is preserved in a safe.

19. **The correct answer is (A).** The analogy is based on activities at different stages of development. The infant plays lying down and gets around by crawling. The child plays by jumping rope, for example, and gets around running. The child in the stroller is getting around passively. It does not fit into the analogy.

20. **The correct answer is (J).** The analogy is that of the rescuer to the rescued. The helicopter comes to the rescue of the people adrift in the lifeboat. The St. Bernard comes to the rescue of the hiker stranded in bad weather.

Section 3. Quantitative Reasoning

1. A	5. C	9. C	13. D	17. B
2. G	6. J	10. F	14. F	18. H
3. B	7. A	11. B	15. D	19. A
4. F	8. J	12. F	16. H	20. F

1. **The correct answer is (A).**

   $2 + 4 = 6$

   $3 + 4 = 7$

   $5 + 4 = 9$

2. **The correct answer is (G).**

   $5 + 1 = 6$

   $2 + 1 = 3$

   $6 + 1 = 7$

3. **The correct answer is (B).**

   $30 - 3 = 27$

   $20 - 3 = 17$

   $10 - 3 = 7$

4. **The correct answer is (F).**

   $8 - 2 = 6$

   $5 - 2 = 3$

   $3 - 2 = 1$

5. **The correct answer is (C).**

   $2 \times 2 = 4$

   $5 \times 2 = 10$

   $9 \times 2 = 18$

6. **The correct answer is (J).**

   $3 \div 3 = 1$

   $6 \div 3 = 2$

   $15 \div 3 = 5$

7. **The correct answer is (A).** There are six squares in the grid. The line is drawn exactly from one corner to the other corner, which means that exactly half the total grid is shaded. Half the grid is $\frac{1}{2}$.

8. **The correct answer is (J).** There are eight squares. Three complete squares and two half-squares are shaded. $3 + \frac{1}{2} + \frac{1}{2}$ is 4. Four squares are shaded. So, 4 over 8 is $\frac{4}{8}$, or $\frac{1}{2}$.

9. **The correct answer is (C).** There are eight squares. One complete square and two half-squares are shaded. $1 + \frac{1}{2} + \frac{1}{2}$ is 2. Two squares are shaded. 2 over 8 is $\frac{2}{8}$, or $\frac{1}{4}$.

10. **The correct answer is (F).** There are eight squares. Four of them are shaded. 4 over 8 is $\frac{4}{8}$, or $\frac{1}{2}$.

11. **The correct answer is (B).** There are eight squares in the grid. Five complete squares and two half-squares are shaded. $5 + \frac{1}{2} + \frac{1}{2}$ is 6. 6 over 8 is $\frac{6}{8}$, or $\frac{3}{4}$.

12. **The correct answer is (F).** There are nine squares. Six complete and two half-squares are shaded. $6 + \frac{1}{2} + \frac{1}{2} = 7$. 7 over 9 is $\frac{7}{9}$.

13. **The correct answer is (D).** There are nine squares. Four squares are shaded. 4 over 9 is $\frac{4}{9}$.

14. **The correct answer is (F).** The scale indicates that 1 cube = 1 cone. The only answer that maintains this relationship is choice (F), since it has 2 cubes = 2 cones.

15. **The correct answer is (D).** The scale indicates that 1 cube = 1 cone. The only answer that maintains this relationship is choice (D), since it has 1 cube + 2 cones = 2 cubes + 1 cone.

16. **The correct answer is (H).** The scale indicates that 1 cube = 1 cone. The only answer that maintains this relationship is choice (H), since it has 2 cubes + 1 cone = 3 cones.

17. **The correct answer is (B).** The scale indicates that 1 cube = 2 cones. The only answer that maintains this relationship is choice (B), since it has 2 cones = 2 cones.

18. **The correct answer is (H).** The scale indicates that 1 cube = 2 cones. The only answer that maintains this relationship is choice (H), since it has 1 cube + 1 cone = 3 cones.

19. **The correct answer is (A).** The scale indicates that 1 cube = 3 cones. The only answer that maintains this relationship is choice (A), since it has 2 cubes + 3 cones = 3 cubes.

20. **The correct answer is (F).** The scale indicates that 1 cube = 4 cones. The only answer that maintains this relationship is choice (F), since it has 1 cube + 4 cones = 2 cubes.

Section 4. Verbal Reasoning—Words

1. C	4. F	7. C	9. A	11. B
2. G	5. B	8. J	10. G	12. J
3. D	6. H			

1. **The correct answer is (C).** A cartoon always involves some sort of drawing. A cartoon usually involves animation, but animation may be lacking in a political cartoon. Humor and a message are common ingredients, but a cartoon may be simply decorative.

2. **The correct answer is (G).** The heroine must be a woman.

3. **The correct answer is (D).** What makes a pump work is pressure. If you were not certain of this answer, you could choose it by elimination. Because both water and air may be pumped, neither can be correct. As for a handle, consider electric pumps.

4. **The correct answer is (F).** The necessary part of a lantern is light. The source of the light might be a bulb, and the light can shine through mica or plastic as well as through glass.

5. **The correct answer is (B).** Information is absolutely necessary to the existence of data. Numbers, words, and charts all constitute information.

6. **The correct answer is (H).** A biography is the story of a life.

7. **The correct answer is (C).** Above the line are the primary colors of the spectrum, in order. Below the line are the mixed colors, also in order of appearance.

8. **The correct answer is (J).** Above the line are natural energy sources. Below the line are fossil fuels. Wood, uranium, and fission are all sources of power, but only oil is a fossil fuel.

9. **The correct answer is (A).** The birds above the line are all fish-eating wading birds. The birds below the line are seed eaters. A woodpecker eats insects; a robin eats worms; and a crane shares characteristics with the birds above the line, not with those below.

10. **The correct answer is (G).** Above the line are degrees of wetness, from left to right most wet to least wet. Below the lines are academic degrees, from left to right the most highly educated doctorate, through the master's degree, to the bachelor's.

11. The correct answer is (B). Above the line are seed fruits; below the line, the common factor is that all are stone fruits.

12. The correct answer is (J). The structures are connected in order.

Section 5. Verbal Reasoning—Context

1. D	5. B	9. A	13. B	17. D
2. H	6. G	10. H	14. H	18. F
3. C	7. A	11. D	15. D	19. D
4. F	8. J	12. F	16. G	20. F

1. The correct answer is (D). Because Bob went into the store alone and walked out empty-handed, we can safely conclude that the clerk did not sell cigarettes to Bob. No other assumption is supported by the facts as presented.

2. The correct answer is (H). If Tara's name was not on the injured list, Tara was not injured. She might have survived unscathed or have been killed. She might have missed the flight. As for choice (J), she might have changed her plans and taken a cruise to Bermuda instead. The possibility of an airline error in compiling the list of injured is not offered. Strictly on the basis of the situation described, you may correctly assume that Tara was not injured.

3. The correct answer is (C). Producers plan lavish stage productions to become long-running shows and always have contingency plans to replace actors as needed. There are many reasons why a show might not draw large audiences, but you can be certain that the reason for the premature closing was that the play was not a box office success.

4. The correct answer is (F). Michelle definitely spent some time at the kennel. We have no way of knowing where the kennel is nor at what point during Bernie's vacation Jack was called out of town. Bernie might have returned while Jack was out of town and might have taken Michelle home himself. And maybe Michelle was perfectly happy at the kennel or with Jack.

5. The correct answer is (B). We know that this is an out-of-place goose. Everything else is conjecture.

6. The correct answer is (G).

adaba means *north*
mikula means *pole*
bomani means *south*
tinkipu means *wind*
gotono means *star*

Therefore, *manitu* must mean *east* and *manitutinkipu* must mean *east wind*.

7. The correct answer is (A). If you study this question carefully, you do not need to actually translate at all. The word that you are trying to identify, *geophysics*, has no elements in common with any of the three words for which you are given translations. You can therefore eliminate any choice that contains any element that appears in any of the three initial words.

8. The correct answer is (J). In this language, the modifiers follow the noun.

eleme means *fruit*
naftama means *vegetable*
hotuto means *red*
zigaru means *green*
bigani means *leafy*

Therefore, *toribuz* must mean *flower*. Remember that in this language, the modifier follows the noun. Choice (A) reverses this order. *Toribuzhotuto* means *red flower*.

9. **The correct answer is (A).** Angela always follows her advisor's recommendations, and her advisor suggests taking the advanced biology course. So, it must be true that Angela takes advanced biology. That is the only answer choice that is definitely true.

10. **The correct answer is (H).** With one brother missing school due to illness, Kim only has to pack lunches for herself and her other brother on Monday. The other answer choices could be true, but based on the statements, we can't know that they must be true.

11. **The correct answer is (D).** Based on the statements, Kelly has to be the new class president. She received five more votes than Peter, the runner up.

12. **The correct answer is (F).** Since Heather leaves school before 3 p.m., she leaves in enough time to make her dance class. We don't have enough information to conclude that the other statements are true.

13. **The correct answer is (B).** The statements tell us that Farm Day cannot be held during bad weather, and the thunderstorms and dark skies indicate bad weather.

14. **The correct answer is (H).** With four hours between Charleston and Charlotte, Renee leaves Charleston at 3 p.m. That puts her in Charlotte at about 7 p.m. The statements don't give us any information about the other answer choices, including her means of travel.

15. **The correct answer is (D).** While any of the statements could be true, the only certain fact is that Button, a St. Bernard, is descended from wolves. We know this because the statements tell us that all dogs have wolves for ancestors.

16. **The correct answer is (G).** Any of the four statements could be true, but the only thing we know for sure is that Abby scores high enough to be allowed to go out with her friends on Saturday. We know that if she earned at least a "C" on the history test, she would score high enough to be allowed to go. She ended up scoring better than a "C."

17. **The correct answer is (D).** We know that the boys obey Rick's parents. So, if they choose to play soccer at Rick's house, they must play outside. While the other choices could be true, there is not enough information to determine that they must be true.

18. **The correct answer is (F).** Because Rob places better than everyone in the spelling contest except Martha, she is the highest placer in the group. We aren't given enough information to know if the other answer choices are true, including the difficulty of the words Nancy and Georgia missed.

19. **The correct answer is (D).** The newspaper staff does not use the school camera on Thursdays. Therefore, the yearbook staff is free to use the camera on Thursdays. Answer choice (D) must be true.

20. **The correct answer is (F).** Since Amber does not work on weekends, she can visit the nursing home on these nights. The other answer choices may or may not be true; we can't tell for sure that they're definitely true.

Section 6. Reading and Language Arts

1. C	11. D	21. C	31. D	41. B
2. H	12. F	22. G	32. F	42. F
3. C	13. A	23. C	33. B	43. D
4. F	14. H	24. G	34. G	44. G
5. A	15. B	25. D	35. C	45. D
6. J	16. J	26. J	36. F	46. H
7. C	17. A	27. A	37. C	47. C
8. G	18. G	28. H	38. J	48. J
9. C	19. D	29. B	39. D	49. B
10. F	20. H	30. G	40. G	50. F

1. **The correct answer is (C).** Choosing the title for this paragraph takes more than one reading of the paragraph. This is not an easy question. After a couple of readings, however, you should be able to conclude that the all-inclusive subject of the paragraph is the remodeling of plants. An equally correct title, not offered here, might be "Uses and Effects of Colchicine."

2. **The correct answer is (H).** Buried in the middle of the paragraph is the sentence: "It creates new varieties with astonishing frequency, whereas such mutations occur but rarely in nature."

3. **The correct answer is (C).** This question becomes easy to answer after you have dealt with the previous question.

4. **The correct answer is (F).** The third sentence states that colchicine is a poisonous drug.

5. **The correct answer is (A).** The answer to this question of fact is in the first sentence.

6. **The correct answer is (J).** Do not be misled by the first sentence, which introduces Reverend Manasseh Cutler, nor by the last portion of the selection, which discusses the naming of Cleveland. The entire selection has to do with the settling of the Northwest Territory.

7. **The correct answer is (C).** In this context, the word *related* means reported or simply told.

8. **The correct answer is (G).** Read carefully. General Cleaveland *quieted the Indian claims*; he did not quiet the Indians. If the Indians were making claims, they were not eager to work with him. The selection suggests that General Cleaveland bought off the Indians with money, cattle, and whiskey.

9. **The correct answer is (C).** Clearly the writer of the selection is an admirer of carrier pigeons, praising their usefulness and reliability.

10. **The correct answer is (F).** G. I. Joe brought the news of an allied victory, but he was rewarded for the results of his bringing the news, for preventing unnecessary loss of life. If the British had not received news that their troops were already in the town of Colvi Vecchia, they would have sent out the raid and bombed their own soldiers. When two answers to a question seem right, you must choose the one that more specifically answers what is asked.

11. **The correct answer is (D).** The Lord Mayor of London gave G. I. Joe the Dickin Medal.

12. **The correct answer is (F).** This sentence is written correctly. The other answer choices contain errors of usage and grammar.

13. **The correct answer is (A).** The context in which it is used should help you to choose this answer. "...veneration due to its sacred origin..." implies something religious and related to worship.

14. **The correct answer is (H).** The speaker probably does celebrate and enjoy Christmas, but the primary reason for this speech is to defend the holiday to Uncle Scrooge by listing its advantages to mankind.

15. **The correct answer is (B).** This is the whole point of the first paragraph.

16. **The correct answer is (J).** Again, use of the word in context should lead you to its meaning. The paragraph speaks of goodwill among all men and women. This *one consent* therefore is *unanimous* good feeling.

17. **The correct answer is (A).** Read the last paragraph carefully. Scrooge is first reacting to the clerk who has just applauded the speech in defense of Christmas. Scrooge threatens the clerk with firing. He then turns and makes a sarcastic remark to his nephew. It can be assumed that he is angry with both characters.

18. **The correct answer is (G).** The harbor police force was established almost a century ago, that is, at the beginning of the twentieth century.

19. **The correct answer is (D).** The first sentence of the second paragraph says that the boats are equipped for various jobs. This means that they vary in function.

20. **The correct answer is (H).** By checking on the operation of the junk boats, the harbor police ensure that the activities of the junk boats are legal.

21. **The correct answer is (C).** Each of the other choices includes some activity that is not mentioned as an activity of the harbor police.

22. **The correct answer is (G).** The 450 disabled boats that were towed and the thousands that were assisted in other ways must surely have included a vast variety of different kinds of boats.

23. **The correct answer is (C).** This is the meaning of the second sentence of the first paragraph. You may be aware that the efforts of conservationists have paid off and that the population of bald eagles has been recovering over the last decade. Remember that your answers to reading comprehension questions must be based on information provided in the passage.

24. **The correct answer is (G).** Because the thrust of the selection is the threatened extinction of the bald eagle, you really do not need to search for the precise words that answer this question. However, you can find them in the second paragraph.

25. **The correct answer is (D).** This definition is given in the second sentence of the third paragraph: "...aeries, the eagles' mammoth nests."

26. **The correct answer is (J).** The bald eagle appears on the Great Seal of the United States, our national emblem. An emblem is a symbol. "Emblematic" is the adjective form of the noun "emblem."

27. **The correct answer is (A).** Any one of the reasons might be accurate, but the author specifically tells you his reason in the second sentence.

28. **The correct answer is (H).** This is a fact question; see the third sentence.

29. **The correct answer is (B).** The old-fashioned language of this selection might require more than one reading, but this detail is found in the fourth sentence.

30. **The correct answer is (G).** The selection says that the garden extended so far that the gardener did not know where it ended, but it does not say that he was unable to care for it because of its size. In the sixth sentence, we learn that the garden led into a lovely forest. The nightingale lived in the forest, not in the garden.

31. **The correct answer is (D).** Great blank spaces on a population map indicate a very sparse or scanty population. The fact that desert populations grow fruits and vegetables does not mean that they restrict their diets to these products.

32. **The correct answer is (F).** You may eat the vegetables at a winter dinner, but the farm only produces the vegetables; it does not cook the dinner.

33. **The correct answer is (B).** Broadcloth is made from silky cotton grown in Egypt.

34. **The correct answer is (G).** The third paragraph makes the statement that desert civilizations have made important cultural contributions, but it does not compare these contributions with those of any other civilizations. The last paragraph tells what these contributions are. It is obvious that these have had an impact on western civilizations.

35. **The correct answer is (C).** This need is explained in the middle of the last paragraph.

36. **The correct answer is (F).** The name of the town is *Ekalaka,* but they call it "Skeleton Flats."

37. **The correct answer is (C).** The answer to this main-idea question should be clear. The article is about the various fossil finds.

38. **The correct answer is (J).** This definition is in the second paragraph: ". . . paleontologists, scientists who use fossils to study prehistoric life forms." Walter Peck's hobby was geology, and in the course of pursuing his hobby, he made the first find.

39. **The correct answer is (D).** The third paragraph discusses the people of Ekalaka in terms of their enthusiasm for digging and fossil discovery. The various exciting finds are described in the fourth paragraph.

40. **The correct answer is (G).** The answer is nothing more than a restatement of the last sentence.

41. **The correct answer is (B).** The first development sentence begins with "these people."

The topic sentence must tell us who these people are. You can immediately eliminate choices (C) and (D). Choice (B) then becomes clearly the best answer because it offers an opinion that contrasts with the bulk of the paragraph.

42. **The correct answer is (F).** Because the first development sentence tells of two dimensions that are not the same, and the remainder of the paragraph proceeds to define these two dimensions, it is reasonable to expect the topic sentence to lead into discussion of at least one of these dimensions.

43. **The correct answer is (D).** What consists only of ordinances with little or no attempt at enforcement? Only "the varying degrees of inspection and control" answers this question, so it must be the topic sentence.

44. **The correct answer is (G).** The topic sentence introduces the structure of the ear and specifically mentions the eardrum. Choice (G) tells of the function of the eardrum and then continues describing the structure of the ear. Choice (H) speaks of "this tube," but the reference is unclear. All other choices lead off on various tangents, all of them ear-related but none of them logically developing the topic sentence.

45. **The correct answer is (D).** The topic sentence promises a history of the development of open-air markets in urban locations. Choice (D) picks right up on the theme. Choices (A) and (B) focus in on the negative aspects of the open-air markets. Choice (C) digresses to the nature of open-air markets in other cultures.

46. **The correct answer is (H).** It is quite clear that a number of sentences must intervene between the topic sentence and choices (G) and (J). The transition from the topic sentence to the first sentence of choice (F) is smooth and logical, but the second sentence of choice (F) does not flow from the first. Choice (H) represents only the beginning of development of a complex paragraph, but it is a reasonable beginning.

47. The correct answer is (C). The paragraph concerns the economies of the Caribbean islands, their resources, produce, and trade. The Mediterranean Sea might make an interesting topic for comparison with the Caribbean, but it has no place in this paragraph.

48. The correct answer is (J). The space should be filled with another sentence cataloging the effects of alcohol on the person who drinks it.

49. The correct answer is (B). The second sentence, telling us that different fuels have different kindling temperatures, sets the stage. What follows should be a discussion of a number of fuels with respect to their kindling temperatures.

50. The correct answer is (F). The next two sentences tell some reasons for which an arsonist might set a fire. Choice (H) also gives a reason, but "another" must come later in the paragraph.

Section 7. Mathematics

1. C	9. A	17. B	25. A	33. B
2. G	10. H	18. G	26. G	34. F
3. A	11. C	19. A	27. D	35. C
4. J	12. G	20. G	28. H	36. H
5. B	13. C	21. C	29. B	37. D
6. F	14. J	22. H	30. H	38. H
7. C	15. C	23. D	31. C	39. C
8. J	16. F	24. H	32. J	40. J

1. The correct answer is (C). The reciprocal of a fraction is the fraction "turned upside down." $1\frac{2}{3}$ is equivalent to $\frac{5}{3}$. The reciprocal of $\frac{5}{3}$ is $\frac{3}{5}$. The correct answer is (C). Choice (D) is a distractor. Because x has a precise value in the problem, we must choose an answer having a precise value.

2. The correct answer is (G). The product of any number and its reciprocal is 1. Therefore, $\frac{7}{16} \times \frac{16}{7} = 1$, and choice (G) is the correct answer. Even if you didn't know this rule, you could have examined the answers and eliminated both choice (F) because the product was greater than 1 and choice (J) because the product was less than 1.

3. The correct answer is (A). This problem looks much harder than it really is. The numerator of this complex fraction is the same as the denominator. When numerator and denominator are equivalent, the fraction is equal to 1.

4. The correct answer is (J). This is a complex fraction requiring all of your skills in working with fractions. To estimate the correct answer, note that the numerator is slightly larger than $1 \left(\frac{2}{3} + \frac{3}{8} > 1 \right)$, and the denominator is equivalent to $\frac{4}{16} - \frac{3}{16}$, or $\frac{1}{16}$. Therefore, a number slightly larger than 1 divided by $\frac{1}{16}$ is slightly larger than 16. The closest is choice (J), $\frac{50}{3}$, which is equivalent to $16\frac{2}{3}$. To solve the problem by calculation, simplify the numerator and denominator, and then divide.

5. **The correct answer is (B).** This is a problem in which you must substitute the values given into the formula. After you do that, it is a simple problem.

$$L = \frac{3}{4} \times 2 \times 7 \times \frac{1}{2}$$

$$\frac{3 \times 2 \times 7 \times 1}{4 \times 2} = \frac{42}{8} = \frac{21}{4}$$

Therefore, choice (B) is the correct answer. The other answers would have resulted if you had forgotten to multiply one of the numbers in the numerator. Choice (D) might have been chosen by someone who didn't know what to do but thought the most difficult-looking answer would be the best.

6. **The correct answer is (F).** The sum of the angles of a triangle is always 180°. The correct answer, therefore, is choice (F) because $45° + 75° + 60° = 180°$.

7. **The correct answer is (C).** Note that the base of the triangle is the same as the diameter of the circle. Because $\triangle ABC$ is isosceles, its altitude is the same length as the radius of the circle. Use the formula for the area of a triangle, and substitute the correct values:

$$A = \frac{1}{2}bh$$
$$= \frac{1}{2} \times 10 \times 5$$
$$= 25 \text{ cm}^2$$

Choice (A) is the area of the circle.

8. **The correct answer is (J).** These measurements describe a large rectangular room 30 feet high. Use the formula $V = l \times w \times h$ to find the volume:

$V = 75$ feet $\times$ 50 feet $\times$ 30 feet

$V = 112,500$ cubic feet

Choices (G) and (H) use the wrong units. Volume is always measured in *cubic* units.

9. **The correct answer is (A).** A store markup of 100% would exactly double the price. An 80% markup almost doubles the price. The $14 jeans are priced at almost double their cost to the store. By estimation, the best answer is choice (A). To figure precisely, remember that an 80% markup is the equivalent of multiplying the cost by 180%, or 1.80.

cost $\times$ 1.80 = 14.00
    cost = 14.00 ÷ 1.80
    cost = $7.78

10. **The correct answer is (H).** The finance charge will be the sum of $1\frac{1}{2}$% of $500, plus 1% of $250. You can write this as follows:

$(0.015 \times 500) + (0.01 \times 250) =$
$7.50 + 2.50 = \$10.00$

You can estimate the answer if you remember that percent means "hundredths of." One hundredth of $500 is $5.00; one hundredth of $250 is $2.50. The only answer near this sum is choice (H). Choices (G) and (J) would have resulted if you had misplaced a decimal point.

11. **The correct answer is (C).** The area of the shaded portion is equal to the area of the square, less the area of the circle. The length of the side of the square is equal to the diameter of the circle. Therefore, using $\frac{22}{7}$ for pi:

$$(4" \times 4") - (\pi 2^2) = 16 \text{ sq. in.} - \frac{88}{7} \text{ sq. in.}$$
$$= 3\frac{3}{7} \text{ sq. in.}$$

The correct answer is (C). If you selected choice (D), $4\frac{3}{7}$, check your skills in subtracting fractions from whole numbers.

12. **The correct answer is (G).** For each teacher, there are 14 students. Because there are 14 teachers, there must be 14 × 14, or 196, students.

13. **The correct answer is (C).** The long way to solve this problem is to multiply both the numerator and denominator out, and then divide. If you notice that 100^4 can also be written as 10^8, the answer is obviously choice (C).

$$100 = 10^2$$
$$100^4 = 10^2 \times 10^2 \times 10^2 \times 10^2 = 10^8$$
$$\frac{100^4}{10^8} = \frac{10^8}{10^8} = 1$$

14. **The correct answer is (J).** In the whole number system, every other number is odd and every other number is even. If x is odd, $x + 1$ is even, $x + 2$ is odd, $x + 3$ is even, and so forth. Also, if x is odd, $x - 1$ is even, $x - 2$ is odd, and $x - 3$ is even. If an even or odd number is doubled, the outcome is even. Therefore, if x is odd, $2x + 1$ is odd, $x - 2$ is odd, and $4x - 3$ is odd.

15. **The correct answer is (C).** Arrange the periods of time in columns and add as you would add whole numbers.

4 hr.	17 min.
3 hr.	58 min.
	45 min.
+ 7 hr.	12 min.
14 hr.	132 min.

We know there are 60 minutes in each hour. Therefore, 132 minutes equal 2 hours 12 minutes. The correct answer for this addition is 16 hours 12 minutes, or choice (C). When working with units that measure time, volume, and length, it is usually best to represent the answer using as many larger units as possible. That's why 16 hours 12 minutes is preferable to 14 hours 132 minutes as an answer.

16. **The correct answer is (F).** You do not have to calculate this answer. If eight people share equally of 8 pounds and some ounces of fruit, each person would receive 1 pound and a few ounces. Only choice (F) is possible.

17. **The correct answer is (B).** This is a subtraction problem. You must find the difference between the lengths of time required to finish the race. As with other problems involving units of measurement, you must work carefully.

3 hr.	2 min.	24 sec.
− 2 hr.	12 min.	38 sec.

Because 38 seconds is larger than 24 seconds and 12 minutes is larger than 2 minutes, borrow from the minutes column and the hour column and rewrite the problem as follows:

2 hr.	61 min.	84 sec.
− 2 hr.	12 min.	38 sec.
0 hr.	49 min.	46 sec.

18. **The correct answer is (G).** If the drawing is at $\frac{1}{16}$ scale, it means that the drawing is $\frac{1}{16}$ the size of the actual wheel. Therefore, multiply the size of the drawing by 16.
$1.8 \times 16 = 28.8$ inches

19. **The correct answer is (A).** This problem asks you to find speed or rate. Speed or rate is found by dividing the distance traveled by the time required. The choice in which distance is divided by time is (A).

20. **The correct answer is (G).** R rooms each with S square feet contain a total of RS square feet. Because there are 144 square inches in each square foot, the rooms contain $144RS$ square inches.

21. **The correct answer is (C).**

Step 1. To find the correct ratio, write it as:

$$\frac{6 \text{ inches}}{6 \text{ feet}}$$

Step 2. Rewrite each quantity in inches.

$$\frac{6 \text{ inches}}{72 \text{ inches}}$$

Step 3. Simplify the ratio.

$$\frac{6}{72} = \frac{1}{12} = 1:12$$

22. **The correct answer is (H).** Here, three events occur periodically, so we must find the LCM of 4, 11, and 33 and add that number to 1950. That year will be the next common occurrence. The LCM of 4, 11, and 33 is 132. 1950 + 132 = 2082.

23. **The correct answer is (D).** This is a two-step problem. First, find the length of the hypotenuse, so you know how far the other person is driving.

$$(AC)^2 = (AB)^2 + (BC)^2$$
$$= (40)^2 + (30)^2$$
$$= 1600 + 900$$
$$(AC) = \sqrt{2500} = 50 \text{ miles}$$

The person driving from C to A must drive 50 miles at 50 mph. He or she will get there in 1 hour. The other must drive 70 miles. To get there first, he or she must drive faster than 70 miles per hour.

24. **The correct answer is (H).** This graph contains a line that has points with coordinates (1,1), (2,2), (3,3) and (4,4). From one point to another, the value of the x-coordinate changes just as much as the value of the y-coordinate. This line is at a 45° angle from the x-axis and will be created whenever the x- and y-coordinates are equal.

25. **The correct answer is (A).** The first 6 is in the billions place; the second, in the hundred-thousands place. If you had trouble with this problem, review the sections on how to read numbers and determine place values in your math textbook.

26. **The correct answer is (G).** A scale of 1:24,000 means that 1 inch on the map equals 24,000 inches on the ground. 24,000 inches equals 2000 feet (24,000 ÷ 12 = 2000).

27. **The correct answer is (D).** This is a *literal problem* requiring you to "think without numbers." Creating mental pictures might help you solve this type of problem. If each person in a group makes L number of things, the group's output will be the product of the number of people in the group and the number of things each makes. Choice (D)

represents the product and is the correct answer.

28. **The correct answer is (H).** Find 300 on the horizontal axis. Draw a vertical line upward until you touch the line. Move horizontally from this point on the line to the vertical axis. Note that you touch the vertical axis at a point roughly equivalent to $20. We suggest you use a ruler to sketch your line.

29. **The correct answer is (B).** To find the perimeter, we add up the dimensions of all of the sides. Note that there are some parts that have not been assigned measurements, so we should infer that they are the same as those corresponding parts whose measurements have been designated because we are told to assume that there are right angles in the figure. Beginning at the bottom and moving clockwise, the dimensions are:

5" + 7" + 1" + 3" + 3" + 3" + 1" + 7"

These equal 30 inches. If you selected choices (A), (C), or (D), you failed to add up all of the segments.

30. **The correct answer is (H).** The ratio of men to women is 15:12, but this ratio must be expressed in simplest form. Because 15 and 12 have 3 as a common factor, the ratio expressed correctly is 5:4. The ratio of women to men is 12:15 or 4:5.

31. **The correct answer is (C).** A straight line represents a "straight angle" of 180°. An angle of 60° is given, so m∠C must be 120° to complete the line. Knowing that all the angles in a triangle added together equal 180°,

$$m\angle A + m\angle B + m\angle C = 180°$$
$$m\angle A + 35° + 120° = 180°$$
$$m\angle A = 180° - 155°$$
$$m\angle A = 25°$$

32. **The correct answer is (J).** This is a simple subtraction problem designed to test how carefully you can subtract. It is possible to calculate the correct answer without pencil and paper. 999,999 is only 1 less than a million, and 1,001,000 is 1000 greater than a

million. The difference, then, is 1000 + 1, or 1001. Or, you may figure the problem in the following way:

$$\begin{array}{r} 1001000 \\ -\;999999 \\ \hline 1001 \end{array}$$

33. **The correct answer is (B).** The surface of a rectangular solid such as a brick is found by calculating the area of each face of the brick and finding the sum of the areas of the faces. The brick has 6 faces:

Two faces 6" × 3"; total 36 sq. in.
Two faces 6" × 2"; total 24 sq. in.
Two faces 3" × 2"; total 12 sq. in.
                    Total 72 sq. in.

Surface area of a solid figure, is expressed in square measure. Only volume is expressed in cubic measure.

34. **The correct answer is (F).**

Step 1. $-3 - [-2 + (5 - 6) - 3]$
Step 2. $-3 - [-2 + (-1) - 3]$
Step 3. $-3 - [-2 - 1 - 3]$
Step 4. $-3 - [-6]$
Step 5. $-3 + 6 = +3$

35. **The correct answer is (C).** By far the easiest way to solve this problem is to rename the fractions as decimals: 0.6 + 1.5 + 0.75 = 2.85. If you were to rename as fractions, the correct answer would be $2\frac{17}{20}$.

36. **The correct answer is (H).** When simplifying, begin with the innermost grouping symbols first, and work your way outward.

Step 1. $-6 - [2 - (3a - b) + b] + a$
Step 2. $-6 - [2 - 3a + b + b] + a$
Step 3. $-6 - [2 - 3a + 2b] + a$
Step 4. $-6 - 2 + 3a - 2b + a$
Step 5. $-8 + 4a - 2b$

37. **The correct answer is (D).** Begin with the innermost parentheses and work your way outward. Note that a negative sign in front of a grouping symbol reverses the signs of all numbers within.

Step 1. $-2 [-4 (2 - 1) + (3 + 2)]$
Step 2. $-2 [-4 (1) + (5)]$
Step 3. $-2 [-4 + 5]$
Step 4. $-2 [+1] = -2$

38. **The correct answer is (H).** The Pythagorean theorem is used to find the length of the sides of right triangles. The square of the length of the longest side (the hypotenuse) is equal to the sum of the squares of the other two sides. Once we know the square of the length of the longest side, it is easy to find the length.

$$(AC)^2 = (AB)^2 + (BC)^2$$
$$(AC)^2 = 3^2 + 4^2$$
$$(AC)^2 = 25$$
$$AC = \sqrt{25} = 5$$

39. **The correct answer is (C).** This proportion asks you to find the missing element. A proportion is a statement of equality between two ratios, so we know that 5 bears the same relationship to 15 as 6 does to the unknown number. Since 3 × 5 equals 15, we know 3 × 6 equals the unknown number. The number, thus, is 18. The completed proportion should read: 5:6 as 15:18. Proportions may also be written with a set of two colons replacing the word "as." In this case, the proportion would read: 5:6::15:18.

40. **The correct answer is (J).** Calculate the surface area of the cube. It has six faces, each 2" × 2". Its surface area, then, is 6 × 4 sq. in., or 24 sq. in. Its volume is found by multiplying its length × width × height, or 2" × 2" × 2" = 8 cu. in. The ratio of surface area to volume is 24:8, or 3:1.

SCORE SHEET

CTB/McGraw-Hill will score your actual exam and send your scaled scores and your percentile scores directly to the schools you indicated. Scaled scores are scores converted by a special formula to make comparable your performance on tests of unequal lengths and unequal importance. Percentile scores compare your performance on each test and the whole exam with the performance of other students who took the same exam at the same time. Your scores will not be reported either as raw scores—that is, number correct—nor as percents. Right now, however, you will find it very useful to convert your own scores on the practice exam into simple percentages. In this way, you can compare your own performance on each test of the exam with your performance on each other test. You can then focus your study where it will do you the most good.

Subject	No. Correct ÷ No. of Questions	× 100 = ____ %
Sequences	____ ÷ 20 =	____ × 100 = ____ %
Analogies	____ ÷ 20 =	____ × 100 = ____ %
Quantitative Reasoning	____ ÷ 20 =	____ × 100 = ____ %
Verbal Reasoning—Words	____ ÷ 12 =	____ × 100 = ____ %
Verbal Reasoning—Context	____ ÷ 20 =	____ × 100 = ____ %
Reading and Language Arts	____ ÷ 50 =	____ × 100 = ____ %
Mathematics	____ ÷ 40 =	____ × 100 = ____ %
TOTAL EXAM	____ ÷ 182 =	____ × 100 = ____ %

Now compare the percentage scores you just earned on the Practice Test 4: COOP with the scores you achieved on the Practice Test 3: COOP. If you have paid attention to the study chapters in this book and if you have concentrated especially on your areas of previous weakness, you should see a marked improvement in your performance. If you still see trouble spots, review the applicable study chapters again and, perhaps, consult a textbook or a teacher for further help and suggestions.

Subject	Practice Test 3	Practice Test 4
Sequences	%	%
Analogies	%	%
Quantitative Reasoning	%	%
Verbal Reasoning--Words	%	%
Verbal Reasoning--Context	%	%
Reading and Language Arts	%	%
Mathematics	%	%
TOTAL EXAM	%	%

ANSWER SHEET PRACTICE TEST 5: HSPT

Verbal Skills

1. Ⓐ Ⓑ Ⓒ Ⓓ   13. Ⓐ Ⓑ Ⓒ Ⓓ   25. Ⓐ Ⓑ Ⓒ Ⓓ   37. Ⓐ Ⓑ Ⓒ Ⓓ   49. Ⓐ Ⓑ Ⓒ
2. Ⓐ Ⓑ Ⓒ Ⓓ   14. Ⓐ Ⓑ Ⓒ Ⓓ   26. Ⓐ Ⓑ Ⓒ Ⓓ   38. Ⓐ Ⓑ Ⓒ   50. Ⓐ Ⓑ Ⓒ Ⓓ
3. Ⓐ Ⓑ Ⓒ Ⓓ   15. Ⓐ Ⓑ Ⓒ   27. Ⓐ Ⓑ Ⓒ Ⓓ   39. Ⓐ Ⓑ Ⓒ Ⓓ   51. Ⓐ Ⓑ Ⓒ Ⓓ
4. Ⓐ Ⓑ Ⓒ   16. Ⓐ Ⓑ Ⓒ Ⓓ   28. Ⓐ Ⓑ Ⓒ Ⓓ   40. Ⓐ Ⓑ Ⓒ Ⓓ   52. Ⓐ Ⓑ Ⓒ
5. Ⓐ Ⓑ Ⓒ Ⓓ   17. Ⓐ Ⓑ Ⓒ Ⓓ   29. Ⓐ Ⓑ Ⓒ Ⓓ   41. Ⓐ Ⓑ Ⓒ Ⓓ   53. Ⓐ Ⓑ Ⓒ Ⓓ
6. Ⓐ Ⓑ Ⓒ Ⓓ   18. Ⓐ Ⓑ Ⓒ Ⓓ   30. Ⓐ Ⓑ Ⓒ Ⓓ   42. Ⓐ Ⓑ Ⓒ Ⓓ   54. Ⓐ Ⓑ Ⓒ Ⓓ
7. Ⓐ Ⓑ Ⓒ Ⓓ   19. Ⓐ Ⓑ Ⓒ Ⓓ   31. Ⓐ Ⓑ Ⓒ Ⓓ   43. Ⓐ Ⓑ Ⓒ Ⓓ   55. Ⓐ Ⓑ Ⓒ
8. Ⓐ Ⓑ Ⓒ Ⓓ   20. Ⓐ Ⓑ Ⓒ Ⓓ   32. Ⓐ Ⓑ Ⓒ Ⓓ   44. Ⓐ Ⓑ Ⓒ Ⓓ   56. Ⓐ Ⓑ Ⓒ Ⓓ
9. Ⓐ Ⓑ Ⓒ Ⓓ   21. Ⓐ Ⓑ Ⓒ Ⓓ   33. Ⓐ Ⓑ Ⓒ   45. Ⓐ Ⓑ Ⓒ Ⓓ   57. Ⓐ Ⓑ Ⓒ Ⓓ
10. Ⓐ Ⓑ Ⓒ Ⓓ   22. Ⓐ Ⓑ Ⓒ   34. Ⓐ Ⓑ Ⓒ Ⓓ   46. Ⓐ Ⓑ Ⓒ Ⓓ   58. Ⓐ Ⓑ Ⓒ Ⓓ
11. Ⓐ Ⓑ Ⓒ Ⓓ   23. Ⓐ Ⓑ Ⓒ Ⓓ   35. Ⓐ Ⓑ Ⓒ Ⓓ   47. Ⓐ Ⓑ Ⓒ Ⓓ   59. Ⓐ Ⓑ Ⓒ Ⓓ
12. Ⓐ Ⓑ Ⓒ Ⓓ   24. Ⓐ Ⓑ Ⓒ   36. Ⓐ Ⓑ Ⓒ Ⓓ   48. Ⓐ Ⓑ Ⓒ Ⓓ   60. Ⓐ Ⓑ Ⓒ

Quantitative Skills

61. Ⓐ Ⓑ Ⓒ Ⓓ   72. Ⓐ Ⓑ Ⓒ Ⓓ   83. Ⓐ Ⓑ Ⓒ Ⓓ   94. Ⓐ Ⓑ Ⓒ Ⓓ   105. Ⓐ Ⓑ Ⓒ Ⓓ
62. Ⓐ Ⓑ Ⓒ Ⓓ   73. Ⓐ Ⓑ Ⓒ Ⓓ   84. Ⓐ Ⓑ Ⓒ Ⓓ   95. Ⓐ Ⓑ Ⓒ Ⓓ   106. Ⓐ Ⓑ Ⓒ Ⓓ
63. Ⓐ Ⓑ Ⓒ Ⓓ   74. Ⓐ Ⓑ Ⓒ Ⓓ   85. Ⓐ Ⓑ Ⓒ Ⓓ   96. Ⓐ Ⓑ Ⓒ Ⓓ   107. Ⓐ Ⓑ Ⓒ Ⓓ
64. Ⓐ Ⓑ Ⓒ Ⓓ   75. Ⓐ Ⓑ Ⓒ Ⓓ   86. Ⓐ Ⓑ Ⓒ Ⓓ   97. Ⓐ Ⓑ Ⓒ Ⓓ   108. Ⓐ Ⓑ Ⓒ Ⓓ
65. Ⓐ Ⓑ Ⓒ Ⓓ   76. Ⓐ Ⓑ Ⓒ Ⓓ   87. Ⓐ Ⓑ Ⓒ Ⓓ   98. Ⓐ Ⓑ Ⓒ Ⓓ   109. Ⓐ Ⓑ Ⓒ Ⓓ
66. Ⓐ Ⓑ Ⓒ Ⓓ   77. Ⓐ Ⓑ Ⓒ Ⓓ   88. Ⓐ Ⓑ Ⓒ Ⓓ   99. Ⓐ Ⓑ Ⓒ Ⓓ   110. Ⓐ Ⓑ Ⓒ Ⓓ
67. Ⓐ Ⓑ Ⓒ Ⓓ   78. Ⓐ Ⓑ Ⓒ Ⓓ   89. Ⓐ Ⓑ Ⓒ Ⓓ   100. Ⓐ Ⓑ Ⓒ Ⓓ   111. Ⓐ Ⓑ Ⓒ Ⓓ
68. Ⓐ Ⓑ Ⓒ Ⓓ   79. Ⓐ Ⓑ Ⓒ Ⓓ   90. Ⓐ Ⓑ Ⓒ Ⓓ   101. Ⓐ Ⓑ Ⓒ Ⓓ   112. Ⓐ Ⓑ Ⓒ Ⓓ
69. Ⓐ Ⓑ Ⓒ Ⓓ   80. Ⓐ Ⓑ Ⓒ Ⓓ   91. Ⓐ Ⓑ Ⓒ Ⓓ   102. Ⓐ Ⓑ Ⓒ Ⓓ
70. Ⓐ Ⓑ Ⓒ Ⓓ   81. Ⓐ Ⓑ Ⓒ Ⓓ   92. Ⓐ Ⓑ Ⓒ Ⓓ   103. Ⓐ Ⓑ Ⓒ Ⓓ
71. Ⓐ Ⓑ Ⓒ Ⓓ   82. Ⓐ Ⓑ Ⓒ Ⓓ   93. Ⓐ Ⓑ Ⓒ Ⓓ   104. Ⓐ Ⓑ Ⓒ Ⓓ

Reading

COMPREHENSION

113. Ⓐ Ⓑ Ⓒ Ⓓ   121. Ⓐ Ⓑ Ⓒ Ⓓ   129. Ⓐ Ⓑ Ⓒ Ⓓ   137. Ⓐ Ⓑ Ⓒ Ⓓ   145. Ⓐ Ⓑ Ⓒ Ⓓ
114. Ⓐ Ⓑ Ⓒ Ⓓ   122. Ⓐ Ⓑ Ⓒ Ⓓ   130. Ⓐ Ⓑ Ⓒ Ⓓ   138. Ⓐ Ⓑ Ⓒ Ⓓ   146. Ⓐ Ⓑ Ⓒ Ⓓ
115. Ⓐ Ⓑ Ⓒ Ⓓ   123. Ⓐ Ⓑ Ⓒ Ⓓ   131. Ⓐ Ⓑ Ⓒ Ⓓ   139. Ⓐ Ⓑ Ⓒ Ⓓ   147. Ⓐ Ⓑ Ⓒ Ⓓ
116. Ⓐ Ⓑ Ⓒ Ⓓ   124. Ⓐ Ⓑ Ⓒ Ⓓ   132. Ⓐ Ⓑ Ⓒ Ⓓ   140. Ⓐ Ⓑ Ⓒ Ⓓ   148. Ⓐ Ⓑ Ⓒ Ⓓ
117. Ⓐ Ⓑ Ⓒ Ⓓ   125. Ⓐ Ⓑ Ⓒ Ⓓ   133. Ⓐ Ⓑ Ⓒ Ⓓ   141. Ⓐ Ⓑ Ⓒ Ⓓ   149. Ⓐ Ⓑ Ⓒ Ⓓ
118. Ⓐ Ⓑ Ⓒ Ⓓ   126. Ⓐ Ⓑ Ⓒ Ⓓ   134. Ⓐ Ⓑ Ⓒ Ⓓ   142. Ⓐ Ⓑ Ⓒ Ⓓ   150. Ⓐ Ⓑ Ⓒ Ⓓ
119. Ⓐ Ⓑ Ⓒ Ⓓ   127. Ⓐ Ⓑ Ⓒ Ⓓ   135. Ⓐ Ⓑ Ⓒ Ⓓ   143. Ⓐ Ⓑ Ⓒ Ⓓ   151. Ⓐ Ⓑ Ⓒ Ⓓ
120. Ⓐ Ⓑ Ⓒ Ⓓ   128. Ⓐ Ⓑ Ⓒ Ⓓ   136. Ⓐ Ⓑ Ⓒ Ⓓ   144. Ⓐ Ⓑ Ⓒ Ⓓ   152. Ⓐ Ⓑ Ⓒ Ⓓ

VOCABULARY

153. Ⓐ Ⓑ Ⓒ Ⓓ   158. Ⓐ Ⓑ Ⓒ Ⓓ   163. Ⓐ Ⓑ Ⓒ Ⓓ   168. Ⓐ Ⓑ Ⓒ Ⓓ   173. Ⓐ Ⓑ Ⓒ Ⓓ
154. Ⓐ Ⓑ Ⓒ Ⓓ   159. Ⓐ Ⓑ Ⓒ Ⓓ   164. Ⓐ Ⓑ Ⓒ Ⓓ   169. Ⓐ Ⓑ Ⓒ Ⓓ   174. Ⓐ Ⓑ Ⓒ Ⓓ
155. Ⓐ Ⓑ Ⓒ Ⓓ   160. Ⓐ Ⓑ Ⓒ Ⓓ   165. Ⓐ Ⓑ Ⓒ Ⓓ   170. Ⓐ Ⓑ Ⓒ Ⓓ
156. Ⓐ Ⓑ Ⓒ Ⓓ   161. Ⓐ Ⓑ Ⓒ Ⓓ   166. Ⓐ Ⓑ Ⓒ Ⓓ   171. Ⓐ Ⓑ Ⓒ Ⓓ
157. Ⓐ Ⓑ Ⓒ Ⓓ   162. Ⓐ Ⓑ Ⓒ Ⓓ   167. Ⓐ Ⓑ Ⓒ Ⓓ   172. Ⓐ Ⓑ Ⓒ Ⓓ

Mathematics

CONCEPTS

175. Ⓐ Ⓑ Ⓒ Ⓓ   180. Ⓐ Ⓑ Ⓒ Ⓓ   185. Ⓐ Ⓑ Ⓒ Ⓓ   190. Ⓐ Ⓑ Ⓒ Ⓓ   195. Ⓐ Ⓑ Ⓒ Ⓓ
176. Ⓐ Ⓑ Ⓒ Ⓓ   181. Ⓐ Ⓑ Ⓒ Ⓓ   186. Ⓐ Ⓑ Ⓒ Ⓓ   191. Ⓐ Ⓑ Ⓒ Ⓓ   196. Ⓐ Ⓑ Ⓒ Ⓓ
177. Ⓐ Ⓑ Ⓒ Ⓓ   182. Ⓐ Ⓑ Ⓒ Ⓓ   187. Ⓐ Ⓑ Ⓒ Ⓓ   192. Ⓐ Ⓑ Ⓒ Ⓓ   197. Ⓐ Ⓑ Ⓒ Ⓓ
178. Ⓐ Ⓑ Ⓒ Ⓓ   183. Ⓐ Ⓑ Ⓒ Ⓓ   188. Ⓐ Ⓑ Ⓒ Ⓓ   193. Ⓐ Ⓑ Ⓒ Ⓓ   198. Ⓐ Ⓑ Ⓒ Ⓓ
179. Ⓐ Ⓑ Ⓒ Ⓓ   184. Ⓐ Ⓑ Ⓒ Ⓓ   189. Ⓐ Ⓑ Ⓒ Ⓓ   194. Ⓐ Ⓑ Ⓒ Ⓓ

PROBLEM-SOLVING

199. Ⓐ Ⓑ Ⓒ Ⓓ   207. Ⓐ Ⓑ Ⓒ Ⓓ   215. Ⓐ Ⓑ Ⓒ Ⓓ   223. Ⓐ Ⓑ Ⓒ Ⓓ   231. Ⓐ Ⓑ Ⓒ Ⓓ
200. Ⓐ Ⓑ Ⓒ Ⓓ   208. Ⓐ Ⓑ Ⓒ Ⓓ   216. Ⓐ Ⓑ Ⓒ Ⓓ   224. Ⓐ Ⓑ Ⓒ Ⓓ   232. Ⓐ Ⓑ Ⓒ Ⓓ
201. Ⓐ Ⓑ Ⓒ Ⓓ   209. Ⓐ Ⓑ Ⓒ Ⓓ   217. Ⓐ Ⓑ Ⓒ Ⓓ   225. Ⓐ Ⓑ Ⓒ Ⓓ   233. Ⓐ Ⓑ Ⓒ Ⓓ
202. Ⓐ Ⓑ Ⓒ Ⓓ   210. Ⓐ Ⓑ Ⓒ Ⓓ   218. Ⓐ Ⓑ Ⓒ Ⓓ   226. Ⓐ Ⓑ Ⓒ Ⓓ   234. Ⓐ Ⓑ Ⓒ Ⓓ
203. Ⓐ Ⓑ Ⓒ Ⓓ   211. Ⓐ Ⓑ Ⓒ Ⓓ   219. Ⓐ Ⓑ Ⓒ Ⓓ   227. Ⓐ Ⓑ Ⓒ Ⓓ   235. Ⓐ Ⓑ Ⓒ Ⓓ
204. Ⓐ Ⓑ Ⓒ Ⓓ   212. Ⓐ Ⓑ Ⓒ Ⓓ   220. Ⓐ Ⓑ Ⓒ Ⓓ   228. Ⓐ Ⓑ Ⓒ Ⓓ   236. Ⓐ Ⓑ Ⓒ Ⓓ
205. Ⓐ Ⓑ Ⓒ Ⓓ   213. Ⓐ Ⓑ Ⓒ Ⓓ   221. Ⓐ Ⓑ Ⓒ Ⓓ   229. Ⓐ Ⓑ Ⓒ Ⓓ   237. Ⓐ Ⓑ Ⓒ Ⓓ
206. Ⓐ Ⓑ Ⓒ Ⓓ   214. Ⓐ Ⓑ Ⓒ Ⓓ   222. Ⓐ Ⓑ Ⓒ Ⓓ   230. Ⓐ Ⓑ Ⓒ Ⓓ   238. Ⓐ Ⓑ Ⓒ Ⓓ

Language

239. Ⓐ Ⓑ Ⓒ Ⓓ	251. Ⓐ Ⓑ Ⓒ Ⓓ	263. Ⓐ Ⓑ Ⓒ Ⓓ	275. Ⓐ Ⓑ Ⓒ Ⓓ	287. Ⓐ Ⓑ Ⓒ Ⓓ
240. Ⓐ Ⓑ Ⓒ Ⓓ	252. Ⓐ Ⓑ Ⓒ Ⓓ	264. Ⓐ Ⓑ Ⓒ Ⓓ	276. Ⓐ Ⓑ Ⓒ Ⓓ	288. Ⓐ Ⓑ Ⓒ Ⓓ
241. Ⓐ Ⓑ Ⓒ Ⓓ	253. Ⓐ Ⓑ Ⓒ Ⓓ	265. Ⓐ Ⓑ Ⓒ Ⓓ	277. Ⓐ Ⓑ Ⓒ Ⓓ	289. Ⓐ Ⓑ Ⓒ Ⓓ
242. Ⓐ Ⓑ Ⓒ Ⓓ	254. Ⓐ Ⓑ Ⓒ Ⓓ	266. Ⓐ Ⓑ Ⓒ Ⓓ	278. Ⓐ Ⓑ Ⓒ Ⓓ	290. Ⓐ Ⓑ Ⓒ Ⓓ
243. Ⓐ Ⓑ Ⓒ Ⓓ	255. Ⓐ Ⓑ Ⓒ Ⓓ	267. Ⓐ Ⓑ Ⓒ Ⓓ	279. Ⓐ Ⓑ Ⓒ Ⓓ	291. Ⓐ Ⓑ Ⓒ Ⓓ
244. Ⓐ Ⓑ Ⓒ Ⓓ	256. Ⓐ Ⓑ Ⓒ Ⓓ	268. Ⓐ Ⓑ Ⓒ Ⓓ	280. Ⓐ Ⓑ Ⓒ Ⓓ	292. Ⓐ Ⓑ Ⓒ Ⓓ
245. Ⓐ Ⓑ Ⓒ Ⓓ	257. Ⓐ Ⓑ Ⓒ Ⓓ	269. Ⓐ Ⓑ Ⓒ Ⓓ	281. Ⓐ Ⓑ Ⓒ Ⓓ	293. Ⓐ Ⓑ Ⓒ Ⓓ
246. Ⓐ Ⓑ Ⓒ Ⓓ	258. Ⓐ Ⓑ Ⓒ Ⓓ	270. Ⓐ Ⓑ Ⓒ Ⓓ	282. Ⓐ Ⓑ Ⓒ Ⓓ	294. Ⓐ Ⓑ Ⓒ Ⓓ
247. Ⓐ Ⓑ Ⓒ Ⓓ	259. Ⓐ Ⓑ Ⓒ Ⓓ	271. Ⓐ Ⓑ Ⓒ Ⓓ	283. Ⓐ Ⓑ Ⓒ Ⓓ	295. Ⓐ Ⓑ Ⓒ Ⓓ
248. Ⓐ Ⓑ Ⓒ Ⓓ	260. Ⓐ Ⓑ Ⓒ Ⓓ	272. Ⓐ Ⓑ Ⓒ Ⓓ	284. Ⓐ Ⓑ Ⓒ Ⓓ	296. Ⓐ Ⓑ Ⓒ Ⓓ
249. Ⓐ Ⓑ Ⓒ Ⓓ	261. Ⓐ Ⓑ Ⓒ Ⓓ	273. Ⓐ Ⓑ Ⓒ Ⓓ	285. Ⓐ Ⓑ Ⓒ Ⓓ	297. Ⓐ Ⓑ Ⓒ Ⓓ
250. Ⓐ Ⓑ Ⓒ Ⓓ	262. Ⓐ Ⓑ Ⓒ Ⓓ	274. Ⓐ Ⓑ Ⓒ Ⓓ	286. Ⓐ Ⓑ Ⓒ Ⓓ	298. Ⓐ Ⓑ Ⓒ Ⓓ

answer sheet

Practice Test 5: HSPT

VERBAL SKILLS

16 MINUTES

Directions: Mark one answer—the answer you think is best—for each problem.

1. Which word does *not* belong with the others?
   - (A) sundial
   - (B) watch
   - (C) time
   - (D) clock

2. Which word does *not* belong with the others?
   - (A) light
   - (B) elated
   - (C) gleeful
   - (D) joyous

3. Red is to pink as black is to
   - (A) beige.
   - (B) white.
   - (C) dark.
   - (D) gray.

4. Ann reads faster than Sue. Karen reads faster than Ann. Karen reads more slowly than Sue. If the first two statements are true, the third is
   - (A) true.
   - (B) false.
   - (C) uncertain.

5. *Create* most nearly means
   - (A) destroy.
   - (B) build.
   - (C) discover.
   - (D) invent.

6. Youth is to young as age is to
   - (A) people.
   - (B) parents.
   - (C) grandmother.
   - (D) old.

7. Which word does *not* belong with the others?
   - (A) quality
   - (B) honesty
   - (C) sincerity
   - (D) integrity

8. Sand is to beach as black dirt is to
   - (A) earth.
   - (B) plants.
   - (C) water.
   - (D) farm.

9. Which word does *not* belong with the others?
   - (A) day
   - (B) time
   - (C) month
   - (D) hour

10. A *salamander* is a(n)
    - (A) amphibian.
    - (B) hammock.
    - (C) spice.
    - (D) fish.

11. *Arrogant* most nearly means
   (A) poised.
   (B) superior.
   (C) fragrant.
   (D) haughty.

12. Square is to circle as rectangle is to
   (A) round.
   (B) triangle.
   (C) oval.
   (D) cube.

13. One is to two as three is to
   (A) two.
   (B) five.
   (C) thirty.
   (D) six.

14. Which word does *not* belong with the others?
   (A) figure
   (B) number
   (C) add
   (D) letter

15. Paul is taller than Peter. Peter is shorter than John. Paul is taller than John. If the first two statements are true, the third is
   (A) true.
   (B) false.
   (C) uncertain.

16. A *mellow* peach is
   (A) ripe.
   (B) rotten.
   (C) yellow.
   (D) green.

17. *Gossamer* most nearly means
   (A) beautiful.
   (B) flimsy.
   (C) eerie.
   (D) supernatural.

18. *Coddle* most nearly means
   (A) handle.
   (B) embrace.
   (C) pamper.
   (D) love.

19. Light is to lamp as heat is to
   (A) furnace.
   (B) light.
   (C) sun.
   (D) room.

20. Choir is to director as team is to
   (A) sport.
   (B) coach.
   (C) player.
   (D) athlete.

21. *Diversify* most nearly means
   (A) vary.
   (B) oppose.
   (C) change.
   (D) strengthen.

22. Harry is more intelligent than George. Sam is more intelligent than Ralph. Harry is more intelligent than Ralph. If the first two statements are true, the third is
   (A) true.
   (B) false.
   (C) uncertain.

23. A *superficial* wound is
   (A) serious.
   (B) deep.
   (C) facial.
   (D) shallow.

24. A is north of B. B is north of C. C is south of A. If the first two statements are true, the third is
   (A) true.
   (B) false.
   (C) uncertain.

25. A *precocious* child is
   (A) precious.
   (B) proper.
   (C) tall.
   (D) quick.

26. A *sadistic* remark is
   (A) sad.
   (B) silly.
   (C) hurtful.
   (D) sudden.

27. Which word does *not* belong with the others?
   (A) college
   (B) university
   (C) school
   (D) dormitory

28. *Truncate* most nearly means
   (A) pack.
   (B) cut.
   (C) sound.
   (D) transport.

29. A *sallow* face is
   (A) ruddy.
   (B) young.
   (C) healthy.
   (D) sickly.

30. An *indigent* person is
   (A) delicate.
   (B) intelligent.
   (C) indignant.
   (D) needy.

31. Table is to leg as automobile is to
   (A) wheel.
   (B) axle.
   (C) door.
   (D) fuel.

32. Which word does *not* belong with the others?
   (A) dungeon
   (B) residence
   (C) dwelling
   (D) domicile

33. All tumps are winged boscs. No blue boscs have wings. No tumps are blue. If the first two statements are true, the third is
   (A) true.
   (B) false.
   (C) uncertain.

34. Which word does *not* belong with the others?
   (A) prison
   (B) jail
   (C) reformatory
   (D) punishment

35. Refuse means the *opposite* of
   (A) reheat.
   (B) accept.
   (C) reveal.
   (D) tidy.

36. Ink is to pen as paint is to
   (A) canvas.
   (B) bucket.
   (C) wall.
   (D) brush.

37. Acquire means the *opposite* of
   (A) solo.
   (B) buy.
   (C) release.
   (D) collect.

38. River A is wider than River B. River B is narrower than River C. River A is wider than River C. If the first two statements are true, the third is
   (A) true.
   (B) false.
   (C) uncertain.

39. Scant means the *opposite* of
   (A) sparse.
   (B) scoundrel.
   (C) abundant.
   (D) straight.

40. Pinnacle means the *opposite* of
   (A) bridge.
   (B) base.
   (C) wall.
   (D) rummy.

41. Team is to captain as office is to
   (A) secretary.
   (B) accountant.
   (C) staff.
   (D) manager.

42. Which word does *not* belong with the others?
   (A) window
   (B) drape
   (C) shade
   (D) curtain

43. Corpulent means the *opposite* of
   (A) bulky.
   (B) singular.
   (C) company.
   (D) slender.

44. Naive means the *opposite* of
   (A) rural.
   (B) dull.
   (C) sophisticated.
   (D) funny.

45. Which word does *not* belong with the others?
   (A) fez
   (B) turban
   (C) glove
   (D) derby

46. Which word does *not* belong with the others?
   (A) gallery
   (B) audience
   (C) congregation
   (D) podium

47. *Pledge* most nearly means
   (A) promise.
   (B) beg.
   (C) join.
   (D) obey.

48. Depression is the *opposite* of
   (A) incline.
   (B) valley.
   (C) hill.
   (D) oppression.

49. Grapes cost more than apples but less than pineapples. Oranges cost more than apples but less than lemons. Apples cost the least of the fruits. If the first two statements are true, the third is
   (A) true.
   (B) false.
   (C) uncertain.

50. Which word does *not* belong with the others?
   (A) oak
   (B) elm
   (C) maple
   (D) fir

51. Diminish is the *opposite* of
   (A) trim.
   (B) augment.
   (C) decorate.
   (D) decrease.

52. Jay's batting average is better than Michael's. Michael's batting average is higher than Tom's. Jay's batting average is lower than Tom's. If the first two statements are true, the third is
    - (A) true.
    - (B) false.
    - (C) uncertain.

53. Abandon is the *opposite* of
    - (A) abdicate.
    - (B) keep.
    - (C) maintain.
    - (D) encourage.

54. Which word does *not* belong with the others?
    - (A) flexible
    - (B) feasible
    - (C) supple
    - (D) malleable

55. A is northeast of B. C is southwest of D but northwest of A. C is north of B. If the first two statements are true, the third is
    - (A) true.
    - (B) false.
    - (C) uncertain.

56. Which word does *not* belong with the others?
    - (A) leather
    - (B) cotton
    - (C) wool
    - (D) fur

57. Which word does *not* belong with the others?
    - (A) zipper
    - (B) button
    - (C) snap
    - (D) seam

58. *Dwindle* most nearly means
    - (A) shrink.
    - (B) ooze.
    - (C) leak.
    - (D) spoil.

59. Which word does *not* belong with the others?
    - (A) oxygen
    - (B) water
    - (C) helium
    - (D) gold

60. Jon ran faster than Carl. Ron ran faster than George but not as fast as Jon. Carl was the fastest runner. If the first two statements are true, the third is
    - (A) true.
    - (B) false.
    - (C) uncertain.

STOP End of Verbal Skills section. If you have any time left, go over your work in this section only. Do not work in any other section of the test.

QUANTITATIVE SKILLS

30 MINUTES

Directions: Mark one answer—the answer you think is best—for each problem.

61. What number is 3 more than 20% of 40?
- **(A)** 11
- **(B)** 8
- **(C)** 5
- **(D)** 9

62. Look at this series: 32, 39, 46, 53, ... What number should come next?
- **(A)** 68
- **(B)** 61
- **(C)** 59
- **(D)** 60

63. Look at this series: 48, 39, 30, 21, ... What number should come next?
- **(A)** 17
- **(B)** 20
- **(C)** 29
- **(D)** 12

64. Examine (A), (B), and (C) and find the best answer.

(A)   (B)   (C)

- **(A)** (A) plus (C) is less than (B).
- **(B)** (C) is equal to (A).
- **(C)** (A) is greater than (C).
- **(D)** (C) is less than (B) and greater than (A).

65. Examine (A), (B), and (C) and find the best answer.
- (A)   0.625
- (B) $\frac{4}{7}$
- (C) 0.297×2.1
- **(A)** (B) is less than (A) but greater than (C).
- **(B)** (A) and (C) are equal and greater than (B).
- **(C)** (C) is greater than (A) and (B).
- **(D)** (B) is less than (A) and (C).

66. What number is the cube of 5 divided by 5?
- **(A)** 15
- **(B)** 25
- **(C)** 75
- **(D)** 125

67. What number is $\frac{1}{2}$ of the average of 7, 18, 5, 39, 11?
- **(A)** 40
- **(B)** 5
- **(C)** 8
- **(D)** 20

68. Examine (A), (B), and (C) and find the best answer.

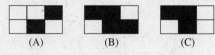

(A)   (B)   (C)

- **(A)** (A) is more shaded than (B).
- **(B)** (B) and (C) are equally shaded.
- **(C)** (C) is less shaded than either (A) or (B).
- **(D)** (A) and (C) are both less shaded than (B).

69. Look at this series: 1, 4, 11, _____, 21, 24, 31, ... What number should fill the blank in the middle of the series?

    (A) 3

    (B) 14

    (C) 20

    (D) 22

70. Examine (A), (B), and (C) and find the best answer.

    (A) 10% of 80

    (B) 80% of 10

    (C) 10% of 80%

    (A) (B) is greater than (A) or (C).

    (B) (A), (B), and (C) are equal.

    (C) (A) is equal to (B) and smaller than (C).

    (D) (A) is greater than (C).

71. Look at this series: 1, 2, 4, 5, 10, 11, ... What number should come next?

    (A) 22

    (B) 12

    (C) 15

    (D) 21

72. Look at this series: 34, 40, 37, 36, 42, 39, 38, ... What three numbers come next?

    (A) 44, 42, 41

    (B) 43, 40, 39

    (C) 44, 41, 40

    (D) 45, 42, 41

73. What number subtracted from 30 leaves 7 more than $\frac{3}{5}$ of 25?

    (A) 8

    (B) 15

    (C) 22

    (D) 23

74. What number is 5 more than $\frac{1}{3}$ of 18?

    (A) 6

    (B) 11

    (C) 1

    (D) 14

75. Examine (A), (B), and (C) and find the best answer.

    (A) $(8 \times 3) - 10$

    (B) $(5 \times 2) + 4$

    (C) $(4 \times 4) - 2$

    (A) (C) is greater than (A) and (B).

    (B) (A) is greater than (B) and equal to (C).

    (C) (A), (B), and (C) are equal.

    (D) (B) is greater than (A) and less than (C).

76. Look at this series: 821, 812, 804, 797, ... What number should come next?

    (A) 791

    (B) 788

    (C) 787

    (D) 790

77. Examine (A), (B), and (C) and find the best answer.

    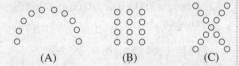

    (A)   (B)   (C)

    (A) (A) has more circles than (B).

    (B) (B) and (C) have the same number of circles.

    (C) (B) and (C) each have more circles than (A).

    (D) (A) and (C) each have fewer circles than (B).

78. Examine (A), (B), and (C) and find the best answer.

    (A)   (B)   (C)

    (A) (C) is more shaded than (B).

    (B) (A) and (C) are equally shaded, and both are more shaded than (B).

    (C) (B) is more shaded than (A) and less shaded than (C).

    (D) (A), (B), and (C) are equally shaded.

79. Look at this series: 95, 99, _____, 107, 111. What number should fill the blank in the middle of the series?

(A) 104

(B) 98

(C) 106

(D) 103

80. What number divided by 4 is $\frac{1}{5}$ of 100?

(A) 400

(B) 20

(C) 80

(D) 200

81. Look at this series: 1, V, 6, X, ... What number should come next?

(A) XV

(B) 11

(C) 10

(D) IX

82. Examine (A), (B), and (C) and find the best answer.

(A) $\frac{1}{3}$ of 15

(B) $\frac{1}{4}$ of 16

(C) $\frac{1}{5}$ of 20

(A) (A) and (B) are each greater than (C).

(B) (A), (B), and (C) are equal.

(C) (C) is greater than (A).

(D) (B) and (C) are equal.

83. $\frac{1}{2}$ of what number is 7 times 3?

(A) 21

(B) 42

(C) 20

(D) 5

84. Examine (A), (B), and (C) and find the best answer.

(A)   (B)   (C)

(A) (A), (B), and (C) are equally shaded.

(B) (B) is less shaded than (C) and more shaded than (A).

(C) (A) is more shaded than (B) or (C).

(D) (C) is more shaded than (A).

85. What number added to 6 is 3 times the product of 5 and 2?

(A) 16

(B) 4

(C) 30

(D) 24

86. Look at this series: 50, 48, 52, 50, 54, 52, ... What number should come next?

(A) 50

(B) 56

(C) 54

(D) 58

87. Examine (A), (B), and (C) and find the best answer.

(A) 0.4

(B) 4%

(C) $\frac{2}{5}$

(A) (A) is greater than (C), which is greater than (B).

(B) (A) is equal to (C) and greater than (B).

(C) (A) is equal to (B) and greater than (C).

(D) (A) is less than (B) and equal to (C).

88. $\frac{3}{4}$ of what number is 6 times 4?

    (A) 18
    (B) 24
    (C) 32
    (D) 8

89. Look at this series: 12, 14, 28, _____, 60, ... What number should fill the blank in this series?

    (A) 19
    (B) 16
    (C) 40
    (D) 30

90. Look at this series: 4, 5, 8, 11, 12, 15, 18, 19, ... What number should come next?

    (A) 20
    (B) 22
    (C) 23
    (D) 21

91. Examine the triangle and find the best answer.

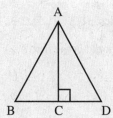

    (A) AD is greater than CD.
    (B) BA and AD are each less than BC.
    (C) AB is equal to BC.
    (D) AB is equal to AC plus BC.

92. What number multiplied by 3 is 5 less than 29?

    (A) 6
    (B) 24
    (C) 8
    (D) 21

93. Look at this series: 23, 29, 32, 38, 41, _____, 50, ... What number should fill the blank in this series?

    (A) 42
    (B) 47
    (C) 44
    (D) 51

94. Examine (A), (B), and (C) and find the best answer.

    (A) $(10 \div 5) \times 10$
    (B) $(5 \div 1) \times 4$
    (C) $(20 \div 5) \times 5$

    (A) (A) is equal to (B), which is equal to (C).
    (B) (A) is equal to (B) and less than (C).
    (C) (B) is equal to (C) and less than (A).
    (D) (C) is greater than (A) and (B).

95. Look at this series: 100, 101, 91, 92, 82, ... What two numbers should come next?

    (A) 72, 74
    (B) 72, 73
    (C) 83, 73
    (D) 84, 74

96. Examine the cube and find the best answer.

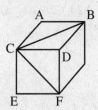

    (A) CF is greater than CB.
    (B) EF is less than AB.
    (C) CB is equal to CE.
    (D) CF is greater than AB.

97. What number divided by 2 leaves 4 more than 6?

    (A) 5
    (B) 10
    (C) 20
    (D) 4

98. Examine (A), (B), and (C) and find the best answer if both x and y are greater than zero.

(A) $5(x + y)$

(B) $5x + y$

(C) $5(x + y) + x$

(A) (A), (B), and (C) are equal.

(B) (B) is less than (A), which is less than (C).

(C) (C) is greater than (A) and less than (B).

(D) (A) and (B) are equal.

99. Look at this series: 14, 28, 32, 64, 68, ... What number should come next?

(A) 136

(B) 138

(C) 72

(D) 76

100. What number subtracted from 7 leaves $\frac{1}{4}$ of 20?

(A) 13

(B) 5

(C) 12

(D) 2

101. Look at this series: A24, C28, E18, G22, ... What comes next?

(A) H26

(B) J14

(C) I12

(D) F20

102. Examine the graph and find the best answer.

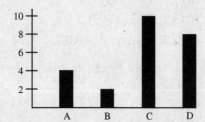

(A) B plus C minus A equals D.

(B) C minus A minus B equals D.

(C) C plus D equals A plus B.

(D) D minus B equals A plus C.

103. What number is 2 less than $\frac{3}{5}$ of 10?

(A) 4

(B) 8

(C) 6

(D) 2

104. Look at this series: 4, 16, 5, 25, 6, ... What number should come next?

(A) 36

(B) 30

(C) 6

(D) 20

105. Examine (A), (B), and (C) and find the best answer.

(A) 5^2

(B) 4^3

(C) 2^4

(A) A > B > C

(B) B > A > C

(C) A = B = C

(D) B > A = C

106. Look at this series: 10, $7\frac{1}{2}$, 5, $2\frac{1}{2}$, ...

What number should come next?

(A) 1

(B) $1\frac{1}{2}$

(C) $\frac{1}{2}$

(D) 0

107. What number is 8 times $\frac{1}{2}$ of 20?

(A) 10

(B) 80

(C) 24

(D) 28

108. Look at this series: 26, 30, 28, 27, 31, 29, 28, ... What three numbers should come next?

    (A) 32, 38, 24

    (B) 30, 28, 27

    (C) 32, 30, 29

    (D) 24, 26, 27

109. $\frac{1}{3}$ of what number added to 6 is 2 times 9?

    (A) 12

    (B) 36

    (C) 18

    (D) 3

110. Examine the parallelogram and find the best answer.

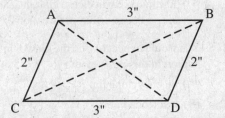

    (A) The perimeter of the parallelogram is 10 inches.

    (B) The area of the parallelogram is 5 square inches.

    (C) The area of triangle ABD is greater than the area of triangle ACD.

    (D) The perimeter of triangle BAC is equal to the perimeter of the parallelogram.

111. What number is 10 more than $\frac{4}{9}$ of 27?

    (A) 37

    (B) 12

    (C) 2

    (D) 22

112. What number is 7 less than 4 squared?

    (A) 9

    (B) 25

    (C) 16

    (D) 11

STOP End of Quantitative Skills section. If you have any time left, go over your work in this section only. Do not work in any other section of the test.

READING

Comprehension

25 MINUTES

Directions: Read each passage carefully. Then mark one answer—the answer you think is best—for each item.

Our planet Earth is divided into seven separate layers. The outer layer is called the crust and appears to be approximately twenty miles thick. Next in line are the four layers of the mantle. These layers vary in thickness from 250 to 1,000 miles. The remaining two layers are divided into the outer core and inner core. The thickness of the outer core has been determined to be slightly more than 1,200 miles, while that of the inner core is slightly less than 800 miles. Scientists calculate the location and depth of these layers by measuring and studying the speed and direction of earthquake waves. They have also determined that both temperature and pressure are much greater at the core than at the crust.

113. The thickest portion of the Earth is the
   (A) crust.
   (B) outer core.
   (C) mantle.
   (D) inner core.

114. How many separate layers does the Earth have?
   (A) Two
   (B) Twenty
   (C) Seven
   (D) Four

115. Which of the following is correct?
   (A) No two sets of earthquake waves ever travel in the same direction.
   (B) Earthquakes usually travel in the same direction.
   (C) Earthquake waves travel at different speeds.
   (D) Earthquake waves travel at the same speed but in different directions.

116. You would expect to find the kind of information in this passage in
   (A) an encyclopedia.
   (B) a science book.
   (C) neither of these.
   (D) both of these.

117. In going from the surface to the center of the Earth, in which order would you pass through the layers?
   (A) crust, outer core, mantle, inner core
   (B) outer core, inner core, crust, mantle
   (C) outer core, crust, inner core, mantle
   (D) crust, mantle, outer core, inner core

118. The word vary, as underlined and used in this passage, most nearly means
   (A) stabilize.
   (B) increase.
   (C) range.
   (D) arbitrate.

119. Which of the following is correct?

    (A) Scientists know the exact thickness of the crust.

    (B) Scientists believe they know the thickness of the crust.

    (C) The thickness of the crust cannot be determined.

    (D) Scientists cannot agree on the thickness of the crust.

120. In comparing the core with the crust, you would find that at the core,

    (A) temperature and pressure are less.

    (B) pressure is greater, temperature is less.

    (C) temperature is greater, pressure is less.

    (D) temperature and pressure are greater.

121. The word slightly, as underlined and used in this passage, most nearly means

    (A) scarcely.

    (B) considerably.

    (C) a little.

    (D) at least.

122. The word remaining, as underlined and used in this passage, most nearly means

    (A) previous.

    (B) outer.

    (C) last.

    (D) prior.

The man is in utter darkness. Only the wavering beam of light from his flashlight pierces the blackness. The air, damp and cold, smells of dank, unseen, decaying material.

The man stumbles over stones, splashes into a hidden puddle. He bangs into a cold rocky wall. The flashlight cocks upward, and suddenly, the air is filled with the flutter of thousands of wings and the piping of tiny animal wails. He ducks, startled, then grins. He's found what he's looking for—bats!

For this man is a spelunker, another name for someone who explores caves for the fun of it. Spelunkers actually enjoy crawling on their stomachs in narrow, rocky tunnels far below the surface of the earth.

Spelunkers have discovered new caves. Some have formed clubs, sharing safety knowledge, developing new techniques, and teaching novices.

Spelunkers believe that Earth's inner spaces are as exciting as the universe's outer spaces.

123. The first two paragraphs of this passage describe a cave's

    (A) rocks.

    (B) depth.

    (C) atmosphere.

    (D) streams.

124. The word wavering, as underlined and used in this passage, most nearly means

    (A) swaying.

    (B) steady.

    (C) strong.

    (D) shining.

125. The author of this passage is most likely a

    (A) spelunker.

    (B) cave scientist.

    (C) medical doctor.

    (D) magazine writer.

126. The cave the man was exploring was probably
    (A) large and dry.
    (B) deep underground.
    (C) near the surface.
    (D) dangerous.

127. According to this passage, what started the bats to suddenly fly about?
    (A) The spelunker
    (B) The damp and cold air
    (C) The flashlight
    (D) The sudden noise

128. The man ducked when the bats flew because he was
    (A) angry.
    (B) afraid.
    (C) surprised.
    (D) hurt.

129. The word utter, as underlined and used in this passage, most nearly means
    (A) bovine.
    (B) unspeakable.
    (C) oppressive.
    (D) great.

130. According to this passage, spelunkers ignore
    (A) safety rules.
    (B) light.
    (C) discomfort.
    (D) other spelunkers.

131. A good title for this passage would be
    (A) "Batty about Bats."
    (B) "Spelunkers—Underground Explorers."
    (C) "Inner Space."
    (D) "The Life of a Spelunker."

132. According to this passage, which word would most nearly describe spelunkers?
    (A) Experimental
    (B) Cautious
    (C) Antisocial
    (D) Adventurous

Litterbugs have a bad reputation, but the biggest litterbugs in history have, in fact, been very helpful to mankind.

For glaciers, in ancient times and today, are the greatest creators and distributors of litter. Of course, they don't drop tin cans, paper cups, and pop bottles; they dump rocks, boulders, sand, gravel, and mud all over the landscape, and it's this glacial debris that has helped create some of the world's most fertile farmland, such as that in America's Midwest.

Geologists describe glacial ice as true rock, different only in that it melts more easily than other rock. Because glacial ice is moving rock, it scrapes, bangs, and tears at the terrain over which it moves, breaking off chunks of all sizes. When the ice melts, the debris drops, and, if it is rich in minerals, creates fertile soil when it erodes.

It's too bad human litterbugs aren't as useful!

133. The richness of the soil in America's Midwest can be attributed, in part, to
    (A) heavy annual rainfalls.
    (B) scientific analysis.
    (C) human litterbugs.
    (D) ancient glacial debris.

134. Although the author of this passage describes glaciers as litterbugs, his attitude toward glaciers is one of
    (A) love.
    (B) gratitude.
    (C) admiration.
    (D) fear.

135. Which of the following is correct?
    (A) Glacial ice is full of pop bottles.
    (B) Glaciers are harmful.
    (C) Glaciers erode the terrain.
    (D) Glacial ice may be full of fertile soil.

136. According to this passage, history's biggest litterbugs are

(A) glaciers.

(B) people.

(C) rocks.

(D) bulldozers.

137. The words most fertile, as underlined and used in this passage, most nearly mean

(A) most icy.

(B) flattest.

(C) most rocky.

(D) best growing.

138. Good soil contains

(A) rocks.

(B) minerals.

(C) vitamins.

(D) melted ice.

139. A good title for this passage might be

(A) "A Lovely Litterbug."

(B) "The Destructive Forces of Glaciers."

(C) "Glaciers—Then and Now."

(D) "The History of Glaciers."

140. This passage implies that the litter human beings drop is

(A) useless.

(B) ugly.

(C) uninteresting.

(D) unimportant.

141. The word terrain, as underlined and used in this passage, most nearly means

(A) rock.

(B) terror.

(C) view.

(D) land.

142. It could be said, on the basis of this passage, that glaciers change the

(A) Earth's atmosphere.

(B) pollution rate.

(C) mineral content of rocks.

(D) Earth's geography.

The superstition of witchcraft, which most people laugh at today, is still a matter of mystery and speculation.

Hundreds of thousands of people in Europe who were accused of being witches were executed during the Middle Ages and even as late as the early eighteenth century. Their deaths probably resulted from hysterical fears. Yet the judges undoubtedly were sincere in their desire to eliminate what they thought was a real danger. Some modern psychologists have theorized that so-called witches actually were dangerous. In essence, they say that a person who believes in the powers of witchcraft can be affected emotionally or physically—may even die—because of a "witch's spell."

When Europeans immigrated to America, they brought their beliefs with them. There were a number of witchcraft trials in Massachusetts during the 1600s; however, after the execution of twenty Salem "witches" in 1692, prosecution for witchcraft didn't survive long in the New World.

Most people in the civilized world no longer believe in witchcraft. Nonetheless, the subject is fascinating for many people. As an example, the TV show *Bewitched* was a very popular program for more than five years.

143. This passage was probably printed in a(n)

(A) history book.

(B) magazine.

(C) psychology book.

(D) encyclopedia.

144. According to this passage, the mystery of witchcraft is

(A) a major problem for psychologists.

(B) of very little interest today.

(C) still unsolved.

(D) a major problem for sincere judges.

practice test

145. One of today's reminders of ancient witch-craft beliefs is
   (A) Halloween.
   (B) April Fools' Day.
   (C) the use of brooms.
   (D) the death penalty for certain crimes.

146. Which group can we be sure has had members who believed in witchcraft?
   (A) Judges
   (B) TV producers
   (C) Psychologists
   (D) Newspaper reporters

147. This passage calls witchcraft a "superstition." Which of these would also be a superstition?
   (A) "Many hands make light work."
   (B) "Breaking a mirror brings bad luck."
   (C) "Eating sweets causes pimples."
   (D) "Great oaks from little acorns grow."

148. According to some psychologists, persons who *do* believe in witchcraft
   (A) can be harmed by it.
   (B) tend to laugh at it today.
   (C) are crazy.
   (D) tend to be dangerous.

149. The phrase In essence, as underlined and used in this passage, most nearly means
   (A) probably.
   (B) basically.
   (C) briefly.
   (D) finally.

150. The word fascinating, as underlined and used in this passage, most nearly means
   (A) frightening.
   (B) enjoyable.
   (C) frustrating.
   (D) interesting.

151. This passage suggests that what you believe
   (A) can hurt you.
   (B) should be based on facts.
   (C) does not affect you.
   (D) changes as you grow older.

152. A good title for this passage might be
   (A) "Witchcraft—Fact or Fiction?"
   (B) "The End of Witchcraft."
   (C) "Witchcraft in the New World."
   (D) "The Powers of Witchcraft."

Vocabulary

Directions: Choose the word that means the same or about the same as the underlined word.

153. a new perspective
(A) receptacle
(B) sight
(C) picture
(D) view

154. impair his vision
(A) test
(B) weaken
(C) improve
(D) destroy

155. the smallest hovel
(A) hut
(B) shovel
(C) house
(D) palace

156. to loathe
(A) hate
(B) love
(C) help
(D) lose

157. to reproach
(A) approach
(B) praise
(C) blame
(D) steal

158. to be elated
(A) happy
(B) akin
(C) moved
(D) upset

159. his brusque manner
(A) foreign
(B) subtle
(C) soft
(D) abrupt

160. depress the key
(A) put away
(B) insert
(C) turn
(D) push down

161. quench your thirst
(A) end
(B) increase
(C) continue
(D) decrease

162. a famous exploit
(A) crime
(B) deed
(C) reputation
(D) game

163. a deft move
(A) skillful
(B) dangerous
(C) thoughtless
(D) final

164. an interesting chronicle
(A) fairy tale
(B) record
(C) time
(D) item

165. that amiable soul
(A) casual
(B) honest
(C) fine
(D) likable

166. her astute mind
(A) shrewd
(B) careful
(C) stupid
(D) astounding

practice test

167. to sever contact
    (A) cut
    (B) maintain
    (C) seek
    (D) establish

168. the eminent man
    (A) wicked
    (B) destitute
    (C) ancient
    (D) outstanding

169. to terminate a contract
    (A) end
    (B) enter
    (C) make
    (D) determine

170. to hinder someone
    (A) assist
    (B) follow
    (C) impede
    (D) slight

171. a spirit of contention
    (A) debate
    (B) content
    (C) inquiry
    (D) calm

172. to concede defeat
    (A) suspect
    (B) admit
    (C) realize
    (D) refuse

173. to forego his rights
    (A) usurp
    (B) insure
    (C) insist on
    (D) give up

174. your canny guess
    (A) uncertain
    (B) mistaken
    (C) clever
    (D) insincere

STOP End of Reading section. If you have any time left, go over your work in this section only. Do not work in any other section of the test.

MATHEMATICS

Concepts

45 MINUTES

Directions: Mark one answer—the answer you think is best—for each problem. You may use scratch paper when working on these problems.

175. Which of the following is *not* a quadrilateral?

(A) Square

(B) Trapezoid

(C) Triangle

(D) Rectangle

176. $\{1, 3, 8, 10\} \cap \{2, 3, 8\} =$

(A) $\{1, 2\}$

(B) $\{1, 2, 3, 8, 10\}$

(C) $\{3, 8\}$

(D) $\{\ \}$

177. To the nearest tenth, 63.594 is written

(A) 63.6

(B) 64

(C) 63.59

(D) 64.5

178. Simplify: $3(-2)^3 =$

(A) −216

(B) −18

(C) 1

(D) −24

179. As a fraction, 0.24 is

(A) $\dfrac{24}{1000}$

(B) $\dfrac{6}{25}$

(C) $\dfrac{1}{4}$

(D) $\dfrac{100}{24}$

180. The measure of angle A is

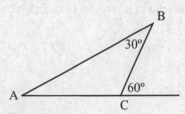

(A) 15°

(B) 20°

(C) 30°

(D) 35°

181. To multiply a number by 100, move the decimal point

(A) one place to the right.

(B) two places to the left.

(C) three places to the right.

(D) two places to the right.

182. Which of the following is a pair of reciprocals?

(A) $(3, -3)$

(B) $\left(3\dfrac{1}{3}, \dfrac{3}{10}\right)$

(C) $(2^3, 3^2)$

(D) $(0, 1)$

183. The circumference of this circle is

(A) 32π
(B) 16
(C) 8π
(D) 4

184. The ratio of 3 yards to 18 inches is

(A) 3 to 18
(B) 1 to 6
(C) 3 to 2
(D) 6 to 1

185. How many integers are between $\frac{33}{7}$ and 8.001?

(A) 3
(B) 6
(C) 5
(D) 4

186. Which of the following is true?

(A) $a \div (b + c) = \frac{a}{b} + \frac{a}{c}$
(B) $a(x + b) = ax + b$
(C) $a(x + b) = a(x) + a(b)$
(D) $a \div b = b\left(\frac{1}{a}\right)$

187. The square root of 198 is between

(A) 19 and 20
(B) 98 and 100
(C) 90 and 100
(D) 14 and 15

188. In a base-five system of numeration, what are the next three counting numbers after $43_{(5)}$?

(A) $44_{(5)}, 45_{(5)}, 50_{(5)}$
(B) $44_{(5)}, 45_{(5)}, 46_{(5)}$
(C) $44_{(5)}, 50_{(5)}, 52_{(5)}$
(D) $44_{(5)}, 100_{(5)}, 101_{(5)}$

189. Which of these is a correctly written scientific notation?

(A) $0.038 = 3.8 \times 10^{-2}$
(B) $380 = 3.8 \times 10^{3}$
(C) $0.38 = 3.8 \times 10^{-2}$
(D) $3800 = 3.8 \times 102$

190. Which fraction shows the greatest value?

(A) $\frac{5}{9}$
(B) $\frac{2}{3}$
(C) $\frac{6}{7}$
(D) $\frac{7}{8}$

191. Which of the following is true?

(A) $8 \le 6$
(B) $6 \ge 6$
(C) $0.080 > 0.08$
(D) $15 < 8$

192. $\triangle ABC$ is similar to $\triangle DBE$. The length of AB is

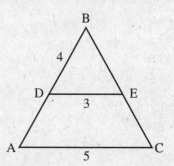

(A) $8\frac{1}{3}$
(B) $6\frac{1}{3}$
(C) $6\frac{2}{3}$
(D) $8\frac{2}{3}$

193. It is possible to have a right triangle that is also
    (A) equilateral.
    (B) equiangular.
    (C) obtuse.
    (D) isosceles.

194. Which one of the following is *not* equal to $62\frac{1}{2}\%$?
    (A) $\frac{10}{16}$
    (B) $\frac{5}{8}$
    (C) 0.625
    (D) 62.5

195. The prime factorization of 12 is
    (A) $2 \cdot 2 \cdot 3$
    (B) $4 + 8$
    (C) $6 \cdot 2$
    (D) $4 \cdot 3$

196. The least common multiple of 2 and 6 is
    (A) 6
    (B) 12
    (C) 3
    (D) 2

197. If Bill can mow a lawn in x hours, what part of the lawn can he mow in 2 hours?
    (A) $\frac{2}{x}$
    (B) $\frac{x}{2}$
    (C) $\frac{1}{2}$
    (D) $\frac{1}{x}$

198. The associative property of addition states that
    (A) $\frac{2}{3}+\left(\frac{1}{4}+\frac{1}{2}\right)=\frac{2}{3}+\left(\frac{1}{2}+\frac{1}{4}\right)$
    (B) $\left(\frac{2}{3}+\frac{1}{2}\right)+\frac{1}{4}=\frac{2}{3}+\left(\frac{1}{2}+\frac{1}{4}\right)$
    (C) $\frac{2}{3}\left(\frac{1}{4}+\frac{1}{2}\right)=\frac{2}{3}\left(\frac{1}{4}\right)+\frac{2}{3}\left(\frac{1}{2}\right)$
    (D) $\frac{2}{3}+\frac{1}{2}=\frac{2}{3}+\frac{1}{2}$

Problem-Solving

199. A movie theater sold 130 student tickets at $1.25 each and 340 adult tickets at $1.90 each. How much was collected?

(A) $798.50

(B) $708.50

(C) $808.50

(D) $818.50

200. Solve: $12 - 2\frac{3}{16} =$

(A) $10\frac{3}{16}$

(B) $9\frac{13}{16}$

(C) $10\frac{13}{16}$

(D) $9\frac{3}{16}$

201. Mr. Allen paid $542.40 for his telephone bills last year. How much did he pay, on average, per month?

(A) $46.20

(B) $54.20

(C) $55.20

(D) $45.20

202. Bob has $10 less than four times the amount Tim has. If Bob has $88, how much does Tim have?

(A) $48

(B) $22

(C) $16

(D) $24.50

203. Solve: $6 + (-12) + 7 + (-3) =$

(A) −2

(B) 2

(C) 28

(D) −8

204. The formula $F = \frac{9}{5}C + 32$ converts temperature from Centigrade to Fahrenheit. What is the Fahrenheit temperature for 85° Centigrade?

(A) 153°

(B) 185°

(C) 175°

(D) 130°

205. If the 5% sales tax on a snowmobile was $42, what was the price of the snowmobile not including the tax?

(A) $840

(B) $210

(C) $820

(D) $640

206. Solve: $4\frac{1}{8} - 2\frac{2}{3} =$

(A) $2\frac{13}{24}$

(B) $2\frac{11}{24}$

(C) $1\frac{13}{24}$

(D) $1\frac{11}{24}$

207. If $-5 + 4x = 21$, $x =$

(A) 6.5

(B) 4

(C) 8.5

(D) 5.75

208. Solve: $3\frac{1}{3} \times 3\frac{3}{4} \times \frac{2}{5} =$

(A) $9\frac{1}{4}$

(B) 6

(C) 5

(D) $6\frac{2}{5}$

209. Mr. Symon paid $58.50 interest on a loan that had a 6% simple interest rate. How much did he borrow?

(A) $975

(B) $351

(C) $898

(D) $410

210. If a flagpole has a shadow 56 feet long when a 6–foot man's shadow is 14 feet long, what is the height of the flagpole?

(A) 24 feet

(B) 28 feet

(C) 20 feet

(D) 32 feet

211. If the perimeter of a rectangular region is 50 units, and the length of one side is 7 units, what is the area of the rectangular region?

(A) 291 square units

(B) 301 square units

(C) 126 square units

(D) 226 square units

212. If $4(3x - 2) = 16$, $x =$

(A) 1.5

(B) −2

(C) 2

(D) −1.5

213. If 18 is added to an integer, and the result is $\frac{5}{4}$ of the integer, what is the integer?

(A) 72

(B) 36

(C) 24

(D) −18

214. If $A = 6$ and $B = 3$, then $7A - 3B =$

(A) 7

(B) 5

(C) 36

(D) 33

215. Four years ago, Jim's father was 5 times as old as Jim. How old is Jim's father now if Jim is 12?

(A) 56

(B) 44

(C) 40

(D) 36

216. Solve: $2\frac{1}{2} + 7\frac{2}{3} + \frac{3}{4} =$

(A) $9\frac{1}{4}$

(B) $11\frac{1}{2}$

(C) $10\frac{11}{12}$

(D) $10\frac{1}{4}$

217. If $N\%$ of 60 is 24, $N =$

(A) 40

(B) 25

(C) 125

(D) 150

218. If $10x - 3 = 2x + 4$, then x equals

(A) $\frac{9}{8}$

(B) $\frac{7}{8}$

(C) $\frac{8}{7}$

(D) $\frac{6}{7}$

219. The ratio of $\frac{3}{4}$ to $\frac{5}{2}$ is

(A) 10 to 3

(B) 15 to 8

(C) 3 to 10

(D) 8 to 15

220. What will a 9 ft. by 15 ft. rectangular rug cost at $5 a square yard?

(A) $75

(B) $60

(C) $675

(D) $225

221. Solve: $6.41\overline{)3.6537}$

(A) 67

(B) 57

(C) 0.57

(D) 0.67

222.

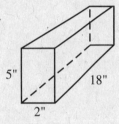

What is the volume of this rectangular solid?

(A) 90 cu. in.

(B) 160 cu. in.

(C) 140 cu. in.

(D) 180 cu. in.

223. If $A = 3$, $B = 2$, and $C = 6$, then $\dfrac{3ABC}{2A} =$

(A) 18

(B) 24

(C) $4\frac{1}{2}$

(D) $4\frac{1}{6}$

224. Simplify: $\dfrac{5\frac{2}{3}}{2\frac{5}{6}}$

(A) $2\frac{1}{2}$

(B) $\frac{1}{2}$

(C) 2

(D) $1\frac{1}{3}$

225. If $\frac{5}{6}x = 30$, then $x =$

(A) 42

(B) 25

(C) 20

(D) 36

226. Solve: 65.14×0.093

(A) 6.05802

(B) 60.5802

(C) 605.602

(D) 6.05602

227. 26.80, 26.86, 26.92, 26.98, _____

What number should come next in this sequence?

(A) 27.04

(B) 27.02

(C) 26.02

(D) 26.04

228. Solve: $72{,}528 \times 109$

(A) 1,377,032

(B) 7,805,452

(C) 1,378,032

(D) 7,905,552

229. The product of 11 and 12 is 3 more than N. What is N?

(A) 135

(B) 129

(C) 132

(D) 126

230. How many boards $1\frac{1}{3}$ feet long can be cut from a board $9\frac{1}{2}$ feet long?

(A) 9

(B) 6

(C) 7

(D) 8

231. Solve for x: $3x + 3 < 9 + x$

(A) $x = 6$

(B) $x > 3$

(C) $x < 3$

(D) $x > 6$

232. Solve: $0.602 + 4.2 + 5.03 =$

(A) 11.47

(B) 9.802

(C) 9.832

(D) 10.441

233. Solve for x: $2.5x + 12.5 = 30$

(A) 7

(B) 9

(C) 17

(D) 70

234. Solve: $28\overline{)54,900}$

(A) 1960 R20

(B) 1858 R20

(C) 1642 R12

(D) 1868 R16

235. Solve: If $\sqrt{x + 36} = 10$, then $x =$

(A) 8

(B) 64

(C) −16

(D) −4

236. Add in base 5:

$$143_{(5)}$$
$$+\quad 33_{(5)}$$

(A) $131_{(5)}$

(B) $221_{(5)}$

(C) $231_{(5)}$

(D) $211_{(5)}$

237. Solve for x: $\left(\dfrac{2}{3} + \dfrac{1}{5}\right) - \left(\dfrac{1}{4} + \dfrac{1}{2}\right) = x$

(A) $\dfrac{13}{30}$

(B) $\dfrac{7}{60}$

(C) $\dfrac{51}{60}$

(D) $\dfrac{37}{60}$

238. If the tax rate is $3.62 per $100, how much tax must be paid on a home assessed at $25,000?

(A) $90.50

(B) $80.50

(C) $805

(D) $905

STOP End of Mathematics section. If you have any time left, go over your work in this section only. Do not work in any other section of the test.

practice test

LANGUAGE

25 MINUTES

Directions: In questions 239–278, look for errors in capitalization, punctuation, or usage. Mark the answer choice that contains the error. If you find no mistake, mark (D) on your answer sheet.

239. (A) Jeff asked, "What color is the Easter bunny?"
(B) Steve won the annual polka contest.
(C) The letter was mailed on Memorial day.
(D) No mistakes

240. (A) Are you coming to my birthday party?
(B) The first snow fell on Sunday October 27.
(C) Jack's father drove us to the movies.
(D) No mistakes

241. (A) We will be vacationing in sunny Italy.
(B) Dave will arrive at Kennedy international airport.
(C) We decided to have Charlie read the report.
(D) No mistakes

242. (A) Dallas is one of the most populous cities in Texas.
(B) Michigan Avenue is a main tourist attraction in Chicago.
(C) New York is the larger city in the United States.
(D) No mistakes

243. (A) Kim's birthday is in June.
(B) Jared was the second person in line.
(C) August falls between july and September.
(D) No mistakes

244. (A) The coach gave instructions to each of the girls on the team.
(B) Just forward the mail to Dan and me.
(C) Will all of us travel on one bus?
(D) No mistakes

245. (A) Where in the world did you leave your gloves?
(B) The dog licked its chops after the meal.
(C) "Oh, that's terrible!" Sally cried.
(D) No mistakes

246. (A) Detroit is the center of the automobile industry.
(B) Governor Jones was an officer in the Navy.
(C) Their making a terrible mistake.
(D) No mistakes

247. (A) How is your cold?
(B) The rabbit got sick and died.
(C) Who's book is this?
(D) No mistakes

248. (A) That is a pretty dress, isn't it, Sheila?
(B) How old is your pet, Alfie?
(C) Why are you so tired?
(D) No mistakes

249. (A) How long has the train been gone?
(B) "Well," Jay said, let's get going."
(C) Jack's uncle is a fireman.
(D) No mistakes

250. (A) Don told us where he'd bought his coat.
(B) What's your name, little girl?
(C) Yellowstone is run by the National Park Service.
(D) No mistakes

251. (A) How are you, Jim?

    (B) I'm fine, thank you.

    (C) Did you notice that John left early?

    (D) No mistakes

252. (A) The teacher asked the child to bring the book home.

    (B) Spring will begin at noon today.

    (C) Let's share the candy with the whole group.

    (D) No mistakes

253. (A) Will, you're parents are very nice.

    (B) Ted's family is buying a boat.

    (C) My father is a textbook publisher.

    (D) No mistakes

254. (A) It was the most beautiful sight I've ever saw.

    (B) Ed's aunt and uncle lived in the South for many years.

    (C) Mattie is the older of the two.

    (D) No mistakes

255. (A) What is the matter with Sam's leg?

    (B) The first show is at 2:30, isn't it?

    (C) How much is your plane ticket?

    (D) No mistakes

256. (A) The award was given jointly to Deirdre and I.

    (B) John asked if he might go home early.

    (C) Cats and dogs sometimes play well together.

    (D) No mistakes

257. (A) Have you seen Marie's new coat?

    (B) Sue said, "I'm taking dancing lessons this year."

    (C) People lay down when they are tired.

    (D) No mistakes

258. (A) Anne said, "we really should go now."

    (B) You can always say Sam eats well— and often!

    (C) I told them my study hall was second period.

    (D) No mistakes

259. (A) The boy threw his shoe in anger.

    (B) I laid in bed all night without sleeping.

    (C) Keep this as a secret between you and me.

    (D) No mistakes

260. (A) Yesterday, Valerie came to visit me.

    (B) The package arrived hear around 5 p.m.

    (C) Arnold and I went to dinner at the Panda Palace, which has great egg rolls.

    (D) No mistakes

261. (A) She and I consider ourselves to be best friends.

    (B) Do you know which of the spellings of <u>too</u> means <u>also</u>?

    (C) There is a narrow path beside the railroad track.

    (D) No mistakes

262. (A) We would have called you if we'd known.

    (B) May I open my eyes now?

    (C) My brother–in–law lives in Butte, Montana.

    (D) No mistakes

263. (A) Actually, ice hockey is exciting to watch.

    (B) Janet plays guitar almost as well as Tom.

    (C) Does Dave like to talk to Debby Ann?

    (D) No mistakes

264. (A) Ken will graduate from Stanford this June.

    (B) Jack is learning Kay to draw.

    (C) Before we knew it, the class was over.

    (D) No mistakes

265. (A) When will you know what the assignment is?

    (B) You should of seen the crowd at Paul's yesterday.

    (C) Joe will be stationed at Fort Benning, Georgia.

    (D) No mistakes

266. (A) Dad's going fishing in Canada next week.

    (B) Barb didn't know whether to laugh or to cry.

    (C) Mom put to much baking powder in the cake.

    (D) No mistakes

267. (A) We have already sold too many tickets.

    (B) If I knew the answer, I would be rich now.

    (C) The artist works less hours than the carpenter.

    (D) No mistakes

268. (A) The tiny kitten sat licking it's wounds.

    (B) If you wish, we will have chicken for dinner.

    (C) It is so cloudy that we cannot see the Milky Way tonight.

    (D) No mistakes

269. (A) Everyone must sign their name on the register.

    (B) I am all ready, but the taxi is not here yet.

    (C) I do not believe that I have only two choices.

    (D) No mistakes

270. (A) If you don't know the answer, don't raise your hand.

    (B) The baby is playing in her crib.

    (C) Jeff is the taller of my three sons.

    (D) No mistakes

271. (A) Neither Lisa nor Liz has made the Honor Roll.

    (B) I have much more free time than you.

    (C) Everyone wants to have his own way.

    (D) No mistakes

272. (A) When he said that, everyone applauded.

    (B) He was much more interesting than I thought he'd be.

    (C) Helen asked Molly and I to come to her party.

    (D) No mistakes

273. (A) The sun set at 5:15 this afternoon.

    (B) Mary set the table for dinner yesterday.

    (C) Please set those books over there, Jim.

    (D) No mistakes

274. (A) The horse ran swiftly and won the race.

    (B) I feel badly that I cannot attend your wedding.

    (C) Most birds and some people fly south for the winter.

    (D) No mistakes

275. (A) This kind of movie may frighten small children.

    (B) I'm glad to hear that you're planning to go to college.

    (C) Myself has bought a new dress for the party.

    (D) No mistakes

276. (A) How many eggs did you use in this cake?

    (B) I can't hardly wait for the school year to be over.

    (C) Neither Shawn nor Sylvia has to work for her spending money.

    (D) No mistakes

277. (A) The childrens' boots got mixed up in the coatroom.

(B) Sheila is trying out for the marching band today.

(C) My sisters and I all went to camp last summer.

(D) No mistakes

278. (A) I'll let you know if my parents can pick us up.

(B) Our whole class sent get–well cards to Hilda.

(C) Harry said he hadn't done nothing wrong.

(D) No mistakes

Directions: For questions 279–288, look for mistakes in spelling only.

279. (A) Clarence Darrow was a distinguished trial lawyer.

(B) Apparantly Suzy couldn't find her umbrella.

(C) Alice will be married next Wednesday.

(D) No mistakes

280. (A) Are you sure you can complete the assignment on time?

(B) The entire crew worked very efficently.

(C) Mary went to the library yesterday.

(D) No mistakes

281. (A) It occured to me that I should write home.

(B) "What a dreadful comparison," Ida remarked.

(C) Bob's temperature was back to normal yesterday.

(D) No mistakes

282. (A) Mary Lou is eligible for the committee.

(B) Discussion and argument are not the same thing.

(C) The chemist analized the solution in his laboratory.

(D) No mistakes

283. (A) My brother's going out for athletics next year.

(B) "This is a small token of my esteem," he told his teacher.

(C) Mary dropped her handkerchief in the corridor.

(D) No mistakes

284. (A) The general spoke of a possible winter offensive.

(B) Ted finally succeded in solving the puzzle.

(C) Thomas Alva Edison was a brilliant inventor.

(D) No mistakes

285. (A) The schedule is posted on the bulletin board in the hall.

(B) Don discribed the play with sweeping gestures.

(C) Occasionally our class runs over into the next period.

(D) No mistakes

286. (A) Pete perfers to sit by the door.

(B) Joy has a very agreeable personality.

(C) We struggle with ourselves to overcome our faults.

(D) No mistakes

287. (A) Did you hear the announcement about the picnic?

(B) While the initial cost is high, maintenance is low.

(C) Jan's coat is similar to mine.

(D) No mistakes

288. (A) Al said it was not neccessary to read all of the plays.

(B) It's disappointing to have missed the picture.

(C) The original order was difficult to decipher.

(D) No mistakes

Directions: For questions 289–298, look for errors in composition. Follow the directions for each question.

289. Choose the best word or words to join the thoughts together.

I left my books at school; _____ I won't be able to do my homework.

(A) therefore,

(B) nevertheless,

(C) however,

(D) None of these

290. Choose the best word or words to join the thoughts together.

That area is experiencing great economic hardship; _____ its unemployment rate is very high.

(A) for example,

(B) in contrast,

(C) suprisingly,

(D) None of these

291. Choose the group of words that best completes this sentence.

After a hard day at work, _____

(A) sleep was something Mary did very well.

(B) Mary slept very well.

(C) Mary slept well afterwards.

(D) sleeping was what Mary did

292. Which of these expresses the idea most clearly?

(A) Tom, every morning at breakfast, the paper he liked to read.

(B) At breakfast every morning it was the paper that Tom liked to read.

(C) At breakfast, reading the paper was what Tom liked to do every morning.

(D) Tom liked to read the paper every morning at breakfast.

293. Which of these expresses the idea most clearly?

(A) In order to hear her favorite musician perform, 50 miles it was that she drove.

(B) She drove 50 miles in order to hear her favorite musician perform.

(C) She drove, in order to hear her favorite musician perform, 50 miles.

(D) Her favorite musician performed, and she drove 50 miles in order to hear him perform.

294. Which of these best fits under the topic "History of the Automobile"?

(A) Cars require a great deal of attention and care in order to prevent problems from developing.

(B) The legal driving age varies from one state to another.

(C) The invention of the automobile cannot be credited to any one person.

(D) None of these

295. Which of these expresses the idea most clearly?

(A) Kim liked the skateboard with the nylon wheels that his father had built.

(B) Kim liked the new skateboard his father had built with the nylon wheels.

(C) The skateboard with the nylon wheels which his father had built new Kim liked.

(D) His father had built a new skateboard which Kim liked with nylon wheels.

296. Which sentence does *not* belong in the paragraph?

(1) Everyone in the class was looking forward to the Halloween party. (2) Five students had difficulty with their math homework from the previous day. (3) Each student had prepared a snack to bring. (4) The costumes included four ghosts, five space creatures, and two pumpkins.

(A) Sentence 1
(B) Sentence 2
(C) Sentence 3
(D) Sentence 4

297. Which topic is best for a one–paragraph theme?

(A) How to Open Your Own Business
(B) Child Psychology
(C) The Geography of Asia and Africa
(D) None of these

298. Where should the sentence, "The government has set up laws restricting or forbidding the hunting of certain animals," be placed in the paragraph below?

(1) Many animal species are now becoming or have recently become extinct. (2) Both government and private efforts are being made to protect those species currently in danger. (3) It has also attempted to educate the public about the problem.

(A) Between sentences 1 and 2
(B) Between sentences 2 and 3
(C) After sentence 3
(D) The sentence does not fit in this paragraph.

STOP End of Language section. If you have any time left, go over your work in this section only. Do not work in any other section of the test.

ANSWER KEYS AND EXPLANATIONS

Verbal Skills

1. C	13. D	25. D	37. C	49. A
2. A	14. C	26. C	38. C	50. D
3. D	15. C	27. D	39. C	51. B
4. B	16. A	28. B	40. B	52. B
5. D	17. B	29. D	41. D	53. B
6. D	18. C	30. D	42. A	54. B
7. A	19. A	31. A	43. D	55. A
8. D	20. B	32. A	44. C	56. B
9. B	21. A	33. A	45. C	57. D
10. A	22. C	34. D	46. D	58. A
11. D	23. D	35. B	47. A	59. B
12. C	24. A	36. D	48. C	60. B

1. **The correct answer is (C).** *Time* is a general classification. The other choices are objects that tell time.

2. **The correct answer is (A).** *Elated, gleeful,* and *joyous* are synonyms.

3. **The correct answer is (D).** Cause-effect relationship. The effect of lightening red is pink; the effect of lightening black is gray.

4. **The correct answer is (B).** Because the first two statements are true and Karen reads faster than Ann, she must also read faster than Sue.

5. **The correct answer is (D).** *Create* means to bring into existence or to invent.

6. **The correct answer is (D).** Noun-adjective relationship.

7. **The correct answer is (A).** *Quality* is a general classification. The other choices are examples of good qualities.

8. **The correct answer is (D).** Part-whole relationship. Sand is part of the beach; black dirt is part of a farm.

9. **The correct answer is (B).** *Time* is a general classification. The other choices are measures of time.

10. **The correct answer is (A).** A *salamander* is an amphibian resembling a lizard.

11. **The correct answer is (D).** *Arrogant* means proud or haughty.

12. **The correct answer is (C).** Cause-effect relationship. Rounding the corners of a square produces a circle; rounding the corners of a rectangle produces an oval.

13. **The correct answer is (D).** Part-whole relationship. 1 is half of 2; 3 is half of 6.

14. **The correct answer is (C).** *Add* is a function. The others are general classifications of symbols.

15. **The correct answer is (C).** From the first two statements, it is only certain that Peter is the shortest of the three boys. The relationship between Paul and John cannot be determined.

16. **The correct answer is (A).** A *mellow* fruit is one that is tender and sweet.

17. **The correct answer is (B).** Other synonyms for *gossamer* are insubstantial, delicate, or tenuous.

18. **The correct answer is (C).** *Coddle* means to treat with extreme care.

19. **The correct answer is (A).** Object-purpose relationship. The purpose of a lamp is to give light; the purpose of a furnace is to give heat.

20. **The correct answer is (B).** Object-purpose relationship. The purpose of a director is to lead a choir; the purpose of a coach is to lead a team.

21. **The correct answer is (A).** *Diversify* means to give variety to.

22. **The correct answer is (C).** The first two statements indicate no relationship between Harry and Ralph; therefore, the third statement is uncertain.

23. **The correct answer is (D).** A *superficial* wound is a surface wound.

24. **The correct answer is (A).** From the first two statements, it is known that B is south of A. Because C is south of B, it must also be south of A.

25. **The correct answer is (D).** A *precocious* child is one who is advanced in development.

26. **The correct answer is (C).** A *sadistic* remark is intended to inflict pain.

27. **The correct answer is (D).** A *dormitory* is only one part of a school, university, or college.

28. **The correct answer is (B).** *Truncate* means to shorten or to cut off.

29. **The correct answer is (D).** A *sallow* complexion is of a sickly yellowish hue.

30. **The correct answer is (D).** An *indigent* person is impoverished.

31. **The correct answer is (A).** Part-whole relationship. A leg is a part of a table on which the table rests; a wheel is a part of a car on which the car rests.

32. **The correct answer is (A).** A *dungeon* is a place where people may be forced to stay. The other choices are places in which people choose to live.

33. **The correct answer is (A).** Because the first two statements are true, all tumps are a part of a larger set of boscs with wings. Blue boscs have no wings; therefore, they cannot be tumps, nor can tumps be blue.

34. **The correct answer is (D).** *Punishment* is a general classification. The other choices describe specific types or places of punishment.

35. **The correct answer is (B).** *Refuse* means to decline; the opposite is *to accept*.

36. **The correct answer is (D).** Object-user relationship. Ink is used in a pen when applied; paint is used on a brush when applied.

37. **The correct answer is (C).** *Acquire* means to gain possession of; the opposite is *to release*.

38. **The correct answer is (C).** Though the first two statements are considered true, they do not provide any information as to the direct relationship between rivers A and C.

39. **The correct answer is (C).** *Scant* means meager; the opposite is *abundant*.

40. **The correct answer is (B).** *Pinnacle* means peak; the opposite is *base*.

41. **The correct answer is (D).** Part-whole relationship. The captain is the part of a team that guides the team; the manager is the part of an office that guides the office.

42. **The correct answer is (A).** A *window* may be covered by the other three choices.

43. The correct answer is (D). *Corpulent* means obese; the opposite is *slender*.

44. The correct answer is (C). *Naive* means artless; the opposite is *sophisticated*.

45. The correct answer is (C). A *glove* is a hand covering; all the other choices are head coverings.

46. The correct answer is (D). A *podium* is positioned at the front of an auditorium or theater. The other choices represent those who face the podium.

47. The correct answer is (A). To *pledge* is to promise.

48. The correct answer is (C). A *depression* is a low spot or a *hollow;* the opposite is a *hill*.

49. The correct answer is (A). Because the first two statements are true and all the fruits cost more than apples, apples must cost the least.

50. The correct answer is (D). A *fir tree* is an evergreen; all of the other trees are deciduous, losing their leaves.

51. The correct answer is (B). *Diminish* means to decrease; the opposite is *to augment*.

52. The correct answer is (B). Because the first two statements are true, Jay's batting average must be higher than Tom's.

53. The correct answer is (B). *Abandon* means to give up; the opposite is *to keep*.

54. The correct answer is (B). *Feasible* is an attribute of abstract things or ideas. The other choices are generally attributes applied to concrete objects.

55. The correct answer is (A). Because the first two statements are true and C is north of A, it must also be north of B.

56. The correct answer is (B). *Cotton* is a vegetable product; leather, wool, and fur are animal products.

57. The correct answer is (D). A *seam* is a type of closing. The other choices are things for opening and closing.

58. The correct answer is (A). *Dwindle* means to grow smaller.

59. The correct answer is (B). Oxygen, helium, and gold are elements; water is a compound of hydrogen and oxygen.

60. The correct answer is (B). Because the first two statements are true and the third statement is in direct opposition to the first, it cannot be true.

Quantitative Skills

61. A	72. C	83. B	93. B	103. A
62. D	73. A	84. A	94. A	104. A
63. D	74. B	85. D	95. C	105. B
64. C	75. C	86. B	96. D	106. D
65. D	76. A	87. B	97. C	107. B
66. B	77. C	88. C	98. B	108. C
67. C	78. D	89. D	99. A	109. B
68. D	79. D	90. B	100. D	110. A
69. B	80. C	91. A	101. C	111. D
70. D	81. B	92. C	102. A	112. A
71. A	82. D			

61. **The correct answer is (A).** Start by finding 20% of 40: $0.20 \times 40 = 8$. Then add 3: $8 + 3 = 11$.

62. **The correct answer is (D).** The pattern in this series is made by adding 7 to each number.

63. **The correct answer is (D).** The pattern in this series is made by subtracting 9 from each number.

64. **The correct answer is (C).** Determine the amount of money for (A), (B), and (C). Then test the alternatives given to see which is correct.

65. **The correct answer is (D).** (A) is 0.625; (B) is 0.571; (C) is 0.6237. Clearly (B) is less than both (A) and (C), which are not equal to each other.

66. **The correct answer is (B).** The cube of 5 is 125. 125 divided by 5 = 25.

67. **The correct answer is (C).** The sum of $7 + 18 + 5 + 39 + 11 = 80$.

$80 \div 5 = 16$. $\frac{1}{2}$ of 16 = 8.

68. **The correct answer is (D).** Determine how much of each box is shaded. Then test each alternative to see which is correct.

69. **The correct answer is (B).** The pattern in this series is $+3, +7, +3, +7$, and so on.

70. **The correct answer is (D).** Determine the amounts for (A), (B), and (C). Here, (A) = 8, (B) = 8, and (C) = 0.08. When you test each alternative to see which is correct, you see that choice (D) is the correct answer: (A) is greater than (C).

71. **The correct answer is (A).** The pattern in this series is $+1, \times 2, +1, \times 2$, and so on.

72. **The correct answer is (C).** The pattern in this series is $+6, -3, -1, +6, -3, -1$, and so on.

73. **The correct answer is (A).** Start this problem from the end and work forward:

$$\frac{3}{5} \times \frac{25}{1} = 15$$
$$15 + 7 = 22$$

The number you're looking for is found by setting up an equation.

$$30 - x = 22$$
$$x = 30 - 22$$
$$x = 8$$

74. The correct answer is (B). Begin with $\frac{1}{3}$ of 18:

$$\frac{1}{3} \times \frac{18}{1} = 6.$$

Then, $6 + 5 = 11$.

75. The correct answer is (C). First determine the amounts of (A), (B), and (C). In this case, (A), (B), and (C) all equal 14. When you test each alternative, you see that choice (C) is the correct answer: (A), (B), and (C) are equal.

76. The correct answer is (A). The pattern in this series is −9, −8, −7, −6, and so on.

77. The correct answer is (C). Count the circles in (A), (B), and (C). Test each alternative to find the one that is true.

78. The correct answer is (D). Determine how much of each figure is shaded. Then test each alternative to find the one that is true.

79. The correct answer is (D). The pattern in this series is made by adding 4 to each number.

80. The correct answer is (C). Determine $\frac{1}{5}$ of 100: $\frac{1}{5} \times \frac{100}{1} = 20$. Multiply this result by 4 to find the answer:

$$20 \times 4 = 80.$$

81. The correct answer is (B). The pattern in this series is +4, +1, +4, +1, and so on. Also, whenever 1 is added, the result is expressed as an Arabic numeral; whenever 4 is added, the result is expressed as a Roman numeral.

82. The correct answer is (D). Determine the amounts for (A), (B), and (C). Here, (A) = 5, (B) = 4, and (C) = 4. When you test each alternative to find the one that is true, you see that choice (D) is the correct answer: (B) and (C) are equal.

83. The correct answer is (B). First find 7 times 3: $7 \times 3 = 21$. Double this result to find the answer: $2 \times 21 = 42$.

84. The correct answer is (A). Each box is shaded by $\frac{1}{2}$. Therefore, only (A) can be true.

85. The correct answer is (D). Figure this problem from the end and work forward:

$$5 \times 2 = 10$$
$$3 \times 10 = 30$$
$$6 + x = 30$$
$$x = 30 - 6 = 24$$

86. The correct answer is (B). The pattern in this series is −2, +4, −2, +4, and so on.

87. The correct answer is (B). If we change (A), (B), and (C) so that they are all the same form—in this case, decimals—we see that (A) = 0.4, (B) = 0.04, and (C) = 0.4. Therefore, choice (B) is the correct answer.

88. The correct answer is (C). You can figure out this problem with algebra:

$$\frac{3}{4} \times x = 6 \times 4$$
$$\frac{3}{4} \times x = 24$$
$$x = \frac{24}{1} \times \frac{4}{3}$$
$$x = 32$$

89. The correct answer is (D). The pattern in this series is +2, ×2, +2, ×2, and so on.

90. The correct answer is (B). The pattern in this series is +1, +3, +3, +1, +3, +3, +1, and so on.

91. The correct answer is (A). The line drawn from point A to the base of triangle ABD divides this triangle into two right triangles, one of which is $\triangle ACD$. AD is the hypotenuse of this right triangle whose length must be greater than the length CD, a leg of $\triangle ACD$.

92. The correct answer is (C). Begin by subtracting 5 from 29. This number divided by 3 will provide the answer:

$$29 - 5 = 24$$
$$24 \div 3 = 8$$

93. **The correct answer is (B).** The pattern in this series is +6, +3, +6, +3, and so on.

94. **The correct answer is (A).** Determine the amounts for (A), (B), and (C). Then choose the best alternative. Be sure to do the operations in the parentheses first when figuring.

95. **The correct answer is (C).** The pattern in this series is +1, –10, +1, –10, and so on.

96. **The correct answer is (D).** Because the figure is a cube, all edges and sides are equal. When a diagonal line is drawn across one side, like CF, it forms a hypotenuse of a right triangle whose length is longer than the length of either of its sides (CE and EF). Because the sides of the cube are all equal, CF must also be longer than AB.

97. **The correct answer is (C).** This can be done with algebra. If x is the number you are looking for:

$$x \div 2 = 6 + 4$$
$$2(x \div 2) = (6 + 4)2$$
$$x = 20$$

98. **The correct answer is (B).** Perform the multiplications as indicated to arrive at these values:

(A) = $5x + 5y$

(B) = $5x + y$

(C) = $5x + 5y + x = 6x + 5y$

It can now be seen that (B) has the least value, (C) has the greatest value, and (A) has a value between these. Therefore, choice (B) is the correct answer.

99. **The correct answer is (A).** The pattern in this series is ×2, +4, ×2, +4, and so on.

100. **The correct answer is (D).** To begin, find $\frac{1}{4}$ of 20. This is the same as saying 20 ÷ 4, which equals 5. If x is the number you are looking for:

$$7 - x = 5$$
$$x = 2$$

101. **The correct answer is (C).** The pattern for the letters in this series is made by using every other letter starting with A. The pattern for the numbers is +4, –10, +4, –10, and so on.

102. **The correct answer is (A).** Determine the values for each bar in the graph by using the number scale to the left. Then choose the correct alternative.

103. **The correct answer is (A).** This can be set up as an algebraic equation. If x is the number you are looking for:

$$x = \frac{3}{5}(10) - 2$$
$$x = 6 - 2$$
$$x = 4$$

104. **The correct answer is (A).** The pattern in this series is made by taking numbers in sequential order (4, 5, 6, and so on) and following each number with its square.

105. **The correct answer is (B).** Determine the amounts for (A), (B), and (C). Then, decide which alternative is true.

(A) $5^2 = 25$

(B) $4^3 = 64$

(C) $2^4 = 16$

106. **The correct answer is (D).** The pattern in this series is made by subtracting $2\frac{1}{2}$ from each number.

107. **The correct answer is (B).** Begin by figuring $\frac{1}{2}$ of 20. This number multiplied by 8 will provide the answer:

$$\frac{1}{2} \times 20 = 10$$
$$8 \times 10 = 80$$

108. **The correct answer is (C).** The pattern in this series is +4, –2, –1, +4, –2, –1, and so on.

109. The correct answer is (B). This can be set up as an algebraic equation. If x is the number you are looking for:

$$6 + \frac{1}{3}x = 2 \times 9$$
$$6 + \frac{1}{3}x = 18$$
$$\frac{1}{3}x = 12$$
$$x = 36$$

110. The correct answer is (A). Test each of the alternatives to find the true one. To find the perimeter, add the length of all four sides together: $2 + 3 + 2 + 3 = 10$.

111. The correct answer is (D). This can be set up as an algebraic equation. If x is the number you are looking for:

$$x = \frac{4}{9}(27) + 10$$
$$x = 12 + 10$$
$$x = 22$$

112. The correct answer is (A). First figure 4 squared. The number 7 less than 16 is 9:

$$4^2 = 4 \times 4 = 16$$
$$16 - 7 = 9$$

Reading

COMPREHENSION

113. B	121. C	129. D	137. D	145. A
114. C	122. C	130. C	138. B	146. A
115. C	123. C	131. B	139. A	147. B
116. D	124. A	132. D	140. A	148. A
117. D	125. D	133. D	141. D	149. B
118. C	126. B	134. B	142. D	150. D
119. B	127. C	135. D	143. B	151. A
120. D	128. C	136. A	144. C	152. A

113. **The correct answer is (B).** See sentence 6.

114. **The correct answer is (C).** See sentence 1.

115. **The correct answer is (C).** This is an inferential question. Based on sentence 7, we know that both the speed and direction of earthquake waves vary. We do not know from this information if choice (A) is true, so we must assume that (C) is the best answer.

116. **The correct answer is (D).** Because of the nature of the information, it would be found in both sources mentioned.

117. **The correct answer is (D).** This answer is determined by the entire passage, which describes the layers in order. The answer can be verified by eliminating choices (A), (B), and (C).

118. **The correct answer is (C).** *Vary* most closely means *range*.

119. **The correct answer is (B).** This is an inferential question. Though not specifically stated, the answer can be assumed based on sentence 2 and the phrase "appears to be."

120. **The correct answer is (D).** See the last sentence of the paragraph.

121. **The correct answer is (C).** In this passage, *slightly* most nearly means *a little*.

122. **The correct answer is (C).** *Remaining* most closely means *last*.

123. **The correct answer is (C).** This answer may be verified by eliminating choices (A), (B), and (D). Though rocks are mentioned, they are only a part of the entire description.

124. **The correct answer is (A).** In this case, *wavering* most nearly means *swaying*.

125. **The correct answer is (D).** This answer may be verified by eliminating choices (A), (B), and (C). A clue to the answer is the way the passage is written—without technical terms and in the third person.

126. **The correct answer is (B).** This is an inferential question. The answer may be verified by eliminating the other choices.

127. **The correct answer is (C).** This is the most specific, direct answer, though the other choices may have been indirectly related. The answer is found in paragraph 2.

128. **The correct answer is (C).** See paragraph 2, sentence 4.

129. **The correct answer is (D).** *Utter* most nearly means *great*.

130. **The correct answer is (C).** This is an inferential question. The answer may be verified by eliminating the other choices. See paragraphs 3 and 4.

131. **The correct answer is (B).** Though the author mentions bats, the passage covers the more general topic of spelunkers.

132. **The correct answer is (D).** The answer may be verified by eliminating the other choices.

133. **The correct answer is (D).** See paragraph 2, sentence 2.

134. **The correct answer is (B).** The answer may be verified by eliminating the other choices.

135. **The correct answer is (D).** See paragraph 3.

136. **The correct answer is (A).** See paragraph 1.

137. **The correct answer is (D).** In the passage, most fertile means *best growing*.

138. **The correct answer is (B).** See paragraph 3, sentence 3.

139. **The correct answer is (A).** This answer may be verified by eliminating the other three choices.

140. **The correct answer is (A).** See paragraph 4.

141. **The correct answer is (D).** In this passage, *terrain* most nearly means *land*.

142. **The correct answer is (D).** This answer may be verified by eliminating the other three choices.

143. **The correct answer is (B).** This answer may be verified by eliminating the other three choices. It covers several aspects of the topic—more than would be contained in just one type of book.

144. **The correct answer is (C).** See paragraph 1.

145. **The correct answer is (A).** This is a question based on your general knowledge.

146. **The correct answer is (A).** See paragraph 2.

147. **The correct answer is (B).** This answer is actually testing your vocabulary.

148. **The correct answer is (A).** See paragraph 3.

149. **The correct answer is (B).** As it is used in the passage, *in essence* most closely means *basically*.

150. **The correct answer is (D).** *Interesting* is the best answer; it could be substituted for *fascinating*.

151. **The correct answer is (A).** This is an inferential question. The answer is implied in paragraph 3.

152. **The correct answer is (A).** This answer may be verified by eliminating the other choices.

Vocabulary

153. D	158. A	163. A	167. A	171. A
154. B	159. D	164. B	168. D	172. B
155. A	160. D	165. D	169. A	173. D
156. A	161. A	166. A	170. C	174. C
157. C	162. B			

153. The correct answer is (D). *Perspective* means "aspect," "attitude," or "view."

154. The correct answer is (B). To *impair* is to "spoil," "damage," or "weaken."

155. The correct answer is (A). A *hovel* is a "cottage," a "hut," or a "cabin."

156. The correct answer is (A). To *loathe* means to "detest," "abhor," or "hate" something or someone.

157. The correct answer is (C). To *reproach* is to "condemn," "chide," or "blame."

158. The correct answer is (A). To be *elated* is to be "jubilant," "exhilarated," or "happy."

159. The correct answer is (D). *Brusque* means to be "curt," "blunt," or "abrupt."

160. The correct answer is (D). To *depress* something is to "squash," "flatten," or "push down."

161. The correct answer is (A). To *quench* is to "allay," "stifle," or "end."

162. The correct answer is (B). An *exploit* is an "escapade," "deed," or "venture."

163. The correct answer is (A). To be *deft* means to be "dexterous," "expert," or "skillful."

164. The correct answer is (B). A *chronicle* is an "account," a "history," or a "record" of something.

165. The correct answer is (D). To be an *amiable* person means to be "likeable."

166. The correct answer is (A). The meaning of the word *astute* is to be "keen," "shrewd," or "clever."

167. The correct answer is (A). To *sever* something means to "divide," "split," or "cut" the object.

168. The correct answer is (D). *Eminent* means to be "distinguished," "important," or "outstanding."

169. The correct answer is (A). To *terminate* is to "end," "cancel," or "stop" something.

170. The correct answer is (C). To *hinder* means to "obstruct," "interfere," or "impede" something.

171. The correct answer is (A). To be in *contention* means to be in "strife," "discord," or "debate."

172. The correct answer is (B). To *concede* means to "admit," "allow," or "acknowledge."

173. The correct answer is (D). To *forego* means to "concede," "give up," or "relinquish."

174. The correct answer is (C). For something to be *canny* means to be "clever."

Mathematics

CONCEPTS

175. C	180. C	185. D	190. D	195. A
176. C	181. D	186. C	191. B	196. A
177. A	182. B	187. D	192. C	197. A
178. D	183. C	188. D	193. D	198. B
179. B	184. D	189. A	194. D	

175. The correct answer is (C). A quadrilateral is defined as a figure with four sides. A triangle has only three sides.

176. The correct answer is (C). The symbol ∩ stands for "intersection." The intersection of two or more sets is the set of elements common to both sets. In this case, the common elements are 3 and 8.

177. The correct answer is (A). This problem requires you to "round off" the given number to the place one digit to the right of the decimal point.

178. The correct answer is (D). Always start with the operations in the parentheses first:

$(-2)^3 = (-2) \times (-2) \times (-2)$

$(-2)^3 = -8$

Then continue with the operations outside the parentheses:

$3 \times (-8) = -24$

Remember, a negative number times a positive number equals a negative number; a negative times a negative equals a positive.

179. The correct answer is (B). The digits 2 and 4 end in the hundredths place. This means $0.24 = \dfrac{24}{100}$. When simplified to simplest form, $\dfrac{24}{100} = \dfrac{6}{25}$.

180. The correct answer is (C). A straight line represents a "straight angle" of 180°. An angle of 60° is given, so m∠C must be 120° to complete the line. All the angles in a triangle added together equal 180°, therefore:

$m\angle A + m\angle B + m\angle C = 180°$

$m\angle A + 30° + 120° = 180°$

$m\angle A = 180° - 150°$

$m\angle A = 30°$

181. The correct answer is (D). When multiplying by 10, 100, 1000, etc., move the decimal point one place to the right for each zero in the multiplier. In this example, 100 has two zeros, so the decimal point would be moved two places to the right.

182. The correct answer is (B). The reciprocal of a fraction is the fraction "reversed." To find the answer, you would have to rename $3\dfrac{1}{3}$ as an improper fraction: $3\dfrac{1}{3} = \dfrac{10}{3}$; $\dfrac{10}{3}$ is the reciprocal of $\dfrac{3}{10}$.

183. The correct answer is (C). The formula for finding the circumference of a circle is π times the diameter. The diameter is 2 times the radius. In this case, $2 \times 4 = 8$ is the diameter. Therefore:

$C = d\pi$

$= 8\pi$

184. The correct answer is (D). The components of this problem must be stated in the same units. Therefore, 3 yards = 108 inches. The ratio of 108 to 18 is simplified to 6 to 1.

185. **The correct answer is (D).** State $\frac{33}{7}$ as a decimal number. $\frac{33}{7} = 4.714$.

An integer is a whole number.

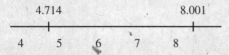

186. **The correct answer is (C).** The distributive property makes choice (C) true.

187. **The correct answer is (D).** $14^2 = 196$; $15^2 = 225$

188. **The correct answer is (D).** The base–five system uses only five symbols: 1, 2, 3, 4, and 0. Because of this, the other three alternatives are eliminated.

189. **The correct answer is (A).** When working with scientific notation, the exponent represents the number of places to move the decimal point in the multiplier. If the exponent of 10 is positive, the decimal point moves to the right. If it is negative, the decimal point moves to the left.

190. **The correct answer is (D).** This problem may be done without computation. The larger the denominator, the smaller the parts of the whole have been divided. The larger the numerator, the more parts are being considered. An alternative to this method is to find a common denominator and compare numerators. The largest numerator in this case shows the greatest value.

191. **The correct answer is (B).** The symbol $\geq$ means "greater than or equal to," and 6 is equal to 6.

192. **The correct answer is (C).** Figures are "similar" when their corresponding angles are equal and their corresponding sides are in proportion.

$$\frac{4}{AB} = \frac{3}{5}$$
$$3AB = 20$$
$$AB = \frac{20}{3} = 6\frac{2}{3}$$

193. **The correct answer is (D).** By definition, an isosceles triangle is any triangle with two sides equal. Therefore, it is the only possible answer.

194. **The correct answer is (D).** For choice (D) to be equal, it would need the percent symbol after it.

195. **The correct answer is (A).** Prime factorization is factoring a number to the point where all factors are prime.

196. **The correct answer is (A).** The least common multiple is the least number divisible by both given numbers.

197. **The correct answer is (A).** This is done by ratios. The relationship between part of the lawn and the whole lawn is the same as the relationship between the time it takes to mow part of the lawn and the time it takes to mow the whole lawn.

198. **The correct answer is (B).** The associative property of addition means that you may group the numbers to be added in different ways and achieve the same sum.

PROBLEM-SOLVING

199. C	207. A	215. B	223. A	231. C
200. B	208. C	216. C	224. C	232. C
201. D	209. A	217. A	225. D	233. A
202. D	210. A	218. B	226. A	234. A
203. A	211. C	219. C	227. A	235. B
204. B	212. C	220. A	228. D	236. C
205. A	213. A	221. C	229. B	237. B
206. D	214. D	222. D	230. C	238. D

199. The correct answer is (C). This involves multiplication and addition.

Student
 tickets $130 \times \$1.25 = \$162.50$
Adult
 tickets $340 \times \$1.90 = \underline{+\ \$646.00}$
    Total $= \ \$808.50$

200. The correct answer is (B). When subtracting fractional numbers, you must first rename the numbers with a common denominator.

$$12 - 2\frac{3}{16} = \frac{192}{16} - \frac{35}{16}$$
$$= \frac{157}{16}$$
$$= 9\frac{13}{16}$$

201. The correct answer is (D). There are 12 months in 1 year. If $542.40 is the total amount paid in a year, the average amount paid per month is $542.40 ÷ 12 = $45.20.

202. The correct answer is (D). First, add $10 to Bob's $88:

$88 + $10 = $98

Then, divide by 4:

$98 ÷ 4 = $24.50

203. The correct answer is (A). When expressed without the parentheses, this equation is $6 - 12 + 7 - 3$. Solve by completing one part at a time:

$$6 - 12 + 7 - 3 = -6 + 7 - 3$$
$$= 1 - 3$$
$$= -2$$

204. The correct answer is (B). Replace the C in the formula with 85 and solve:

$$F = \frac{9}{5}(85) + 32 = 153 + 32$$
$$= 185$$

205. The correct answer is (A). This can be set up as an algebraic equation. If n equals the price of the snowmobile, 5% of n equals $42, or

$$0.05n = \$42$$
$$n = \$42 \div 0.05$$
$$n = \$840$$

206. The correct answer is (D). Rename the fractions of the equation with a common denominator.

$$4\frac{1}{8} - 2\frac{2}{3} = \frac{33}{8} - \frac{8}{3}$$
$$= \frac{99}{24} - \frac{64}{24}$$
$$= \frac{35}{24}$$
$$= 1\frac{11}{24}$$

207. The correct answer is (A). Solve for x:

$$-5 + 4x = 21$$
$$4x = 21 + 5$$
$$4x = 26$$
$$x = \frac{26}{4}$$
$$x = 6.5$$

208. The correct answer is (C). Before multiplying, rename the mixed numbers as improper fractions:

$$3\frac{1}{3} \times 3\frac{3}{4} \times \frac{2}{5} = \frac{10}{3} \times \frac{15}{4} \times \frac{2}{5}$$
$$= \frac{300}{60} = 5$$

209. The correct answer is (A). This can be set up as an algebraic equation. If n is the amount Mr. Symon borrowed:

$$6\%(n) = 58.50$$
$$n = \frac{58.50}{6\%}$$
$$= \frac{58.50}{0.06}$$
$$= 975$$

210. The correct answer is (A). This problem is done by ratios:

$$\frac{n}{6} = \frac{56}{14}$$
$$336 = 14n$$
$$\frac{336}{14} = n$$
$$24 = n$$

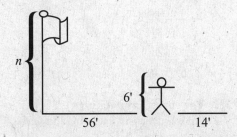

211. The correct answer is (C). By definition, the opposite sides of a rectangle are equal to each other. Because of this, if one side is 7 units, the opposite side is also 7 units. Consequently, 14 units account for two sides (7 + 7). The other two sides are each

equal to $(50 - 14) \div 2$, or 18 units. Area is length times width—in this case: $7 \times 18 = 126$ square units.

212. The correct answer is (C). Solve for x:

$$4(3x - 2) = 16$$
$$12x - 8 = 16$$
$$12x = 24$$
$$x = \frac{24}{12}$$
$$x = 2$$

213. The correct answer is (A). Solve this as an algebraic equation with n as the unknown integer:

$$n + 18 = \frac{5}{4}n$$
$$18 = \frac{5}{4}n - n$$
$$18 = \frac{1}{4}n$$
$$72 = n$$

214. The correct answer is (D). Replace the letters with the given numbers and solve:

$$7A - 3B =$$
$$7(6) - 3(3) =$$
$$42 - 9 = 33$$

215. The correct answer is (B). Because Jim is now 12, four years ago he was 8. His father was then 5 times older, or 40. Now, 4 years later, Jim's father is 44.

216. The correct answer is (C). Convert the mixed numbers into improper fractions, then find the common denominator and add:

$$2\frac{1}{2} + 7\frac{2}{3} + \frac{3}{4} = \frac{5}{2} + \frac{23}{3} + \frac{3}{4}$$
$$= \frac{30}{12} + \frac{92}{12} + \frac{9}{12}$$
$$= \frac{131}{12}$$
$$= 10\frac{11}{12}$$

217. The correct answer is (A).

$$N\% \times 60 = 24$$

$$N\% = \frac{24}{60}$$

$$N\% = \frac{2}{5}$$

$$N\% = 0.4$$

$$N = 40$$

218. The correct answer is (B). Solve for x:

$$10x - 3 = 2x + 4$$

$$10x - 2x = 4 + 3$$

$$8x = 7$$

$$x = \frac{7}{8}$$

219. The correct answer is (C). To determine ratios, multiply the first numerator by the second denominator and the first denominator by the second numerator. Then reduce:

$$\frac{3}{4} \text{ to } \frac{5}{2}$$

6 to 20

3 to 10

220. The correct answer is (A). First convert the dimensions of the rug to yards. Multiply these to obtain the area. Multiply the area by $5 to determine the total cost.

A = 9 ft. × 15 ft.

   = 3 yd. × 5 yd. = 15 sq. yards

15 sq. yds. × $5 = $75

221. The correct answer is (C).

$$
\begin{array}{r}
0.57 \\
6.41)\overline{3.6537} \\
3205 \\
\hline
4487 \\
\underline{4487} \\
0
\end{array}
$$

222. The correct answer is (D).

$$V = lwh$$

$$V = 18 \times 2 \times 5$$

$$V = 180 \text{ cu. in.}$$

223. The correct answer is (A). Replace the letters in the problem with the given numbers.

$$\frac{3ABC}{2A} = \frac{3 \times 3 \times 2 \times 6}{2 \times 3}$$

$$= \frac{108}{6}$$

$$= 18$$

224. The correct answer is (C). Convert the mixed numbers into improper fractions. Then divide.

$$\frac{5\frac{2}{3}}{2\frac{5}{6}} = \frac{\frac{17}{3}}{\frac{17}{6}}$$

$$= \frac{17}{3} \div \frac{17}{6}$$

$$= \frac{17}{3} \times \frac{6}{17} = \frac{6}{3} = 2$$

225. The correct answer is (D).

$$\frac{5}{6}x = 30$$

$$x = \frac{30}{1} \cdot \frac{6}{5}$$

$$x = \frac{180}{5}$$

$$x = 36$$

226. The correct answer is (A). When solving this problem, remember that the number of decimal places to the right of the decimal point in the answer should equal the total number of places to the right of the decimal points in the two factors being multiplied.

$$
\begin{array}{r}
65.14 \\
\times 0.093 \\
\hline
19542 \\
586260 \\
\hline
6.05802
\end{array}
$$

227. The correct answer is (A). The pattern in this sequence is made by adding 0.06 to each number.

228. The correct answer is (D).

$$
\begin{array}{r}
72528 \\
\times\ 109 \\
\hline
652\,752 \\
000\ 00 \\
7\ 252\ 8 \\
\hline
7,905,552
\end{array}
$$

229. The correct answer is (B). Set this problem up as an algebraic equation.

$$11 \times 12 = N + 3$$
$$132 = N + 3$$
$$132 - 3 = N$$
$$129 = N$$

230. The correct answer is (C). Convert the mixed numbers into improper fractions. Then, divide the total length of the board by the length into which it will be cut.

$$9\frac{1}{2} \div 1\frac{1}{3} = \frac{19}{2} \div \frac{4}{3}$$
$$= \frac{19}{2} \times \frac{3}{4}$$
$$= \frac{57}{8}$$
$$= 7\frac{1}{8}$$

Though $\frac{1}{8}$ of a board is left, only 7 full-size boards can be made.

231. The correct answer is (C).

$$3x + 3 < 9 + x$$
$$3x - x < 9 - 3$$
$$2x < 6$$
$$x < \frac{6}{2}$$
$$x < 3$$

232. The correct answer is (C). When adding decimal numbers, line up the decimal points.

$$
\begin{array}{r}
0.602 \\
4.200 \\
+\ 5.030 \\
\hline
9.832
\end{array}
$$

233. The correct answer is (A).

$$2.5x + 12.5 = 30$$
$$2.5x = 30 - 12.5$$
$$2.5x = 17.5$$
$$x = \frac{17.5}{2.5}$$
$$x = 7$$

234. The correct answer is (A).

$$
\begin{array}{r}
1960 \\
28\overline{)54900} \\
28 \\
\hline
269 \\
252 \\
\hline
170 \\
168 \\
\hline
20
\end{array}
$$

235. The correct answer is (B).

$$\sqrt{x + 36} = 10$$
$$x + 36 = 10^2$$
$$x + 36 = 100$$
$$x = 100 - 36$$
$$x = 64$$

236. The correct answer is (C).

$$
\begin{array}{r}
143_{(5)} \\
+\ 33_{(5)} \\
\hline
231_{(5)}
\end{array}
$$

237. The correct answer is (B). Rename the fractions with a common denominator. Do the operations in parentheses first.

$$\left(\frac{2}{3} + \frac{1}{5}\right) - \left(\frac{1}{4} + \frac{1}{2}\right) = x$$
$$\left(\frac{10}{15} + \frac{3}{15}\right) - \left(\frac{1}{4} + \frac{2}{4}\right) = x$$
$$\frac{13}{15} - \frac{3}{4} = x$$
$$\frac{52}{60} - \frac{45}{60} = \frac{7}{60}$$

238. The correct answer is (D). First determine how many times 25,000 can be divided by 100: $25,000 \div 100 = 250$.

For *every* \$100 in 25,000, \$3.62 must be paid in taxes: $250 \times 3.62 = \$905.00$.

Like us at facebook.com/petersonspublishing

Language

239. C	251. D	263. D	275. C	287. D
240. B	252. A	264. B	276. B	288. A
241. B	253. A	265. B	277. A	289. A
242. C	254. A	266. C	278. C	290. A
243. C	255. D	267. C	279. B	291. B
244. D	256. A	268. A	280. B	292. D
245. D	257. C	269. A	281. A	293. B
246. C	258. A	270. C	282. C	294. C
247. C	259. B	271. D	283. D	295. A
248. D	260. B	272. C	284. B	296. B
249. B	261. D	273. D	285. B	297. D
250. D	262. D	274. B	286. A	298. B

239. **The correct answer is (C).** *Day* should be capitalized.

240. **The correct answer is (B).** There should be a comma after *Sunday.*

241. **The correct answer is (B).** *International* and *Airport* should both be capitalized.

242. **The correct answer is (C).** The use of the word *larger* is incorrect since New York is being compared with more than one city

in the United States. The correct word is *largest.*

243. **The correct answer is (C).** The first letter of the word *July* should be capitalized.

244. **The correct answer is (D).** No mistakes.

245. **The correct answer is (D).** No mistakes.

246. **The correct answer is (C).** The word *their* is incorrect in this context. The word should be *They're* (they are).

247. **The correct answer is (C).** The word *Who's* (who is) is incorrect in this context. The word should be *Whose.*

248. **The correct answer is (D).** No mistakes.

249. **The correct answer is (B).** There should be quotation marks before *let's* because it is a continuation of a direct quote.

250. **The correct answer is (D).** No mistakes.

251. **The correct answer is (D).** No mistakes.

252. **The correct answer is (A).** Because the action is from the teacher toward another place, the correct word is *take.*

253. **The correct answer is (A).** The word *you're* (you are) is incorrect in this context. The word should be *your.*

254. **The correct answer is (A).** The tense is incorrect. The last part of the sentence should read *I'd ever seen.*

255. **The correct answer is (D).** No mistakes.

256. **The correct answer is (A).** The object of the preposition *to* is Deirdre and *me.*

257. **The correct answer is (C).** The word *lay* is incorrect in this context. The word should be *lie.*

258. **The correct answer is (A).** The word *we* should be capitalized.

259. The correct answer is (B). The past tense of the verb *to lie* is *lay.*

260. The correct answer is (B). This sentence contains a misspelled word. The word *hear,* which means the act of hearing, should be replaced with the word *here,* which means a place.

261. The correct answer is (D). No mistakes.

262. The correct answer is (D). No mistakes.

263. The correct answer is (D). No mistakes.

264. The correct answer is (B). The word *learning* is incorrect in this context. The word should be *teaching.*

265. The correct answer is (B). The word *of* is incorrect in this context. The word should be *have.*

266. The correct answer is (C). The preposition *to* is incorrect in this context. The word should be *too,* meaning excessive.

267. The correct answer is (C). The number of hours can be counted—therefore, *fewer.*

268. The correct answer is (A). The possessive of *it* is *its. It's* is the contraction for *it is.*

269. The correct answer is (A). *Everyone* is singular. The pronoun must be singular as well. Either *his* or *her* would be correct.

270. The correct answer is (C). There are three, so the comparative term must be *tallest.*

271. The correct answer is (D). No mistakes.

272. The correct answer is (C). The subjective *I* is incorrect in this context. The correct word is *me,* the object of the verb *asked.*

273. The correct answer is (D). No mistakes.

274. The correct answer is (B). I feel *bad.* I would feel *badly* if something were wrong with my hands.

275. The correct answer is (C). The subject/verb of the sentence is *I have.*

276. The correct answer is (B). I *can hardly* wait. The double negative is incorrect.

277. The correct answer is (A). The apostrophe in *childrens'* should be placed before the *s* since *children* is a plural word.

278. The correct answer is (C). The word *nothing* is incorrect in this context. The correct word is *anything.* The double negative is unacceptable.

279. The correct answer is (B). The correct spelling is *apparently.*

280. The correct answer is (B). The correct spelling is *efficiently.*

281. The correct answer is (A). The correct spelling is *occurred.* (See Spelling—Rule 9.)

282. The correct answer is (C). The correct spelling is *analyzed.*

283. The correct answer is (D). No mistakes.

284. The correct answer is (B). The correct spelling is *succeeded.*

285. The correct answer is (B). The correct spelling is *described.*

286. The correct answer is (A). The correct spelling is *prefers.*

287. The correct answer is (D). No mistakes.

288. The correct answer is (A). The correct spelling is *necessary.*

289. The correct answer is (A). *Therefore* indicates the cause-and-effect relationship of the two clauses.

290. The correct answer is (A). The second clause provides an example.

291. The correct answer is (B). The subject (*Mary*) must follow the introductory phrase.

292. The correct answer is (D). This sentence expresses the idea most clearly.

293. The correct answer is (B). The second clause offers the reason why she drove 50 miles.

294. The correct answer is (C). The invention of the automobile definitely belongs in a discussion of the history of the automobile.

295. The correct answer is (A). The clause *with the nylon wheels* modifies *skateboard*.

296. The correct answer is (B). Sentences 1, 3, and 4 all concern preparation for the Halloween party.

297. The correct answer is (D). All of these topics are too broad for a one-paragraph theme.

298. The correct answer is (B). The given sentence should fall before sentence 3, because it refers to a singular noun and sentence 2 contains a plural noun. By placing the sentence between 2 and 3, the paragraph makes sense.

SCORE SHEET

Although your actual exam scores will not be reported as percentages, it might be helpful to convert your test scores to percentages so that you can see at a glance where your strengths and weaknesses lie. The numbers in parentheses represent the questions that test each skill.

Subject	No. Correct ÷ No. of Questions	× 100 = _____ %
Verbal Analogies (3, 6, 8, 12, 13, 19, 20, 31, 36, 41)	_____ ÷ 10 = _____	× 100 = _____ %
Synonyms (5, 10, 11, 16, 17, 18, 21, 23, 25, 26, 28, 29, 30, 47, 58)	_____ ÷ 15 = _____	× 100 = _____ %
Logic (4, 15, 22, 24, 33, 38, 49, 52, 55, 60)	_____ ÷ 10 = _____	× 100 = _____ %
Verbal Classification (1, 2, 7, 9, 14, 27, 32, 34, 42, 45, 46, 50, 54, 56, 57, 59)	_____ ÷ 16 = _____	× 100 = _____ %
Antonyms (35, 37, 39, 40, 43, 44, 48, 51, 53)	_____ ÷ 9 = _____	× 100 = _____ %
TOTAL VERBAL SKILLS	_____ ÷ 60 = _____	× 100 = _____ %
Number Series (62, 63, 69, 71, 72, 76, 79, 81, 86, 89, 90, 93, 95, 99, 101, 104, 106, 108)	_____ ÷ 18 = _____	× 100 = _____ %
Geometric Comparisons (64, 68, 77, 78, 84, 91, 96, 102, 110)	_____ ÷ 9 = _____	× 100 = _____ %
Nongeometric Comparisons (65, 70, 75, 82, 87, 94, 98, 105)	_____ ÷ 8 = _____	× 100 = _____ %
Number Manipulation (61, 66, 67, 73, 74, 80, 83, 85, 88, 92, 97, 100, 103, 107, 109, 111, 112)	_____ ÷ 17 = _____	× 100 = _____ %
TOTAL QUANTITATIVE SKILLS	_____ ÷ 52 = _____	× 100 = _____ %
Reading—Comprehension (113–152)	_____ ÷ 40 = _____	× 100 = _____ %
Reading—Vocabulary (153–174)	_____ ÷ 22 = _____	× 100 = _____ %
TOTAL READING	_____ ÷ 62 = _____	× 100 = _____ %
Mathematics—Concepts (175–198)	_____ ÷ 24 = _____	× 100 = _____ %
Mathematics—Problem-Solving (199–238)	_____ ÷ 40 = _____	× 100 = _____ %
TOTAL MATHEMATICS	_____ ÷ 64 = _____	× 100 = _____ %
Punctuation and Capitalization (239–242, 248–251, 255, 258, 260, 277)	_____ ÷ 12 = _____	× 100 = _____ %
Usage (243–247, 252–254, 256, 257, 259, 261–276, 278)	_____ ÷ 28 = _____	× 100 = _____ %
Spelling (279–288)	_____ ÷ 10 = _____	× 100 = _____ %
Composition (289–298)	_____ ÷ 10 = _____	× 100 = _____ %
TOTAL LANGUAGE	_____ ÷ 60 = _____	× 100 = _____ %
TOTAL EXAM	_____ ÷ 298 = _____	× 100 = _____ %

ANSWER SHEET PRACTICE TEST 6: HSPT

Verbal Skills

1. Ⓐ Ⓑ Ⓒ Ⓓ   13. Ⓐ Ⓑ Ⓒ Ⓓ   25. Ⓐ Ⓑ Ⓒ Ⓓ   37. Ⓐ Ⓑ Ⓒ Ⓓ   49. Ⓐ Ⓑ Ⓒ Ⓓ
2. Ⓐ Ⓑ Ⓒ Ⓓ   14. Ⓐ Ⓑ Ⓒ Ⓓ   26. Ⓐ Ⓑ Ⓒ Ⓓ   38. Ⓐ Ⓑ Ⓒ Ⓓ   50. Ⓐ Ⓑ Ⓒ Ⓓ
3. Ⓐ Ⓑ Ⓒ   15. Ⓐ Ⓑ Ⓒ   27. Ⓐ Ⓑ Ⓒ   39. Ⓐ Ⓑ Ⓒ Ⓓ   51. Ⓐ Ⓑ Ⓒ
4. Ⓐ Ⓑ Ⓒ Ⓓ   16. Ⓐ Ⓑ Ⓒ Ⓓ   28. Ⓐ Ⓑ Ⓒ Ⓓ   40. Ⓐ Ⓑ Ⓒ Ⓓ   52. Ⓐ Ⓑ Ⓒ Ⓓ
5. Ⓐ Ⓑ Ⓒ Ⓓ   17. Ⓐ Ⓑ Ⓒ Ⓓ   29. Ⓐ Ⓑ Ⓒ Ⓓ   41. Ⓐ Ⓑ Ⓒ Ⓓ   53. Ⓐ Ⓑ Ⓒ Ⓓ
6. Ⓐ Ⓑ Ⓒ Ⓓ   18. Ⓐ Ⓑ Ⓒ Ⓓ   30. Ⓐ Ⓑ Ⓒ   42. Ⓐ Ⓑ Ⓒ Ⓓ   54. Ⓐ Ⓑ Ⓒ Ⓓ
7. Ⓐ Ⓑ Ⓒ Ⓓ   19. Ⓐ Ⓑ Ⓒ Ⓓ   31. Ⓐ Ⓑ Ⓒ Ⓓ   43. Ⓐ Ⓑ Ⓒ Ⓓ   55. Ⓐ Ⓑ Ⓒ
8. Ⓐ Ⓑ Ⓒ Ⓓ   20. Ⓐ Ⓑ Ⓒ   32. Ⓐ Ⓑ Ⓒ Ⓓ   44. Ⓐ Ⓑ Ⓒ   56. Ⓐ Ⓑ Ⓒ Ⓓ
9. Ⓐ Ⓑ Ⓒ Ⓓ   21. Ⓐ Ⓑ Ⓒ Ⓓ   33. Ⓐ Ⓑ Ⓒ Ⓓ   45. Ⓐ Ⓑ Ⓒ Ⓓ   57. Ⓐ Ⓑ Ⓒ Ⓓ
10. Ⓐ Ⓑ Ⓒ   22. Ⓐ Ⓑ Ⓒ Ⓓ   34. Ⓐ Ⓑ Ⓒ Ⓓ   46. Ⓐ Ⓑ Ⓒ Ⓓ   58. Ⓐ Ⓑ Ⓒ
11. Ⓐ Ⓑ Ⓒ Ⓓ   23. Ⓐ Ⓑ Ⓒ Ⓓ   35. Ⓐ Ⓑ Ⓒ Ⓓ   47. Ⓐ Ⓑ Ⓒ Ⓓ   59. Ⓐ Ⓑ Ⓒ Ⓓ
12. Ⓐ Ⓑ Ⓒ Ⓓ   24. Ⓐ Ⓑ Ⓒ Ⓓ   36. Ⓐ Ⓑ Ⓒ   48. Ⓐ Ⓑ Ⓒ Ⓓ   60. Ⓐ Ⓑ Ⓒ Ⓓ

Quantitative Skills

61. Ⓐ Ⓑ Ⓒ Ⓓ   72. Ⓐ Ⓑ Ⓒ Ⓓ   83. Ⓐ Ⓑ Ⓒ Ⓓ   94. Ⓐ Ⓑ Ⓒ Ⓓ   105. Ⓐ Ⓑ Ⓒ Ⓓ
62. Ⓐ Ⓑ Ⓒ Ⓓ   73. Ⓐ Ⓑ Ⓒ Ⓓ   84. Ⓐ Ⓑ Ⓒ Ⓓ   95. Ⓐ Ⓑ Ⓒ Ⓓ   106. Ⓐ Ⓑ Ⓒ Ⓓ
63. Ⓐ Ⓑ Ⓒ Ⓓ   74. Ⓐ Ⓑ Ⓒ Ⓓ   85. Ⓐ Ⓑ Ⓒ Ⓓ   96. Ⓐ Ⓑ Ⓒ Ⓓ   107. Ⓐ Ⓑ Ⓒ Ⓓ
64. Ⓐ Ⓑ Ⓒ Ⓓ   75. Ⓐ Ⓑ Ⓒ Ⓓ   86. Ⓐ Ⓑ Ⓒ Ⓓ   97. Ⓐ Ⓑ Ⓒ Ⓓ   108. Ⓐ Ⓑ Ⓒ Ⓓ
65. Ⓐ Ⓑ Ⓒ Ⓓ   76. Ⓐ Ⓑ Ⓒ Ⓓ   87. Ⓐ Ⓑ Ⓒ Ⓓ   98. Ⓐ Ⓑ Ⓒ Ⓓ   109. Ⓐ Ⓑ Ⓒ Ⓓ
66. Ⓐ Ⓑ Ⓒ Ⓓ   77. Ⓐ Ⓑ Ⓒ Ⓓ   88. Ⓐ Ⓑ Ⓒ Ⓓ   99. Ⓐ Ⓑ Ⓒ Ⓓ   110. Ⓐ Ⓑ Ⓒ Ⓓ
67. Ⓐ Ⓑ Ⓒ Ⓓ   78. Ⓐ Ⓑ Ⓒ Ⓓ   89. Ⓐ Ⓑ Ⓒ Ⓓ   100. Ⓐ Ⓑ Ⓒ Ⓓ   111. Ⓐ Ⓑ Ⓒ Ⓓ
68. Ⓐ Ⓑ Ⓒ Ⓓ   79. Ⓐ Ⓑ Ⓒ Ⓓ   90. Ⓐ Ⓑ Ⓒ Ⓓ   101. Ⓐ Ⓑ Ⓒ Ⓓ   112. Ⓐ Ⓑ Ⓒ Ⓓ
69. Ⓐ Ⓑ Ⓒ Ⓓ   80. Ⓐ Ⓑ Ⓒ Ⓓ   91. Ⓐ Ⓑ Ⓒ Ⓓ   102. Ⓐ Ⓑ Ⓒ Ⓓ
70. Ⓐ Ⓑ Ⓒ Ⓓ   81. Ⓐ Ⓑ Ⓒ Ⓓ   92. Ⓐ Ⓑ Ⓒ Ⓓ   103. Ⓐ Ⓑ Ⓒ Ⓓ
71. Ⓐ Ⓑ Ⓒ Ⓓ   82. Ⓐ Ⓑ Ⓒ Ⓓ   93. Ⓐ Ⓑ Ⓒ Ⓓ   104. Ⓐ Ⓑ Ⓒ Ⓓ

Reading

COMPREHENSION

113. Ⓐ Ⓑ Ⓒ Ⓓ   121. Ⓐ Ⓑ Ⓒ Ⓓ   129. Ⓐ Ⓑ Ⓒ Ⓓ   137. Ⓐ Ⓑ Ⓒ Ⓓ   145. Ⓐ Ⓑ Ⓒ Ⓓ
114. Ⓐ Ⓑ Ⓒ Ⓓ   122. Ⓐ Ⓑ Ⓒ Ⓓ   130. Ⓐ Ⓑ Ⓒ Ⓓ   138. Ⓐ Ⓑ Ⓒ Ⓓ   146. Ⓐ Ⓑ Ⓒ Ⓓ
115. Ⓐ Ⓑ Ⓒ Ⓓ   123. Ⓐ Ⓑ Ⓒ Ⓓ   131. Ⓐ Ⓑ Ⓒ Ⓓ   139. Ⓐ Ⓑ Ⓒ Ⓓ   147. Ⓐ Ⓑ Ⓒ Ⓓ
116. Ⓐ Ⓑ Ⓒ Ⓓ   124. Ⓐ Ⓑ Ⓒ Ⓓ   132. Ⓐ Ⓑ Ⓒ Ⓓ   140. Ⓐ Ⓑ Ⓒ Ⓓ   148. Ⓐ Ⓑ Ⓒ Ⓓ
117. Ⓐ Ⓑ Ⓒ Ⓓ   125. Ⓐ Ⓑ Ⓒ Ⓓ   133. Ⓐ Ⓑ Ⓒ Ⓓ   141. Ⓐ Ⓑ Ⓒ Ⓓ   149. Ⓐ Ⓑ Ⓒ Ⓓ
118. Ⓐ Ⓑ Ⓒ Ⓓ   126. Ⓐ Ⓑ Ⓒ Ⓓ   134. Ⓐ Ⓑ Ⓒ Ⓓ   142. Ⓐ Ⓑ Ⓒ Ⓓ   150. Ⓐ Ⓑ Ⓒ Ⓓ
119. Ⓐ Ⓑ Ⓒ Ⓓ   127. Ⓐ Ⓑ Ⓒ Ⓓ   135. Ⓐ Ⓑ Ⓒ Ⓓ   143. Ⓐ Ⓑ Ⓒ Ⓓ   151. Ⓐ Ⓑ Ⓒ Ⓓ
120. Ⓐ Ⓑ Ⓒ Ⓓ   128. Ⓐ Ⓑ Ⓒ Ⓓ   136. Ⓐ Ⓑ Ⓒ Ⓓ   144. Ⓐ Ⓑ Ⓒ Ⓓ   152. Ⓐ Ⓑ Ⓒ Ⓓ

answer sheet

VOCABULARY

153. Ⓐ Ⓑ Ⓒ Ⓓ   158. Ⓐ Ⓑ Ⓒ Ⓓ   163. Ⓐ Ⓑ Ⓒ Ⓓ   168. Ⓐ Ⓑ Ⓒ Ⓓ   173. Ⓐ Ⓑ Ⓒ Ⓓ
154. Ⓐ Ⓑ Ⓒ Ⓓ   159. Ⓐ Ⓑ Ⓒ Ⓓ   164. Ⓐ Ⓑ Ⓒ Ⓓ   169. Ⓐ Ⓑ Ⓒ Ⓓ   174. Ⓐ Ⓑ Ⓒ Ⓓ
155. Ⓐ Ⓑ Ⓒ Ⓓ   160. Ⓐ Ⓑ Ⓒ Ⓓ   165. Ⓐ Ⓑ Ⓒ Ⓓ   170. Ⓐ Ⓑ Ⓒ Ⓓ
156. Ⓐ Ⓑ Ⓒ Ⓓ   161. Ⓐ Ⓑ Ⓒ Ⓓ   166. Ⓐ Ⓑ Ⓒ Ⓓ   171. Ⓐ Ⓑ Ⓒ Ⓓ
157. Ⓐ Ⓑ Ⓒ Ⓓ   162. Ⓐ Ⓑ Ⓒ Ⓓ   167. Ⓐ Ⓑ Ⓒ Ⓓ   172. Ⓐ Ⓑ Ⓒ Ⓓ

Mathematics

CONCEPTS

175. Ⓐ Ⓑ Ⓒ Ⓓ   180. Ⓐ Ⓑ Ⓒ Ⓓ   185. Ⓐ Ⓑ Ⓒ Ⓓ   190. Ⓐ Ⓑ Ⓒ Ⓓ   195. Ⓐ Ⓑ Ⓒ Ⓓ
176. Ⓐ Ⓑ Ⓒ Ⓓ   181. Ⓐ Ⓑ Ⓒ Ⓓ   186. Ⓐ Ⓑ Ⓒ Ⓓ   191. Ⓐ Ⓑ Ⓒ Ⓓ   196. Ⓐ Ⓑ Ⓒ Ⓓ
177. Ⓐ Ⓑ Ⓒ Ⓓ   182. Ⓐ Ⓑ Ⓒ Ⓓ   187. Ⓐ Ⓑ Ⓒ Ⓓ   192. Ⓐ Ⓑ Ⓒ Ⓓ   197. Ⓐ Ⓑ Ⓒ Ⓓ
178. Ⓐ Ⓑ Ⓒ Ⓓ   183. Ⓐ Ⓑ Ⓒ Ⓓ   188. Ⓐ Ⓑ Ⓒ Ⓓ   193. Ⓐ Ⓑ Ⓒ Ⓓ   198. Ⓐ Ⓑ Ⓒ Ⓓ
179. Ⓐ Ⓑ Ⓒ Ⓓ   184. Ⓐ Ⓑ Ⓒ Ⓓ   189. Ⓐ Ⓑ Ⓒ Ⓓ   194. Ⓐ Ⓑ Ⓒ Ⓓ

PROBLEM-SOLVING

199. Ⓐ Ⓑ Ⓒ Ⓓ   207. Ⓐ Ⓑ Ⓒ Ⓓ   215. Ⓐ Ⓑ Ⓒ Ⓓ   223. Ⓐ Ⓑ Ⓒ Ⓓ   231. Ⓐ Ⓑ Ⓒ Ⓓ
200. Ⓐ Ⓑ Ⓒ Ⓓ   208. Ⓐ Ⓑ Ⓒ Ⓓ   216. Ⓐ Ⓑ Ⓒ Ⓓ   224. Ⓐ Ⓑ Ⓒ Ⓓ   232. Ⓐ Ⓑ Ⓒ Ⓓ
201. Ⓐ Ⓑ Ⓒ Ⓓ   209. Ⓐ Ⓑ Ⓒ Ⓓ   217. Ⓐ Ⓑ Ⓒ Ⓓ   225. Ⓐ Ⓑ Ⓒ Ⓓ   233. Ⓐ Ⓑ Ⓒ Ⓓ
202. Ⓐ Ⓑ Ⓒ Ⓓ   210. Ⓐ Ⓑ Ⓒ Ⓓ   218. Ⓐ Ⓑ Ⓒ Ⓓ   226. Ⓐ Ⓑ Ⓒ Ⓓ   234. Ⓐ Ⓑ Ⓒ Ⓓ
203. Ⓐ Ⓑ Ⓒ Ⓓ   211. Ⓐ Ⓑ Ⓒ Ⓓ   219. Ⓐ Ⓑ Ⓒ Ⓓ   227. Ⓐ Ⓑ Ⓒ Ⓓ   235. Ⓐ Ⓑ Ⓒ Ⓓ
204. Ⓐ Ⓑ Ⓒ Ⓓ   212. Ⓐ Ⓑ Ⓒ Ⓓ   220. Ⓐ Ⓑ Ⓒ Ⓓ   228. Ⓐ Ⓑ Ⓒ Ⓓ   236. Ⓐ Ⓑ Ⓒ Ⓓ
205. Ⓐ Ⓑ Ⓒ Ⓓ   213. Ⓐ Ⓑ Ⓒ Ⓓ   221. Ⓐ Ⓑ Ⓒ Ⓓ   229. Ⓐ Ⓑ Ⓒ Ⓓ   237. Ⓐ Ⓑ Ⓒ Ⓓ
206. Ⓐ Ⓑ Ⓒ Ⓓ   214. Ⓐ Ⓑ Ⓒ Ⓓ   222. Ⓐ Ⓑ Ⓒ Ⓓ   230. Ⓐ Ⓑ Ⓒ Ⓓ   238. Ⓐ Ⓑ Ⓒ Ⓓ

Language

239. Ⓐ Ⓑ Ⓒ Ⓓ   251. Ⓐ Ⓑ Ⓒ Ⓓ   263. Ⓐ Ⓑ Ⓒ Ⓓ   275. Ⓐ Ⓑ Ⓒ Ⓓ   287. Ⓐ Ⓑ Ⓒ Ⓓ
240. Ⓐ Ⓑ Ⓒ Ⓓ   252. Ⓐ Ⓑ Ⓒ Ⓓ   264. Ⓐ Ⓑ Ⓒ Ⓓ   276. Ⓐ Ⓑ Ⓒ Ⓓ   288. Ⓐ Ⓑ Ⓒ Ⓓ
241. Ⓐ Ⓑ Ⓒ Ⓓ   253. Ⓐ Ⓑ Ⓒ Ⓓ   265. Ⓐ Ⓑ Ⓒ Ⓓ   277. Ⓐ Ⓑ Ⓒ Ⓓ   289. Ⓐ Ⓑ Ⓒ Ⓓ
242. Ⓐ Ⓑ Ⓒ Ⓓ   254. Ⓐ Ⓑ Ⓒ Ⓓ   266. Ⓐ Ⓑ Ⓒ Ⓓ   278. Ⓐ Ⓑ Ⓒ Ⓓ   290. Ⓐ Ⓑ Ⓒ Ⓓ
243. Ⓐ Ⓑ Ⓒ Ⓓ   255. Ⓐ Ⓑ Ⓒ Ⓓ   267. Ⓐ Ⓑ Ⓒ Ⓓ   279. Ⓐ Ⓑ Ⓒ Ⓓ   291. Ⓐ Ⓑ Ⓒ Ⓓ
244. Ⓐ Ⓑ Ⓒ Ⓓ   256. Ⓐ Ⓑ Ⓒ Ⓓ   268. Ⓐ Ⓑ Ⓒ Ⓓ   280. Ⓐ Ⓑ Ⓒ Ⓓ   292. Ⓐ Ⓑ Ⓒ Ⓓ
245. Ⓐ Ⓑ Ⓒ Ⓓ   257. Ⓐ Ⓑ Ⓒ Ⓓ   269. Ⓐ Ⓑ Ⓒ Ⓓ   281. Ⓐ Ⓑ Ⓒ Ⓓ   293. Ⓐ Ⓑ Ⓒ Ⓓ
246. Ⓐ Ⓑ Ⓒ Ⓓ   258. Ⓐ Ⓑ Ⓒ Ⓓ   270. Ⓐ Ⓑ Ⓒ Ⓓ   282. Ⓐ Ⓑ Ⓒ Ⓓ   294. Ⓐ Ⓑ Ⓒ Ⓓ
247. Ⓐ Ⓑ Ⓒ Ⓓ   259. Ⓐ Ⓑ Ⓒ Ⓓ   271. Ⓐ Ⓑ Ⓒ Ⓓ   283. Ⓐ Ⓑ Ⓒ Ⓓ   295. Ⓐ Ⓑ Ⓒ Ⓓ
248. Ⓐ Ⓑ Ⓒ Ⓓ   260. Ⓐ Ⓑ Ⓒ Ⓓ   272. Ⓐ Ⓑ Ⓒ Ⓓ   284. Ⓐ Ⓑ Ⓒ Ⓓ   296. Ⓐ Ⓑ Ⓒ Ⓓ
249. Ⓐ Ⓑ Ⓒ Ⓓ   261. Ⓐ Ⓑ Ⓒ Ⓓ   273. Ⓐ Ⓑ Ⓒ Ⓓ   285. Ⓐ Ⓑ Ⓒ Ⓓ   297. Ⓐ Ⓑ Ⓒ Ⓓ
250. Ⓐ Ⓑ Ⓒ Ⓓ   262. Ⓐ Ⓑ Ⓒ Ⓓ   274. Ⓐ Ⓑ Ⓒ Ⓓ   286. Ⓐ Ⓑ Ⓒ Ⓓ   298. Ⓐ Ⓑ Ⓒ Ⓓ

Practice Test 6: HSPT

VERBAL SKILLS

16 MINUTES

Directions: Mark one answer—the answer you think is best—for each problem.

1. Which word does *not* belong with the others?
   - (A) one
   - (B) three
   - (C) fourth
   - (D) nine

2. Arouse is to pacify as agitate is to
   - (A) smooth.
   - (B) ruffle.
   - (C) understand.
   - (D) ignore.

3. Bagels are less expensive than muffins. Rolls are less expensive than bagels. Muffins are less expensive than rolls. If the first two statements are true, the third is
   - (A) true.
   - (B) false.
   - (C) uncertain.

4. Query means the *opposite* of
   - (A) argument.
   - (B) answer.
   - (C) square.
   - (D) loner.

5. *Impair* most nearly means
   - (A) direct.
   - (B) improve.
   - (C) stimulate.
   - (D) weaken.

6. Which word does *not* belong with the others?
   - (A) robbery
   - (B) murder
   - (C) death
   - (D) burglary

7. If the wind is *variable,* it is
   - (A) shifting.
   - (B) mild.
   - (C) chilling.
   - (D) steady.

8. Egg is to beat as potato is to
   - (A) yam.
   - (B) bake.
   - (C) eye.
   - (D) mash.

9. If you *obstruct* the entrance to a building, you
   - (A) block it.
   - (B) enter it.
   - (C) leave it.
   - (D) cross it.

10. Barbara has five nickels more than Barry. Jane has 15¢ less than Barbara. Barry has more money than Jane. If the first two statements are true, the third is
    (A) true.
    (B) false.
    (C) uncertain.

11. Which word does *not* belong with the others?
    (A) tuberculosis
    (B) measles
    (C) fever
    (D) flu

12. Cause means the *opposite* of
    (A) affect.
    (B) result.
    (C) question.
    (D) accident.

13. Skillful is to clumsy as deft is to
    (A) alert.
    (B) awkward.
    (C) dumb.
    (D) agile.

14. Which word does *not* belong with the others?
    (A) tent
    (B) igloo
    (C) cabin
    (D) cave

15. Pepper is the shaggiest dog in the obedience school class. Pretzel is a dachshund. Pepper and Pretzel are in the same obedience school class. If the first two statements are true, the third is
    (A) true.
    (B) false.
    (C) uncertain.

16. Pit is to peach as sun is to
    (A) planet.
    (B) moon.
    (C) orbit.
    (D) solar system.

17. *Revenue* most nearly means
    (A) taxes.
    (B) income.
    (C) expenses.
    (D) produce.

18. Which word does *not* belong with the others?
    (A) trapeze
    (B) wedge
    (C) lever
    (D) pulley

19. Which word does *not* belong with the others?
    (A) joy
    (B) sadness
    (C) tears
    (D) glee

20. Linda jumps rope faster than Mary but slower than Inez. Lori jumps faster than Inez but slower than Cleo. Mary is the slowest jumper in the group. If the first two statements are true, the third is
    (A) true.
    (B) false.
    (C) uncertain.

21. If a machine has *manual* controls, the machine is
    (A) self-acting.
    (B) simple.
    (C) hand-operated.
    (D) handmade.

22. *Marshy* most nearly means
    (A) swampy.
    (B) sandy.
    (C) wooded.
    (D) rocky.

23. Seal is to fish as bird is to
   (A) wing.
   (B) minnow.
   (C) worm.
   (D) snail.

24. Profit means the *opposite* of
   (A) ratio.
   (B) gross.
   (C) net.
   (D) loss.

25. Rest means the *opposite* of
   (A) sleep.
   (B) activity.
   (C) wake.
   (D) speak.

26. Which word does *not* belong with the others?
   (A) wind
   (B) gale
   (C) hurricane
   (D) zephyr

27. All people eaters are purple. No cyclops eat people. No cyclops are purple. If the first two statements are true, the third is
   (A) true.
   (B) false.
   (C) uncertain.

28. *Stench* most nearly means
   (A) puddle of slimy water.
   (B) pile of debris.
   (C) foul odor.
   (D) dead animal.

29. The judge who rules evidence to be *immaterial* means it is
   (A) unclear.
   (B) unimportant.
   (C) unpredictable.
   (D) not debatable.

30. Green books are heavier than red books but not as heavy as orange books. Orange books are lighter than blue books but not as light as yellow books. Yellow books are heavier than green books. If the first two statements are true, the third is
   (A) true.
   (B) false.
   (C) uncertain.

31. Shoe is to leather as highway is to
   (A) passage.
   (B) road.
   (C) trail.
   (D) asphalt.

32. Mend means the *opposite* of
   (A) give back.
   (B) change.
   (C) destroy.
   (D) clean.

33. Abstract means the *opposite* of
   (A) art.
   (B) absurd.
   (C) sculpture.
   (D) concrete.

34. A computer that does not *function* does not
   (A) operate.
   (B) finish.
   (C) stop.
   (D) overheat.

35. Which word does *not* belong with the others?
   (A) vitamin
   (B) protein
   (C) meat
   (D) calcium

36. All Ts are either green-eyed Ys or blue-tailed Gs. All blue-tailed Gs have brown eyes and red noses. Some Ts have red noses. If the first two statements are true, the third is
    (A) true.
    (B) false.
    (C) uncertain.

37. A *sullen* child is
    (A) grayish yellow.
    (B) soaking wet.
    (C) very dirty.
    (D) angrily silent.

38. Which word does *not* belong with the others?
    (A) stag
    (B) monkey
    (C) bull
    (D) ram

39. Taste is to tongue as touch is to
    (A) finger.
    (B) eye.
    (C) feeling.
    (D) borrow.

40. Discord means the *opposite* of
    (A) reward.
    (B) record.
    (C) harmony.
    (D) music.

41. Which word does *not* belong with the others?
    (A) aroma
    (B) odor
    (C) scent
    (D) fumes

42. Which word does *not* belong with the others?
    (A) ride
    (B) creep
    (C) hop
    (D) run

43. *Fatal* most nearly means
    (A) accidental.
    (B) deadly.
    (C) dangerous.
    (D) beautiful.

44. Terry has won more races than Bill. Bill has won more races than Luis. Terry has won fewer races than Luis. If the first two statements are true, the third is
    (A) true.
    (B) false.
    (C) uncertain.

45. Which word does *not* belong with the others?
    (A) glass
    (B) gauze
    (C) brick
    (D) lattice

46. If the packages were kept in a *secure* place, the place was
    (A) distant.
    (B) safe.
    (C) convenient.
    (D) secret.

47. Garish means the *opposite* of
    (A) dull.
    (B) damp.
    (C) sweet.
    (D) closed.

48. Horse is to foal as mother is to
    (A) mare.
    (B) son.
    (C) stallion.
    (D) father.

49. Which word does *not* belong with the others?
    (A) gelatin
    (B) tofu
    (C) gum
    (D) sourball

50. *Counterfeit* most nearly means
    (A) mysterious.
    (B) false.
    (C) unreadable.
    (D) priceless.

51. The thruway has more lanes than the parkway. The parkway has fewer lanes than the highway. The thruway has more lanes than the highway. If the first two statements are true, the third is
    (A) true.
    (B) false.
    (C) uncertain.

52. Dog is to flea as horse is to
    (A) rider.
    (B) mane.
    (C) fly.
    (D) shoe.

53. The foghorn that sounded *intermittently* sounded
    (A) constantly.
    (B) annually.
    (C) using intermediaries.
    (D) at intervals.

54. Which word does *not* belong with the others?
    (A) Greek
    (B) Acrylic
    (C) Latin
    (D) Arabic

55. Diverse means the *opposite* of
    (A) definite.
    (B) understandable.
    (C) similar.
    (D) boring.

56. Finder is to reward as repenter is to
    (A) religion.
    (B) sin.
    (C) absolution.
    (D) contrition.

57. Which word does *not* belong with the others?
    (A) bend
    (B) explode
    (C) shatter
    (D) burst

58. The grocery store is south of the drugstore, which is between the gas station and the dry cleaner. The bookstore is north of the gas station. The grocery store is north of the dry cleaner. If the first two statements are true, the third is
    (A) true.
    (B) false.
    (C) uncertain.

59. *Deception* most nearly means
    (A) secrets.
    (B) fraud.
    (C) mistrust.
    (D) hatred.

60. Which word does *not* belong with the others?
    (A) cotton
    (B) linen
    (C) silk
    (D) nylon

STOP End of Verbal Skills section. If you have any time left, go over your work in this section only. Do not work in any other section of the test.

QUANTITATIVE SKILLS

30 MINUTES

Directions: Mark one answer—the answer you think is best—for each problem.

61. Look at this series: 23, 22, 20, 19, 16, 15, 11, ... What number should come next?

(A) 9

(B) 10

(C) 7

(D) 6

62. Examine (A), (B), (C), and (D) and find the best answer.

(A) ▭

(B) ▭

(C) ▭

(D) ▭

(A) (A) is longer than (C) but shorter than (D).

(B) (C) is shorter than (A) minus (D).

(C) (B) and (D) together are longer than (A).

(D) (C) plus (D) are longer than (A) plus (B).

63. Examine (A), (B), and (C) and find the best answer.

(A) $3(2 + 3)$

(B) $(2 + 3)^3$

(C) $3(2) + 3$

(A) (A) plus (C) is greater than (B).

(B) (C) is greater than (A), which is smaller than (B).

(C) (A) and (B) are equal.

(D) (B) is greater than (A) or (C).

64. What number is 5 less than 60% of 40?

(A) 24

(B) 19

(C) 29

(D) 20

65. Look at this series: 50, 52, 48, 50, 46, 48, 44, ... What number should come next?

(A) 46

(B) 40

(C) 50

(D) 48

66. What number is 3 more than the cube of 4 divided by 4?

(A) 61

(B) 39

(C) 67

(D) 19

67. What number is 2 times the average of 6 + 12 + 4 + 41 + 7?

(A) 140

(B) 14

(C) 28

(D) 30

68. Look at this series: 42, 40, 38, 35, 32, 28, 24, ... What two numbers should come next?

(A) 20, 18

(B) 18, 14

(C) 19, 14

(D) 20, 16

69. Look at this series: 27, 33, 25, _____, 23, 29, 21, ... What number should fill the blank in the middle of the series?

(A) 31

(B) 24

(C) 28

(D) 30

70. Examine the triangle and find the best answer.

(A) AB is equal to AC.

(B) m∠B is greater than m∠C.

(C) AB minus AC is equal to BC.

(D) m∠A + m∠B = m∠C.

71. $\frac{2}{3}$ of what number is 6 times 4?

(A) 16

(B) 36

(C) 48

(D) 32

72. What number multiplied by 9 is 3 more than 42?

(A) 27

(B) 45

(C) 7

(D) 5

73. Examine (A), (B), and (C) and find the best answer.

(A)   (B)   (C)

(A) (B) is less shaded than (A).

(B) (B) and (C) are equally shaded.

(C) (A) and (B) are both less shaded than (C).

(D) (A) and (C) are both more shaded than (B).

74. Look at this series: 2, 11, 21, 32, 44, 57, ... What three numbers should come next?

(A) 71, 86, 102

(B) 68, 72, 94

(C) 70, 85, 101

(D) 72, 85, 105

75. Examine (A), (B), and (C) and find the best answer.

(A) 0.875

(B) 0.33 × 2.6

(C) $\frac{7}{8}$

(A) (A), (B), and (C) are all equal.

(B) (B) is greater than (C).

(C) (B) is less than (A).

(D) (A) is greater than (C).

76. The number that is 6 less than 69 is the product of 7 and what other number?

(A) 9

(B) 12

(C) 8

(D) 6

77. Examine (A), (B), and (C) and find the best answer.

(A) $\frac{1}{5}$ of 20

(B) $\frac{1}{4}$ of 24

(C) $\frac{1}{8}$ of 32

(A) (B) is equal to (C).

(B) (A) is less than (B) and equal to (C).

(C) (A) plus (C) equals (B).

(D) (B) minus (A) equals (C).

78. Examine the pictograph and find the best answer.

Number of New Houses Built in XYZ Town, Years A to D

(A)

(B) (three houses)

(C) (five houses)

(D) (four houses) Each house represents 100 houses.

(A) One-half as many houses were built in year (A) as in year (B).

(B) More houses were built in years (A) and (B) combined than in year (C).

(C) Fewer houses were built in years (A) and (D) combined than in year (C).

(D) An equal number of houses were built in years (A) and (B) combined as in year (D).

79. Look at this series: 8, 16, 9, 18, 11, _____, 15, 30, ... What number should fill the blank in this series?

(A) 12
(B) 22
(C) 19
(D) 7

80. Look at this series: 6, 7, 8, 10, 12, 15, 18, ... What number should come next?

(A) 20
(B) 21
(C) 22
(D) 23

81. The sum of 30% of a number and 50% of the same number is 96. What is the number?

(A) 60
(B) 120
(C) 136
(D) 150

82. By how much does the average of 12, 87, 72, and 41 exceed 25?

(A) 28
(B) 78
(C) 53
(D) 25

83. Look at this series: 24, 25, 23, 24, 21, 22, 18, ... What number should come next?

(A) 17
(B) 23
(C) 21
(D) 19

84. Examine (A), (B), (C), and (D) and find the best answer.

(A)   (B)   (C)   (D)

(A) (A) has fewer paddles than (B) but more than (D).

(B) (A) and (D) together are equal to (B) and (C) together.

(C) (B) has fewer paddles than (A) and (C) together.

(D) (B) has more paddles than (C) and (D) together.

85. What number subtracted from 82 leaves 3 more than $\frac{4}{5}$ of 80?

(A) 64
(B) 5
(C) 15
(D) 67

86. Look at this series: 5, 15, 24, 32, _____, 45, 50, ... What number should fill the blank in this series?

(A) 39
(B) 40
(C) 37
(D) 55

87. Examine (A), (B), and (C) and find the best answer.

    (A) 6^2

    (B) 2^6

    (C) $(2 \times 6)(6 \times 2)$

    (A) (A) + (B) = (C).

    (B) (C) − (B) = (A).

    (C) (A) = (B) and both are smaller than (C).

    (D) (C) is greater than either (A) or (B).

88. Examine (A), (B), and (C) and find the best answer.

    (A) $(9 \times 5) + 6$

    (B) $(7 \times 8) - 5$

    (C) $(15 \times 3) + (2 \times 3)$

    (A) (A) is equal to (B), which is equal to (C).

    (B) (C) is greater than (B) but equal to (A).

    (C) (A) is greater than (B), which is less than (C).

    (D) (C) is greater than (A).

89. What number added to 30 is 3 times the product of 8 and 4?

    (A) 63

    (B) 93

    (C) 39

    (D) 66

90. What number divided by 6 is $\frac{1}{8}$ of 96?

    (A) 48

    (B) 72

    (C) 12

    (D) 84

91. Look at this series: 0.125, 0.250, 0.375, 0.500, ... What number should come next?

    (A) 0.620

    (B) 0.625

    (C) 0.728

    (D) 0.875

92. Examine (A), (B), and (C) and find the best answer.

    (A)   (B)   (C)

    (A) (C) is more shaded than (A).

    (B) (A) and (B) are equally shaded and are more shaded than (C).

    (C) (A) is less shaded than (B) and more shaded than (C).

    (D) (A) and (C) are equally shaded.

93. What number is 15 more than $\frac{5}{9}$ of 99?

    (A) 45

    (B) 60

    (C) 70

    (D) 81

94. What number divided by $\frac{3}{4}$ yields a quotient that is equal to the divisor?

    (A) $\frac{5}{8}$

    (B) $\frac{7}{16}$

    (C) $\frac{9}{16}$

    (D) $\frac{3}{4}$

95. Examine (A), (B), and (C) and find the best answer.

    (A) 0.8

    (B) 80%

    (C) $\frac{8}{10}\%$

    (A) (B) is greater than (A) or (C).

    (B) (A) is greater than (B) plus (C).

    (C) (A), (B), and (C) are equal.

    (D) (C) is smaller than both (A) and (B).

96. Examine the figure and find the best answer.

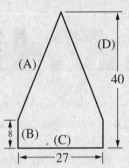

(A) Line segment (A) is shorter than line segment (D), which is longer than line segment (C).

(B) Line segment (B) is shorter than line segment (A), which is longer than line segment (D).

(C) Line segment (C) is longer than line segment (D), which is longer than line segment (B).

(D) Line segment (B) plus line segment (C) together equal the length of line segment (D).

97. Look at this series: 81, 9, 64, 8, _____ , 7, 36, ... What number should fill the blank in this series?

(A) 9

(B) 56

(C) 63

(D) 49

98. Look at this series: B25, E21, H17, K13, ... What comes next?

(A) M9

(B) N9

(C) N10

(D) O8

99. Look at this series: 1, 3, 3, 9, 9, 27, 27, ... What three numbers should come next?

(A) 81, 81, 729

(B) 27, 36, 36

(C) 27, 81, 81

(D) 81, 81, 243

100. If $\frac{3}{8}$ of a number is 9, then $83\frac{1}{3}\%$ of the number is

(A) 20

(B) 27

(C) 14

(D) 54

101. Examine the figure and choose the best answer.

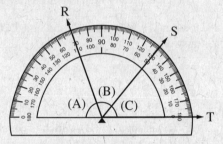

(A) Angle (B) plus angle (C) equals a right angle.

(B) Angle (A) is greater than angle (C), which is smaller than angle (B).

(C) Angle (B) minus angle (C) equals angle (A).

(D) Angle (A) is equal to angle (C).

102. Examine (A), (B), and (C) and choose the best answer.

(A) $\frac{1}{5}$ of 200

(B) 2^2 times 10

(C) $\frac{1}{2}$ of 8^2

(A) (A) is equal to (B) and greater than (C).

(B) (A), (B), and (C) are all equal.

(C) (B) is greater than (A), which is equal to (C).

(D) (A) is greater than (C), which is greater than (B).

103. Look at this series: −19, −14, −12, −7, −5 . . . .

What number should come next?

(A) 0

(B) 5

(C) −1

(D) 1

104. What number added to 60 is 3 times the product of 4 and 5?

(A) 10

(B) 0

(C) 15

(D) 5

105. Look at this series: 0.2, 0.1, 0.05, 0.025, ... What number should come next?

(A) 0.00625

(B) 0.0025

(C) 0.0125

(D) 0.055

106. What number is 12 less than $\frac{5}{8}$ of 96?

(A) 56

(B) 65

(C) 60

(D) 48

107. Examine (A), (B), and (C) and find the best answer.

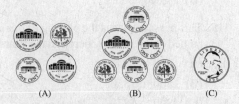

(A)   (B)   (C)

(A) (A) is equal to (C).

(B) (B) is greater than (A) and less than (C).

(C) (A) is not greater than (C), which is not greater than (B).

(D) (A) plus (B) is not greater than (C).

108. Look at this series: VI, IX, 12, 15, XVIII, ... What should come next?

(A) XXI

(B) 21

(C) XXII

(D) 22

109. Look at this series: $\frac{16}{2}$, $\frac{8}{2}$, $\frac{8}{4}$, $\frac{8}{8}$, $\frac{8}{16}$, ... What number should come next?

(A) $\frac{16}{16}$

(B) $\frac{8}{32}$

(C) $\frac{16}{32}$

(D) $\frac{4}{8}$

110. Examine (A), (B), and (C) and find the best answer.

(A)   100% of 95

(B)   100% of 195%

(C)   95% of 100

(A) (B) is greater than (A).

(B) (C) is greater than (A) plus (B).

(C) (A) and (C) are equal and are greater than (B).

(D) (A) and (C) are equal and are smaller than (B).

111. What number decreased by 40% of itself is 90?

(A) 150

(B) 36

(C) 60

(D) 145

112. Look at this series: 26, 18, 18, 12, 12, 8, 8, ... What two numbers should come next?

(A) 7, 7

(B) 8, 6

(C) 6, 4

(D) 6, 6

STOP   End of Quantitative Skills section. If you have any time left, go over your work in this section only. Do not work in any other section of the test.

READING

Comprehension

25 MINUTES

Early in the nineteenth century, American youth was playing a game, somewhat like the English game of rounders, that contained all the elements of modern baseball. It was neither scientifically planned nor skillfully played, but it furnished considerable excitement for players and spectators alike. The playing field was a sixty-foot square with goals, or bases, at each of its four corners. A pitcher stationed himself at the center of the square, and a catcher and an indefinite number of fielders supported the pitcher and completed the team. None of these players, usually between 8 and 20 on a side, covered the bases. The batter was out on balls caught on the fly or the first bounce, and a base runner was out if he was hit by a thrown ball while off base. The bat was nothing more than a <u>stout</u> paddle with a two-inch-thick handle. The ball was apt to be an <u>impromptu</u> affair composed of a bullet, cork, or metal slug tightly wound with wool yarn and string. With its simple equipment and only a few rules, this game steadily increased in popularity during the first half of the century.

113. The title that best expresses the main idea of this selection is
    (A) "Baseball Rules."
    (B) "An English Game."
    (C) "Baseball's Predecessor."
    (D) "American Pastimes."

114. The rules of this game required
    (A) 8 fielders.
    (B) a pitcher, a catcher, and one fielder for each base.
    (C) 20 fielders.
    (D) no specific number of players.

115. The shape of the playing field was
    (A) oblong.
    (B) irregular.
    (C) square.
    (D) subject to no rules.

116. The game was
    (A) scientifically planned.
    (B) exciting for the players but boring to watch.
    (C) boring for the players but exciting to watch.
    (D) similar to an English game called "rounders."

117. The word <u>impromptu</u>, as underlined and used in this passage, most nearly means
    (A) proven.
    (B) unrehearsed.
    (C) improvised.
    (D) argued about.

118. This passage places the playing of this unnamed game roughly between the years of
    (A) 1900 to 1950.
    (B) 1800 to 1850.
    (C) 1800 to 1830.
    (D) 1900 to 1925.

119. This selection suggests that

    (A) the game of baseball has grown more complicated over the years.

    (B) the game described was very dangerous.

    (C) baseball originated in the United States.

    (D) the game described required skilled players.

120. According to the author, the popularity of this game was based largely upon

    (A) the excitement of watching skillful players.

    (B) the low cost of equipment.

    (C) the fact that none of the players covered the bases.

    (D) its being a new, strictly American game.

121. The word stout, as underlined and used in this passage, most nearly means

    (A) courageous.

    (B) fat.

    (C) that the bat was made from a stave of a beer barrel.

    (D) sturdy.

122. The writer of this selection

    (A) disdains this game because of its unprofessional aspects.

    (B) is nostalgic for days when games were simpler.

    (C) has prepared a factual report.

    (D) admires the ingenuity of American youth.

John J. Audubon, a bird watcher, once noticed that a pair of phoebes nested in the same place year after year, and he wondered if they might be the same birds. He put tiny silver bands on their legs, and the next spring the banded birds returned to the same nesting place.

This pair of phoebes were the first birds to be banded. Since that time, naturalists, with the aid of the federal government's Fish and Wildlife Department, band birds in an effort to study them. The bands, which are made of lightweight aluminum so as not to harm the birds, bear a message requesting finders to notify the department. Careful records of these notifications are kept and analyzed. In this way, naturalists have gained a great deal of knowledge about the nesting habits, migration patterns, and populations of a large variety of bird species. Most importantly, they are able to identify those species that are in danger of extinction.

123. Audubon banded phoebes because

    (A) he noticed that a pair of phoebes nested in the same place each year.

    (B) phoebes are in danger of extinction.

    (C) the federal government asked him to observe phoebes.

    (D) phoebes are easy to catch and band.

124. The message on bird bands is

    (A) "Do not harm this bird."

    (B) "Kill this bird and send it to the Fish and Wildlife Department."

    (C) "Remove the band and send it to the Fish and Wildlife Department."

    (D) "Please notify the Fish and Wildlife Department as to where and when you saw this bird."

125. The word naturalists, as underlined and used in this passage, refers to a(n)

    (A) employee of the Fish and Wildlife Department.

    (B) person who loves birds.

    (C) person who observes and studies nature.

    (D) person who develops theories about extinction of bird species.

practice test

126. The title below that best expresses the main idea of this passage is

(A) "The Migration of Birds."

(B) "One Method of Studying Birds."

(C) "The Habits of Birds."

(D) "The Work of John Audubon."

127. Audubon's purpose in banding the phoebes was to

(A) satisfy his own curiosity.

(B) start a government study of birds.

(C) gain fame as the first birdbander.

(D) chart the phoebes' migration patterns.

128. Audubon proved his theory that

(A) silver and aluminum are the best metals for birdbands.

(B) the government should study birds.

(C) phoebes are the most interesting bird to study.

(D) at least some birds return to the same nesting place each spring.

129. The Fish and Wildlife Department is

(A) a branch of the Audubon Society.

(B) a group of naturalists.

(C) an agency of the federal government.

(D) a bird-banding organization.

130. The words migration patterns, as underlined and used in this passage, most nearly mean

(A) random wanderings.

(B) periodic movements.

(C) food-gathering habits.

(D) wintertime behavior.

131. The word extinction, as underlined and used in this passage, most nearly means

(A) darkness.

(B) resettlement.

(C) inactivity.

(D) disappearance.

132. The author's purpose in writing this selection was most probably to

(A) convince readers to join in bird-banding efforts.

(B) save birds from extinction.

(C) encourage readers to cooperate with the Fish and Wildlife Department by reporting as requested.

(D) praise John J. Audubon for his vision.

A vast stretch of land lies untouched by civilization in the back country of the Eastern portion of the African continent. With the occasional exception of a big-game hunter, foreigners never penetrate this area. Aside from the Wandorobo tribe, even the natives shun its confines because it harbors the deadly tsetse fly. The Wandorobo nomads depend on the forest for their lives, eating its roots and fruits, and making their homes wherever they find themselves at the end of the day.

One of the staples of their primitive diet, and their only sweet, is honey. They obtain it through an ancient, symbiotic relationship with a bird known as the Indicator. The scientific community finally confirmed the report, at first discredited, that this bird purposefully led the natives to trees containing the honeycombs of wild bees. Other species of honey guides are also known to take advantage of the foraging efforts of some animals in much the same way that the Indicator uses men.

This amazing bird settles in a tree near a Wandorobo encampment and chatters incessantly until the men answer it with whistles. It then begins its leading flight. Chattering, it hops from tree to tree, while the men continue their musical answering call. When the bird reaches the tree, its chatter becomes shriller and its followers examine the tree carefully. The Indicator usually perches just over the honeycomb, and the men hear the humming of the bees in the hollow trunk. Using torches, they smoke most of the bees out of the tree, but those that escape the nullifying effects of the smoke sting the men viciously. Undaunted, the Wandorobos free the nest, gather the honey, and leave a small offering for their bird guide.

133. The title that best expresses the topic of this selection is
   (A) "Life in the African Backwoods."
   (B) "The Wandorobo Tribe."
   (C) "Locating a Honeycomb."
   (D) "Men and Birds Work Together."

134. Most people avoid the back country of Eastern Africa because they
   (A) dislike honey.
   (B) fear the cannibalistic Wandorobo.
   (C) fear bee stings.
   (D) fear the tsetse fly.

135. The Wandorobo communicate with the Indicator bird by
   (A) whistling.
   (B) chattering.
   (C) playing musical instruments.
   (D) smoke signals.

136. The Indicator bird's name stems from the fact that it
   (A) always flies in a northward line.
   (B) points out locations of tsetse fly nests.
   (C) leads men to honey trees.
   (D) uses smoke to indicate the location of bees.

137. The reward of the Indicator bird is
   (A) a symbiotic relationship.
   (B) a musical concert.
   (C) roots and fruits.
   (D) some honey.

138. Smoke causes bees to
   (A) fly away.
   (B) sting viciously.
   (C) hum.
   (D) make honey.

139. Scientists at first discredited reports of the purposeful behavior of the Indicator bird because
   (A) the Wandorobo are known to exaggerate in their stories.
   (B) birds do not eat honey.
   (C) honey guides take advantage of others of their own species only.
   (D) the arrangement seemed so farfetched that they waited to confirm the reports scientifically.

140. The response of the Wandorobo toward bee stings is to
   (A) ignore them.
   (B) smoke the bees out.
   (C) eat roots to nullify the effects of the stings.
   (D) fear them.

141. The word incessantly, as underlined and used in the passage, most nearly means
   (A) meaninglessly.
   (B) continuously.
   (C) raucously.
   (D) softly.

142. According to the selection, one characteristic of the Wandorobo tribe is that its members
   (A) avoid the country of the tsetse fly.
   (B) have no permanent homes.
   (C) lack physical courage.
   (D) live entirely on a diet of honey.

"Sophistication by the reel" is the motto of Peretz Johannes, who selects juvenile films for Saturday viewing at the Museum of the City of New York. Sampling the intellectual climate of the young fans in this city for the past two years has convinced him that many people underestimate the taste level of young New Yorkers. Consequently, a year ago he began to show films ordinarily restricted to art movie distribution. The series proved enormously successful, and in September, when the program commenced for this season, youngsters from the five boroughs filled the theater.

As a student of history, Mr. Johannes has not confined himself to productions given awards in recent years, but has spent many hours among dusty reels ferreting out such prewar favorites as the silhouette films Lotte Reiniger made in Germany. One program included two films based on children's stories, "The Little Red Lighthouse" and "Mike Mulligan and His Steam Shovel." The movies are shown at 11 a.m. and 3 p.m., with a short program of stories and a demonstration of toys presented during the intermission.

143. Mr. Johannes is a
    (A) filmmaker.
    (B) film critic.
    (C) film selector.
    (D) student of film.

144. Admission to the program described is
    (A) limited to children in the neighborhood of the museum.
    (B) for Manhattan only.
    (C) available for all the city.
    (D) for teenagers only.

145. By his motto, "sophistication by the reel," Mr. Johannes means to imply that he
    (A) can convince students to remain in school through the lessons taught by his films.
    (B) introduces complex ideas and new perceptions by means of the movies.

    (C) considers all moviegoers to be immature.
    (D) feels that education on film is more effective than education in the classroom.

146. The words ferreting out, as underlined and used in the passage, most nearly mean
    (A) searching out.
    (B) dusting off.
    (C) editing.
    (D) protesting against.

147. The films are shown
    (A) year-round.
    (B) twice every day.
    (C) at the Museum of Modern Art.
    (D) on Saturday.

148. Mr. Johannes
    (A) followed an established policy in planning his programs.
    (B) has failed so far to secure a good audience.
    (C) limits his programs to the newest award-winning pictures.
    (D) evidently is a good judge of children's tastes.

149. Mr. Johannes found that children's taste in motion pictures
    (A) was more varied than had been thought.
    (B) ruled out pictures made before their own day.
    (C) was limited to cartoons.
    (D) was even poorer than adults had suspected.

150. Mr. Johannes would probably not choose to show a(n)
    (A) film about a ballet dancer.
    (B) X-rated film.
    (C) film about the plight of migrant farmers.
    (D) silent movie.

151. In the first sentence of the second paragraph, the reels are described as "dusty." The writer chose this word because

  (A) the cans in which the films were kept were very dirty.

  (B) the movies had not been shown in a long time.

  (C) many of the prewar films were about the plight of the farmers in the dust bowl of the Southwest.

  (D) the word *dusty* is a synonym for *stuffy*.

152. The silhouette films were probably popular with children because they

  (A) were made in Germany.

  (B) were not very colorful.

  (C) allowed for free run of the imagination to fill details.

  (D) had lively background music.

Vocabulary

Directions: Choose the word that means the same or about the same as the underlined word.

153. tedious work

  (A) technical

  (B) interesting

  (C) tiresome

  (D) confidential

154. to rescind an order

  (A) revise

  (B) cancel

  (C) misinterpret

  (D) confirm

155. diversity in the suggestions

  (A) similarity

  (B) value

  (C) triviality

  (D) variety

156. the problem of indigence

  (A) poverty

  (B) corruption

  (C) intolerance

  (D) laziness

157. a vindictive person

  (A) prejudiced

  (B) unpopular

  (C) petty

  (D) revengeful

158. unsatisfactory remuneration

  (A) payment

  (B) summary

  (C) explanation

  (D) estimate

159. a deficient program

  (A) excellent

  (B) inadequate

  (C) demanding

  (D) interrupted

160. a detrimental influence

  (A) favorable

  (B) lasting

  (C) harmful

  (D) restraining

161. accurate information
    (A) correct
    (B) good
    (C) ample
    (D) useful

162. to amplify one's remarks
    (A) soften
    (B) simplify
    (C) enlarge upon
    (D) repeat

163. to be legally competent
    (A) expert
    (B) ineligible
    (C) accused
    (D) able

164. infraction of the rules
    (A) violation
    (B) use
    (C) interpretation
    (D) part

165. a relevant magazine article
    (A) applicable
    (B) controversial
    (C) miscellaneous
    (D) recent

166. an office manual
    (A) laborer
    (B) handbook
    (C) typewriter
    (D) handle

167. a computational device
    (A) calculator
    (B) adder
    (C) mathematician
    (D) machine

168. a conventional test
    (A) agreeable
    (B) public
    (C) large-scale
    (D) ordinary

169. the subject of controversy
    (A) annoyance
    (B) debate
    (C) envy
    (D) review

170. a diplomatic person
    (A) well-dressed
    (B) tactful
    (C) domineering
    (D) tricky

171. an irate student
    (A) irresponsible
    (B) untidy
    (C) insubordinate
    (D) angry

172. durable paint
    (A) cheap
    (B) long-lasting
    (C) easily applied
    (D) quick-drying

173. an extensive search
    (A) complicated
    (B) superficial
    (C) thorough
    (D) leisurely

174. the inception of the program
    (A) beginning
    (B) discussion
    (C) rejection
    (D) purpose

STOP   End of Reading section. If you have any time left, go over your work in this section only. Do not work in any other section of the test.

MATHEMATICS

Concepts

45 MINUTES

Directions: Mark one answer—the answer you think is best—for each problem. You may use scratch paper when working on these problems.

175. Three hundred twenty-six million nine hundred thousand six hundred nineteen =
    (A) 3,269,619
    (B) 32,690,619
    (C) 326,960,019
    (D) 326,900,619

176. A number is changed if
    (A) 0 is added to it.
    (B) 1 is subtracted from it.
    (C) it is divided by 1.
    (D) it is multiplied by 1.

177. In the number 4,000,400,000, there are
    (A) 4 billions and 4 hundred thousands.
    (B) 4 millions and 4 thousands.
    (C) 4 billions and 4 millions.
    (D) 4 millions and 40 thousands.

178. Which is the longest time?
    (A) 1,440 minutes
    (B) 25 hours
    (C) $\frac{1}{2}$ day
    (D) 3,600 seconds

179. $5^3 \times 3^4 =$
    (A) $5 \times 3 \times 3 \times 4$
    (B) $5 \times 5 \times 5 \times 3 \times 3 \times 3$
    (C) $5 \times 5 \times 5 \times 3 \times 3 \times 3 \times 3$
    (D) $5 \times 5 \times 5 \times 5 \times 3 \times 3 \times 3$

180. $\frac{3 \times 8}{6 \times 5} =$
    (A) $\frac{2}{3}$
    (B) $\frac{1}{6}$
    (C) $\frac{3}{4}$
    (D) $\frac{4}{5}$

181. Which of the following has the same value as 0.5%?
    (A) 0.005%
    (B) $\frac{1}{2}\%$
    (C) $\frac{1}{50}\%$
    (D) $\frac{1}{500}\%$

182. What is the total number of degrees found in angles A and C in the triangle below?

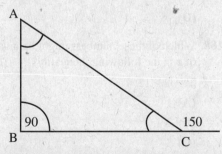

    (A) 100°
    (B) 180°
    (C) 90°
    (D) 60°

183. If $x > 9$, then

(A) $x^2 > 80$

(B) $x^2 - 2 = 47$

(C) $x^2 < 65$

(D) $x^2 - 2 < 90$

184. Any number that is divisible by both 3 and 4 is also divisible by

(A) 8

(B) 9

(C) 12

(D) 16

185. Which symbol belongs in the circle? 0.023 ○ 0.0086

(A) $>$

(B) $<$

(C) $=$

(D) $\cong$

186. The greatest common factor of 50 and 10 is

(A) 1

(B) 5

(C) 10

(D) 25

187. What number belongs in the box?

$+ 5 + \Box = -3$

(A) $+3$

(B) -3

(C) $+8$

(D) -8

188. Which of these numbers might be a value of x in the following inequality?

$3x + 2 > 12$

(A) 1

(B) 2

(C) 3

(D) 4

189. The area of the circle is

(A) 3π cm.

(B) 6π sq. cm.

(C) 9π sq. cm.

(D) 36π sq. cm.

190. If $x - 3 < 12$, x is

(A) less than 15

(B) greater than 16

(C) equal to 15

(D) less than 18

191. The ratio of 3 quarts to 3 gallons is

(A) 3:1

(B) 1:4

(C) 6:3

(D) 4:1

192. Which pair of values for x and $\Box$ will make the following statement true?

$2x \Box 8$

(A) $(6, <)$

(B) $(4, >)$

(C) $(0, <)$

(D) $(-3, >)$

193. How many sixths are there in $\frac{4}{5}$?

(A) $4\frac{4}{5}$

(B) $5\frac{1}{5}$

(C) 6

(D) $2\frac{2}{5}$

194. Set M = {1,2,3,4}; Set N = {2,5,6}. The intersection $\cap$ of the two sets is

(A) {2}

(B) {1,2,3,4,5}

(C) {3}

(D) {26}

195. If Mary is x years old now and her sister is 3 years younger, then 5 years from now her sister will be what age?

(A) $x + 5$ years

(B) $x + 3$ years

(C) $x + 2$ years

(D) 8 years

196. Write 493 in expanded form, using exponents.

(A) $(4 \times 10^2) + (9 \times 10) + 3$

(B) $(4 \times 10^3) + (9 \times 10^2) + (3 \times 10)$

(C) $(4 \times 10^1) + (9 \times 10) + 3$

(D) None of the above

197. Which of the following statements is true?

(A) $7 \times 11 > 78$

(B) $6 + 4 < 10.5$

(C) $8 - 3 = 7 + 4$

(D) $16 \div 2 > 9$

198.

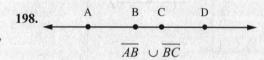

$$\overline{AB} \cup \overline{BC}$$

(A) $\overline{BD}$

(B) $\overline{BC}$

(C) $\overline{AD}$

(D) $\overline{AC}$

Problem-Solving

199. The ratio of teachers to students in a certain school is 1:12. If there are 16 teachers in the school, how many students are there?

(A) 16

(B) 192

(C) 202

(D) 176

200. On a blueprint, 3 inches represent 24 feet. How long must a line be to represent 96 feet?

(A) 36 inches

(B) 12 inches

(C) 6 inches

(D) 4 inches

201. A department store marks up its clothing 75% over cost. If it sells khaki pants for $17, how much did the store pay for them?

(A) $9.71

(B) $17.50

(C) $11.20

(D) $1.12

202. The same store puts the same $17 pants on sale at a 20% discount. What is the new selling price?

(A) $16.80

(B) $13.60

(C) $3.40

(D) $16.75

203.

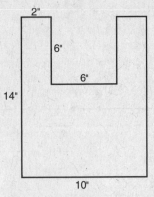

Note: In the figure above, assume that any angle which appears to be a right angle is a right angle.

The perimeter of the figure above is

(A) 38 in.

(B) 60 in.

(C) 46 sq. in.

(D) 38 sq. in.

204. The area of the figure above is

(A) 104 sq. in.

(B) 120 sq. in.

(C) 276 sq. in.

(D) 240 sq. in.

205. The charge for a particular long-distance call was $1.56 for the first 3 minutes and $0.22 for each additional minute. What was the total charge for a 16-minute call?

(A) $5.80

(B) $5.08

(C) $2.86

(D) $4.42

206. The winner of a race received $\frac{1}{3}$ of the total purse. The third-place finisher received $\frac{1}{3}$ of the winner's share. If the winner's share was $2700, what was the total purse?

(A) $2700

(B) $8100

(C) $900

(D) $1800

207. As a train departs from station A, it has 12 empty seats, 14 seated passengers, and 4 standing passengers. At the next stop, 8 passengers get off, 13 passengers get on, and everyone takes a seat. How many empty seats are there?

(A) 1

(B) 2

(C) 3

(D) 4

208. In order to increase revenues, a municipality considers raising its sales tax from 5% to 8%. How much more will it cost to buy a $250 television set if the 8% sales tax is approved?

(A) $7.50

(B) $10.00

(C) $12.50

(D) $15.50

209. Solve: $\dfrac{1\frac{3}{4} - \frac{1}{8}}{\frac{1}{8}} =$

(A) 12

(B) 13

(C) 14

(D) 1

210. Solve: $2.01 \div 1.02 =$

(A) 1.97

(B) 0.507

(C) 3.03

(D) 2.0001

211. Solve: $-3 - [(2 - 1) - (3 + 4)] =$

(A) 3

(B) 12

(C) –6

(D) –9

212. 140% of 70 is

(A) 150

(B) 9.8

(C) 9800

(D) 98

213. 5 gallons 2 quarts 1 pint
     −1 gallon 3 quarts
     _____

     (A) 4 gal. 9 qt. 1 pt.
     (B) 2 gal. 2 qt. 1 pt.
     (C) 3 gal. 3 qt. 1 pt.
     (D) 2 gal. 6 qt. 2 pt.

214. Solve: $6 \div \frac{1}{3} + \frac{2}{3} \times 9 =$

     (A) $\frac{2}{3}$
     (B) 24
     (C) 168
     (D) 54

215. If $a = 9$, $b = 2$, and $c = 1$, the value of $\sqrt{a + 3b + c}$ is

     (A) 7
     (B) 16
     (C) 6
     (D) 4

216. 7 is to 21 as $\frac{2}{3}$ is to

     (A) 2
     (B) 1
     (C) $\frac{4}{3}$
     (D) 3

217. The average of −10, 6, 0, −3, and 22 is

     (A) 2
     (B) −3
     (C) −6
     (D) 3

218. The number of phones in Adelaide, Australia, is 48,000. If this represents 12.8 phones per 100 persons, the population of Adelaide to the nearest thousand is

     (A) 128,000
     (B) 375,000
     (C) 378,000
     (D) 556,000

219. A carpenter needs four boards, each 2 feet 9 inches long. If wood is sold only by the foot, how many feet must he buy?

     (A) 9
     (B) 10
     (C) 11
     (D) 12

220. What is the difference between $(4 \times 10^3) + 6$ and $(2 \times 10^3) + (3 \times 10) + 8$?

     (A) 168
     (B) 55,968
     (C) 3765
     (D) 1968

221. A square has an area of 49 sq. in. The number of inches in its perimeter is

     (A) 7
     (B) 28
     (C) 14
     (D) 98

222. $r = 35 - (3 + 6)(-n)$
     $n = 2$
     $r =$

     (A) 53
     (B) 17
     (C) −53
     (D) −17

223. $(3 + 4)^3 =$

     (A) 21
     (B) 91
     (C) 343
     (D) 490

224. Aluminum bronze consists of copper and aluminum, usually in the ratio of 10:1 by weight. If an object made of this alloy weighs 77 pounds, how many pounds of aluminum does it contain?

     (A) 7.7
     (B) 7.0
     (C) 70.0
     (D) 10

225. Mr. Wilson makes a weekly salary of $175 plus 8% commission on his sales. What will his income be for a week in which he makes sales totaling $1025?

    (A) $257.00
    (B) $260.50
    (C) $247.00
    (D) $267.00

226. Solve for x: $x^2 + 5 = 41$

    (A) ±6
    (B) ±7
    (C) ± 8
    (D) ± 9

227. If 5 pints of water are needed to water each square foot of lawn, the minimum number of gallons of water needed for a lawn 8' by 12' is

    (A) 60
    (B) 56
    (C) 80
    (D) 30

228. Solve for x: $\frac{x}{2} + 36 = 37.25$

    (A) 18.5
    (B) 3.5
    (C) 2.5
    (D) 12.5

229.

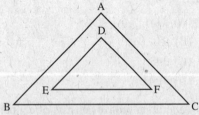

In the figure above, the sides of △ABC are respectively parallel to the sides of △DEF. If the complement of ∠A is 40°, then the complement of ∠D is

    (A) 20°
    (B) 50°
    (C) 60°
    (D) 40°

230. Find the area of a rectangle with a length of 168 feet and a width of 82 feet.

    (A) 13,776 sq. ft.
    (B) 13,856 sq. ft.
    (C) 13,306 sq. ft.
    (D) 13,706 sq. ft.

231. Solve: $63 \div \frac{1}{9} =$

    (A) 56
    (B) 67
    (C) 7
    (D) 567

232. A house was valued at $83,000 and insured for 80% of that amount. Find the yearly premium if it is figured at $0.45 per $100 of value.

    (A) $298.80
    (B) $252.63
    (C) $664.00
    (D) $83.80

233. Solve: $72.61 \div 0.05 =$

    (A) 1.45220
    (B) 145.220
    (C) 1452.20
    (D) 14.522

234. Find the area of a triangle whose dimensions are $b = 12'$, $h = 14'$.

    (A) 168 sq. ft.
    (B) 84 sq. ft.
    (C) 42 sq. ft.
    (D) 24 sq. ft.

235. Increased by 150%, the number 72 becomes

    (A) 188
    (B) 108
    (C) 180
    (D) 170

236. If $14x - 2y = 32$ and $x + 2y = 13$, then $x =$

    (A) 5

    (B) 8

    (C) 3

    (D) 4

237. If $ab + 4 = 52$, and $a = 6$, $b =$

    (A) 42

    (B) 8

    (C) 21

    (D) 4

238. A group left on a trip at 8:50 a.m. and reached its destination at 3:30 p.m. How long, in hours and minutes, did the trip take?

    (A) 3 hours 10 minutes

    (B) 4 hours 40 minutes

    (C) 5 hours 10 minutes

    (D) 6 hours 40 minutes

STOP End of Mathematics section. If you have any time left, go over your work in this section only. Do not work in any other section of the test.

LANGUAGE

25 MINUTES

Directions: In questions 239–278, look for errors in capitalization, punctuation, or usage. Mark the answer choice that contains the error. If you find no error, mark (D) on your answer sheet.

239. (A) We had swum across the lake before the sun rose.
(B) Clearly visible on the desk were those letters he claimed to have mailed yesterday.
(C) John Kennedy effected many executive reforms during the tragically few years that he served as president of the United States.
(D) No mistakes

240. (A) John and I are meeting friends on Sunday afternoon to shop for prom wear.
(B) We are going to Milner Farms on Saturday.
(C) He hadn't seen none of the movies the others talked about.
(D) No mistakes

241. (A) Rather than go with John, he decided to stay at home.
(B) Each of the nurses were scrupulously careful about personal cleanliness.
(C) His education had filled him with anger against those who he believed had hurt or humiliated him.
(D) No mistakes

242. (A) The Fourth of July is also known as Independence day.
(B) Many Americans enjoy swimming.
(C) Abby left Jen's house after dinner.
(D) No mistakes

243. (A) Neither tears nor protests effected the least change in their parents' decision.
(B) Being able to trust one's sources is indispensable for the investigative reporter.
(C) When you go to the library tomorrow, please take this book to the librarian who sits in the reference room.
(D) No mistakes

244. (A) The government, announcing a bill of rights for its citizens, promised them equal rights under the law.
(B) Martin Luther King's birthday was recently designated a federal holiday.
(C) Remember that our Constitution is not self-executing; it must be interpreted and applied by the Supreme Court.
(D) No mistakes

245. (A) If you prepare systematically and diligently for the examination, one can be confident of passing it.
(B) Mary was so uninterested in the baseball game that she yawned unashamedly.
(C) If he had had the forethought to arrange an appointment, his reception might have been more friendly.
(D) No mistakes

246. **(A)** Carlie, Gracie, and Sammie are members of the swim team.

  (B) Sheila and Margie are the school's best pitchers.

  (C) My favorite zoo exhibit is the snake house.

  (D) No mistakes

247. **(A)** For conscience's sake he gave himself up, though no suspicion had been directed toward him.

  (B) Because they were unaware of his interest in the building, they did not understand why he felt so bad about it's being condemned.

  (C) "I truly think," he said, "that we are entitled to have the day off in this snowstorm."

  (D) No mistakes

248. **(A)** Was it really she whom you saw last night?

  (B) The distraught traveler asked Tom and I to give her directions to the nearest bus stop.

  (C) Making friends is more rewarding than being antisocial.

  (D) No mistakes

249. **(A)** In his tales of adventure and romance, he predicted many scientific achievements of the twentieth century.

  (B) Today's *Times* has headlines about another woman who has just swum the English Channel.

  (C) Some Third World Countries have suggested that they be given the right to regularly censor what foreign journalists tell about their countries.

  (D) No mistakes

250. **(A)** Even if history does not repeat itself, knowledge of history can give current problems a familiar look.

  (B) He proved to his own satisfaction that he was as clever as, if not more clever than, she.

  (C) The citizens of Washington, like Los Angeles, prefer to commute by automobile.

  (D) No mistakes

251. **(A)** I have found one of those books that teaches how to build a model airplane.

  (B) There are less derelicts in the downtown area since the crumbling building was razed.

  (C) The ceremonies were opened by a colorful drum and bugle corps.

  (D) No mistakes

252. **(A)** Do not make a choice that changed the meaning of the original sentence.

  (B) I would appreciate your treating me as if I were your sister.

  (C) The contract should not have been awarded to the secretary's nephew.

  (D) No mistakes

253. **(A)** "To eat sparingly is advisable," said the doctor.

  (B) "Which is the way to the science building?" asked the new student.

  (C) She inquired, "Are you going to hand in your report before lunch?"

  (D) No mistakes

254. **(A)** A portion of the rental cost of the building, is based on the office space used by the agency.

  (B) It is in everyone's interest for the poor to be assisted with heating costs.

  (C) Do you understand the meaning of the expression, "full faith and credit"?

  (D) No mistakes

255. (A) You must explain that in the United States, there is no government interference with the arts.

(B) The failure to pay back loans is a major cause of the failure of banks.

(C) The former Soviet Union was unsuccessful in curbing youth's "addiction" to hard rock and heavy metal.

(D) No mistakes

256. (A) The convicted spy was hanged at sunrise.

(B) The lady looked well in her new boots.

(C) Neither the manager nor the employees want to work overtime.

(D) No mistakes

257. (A) The town consists of three distinct sections, of which the western one is by far the larger.

(B) His speech is so precise as to seem affected.

(C) The door opens, and in walk John and Mary.

(D) No mistakes

258. (A) His testimony today is different from that of yesterday.

(B) If you had studied the problem carefully, you would have found the solution more quickly.

(C) The flowers smelled so sweet that the whole house was perfumed.

(D) No mistakes

259. (A) Band practice is every other Tuesday.

(B) Charlotte and Kelly are planning a Memorial Day tribute with the local Firefighters.

(C) The deadline for signing up for soccer is next Friday.

(D) No mistakes

260. (A) My parents love to go on vacations with my sister and me.

(B) Last year, we went to Honolulu, Hawaii.

(C) We went to a luau and watched fire eaters.

(D) No mistakes

261. (A) That business is good appears to be true.

(B) The school secretary was pleased that the courses she had taken were relevant to her work.

(C) Strict accuracy is a necessary requisite in record keeping.

(D) No mistakes

262. (A) The expression "Thanking you in advance" is unacceptable in modern practice.

(B) I like Burns's poem "To a Mountain Daisy."

(C) Venetian blinds—called that even though they probably did not originate in Venice, are no longer used in most homes.

(D) No mistakes

263. (A) You see, you did mail the letter to yourself!

(B) Your introduction to your new classmates has been a pleasant experience, has it not.

(C) During the broadcast, you are expected to stand, to salute, and to sing the fourth stanza of "America."

(D) No mistakes

264. (A) Participation in active sports produces both release from tension as well as physical well-being.

(B) One or the other of those clerks is responsible for these errors.

(C) None of the rocks that form the solid crust of our planet is more than two billion years old.

(D) No mistakes

265. **(A)** We all prefer those other kinds of candy.

(B) The law prescribes when, where, and to whom the tax should be paid.

(C) Everything would have turned out right if she had only waited.

(D) No mistakes

266. **(A)** Yesterday they laid their uniforms aside with the usual end-of-the-season regret.

(B) John told William that he was sure he had seen it.

(C) He determined to be guided by the opinion of whoever spoke first.

(D) No mistakes

267. **(A)** Because a man understands a woman does not mean they are necessarily compatible.

(B) After much talk and haranguing, the workers received an increase in wages.

(C) If I am chosen, I will try and attend every meeting that is called.

(D) No mistakes

268. **(A)** While driving through the mountain pass, the breathtaking scenes awed the travelers.

(B) I do not understand why mother should object to my playing the piano at the party.

(C) My experience in South Africa taught me that the climate there is quite different from ours.

(D) No mistakes

269. **(A)** To learn to speak a foreign language fluently requires much practice.

(B) Buzzing around the picnic basket, a bumblebee flew into Sam's open mouth.

(C) It would be interesting to compare the interior of one of the pyramids in Mexico with that of one of the pyramids in Egypt.

(D) No mistakes

270. **(A)** "Complaints from the public," reports a government official, "are no longer considered to be a mere nuisance."

(B) Statistics tell us, "that heart disease kills more people than any other illness."

(C) According to a report released by the Department of Agriculture, the labor required to produce a bushel of wheat in 1830 was 3 hours.

(D) No mistakes

271. **(A)** His written work has been done in so careless a manner that I refuse to read it.

(B) I never feel badly if after trying hard I fail to win a prize; the effort gives me satisfaction.

(C) Neither the United States nor, for that matter, any other country has seriously regretted having joined the United Nations.

(D) No mistakes

272. **(A)** My landlord does not approve of my sending that letter to the local rent control agency.

(B) My artist friend and myself were the only guests in the gallery to truly appreciate the abstract paintings on display.

(C) The messenger will have gone to the airport before the package can be sent to the shipping room.

(D) No mistakes

273. **(A)** Between you and me, I must say that I find this whole situation to be ridiculous.

(B) The dimensions of the envelope determine the quantity of material that can be enclosed.

(C) The reason why the train was so late today was because the previous train had been derailed.

(D) No mistakes

274. (A) Due to the impending snowstorm, we will go directly home instead of stopping for ice cream.

(B) The eraser was lost after it had lain alongside the typewriter for weeks.

(C) Please distribute these newly arrived booklets among all the teachers in the building.

(D) No mistakes

275. (A) The lecture was interrupted by the whirring, often much too loud, of the street-repair machinery right outside the window.

(B) Mandated school courses include mathematics, literature, history, and science; optional subjects include drama, marching band, and weaving.

(C) The pupil's account of his lateness is incredible, I will not give him a classroom pass.

(D) No mistakes

276. (A) Winter came before the archaeologists could do anything more than mark out the burial site.

(B) Since her concentration was disrupted by the loud noise, she decided to wash her hair.

(C) Let's you and me settle the matter between ourselves.

(D) No mistakes

277. (A) I recommend that you participate in all the discussions and heed the council of your elders.

(B) Upon graduation from the training course, my friend will be assigned to a permanent position.

(C) He finally realized that the extra practice had had a visible effect on his accuracy at the foul line.

(D) No mistakes

278. (A) That unfortunate family faces the problem of adjusting itself to a new way of life.

(B) The secretary promptly notified the principal of the fire for which he was highly praised.

(C) All questions regarding procedure should be referred to a disinterested expert.

(D) No mistakes

Directions: For questions 279–288, look for mistakes in spelling only.

279. (A) A novocaine shot promises only transient pain in place of agony from prolonged drilling.

(B) I will join the theater party next week if I am able to locate a responseble babysitter.

(C) That painting is so valuable that it is described as priceless.

(D) No mistakes

280. (A) The cirkumference of a circle is the distance around its outer edge.

(B) Every accused is entitled to trial before an impartial jury.

(C) Now that the snow has been cleared from the streets, the mayor is able to rescind the no-parking order.

(D) No mistakes

281. (A) A timid person is likely to be terrified of weird noises in the night.

(B) Persons who are taking certain medicines should confine themselves to drinking caffeine-free coffee.

(C) Examinations such as this one are, unfortunately, a necessary evil.

(D) No mistakes

282. (A) The eager young politician stood at the street corner handing out political pamphlets.
(B) If you do not watch your eating habits in a foreign country, you may return with an intestinal paresite.
(C) My childhood heroes were mainly cartoon characters.
(D) No mistakes

283. (A) Begin to descend into the cave by way of the staircase just beyond the huge copper beech tree.
(B) Admissible evidence is evidence that has been collected in entirely legal ways.
(C) Since our army is so outnumbered, we might as well conceed defeat and limit our casualties.
(D) No mistakes

284. (A) The scavengers desecrated many native graves.
(B) Be sure you enter your figures in a straight column.
(C) Even an exorbitant charge does not guarantee that the doctor will perform a thorough examination.
(D) No mistakes

285. (A) The prologue to the play greatly enhanced its meaning.
(B) Handicapped students may sometimes join their classmates for assembly programs and physical education classes.
(C) The error on the scoreboard was immediately noticable to all.
(D) No mistakes

286. (A) The union and management agreed that the reccomendation of the arbitrator would be binding.
(B) Parallel lines never meet.
(C) Drinking and driving often combine to conclude with a tragic accident.
(D) No mistakes

287. (A) The hospital issued a daily bulletin regarding the movie star's medical condition.
(B) Please do not interrup my telephone conversation.
(C) The newest soft contact lenses allow for extended wear.
(D) No mistakes

288. (A) The manufacturer's reply was terse but cordial.
(B) Every student who was questioned gave a similar explanation.
(C) The writer has created a clever psuedonym for himself.
(D) No mistakes

Directions: For questions 289–298, look for errors in composition. Follow the directions for each question.

289. Choose the best word or words to join the thoughts together.
The soldiers will not come home _____ the war is over.
(A) while
(B) since
(C) before
(D) None of these

290. Choose the best word or words to join the thoughts together.
We enjoyed the movie _____ the long wait in line.
(A) during
(B) despite
(C) because of
(D) None of these

291. Choose the group of words that best completes this sentence.

She avoided my look of surprise by _____

- **(A)** staring at the ceiling steadily.
- **(B)** staring up at the steady ceiling.
- **(C)** staring up steadily at the ceiling.
- **(D)** steadily staring at the ceiling.

292. Which of these expresses the idea most clearly?

- **(A)** You can swim in tropical waters and see glass-bottomed boats, colorful fish, and coral reefs.
- **(B)** You can see glass-bottomed fish swimming among coral reefs and colorful boats in tropical waters.
- **(C)** In tropical waters you can see glass-bottomed boats, colorful fish, and coral reefs swimming.
- **(D)** From glass-bottomed boats you can see colorful fish swimming in tropical waters among coral reefs.

293. Which of these expresses the idea most clearly?

- **(A)** Backgammon is a complex game, and you must change strategies often to learn it well.
- **(B)** Though backgammon is easy to learn, it is a complex game which requires frequent shifts of strategy when played well.
- **(C)** To learn to play backgammon you must shift complex strategies easily.
- **(D)** You must easily learn to shift strategies to play the complex game of backgammon well.

294. Choose the pair of sentences that best develops this topic sentence.

Computers came along at just the right moment.

- **(A)** Cities were growing larger and spreading farther. People found they couldn't gather facts fast enough to make needed decisions.
- **(B)** The computer is a mass of complex parts and flashing lights. However, it is still just a machine made by humans to serve humans.
- **(C)** The most unusual use for computers lately has been in the supermarket. At the wave of a wand, the computer can read what a person has bought.
- **(D)** The computer aids business by storing information. It is able to provide this information almost as soon as a problem comes up.

295. Which of the following sentences offers *least* support to the topic "The Need to Protect the Bald Eagle"?

- **(A)** In flight, the bald eagle is beautiful.
- **(B)** Today, it enjoys the full protection of the law and seems to be slowly increasing.
- **(C)** It is so plentiful that it is seen as a dangerous rival to the fishing industry.
- **(D)** The game laws of Alaska are under local jurisdiction.

296. Which of these best fits under the topic "The Squid—A Master of Disguise"?

- **(A)** Because the squid is shy, it is often misunderstood.
- **(B)** Little sacs of pigment enable the squid to change its color.
- **(C)** In reality, they are adaptable, intelligent, and often beautiful.
- **(D)** They propel themselves backward by squirting water out of a nozzle located near their heads.

297. Which sentence does *not* belong in the paragraph?

(1) Intense religious zeal was the main reason for the Crusades, but it was not the only reason. (2) The Crusades weakened feudalism. (3) Businessmen saw good opportunities to set up new markets in the East. (4) Some knights hoped to win military glory, and many just sought adventure.

(A) Sentence 1

(B) Sentence 2

(C) Sentence 3

(D) Sentence 4

298. Where should the sentence "Man is learning" be placed in the paragraph below?

(1) His past experiences have taught him well. (2) He imports ladybugs to destroy aphids. (3) He irrigates, fertilizes, and rotates his crops.

(A) Before sentence 1

(B) Between sentences 1 and 2

(C) Between sentences 2 and 3

(D) The sentence does not fit in this paragraph.

STOP End of Language section. If you have any time left, go over your work in this section only. Do not work in any other section of the test.

ANSWER KEYS AND EXPLANATIONS

Verbal Skills

1. C	13. B	25. B	37. D	49. D
2. A	14. D	26. A	38. B	50. B
3. B	15. C	27. C	39. A	51. C
4. B	16. D	28. C	40. C	52. C
5. D	17. B	29. B	41. D	53. D
6. C	18. A	30. C	42. A	54. B
7. A	19. C	31. D	43. B	55. C
8. D	20. A	32. C	44. B	56. C
9. A	21. C	33. D	45. C	57. A
10. B	22. A	34. A	46. B	58. C
11. C	23. C	35. C	47. A	59. B
12. B	24. D	36. A	48. B	60. D

1. **The correct answer is (C).** *Fourth* is an ordinal number. The other three are cardinal numbers.

2. **The correct answer is (A).** *Arouse* and *pacify* are antonyms, as are *agitate* and *smooth. Ruffle* is a synonym for *agitate.*

3. **The correct answer is (B).** From the least expensive to the most expensive: rolls—bagels—muffins. Muffins are more expensive than rolls, not less.

4. **The correct answer is (B).** A query is a question.

5. **The correct answer is (D).** To *impair* is to damage or to *weaken.*

6. **The correct answer is (C).** *Death* is the fact of dying. The other choices are crimes, one of which just happens to cause death.

7. **The correct answer is (A).** That which is *variable* is changeable, fluctuating, or *shifting.*

8. **The correct answer is (D).** The relationship is that of object to action. When one *beats* an *egg,* one performs a violent act upon the substance of the egg in preparation for eating. When one *mashes* a *potato,* one performs an analogous act upon the potato. Baking a potato prepares it for eating, but the act of baking is not analogous to the act of beating. If *mash* were not offered as a choice, *bake* might have served as the answer. You must always choose the best answer available.

9. **The correct answer is (A).** To *obstruct* is to "clog" or to *block.*

10. **The correct answer is (B).** Jane has 15¢ less than Barbara; Barry has 25¢ less than Barbara. Barry has less money than Jane, not more.

11. **The correct answer is (C).** *Fever* is a symptom. All the other choices are diseases.

12. **The correct answer is (B).** The *result* is the end product of a *cause.* A synonym for *result* is "effect." Do not confuse "effect" with *affect,* which means "influence."

13. The correct answer is (B). The analogy is one of opposites or antonyms. *Clumsy* is the opposite of *skillful; awkward* is the opposite of *deft. Agile* is a synonym for *deft.*

14. The correct answer is (D). A cave is a naturally occurring shelter that might be used as a dwelling place. All the other choices are man-made.

15. The correct answer is (C). Pretzel, the dachshund, is clearly less shaggy than Pepper and so could be in the same dog obedience class, but there is no information to suggest that Pretzel even goes to obedience school.

16. The correct answer is (D). The relationship is that of part to whole or, more specifically, that of the center to its surroundings. The *pit* is at the center of the *peach;* the *sun* is at the center of the *solar system.*

17. The correct answer is (B). *Revenue* means *income.* Taxes produce revenue, but they are not in themselves revenue.

18. The correct answer is (A). A *trapeze* is a short horizontal bar that gymnasts and aerialists swing from and upon which they perform. All the other choices are tools that make work easier.

19. The correct answer is (C). *Tears* may well come as a sign of emotion. All the other choices are emotions themselves.

20. The correct answer is (A). From fastest to slowest jumper, we have: Cleo—Lori—Inez—Linda—Mary.

21. The correct answer is (C). *Manual,* as opposed to automatic or mechanical, means *hand-operated.*

22. The correct answer is (A). *Marshy* means "boggy" or *swampy.*

23. The correct answer is (C). The relationship is that of actor to object or, if you like, eater to eaten. A *seal* eats *fish;* a *bird* eats *worms.*

24. The correct answer is (D). *Loss* is the opposite of *profit.*

25. The correct answer is (B). *Activity* is motion. *Rest* is freedom from activity.

26. The correct answer is (A). *Wind* is the general term for air in motion. All the other choices are descriptions of winds based upon wind speed.

27. The correct answer is (C). All people eaters are purple, but it does not necessarily follow that all things purple eat people. We cannot tell whether or not there are some cyclops that are purple even though they do not eat people.

28. The correct answer is (C). A *stench* is an offensive smell, or *foul odor.*

29. The correct answer is (B). The word *immaterial* means *unimportant.*

30. The correct answer is (C). From the heaviest to the lightest books, the order is blue, orange, green, and red. Although we are told that orange books are not as light as yellow books, we cannot tell whether yellow books are heavier or lighter than the green books.

31. The correct answer is (D). A *shoe* is made of *leather;* a *highway* is made of *asphalt.*

32. The correct answer is (C). To *mend* is to *repair,* which is the opposite of *destroy.*

33. The correct answer is (D). *Concrete* means "specific" or "particular." *Abstract* means "general" or "theoretical."

34. The correct answer is (A). To *function* is to *operate* or to "work."

35. The correct answer is (C). *Meat* is food. All the other choices are nutrients found in food.

36. The correct answer is (A). Because all Ts are either green-eyed Ys or blue-tailed Gs, it is reasonable to assume that some are blue-tailed Gs. Because all blue-tailed Gs have red noses, we can safely assume that some Ts, at least those that are blue-tailed Gs, have red noses.

37. The correct answer is (D). *Sullen* means "morose" or *angrily silent.* The word meaning "grayish yellow" is "sallow"; that meaning "soaking wet" is "sodden"; that meaning "very dirty" is "sordid."

38. The correct answer is (B). *Monkey* is the general term describing a whole class of primates, regardless of gender. All the other choices are specifically male animals.

39. The correct answer is (A). You *taste* with your *tongue;* you *touch* with your *finger.* The sense of touch has to do with feeling, but the organ of touch to be found among the choices is *finger,* which is analogous to *tongue* in its relation to *taste.*

40. The correct answer is (C). *Discord* means "deep disagreement." Music may be either harmonious or discordant.

41. The correct answer is (D). *Fumes* are gas, smoke, or vapor emanations. The other choices describe the smell of fumes.

42. The correct answer is (A). *Riding* is a passive act; an animal or machine does the transporting. All the other choices are active ways in which to move from one place to another.

43. The correct answer is (B). *Fatal* means "causing death" or *deadly.*

44. The correct answer is (B). Terry has won the most races of all.

45. The correct answer is (C). A *brick* is opaque. All the other choices are translucent.

46. The correct answer is (B). *Secure* means *safe,* as in "not exposed to danger."

47. The correct answer is (A). *Garish* means "gaudy" and "glaring."

48. The correct answer is (B). This is a sequential relationship. The sequence is from parent to child. *Horse* is the parent; *foal* the child. *Mother* is the parent; *son* the child. The gender of the parent and child is irrelevant to this analogy.

49. The correct answer is (D). A *sourball* is a very hard food. All the other choices are soft foods.

50. The correct answer is (B). That which is *counterfeit* is an "imitation made with intent to defraud" and, hence, *false.*

51. The correct answer is (C). All you know is that the thruway and the highway have more lanes then the parkway.

52. The correct answer is (C). In this actor-and-object relationship, the actor serves as an irritant to the object. Thus, a *flea* irritates a *dog;* a *fly* irritates a *horse.* A rider might at times irritate a horse but not with such consistency as a fly.

53. The correct answer is (D). The word *intermittently* means "recurring from time to time."

54. The correct answer is (B). *Acrylic* refers to a resin product—fiber, paint, or adhesive. The other choices refer to languages that are printed in different alphabets. If you had trouble with this, you were probably thinking of *Cyrillic,* the alphabet in which the Russian language is written.

55. The correct answer is (C). *Diverse* means "different."

56. The correct answer is (C). The *finder* seeks and receives a *reward;* the *repenter* seeks and receives *absolution* (from sin). *Contrition* is the feeling the repenter must have in order to repent. *Religion* may be associated with *repentance* but without the same essential actor-to-object relationship.

57. The correct answer is (A). When an object *bends,* it changes shape or orientation but remains intact. All the other choices refer to breaking apart.

58. The correct answer is (C). We are told only relative positions with regard to north and south but have no information as to proximity or what is adjacent to what. We cannot tell from this information exactly where the grocery store is in relation to the dry cleaner.

59. The correct answer is (B). *Deception* means *fraud* or "subterfuge."

60. The correct answer is (D). *Nylon* is a synthetic fiber. All the other choices are natural fibers.

Quantitative Skills

61. B	72. D	83. D	93. C	103. A
62. C	73. C	84. B	94. C	104. B
63. D	74. A	85. C	95. D	105. C
64. B	75. C	86. A	96. A	106. D
65. A	76. A	87. D	97. D	107. C
66. D	77. B	88. A	98. B	108. A
67. C	78. A	89. D	99. D	109. B
68. C	79. B	90. B	100. A	110. C
69. A	80. C	91. B	101. B	111. A
70. D	81. B	92. D	102. A	112. D
71. B	82. A			

61. The correct answer is (B). If you write the direction and amount of change between the numbers of the series, you see that the pattern of the series is –1, –2, –1, –3, –1, –4, ... The next step is –1. 11 – 1 = 10.

62. The correct answer is (C). The relationships are clearly visible. Just read and examine carefully.

63. The correct answer is (D). First do the arithmetic. (A) is 15; (B) is 125; and (C) is 9. Obviously, (B) is greater than either (A) or (C).

64. The correct answer is (B). 60% of 40 = 24 – 5 = 19.

65. The correct answer is (A). The pattern is +2, –4, +2, –4, and so on. 44 + 2 = 46.

66. The correct answer is (D). The cube of 4 divided by 4 is the square of 4 = 16. 16 + 3 = 19.

67. The correct answer is (C). 6 + 12 + 4 + 41 + 7 = 70 ÷ 5 = 14 × 2 = 28.

68. The correct answer is (C). The series so far is: –2, –2, –3, –3, –4, –4; next should come –5, –5. 24 – 5 = 19 – 5 = 14.

69. The correct answer is (A). The series on both sides of the blank reads +6, –8. 25 + 6 = 31. Then, to confirm, 31 – 8 = 23.

70. The correct answer is (D). Angle C is a right angle (90°). The three angles of a triangle must add up to 180°. Therefore, the sum of the other two angles is equal to 90°.

71. The correct answer is (B). $6 \times 4 = 24$. 24 is $\frac{2}{3}$ of 36.

72. The correct answer is (D). 42 + 3 = 45. 45 ÷ 9 = 5.

73. The correct answer is (C). Count up the shaded areas, taking note of the fact that some areas are larger than others. Then choose your answer by inspection and careful reading.

74. The correct answer is (A). The series reads: +9, +10, +11, +12, +13. Continue: 57 + 14 = 71 + 15 = 86 + 16 = 102.

75. The correct answer is (C). Doing the math, (B) = 0.858. The decimal form of (C) = 0.875, which makes it equal to (A). Now you can see that there is only one true statement.

76. The correct answer is (A). $69 - 6 = 63 \div 7 = 9$.

77. The correct answer is (B). (A) is 4; (B) is 6; (C) is 4. Now just be careful.

78. The correct answer is (A). (A) is 150; (B) is 300; (C) is 500; and (D) is 350.

79. The correct answer is (B). Sometimes you must shift gears. Most series are based upon addition and subtraction but not all. You cannot make sense of this series if you stick to the $+8$ with which you probably started out. The relationship between 9 and 18 and between 15 and 30 should make you think of multiplication. The series reads: $\times 2, -7, \times 2, -7, \times 2, -7, \ldots$ $11 \times 2 = 22$. To confirm: $22 - 7 = 15$.

80. The correct answer is (C). You should see that the pattern is developing: $+1, +1, +2, +2, +3, +3, +4, \ldots$ $18 + 4 = 22$.

81. The correct answer is (B). Let x equal the number.

$30\% + 50\% = 80\% = 0.80$
$0.80x = 96; x = 96 \div 0.80 = 120$

82. The correct answer is (A). $12 + 87 + 72 + 41 = 212 \div 4 = 53 - 25 = 28$.

83. The correct answer is (D). The series $+1, -2, +1, -3, +1, -4$ now continues with $+1$. $18 + 1 = 19$.

84. The correct answer is (B). Read, count, and reason carefully.

85. The correct answer is (C). $\frac{4}{5}$ of $80 = 64 + 3 = 67$. $82 - 67 = 15$.

86. The correct answer is (A). The series as we see it reads $+10, +9, +8, \underline{\hspace{1cm}}, +6, +5$. Fill in with $32 + 7 = 39$.

87. The correct answer is (D). (A) is 36; (B) is 64; and (C) is 144. Plug in the numbers and find the answer.

88. The correct answer is (A). Work out the arithmetic and learn that (A), (B), and (C) all are equal to 51. Now there is only one true statement.

89. The correct answer is (D). $8 \times 4 = 32 \times 3 = 96 - 30 = 66$.

90. The correct answer is (B). $\frac{1}{8}$ of $96 = 12 \times 6 = 72$.

91. The correct answer is (B). The series may be interpreted as a repetition of $+0.125$ or as increasing decimals of $\frac{1}{8}, \frac{2}{8}, \frac{3}{8}$ and so on.

92. The correct answer is (D). Count, then read carefully.

93. The correct answer is (C). $\frac{5}{9}$ of $99 = 55 + 15 = 70$.

94. The correct answer is (C). The easiest way to find the solution is to try out each of the answers.

$$\frac{9}{16} \div \frac{3}{4} = \frac{9}{16} \times \frac{4}{3} = \frac{3}{4}; \frac{5}{8} \div \frac{3}{4} = \frac{5}{6};$$
$$\frac{7}{16} \div \frac{3}{4} = \frac{7}{12}; \frac{3}{4} \div \frac{3}{4} = 1.$$

95. The correct answer is (D). 0.8 and 80% are equal, but $\frac{8}{10}\%$ is only 0.008. Now it's easy.

96. The correct answer is (A). The order of the lengths of the line segments, shortest to longest, is (B), (C), (A), (D).

97. The correct answer is (D). You should see quite readily that the series is based on squares followed by their positive number square roots in descending order. The missing number is the square of 7.

98. The correct answer is (B). The letters progress by $+3$. The numbers progress by -4. Three letters after K is N. $13 - 4 = 9$.

99. The correct answer is (D). After you look beyond the first two numbers, you can see that the progression is $\times 3$, repeat the number, $\times 3$, repeat the number, $\times 3$, repeat the number. We pick up the series at $27 \times 3 = 81$. Then repeat the number 81. Then, $81 \times 3 = 243$.

100. The correct answer is (A). If $\frac{3}{8}x = 9$, then

$3x = 72$ and $x = \frac{72}{3}$. So, $x = 24$.

$83\frac{1}{3}\%$, or $\frac{5}{6}$, of $24 = 20$.

101. The correct answer is (B). The size of the angle is easily read on the arc of the protractor. (A) = 70°; (B) = 60°; and (C) = 50°. A right angle is 90°. Now, plug the angle sizes into the statements to find the answer.

102. The correct answer is (A). (A) is 40; (B) is 40; and (C) is 32. Use numbers in place of the letters and solve.

103. The correct answer is (A). Don't be thrown by the negative numbers. The series is: +5, +2, +5, +2. Next comes +5. –5 + 5 = 0.

104. The correct answer is (B). $4 \times 5 = 20 \times 3 = 60$. We need to add nothing at all (0) to 60 to get 60.

105. The correct answer is (C). This is a simple ÷ 2 series; the decimals make it a bit confusing. $0.025 \div 2 = 0.0125$

106. The correct answer is (D). $\frac{5}{8}$ of $96 = 60$

$-12 = 48$.

107. The correct answer is (C). (A) is 21¢; (B) is 28¢; and (C) is 25¢. Replace letters with money amounts and answer the question.

108. The correct answer is (A). The progress of the series is +3. 18 + 3 = 21. However, in the small segment that we see, the series alternates two Roman numerals and two Arabic numbers. Having no reason to suppose that this alternation will change later in the series, we must assume that the next entry will be a Roman numeral. Hence, XXI is the correct form for the next number in the series.

109. The correct answer is (B). This is a ÷2 series, which you might find somewhat hard to visualize in the fraction form. Rename the improper fractions as whole numbers to make this clear:

$\frac{16}{2} = 8; \frac{8}{2} = 4; \frac{8}{4} = 2; \frac{8}{8} = 1; \frac{8}{16} = \frac{1}{2}.$

The correct answer, $\frac{8}{32}$, is $\frac{8}{16} \div 2$.

$\frac{8}{16} \div 2 = \frac{8}{16} \times \frac{1}{2} = \frac{8}{32}$

110. The correct answer is (C). (A) is 95; (B) is 1.95; (C) is 95. Work with the numbers instead of the letters to find the answer.

111. The correct answer is (A). This is another instance in which it is easiest to try out the answers. 40% of 150 = 60. 150 – 60 = 90. Because the first choice works, there is no reason to continue. Choices (B) and (C), being less than 90, could not possibly be correct. If you wanted to be doubly sure (and if you had spare time), you could try 40% of 145 = 58. 145 – 58 = 87, which is not 90.

112. The correct answer is (D). The pattern being established is: –8, repeat the number, –6, repeat the number, –4, repeat the number. Logically, the next step is –2, repeat the number. 8 – 2 = 6; then repeat the 6.

Reading

COMPREHENSION

113. C	121. D	129. C	137. D	145. B
114. D	122. C	130. B	138. A	146. A
115. C	123. A	131. D	139. D	147. D
116. D	124. D	132. C	140. A	148. D
117. C	125. C	133. D	141. B	149. A
118. B	126. B	134. D	142. B	150. B
119. A	127. A	135. A	143. C	151. B
120. B	128. D	136. C	144. C	152. C

113. The correct answer is (C). The selection is about a game that appears to be an early version of modern baseball.

114. The correct answer is (D). There were "usually between 8 and 20 players." The number of players was not fixed by rule. In fact, according to the last sentence, there were very few rules.

115. The correct answer is (C). One of the few rules defined the playing field as a 60-foot square.

116. The correct answer is (D). The first sentence tells us that the game was similar to the English game of rounders. The game probably derived its name from the fact that players ran around the bases. The second sentence assures us that the game was exciting for both players and spectators.

117. The correct answer is (C). The ball is described as a bullet, cork, or metal slug wound with yarn and string, obviously improvised to be put into service by that moment's group of players.

118. The correct answer is (B). The nineteenth century consists of the years in the 1800s. The game is placed in the early nineteenth century, from 1800 on. Its popularity increased throughout the first half of the century, so it clearly was played at least until 1850—and probably beyond.

119. The correct answer is (A). Compare your knowledge of the game of baseball as it is played today with the description of the game in the selection. You can readily see how much more complicated the game is today.

120. The correct answer is (B). The simple, improvised equipment made this a low-cost pastime. The players were not exceptionally skillful, and the game was only an American adaptation of an English game.

121. The correct answer is (D). The paddle with the thick handle was sturdy.

122. The correct answer is (C). The writer of the passage expresses no feeling whatsoever. This is nothing more than a clear, factual report.

123. The correct answer is (A). Phoebes might be easy to catch and band, but the reason that Audubon chose them was that it was a pair of phoebes that had piqued his curiosity.

124. The correct answer is (D). The selection says that the message on the band requests that the finder notify the Fish and Wildlife Department.

125. The correct answer is (C). Any one of the answer choices could be true, but as used in this passage, a naturalist is specifically a person who studies birds and nature in general.

126. The correct answer is (B). The selection describes birdbanding as one method of studying the nesting habits, migration patterns, and populations of birds.

127. The correct answer is (A). The clue to this answer is in the first sentence: ". . . he wondered if they might be the same birds."

128. The correct answer is (D). The second sentence tells us that Audubon's banded phoebes returned to the same nesting place. He could legitimately assume that at least some other birds behaved in the same way.

129. The correct answer is (C). See the second sentence of the second paragraph.

130. The correct answer is (B). *Migration* refers to group movements. *Patterns* implies some form of organization in the movements, that the movements might be periodic rather than random. Migration patterns tend to be seasonal and dictated by the need for food-gathering, but the question asks for a definition, not a reason.

131. The correct answer is (D). *Extinction* is the dying out and total disappearance of a species.

132. The correct answer is (C). In explaining the value of the Fish and Wildlife Department's endeavors in its studies of birds, the author is encouraging the public to cooperate in reporting sightings of banded birds.

133. The correct answer is (D). Although the selection does describe the Wandorobo tribe in some detail, the main topic of the selection is the manner in which birds and men work together in their quest for honey.

134. The correct answer is (D). People fear the tsetse fly because it carries the blood parasite that causes the often fatal African sleeping sickness.

135. The correct answer is (A). The Wandorobo whistle. The bird chatters.

136. The correct answer is (C). The Indicator bird indicates the location of honey trees. Men use the smoke to dislodge the bees.

137. The correct answer is (D). The small offering of honey left by the Wandorobo is the bird's reward. A symbiotic relationship is the association of two dissimilar organisms for their mutual benefit.

138. The correct answer is (A). Bees do not like smoke. Smoke causes them to fly away to escape from the smoky area. When the bees leave, the Wandorobo collect the honey. Those few bees that somehow avoid the effects of the smoke, perhaps by being outside the tree trunk at the time, sting viciously.

139. The correct answer is (D). Would you believe this account if scientists had not confirmed it? It does sound unbelievable. There is no support for the other choices in this passage.

140. The correct answer is (A). If the Wandorobo are undaunted by bee stings, they ignore the stings.

141. The correct answer is (B). The bird chatters without stopping until the men answer it with whistles and begin to follow.

142. The correct answer is (B). The last sentence of the first paragraph tells us that the Wandorobo are nomads who make their homes wherever they find themselves at the end of the day. The Wandorobo are the only tribe that travels in the forest infested with the tsetse fly. Their diet is roots and fruits. They are very courageous, even in the face of stinging bees.

143. The correct answer is (C). Mr. Johannes selects films for showing. He is a student of history.

144. The correct answer is (C). The last sentence of the first paragraph tells us that youngsters from all five boroughs of the City of New York attend the program.

145. The correct answer is (B). Mr. Johannes makes no far-reaching claims for long-term effects of his films. All he claims is that children are open to a broader range of concepts and visual presentations than those of their daily experience.

answers practice test 6

146. The correct answer is (A). To *ferret out* is to "dig" or to "search out." A ferret is a weasel-like animal that hunts out small rodents by flushing them out of their burrows.

147. The correct answer is (D). Read carefully. The film series begins in September. The films are shown at the Museum of the City of New York at 11 a.m. and 3 p.m. on Saturdays only.

148. The correct answer is (D). Because Mr. Johannes chooses a wide variety of films and regularly fills his theater, he is obviously a good judge of children's tastes.

149. The correct answer is (A). The answer is in the first paragraph.

150. The correct answer is (B). The audience consists of children.

151. The correct answer is (B). The word *dusty* is a metaphor for "long-unused" or "almost forgotten." The cans may well have been dust-laden from long disuse, but the reels were well preserved if he was able to show them. At any rate, choice (B) is certainly true while choice (A) only possibly might be true. Without (B) as a choice, (A) might have been correct. You must always choose the best answer.

152. The correct answer is (C). Silhouettes are one-color dark outline shapes against a light background. As such, the shapes present motion, form, and limited features, mainly profiles. Details can be filled by an active imagination. Choice (B), if anything, would argue against popularity.

Vocabulary

153. C	158. A	163. D	167. D	171. D
154. B	159. B	164. A	168. D	172. B
155. D	160. C	165. A	169. B	173. C
156. A	161. A	166. B	170. B	174. A
157. D	162. C			

153. The correct answer is (C). *Tedious* means "monotonous," "boring," or *"tiresome."*

154. The correct answer is (B). To *rescind* is "to take back," "to revoke," or *to cancel.*

155. The correct answer is (D). *Diversity* is "difference," or *variety.*

156. The correct answer is (A). *Indigence* is "destitution," or *poverty.* The word that means "laziness" is "indolence."

157. The correct answer is (D). *Vindictive* means "eager to get even," or *revengeful.*

158. The correct answer is (A). *Remuneration* is "compensation," "reward," or *payment.*

159. The correct answer is (B). *Deficient* means "lacking," "incomplete," or *inadequate.*

160. The correct answer is (C). *Detrimental* means "causing damage," or *harmful.*

161. The correct answer is (A). *Accurate* means "precise," or *correct.*

162. The correct answer is (C). To *amplify* is "to make larger or stronger" or "to develop more fully," as with details and examples.

163. The correct answer is (D). To be *competent* is to be "sufficient," "permissible," "authorized," or *able.*

164. The correct answer is (A). *Infraction* is "breaking of the rules" or *violation*.

165. The correct answer is (A). *Relevant* means "related to the matter at hand," or *applicable*.

166. The correct answer is (B). A *manual* is a "book of instructions," or a *handbook*.

167. The correct answer is (D). A *device* is a machine devised for a specific purpose. Be careful to define only the underscored word. A *calculator* is a "computational device."

168. The correct answer is (D). *Conventional* means "customary," "usual," or *ordinary*.

169. The correct answer is (B). *Controversy* is "difference of opinion," "argument," or *debate*.

170. The correct answer is (B). *Diplomatic* means *tactful* when dealing with people.

171. The correct answer is (D). *Irate* means *angry*.

172. The correct answer is (B). *Durable* means *long-lasting,* even under conditions of hard use.

173. The correct answer is (C). *Extensive* means "comprehensive," "intensive," or *thorough*.

174. The correct answer is (A). The *inception* is the *beginning*.

Mathematics

CONCEPTS

175. D	180. D	185. A	190. A	195. C
176. B	181. B	186. C	191. B	196. A
177. A	182. C	187. D	192. C	197. B
178. B	183. A	188. D	193. A	198. D
179. C	184. C	189. C	194. A	

175. The correct answer is (D). The millions begin with the seventh digit to the left of the decimal place. Because you need 326 million, you can immediately eliminate choices (A) and (B). Read on: 900 thousand. You need look no further for the correct answer.

176. The correct answer is (B). You should know this answer instantly. If you do not, try out each option.

177. The correct answer is (A). The first 4 is in the billions place; the second, in the hundred-thousands place. If you had trouble with this problem, review the sections on how to read numbers and determine place values in your math textbook.

178. The correct answer is (B). You should recognize immediately that $\frac{1}{2}$ day is shorter than 25 hours and that 3,600 seconds is far shorter than 1,440 minutes. Narrowing down to the first two choices, you probably know that there are 1,440 minutes in a day. If you do not know this, multiply 24 by 60 to see for yourself.

179. The correct answer is (C). You should know what the exponents mean. Count the 5s and 3s carefully.

180. **The correct answer is (D).** Multiply and simplify.

$$\frac{3 \times 8}{6 \times 5} = \frac{24}{30} = \frac{4}{5}$$

181. **The correct answer is (B).** $0.5 = \frac{1}{2}$. Therefore, 0.5% must equal $\frac{1}{2}\%$.

182. **The correct answer is (C).** Because the sum of the angles of a triangle must always equal 180°, and because m∠B = 90°, angles A and C together must equal 90°. Do not allow yourself to be diverted by extra information. m∠C of the triangle is equal to 30°, so m∠A = 60°, but this knowledge is irrelevant to the question being asked. Do not waste time on unnecessary calculations.

183. **The correct answer is (A).** $9^2 = 81$. Because x is greater than 9, x^2 would have to be greater than 81. Obviously, then, x^2 is greater than 80.

184. **The correct answer is (C).** Many numbers are divisible by either 3 or 4 but not by both. All numbers that are divisible by both 3 and 4 are also divisible by their multiple, 12.

185. **The correct answer is (A).** Compare the digit in the hundredths place.

186. **The correct answer is (C).** The *greatest* common factor of 50 and 10 is 10 itself. 1 and 5 are also common factors, but they are smaller.

187. **The correct answer is (D).** For the sum to be smaller than the given number of an addition problem, the missing number must be negative.

188. **The correct answer is (D).** Begin as if you were solving an equation; subtract 2 from both sides. Now $3x > 10$. Quick inspection will show you that only 3×4 is greater than 10.

189. **The correct answer is (C).** The formula for determining the area of a circle is πr^2. $r = 3$; $r^2 = 3^2 = 9$.

190. **The correct answer is (A).** Because $x - 3 < 12$, x can be any number less than 15.

191. **The correct answer is (B).** Three gallons contain 12 quarts. The ratio is 3:12, or, in simplest form, 1:4.

192. **The correct answer is (C).** If $x = 0$, then $2x < 8$ because $2(0) < 8$. None of the other pairs results in a true statement.

193. **The correct answer is (A).** Simply divide $\frac{4}{5}$ by $\frac{1}{6}$ to find the answer. $\frac{4}{5} \div \frac{1}{6} = \frac{4}{5} \times \frac{6}{1} = \frac{24}{5} = 4\frac{4}{5}$.

194. **The correct answer is (A).** The intersection (∩) of two sets has as its elements only those numbers that are in both original sets.

195. **The correct answer is (C).** Mary's age now = x. Her sister's age now $x - 3$. In 5 years, her sister's age will be $x - 3 + 5 = x + 2$.

196. **The correct answer is (A).** Choice (B) is 4930; choice (C) is 133.

197. **The correct answer is (B).** $10 < 10.5$.

198. **The correct answer is (D).** The union of the two adjacent line segments creates one continuous line segment.

Problem-Solving

199. B	207. C	215. D	223. C	231. D
200. B	208. A	216. A	224. B	232. A
201. A	209. B	217. D	225. A	233. C
202. B	210. A	218. B	226. A	234. B
203. B	211. A	219. C	227. A	235. C
204. A	212. D	220. D	228. C	236. C
205. D	213. C	221. B	229. D	237. B
206. B	214. B	222. A	230. A	238. D

199. **The correct answer is (B).** For each teacher, there are 12 students. Because there are 16 teachers, there must be 12 × 16, or 192, students.

200. **The correct answer is (B).** If 3 inches equal 24 feet, 1 inch equals 8 feet. A line representing 96 feet, therefore, must be 12 inches long (96 ÷ 8 = 12).

201. **The correct answer is (A).** A store markup of 100% would exactly double the price. A 75% markup almost doubles the price. The $17 pants are priced at almost double their cost to the store. By estimation, the best answer is (A). To figure precisely, remember that a 75% markup is the equivalent of multiplying the cost by 175%, or 1.75.

$$\text{cost} \times 1.75 = 17.00$$
$$\text{cost} = 17.00 \div 1.75$$
$$\text{cost} = \$9.71$$

202. **The correct answer is (B).** Reduce the $17.00 price by 20%.

$$20\% \text{ of } 17.00 = \$17 \times 0.20 = \$3.40$$
$$\$17.00 - 3.40 = \$13.60 \text{ (new price)}$$

Therefore, (B) is the correct answer. Choice (A) indicates a reduction of only 20 cents. Choice (C) represents a reduction *to* 20% of the original price, or an 80% decrease in price.

203. **The correct answer is (B).** To find the perimeter, we add up the dimensions of all of the sides. Note that there are some parts that have not been assigned measurements, so we should infer that they are the same as those corresponding parts whose measurements have been designated because we are told to assume that there are right angles in the figure. Beginning at the bottom and moving clockwise, the dimensions are:

$$10" + 14" + 2" + 6" + 6" + 6" + 2" + 14"$$

These equal 60 inches. The correct answer is (B). If you selected choices (A), (C), or (D), you failed to add up all of the segments.

204. **The correct answer is (A).** The area is most easily found by multiplying the length of the figure by its width, and then subtracting the area of the small 6" × 6" square.

$$(14" \times 10") - (6" \times 6") = \text{area}$$
$$140 \text{ sq. in.} - 36 \text{ sq. in.} = 104 \text{ sq. in.}$$

Shapes such as this are often used for irregular pieces of carpeting or covering.

205. **The correct answer is (D).** A 16-minute call would cost $1.56 for the first 3 minutes, plus 22¢ for each of the 13 additional minutes. The total cost is found by $1.56 + 13(0.22) = $4.42.

206. **The correct answer is (B).** You have to read only the first and third sentences of the problem. The information in the second sentence is not relevant to the problem. The

winner received $\frac{1}{3}$ of the total, or $2700.

Thus, the total purse was $2700 \times 3 = \$8100$.

207. The correct answer is (C). Number of seats = 12 + 14 = 26

Number of passengers at station A = 14 + 4 = 18

Number of passengers at next stop = 18 − 8 + 13 = 23

Number of empty seats = 26 − 23 = 3

208. The correct answer is (A). Raising the sales tax from 5% to 8% is a raise of 3%. 3% of $250 = 0.03 × \$250 = \$7.50$.

209. The correct answer is (B). Simplify the numerator of the fraction, and then divide.

$$\frac{1\frac{3}{4} - \frac{1}{8}}{\frac{1}{8}} = \frac{1\frac{6}{8} - \frac{1}{8}}{\frac{1}{8}}$$

$$= \frac{1\frac{5}{8}}{\frac{1}{8}} = 1\frac{5}{8} \cdot \frac{8}{1}$$

$$= \frac{13}{8} \cdot \frac{8}{1} = 13$$

210. The correct answer is (A).

$$
\begin{array}{r}
1.970 \\
1.02\overline{)2.01000} \\
\underline{1\,02} \\
99\,0 \\
\underline{91\,8} \\
7\,20 \\
\underline{7\,14} \\
60
\end{array}
$$

211. The correct answer is (A). Begin working with the innermost parentheses and work your way out.

$-3 - [(2-1) - (3+4)] = -3 - [(1) - (7)]$

$= -3 - [1 - 7]$

$= -3 - [-6]$

$= -3 + 6$

$= 3$

212. The correct answer is (D). This is a good problem to do in your head. Note that 10% of 70 is 7. 140%, then, is 14 × 7, or 98.

213. The correct answer is (C). Borrow a gallon and add it to 2 quarts. Rewrite the problem. Remember that you borrowed.

$$
\begin{array}{r}
4 \text{ gallons } 6 \text{ quarts } 1 \text{ pint} \\
- \; 1 \text{ gallon } \;\; 3 \text{ quarts } 0 \text{ pints} \\
\hline
3 \text{ gallons } 3 \text{ quarts } 1 \text{ pint}
\end{array}
$$

214. The correct answer is (B). Bracket the multiplication and division first, and solve the problem.

$$\left(6 \div \frac{1}{3}\right) + \left(\frac{2}{3} \times 9\right)$$

$= 18 + 6$

$= 24$

215. The correct answer is (D). Substitute the values into the expression.

$$\sqrt{9 + 3(2) + 1}$$

$= \sqrt{9 + 6 + 1}$

$= \sqrt{16}$

$= 4$

216. The correct answer is (A). 7 is one-third of 21, and $\frac{2}{3}$ is one-third of 2.

217. The correct answer is (D). To find the average, find the sum of the addends and divide that sum by the number of addends.

$-10 + 6 + 0 + -3 + 22 = 15$

$15 \div 5 = 3$

218. The correct answer is (B). By knowing how many phones are in Adelaide (48,000) and how many serve each group of 100 in the population (12.8), we can find how many groups of 100 are in the population. 48,000 phones ÷ 12.8 phones per 100 of population = 3,750 groups of 100 in the population. $3,750 \times 100 = 375,000$ people.

219. The correct answer is (C). Four boards, each 2'9" long, total 11 feet. The carpenter must buy 11 feet of wood.

220. The correct answer is (D).

$$(4 \times 10^3) + 6 = 4006$$
$$(2 \times 10^3) + (3 \times 10) + 8 = 2038$$

The difference is 1968.

221. The correct answer is (B).

Area of a square $= s^2$
$$49 = 7^2$$
one side = 7 inches
$$P = 4s$$
$$P = 4 \times 7" = 28 \text{ inches}$$

222. The correct answer is (A).

$$r = 35 - (9)(-n)$$
$$r = 35 - (9)(-2)$$
$$r = 35 - (-18)$$
$$r = 35 + 18 = 53$$

To subtract signed numbers, change the sign of the subtrahend and proceed as in algebraic addition.

223. The correct answer is (C). First perform the operation within the parentheses. To cube a number, multiply it by itself, two times.

$$(3 + 4)^3 = (7)^3 = 7 \times 7 \times 7 = 343$$

224. The correct answer is (B). Copper and aluminum in the ratio of 10:1 means 10 parts copper to 1 part aluminum.

Let x = weight of aluminum, then $10x$ = weight of copper

$$10x + x = 77$$
$$11x = 77$$
$$x = 7$$

225. The correct answer is (A). His total income is equal to 8% of his sales plus $175. 8% of his sales is $1025 \times 0.08 = $82: $82 + $175 = $257.

226. The correct answer is (A).

$$x^2 + 5 = 41$$
$$x^2 = 41 - 5$$
$$x^2 = 36$$
$$x = \pm 6$$

227. The correct answer is (A). The lawn is $8' \times 12' = 96$ sq. ft.

$96 \times 5 = 480$ pints of water needed

8 pts. in 1 gal.; $480 \div 8 = 60$ gallons needed

228. The correct answer is (C).

$$\frac{x}{2} + 36 = 37.25$$
$$\frac{x}{2} = 37.25 - 36$$
$$\frac{x}{2} = 1.25$$
$$x = 2.50$$

229. The correct answer is (D). If the sides are parallel, the angles are congruent.

230. The correct answer is (A).

Area = length × width
Area = 168 ft. × 82 ft.
Area = 13,776 sq. ft.

231. The correct answer is (D).
$$63 \div \frac{1}{9} = 63 \times \frac{9}{1} = 567$$

This is a good answer to estimate. By dividing a number by $\frac{1}{9}$, you are, in effect, multiplying it by 9. Only one of the suggested answers is close.

232. The correct answer is (A). The amount the house was insured for is 80% of $83,000, or $66,400. The insurance is calculated at

45¢ per hundred, or $4.50 per thousand of value. Because there are 66.4 thousands of value, 66.4 × $4.50 per thousand equals the yearly premium of $298.80.

233. **The correct answer is (C).** Move the decimal point of the divisor two places to the right; do the same for the dividend. Then divide.

234. **The correct answer is (B).** The formula for the area of a triangle is

$A = \frac{1}{2}bh$. Plug in the numbers:

$A = \frac{1}{2} \cdot 12 \cdot 14$

$A = 84$ sq. ft.

235. **The correct answer is (C).** This is a tricky question. It doesn't ask for 150% of 72, but rather to increase 72 by 150%. Because 150% of 72 = 108, we add 72 and 108 for the correct answer. Careful reading is an important factor in test success.

236. **The correct answer is (C).** Write down both equations and add them together.

$$14x - 2y = 32$$
$$+ \quad x + 2y = 13$$
$$\overline{15x = 45}$$
$$x = 3$$

237. **The correct answer is (B).** If $a = 6$, $ab + 4 = 52$ becomes $6b + 4 = 52$.

If $6b + 4 = 52$

$6b = 52 - 4$

$6b = 48$

$b = 8$

238. **The correct answer is (D).** First convert to a 24-hour clock.

3:30 p.m. = 5:30

$$\begin{array}{r} 15:30 \\ - 8:50 \\ \hline 6:40 \end{array} = 6 \text{ hours } 40 \text{ minutes}$$

To subtract a greater number of minutes from a lesser number of minutes, "borrow" 60 minutes from the hour to enlarge the lesser number.

Language

239. C	251. B	263. B	275. C	287. B
240. C	252. A	264. A	276. D	288. C
241. B	253. D	265. D	277. A	289. C
242. A	254. A	266. B	278. B	290. B
243. D	255. D	267. C	279. B	291. D
244. D	256. B	268. A	280. A	292. D
245. A	257. A	269. D	281. D	293. B
246. D	258. D	270. B	282. B	294. A
247. B	259. B	271. B	283. C	295. C
248. B	260. D	272. B	284. D	296. B
249. C	261. C	273. C	285. C	297. B
250. C	262. C	274. A	286. A	298. A

239. **The correct answer is (C).** *President of the United States* must be capitalized.

240. **The correct answer is (C).** The use of double negatives, *hadn't* and *none*, makes this sentence incorrect. It should read *hadn't seen any*.

241. **The correct answer is (B).** Each of the nurses, one at a time, *was* careful. In choice (C), *who*, rather than *whom*, is correctly the subject of the clause "who had hurt or . . . ."

242. **The correct answer is (A).** The letter *d* should be capitalized in *Day*, because Independence Day is a proper noun.

243. **The correct answer is (D).** No mistakes.

244. **The correct answer is (D).** No mistakes.

245. **The correct answer is (A).** Maintain the same voice throughout the sentence. "If *you* prepare, *you* can be confident." The statement, "If *one* prepares, *one* can be confident" would also be correct.

246. **The correct answer is (D).** No mistakes.

247. **The correct answer is (B).** The possessive form of *it* is *its*. *It's* is the contraction for *it is*.

248. **The correct answer is (B).** Tom and *me* are the objects of the verb *asked*.

249. **The correct answer is (C).** There is no reason for the word *countries* to begin with a capital letter.

250. **The correct answer is (C).** You cannot compare people with a city. "The citizens of Washington, like *those* of Los Angeles . . . ."

251. **The correct answer is (B).** *Less* is a measure of bulk amount. *Fewer* gives the count of individuals.

252. **The correct answer is (A).** The choice that you have not yet made cannot have already changed the meaning of the sentence "Do not make a choice that *changes* . . . ."

253. **The correct answer is (D).** No mistakes.

254. **The correct answer is (A).** The comma that separates subject from predicate does not belong there. The entire sentence at choice (C) is a question, so the question mark is correctly placed outside the quotation marks.

255. The correct answer is (D). No mistakes.

256. The correct answer is (B). It is unlikely that the new boots made the lady look healthy; they made her look *good,* that is, attractive.

257. The correct answer is (A). Three sections are being compared, so the superlative, *largest,* must be used. Choice (C) might sound awkward, but both verbs are in the present tense, and the sentence is correct.

258. The correct answer is (D). No mistakes.

259. The correct answer is (B). The word *fire-fighters* is not a proper noun, so it should not be capitalized.

260. The correct answer is (D). No mistakes.

261. The correct answer is (C). A *requisite* is a *necessity.* "Necessary requisite" is redundant.

262. The correct answer is (C). Dashes used to set apart amplifying but extraneous information must be used in pairs. The comma after *Venice* should be replaced by a dash.

263. The correct answer is (B). This direct question should end with a question mark. In choice (C), a period *always* goes inside the quotation marks, regardless of meaning.

264. The correct answer is (A). "Both" requires two objects connected by "and." Sports produce both release from tension *and* physical well-being.

265. The correct answer is (D). No mistakes.

266. The correct answer is (B). This sentence is ambiguous. To whom does the second *he* refer? Is John sure that John had seen it, or is John sure that William had seen it? In choice (A), *laid* is correctly used as the past tense of lay. In choice (C), *whoever* is the subject of the clause.

267. The correct answer is (C). Proper idiomatic form demands *try to attend.*

268. The correct answer is (A). The breathtaking scenes did not drive, but that is what the sentence implies. The *travelers* must be cast

as the subject of the sentence. "While driving . . ., the travelers were awed by . . . ."

269. The correct answer is (D). No mistakes.

270. The correct answer is (B). There is no direct quote here, so quotation marks are inappropriate, as is the comma following "us."

271. The correct answer is (B). Feeling *badly* refers to one's sense of touch. When referring to health or emotions, one feels *bad.*

272. The correct answer is (B). The correct subject of the sentence is "my artist friend and *I.*" The reflexive *myself* is used only when something is reflecting back on me as, for instance, "I was beside myself with grief."

273. The correct answer is (C). The *reason why* is not *because;* The *reason why is* that . . . . Or the *reason that* is *because* . . . . In choice (A), *you and me* are correctly the objects of the preposition *between.*

274. The correct answer is (A). It is poor form to begin a sentence with "due to." The correct introduction to such an explanatory statement is "because of." In choice (B), the past participle of the verb *to lie* is *lain.*

275. The correct answer is (C). This error is called a "comma splice." The cure might be to create two sentences, with a period at the end of the first, or to join the two independent clauses with either a semicolon or a conjunction such as "so."

276. The correct answer is (D). No mistakes.

277. The correct answer is (A). The wrong word has been used. A "council" is a group; *counsel,* the required word, means "advice."

278. The correct answer is (B). Was the secretary highly praised for the fire? Was the principal highly praised for the fire? If the sentence means to say that the secretary was highly praised for promptly notifying the principal, then that is what the sentence should say.

279. The correct answer is (B). The correct spelling is *responsible*.

280. The correct answer is (A). The correct spelling is *circumference*.

281. The correct answer is (D). No mistakes.

282. The correct answer is (B). The correct spelling is *parasite*.

283. The correct answer is (C). The correct spelling is *concede*.

284. The correct answer is (D). No mistakes.

285. The correct answer is (C). The correct spelling is *noticeable*. (See Spelling—Rule 4.)

286. The correct answer is (A). The correct spelling is *recommendation*.

287. The correct answer is (B). The correct spelling is *interrupt*.

288. The correct answer is (C). The correct spelling is *pseudonym*.

289. The correct answer is (C). The point is that the soldiers are busy fighting a war but will return when the war is over. They will not return before the war is over because they are busy fighting it.

290. The correct answer is (B). Choice (A) represents an impossibility, and choice (C) is ridiculous. If the movie is very good, one might consider it to have been worth the wait.

291. The correct answer is (D). The ceiling is "up," so choices (B) and (C) can be eliminated as containing redundancies. "Steadily" describes the manner in which she stared and so should be placed next to the word it describes.

292. The correct answer is (D). "Glass-bottomed fish" and "coral reefs swimming" make no sense at all. Choice (A) is technically correct, but the whole purpose of glass-bottomed boats is to peer down to observe the fish swimming among the coral reefs.

293. The correct answer is (B). Choice (D) is totally garbled. Choices (A) and (C) suggest that changing strategies is part of the learning process. The statement made by choice (B) is more reasonable.

294. The correct answer is (A). The growth of cities and the information explosion define the moment at which computers were needed.

295. The correct answer is (C). The threat that the bald eagle poses to the fishing industry counters the need to protect the bird.

296. The correct answer is (B). Changing one's color is a means for disguise.

297. The correct answer is (B). This sentence is an effect, not a reason.

298. The correct answer is (A). This sentence serves as a topic sentence and provides a subject. All the other sentences begin with pronouns referring to "man" and offer examples to bolster the topic sentence.

answers practice test 6

SCORE SHEET

Although your actual exam scores will not be reported as percentages, it may be helpful to convert your test scores to percentages so that you can see at a glance where your strengths and weaknesses lie. The numbers in parentheses represent the questions that test each skill area.

Subject	No. Correct ÷ No. of Questions	× 100 = _____ %
Verbal Analogies (2, 8, 13, 16, 23, 31, 39, 48, 52, 56)	_____ ÷ 10 = _____	× 100 = _____ %
Synonyms (5, 7, 9, 17, 21, 22, 28, 29, 34, 37, 43, 46, 50, 53, 59)	_____ ÷ 15 = _____	× 100 = _____ %
Logic (3, 10, 15, 20, 27, 30, 36, 44, 51, 58)	_____ ÷ 10 = _____	× 100 = _____ %
Verbal Classification (1, 6, 11, 14, 18, 19, 26, 35, 38, 41, 42, 45, 49, 54, 57, 60)	_____ ÷ 16 = _____	× 100 = _____ %
Antonyms (4, 12, 24, 25, 32, 33, 40, 47, 55)	_____ ÷ 9 = _____	× 100 = _____ %
TOTAL VERBAL SKILLS	_____ ÷ 60 = _____	× 100 = _____ %
Number Series (61, 65, 68, 69, 74, 79, 80, 83, 86, 91, 97, 98, 99, 103, 105, 108, 109, 112)	_____ ÷ 18 = _____	× 100 = _____ %
Geometric Comparisons (62, 70, 73, 78, 84, 92, 96, 101, 107)	_____ ÷ 9 = _____	× 100 = _____ %
Nongeometric Comparisons (63, 75, 77, 87, 88, 95, 102, 110)	_____ ÷ 8 = _____	× 100 = _____ %
Number Manipulation (64, 66, 67, 71, 72, 76, 81, 82, 85, 89, 90, 93, 94, 100, 104, 106, 111)	_____ ÷ 17 = _____	× 100 = _____ %
TOTAL QUANTITATIVE SKILLS	_____ ÷ 52 = _____	× 100 = _____ %
Reading—Comprehension (113–152)	_____ ÷ 40 = _____	× 100 = _____ %
Reading—Vocabulary (153–174)	_____ ÷ 22 = _____	× 100 = _____ %
TOTAL READING	_____ ÷ 62 = _____	× 100 = _____ %
Mathematics—Concepts (175–198)	_____ ÷ 22 = _____	× 100 = _____ %
Mathematics—Problem-Solving (199–238)	_____ ÷ 40 = _____	× 100 = _____ %
TOTAL MATHEMATICS	_____ ÷ 64 = _____	× 100 = _____ %
Punctuation and Capitalization (239, 242, 244, 247, 249, 253–255, 262, 263, 270, 275)	_____ ÷ 12 = _____	× 100 = _____ %
Usage (240, 241, 243, 245, 246, 248, 250–252, 256–261, 264–269, 271–274, 276–278)	_____ ÷ 28 = _____	× 100 = _____ %
Spelling (279–288)	_____ ÷ 10 = _____	× 100 = _____ %
Composition (289–298)	_____ ÷ 10 = _____	× 100 = _____ %
TOTAL LANGUAGE	_____ ÷ 60 = _____	× 100 = _____ %
TOTAL EXAM	_____ ÷ 298 = _____	× 100 = _____ %

ANSWER SHEET PRACTICE TEST 7: SSAT (UPPER LEVEL)

Part I: Writing Sample

_____

_____

_____

_____

_____

_____

_____

_____

_____

_____

_____

_____

_____

_____

_____

_____

_____

_____

_____

answer sheet

Part II: Multiple Choice

SECTION 1: VERBAL

1. Ⓐ Ⓑ Ⓒ Ⓓ Ⓔ	16. Ⓐ Ⓑ Ⓒ Ⓓ Ⓔ	31. Ⓐ Ⓑ Ⓒ Ⓓ Ⓔ	46. Ⓐ Ⓑ Ⓒ Ⓓ Ⓔ
2. Ⓐ Ⓑ Ⓒ Ⓓ Ⓔ	17. Ⓐ Ⓑ Ⓒ Ⓓ Ⓔ	32. Ⓐ Ⓑ Ⓒ Ⓓ Ⓔ	47. Ⓐ Ⓑ Ⓒ Ⓓ Ⓔ
3. Ⓐ Ⓑ Ⓒ Ⓓ Ⓔ	18. Ⓐ Ⓑ Ⓒ Ⓓ Ⓔ	33. Ⓐ Ⓑ Ⓒ Ⓓ Ⓔ	48. Ⓐ Ⓑ Ⓒ Ⓓ Ⓔ
4. Ⓐ Ⓑ Ⓒ Ⓓ Ⓔ	19. Ⓐ Ⓑ Ⓒ Ⓓ Ⓔ	34. Ⓐ Ⓑ Ⓒ Ⓓ Ⓔ	49. Ⓐ Ⓑ Ⓒ Ⓓ Ⓔ
5. Ⓐ Ⓑ Ⓒ Ⓓ Ⓔ	20. Ⓐ Ⓑ Ⓒ Ⓓ Ⓔ	35. Ⓐ Ⓑ Ⓒ Ⓓ Ⓔ	50. Ⓐ Ⓑ Ⓒ Ⓓ Ⓔ
6. Ⓐ Ⓑ Ⓒ Ⓓ Ⓔ	21. Ⓐ Ⓑ Ⓒ Ⓓ Ⓔ	36. Ⓐ Ⓑ Ⓒ Ⓓ Ⓔ	51. Ⓐ Ⓑ Ⓒ Ⓓ Ⓔ
7. Ⓐ Ⓑ Ⓒ Ⓓ Ⓔ	22. Ⓐ Ⓑ Ⓒ Ⓓ Ⓔ	37. Ⓐ Ⓑ Ⓒ Ⓓ Ⓔ	52. Ⓐ Ⓑ Ⓒ Ⓓ Ⓔ
8. Ⓐ Ⓑ Ⓒ Ⓓ Ⓔ	23. Ⓐ Ⓑ Ⓒ Ⓓ Ⓔ	38. Ⓐ Ⓑ Ⓒ Ⓓ Ⓔ	53. Ⓐ Ⓑ Ⓒ Ⓓ Ⓔ
9. Ⓐ Ⓑ Ⓒ Ⓓ Ⓔ	24. Ⓐ Ⓑ Ⓒ Ⓓ Ⓔ	39. Ⓐ Ⓑ Ⓒ Ⓓ Ⓔ	54. Ⓐ Ⓑ Ⓒ Ⓓ Ⓔ
10. Ⓐ Ⓑ Ⓒ Ⓓ Ⓔ	25. Ⓐ Ⓑ Ⓒ Ⓓ Ⓔ	40. Ⓐ Ⓑ Ⓒ Ⓓ Ⓔ	55. Ⓐ Ⓑ Ⓒ Ⓓ Ⓔ
11. Ⓐ Ⓑ Ⓒ Ⓓ Ⓔ	26. Ⓐ Ⓑ Ⓒ Ⓓ Ⓔ	41. Ⓐ Ⓑ Ⓒ Ⓓ Ⓔ	56. Ⓐ Ⓑ Ⓒ Ⓓ Ⓔ
12. Ⓐ Ⓑ Ⓒ Ⓓ Ⓔ	27. Ⓐ Ⓑ Ⓒ Ⓓ Ⓔ	42. Ⓐ Ⓑ Ⓒ Ⓓ Ⓔ	57. Ⓐ Ⓑ Ⓒ Ⓓ Ⓔ
13. Ⓐ Ⓑ Ⓒ Ⓓ Ⓔ	28. Ⓐ Ⓑ Ⓒ Ⓓ Ⓔ	43. Ⓐ Ⓑ Ⓒ Ⓓ Ⓔ	58. Ⓐ Ⓑ Ⓒ Ⓓ Ⓔ
14. Ⓐ Ⓑ Ⓒ Ⓓ Ⓔ	29. Ⓐ Ⓑ Ⓒ Ⓓ Ⓔ	44. Ⓐ Ⓑ Ⓒ Ⓓ Ⓔ	59. Ⓐ Ⓑ Ⓒ Ⓓ Ⓔ
15. Ⓐ Ⓑ Ⓒ Ⓓ Ⓔ	30. Ⓐ Ⓑ Ⓒ Ⓓ Ⓔ	45. Ⓐ Ⓑ Ⓒ Ⓓ Ⓔ	60. Ⓐ Ⓑ Ⓒ Ⓓ Ⓔ

SECTION 2: QUANTITATIVE (MATH)

1. Ⓐ Ⓑ Ⓒ Ⓓ Ⓔ	8. Ⓐ Ⓑ Ⓒ Ⓓ Ⓔ	14. Ⓐ Ⓑ Ⓒ Ⓓ Ⓔ	20. Ⓐ Ⓑ Ⓒ Ⓓ Ⓔ
2. Ⓐ Ⓑ Ⓒ Ⓓ Ⓔ	9. Ⓐ Ⓑ Ⓒ Ⓓ Ⓔ	15. Ⓐ Ⓑ Ⓒ Ⓓ Ⓔ	21. Ⓐ Ⓑ Ⓒ Ⓓ Ⓔ
3. Ⓐ Ⓑ Ⓒ Ⓓ Ⓔ	10. Ⓐ Ⓑ Ⓒ Ⓓ Ⓔ	16. Ⓐ Ⓑ Ⓒ Ⓓ Ⓔ	22. Ⓐ Ⓑ Ⓒ Ⓓ Ⓔ
4. Ⓐ Ⓑ Ⓒ Ⓓ Ⓔ	11. Ⓐ Ⓑ Ⓒ Ⓓ Ⓔ	17. Ⓐ Ⓑ Ⓒ Ⓓ Ⓔ	23. Ⓐ Ⓑ Ⓒ Ⓓ Ⓔ
5. Ⓐ Ⓑ Ⓒ Ⓓ Ⓔ	12. Ⓐ Ⓑ Ⓒ Ⓓ Ⓔ	18. Ⓐ Ⓑ Ⓒ Ⓓ Ⓔ	24. Ⓐ Ⓑ Ⓒ Ⓓ Ⓔ
6. Ⓐ Ⓑ Ⓒ Ⓓ Ⓔ	13. Ⓐ Ⓑ Ⓒ Ⓓ Ⓔ	19. Ⓐ Ⓑ Ⓒ Ⓓ Ⓔ	25. Ⓐ Ⓑ Ⓒ Ⓓ Ⓔ
7. Ⓐ Ⓑ Ⓒ Ⓓ Ⓔ			

SECTION 3: READING COMPREHENSION

1. Ⓐ Ⓑ Ⓒ Ⓓ Ⓔ	11. Ⓐ Ⓑ Ⓒ Ⓓ Ⓔ	21. Ⓐ Ⓑ Ⓒ Ⓓ Ⓔ	31. Ⓐ Ⓑ Ⓒ Ⓓ Ⓔ
2. Ⓐ Ⓑ Ⓒ Ⓓ Ⓔ	12. Ⓐ Ⓑ Ⓒ Ⓓ Ⓔ	22. Ⓐ Ⓑ Ⓒ Ⓓ Ⓔ	32. Ⓐ Ⓑ Ⓒ Ⓓ Ⓔ
3. Ⓐ Ⓑ Ⓒ Ⓓ Ⓔ	13. Ⓐ Ⓑ Ⓒ Ⓓ Ⓔ	23. Ⓐ Ⓑ Ⓒ Ⓓ Ⓔ	33. Ⓐ Ⓑ Ⓒ Ⓓ Ⓔ
4. Ⓐ Ⓑ Ⓒ Ⓓ Ⓔ	14. Ⓐ Ⓑ Ⓒ Ⓓ Ⓔ	24. Ⓐ Ⓑ Ⓒ Ⓓ Ⓔ	34. Ⓐ Ⓑ Ⓒ Ⓓ Ⓔ
5. Ⓐ Ⓑ Ⓒ Ⓓ Ⓔ	15. Ⓐ Ⓑ Ⓒ Ⓓ Ⓔ	25. Ⓐ Ⓑ Ⓒ Ⓓ Ⓔ	35. Ⓐ Ⓑ Ⓒ Ⓓ Ⓔ
6. Ⓐ Ⓑ Ⓒ Ⓓ Ⓔ	16. Ⓐ Ⓑ Ⓒ Ⓓ Ⓔ	26. Ⓐ Ⓑ Ⓒ Ⓓ Ⓔ	36. Ⓐ Ⓑ Ⓒ Ⓓ Ⓔ
7. Ⓐ Ⓑ Ⓒ Ⓓ Ⓔ	17. Ⓐ Ⓑ Ⓒ Ⓓ Ⓔ	27. Ⓐ Ⓑ Ⓒ Ⓓ Ⓔ	37. Ⓐ Ⓑ Ⓒ Ⓓ Ⓔ
8. Ⓐ Ⓑ Ⓒ Ⓓ Ⓔ	18. Ⓐ Ⓑ Ⓒ Ⓓ Ⓔ	28. Ⓐ Ⓑ Ⓒ Ⓓ Ⓔ	38. Ⓐ Ⓑ Ⓒ Ⓓ Ⓔ
9. Ⓐ Ⓑ Ⓒ Ⓓ Ⓔ	19. Ⓐ Ⓑ Ⓒ Ⓓ Ⓔ	29. Ⓐ Ⓑ Ⓒ Ⓓ Ⓔ	39. Ⓐ Ⓑ Ⓒ Ⓓ Ⓔ
10. Ⓐ Ⓑ Ⓒ Ⓓ Ⓔ	20. Ⓐ Ⓑ Ⓒ Ⓓ Ⓔ	30. Ⓐ Ⓑ Ⓒ Ⓓ Ⓔ	40. Ⓐ Ⓑ Ⓒ Ⓓ Ⓔ

answer sheet

SECTION 4: QUANTITATIVE (MATH)

1. Ⓐ Ⓑ Ⓒ Ⓓ Ⓔ   8. Ⓐ Ⓑ Ⓒ Ⓓ Ⓔ   14. Ⓐ Ⓑ Ⓒ Ⓓ Ⓔ   20. Ⓐ Ⓑ Ⓒ Ⓓ Ⓔ
2. Ⓐ Ⓑ Ⓒ Ⓓ Ⓔ   9. Ⓐ Ⓑ Ⓒ Ⓓ Ⓔ   15. Ⓐ Ⓑ Ⓒ Ⓓ Ⓔ   21. Ⓐ Ⓑ Ⓒ Ⓓ Ⓔ
3. Ⓐ Ⓑ Ⓒ Ⓓ Ⓔ   10. Ⓐ Ⓑ Ⓒ Ⓓ Ⓔ   16. Ⓐ Ⓑ Ⓒ Ⓓ Ⓔ   22. Ⓐ Ⓑ Ⓒ Ⓓ Ⓔ
4. Ⓐ Ⓑ Ⓒ Ⓓ Ⓔ   11. Ⓐ Ⓑ Ⓒ Ⓓ Ⓔ   17. Ⓐ Ⓑ Ⓒ Ⓓ Ⓔ   23. Ⓐ Ⓑ Ⓒ Ⓓ Ⓔ
5. Ⓐ Ⓑ Ⓒ Ⓓ Ⓔ   12. Ⓐ Ⓑ Ⓒ Ⓓ Ⓔ   18. Ⓐ Ⓑ Ⓒ Ⓓ Ⓔ   24. Ⓐ Ⓑ Ⓒ Ⓓ Ⓔ
6. Ⓐ Ⓑ Ⓒ Ⓓ Ⓔ   13. Ⓐ Ⓑ Ⓒ Ⓓ Ⓔ   19. Ⓐ Ⓑ Ⓒ Ⓓ Ⓔ   25. Ⓐ Ⓑ Ⓒ Ⓓ Ⓔ
7. Ⓐ Ⓑ Ⓒ Ⓓ Ⓔ

Practice Test 7: SSAT (Upper Level)

PART I: WRITING SAMPLE

25 MINUTES

Directions: Read the topic choose your position and organize your essay before writing. Write a convincing' legible essay on the paper provided.

Topic: High schools should require students to maintain a certain grade point level in order to play on competitive sports teams.

Do you agree or disagree with this statement? Support your position with examples from your own experience the experience of others current events or your reading.

PART II: MULTIPLE CHOICE

Section 1: Verbal

30 MINUTES

The Verbal section consists of two different types of questions. There are directions for each type of question.

Directions: Each question shows a word in capital letters followed by five words or phrases. Choose the word or phrase whose meaning is most similar to the word in capital letters.

1. AGENDA
   - (A) receipt
   - (B) agent
   - (C) combination
   - (D) correspondence
   - (E) schedule

2. CREDIBLE
   - (A) believable
   - (B) untrue
   - (C) correct
   - (D) suitable
   - (E) fortunate

3. PLACID
   - (A) explosive
   - (B) quiet
   - (C) public
   - (D) lenient
   - (E) crystalline

4. INTERVENE
   - (A) induce
   - (B) invert
   - (C) interfere
   - (D) solve
   - (E) intermediary

5. MUNDANE
   - (A) stupid
   - (B) extraordinary
   - (C) weekly
   - (D) immense
   - (E) common

6. DEHYDRATED
   - (A) airless
   - (B) deflated
   - (C) pointless
   - (D) worthless
   - (E) waterless

7. PREVALENT
   - (A) predating
   - (B) predominant
   - (C) preeminent
   - (D) prior
   - (E) predictive

8. SUCCINCT
   - (A) concise
   - (B) superfluous
   - (C) alert
   - (D) despicable
   - (E) fearful

9. NOCTURNAL
   (A) by night
   (B) by day
   (C) revolving
   (D) alternating
   (E) frequent

10. EQUITABLE
    (A) preferential
    (B) fair
    (C) unreasonable
    (D) biased
    (E) prejudiced

11. EXPEDITE
    (A) hinder
    (B) harm
    (C) send
    (D) hasten
    (E) block

12. TURBULENT
    (A) authentic
    (B) tranquil
    (C) tamed
    (D) fatal
    (E) violent

13. TENACIOUS
    (A) timid
    (B) thin
    (C) unyielding
    (D) divisive
    (E) stranded

14. PERTINENT
    (A) applicable
    (B) prudent
    (C) irreverent
    (D) irrelevant
    (E) truthful

15. DOGMATIC
    (A) bovine
    (B) canine
    (C) opinionated
    (D) individualistic
    (E) traditional

16. UNSCRUPULOUS
    (A) filthy
    (B) honest
    (C) austere
    (D) unprincipled
    (E) unresolved

17. WILY
    (A) crooked
    (B) narrow
    (C) cunning
    (D) blunt
    (E) broken

18. BLATANT
    (A) insipid
    (B) obvious
    (C) shining
    (D) closed
    (E) secret

19. PRETEXT
    (A) excuse
    (B) reason
    (C) preface
    (D) fit
    (E) doubt

20. ACUMEN
    (A) beauty
    (B) poise
    (C) keenness
    (D) illness
    (E) courtesy

21. EVASION
    (A) attack
    (B) displeasure
    (C) enjoyment
    (D) avoidance
    (E) fatigue

22. INDISPENSABLE
    (A) incontrovertible
    (B) essential
    (C) impetuous
    (D) ungovernable
    (E) confused

23. OBLITERATE
    (A) obligate
    (B) subjugate
    (C) exhibit
    (D) maintain
    (E) erase

24. AMIABLE
    (A) allied
    (B) disjointed
    (C) indignant
    (D) friendly
    (E) introverted

25. WRITHE
    (A) strangle
    (B) topple
    (C) trouble
    (D) slide
    (E) twist

26. ABATE
    (A) let up
    (B) continue
    (C) forego
    (D) placate
    (E) intimidate

27. ENDORSEMENT
    (A) inscription
    (B) approval
    (C) standard
    (D) editorial
    (E) article

28. CONVERT
    (A) reform
    (B) predict
    (C) weave
    (D) transform
    (E) translate

29. ERUDITE
    (A) knowledgeable
    (B) meddlesome
    (C) eroded
    (D) careless
    (E) intrusion

30. ENDEAVOR
    (A) expectation
    (B) attempt
    (C) tack
    (D) necessity
    (E) ability

Directions: The following questions ask you to find relationships between words. Read each question, and then choose the answer that best completes the meaning of the sentence.

31. None is to little as never is to
    (A) nothing
    (B) infrequently
    (C) negative
    (D) much
    (E) often

32. Receive is to admit as settle is to
    (A) resist
    (B) anger
    (C) remain
    (D) adjust
    (E) mediate

33. Dishonesty is to distrust as
    (A) violin is to bow
    (B) hand is to paper
    (C) money is to thief
    (D) strange is to odd
    (E) carelessness is to accident

34. Sociologist is to group as
    (A) psychologist is to individual
    (B) doctor is to nurse
    (C) children is to pediatrician
    (D) biologist is to frog
    (E) mathematician is to algebra

35. Generous is to frugal as
    (A) wasteful is to squander
    (B) philanthropist is to miser
    (C) tasteful is to garish
    (D) gratify is to desire
    (E) important is to nonessential

36. Transparent is to translucent as
    (A) water is to milk
    (B) glass is to crystal
    (C) translucent is to opaque
    (D) muddy is to clear
    (E) suspension is to mixture

37. Discontent is to rebellion as
    (A) friction is to spark
    (B) complacent is to revolt
    (C) success is to study
    (D) employment is to retirement
    (E) surgeon is to operation

38. Beaker is to chemist as hammer is to
    (A) nails
    (B) geologist
    (C) construction
    (D) architect
    (E) noise

39. Follow is to lead as dependent is to
    (A) subservient
    (B) supportive
    (C) child
    (D) autonomous
    (E) anonymous

40. State is to country as country is to
    (A) island
    (B) capitol
    (C) continent
    (D) planet
    (E) ocean

41. Accelerator is to motion as
    (A) catalyst is to change
    (B) inertia is to immobile
    (C) ignition is to speed
    (D) automobile is to vehicle
    (E) experiment is to hypothesis

42. Probable is to certain as
    (A) approach is to reproach
    (B) steady is to rocky
    (C) correct is to accurate
    (D) save is to record
    (E) plausible is to definite

43. Obstruct is to impede as impenetrable is to
    (A) impervious
    (B) hidden
    (C) merciful
    (D) porous
    (E) transparent

44. Include is to omit as acknowledge is to
    (A) notice
    (B) ignore
    (C) recognize
    (D) greet
    (E) know

45. Nucleus is to electron as
    (A) Earth is to satellite
    (B) Earth is to Sun
    (C) constellation is to Sun
    (D) neutron is to proton
    (E) atom is to neutron

46. Sculptor is to statue as
    (A) actor is to play
    (B) paint is to artist
    (C) composer is to music
    (D) orchestra is to conductor
    (E) programmer is to computer

47. Dreary is to happy as
    (A) light is to graceful
    (B) close is to narrow
    (C) dearth is to surplus
    (D) curtain is to play
    (E) interdict is to expect

48. Allow is to restrict as
    (A) gain is to success
    (B) seeing is to believing
    (C) heart is to soul
    (D) encourage is to prevent
    (E) terrible is to worse

49. Interrupt is to speak as
    (A) telephone is to telegraph
    (B) interfere is to assist
    (C) shout is to yell
    (D) intercede is to interfere
    (E) intrude is to enter

50. Modesty is to arrogance as
    (A) debility is to strength
    (B) cause is to purpose
    (C) hate is to emotion
    (D) finance is to poverty
    (E) agility is to stamina

51. Adversity is to happiness as
    (A) fear is to misfortune
    (B) solace is to sorrow
    (C) graduation is to superfluous
    (D) vehemence is to serenity
    (E) troublesome is to petulant

52. Extortionist is to blackmail as
    (A) kleptomaniac is to steal
    (B) criminal is to arrest
    (C) kidnapper is to crime
    (D) businessman is to profit
    (E) clerk is to stock

53. Monsoon is to rain as
    (A) hurricane is to destruction
    (B) tornado is to wind
    (C) sun is to spring
    (D) famine is to drought
    (E) morning is to dew

54. Introspective is to withdrawn as
    (A) hesitant is to hasty
    (B) quick is to feelings
    (C) introvert is to extrovert
    (D) import is to export
    (E) gregarious is to social

55. Equator is to world as
   (A) boundary is to country
   (B) capital is to state
   (C) fur is to animal
   (D) waist is to man
   (E) latitude is to longitude

56. Superficial is to surface as
   (A) probing is to deep
   (B) subway is to subterranean
   (C) crust is to Earth
   (D) tepid is to warm
   (E) internal is to external

57. Stagnant is to pond as
   (A) sandy is to river
   (B) noisy is to sheep
   (C) flowing is to stream
   (D) oceanic is to tide
   (E) tidal is to wave

58. Sanctuary is to fortress as
   (A) sanctum is to inner
   (B) shelter is to house
   (C) violent is to peaceful
   (D) guns is to fort
   (E) sanction is to assassinate

59. Mentor is to professor as
   (A) advisor is to counselor
   (B) child is to parent
   (C) learning is to teacher
   (D) mental is to physical
   (E) tooth is to dentist

60. Lucid is to clear as
   (A) sullen is to gloomy
   (B) furtive is to clever
   (C) potent is to weak
   (D) droll is to serious
   (E) pensive is to hanging

STOP END OF SECTION 1. IF YOU HAVE ANY TIME LEFT, GO OVER YOUR WORK IN THIS SECTION ONLY. DO NOT WORK IN ANY OTHER SECTION OF THE TEST.

Section 2: Quantitative (Math)

30 MINUTES

Directions: Calculate the answer to each of the following questions. Select the answer choice that is best and mark the appropriate letter on your answer sheet.

1. $\frac{3}{5} + 1.25 + 0.004 =$
   - (A) 1.750
   - (B) 1.854
   - (C) 1.9
   - (D) 2.25
   - (E) 2.35

2. Evaluate: $\frac{10^6}{10^3}$
   - (A) 1 billion
   - (B) 1 million
   - (C) 1000
   - (D) 100
   - (E) 1^3

3. $71.4 \times 98.2 =$
   - (A) 4011.38
   - (B) 5321.48
   - (C) 6921.38
   - (D) 7011.48
   - (E) 8231.48

4. $\dfrac{4\frac{2}{3} + \frac{1}{6}}{\frac{1}{3}} =$
   - (A) 9
   - (B) $10\frac{1}{3}$
   - (C) $12\frac{3}{24}$
   - (D) $14\frac{1}{2}$
   - (E) 23

5. $(0.25)^2 =$
   - (A) 0.00625
   - (B) 0.0625
   - (C) 0.625
   - (D) 1.625
   - (E) 16.25

6. $(3 + 1) + [(2 - 3) - (4 - 1)] =$
   - (A) 6
   - (B) 2
   - (C) 0
   - (D) −2
   - (E) −4

7. $10,001 - 8093 =$
   - (A) 1908
   - (B) 1918
   - (C) 2007
   - (D) 18,094
   - (E) 20,007

8. The ratio of 3 quarts to 3 gallons is
   - (A) 3:1
   - (B) 1:4
   - (C) 6:3
   - (D) 4:1
   - (E) 1:3

9. 10% of $\frac{1}{5}$ of $50 is
   - (A) $100
   - (B) $5
   - (C) $1
   - (D) 103
   - (E) $\frac{3}{5}$

10.   4 hours 12 minutes 10 seconds
    − 2 hours 48 minutes 35 seconds

(A) 2 hr. 23 min. 25 sec.

(B) 2 hr. 12 min. 40 sec.

(C) 1 hr. 23 min. 35 sec.

(D) 1 hr. 23 min. 25 sec.

(E) 1 hr. 12 min. 35 sec.

11. If we double the value of a and c in the fraction $\frac{ab}{c}$, the value of the fraction is

(A) doubled.

(B) tripled.

(C) multiplied by 4.

(D) halved.

(E) unchanged.

12. What percentage of 220 is 24.2?

(A) 909%

(B) 99%

(C) 40%

(D) 27%

(E) 11%

13. 98 reduced by $\frac{5}{7}$ is equivalent to

(A) 28

(B) 33

(C) 66

(D) 70

(E) 85

14. How long should an object $6\frac{1}{2}$ feet long be drawn, if according to the scale, $\frac{1}{4}$ inch in the drawing equals 1 foot?

(A) $1\frac{3}{4}$ inches

(B) $1\frac{5}{8}$ inches

(C) $\frac{7}{8}$ inches

(D) $\frac{5}{8}$ inches

(E) $\frac{17}{32}$ inches

15. $12\frac{1}{2} \div \frac{1}{2} + \frac{3}{2} \times 4 - 3 =$

(A) 1

(B) $4\frac{3}{4}$

(C) 20

(D) 28

(E) $32\frac{1}{2}$

16. If $y + 2 > 10$, then y is

(A) larger than 8.

(B) larger than 6.

(C) larger than 0.

(D) equal to 0.

(E) unknown.

17. The shadow of a man 6 feet tall is 12 feet long. How tall is a tree that casts a 50-foot shadow?

(A) 100'

(B) 50'

(C) 25'

(D) 15'

(E) 10'

18. In the fraction $\frac{1}{\Delta}$, Δ could be replaced by all of the following EXCEPT

(A) 0

(B) 1

(C) 4.2

(D) 9

(E) 10

19. 0.0515×100 is equivalent to

(A) $5{,}150 \div 100$

(B) 5.15×10

(C) $0.00515 \times 1{,}000$

(D) $510{,}000 \div 10$

(E) $5{,}150 \div 10{,}000$

20.

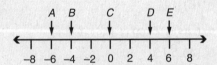

m∠2 = 60°

NOTE: Figure not drawn to scale.

Which of the following is true?

(A) m∠1 + m∠3 > 180°

(B) m∠1 > m∠3

(C) m∠1 = m∠3

(D) m∠1 − m∠3 > m∠2

(E) m∠1 + m∠3 = 120°

21. 45 is to _____ as 90 is to 0.45.

(A) 0.225

(B) 0.900

(C) 4.50

(D) 9.00

(E) 22.5

22. If $n = \sqrt{20}$, then

(A) $\sqrt{5} > n > \sqrt{3}$

(B) $3 > n > 2$.

(C) $n = 4.5$.

(D) $4 < n < 5$.

(E) $n > 5$.

23.

How would you move along the number line above to find the difference between 4 and −6?

(A) From *E* to *B*

(B) From *A* to *D*

(C) From *B* to *D*

(D) From *D* to *A*

24. How many sixths are there in $\frac{4}{5}$?

(A) $2\frac{3}{8}$

(B) 3

(C) $4\frac{4}{5}$

(D) $5\frac{1}{5}$

(E) 6

25. Four games drew an average of 36,500 people per game. If the attendance at the first three games was 32,000, 35,500, and 38,000, how many people attended the fourth game?

(A) 36,500

(B) 37,000

(C) 39,000

(D) 40,500

(E) 43,000

STOP   END OF SECTION 2. IF YOU HAVE ANY TIME LEFT, GO OVER YOUR WORK IN THIS SECTION ONLY. DO NOT WORK IN ANY OTHER SECTION OF THE TEST.

Section 3: Reading Comprehension

40 MINUTES

Directions: Read each passage carefully. Then decide which of the possible responses is the best answer to each question.

Line Back in the seventeenth century, when
Abraham Rycken owned it, Rikers Island
was a tiny spit of land in the East River.
It became part of New York City in the
5 1890s and was used as a convenient place
to deposit the rock and soil debris of subway
construction. Later, the island became the
end of the line for the discards of city households, in a landfill operation that went on
10 until Rikers Island reached its present size
of 400 acres.

　　Robert Moses, then New York's Park
Commissioner, was looking for ways to
supply city parks with shade trees and
15 eliminate the expense of buying them from
commercial nurseries. He noted that weeds
grew prodigiously in the landfill, thought
that trees and plants might do the same,
and arranged to clear a few acres for a trial
20 planting. In 1944, the first 287 shrubs and
trees were transplanted from the fledgling
nursery to the city's parks. The nursery now
covers some 115 acres of the island, and
several hundred thousand of its shrubs and
25 trees have been planted along city streets, in
parks, around housing projects, and around
the malls and paths of the United Nations.

1. To obtain plantings for New York City,
authorities
(A) buy them from the United Nations.
(B) purchase them from commercial
nurseries.
(C) transplant them from city-owned
property.
(D) buy them from Robert Moses.
(E) grow them in Central Park.

2. Rikers Island is currently
(A) 115 acres in area.
(B) a landfill operation.
(C) owned by Abraham Rycken.
(D) 400 acres in area.
(E) a dumping ground for subway
debris.

3. The soil of the island
(A) is volcanic.
(B) was enriched by discarded rubbish.
(C) was brought in from commercial
nurseries.
(D) is a combination of mud and rock.
(E) was brought in on subways.

4. The first plantings were taken from Rikers
Island
(A) a decade ago.
(B) about 1890.
(C) in the seventeenth century.
(D) quite recently.
(E) in 1944.

Line America's national bird, the bald eagle,
which has flown high since the Revolutionary War, may soon be grounded. The
eagle population of the United States is
5 decreasing at an alarming rate, and the
National Audubon Society has just launched
a full-scale survey to find out how many
bald eagles are left and what measures are
necessary to protect them from extinction.
10 The survey, a year-long project, focuses
attention on the bird chosen to appear on
the Great Seal of the United States.

　　When it gained its official status over 200
years ago, the bald eagle was undisputed
15 king of America's skies. Many thousands
of the great birds roamed the country, and

both the sight of the bald eagle and its piercing scream were familiar to almost every American. Today, naturalists fear that
20 there are less than a thousand of them still in this country.

Nature is partly to blame. Our severe hurricanes have destroyed many eggs, fledglings, and aeries, the eagles' mammoth
25 nests. But man is the chief culprit. Despite legislation passed by Congress in 1940 to protect the *emblematic birds,* thousands of them have been gunned out of the skies by over-eager shooters who perhaps mistook
30 them for large hawks.

The bald eagle was known as the bald-headed eagle when Congress began the search for a seal in 1776. The archaic meaning of bald—white or streaked with
35 white—refers to his head, neck, and tail coloring rather than to any lack of plumage in our fine-feathered friend.

5. The Audubon Society is trying to

(A) rid the country of the bald eagle.

(B) have the bald eagle chosen as the national bird of the United States.

(C) prevent the extinction of the bald eagle in this country.

(D) have Congress pass a law forbidding the shooting of eagles.

(E) band more eagles.

6. There are now

(A) more eagles in this country than in 1776.

(B) fewer eagles here than there were over 200 years ago.

(C) many thousands of bald eagles.

(D) eagles whose scream is familiar to every American.

(E) too many eagles.

7. *Aeries* are

(A) fledglings.

(B) eggs.

(C) young mammoths.

(D) nests.

(E) mating areas.

8. The eagle is called an *emblematic bird* (line 27) because it is

(A) bald.

(B) decreasing.

(C) handsome and powerful.

(D) prized by hunters.

(E) a symbol of a nation.

9. The design for the Great Seal of the United States was first considered

(A) in 1776.

(B) in 1783.

(C) in 1840.

(D) in 1876.

(E) at an unknown date.

Line You know, of course, that in China the Emperor is a Chinaman, and all the people around him are Chinamen too. It happened a good many years ago but that's just why
5 it's worthwhile to hear the story, before it is forgotten. The Emperor's palace was the most splendid in the world; entirely and altogether made of porcelain, so costly, but so brittle, so difficult to handle that one had
10 to be terribly careful. In the garden were to be seen the strangest flowers, and to the most splendid of them silver bells were tied, which tinkled so that nobody should pass by without noticing the flowers. Oh,
15 the Emperor's garden had been laid out very smartly, and it extended so far that the gardener himself didn't know where the end was. If you went on and on, you came into the loveliest forest with high trees and
20 deep lakes. The forest went right down to the sea, which was blue and deep; tall ships could sail right in under the branches of the trees; and in the trees lived a nightingale, which sang so sweetly that even the poor
25 fisherman, who had many other things to do, stopped still and listened when he had gone out at night to take up his nets and then heard the nightingale.

—from *The Nightingale*
by Hans Christian Andersen

10. The author wants to tell this story
    - (A) because he can't forget the nightingale.
    - (B) before it is forgotten.
    - (C) to teach us about China.
    - (D) because he is a writer and storyteller.
    - (E) in order to describe the garden.

11. The Emperor's palace was made of
    - (A) brick.
    - (B) silver bells.
    - (C) high trees.
    - (D) large stones and boulders.
    - (E) porcelain.

12. Silver bells were tied to flowers in the garden to
    - (A) draw attention to their beauty.
    - (B) frighten birds and mice away.
    - (C) play soft melodies.
    - (D) remind the gardener not to pick them.
    - (E) sparkle in the sun.

13. The Emperor's garden
    - (A) was very strange.
    - (B) was too large to care for.
    - (C) led into a lovely forest.
    - (D) housed a rare nightingale.
    - (E) was a source of pleasure for all in the kingdom.

14. The forest
    - (A) was dark and threatening.
    - (B) contained many rare animals.
    - (C) was an easy place in which to get lost.
    - (D) housed the nightingale.
    - (E) was a fisherman's hiding place.

Line An excerpt from a Dead Sea Scroll describing Abraham's *sojourn* in Egypt and the beauty of Sarah, his wife, was recently made public for the first time. The 2,000-year-old scroll,
5 badly preserved and extremely brittle, is the last of seven scrolls found in 1947 in the caves of the Judean desert south of Jericho. Scholars say that this scroll enlarges on the hitherto known Biblical tales of Lamech,
10 Enoch, Noah, and Abraham.

   This document of Hebrew University yielded *decipherable* contents only after months of exposure to controlled humidity. The centuries had compressed the leather
15 scroll into a brittle, glued-together mass. After it had been rendered flexible, the scroll was folded into pages. Four complete pages, each with 34 lines of writing, resulted. Besides this, scholars had for their studies
20 large sections of the decipherable writing on five other pages, and readable lines and words on additional pages. Scholars were delighted, for they had almost despaired of recovering the scroll as a readable document.
25 The work of giving new life to the desiccated parchment and of unrolling it was done by an old German expert on ancient materials, under the supervision of two Israeli scholars.

15. The word *sojourn* (line 2) means
    - (A) servitude.
    - (B) stay.
    - (C) congruent.
    - (D) flight.
    - (E) difficulties.

16. *Decipherable* (line 12) as used in the second paragraph means
    - (A) intelligible.
    - (B) durable.
    - (C) exciting.
    - (D) scholarly.
    - (E) practical.

practice test

17. The scroll

    (A) was found in Egypt.

    (B) gives new details about people already known of.

    (C) is limited to an account of Abraham and Sarah.

    (D) tells of Abraham's life in the Judean desert.

    (E) is the first of seven found in 1947.

18. The scroll

    (A) belongs to an Israeli university.

    (B) is in Germany.

    (C) was deciphered by a German specialist.

    (D) was taken to Jericho.

    (E) was beautifully preserved.

19. The writing on the scroll

    (A) was finally legible throughout the document.

    (B) was legible on only four pages.

    (C) could be read on several pages.

    (D) was too damaged by age to be deciphered.

    (E) was irreparable.

Line The police department of New York City has
one branch that many do not know about,
although it was established almost a century
ago. This is the harbor precinct's 14-boat
5   fleet of police launches, which patrols 578
miles of waters around the city, paying
particular attention to the areas containing
500 piers and some 90 boat clubs.

The boats are equipped for various
10 jobs. One boat is an ice-breaker; another
is equipped to render aid in the event of an
airplane crash at La Guardia Airport. All of
the boats are equipped with lifeline guns,
heavy grappling irons to raise sunken auto-
15 mobiles, and lasso-sticks to rescue animals
in the water. They have power pumps to bail
out sinking craft, first-aid kits, extra life
preservers, signal flags, and searchlights.

The force of 183 officers have all had
20 previous experience with boats. Some of the
officers are Navy and Coast Guard veterans.

Many of the harbor police officers have
oceangoing Master's or Harbor Captain's
licenses. All are highly trained in the care
25 and handling of engines and in navigation.
All are skilled in giving first aid, and each
officer is a qualified radio operator and a
trained marksman with a revolver.

The work of the police includes many
30 tasks. One duty of this force is to check the
operation of the fleet of 43 junk boats that
ply their trade in the harbor, buying scrap,
rope, and other items for resale ashore.
These boats could just as easily be used to
35 smuggle narcotics, gems, aliens, or spies
into the country, so they are watched closely
by the city's harbor police force. During
the last summer, the police launches towed
450 disabled boats and gave some kind of
40 help to thousands of others. The officers
also arrest those who break navigation
laws or who endanger the safety of bathers
by approaching too near the shore in speed
boats.

20. The harbor police were

    (A) introduced by order of the mayor.

    (B) first used in the twentieth century.

    (C) in use before the Civil War.

    (D) introduced by veterans of World War II.

    (E) in full force almost 100 years ago.

21. The boats used

    (A) are uniform in design.

    (B) can all serve as ice-breakers.

    (C) are all equipped with deck guns.

    (D) work at Kennedy Airport.

    (E) vary in function.

22. The harbor police

    (A) arrest any man found on a junk boat.

    (B) prevent the resale of scrap material.

    (C) regulate the admission of spies.

    (D) ensure legal traffic in junk.

    (E) regulate disabled boats.

23. Their services include
    (A) towing, life-saving, and salvage.
    (B) customs collection, towing, and the sending of radio messages.
    (C) first aid, the rescue of animals, and fire patrol.
    (D) ice-breaking, the collection of junk, and the transportation of aliens.
    (E) smuggling, first aid, and rescue.

24. The police boats
    (A) have no responsibility for bathers.
    (B) unload ships at the piers.
    (C) assist boats of all kinds.
    (D) warn offenders but do not make arrests.
    (E) cannot detain other boats.

Line "There are many things from which I might have derived good, by which I have not profited, I dare say, Christmas among the rest. But I am sure I have always thought of
5 Christmas-time, when it has come round— apart from the *veneration* due to its sacred origin, if anything belonging to it can be apart from that—as a good time; a kind, forgiving, charitable, pleasant time; the only
10 time I know of, in the long calendar of the year, when men and women seem by one consent to open their shut-up hearts freely and to think of people below them as if they really were fellow travelers to the grave,
15 and not another race of creatures bound on other journeys. And therefore, Uncle, though it has never put a scrap of gold or silver in my pocket, I believe that it *has* done me good, and *will* do me good; and I
20 say, God bless it!"
    The clerk in the tank involuntarily applauded.
    "Let me hear another sound from *you,*" said Scrooge, "and you'll keep your
25 Christmas by losing your situation! You're quite a powerful speaker, sir," he added, turning to his nephew. "I wonder you don't go into Parliament."

　　　　—from *A Christmas Carol*
　　　　by Charles Dickens

25. The word *veneration* (line 6) probably means
    (A) worship.
    (B) disapproval.
    (C) agreement.
    (D) love.
    (E) participation.

26. The first speaker
    (A) is a very religious person.
    (B) enjoys and celebrates Christmas.
    (C) is defending Christmas.
    (D) has been fired by Scrooge.
    (E) is obviously frightened of Scrooge.

27. The first speaker believes that Christmas
    (A) is a pleasant nuisance.
    (B) is an excuse for people to throw wild parties.
    (C) has been separated from its religious origin.
    (D) could be a profitable time of year.
    (E) brings out the best in people.

28. The phrase "by one consent" (lines 11–12) is synonymous with
    (A) affirmation.
    (B) reaffirmation.
    (C) partially.
    (D) unanimously.
    (E) contractual.

29. Scrooge probably is angry with
    (A) the speaker and the clerk.
    (B) only the speaker.
    (C) only the clerk.
    (D) people who celebrate Christmas.
    (E) no one.

Line One day recently, a man in a ten-gallon hat appeared at the gate of New York's famous Bronx Zoo. "Just stopped by on my way through town," he told zoo officials. "I've
5 got an animal outside I think you might like to see."

The officials raised their eyebrows and looked at each other meaningfully, but the man in the hat didn't seem to notice. He went
10 on to introduce himself as Gene Holter. "I call it a Zonkey," he said calmly, "because it's a cross between a donkey and a zebra. I've got his parents out there, too."

The zoo officials didn't wait to hear about
15 the parents. They left their desks and started for the gate. Outside, Mr. Holter opened the side door of a huge truck and reached inside. Calmly, he pulled out a gibbon, and hung it, by its tail, from a tree. Then he walked
20 past five ostriches and carried out the baby Zonkey.

Just three weeks old, the only Zonkey in the world had long ears, a face and legs covered with candy stripes, and a body
25 covered with brown baby fuzz. The parents were on hand, too. The father was no ordinary zebra. He was broken to ride, and one of the zoo officials realized a lifelong dream when he jumped on the zebra's back and cantered
30 around.

When last seen, Mr. Holter and his caravan were on their way to Dayton and then to Anaheim, California, where they live year-round.

30. Mr. Holter's manner was

(A) boastful.

(B) excitable.

(C) demanding.

(D) matter-of-fact.

(E) personable.

31. When Mr. Holter first approached the zoo officials, they

(A) were excited about his announcement.

(B) thought he was telling a tall tale.

(C) thought he was an interesting person.

(D) couldn't wait to realize a lifelong dream.

(E) laughed behind his back.

32. Mr. Holter probably made a living

(A) as a veterinarian.

(B) traveling and showing his animals.

(C) breeding animals for scientific experiments.

(D) working as a zoo official.

(E) filming animals.

Line There is evidence that the usual variety of high blood pressure is, in part, a familial disease. Since families have similar genes as well as similar environment, familial
5 diseases could be due to shared genetic influences, to shared environmental factors, or both. For some years, the role of one environmental factor commonly shared by families, namely dietary salt, has been
10 studied at Brookhaven National Laboratory. The studies suggest that excessive ingestion of salt can lead to high blood pressure in man and animals. Some individuals and some rats, however, consume large amounts of salt
15 without developing high blood pressure. No matter how strictly all environmental factors were controlled in these experiments, some salt-fed animals never developed hypertension, whereas a few rapidly developed
20 very severe hypertension followed by early death. These marked variations were interpreted to result from differences in genetic makeup.

33. The main idea of this article is that

(A) research is desperately needed in the field of medicine.

(B) a cure for high blood pressure is near.

(C) research shows salt to be a major cause of high blood pressure.

(D) a tendency toward high blood pressure may be inherited.

(E) some animals never develop high blood pressure.

34. According to the article, high blood pressure is
    (A) strictly a genetic disease.
    (B) strictly an environmental disease.
    (C) due to both genetic and environmental factors.
    (D) caused only by dietary salt.
    (E) a more severe form of hypertension.

Line The dark and the sea are full of dangers to the fishermen of Norway. A whale may come and destroy the floating chain of corks that edge the nets, break it, and carry it off. Or a storm
5 may come suddenly, unexpectedly, out of the night. The sea seems to turn somersaults. It opens and closes immense caverns with terrible clashes, chasing boats and men who must flee from their nets and the expected
10 catch. Then the men may lift their nets as empty as they set them. At other times the herring may come in such masses that the lines break from the weight when lifted, and the men must return home empty-handed,
15 without lines, nets, or the herring.
    But often the nets are full of herring that shine and glisten like silver. Once in a while, a couple of men will venture in their boats along the net lines to see whether the herring
20 are coming, and when the corks begin to bob and jerk, as if something were hitting the nets to which they are attached, then they know that the herring are there. The nets are being filled, and all the men sit in
25 quiet excitement. They dare only to whisper to each other, afraid to disturb, and quite overcome by the overwhelming generosity of the sea. Eyes shine in happy anticipation; hands are folded in thanks. Then muscles
30 strain with power. It is as though the strength of the body doubled. They can workday and night without a thought of weariness. They need neither food nor rest; the thought of success keeps their vigor up almost end-
35 lessly. They will take food and rest when it is all over.

35. The best title for this passage is
    (A) "Whaling in Norway."
    (B) "The Perils and Rewards of Fishing."
    (C) "Hard Work in Norway."
    (D) "Risky Business."
    (E) "The Generosity of the Sea."

36. The fishermen's difficulties include
    (A) the eating of the herring by whales.
    (B) becalming.
    (C) an attack on the men by the herring.
    (D) the jerking of the corks.
    (E) interference by rough seas.

37. At the first indication that herring are entering the nets, the men
    (A) try not to frighten the fish away.
    (B) strain every muscle to haul in the catch.
    (C) glisten like silver.
    (D) collect the nets quickly.
    (E) row quickly along the edge of the nets.

38. Which quality of the sea is NOT mentioned?
    (A) Its sudden changes
    (B) Its generosity
    (C) Its beauty
    (D) Its power
    (E) Its destroying strength

39. The fishermen are described as
    (A) patient, brave, and cautious.
    (B) angry, weary, and sickly.
    (C) strong, angry, and reckless.
    (D) skillful, impatient, and weary.
    (E) hardworking, surly, and excitable.

40. Which is NOT mentioned as a problem to fishermen?
    (A) Destruction of the nets
    (B) Too large a catch
    (C) Rough seas
    (D) Unexpected storms
    (E) Theft of the nets by other fishermen

STOP END OF SECTION 3. IF YOU HAVE ANY TIME LEFT, GO OVER YOUR WORK IN THIS SECTION ONLY. DO NOT WORK IN ANY OTHER SECTION OF THE TEST.

Like us at facebook.com/petersonspublishing

Section 4: Quantitative (Math)

30 MINUTES

Directions: Each question below is followed by five possible answers. Select the one that is best, and mark the appropriate letter on your answer sheet.

1. In two days a point on the Earth's surface rotates through an angle of approximately

   (A) 90°
   (B) 180°
   (C) 360°
   (D) 480°
   (E) 720°

2. Which of the following groups is arranged in order from smallest to largest?

   (A) $\frac{3}{7}, \frac{11}{23}, \frac{15}{32}, \frac{1}{2}, \frac{9}{16}$

   (B) $\frac{3}{7}, \frac{15}{32}, \frac{11}{23}, \frac{1}{2}, \frac{9}{16}$

   (C) $\frac{11}{23}, \frac{3}{7}, \frac{15}{32}, \frac{1}{2}, \frac{9}{16}$

   (D) $\frac{15}{32}, \frac{1}{2}, \frac{3}{7}, \frac{11}{23}, \frac{9}{16}$

   (E) $\frac{1}{2}, \frac{15}{32}, \frac{3}{7}, \frac{11}{23}, \frac{9}{16}$

3. The rectangle below has a length twice as long as its width. If its width is x, its perimeter is

   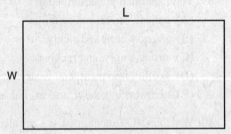

   (A) 6
   (B) $2x^2$
   (C) $4x$
   (D) $6x$
   (E) $8x$

4. This square has a side of 1". The diagonal distance from one corner to another is

   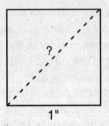

   (A) 1 inch.
   (B) $\sqrt{2}$ inches.
   (C) $\sqrt{3}$ inches.
   (D) 2 inches.
   (E) 3 inches.

5. A plumber needs eight sections of pipe, each 3'2" long. If pipe is sold only by the 10' section, how many sections must he buy?

   (A) 1
   (B) 2
   (C) 3
   (D) 4
   (E) 5

6. In the square below, the ratio of the area of the shaded part to the unshaded part is

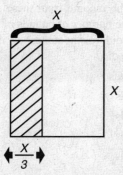

(A) $x : \dfrac{x}{3}$

(B) 2:1

(C) 1:3

(D) 1:2

(E) 3:1

7. An airplane on a transatlantic flight took 4 hours 20 minutes to get from New York to its destination, a distance of 3,000 miles. To avoid a storm, however, the pilot went off his course, adding a distance of 200 miles to the flight. Approximately how fast did the plane travel?

(A) 640 mph

(B) 710 mph

(C) 738 mph

(D) 750 mph

(E) 772 mph

8. A photograph measuring 5" wide × 7" long must be reduced in size to fit a space 4 inches long in an advertising brochure. How wide must the space be so that the picture remains in proportion?

(A) $1\dfrac{4}{7}$"

(B) $2\dfrac{6}{7}$"

(C) $4\dfrac{3}{5}$"

(D) $5\dfrac{3}{5}$"

(E) $8\dfrac{3}{4}$"

9. Find the total area of the shaded part of the figure. (Use $\dfrac{22}{7}$ for π.)

(A) $\dfrac{2}{7}$ in.²

(B) $\dfrac{1}{2}$ in.²

(C) $\dfrac{6}{7}$ in.²

(D) $1\dfrac{3}{7}$ in.²

(E) $2\dfrac{1}{3}$ in.²

10. A certain population of microbes grows according to the formula $P = A \times 2^n$, where P is the final size of the population A is the initial size of the population and n is the number of times the population reproduces itself. If each microbe reproduces itself every 20 minutes how large would a population of only one microbe become after 4 hours?

(A) 16

(B) 64

(C) 128

(D) 1,028

(E) 4,096

11. If x is a positive number and $y = \dfrac{1}{x}$, as x increases in value, what happens to y?

(A) y increases

(B) y decreases

(C) y is unchanged

(D) y increases then decreases

(E) y decreases then increases

12. A box was made in the form of a cube. If a second cubical box has inside dimensions three times those of the first box how many times as much volume does it contain?

    (A) 3
    (B) 9
    (C) 12
    (D) 27
    (E) 33

13. Mr. Adams has a circular flower bed with a diameter of 4 feet. He wishes to increase the size of this bed so that it will have four times as much planting area. What must be the diameter of the new bed?

    (A) 6 feet
    (B) 8 feet
    (C) 12 feet
    (D) 16 feet
    (E) 20 feet

14. A train left Albany for Buffalo, a distance of 290 miles, at 10:10 a.m. The train was scheduled to reach Buffalo at 3:45 p.m. If the average rate of the train on this trip was 50 mph, it arrived in Buffalo

    (A) about 5 minutes early.
    (B) on time.
    (C) about 5 minutes late.
    (D) about 13 minutes late.
    (E) more than 15 minutes late.

15. If $3x - 2 = 13$, what is the value of $12x + 20$?

    (A) 5
    (B) 20
    (C) 30
    (D) 37
    (E) 80

16. A bakery shop sold three kinds of cake. The prices of these were 25¢, 30¢, and 35¢ per pound. The income from these sales was $36. If the number of pounds of each kind of cake sold was the same, how many pounds were sold?

    (A) 120 pounds
    (B) 90 pounds
    (C) 60 pounds
    (D) 45 pounds
    (E) 36 pounds

17. How many more 9" × 9" linoleum tiles than 1' × 1' tiles will it take to cover a 12' × 12' floor?

    (A) 63
    (B) 98
    (C) 112
    (D) 120
    (E) 144

18. If p pencils cost c cents, n pencils at the same rate will cost

    (A) $\dfrac{pc}{n}$ cents

    (B) $\dfrac{cn}{p}$ cents

    (C) npc cents

    (D) $\dfrac{np}{c}$ cents

    (E) $n + p + c$ cents

19. Which, if any, of the following statements is always true?

    (A) If the numerator and denominator of a fraction are increased or decreased by the same amount, the value of the fraction is unchanged.

    (B) If the numerator and denominator of a fraction are squared, the value of the fraction is unchanged.

    (C) The square of any number is greater than that number.

    (D) If unequal quantities are added to unequal quantities, the sums are unequal.

    (E) None of the above

20. If the length and width of a rectangle are each doubled, by what percent is the area increased?

    (A) 50%

    (B) 75%

    (C) 100%

    (D) 300%

    (E) 400%

21. If one pipe can fill a tank in $1\frac{1}{2}$ hours, and another can fill the same tank in 45 minutes, how long will it take for the two pipes to fill the tank together?

    (A) $\frac{1}{3}$ hour

    (B) $\frac{1}{2}$ hour

    (C) $\frac{5}{6}$ hour

    (D) 1 hour

    (E) $1\frac{1}{2}$ hours

22. A baseball team has won 50 games out of 75 played. It has 45 games still to play. How many of these must the team win to make its record for the season 60%?

    (A) 20

    (B) 22

    (C) 25

    (D) 30

    (E) 35

23. If 9 million barrels of oil are consumed daily in the United States, how many barrels are required to meet commercial and industrial needs?

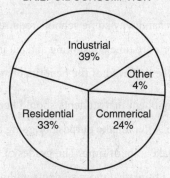

DAILY OIL CONSUMPTION

    (A) 2,840,000

    (B) 3,420,000

    (C) 4,750,000

    (D) 5,670,000

    (E) 7,400,000

24. A real estate investor buys a house and lot for $44,000. He pays $1250 to have it painted, $1750 to fix the plumbing, and $1000 for grading a driveway. At what price must he sell the property to make a 12% profit?

    (A) $53,760

    (B) $52,800

    (C) $52,000

    (D) $49,760

    (E) $44,480

25. If $a = 1$, $b = 2$, $c = 3$, and $d = 5$, the value of $\sqrt{b(d + a) - b(c + a)}$ is

    (A) 2

    (B) 3.5

    (C) 4

    (D) $\sqrt{20}$

    (E) 50

STOP END OF SECTION 4. IF YOU HAVE ANY TIME LEFT, GO OVER YOUR WORK IN THIS SECTION ONLY. DO NOT WORK IN ANY OTHER SECTION OF THE TEST.

ANSWER KEYS AND EXPLANATIONS

Part I: Writing Sample

Example of a well-written essay.

I can understand why some schools require students to maintain their grades if they want to be in sports. Sports are time consuming and cut into study time. But, I think that less competent students should not be deprived of the benefits of sports participation.

The argument that students should keep up their grades if they want to be in sports is worth listening to. After all, the purpose of going to school is to get an education. And sports practice and games do take a lot of time. The grades of a few students might in fact suffer from sports participation, but I think that more students will work harder and will learn to manage time better if they are allowed to play on the team. Learning to organize time is also an important lesson to be gained from school. Happy people tend to reach to meet expectations, and less capable students may even do better in school to prove that being in sports did not do them any harm.

An equally good argument is that everyone must succeed at something. If a poor student an excel at sports, that student will develop self-esteem. Once that student feels good about himself or herself, the student may transfer that confidence to schoolwork and actually get better grades. The old adage that success breeds success applies here.

While the attitude that schoolwork comes first does make a good point, I think that permitting a student to participate in sports and to develop a good self-image is more important. The school should give extra help to the less competent student, especially help in learning time management. Then it should let that student contribute to school spirit on the laying fields as well as in the classroom.

Part II: Multiple Choice

Section 1: Verbal

1. E	13. C	25. E	37. A	49. E
2. A	14. A	26. A	38. B	50. A
3. B	15. C	27. B	39. D	51. D
4. C	16. D	28. D	40. C	52. A
5. E	17. C	29. A	41. A	53. B
6. E	18. B	30. B	42. E	54. E
7. B	19. A	31. B	43. A	55. D
8. A	20. C	32. C	44. B	56. A
9. A	21. D	33. E	45. A	57. C
10. B	22. B	34. A	46. C	58. B
11. D	23. E	35. B	47. C	59. A
12. E	24. D	36. C	48. D	60. A

1. **The correct answer is (E).** The AGENDA is the *program of things to be done* or the *schedule*. Preparation of next year's budget was the top item on the agenda for the meeting.

2. **The correct answer is (A).** CREDIBLE means *plausible, reliable,* or *believable*. The presence of many squirrels in my yard is a credible explanation for the many holes.

3. **The correct answer is (B).** PLACID means *tranquil, calm,* or *peaceful*. Lake Placid in New York is so placid that its waters are seldom stormy.

4. **The correct answer is (C).** To INTERVENE is to *come between two people or things* either to *interfere* or to influence positively. *Intervene* is a verb. An *intermediary* (noun) may intervene in a dispute.

5. **The correct answer is (E).** MUNDANE means *commonplace, earthly,* or *ordinary*. Every morning I perform the mundane tasks of brushing my teeth and making my bed.

6. **The correct answer is (E).** To dehydrate is to remove water therefore DEHYDRATED means *waterless*. The root *hydr-* refers to water and the prefix *de-* is a negative prefix. Dehydrated foods are lightweight and are easy to store for long periods of time.

7. **The correct answer is (B).** PREVALENT means *widely existing, prevailing,* or *generally accepted*. *Preeminent* means *excelling*. The prevalent mood among the Boy Scouts was one of eager anticipation.

8. **The correct answer is (A).** SUCCINCT means *brief* and *to the point*. The legislator gave a succinct background of the reasons for the proposed law.

9. **The correct answer is (A).** That which is NOCTURNAL *happens at night*. Bats do not fly about in the daytime because they are nocturnal creatures.

10. **The correct answer is (B).** EQUITABLE means *fair* and *just*. You should see the root *equal* in this word. The will provided for an equitable distribution of the property.

answers practice test 7

11. **The correct answer is (D).** To EXPEDITE is to *speed up the action* or to *send quickly*. The Latin derivation of this word is "to free one caught by the feet." You can expedite the delivery of mail by using ZIP Code plus four.

12. **The correct answer is (E).** TURBULENT means *unruly* or *agitated*. As the airplane passed through turbulent air we all felt rather queasy.

13. **The correct answer is (C).** TENACIOUS means *holding on tightly* or persistent. The tenacious salesman calls twice a week between 5 and 7 p.m.

14. **The correct answer is (A).** PERTINENT means *relevant*. Testimony is admitted in court only if it is pertinent to the charges in the case.

15. **The correct answer is (C).** DOGMATIC means *dictatorial* or *opinionated*. The word has to do with *doctrine* or *dogma*, not with *dogs*. My uncle is so dogmatic that he refuses to even listen to my point of view.

16. **The correct answer is (D).** One who is UNSCRUPULOUS is *not restrained by ideas of right and wrong*. The unscrupulous stockbroker used inside information to sell before the stock price plummeted.

17. **The correct answer is (C).** WILY means *crafty* or *sly*. The wily wolf outwitted Red Riding Hood.

18. **The correct answer is (B).** BLATANT means *loud* and *obtrusive*. The misspelling in the address was a blatant error in an otherwise excellent letter.

19. **The correct answer is (A).** A PRETEXT is a *false reason* or *an excuse*. Illness was his pretext for absence from school; actually he went to the beach.

20. **The correct answer is (C).** ACUMEN is *keenness and quickness in understanding and dealing with a situation*. Acumen with respect to foreign cultures is a great asset in the diplomatic corps.

21. **The correct answer is (D).** EVASION is *subterfuge* or *avoidance*. His manner of evasion of embarrassing questions was to make a long speech on another topic.

22. **The correct answer is (B).** That which is INDISPENSABLE *cannot be dispensed with*, that is it is *absolutely essential*. The president of the company refused to take a vacation because he had the mistaken notion that his presence was indispensable.

23. **The correct answer is (E).** To OBLITERATE is to *destroy without leaving a trace*. The washing waves obliterated our footsteps in the sand.

24. **The correct answer is (D).** AMIABLE means *pleasant, friendly,* and *good-natured*. The amiable shopkeeper allowed us to continue trying on shoes even though it was already past closing time.

25. **The correct answer is (E).** To WRITHE is to *twist, squirm,* or *contort,* usually in discomfort. The skier writhed in pain when she broke her ankle.

26. **The correct answer is (A).** To ABATE is to *diminish*. We will stay tied up in port until the winds abate.

27. **The correct answer is (B).** An ENDORSEMENT is a *statement of approval*. The governor gave his endorsement to the candidate for mayor of the city.

28. **The correct answer is (D).** To CONVERT is to *change* from one form to another. Use a transformer to convert DC current to AC current.

29. **The correct answer is (A).** ERUDITE means *learned* or *scholarly*. He has little information, but his beautiful command of the English language makes him appear to be erudite.

30. **The correct answer is (B).** To ENDEAVOR is to *attempt* or to *try*. The expedition endeavored to reach the mountaintop before the thunderstorm.

31. The correct answer is (B). The relationship of the terms is one of degree. *None* is the ultimate the empty set of *little; never* bears the same relationship to *infrequently.*

32. The correct answer is (C). If you think in terms of a house, you can see that the terms on each side of the relationship are synonymous. You can *receive* a person into your home or *admit* the person. Once the person decides to *remain,* that person *settles* in.

33. The correct answer is (E). Here the cause-and-effect relationship is clear. Recognized *dishonesty* leads to *distrust; carelessness* leads to *accidents.*

34. The correct answer is (A). The relationship is that of actor to object. A *sociologist* studies *groups;* a *psychologist* studies *individuals.* The relationship of the children to the pediatrician is in reverse order.

35. The correct answer is (B). The terms are antonyms. *Generous* is the opposite of *frugal;* a *philanthropist* is truly the opposite of a *miser.* The terms in choices (C) and (E) are also antonyms. When faced with questions in which the same relationship is maintained by a number of the choices, you must look for a relationship among all four terms. In this case, the theme to be carried through among the choices of the correct analogy is "money."

36. The correct answer is (C). The relationship is one of degree. *Translucent* is denser than *transparent,* that is, one can actually see through something that is transparent whereas only light passes through a translucent medium. Carrying on to the next degree, *opaque* is denser than *translucent.* Not even light can pass through something that is opaque. Choice (A) is incorrect because it skips a degree and jumps from transparent to opaque. Choice (D) reverses the order. Glass and crystal, choice (B), may both be transparent.

37. The correct answer is (A). This is a classic cause-and-effect relationship. *Discontent* leads to *rebellion; friction* creates a *spark.*

38. The correct answer is (B). The relationship is that of worker to tool. A *chemist* uses a *beaker* in the laboratory; a *geologist* uses a *hammer* to chip at rocks in the field or laboratory. Avoid the "trap" of choice (C). A hammer is certainly used in construction, but the relationship of the first two terms requires that a person be involved to complete the analogy.

39. The correct answer is (D). The basis of the analogy is antonyms.

40. The correct answer is (C). This is a part-to-whole analogy. A *state* is part of a *country;* a *country* is part of a *continent.*

41. The correct answer is (A). Cause and effect. An *accelerator* causes the motion of the *car;* a *catalyst* causes the chemical *change.*

42. The correct answer is (E). The relationship is one of degree. *Probable* is likely but less likely than *certain; plausible* is possible but less likely than *definite.*

43. The correct answer is (A). The relationship is one of true synonyms.

44. The correct answer is (B). This analogy involves true antonyms.

45. The correct answer is (A). The relationship is that of object to actor. The *nucleus* is the object that is orbited by an *electron; Earth* is the object that is orbited by a *satellite.* Choice (B) reverses the order of the relationship.

46. The correct answer is (C). Here the relationship is that of actor to object. A *sculptor* creates a *statue;* a *composer* creates *music.* An actor performs in a play but does not create it. A programmer creates a program while working at a computer.

47. The correct answer is (C). The analogy is based on an antonym relationship.

48. The correct answer is (D). This analogy is also based on antonyms.

49. The correct answer is (E). It is hard to categorize this relationship. One *interrupts* by *speaking* out of turn; one *intrudes* by *entering* out of turn. The relationship in choice (B) might be that of opposites.

50. The correct answer is (A). The first two terms are true opposites. Only choice (A) offers true opposites. *Financial stability* is the opposite of *poverty,* but finance bears no relationship to poverty at all.

51. The correct answer is (D). This analogy is best understood as a negative cause and effect. *Adversity* leads to a lack of *happiness; vehemence* leads to a lack of *serenity.*

52. The correct answer is (A). The relationship is that of actor to action. An *extortionist blackmails;* a *kleptomaniac steals.*

53. The correct answer is (B). This is a whole-to-part relationship. A *monsoon* is a major storm of which *rain* is a crucial component; a *tornado* is a major storm of which *wind* is a crucial component.

54. The correct answer is (E). The relationship between the two sets of words is that the words in each half of the analogy are synonyms. Don't worry that the words in the first half are antonyms of the second. You aren't looking at how all four words relate to one another in this analogy just at how the words in each half relate to one another.

55. The correct answer is (D). You needn't categorize an analogy; you only need to understand it. The *equator* is the midline that circles the *world;* the *waist* is the midline that circles the *man.*

56. The correct answer is (A). On each side of the analogy the first term is a characteristic of the second.

57. The correct answer is (C). This analogy is based on characteristics of bodies of water. A *pond* may be *stagnant;* a *stream* is likely to *flow.* Sheep may be noisy but since there are two choices that involve characteristics you must choose the one that is closest in other aspects to the first set of terms that is the one involving *water.*

58. The correct answer is (B). This is a purposeful or functional relationship. A *fortress* gives *sanctuary;* a *house* gives *shelter.*

59. The correct answer is (A). The terms are synonyms.

60. The correct answer is (A). This analogy is also based on synonyms. Choice (E) is incorrect because pensive means thoughtful. If you made this choice, you were mistaking pensive for pendant, which does mean hanging.

Section 2: Quantitative (Math)

1. B	6. C	11. E	16. A	21. A
2. C	7. A	12. E	17. C	22. D
3. D	8. B	13. A	18. A	23. B
4. D	9. C	14. B	19. C	24. C
5. B	10. C	15. D	20. E	25. D

1. **The correct answer is (B).** Rename $\frac{3}{5}$ as

   a decimal: $\frac{3}{5} = 0.6$.

   $0.6 + 1.25 + 0.004 = 1.854$

2. **The correct answer is (C).**

   $$\frac{10^6}{10^3} = 10^{6-3} = 1000$$

   or $10^6 = 1,000,000$ and $10^3 = 1000$
   Therefore, $1,000,000 \div 1000 = 1000$.

3. **The correct answer is (D).**

   $$\begin{array}{r} 71.4 \\ \times\ 98.2 \\ \hline 1428 \\ 5712 \\ 6426 \\ \hline 7011.48 \end{array}$$

4. **The correct answer is (D).** Simplify the numerator.

   $$\frac{4\frac{2}{3} + \frac{1}{6}}{\frac{1}{3}} = \frac{4\frac{4}{6} + \frac{1}{6}}{\frac{1}{3}} = \frac{4\frac{5}{6}}{\frac{1}{3}}$$

   Proceed as you would to divide any fraction:

   $$4\frac{5}{6} \div \frac{1}{3} = \frac{29}{\underset{2}{6}} \bullet \frac{\overset{1}{3}}{1} = 14\frac{1}{2}$$

5. **The correct answer is (B).** $(0.25)^2 = 0.25$
   $\times\ 0.25 = 0.0625$

6. **The correct answer is (C).** Begin with the innermost group and work outward:

   $(3 + 1) + [(2 - 3) - (4 - 1)]$
   $= (3 + 1) + [(-1) - (3)]$
   $= (3 + 1) + [-1 - 3]$
   $= (3 + 1) + [-4]$
   $= 4 + [-4]$
   $= 0$

7. **The correct answer is (A).** Try to estimate the answer rather than calculate:

   $$\begin{array}{r} 10001 \\ -\ \ \ 8093 \\ \hline 1908 \end{array}$$

8. **The correct answer is (B).** 3 gallons contain 12 quarts. The ratio is 3 quarts:12 quarts, or, in simplest form, 1:4.

9. **The correct answer is (C).** One fifth of $50 is $10. Ten percent, or $\frac{1}{10}$ of $10 is $1.

10. **The correct answer is (C).** Borrow 1 minute from the minutes column, and 1 hour from the hours column. Then subtract:

    $$\begin{array}{r} 3 \text{ hr. } 71 \text{ min. } 70 \text{ sec.} \\ -\ 2 \text{ hr. } 48 \text{ min. } 35 \text{ sec.} \\ \hline 1 \text{ hr. } 23 \text{ min. } 35 \text{ sec.} \end{array}$$

11. **The correct answer is (E).** By doubling the size of one of the factors of the numerator and the size of the denominator, we do not change the value of the fraction. We are actually writing an equivalent fraction. Try

this with fractions having numerical values for the numerator and denominator.

12. **The correct answer is (E).** This is a good problem for estimation. Note that 10% of 220 = 22. One percent of 220 = 2.2 and 24.2 = 22 (10 percent) + 2.2 (1 percent). Or, $\frac{24.2}{220} = 0.11$.

13. **The correct answer is (A).** Be careful. This problem asks you to reduce 98 by $\frac{5}{7}$. In other words, find $\frac{2}{7}$ of 98.

$$98 \bullet \frac{2}{7} = \frac{\cancel{98}^{14}}{1} \bullet \frac{2}{\cancel{7}_1} = 28$$

14. **The correct answer is (B).** Since one foot corresponds to $\frac{1}{4}$ inch in the drawing, the drawing should be $6\frac{1}{2} \bullet \frac{1}{4}$ inches long.

$$6\frac{1}{2} \bullet \frac{1}{4} =$$
$$= \frac{13}{2} \bullet \frac{1}{4}$$
$$= \frac{13}{8} = 1\frac{5}{8} \text{ inches}$$

15. **The correct answer is (D).** Bracket the multiplication and division operations from left to right. Then calculate.

$$\left[12\frac{1}{2} \div \frac{1}{2}\right] + \left[\frac{3}{2} \times 4\right] - 3$$
$$= [25] + 6 - 3$$
$$= 28$$

16. **The correct answer is (A).** Since $y + 2 > 10$, $y > 10 - 2$, or $y > 8$.

17. **The correct answer is (C).** This is a simple proportion. A man casts a shadow twice as long as his height. Therefore, so does the tree. Therefore, a tree that casts a shadow 50' long is 25' tall.

18. **The correct answer is (A).** The denominator of a fraction can never be equivalent to zero. Division by zero is undefined in mathematics.

19. **The correct answer is (C).** $0.0515 \times 100 = 5.15$, and so does 0.00515×1000. You should be able to do this problem by moving

decimal points and not by multiplying out. To divide by 10, move the decimal point one place to the left. Move it two places to the left to divide by 100, three places to divide by 1000, and so forth. To multiply by 10, 100, 1000, and so forth, move the decimal point the corresponding number of places to the right. This is an important skill to review.

20. **The correct answer is (E).** This is a tricky problem. Choices (B), (C), and (D) might be true in some cases depending upon the exact measurements of $\angle 1$ and $\angle 3$. The only answer that is true no matter what the measures of $\angle 1$ and $\angle 3$ is the one in which their sum is equal to 120°.

21. **The correct answer is (A).** This can be set up as a proportion where x is the unknown number:

$$\frac{45}{x} = \frac{90}{0.45}$$

This is a good problem for estimation. Study the numerators of the fractions and note that 45 is one half of 90. Therefore, the denominators of the fractions must have the same relationship. One half of 0.45 is 0.225.

22. **The correct answer is (D).** The square root of 20 is less than the square root of 25, which is 5, and greater than the square root of 16, which is 4. Therefore, n is between 4 and 5.

23. **The correct answer is (B).** To find the difference, we subtract –6 from 4 and move from –6 to 4, a distance of +10 units.

24. **The correct answer is (C).** Simply divide $\frac{4}{5}$ by $\frac{1}{6}$ to find the answer.

$$\frac{4}{5} \div \frac{1}{6} = \frac{4}{5} \bullet \frac{6}{1} = \frac{24}{5} = 4\frac{4}{5}$$

25. **The correct answer is (D).** Four games averaging 36,500 people per game total 146,000 attendance. The total for the first three games was 105,500. The fourth game attracted 40,500 people.

Section 3: Reading Comprehension

1. C	9. A	17. B	25. A	33. D
2. D	10. B	18. A	26. C	34. C
3. B	11. E	19. C	27. E	35. B
4. E	12. A	20. E	28. D	36. E
5. C	13. C	21. E	29. A	37. A
6. B	14. D	22. D	30. D	38. C
7. D	15. B	23. A	31. B	39. A
8. E	16. A	24. C	32. B	40. E

1. **The correct answer is (C).** You will find the answer to this detail question in the last two sentences of the selection.

2. **The correct answer is (D).** This detail is given in the last sentence of the first paragraph. All the other answer choices were true of the history of Riker's Island but are not true at the present time.

3. **The correct answer is (B).** You can infer that the discards of city households included garbage. Decayed garbage is an excellent fertilizer.

4. **The correct answer is (E).** See the next-to-last sentence of the selection.

5. **The correct answer is (C).** This is the meaning of the second sentence of the first paragraph.

6. **The correct answer is (B).** Since the thrust of the selection is the threatened extinction of the bald eagle, you really do not need to search for the precise words that answer this question. However, you can find them in the second paragraph.

7. **The correct answer is (D).** This definition is given in the second sentence of the third paragraph: ". . . aeries, the eagles' mammoth nests."

8. **The correct answer is (E).** The selection tells us that the bald eagle appears on the Great Seal of the United States, our

national emblem. An *emblem* is a symbol. *Emblematic* is the adjective form of the noun, *emblem*.

9. **The correct answer is (A).** This detail may be found in the first sentence of the last paragraph.

10. **The correct answer is (B).** The author tells you his reason in the second sentence.

11. **The correct answer is (E).** See the third sentence.

12. **The correct answer is (A).** The fourth sentence gives this detail.

13. **The correct answer is (C).** The sixth sentence tells that the garden led to a forest. The selection says that the garden extended so far that the gardener did not know where it ended, but it does not say that he was unable to care for it because of its size.

14. **The correct answer is (D).** In the last sentence we learn that the forest went down to the sea, and in the trees of the forest at seaside lived a nightingale.

15. **The correct answer is (B).** This really is a vocabulary question. A *sojourn* is a visit or a *temporary stay*.

16. **The correct answer is (A).** The context of the second paragraph should help you to figure out the meaning of this word. In other contexts, *decipher* may mean to *decode*. Here it means to *make out the meaning of*

ancient, nearly illegible, inscriptions or writings.

17. The correct answer is (B). See the last sentence of the first paragraph. By enlarging on hitherto known tales of the named persons, the scroll is giving new details about persons already known of. The scroll is the last of the seven found in 1947, not the first. It tells of Abraham's stay in Egypt, but it was found in the Judean desert of Israel.

18. The correct answer is (A). The second paragraph opens by telling us that the scroll belongs to Hebrew University. If you were not certain that Hebrew University is an Israeli university, the statement that the work is being done under the supervision of Israeli scholars (last sentence) should confirm this.

19. The correct answer is (C). If this question gives you trouble, reread the middle of the second paragraph. The readable material included: four full pages, legible parts of five other pages, and some lines and words on additional pages.

20. The correct answer is (E). See the first sentence. A century ago was 100 years ago.

21. The correct answer is (E). The first sentence of the second paragraph says that the boats are equipped for various jobs, which means that they vary in function.

22. The correct answer is (D). By checking on the operation of the junk boats, the harbor police ensure that their activities are legal.

23. The correct answer is (A). The other choices all include some activity that is not mentioned as an activity of the harbor police.

24. The correct answer is (C). The 450 disabled boats that were towed and the thousands that needed some sort of help (next-to-last sentence) could not possibly have all been of the same kind.

25. The correct answer is (A). Context should help you here. ". . . *veneration* due to

its sacred origin . . ." implies something religious and related to worship.

26. The correct answer is (C). This is an inferential question. The speaker probably enjoys and celebrates Christmas, choice (B), as well but the primary reason for this speech is defending the holiday to his Uncle Scrooge by listing its advantages to mankind.

27. The correct answer is (E). This is the whole point of the first paragraph.

28. The correct answer is (D). Again, use of the word in context should lead you to its meaning. The paragraph speaks of good will among all men and women. This *one consent,* therefore, is *unanimous* good feeling.

29. The correct answer is (A). Read the last paragraph carefully. Scrooge is first reacting to the clerk who has just applauded the speech in defense of Christmas. Scrooge threatens the clerk with firing. He then turns and makes a sarcastic remark to his nephew. It can be assumed that he is angry with both characters.

30. The correct answer is (D). "Just stopped by . . ." is quite a matter-of-fact way of speaking.

31. The correct answer is (B). The raised eyebrows of the first sentence of the second paragraph imply disbelief.

32. The correct answer is (B). Mr. Holter had a caravan of animals; was in New York on his way to Dayton, Ohio; and actually lived in Anaheim, California. You can infer that he made his living traveling and showing his animals.

33. The correct answer is (D). The article discusses high blood pressure as a familial disease, a disease that runs in families. It goes on to discuss the role of genetic makeup in determining reaction to dietary factors. Genetic makeup refers to hereditary factors.

34. The correct answer is (C). This is a main-idea question. The main point of the selection is that there is an interplay of genetic and environmental factors influencing the development of high blood pressure.

35. **The correct answer is (B).** The first paragraph speaks of the perils of fishing, the second about its rewards.

36. **The correct answer is (E).** The middle of the first paragraph discusses the problems created by rough seas. None of the other choices is a mentioned difficulty.

37. **The correct answer is (A).** In the middle of the second paragraph we learn that when the fishermen note that herring are entering the nets they sit in quiet excitement so

as not to frighten the fish away. They row along the net, choice (E), in order to find out if the net is filling, and haul in the nets, choices (B) and (D), when the nets are full. It is the fish that glisten, not the fishermen.

38. **The correct answer is (C).** Everything is mentioned except the beauty of the sea.

39. **The correct answer is (A).** All other choices contain at least one trait that is not ascribed to the fishermen.

40. **The correct answer is (E).** One might add honesty to the traits of the fishermen. Theft is not mentioned as a problem.

Section 4: Quantitative (Math)

1. E	6. D	11. B	16. A	21. B
2. B	7. C	12. D	17. C	22. B
3. D	8. B	13. B	18. B	23. D
4. B	9. C	14. D	19. E	24. A
5. C	10. E	15. E	20. D	25. A

1. **The correct answer is (E).** Any point on the surface rotates once each day relative to a point in space. Each revolution is an angle of 360°. In two days, two revolutions take place, $360° \times 2 = 720°$.

2. **The correct answer is (B).** $\frac{3}{7}$, $\frac{15}{32}$, and $\frac{11}{23}$ are all less than $\frac{1}{2}$; $\frac{9}{16}$ is larger than $\frac{1}{2}$. Compare the size of fractions this way:
$$\frac{3}{7} \times \frac{15}{32}$$
Because the product of 7 and 15 is larger than the product of 32 and 3, $\frac{15}{32}$ will be found to be larger. Using the same method, $\frac{15}{32} < \frac{11}{23}$.

3. **The correct answer is (D).** If the width is x, the length, which is twice as long, is $2x$. The perimeter is equal to the sum of the four sides: $2x + 2x + x + x = 6x$.

4. **The correct answer is (B).** Use the Pythagorean theorem $c^2 = a^2 + b^2$ to find the length of the diagonal:
$$c^2 = 1^2 + 1^2$$
$$c^2 = 2$$
$$c = \sqrt{2}$$

5. **The correct answer is (C).** Eight sections, each 3'2" long, is equivalent to $8 \times 38" = 304"$.

$304" = 25\frac{1}{3}$ feet; therefore, three 10-foot sections are needed.

6. **The correct answer is (D).** The width of the shaded area is $\frac{1}{3}$ of the width of the square. Therefore, the area of the shaded part is $\frac{1}{3}$ the area of the whole square. The unshaded part is twice as large as the shaded part. The ratio of the shaded part to the unshaded, therefore, is 1:2.

7. **The correct answer is (C).** Since distance = rate × time, rate = distance ÷ time. Total distance traveled is 3,200 miles. Total time is 4 hours 20 minutes.

   Rate = 3,200 miles ÷ 4 hrs. 20 min.

   $= 3,200$ miles $\div 4\frac{1}{3}$ hours

   $= 738$ mph, approximately

8. **The correct answer is (B).** This is a simple proportion: $\frac{7}{4} = \frac{5}{x}$. x is the unknown width. Cross-multiply:

   $7x = 20$

   $x = \frac{20}{7}$, or $2\frac{6}{7}$"

9. **The correct answer is (C).** Subtract the area of the circle from the area of the square to find the area of just the shaded part.

   Note that the diameter of the circle equals the width of the square.

   Area of square = s^2 = 4 sq. in.
   Area of circle = $\pi r^2 = \pi(1)^2 = \pi$ sq. in.
   Area of square – Area of circle

   $= 4$ sq. in. $- \frac{22}{7}$ sq. in.

   $= \frac{6}{7}$ sq. in., or $\frac{6}{7}$ in.^{2}

10. **The correct answer is (E).** The population would reproduce 12 times in 4 hours. The size, then, is $P = 1 \times 2^{12} = 2 \cdot 2 \cdot 2 \cdot 2 \cdot 2 \cdot 2 \cdot 2 \cdot 2 \cdot 2 \cdot 2 \cdot 2 \cdot 2 = 4,096$.

11. **The correct answer is (B).** The larger the number of the denominator of a fraction,

the smaller the quantity represented. For example, $\frac{1}{4}$ represents a lesser quantity than $\frac{1}{2}$. Therefore, as x becomes greater, y becomes smaller.

12. **The correct answer is (D).** If the second box has each dimension 3 times that of the first box, then its volume is $3 \times 3 \times 3 = 27$ times as great.

13. **The correct answer is (B).** The area of the flower bed is 4π sq. ft. $(A = \pi r^2)$. The area of the new bed is to be four times as great, or 16π sq. ft. A bed with an area of 16π sq. ft. must have a diameter of 8', and a radius of 4', since $A = \pi r^2$.

14. **The correct answer is (D).** Use the formula $D = R \times T$ to find the time it actually took to get to Buffalo: time = distance ÷ rate. Travel time of trip was equal to 290 miles ÷ 50 mph.

   Travel time = $5\frac{4}{5}$ hours, or 5 hours 48 minutes. Scheduled travel time was between 10:10 a.m. and 3:45 p.m., an interval of 5 hours 35 minutes. Therefore, the train took about 13 minutes longer than scheduled.

15. **The correct answer is (E).** Solve the equation for x:

   $3x - 2 = 13$
   $3x = 15$
   $x = 5$

   If $x = 5$, then $12x + 20 = 12(5) + 20 = 80$.

16. **The correct answer is (A).** Since the number of pounds of each kind of cake sold was the same, we can say that a pound of cake sold for an average price of 30¢ per pound.

   25¢ + 30¢ + 35¢ = 90¢ ÷ 3 = 30¢ per lb.

   Divide the total sales income of $36 by 30¢ to find how many pounds were sold.

   $36 ÷ 0.30 = 120

17. The correct answer is (C). A floor 12' × 12' is 144 sq. ft. in area, and would require 144 tiles that are each one foot by one foot. Twelve tiles would be placed along the width and length of the room. If 9" tiles are used, it requires 16 of them placed end to end to cover the length of the room. Therefore, it requires 16 × 16 tiles to cover the floor, or 256 tiles. It requires 112 more 9" tiles than 12" tiles to cover the floor.

18. The correct answer is (B). If p pencils cost c cents the cost of each pencil is $\frac{c}{p}$ cents. To find the cost of n pencils we multiply the cost of each times n:

$$\frac{c}{p} \bullet n = \frac{cn}{p}$$

19. The correct answer is (E). If necessary, try each of the answers for yourself to see that each is false. Choice (C) is untrue for the number 1.

20. The correct answer is (D). Think of a rectangle with the dimensions 1" by 2". Its area is 2 square inches. If we double each dimension to 2" by 4", the area becomes 8 square inches, which is four times the area of the first rectangle. This is equal to an increase of 300%.

21. The correct answer is (B). The first pipe can fill the tank in $1\frac{1}{2}$, or $\frac{3}{2}$, hours; that is, it can do $\frac{2}{3}$ of the job in 1 hour. The second pipe can fill the tank in 45 minutes, or $\frac{3}{4}$ of an hour, or it can do $\frac{4}{3}$ of the job in 1 hour. Together the pipes can complete $\frac{4}{3} + \frac{2}{3} = \frac{6}{3}$ of the job in one hour. $\frac{6}{3} = 2$, or twice the job in one hour. There-

fore, together the two pipes could fill the tank in $\frac{1}{2}$ hour.

22. The correct answer is (B). The whole season consists of 120 games. For a season record of 60%, the team must win 72 games. Since it has already won 50, it must win 22 more games out of those left.

23. The correct answer is (D). Commercial and industrial needs total 63% of daily oil consumption. Since consumption is 9 million barrels, 63% of 9 million is 5,670,000 barrels.

24. The correct answer is (A). Add the cost of the house, driveway, painting, and plumbing:

$44,000 + $1250 + $1750 + $1000 = $48,000

If he wants to make a 12% profit when reselling the house, he should increase the total cost by 12% to find the new selling price:

12% of $48,000 = $5760
$48,000 + $5760 = $53,760

25. The correct answer is (A). This is a problem that must be done carefully.

$a = 1, b = 2, c = 3, d = 5$

$$\sqrt{b(d+a) - b(c+a)}$$
$$= \sqrt{2(5+1) - 2(3+1)}$$
$$= \sqrt{2(6) - 2(4)}$$
$$= \sqrt{12 - 8}$$
$$= \sqrt{4}$$
$$= 2$$

SCORE YOURSELF

Check your answers against the answer key. Count up the number of answers you got right and the number you got wrong.

Section	No. Right	No. Wrong
Quantitative (Math)		
Reading Comprehension		
Verbal		

Now calculate your raw scores:

Quantitative (Math): $\dfrac{(\qquad)}{\text{No. Right}} - \left(\dfrac{1}{4}\right)\dfrac{(\qquad)}{\text{No. Wrong}} = \dfrac{(\qquad)}{\text{Raw Score}}$

Reading Comprehension: $\dfrac{(\qquad)}{\text{No. Right}} - \left(\dfrac{1}{4}\right)\dfrac{(\qquad)}{\text{No. Wrong}} = \dfrac{(\qquad)}{\text{Raw Score}}$

Verbal: $\dfrac{(\qquad)}{\text{No. Right}} - \left(\dfrac{1}{4}\right)\dfrac{(\qquad)}{\text{No. Wrong}} = \dfrac{(\qquad)}{\text{Raw Score}}$

Now check your Raw Score against the conversion chart to get an idea of the range in which your test scores fall:

Raw Score	Quantitative (Math)	Reading Comprehension	Verbal
60			350
55			350
50	350		343
45	344		334
40	335	348	325
35	325	324	316
30	316	314	307
25	306	304	298
20	297	294	289
15	288	284	280
10	278	274	271
5	269	264	261
0	260	254	252
−5 or lower	250	250	250

Remember:

- The same exam is given to students in grades 8 through 11. You are not expected to know what you have not been taught.

- You will be compared only with students in your own grade.

Use your scores to plan further study if you have time.

ANSWER SHEET PRACTICE TEST 8: ISEE (UPPER LEVEL)

Section 1: Verbal Reasoning

1. Ⓐ Ⓑ Ⓒ Ⓓ   9. Ⓐ Ⓑ Ⓒ Ⓓ   17. Ⓐ Ⓑ Ⓒ Ⓓ   25. Ⓐ Ⓑ Ⓒ Ⓓ   33. Ⓐ Ⓑ Ⓒ Ⓓ
2. Ⓐ Ⓑ Ⓒ Ⓓ   10. Ⓐ Ⓑ Ⓒ Ⓓ   18. Ⓐ Ⓑ Ⓒ Ⓓ   26. Ⓐ Ⓑ Ⓒ Ⓓ   34. Ⓐ Ⓑ Ⓒ Ⓓ
3. Ⓐ Ⓑ Ⓒ Ⓓ   11. Ⓐ Ⓑ Ⓒ Ⓓ   19. Ⓐ Ⓑ Ⓒ Ⓓ   27. Ⓐ Ⓑ Ⓒ Ⓓ   35. Ⓐ Ⓑ Ⓒ Ⓓ
4. Ⓐ Ⓑ Ⓒ Ⓓ   12. Ⓐ Ⓑ Ⓒ Ⓓ   20. Ⓐ Ⓑ Ⓒ Ⓓ   28. Ⓐ Ⓑ Ⓒ Ⓓ   36. Ⓐ Ⓑ Ⓒ Ⓓ
5. Ⓐ Ⓑ Ⓒ Ⓓ   13. Ⓐ Ⓑ Ⓒ Ⓓ   21. Ⓐ Ⓑ Ⓒ Ⓓ   29. Ⓐ Ⓑ Ⓒ Ⓓ   37. Ⓐ Ⓑ Ⓒ Ⓓ
6. Ⓐ Ⓑ Ⓒ Ⓓ   14. Ⓐ Ⓑ Ⓒ Ⓓ   22. Ⓐ Ⓑ Ⓒ Ⓓ   30. Ⓐ Ⓑ Ⓒ Ⓓ   38. Ⓐ Ⓑ Ⓒ Ⓓ
7. Ⓐ Ⓑ Ⓒ Ⓓ   15. Ⓐ Ⓑ Ⓒ Ⓓ   23. Ⓐ Ⓑ Ⓒ Ⓓ   31. Ⓐ Ⓑ Ⓒ Ⓓ   39. Ⓐ Ⓑ Ⓒ Ⓓ
8. Ⓐ Ⓑ Ⓒ Ⓓ   16. Ⓐ Ⓑ Ⓒ Ⓓ   24. Ⓐ Ⓑ Ⓒ Ⓓ   32. Ⓐ Ⓑ Ⓒ Ⓓ   40. Ⓐ Ⓑ Ⓒ Ⓓ

Section 2: Quantitative (Reasoning)

1. Ⓐ Ⓑ Ⓒ Ⓓ   8. Ⓐ Ⓑ Ⓒ Ⓓ   15. Ⓐ Ⓑ Ⓒ Ⓓ   22. Ⓐ Ⓑ Ⓒ Ⓓ   29. Ⓐ Ⓑ Ⓒ Ⓓ
2. Ⓐ Ⓑ Ⓒ Ⓓ   9. Ⓐ Ⓑ Ⓒ Ⓓ   16. Ⓐ Ⓑ Ⓒ Ⓓ   23. Ⓐ Ⓑ Ⓒ Ⓓ   30. Ⓐ Ⓑ Ⓒ Ⓓ
3. Ⓐ Ⓑ Ⓒ Ⓓ   10. Ⓐ Ⓑ Ⓒ Ⓓ   17. Ⓐ Ⓑ Ⓒ Ⓓ   24. Ⓐ Ⓑ Ⓒ Ⓓ   31. Ⓐ Ⓑ Ⓒ Ⓓ
4. Ⓐ Ⓑ Ⓒ Ⓓ   11. Ⓐ Ⓑ Ⓒ Ⓓ   18. Ⓐ Ⓑ Ⓒ Ⓓ   25. Ⓐ Ⓑ Ⓒ Ⓓ   32. Ⓐ Ⓑ Ⓒ Ⓓ
5. Ⓐ Ⓑ Ⓒ Ⓓ   12. Ⓐ Ⓑ Ⓒ Ⓓ   19. Ⓐ Ⓑ Ⓒ Ⓓ   26. Ⓐ Ⓑ Ⓒ Ⓓ   33. Ⓐ Ⓑ Ⓒ Ⓓ
6. Ⓐ Ⓑ Ⓒ Ⓓ   13. Ⓐ Ⓑ Ⓒ Ⓓ   20. Ⓐ Ⓑ Ⓒ Ⓓ   27. Ⓐ Ⓑ Ⓒ Ⓓ   34. Ⓐ Ⓑ Ⓒ Ⓓ
7. Ⓐ Ⓑ Ⓒ Ⓓ   14. Ⓐ Ⓑ Ⓒ Ⓓ   21. Ⓐ Ⓑ Ⓒ Ⓓ   28. Ⓐ Ⓑ Ⓒ Ⓓ   35. Ⓐ Ⓑ Ⓒ Ⓓ

answer sheet

Section 3: Reading Comprehension

1. Ⓐ Ⓑ Ⓒ Ⓓ	9. Ⓐ Ⓑ Ⓒ Ⓓ	17. Ⓐ Ⓑ Ⓒ Ⓓ	25. Ⓐ Ⓑ Ⓒ Ⓓ	33. Ⓐ Ⓑ Ⓒ Ⓓ
2. Ⓐ Ⓑ Ⓒ Ⓓ	10. Ⓐ Ⓑ Ⓒ Ⓓ	18. Ⓐ Ⓑ Ⓒ Ⓓ	26. Ⓐ Ⓑ Ⓒ Ⓓ	34. Ⓐ Ⓑ Ⓒ Ⓓ
3. Ⓐ Ⓑ Ⓒ Ⓓ	11. Ⓐ Ⓑ Ⓒ Ⓓ	19. Ⓐ Ⓑ Ⓒ Ⓓ	27. Ⓐ Ⓑ Ⓒ Ⓓ	35. Ⓐ Ⓑ Ⓒ Ⓓ
4. Ⓐ Ⓑ Ⓒ Ⓓ	12. Ⓐ Ⓑ Ⓒ Ⓓ	20. Ⓐ Ⓑ Ⓒ Ⓓ	28. Ⓐ Ⓑ Ⓒ Ⓓ	36. Ⓐ Ⓑ Ⓒ Ⓓ
5. Ⓐ Ⓑ Ⓒ Ⓓ	13. Ⓐ Ⓑ Ⓒ Ⓓ	21. Ⓐ Ⓑ Ⓒ Ⓓ	29. Ⓐ Ⓑ Ⓒ Ⓓ	37. Ⓐ Ⓑ Ⓒ Ⓓ
6. Ⓐ Ⓑ Ⓒ Ⓓ	14. Ⓐ Ⓑ Ⓒ Ⓓ	22. Ⓐ Ⓑ Ⓒ Ⓓ	30. Ⓐ Ⓑ Ⓒ Ⓓ	38. Ⓐ Ⓑ Ⓒ Ⓓ
7. Ⓐ Ⓑ Ⓒ Ⓓ	15. Ⓐ Ⓑ Ⓒ Ⓓ	23. Ⓐ Ⓑ Ⓒ Ⓓ	31. Ⓐ Ⓑ Ⓒ Ⓓ	39. Ⓐ Ⓑ Ⓒ Ⓓ
8. Ⓐ Ⓑ Ⓒ Ⓓ	16. Ⓐ Ⓑ Ⓒ Ⓓ	24. Ⓐ Ⓑ Ⓒ Ⓓ	32. Ⓐ Ⓑ Ⓒ Ⓓ	40. Ⓐ Ⓑ Ⓒ Ⓓ

Section 4: Mathematics Achievement

1. Ⓐ Ⓑ Ⓒ Ⓓ	10. Ⓐ Ⓑ Ⓒ Ⓓ	19. Ⓐ Ⓑ Ⓒ Ⓓ	28. Ⓐ Ⓑ Ⓒ Ⓓ	37. Ⓐ Ⓑ Ⓒ Ⓓ
2. Ⓐ Ⓑ Ⓒ Ⓓ	11. Ⓐ Ⓑ Ⓒ Ⓓ	20. Ⓐ Ⓑ Ⓒ Ⓓ	29. Ⓐ Ⓑ Ⓒ Ⓓ	38. Ⓐ Ⓑ Ⓒ Ⓓ
3. Ⓐ Ⓑ Ⓒ Ⓓ	12. Ⓐ Ⓑ Ⓒ Ⓓ	21. Ⓐ Ⓑ Ⓒ Ⓓ	30. Ⓐ Ⓑ Ⓒ Ⓓ	39. Ⓐ Ⓑ Ⓒ Ⓓ
4. Ⓐ Ⓑ Ⓒ Ⓓ	13. Ⓐ Ⓑ Ⓒ Ⓓ	22. Ⓐ Ⓑ Ⓒ Ⓓ	31. Ⓐ Ⓑ Ⓒ Ⓓ	40. Ⓐ Ⓑ Ⓒ Ⓓ
5. Ⓐ Ⓑ Ⓒ Ⓓ	14. Ⓐ Ⓑ Ⓒ Ⓓ	23. Ⓐ Ⓑ Ⓒ Ⓓ	32. Ⓐ Ⓑ Ⓒ Ⓓ	41. Ⓐ Ⓑ Ⓒ Ⓓ
6. Ⓐ Ⓑ Ⓒ Ⓓ	15. Ⓐ Ⓑ Ⓒ Ⓓ	24. Ⓐ Ⓑ Ⓒ Ⓓ	33. Ⓐ Ⓑ Ⓒ Ⓓ	42. Ⓐ Ⓑ Ⓒ Ⓓ
7. Ⓐ Ⓑ Ⓒ Ⓓ	16. Ⓐ Ⓑ Ⓒ Ⓓ	25. Ⓐ Ⓑ Ⓒ Ⓓ	34. Ⓐ Ⓑ Ⓒ Ⓓ	43. Ⓐ Ⓑ Ⓒ Ⓓ
8. Ⓐ Ⓑ Ⓒ Ⓓ	17. Ⓐ Ⓑ Ⓒ Ⓓ	26. Ⓐ Ⓑ Ⓒ Ⓓ	35. Ⓐ Ⓑ Ⓒ Ⓓ	44. Ⓐ Ⓑ Ⓒ Ⓓ
9. Ⓐ Ⓑ Ⓒ Ⓓ	18. Ⓐ Ⓑ Ⓒ Ⓓ	27. Ⓐ Ⓑ Ⓒ Ⓓ	36. Ⓐ Ⓑ Ⓒ Ⓓ	45. Ⓐ Ⓑ Ⓒ Ⓓ

Practice Test 8: ISEE (Upper Level)

SECTION 1: VERBAL REASONING

20 MINUTES

Directions: Each question is made up of a word in CAPITAL letters followed by four choices. Choose the one word that is most nearly the same in meaning as the word in CAPITAL letters, and mark its letter on your answer sheet.

1. FEINT
   (A) fool
   (B) proclaim
   (C) penalize
   (D) scavenge

2. PEER
   (A) officer
   (B) beginner
   (C) equal
   (D) patient

3. TRITE
   (A) unskilled
   (B) common
   (C) unlikely
   (D) ignorant

4. AMIABLE
   (A) forgetful
   (B) friendly
   (C) strange
   (D) great

5. GRIMACE
   (A) sneer
   (B) grindstone
   (C) journal
   (D) treasure

6. COMPELLED
   (A) calculated
   (B) combined
   (C) collected
   (D) forced

7. ALLY
   (A) opponent
   (B) passage
   (C) friend
   (D) preference

8. SOLICIT
   (A) consent
   (B) comfort
   (C) request
   (D) help

9. REFUTE
   (A) demolish
   (B) postpone
   (C) disprove
   (D) assist

10. EXPLICIT
    (A) ambiguous
    (B) clearly stated
    (C) give information about
    (D) to blow out

11. RETAIN
    (A) pay out
    (B) play
    (C) keep
    (D) inquire

12. CORRESPONDENCE
    (A) letters
    (B) files
    (C) testimony
    (D) response

13. LEGITIMATE
    (A) democratic
    (B) legal
    (C) genealogical
    (D) underworld

14. DEDUCT
    (A) conceal
    (B) understand
    (C) subtract
    (D) terminate

15. EGRESS
    (A) extreme
    (B) extra supply
    (C) exit
    (D) high price

16. HORIZONTAL
    (A) marginal
    (B) in a circle
    (C) left and right
    (D) up and down

17. CONTROVERSY
    (A) publicity
    (B) debate
    (C) revolution
    (D) revocation

18. PREEMPT
    (A) steal
    (B) empty
    (C) preview
    (D) appropriate

19. PER CAPITA
    (A) for an entire population
    (B) by income
    (C) for each person
    (D) for every adult

20. OPTIONAL
    (A) not required
    (B) infrequent
    (C) choosy
    (D) for sale

Directions: Each of the following questions is made up of a sentence containing one or two blanks. The sentences with one blank indicate that one word is missing. Sentences with two blanks have two missing words. Each sentence is followed by four choices. Choose the one word or pair of words that will best complete the meaning of the sentence as a whole, and mark the letter of your choice on your answer sheet.

21. Custom has so _____ our language that we can _____ only what has been said before.

    (A) improved .. repeat

    (B) changed .. understand

    (C) enslaved .. say

    (D) dominated .. hear

22. A few of the critics _____ the play, but in general they either disregarded or ridiculed it.

    (A) discredited

    (B) criticized

    (C) denounced

    (D) appreciated

23. Politicians are not the only ones who have made _____; being human, we have all blundered at some time in our lives.

    (A) explanations

    (B) arguments

    (C) errors

    (D) excuses

24. Because of his _____ nature, he often acts purely on impulse.

    (A) stoic

    (B) reflective

    (C) passionate

    (D) wistful

25. A system of education should be _____ by the _____ of students it turns out, for quality is preferred to quantity.

    (A) controlled .. intelligence

    (B) justified .. number

    (C) examined .. wealth

    (D) judged .. caliber

26. We seldom feel _____ when we are allowed to speak freely, but any _____ of our free speech brings anger.

    (A) angry .. defense

    (B) blessed .. restriction

    (C) scholarly .. understanding

    (D) enslaved .. misuse

27. The worst team lost because it had many players who though not completely _____ were also not really _____.

    (A) qualified .. agile

    (B) clumsy .. incompetent

    (C) inept .. proficient

    (D) ungraceful .. amateurish

28. Although the _____ of the legislature become law, the exact _____ of the law is the result of judicial interpretation.

    (A) ideas .. enforcement

    (B) bills .. wording

    (C) works .. punishment

    (D) words .. meaning

29. Since movies have become more _____, many people believe television to be _____.

    (A) helpful .. utilitarian

    (B) expensive .. necessary

    (C) common .. inadequate

    (D) costly .. useless

30. Spores are a form of life that remain _____ until environmental conditions exist in which they can become _____.

    (A) inactive .. vibrant

    (B) hidden .. dangerous

    (C) suppressed .. visible

    (D) controlled .. rampant

31. The spirit of science is always trying to lead people to the study of _____ and away from the spinning of fanciful theories out of their own minds.
   (A) tradition
   (B) order
   (C) legalities
   (D) literature

32. The _____ child thought old people should be polite to him!
   (A) submissive
   (B) impertinent
   (C) alternate
   (D) classless

33. The fame of the author does not _____ the quality of his or her works. We must avoid equating success with infallibility.
   (A) prejudice
   (B) assure
   (C) dignify
   (D) extol

34. The mechanisms that develop hatred in man are most potent, since there is more _____ than _____ in the world.
   (A) tolerance .. prejudice
   (B) joy .. rapture
   (C) love .. hatred
   (D) strife .. tranquility

35. Mining is often called the _____ industry, since it neither creates nor replenishes what it takes.
   (A) robber
   (B) ecology
   (C) natural
   (D) evil

36. The racial problem is of such _____ that it makes going to the moon seem _____.
   (A) complexity .. helpful
   (B) certainty .. problematic
   (C) magnitude .. child's play
   (D) docility .. effortless

37. To be _____ a theatrical setting must resemble _____.
   (A) believable .. home
   (B) effective .. reality
   (C) reasonable .. beauty
   (D) respectable .. ideas

38. The _____ mob roamed through the streets of the city, shouting their _____ of law and order.
   (A) influential .. fear
   (B) indifferent .. horror
   (C) disciplined .. disrespect
   (D) hysterical .. hatred

39. Errors in existing theories are discovered, and the theories are either _____ or _____.
   (A) improved .. obeyed
   (B) removed .. followed
   (C) altered .. discarded
   (D) explained .. excused

40. In observing the _____ society of the ant, the scientist can learn much about the more _____ society of man.
   (A) hostile .. evil
   (B) elementary .. complicated
   (C) plain .. homogeneous
   (D) unadorned .. unsophisticated

STOP   END OF SECTION 1. IF YOU HAVE ANY TIME LEFT, GO OVER YOUR WORK IN THIS SECTION ONLY. DO NOT WORK IN ANY OTHER SECTION OF THE TEST.

SECTION 2: QUANTITATIVE REASONING

35 MINUTES

You may assume that all figures accompanying Quantitative Reasoning questions have been drawn as accurately as possible EXCEPT when it is specifically stated that a particular figure is not drawn to scale. Letters such as *x*, *y*, and *n* stand for real numbers. The Quantitative Reasoning Test includes two types of questions. There are separate directions for each type of question.

Directions: For questions 1–17 work each problem in your head or in the margins of the test booklet. Mark the letter of your answer choice on the answer sheet.

1. Which pair of values for *x* and □ will make the following statement true?

   $2x$ □ 8

   (A) $(6, <)$
   (B) $(4, >)$
   (C) $(0, <)$
   (D) $(-3, >)$

2. Complete the following statement:

   $7(3 \times \underline{\quad}) + 4 = 2104$

   (A) 10
   (B) $10 + 2$
   (C) 10^2
   (D) 10^3

3. 0.5% is equal to

   (A) 0.005
   (B) 0.05
   (C) $\dfrac{1}{2}$
   (D) 0.5

4. A scalene triangle has

   (A) two equal sides.
   (B) two equal sides and one right angle.
   (C) no equal sides.
   (D) three equal sides.

5. A millimeter is what part of a meter?

   (A) $\dfrac{1}{10}$
   (B) $\dfrac{1}{100}$
   (C) $\dfrac{1}{1,000}$
   (D) $\dfrac{1}{10,000}$

6. What is the least common denominator for $\dfrac{2}{3}, \dfrac{1}{2}, \dfrac{5}{6}$, and $\dfrac{7}{9}$?

   (A) 36
   (B) 32
   (C) 24
   (D) 18

7. Find the area of a triangle whose dimensions are: $b = 14$ inches, $h = 20$ inches.

   (A) 140 square inches
   (B) 208 square inches
   (C) 280 square inches
   (D) 288 square inches

8. What is the difference between $(4 \times 10^3) + 6$ and $(2 \times 10^3) + (3 \times 10) + 8$?

   (A) 168
   (B) $1,968$
   (C) $3,765$
   (D) $55,968$

9. The set of common factors for 30 and 24 is

(A) {1, 2, 3, 6}

(B) {1, 2, 3, 4, 6}

(C) {1, 2, 4, 6}

(D) {1, 2, 4, 6, 12}

10.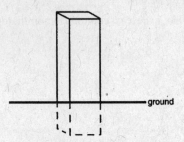

$\overline{AC} \cap \overline{BD}$ is equal to

(A) $\overline{BC}$

(B) $\overline{BD}$

(C) $\overline{AC}$

(D) $\overline{AD}$

11. The board shown below is six feet long, four inches wide, and two inches thick. One-third of it will be driven into the ground. How much surface area remains above ground?

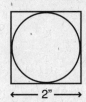

(A) About 4 sq. ft.

(B) Slightly less than 5 sq. ft.

(C) Slightly more than 5 sq. ft.

(D) About 8 sq. ft.

12. One runner can run M miles in H hours. Another faster runner can run N miles in L hours. The difference in their rates can be expressed as

(A) $\dfrac{M - N}{H}$

(B) $MH - HL$

(C) $\dfrac{HN}{M - L}$

(D) $\dfrac{N}{L} - \dfrac{M}{H}$

13. If Mary is x years old now and her sister is 3 years younger, then 5 years from now her sister will be what age?

(A) $x + 5$ years

(B) $x + 3$ years

(C) $x + 2$ years

(D) 8 years

14. In the figure below, the largest possible circle is cut out of a square piece of tin. The area of the remaining piece of tin is approximately (in square inches)

(A) 0.14

(B) 0.75

(C) 0.86

(D) 3.14

15. A square has an area of 49 sq. in. The number of inches in its perimeter is

(A) 7

(B) 14

(C) 28

(D) 98

16. If an engine pumps G gallons of water per minute, then the number of gallons pumped in half an hour may be found by

    (A) taking one half of G.

    (B) dividing 60 by G.

    (C) multiplying G by 30.

    (D) dividing 30 by G.

17. Two cars start from the same point at the same time. One drives north at 20 miles per hour and the other drives south on the same straight road at 36 miles per hour. How many miles apart are they after 30 minutes?

    (A) Less than 10

    (B) Between 10 and 20

    (C) Between 20 and 30

    (D) Between 30 and 40

Directions: For questions 18–35, two quantities are given—one in Column A and the other in Column B. In some questions, additional information concerning the quantities to be compared is centered above the entries in the two columns. Compare the quantities in the two columns, and mark your answer sheet as follows:

(A) if the quantity in Column A is greater

(B) if the quantity in Column B is greater

(C) if the quantities are equal

(D) if the relationship cannot be determined from the information given

Column A	Column B

18.

$$s = 1$$
$$t = 3$$
$$a = -2$$

$[5a(4t)]^3$	$[4a(5s)]^2$

19. $4 > x > -3$

$\dfrac{x}{3}$	$\dfrac{3}{x}$

Column A	Column B

20.

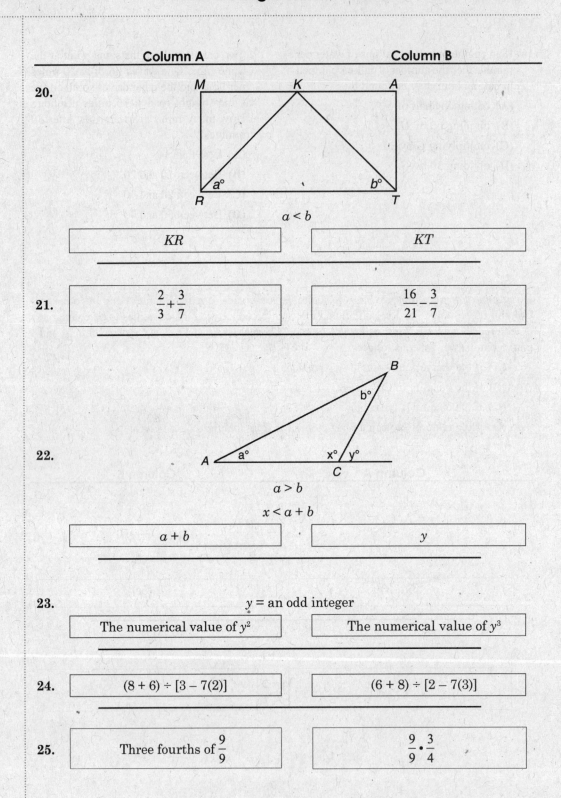

$a < b$

KR	KT

21.

$\dfrac{2}{3} + \dfrac{3}{7}$	$\dfrac{16}{21} - \dfrac{3}{7}$

22.

$a > b$

$x < a + b$

$a + b$	y

23. y = an odd integer

The numerical value of y^2	The numerical value of y^3

24.

$(8 + 6) \div [3 - 7(2)]$	$(6 + 8) \div [2 - 7(3)]$

25.

Three fourths of $\dfrac{9}{9}$	$\dfrac{9}{9} \cdot \dfrac{3}{4}$

Column A	Column B

26.

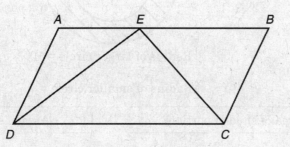

$$NC = NY$$
$$\angle N > \angle C$$

NC	CY

27.

$\dfrac{1}{\sqrt{9}}$	$\dfrac{1}{3}$

28.

$5\left(\dfrac{2}{3}\right)$	$\left(\dfrac{5}{3}\right)2$

29.

Parallelogram $ABCD$

E is a point on AB

Area of $\triangle\ DEC$	Area of $\triangle\ AED +$ Area $\triangle\ EBC$

30. $x = -1$

$x^3 + x^2 - x + 1$	$x^3 - x^2 + x - 1$

Column A	Column B

31. | The edge of a cube whose volume is 27 | The edge of a cube whose total surface area is 54 |

32. | $\dfrac{\frac{1}{2}+\frac{1}{3}}{\frac{2}{3}}$ | $\dfrac{\frac{2}{3}}{\frac{1}{2}+\frac{1}{3}}$ |

33. | Area of a circle whose radius is x^3 | Area of a circle whose radius is $3x$ |

34.

Radius of larger circle = 10

Radius of smaller circle = 7

| Area of shaded portion | Area of smaller circle |

35. $a < 0 < b$

| a^2 | $\dfrac{b}{2}$ |

STOP END OF SECTION 2. IF YOU HAVE ANY TIME LEFT, GO OVER YOUR WORK IN THIS SECTION ONLY. DO NOT WORK IN ANY OTHER SECTION OF THE TEST.

SECTION 3: READING COMPREHENSION

40 MINUTES

Directions: Each reading passage is followed by questions based on its content. Answer the questions on the basis of what is stated or implied in the passage. On your answer sheet, mark the letter of the answer you choose.

Line When we say a snake "glides," we have already persuaded ourselves to shiver a little. If we say that it "slithers," we are as good as undone. To avoid unsettling ourselves, we
5 should state the simple fact—a snake walks.
A snake doesn't have any breastbone. The tips of its ribs are free-moving and amount, so to speak, to its feet. A snake walks along on its rib tips, pushing forward its ventral
10 scutes at each "step," and it speeds up this mode of progress by undulating from side to side and by taking advantage of every rough "toehold" it can find in the terrain. Let's look at it this way: A human or other
15 animal going forward on all fours is using a sort of locomotion that's familiar enough to all of us and isn't at all dismaying. Now: Suppose this walker is enclosed inside some sort of pliable encasement like a sacking.
20 The front "feet" will still step forward, the "hind legs" still hitch along afterward. It will still be a standard enough sort of animal walking, only all we'll see now is a sort of wiggling of the sacking without visible
25 feet. That's the snake way. A snake has its covering outside its feet, as an insect has its skeleton on its outside with no bones in the interior. There's nothing more "horrid" about the one arrangement than about the
30 other.

1. The title below that expresses the main idea of this selection is
   (A) "Snake's Legs."
   (B) "Comparing Snakes to People."
   (C) "The Movement of a Snake."
   (D) "A Slimy Animal."

2. A snake's "feet" are its
   (A) toes.
   (B) ribs.
   (C) side.
   (D) breastbone.

3. The word *terrain* (line 13) means
   (A) terraced.
   (B) rocky ledge.
   (C) vertical hole.
   (D) ground areas.

4. We may conclude that the author
   (A) raises reptiles.
   (B) dislikes snakes.
   (C) is well informed about snakes.
   (D) thinks snakes move better than humans.

Line When a luxury liner or a cargo ship nudges into her slip after an ocean crossing, her first physical contact with land is a heaving line. These streamers with a weight at the end
5 called a "monkey fist" arch gracefully from deck to pier. On board the ship the heaving lines are tied to heavy, golden yellow manila mooring lines. Longshoremen quickly pull in the heaving lines until they can fasten
10 the mooring lines to iron bollards (posts). Soon the ship is strung to her pier by four, eight, or as many as twenty-one nine-inch or ten-inch manila lines with perhaps a few wire ropes to stay motion fore and aft. The
15 ship is secure against even the wrath of the storm or hurricane. A ship could dock without the aid of tugboats—and may have in New York in maritime strikes—but not without the lines to moor her to her berth.

20   The maritime and the related fishing industry find perhaps 250 applications for rope and cordage. There are hundreds of different sizes, constructions, tensile strengths, and weights in rope and twine. Rope is sold 25 by the pound but ordered by length, and is measured by circumference rather than by diameter. The maritime variety is made chiefly from fiber of the abaca, or manila plant, which is imported from the Philip- 30 pines and Central America. Henequen from Mexico and Cuba, and sisal from Africa, the Netherlands East Indies, and other areas, are also used, but chiefly for twine. Nylon is coming into increasing use, particularly 35 by towing companies. But it is six times more expensive than manila. However, nylon is much stronger, lighter in weight, and longer-wearing than manila. It is also more elastic and particularly adaptable for 40 ocean towing.

5. In docking a ship, rope is

    (A) only a little less important than a tugboat.

    (B) essential.

    (C) helpful but not necessary.

    (D) seldom used.

6. A *monkey fist* (line 5) is a

    (A) device for weaving rope.

    (B) slang term for a longshoreman.

    (C) rope streamer.

    (D) weight at the end of a rope.

7. Mooring ropes are

    (A) ten inches in diameter.

    (B) twenty-one inches in circumference.

    (C) six times thicker than heaving ropes.

    (D) nine inches in circumference.

8. Which of the following are NOT correctly paired?

    (A) Sisal from the Philippines

    (B) Henequen from Cuba

    (C) Abaca from Central America

    (D) Sisal from the Netherlands East Indies

Line   In August of 1814, when news came that the British were advancing on Washington, three State Department clerks stuffed all records and valuable papers—including the Articles 5 of Confederation, the Declaration of Independence, and the Constitution—into coarse linen sacks and smuggled them in carts to an unoccupied gristmill on the Virginia side of the Potomac. Later, fearing that a cannon 10 factory nearby might attract a raiding party of the enemy, the clerks procured wagons from neighboring farmers, took the papers 35 miles away to Leesburg, and locked them in an empty house. It was not until 15 the British fleet had left the waters of the Chesapeake that it was considered safe to return the papers to Washington.

     On December 26, 1941, the five pages of the Constitution together with the single 20 leaf of the Declaration of Independence were taken from the Library of Congress, where they had been kept for many years and we restored in the vaults of the United States Bullion Depository at Fort Knox, Kentucky. 25 Here they "rode out the war" safely.

     Since 1952, visitors to Washington may view these historic documents at the Exhibition Hall of the National Archives. Sealed in bronze and glass cases filled with 30 helium, the documents are protected from touch, light, heat, dust, and moisture. At a moment's notice, they can be lowered into a large safe that is bombproof, shockproof, and fireproof.

9. Before the War of 1812, the Constitution and the Declaration of Independence were apparently kept in

    (A) Independence Hall.

    (B) Fort Knox, Kentucky.

    (C) an office of the State Department.

    (D) a gristmill in Virginia.

10. Nowadays, these documents are on view in the

    (A) National Archives Exhibition Hall.

    (B) Library of Congress.

    (C) United States Bullion Depository.

    (D) United States Treasury Building.

11. An important reason for the installation of a device to facilitate the quick removal of the documents is the

(A) possibility of a sudden disaster.

(B) increasing number of tourists.

(C) need for more storage space.

(D) lack of respect for the documents.

12. The documents have been removed from Washington at least twice in order to preserve them from

(A) dust, heat, and moisture.

(B) careless handling.

(C) possible war damage.

(D) sale to foreign governments.

Line On a population map of the world, deserts are shown as great blank spaces, but in fact, these areas contribute many things to our lives.

5   When you go to the market to buy a box of dates, you are buying a bit of sunshine and dry air from the oases of the Sahara Desert or the Coachella Valley. Fresh peas or a lettuce salad for your winter dinner might

10 be the product of an irrigation farmer in the Salt River Valley or the Imperial Valley. That fine broadcloth shirt you received for your birthday was made from silky, long-fibered cotton grown in Egypt. A half-wool,

15 half-cotton sweater might contain Australian wool and Peruvian cotton, which are steppe and desert products.

    These are only a few of the contributions these desert areas make to the quality of

20 our lives. They have also made important cultural contributions.

    Our number system is derived from the system used by the ancient civilizations of Arabia. The use of irrigation to make

25 farming of dry areas possible was developed by the inhabitants of desert regions. The necessity of measuring water levels and noting land boundaries following flooding by the Nile River led to the development of

30 mathematics and the practice of surveying and engineering. The desert people were also our early astronomers. They studied the locations of the stars in order to find their way across the limitless expanse of

35 the desert at night.

13. The population of the world's deserts is

(A) scattered.

(B) starving.

(C) large.

(D) small.

14. The Imperial Valley produces

(A) vegetables.

(B) winter dinners.

(C) shirts.

(D) irrigation.

15. According to this passage, broadcloth is made of

(A) wool.

(B) cotton.

(C) silk.

(D) half wool, half cotton.

16. Culturally, desert civilizations have

(A) made no contributions.

(B) made important contributions.

(C) not influenced western civilizations.

(D) been blank spaces.

17. Surveying was developed because people needed to

(A) study astronomy.

(B) find their way across the deserts.

(C) determine land boundaries after floods.

(D) irrigate their crops.

Line Residents of Montana laughingly refer to
the small, windblown settlement of Ekalaka
in the Eastern badlands as "Skeleton Flats,"
but as curious as it may sound, the name is
5 appropriate.

    So many fossils have been dug up in
this otherwise unremarkable town that it
has become a paradise for paleontologists,
scientists who use fossils to study prehis-
10 toric life forms. In fact, dinosaur bones are
so plentiful in this area that ranchers have
been known to use them as doorstops!

    Ekalaka's fame began to grow more than
50 years ago when Walter H. Peck, whose
15 hobby was geology, found the bones of a
Stegosaurus, a huge, plant-eating dinosaur.
The entire community soon became infected
with Peck's enthusiasm for his find, and
everyone began digging for dinosaur bones.
20 Led by the local science teacher, groups of
people would go out looking for new finds
each weekend, and they rarely returned
empty-handed. It would seem there is no end
to the fossil riches to be found in Ekalaka.

25   Among the most prized finds were the
remains of a Brontosaurus, an 80-foot-long
monster that probably weighed 40 tons. The
skeleton of a Triceratops was also found. The
head of this prehistoric giant alone weighed
30 more than 1,000 pounds. Careful searching
also yielded small fossilized fish, complete
with stony scales, and the remains of a huge
sea reptile.

    The prize find was a *Pachycephalo-*
35 *saurus,* a dinosaur whose peculiar skull was
several inches thick. When descriptions of
it reached scientific circles in the east, there
was great excitement because this particular
prehistoric animal was then completely
40 unknown to scientists.

18. In the first sentence, the author places
"Skeleton Flats" in quotation marks to
show that this phrase is

  (A) a nickname given to the town by
Montana residents, not the actual
name of the town.

  (B) spelled incorrectly.

  (C) being spoken by someone other than
the author.

  (D) a scientific term.

19. This article is primarily about

  (A) paleontology.

  (B) products of the state of Montana.

  (C) fossil finds in Ekalaka.

  (D) the *Pachycephalosaurus.*

20. According to this passage, a paleontologist
is

  (A) someone whose hobby is geology.

  (B) a paradise.

  (C) a plant-eating dinosaur.

  (D) someone who studies fossils.

21. In the third paragraph, the author is describing the

  (A) bones of a Stegosaurus.

  (B) discovery of the first fossil finds in
Ekalaka.

  (C) town of Ekalaka.

  (D) people of Ekalaka.

22. Discovery of the *Pachycephalosaurus*
caused excitement because

  (A) its skull was several inches thick.

  (B) it was the first evidence of this
creature ever found and reported to
scientists.

  (C) news of it reached eastern scientific
circles.

  (D) it received a prize.

Line Powdered zirconium is more fiery and violent than the magnesium powder that went into wartime incendiary bombs. Under some conditions, it can be ignited with a
5 kitchen match, and it cannot be extinguished with water. Munitions makers once tried to incorporate it into explosives, but turned it down as too dangerous for even them to handle.
10 But when this strange metal is transformed into a solid bar or sheet or tube, as lustrous as burnished silver, its temper changes. It is so docile that it can be used by surgeons as a safe covering plate for sensitive
15 brain tissues. It is almost as strong as steel, and it can be exposed to hydrochloric acid or nitric acid without corroding.

Zirconium is also safe and stable when it is bound up with other elements to form
20 mineral compounds which occur in abundant deposits in North and South America, India, and Australia. Although it is classified as a rare metal, it is more abundant in the earth's crust than nickel, copper, tungsten, tin, or
25 lead. Until a few years ago, scarcely a dozen people had ever seen zirconium in pure form, but today it is the wonder metal of a fantastic new industry, a vital component of television, radar, and radio sets, an exciting
30 structural material for chemical equipment and for super rockets and jet engines, and a key metal for atomic piles.

23. The title that best expresses the main idea of this selection is

(A) "A Vital Substance."

(B) "A Safe, Stable Substance."

(C) "Zirconium's Uses in Surgery."

(D) "Characteristics of Zirconium."

24. The word *docile* in line 13 means

(A) calm.

(B) pliable.

(C) strong.

(D) profuse.

25. The selection emphasizes that

(A) zirconium rusts easily.

(B) chemists are finding uses for zirconium.

(C) keys are often made of zirconium nowadays.

(D) zirconium is less abundant in the earth's crust than lead.

26. Zirconium is NOT safe to handle when it is

(A) lustrous.

(B) powdered.

(C) in tubes.

(D) in bar form.

27. The selection tells us that zirconium

(A) is a metal.

(B) is fireproof.

(C) dissolves in water.

(D) is stronger than steel.

28. Zirconium is likely to be useful in all of these fields EXCEPT

(A) surgery.

(B) television.

(C) atomic research.

(D) the manufacture of fireworks.

Line About the year 1812 two steam ferryboats were built under the direction of Robert Fulton for crossing the Hudson River, and one of the same description was built
5 for service on the East River. These boats were what are known as twin boats, each of them having two complete hulls united by a deck or bridge. Because these boats were pointed at both ends and moved equally
10 well with either end foremost, they crossed and recrossed the river without losing any time in turning about. Fulton also contrived, with great ingenuity, floating docks for the reception of the ferryboats and a means by
15 which they were brought to the docks without a shock. These boats were the first of a fleet that has since carried hundreds of millions of passengers to and from New York.

29. The title that best expresses the main idea of this selection is

(A) "Crossing the Hudson River by Boat."

(B) "Transportation of Passengers."

(C) "The Invention of Floating Docks."

(D) "The Beginning of Steam Ferryboat Service."

30. The steam ferryboats were known as twin boats because

(A) they had two complete hulls united by a bridge.

(B) they could move as easily forward as backward.

(C) each ferryboat had two captains.

(D) two boats were put into service at the same time.

31. Which statement is *true* according to the selection?

(A) Boats built under Fulton's direction are still in use.

(B) Fulton planned a reception to celebrate the first ferryboat.

(C) Fulton piloted the first steam ferryboats across the Hudson.

(D) Fulton developed a satisfactory way of docking the ferryboats.

32. Robert Fulton worked in the

(A) seventeenth century.

(B) eighteenth century.

(C) nineteenth century.

(D) twentieth century.

33. In line 16, the word *shock* is used to mean an

(A) unpleasant surprise.

(B) impact.

(C) illness following an accident.

(D) electrical impulse.

Line Between 1780 and 1790, in piecemeal fashion, a trail was established between Catskill on the Hudson and the frontier outpost, Ithaca, in the Finger Lakes country.
5 This path, by grace of following the valleys, managed to thread its way through the mountains by what are on the whole surprisingly easy grades. Ultimately, this route became the Susquehanna Turnpike, but in popular
10 speech it was just the Ithaca Road. It was, along with the Mohawk Turnpike and the Great Western Turnpike, one of the three great east-west highways of the state. Eventually it was the route taken by thousands
15 of Yankee farmers, more especially Connecticut Yankees, seeking new fortunes in southwestern New York. Along it, the tide of pioneer immigration flowed at flood crest for a full generation.
20   As the road left Catskill, there was no stream that might not be either forded or crossed on a crude bridge until the traveler reached the Susquehanna, which was a considerable river and a real obstacle to
25 his progress. The road came down out of the Catskills via the valley of the Ouleout Creek and struck the Susquehanna just above the present village of Unadilla. Hither about the year 1784 came a Connecticut
30 man, Nathaniel Wattles. He provided both a skiff and a large flat-bottomed scow so that the homeseeker, his family, team, and household baggage, and often times a little caravan of livestock, might be set across the
35 river dry-shod and in safety. Wattles here established an inn where one might find lodging and entertainment, and a general store where might be purchased such staples as were essential for the journey. So it was
40 that Wattles' Ferry became the best known landmark on the Ithaca Road.

34. The author indicates that the Susquehanna Turnpike

(A) began as a narrow trail.

(B) was the most important north-south highway in the state.

(C) furnished travelers with surprising obstacles.

(D) went out of use after a generation.

35. The western end of the Susquehanna Turn-
    pike was located at
    (A) the Hudson River.
    (B) the Connecticut border.
    (C) Ithaca.
    (D) Catskill.

36. The Susquehanna Turnpike was also known
    as
    (A) the Ithaca Road.
    (B) Wattles' Ferry.
    (C) the Catskill Trail.
    (D) the Mohawk Turnpike.

37. According to this selection, Nathaniel
    Wattles was prepared to offer travelers all
    of the following EXCEPT
    (A) guides.
    (B) a place to sleep.
    (C) entertainment.
    (D) groceries.

Line As of December, 1983, there were 391
    species listed as endangered. Today over 650
    have been listed including 282 mammals,
    214 birds, 59 reptiles, 49 fish, 26 mollusks,
5 16 amphibians, and 8 insects. We hope to
    provide protection to another 600 species
    by the end of 1988. Although only four
    species of plants have been designated as
    endangered, with the establishment of five
10 botanist positions in 1985, it is expected
    that 200 will be listed by the end of 1987.
      Success should not be measured by the
    number of species listed; the goal is to return
    the species to the point where they are no
15 longer endangered. This Department would
    be just as negligent in the performance of
    its duties under the Act for not delisting a
    species that has recovered as it would be for
    not listing a critical species. We have not had
20 the staffing or funding to review all of the
    species listed at the time of the 1983 Act.

38. It can be inferred that very few plants had
    been listed by 1983 because
    (A) very few are close to extinction.
    (B) the Department doesn't classify
        plants.
    (C) no botanists were on the staff at the
        time.
    (D) some endangered mammals eat
        plants.

39. Which of the following is NOT stated in
    the passage?
    (A) Eight insects have been listed as
        endangered.
    (B) By the end of 1987, many plants will
        be added to the list.
    (C) The Department considers listing
        species more important than
        delisting them.
    (D) The Department lacked staffing to
        review all listed species.

40. "Success should not be measured by the
    number . . ." What is a reasonable inference
    concerning the purpose of this statement?
    (A) To avoid mentioning that
        the computer that kept count
        malfunctioned
    (B) Because measurement is always
        statistically difficult
    (C) Because the concept of success has
        been abused in recent years
    (D) To counteract criticism that the
        Department was not listing enough
        species

STOP END OF SECTION 3. IF YOU HAVE ANY TIME LEFT, GO OVER YOUR WORK IN THIS SECTION ONLY. DO NOT WORK IN ANY OTHER SECTION OF THE TEST.

SECTION 4: MATHEMATICS ACHIEVEMENT

40 MINUTES

Directions: Each question is followed by four answer choices. Choose the correct answer to each question, and mark its letter on your answer sheet.

1. A square measures 8 inches on one side. By how much will the area be increased if its length is increased by 4 inches and its width decreased by 2 inches?
   (A) 14 sq. in.
   (B) 12 sq. in.
   (C) 10 sq. in.
   (D) 8 sq. in.

2. $r = 35 - (3 + 6)(-n)$
   $n = 2$
   $r =$
   (A) 53
   (B) 17
   (C) −17
   (D) −53

3. $(3 + 4)^3 =$
   (A) 21
   (B) 91
   (C) 343
   (D) 490

4. Aluminum bronze consists of copper and aluminum, usually in the ratio of 10:1 by weight. If an object made of this alloy weighs 77 pounds, how many pounds of aluminum does it contain?
   (A) 7
   (B) 7.7
   (C) 10
   (D) 70

5. How many boxes 2 inches × 3 inches × 4 inches can fit into a carton 2 feet × 3 feet × 4 feet?
   (A) 100
   (B) 144
   (C) 1,000
   (D) 1,728

6. A clerk can add 40 columns of figures an hour by using an adding machine and 20 columns of figures an hour without using an adding machine. What is the total number of hours it will take the clerk to add 200 columns of figures if $\frac{3}{5}$ of the work is done by machine and the rest without the machine?
   (A) 6 hours
   (B) 7 hours
   (C) 8 hours
   (D) 9 hours

7. Mr. Lawson makes a weekly salary of $150 plus 7% commission on his sales. What will his income be for a week in which he makes sales totaling $945?
   (A) $196.15
   (B) $206.15
   (C) $216.15
   (D) $226.15

8. Solve for x: $x^2 + 5 = 41$
   (A) ± 6
   (B) ± 7
   (C) ± 8
   (D) ± 9

9. Two rectangular boards each measuring 5 feet by 3 feet are placed together to make one large board. How much shorter will the perimeter be if the two long sides are placed together than if the two short sides are placed together?

(A) 2 feet

(B) 4 feet

(C) 6 feet

(D) 8 feet

10. If a plane travels 1,000 miles in 5 hours 30 minutes, what is its average speed in miles per hour?

(A) $181\frac{9}{11}$

(B) $191\frac{1}{2}$

(C) 200

(D) 215

11. Two years ago a company purchased 500 dozen pencils at 40 cents per dozen. This year only 75 percent as many pencils were purchased as were purchased two years ago, but the price was 20 percent higher than the old price. What was the total cost of pencils purchased by the company this year?

(A) $180

(B) $187.50

(C) $240

(D) $257.40

12. An adult's ski lift ticket costs twice as much as a child's. If a family of three children and two adults can ski for $49, what is the cost of an adult ticket?

(A) $7

(B) $10

(C) $12

(D) $14

13. Solve for $x : \frac{x}{2} + 36 = 37.25$

(A) 2.5

(B) 3.5

(C) 12.5

(D) 18.5

14. A group of 6 people raised $690 for charity. One of the people raised 35% of the total. What was the amount raised by the other 5 people?

(A) $448.50

(B) $241.50

(C) $89.70

(D) $74.75

15. If the scale on a blueprint is $\frac{1}{4}$ inch = 1 foot, give the blueprint dimensions of a room that is actually 29 feet long and 23 feet wide.

(A) $6\frac{3}{4}" \times 6"$

(B) $7\frac{1}{4}" \times 5\frac{1}{2}"$

(C) $7\frac{1}{4}" \times 5\frac{3}{4}"$

(D) $7\frac{1}{2}" \times 5\frac{1}{2}"$

16. Find the area of a rectangle with a length of 176 feet and a width of 79 feet.

(A) 13,904 sq. ft.

(B) 13,854 sq. ft.

(C) 13,804 sq. ft.

(D) 13,304 sq. ft.

17. $63 \div \frac{1}{9} =$

(A) 7

(B) 56

(C) 67

(D) 567

18. With an 18% discount, John was able to save $13.23 on a coat. What was the original price of the coat?

(A) $69.75

(B) $71.50

(C) $73.50

(D) $74.75

19. If it takes three men 56 minutes to fill a trench $4' \times 6' \times 5'$, and two of the men work twice as rapidly as the third, how many minutes will it take the two faster men alone to fill this trench?

    (A) 70 minutes
    (B) 60 minutes
    (C) 50 minutes
    (D) 40 minutes

20. Population figures for a certain area show there are $1\frac{1}{2}$ times as many single men as single women in the area. The total population is 18,000. There are 1,122 married couples, with 756 children. How many single men are there in the area?

    (A) 3,000
    (B) 6,000
    (C) 9,000
    (D) It cannot be determined from the information given.

21. If a vehicle is to complete a 20-mile trip at an average rate of 30 miles per hour, it must complete the trip in

    (A) 20 minutes.
    (B) 30 minutes.
    (C) 40 minutes.
    (D) 50 minutes.

22. Solve for x: $2x^2 + 3 = 21$

    (A) ± 3
    (B) ± 5
    (C) ± 9
    (D) ± 10

23. Find the approximate area of a circle whose diameter is 6".

    (A) 29.26
    (B) 28.26
    (C) 27.96
    (D) 27.26

24. The scale on a map is $\frac{1}{8}" = 25$ miles . If two cities are $3\frac{7}{8}"$ apart on the map, what is the actual distance between them?

    (A) 31 miles
    (B) 56 miles
    (C) 675 miles
    (D) 775 miles

25. A house was valued at $83,000 and insured for 80% of that amount. Find the yearly premium if it is figured at $0.45 per hundred dollars of value.

    (A) $83.80
    (B) $252.63
    (C) $298.80
    (D) $664.00

26. If a certain job can be performed by 18 clerks in 26 days, the number of clerks needed to perform the job in 12 days is

    (A) 24 clerks.
    (B) 30 clerks.
    (C) 39 clerks.
    (D) 52 clerks.

27. $72.61 \div 0.05 =$

    (A) 1.45220
    (B) 14.522
    (C) 145.220
    (D) 1452.20

28. A car dealer sold three different makes of cars. The price of the first make was $4200; the second, $4800; and the third, $5400. The total sales were $360,000. If three times as many of the third make were sold as the first, and twice as many of the second make were sold as the first, how many cars of the third make were sold?

    (A) 15
    (B) 24
    (C) 36
    (D) It cannot be determined by the information given.

29. One third of the number of people attending a football game were admitted at the normal price of admission. How many people paid full price, if the gate receipts were $42,000?

(A) 2,800 people

(B) 3,500 people

(C) 5,000 people

(D) It cannot be determined by the information given.

30. 7 days 3 hours 20 minutes – 4 days 9 hours 31 minutes =

(A) 2 days 17 hours 49 minutes

(B) 2 days 17 hours 69 minutes

(C) 3 days 10 hours 49 minutes

(D) 3 days 10 hours 69 minutes

31. Find the area of a triangle whose dimensions are $b = 12'$, $h = 14'$.

(A) 168 sq. ft.

(B) 84 sq. ft.

(C) 42 sq. ft.

(D) 24 sq. ft.

32. Increased by 150%, the number 72 becomes

(A) 108

(B) 170

(C) 180

(D) 188

33. Which equation represents the statement four times a certain number divided by three, minus six, equals two?

(A) $\dfrac{4n}{3} - 6 = 2$

(B) $4n^2 - 6 = 2$

(C) $4n^2 \div 3 - 6 = 2$

(D) $\left(\dfrac{1}{4}n \div 3\right) - 6 = 2$

34. If $14x - 2y = 32$ and $x + 2y = 13$, then $x =$

(A) 8

(B) 5

(C) 4

(D) 3

35. An ordinary die is thrown. What are the odds that it will come up 1?

(A) $\dfrac{1}{4}$

(B) $\dfrac{1}{6}$

(C) $\dfrac{1}{8}$

(D) $\dfrac{1}{12}$

36. Which is the longest time?

(A) 25 hours

(B) 1,440 minutes

(C) 1 day

(D) 3,600 seconds

37. Two cars are 550 miles apart, both traveling on the same straight road. If one travels at 50 miles per hour, the other at 60 miles per hour, and they both leave at 1 p.m., what time will they meet?

(A) 4 p.m.

(B) 4:30 p.m.

(C) 5:45 p.m.

(D) 6 p.m.

38. Write 493 in expanded form, using exponents.

(A) $(4 \times 10^3) + (9 \times 10^2) + (3 \times 10)$

(B) $(4 \times 10^2) + (9 \times 10) + 3$

(C) $(4 \times 10^2) + (9 \times 10) - 7$

(D) $(4 \times 10^1) + (9 \times 10) + 3$

39. If 10 workers earn $5400 in 12 days, how much will 6 workers earn in 15 days?

(A) $10,500

(B) $5400

(C) $4050

(D) $2025

40. The scale of a particular map is $\frac{3}{8}$ " = 5 miles. If the distance between points A and B is $4\frac{1}{2}$ " on the map, what is the distance in actuality?

    (A) 12 miles
    (B) 36 miles
    (C) 48 miles
    (D) 60 miles

41. Find the approximate diameter of a circle whose area is 78.5 sq. in.

    (A) 25 feet
    (B) 10 feet
    (C) 25 inches
    (D) 10 inches

42. If $ab + 4 = 52$, and $a = 6$, $b =$

    (A) 4
    (B) 8
    (C) 21
    (D) 42

43. If $\frac{2}{3}$ of a jar is filled with water in 1 minute, how many minutes longer will it take to fill the remainder of the jar?

    (A) $\frac{1}{4}$
    (B) $\frac{1}{3}$
    (C) $\frac{1}{2}$
    (D) $\frac{2}{3}$

44. A group left on a trip at 8:50 a.m. and reached its destination at 3:30 p.m. How long, in hours and minutes, did the trip take?

    (A) 3 hours 10 minutes
    (B) 4 hours 40 minutes
    (C) 5 hours 10 minutes
    (D) 6 hours 40 minutes

45. A square is changed into a rectangle by increasing its length 10% and decreasing its width 10%. Its area

    (A) remains the same.
    (B) decreases by 10%.
    (C) increases by 1%.
    (D) decreases by 1%.

STOP   END OF SECTION 4. IF YOU HAVE ANY TIME LEFT, GO OVER YOUR WORK IN THIS SECTION ONLY. DO NOT WORK IN ANY OTHER SECTION OF THE TEST.

SECTION 5: ESSAY

30 MINUTES

Directions: Write a legible, coherent, and correct essay on the following topic.

Topic: If you could spend an afternoon with any author, living or dead, with whom would you spend it? What would you talk about?

_____

_____

_____

_____

_____

_____

_____

_____

_____

_____

_____

_____

_____

_____

_____

_____

_____

_____

_____

_____

_____

_____

_____

_____

practice test

ANSWER KEYS AND EXPLANATIONS

Section 1: Verbal Reasoning

1. A	9. C	17. B	25. D	33. B
2. C	10. B	18. D	26. B	34. D
3. B	11. C	19. C	27. C	35. A
4. B	12. A	20. A	28. D	36. C
5. A	13. B	21. C	29. B	37. B
6. D	14. C	22. D	30. A	38. D
7. C	15. C	23. C	31. B	39. C
8. C	16. C	24. C	32. B	40. B

1. **The correct answer is (A).** To FEINT is *to deceive* or *make a pretense of.* One of the skills our soccer coach taught us was how to elude opponents by feinting in the opposite direction of where we planned to pass the ball.

2. **The correct answer is (C).** A PEER is *someone or something that is of equal standing to another.* In a democratic society, each citizen is the peer of all the other citizens.

3. **The correct answer is (B).** TRITE means *boring from too much use.* Her essay was riddled with trite expressions, such as "a penny saved is a penny earned" and "all good things come to those who wait."

4. **The correct answer is (B).** AMIABLE means *good-natured* and *loveable.* The amiable dog wagged its tail at the letter carrier.

5. **The correct answer is (A).** A GRIMACE is *a facial expression of disgust or displeasure.* The first time the baby ate spinach, she screwed up her mouth in a grimace and spit out the food.

6. **The correct answer is (D).** To COMPEL is *to force.* Our government compels us to pay income taxes each year on April 15.

7. **The correct answer is (C).** An ALLY is *another with a common purpose, an associate,* or *a helper.* The word meaning "passage" is "alley." Great Britain was our ally during World War II.

8. **The correct answer is (C).** To SOLICIT means *to approach with a request or plea.* Our teacher wants us to solicit help from her whenever we don't understand the math concepts she presents to the class.

9. **The correct answer is (C).** To REFUTE is *to show something to be false.* The lawyer refuted the witness's testimony by presenting contradictory evidence.

10. **The correct answer is (B).** EXPLICIT means *distinct, observable,* or *clearly stated.* The explicit instructions on the package left no opportunity for misunderstanding or error.

11. **The correct answer is (C).** To RETAIN is *to hold on to* or *to keep.* Retain the receipt as proof of payment.

12. **The correct answer is (A).** CORRESPONDENCE is *an exchange of letters* or *the letters themselves.* I save all my correspondence with the schools to which I have applied in an envelope marked "High Schools." **Note:** "Correspondence" can also mean "agreement" or "conformity." Your

exam will never offer you a choice of two correct meanings for the same word.

13. **The correct answer is (B).** LEGITIMATE means c*onforming to the law* or *abiding by the rules*. Since his name is on the deed, he has a legitimate claim to ownership of the property.

14. **The correct answer is (C).** To DEDUCT is *to subtract*. The word with a meaning close to "understand" is "deduce." Each week, my employer deducts social security taxes from my paycheck.

15. **The correct answer is (C).** The EGRESS is the *way out*. The egress is marked with a red "EXIT" sign.

16. **The correct answer is (C).** HORI-ZONTAL, parallel to the horizon, means *left-to-right* as opposed to "vertical." Place the large books horizontally on the shelf so that they do not topple over.

17. **The correct answer is (B).** CON-TROVERSY is *exchange of opposing opinions or argument*. The choice of new wallpaper is a subject of controversy.

18. **The correct answer is (D).** To PREEMPT is *to seize before anyone else can or to appropriate*. No dishonesty is implied, just speed or privilege. The president's speech will preempt the time slot usually taken by my favorite game show.

19. **The correct answer is (C).** PER CAPITA literally *means for each head, therefore for each person,* one-by-one, with age irrelevant. The per capita consumption of red meat has dropped to 2 pounds per week.

20. **The correct answer is (A).** That which is OPTIONAL is *left to one's choice* and is therefore *not required*. You must study English and history, but study of a musical instrument is optional.

21. **The correct answer is (C).** The sense of the sentence calls for a word with a negative connotation in the first blank; therefore, we need consider only choices (C) and (D). Of these choices, ENSLAVED . . . SAY, choice (C), is clearly the better completion.

22. **The correct answer is (D).** Since it is stated that most critics disregarded or ridiculed the play, the few critics remaining must have done the opposite, or APPRECIATED the work.

23. **The correct answer is (C).** The word that is needed must be a synonym for blunder (a stupid or gross mistake). That word is ERROR.

24. **The correct answer is (C).** One who acts purely on impulse is most likely to have a PASSIONATE (emotional or intense) nature.

25. **The correct answer is (D).** If "quality is preferred to quantity" in an educational system, then the measure by which that system should be JUDGED is the CALIBER (degree of ability or merit) of the students it produces.

26. **The correct answer is (B).** Freedom of speech is something we take for granted, so we do not feel BLESSED when allowed to exercise this freedom; however, we do become angry when any RESTRICTION (limit) is imposed on our right to speak freely.

27. **The correct answer is (C).** The qualities attributed to the players on the worst team must be opposites for comparison and adjectives for parallelism within the sentence. INEPT, which means awkward, and PROFICIENT, which means skilled, make up the only choice that meets both requirements.

28. **The correct answer is (D).** It is the function of the legislature to write laws (their WORDS become law). It is the function of the judiciary to interpret the words of the law (to determine their MEANING).

29. **The correct answer is (B).** Movies and television are both media of entertainment. The sentence compares the two media in terms of their cost, stating that many people believe television (which is free after the initial investment in the set) is NEC-ESSARY because movies have become so

EXPENSIVE (and therefore out of reach for many people).

30. **The correct answer is (A).** The sense of the sentence calls for two words that are opposites and that can both be applied to life forms. Spores are the tiny particles in certain plants that act as seeds in the production of new plants. These spores remain dormant or INACTIVE until the proper conditions exist to render them vigorous or VIBRANT, thus creating a new generation of plants.

31. **The correct answer is (B).** The completion needed is a word that is opposite in meaning to "the spinning of fanciful theories." Of the choices given, the study of ORDER best fulfills this requirement.

32. **The correct answer is (B).** This sentence describes a rebellious attitude. Impertinence means "insolence."

33. **The correct answer is (B).** The second sentence provides the clue to the meaning of the first. If success does not mean infallibility (certainty), then the fame of an author does not ASSURE the quality of his or her work.

34. **The correct answer is (D).** The completion here demands words that are opposites. In addition, the first blank requires a word that would promote hatred. Only STRIFE, meaning conflict, and TRANQUILITY, meaning peace, fulfill these requirements and complete the meaning of the sentence.

35. **The correct answer is (A).** Since mining takes away without replacing what it takes, it may be called a ROBBER industry. With these characteristics, mining might also be considered to be evil, but ROBBER is the most specific completion. It is the adjective that best describes an industry that does not replenish what it takes.

36. **The correct answer is (C).** This sentence presents two problems that are being compared in terms of the ease of their solution. The only choices that fulfill the requirements of such a comparison are MAGNITUDE and CHILD'S PLAY.

37. **The correct answer is (B).** A theatrical setting serves to create a mood or a feeling of being in another time or place. If the setting is to be EFFECTIVE (to make the desired impression on the audience), it must have some semblance of REALITY.

38. **The correct answer is (D).** The word "mob" has a negative connotation and requires an adjective that is also negative. HYSTERICAL (emotional and unmanageable) best meets this requirement. The emotion that a shouting mob is most likely to show is HATRED of law and order.

39. **The correct answer is (C).** When errors are discovered in existing theories, those theories must either be ALTERED (changed) in the light of the new information or they must be DISCARDED altogether, if the new information renders the old theories false.

40. **The correct answer is (B).** The sentence compares two different societies and therefore requires completions that are both parallel and opposite. ELEMENTARY (simple) and COMPLICATED (intricate) best meet these requirements.

Section 2: Quantitative Reasoning

1. C	8. B	15. C	22. C	29. C
2. C	9. A	16. C	23. D	30. A
3. A	10. A	17. C	24. B	31. C
4. C	11. A	18. B	25. C	32. A
5. C	12. D	19. D	26. B	33. D
6. D	13. C	20. A	27. C	34. A
7. A	14. C	21. A	28. C	35. D

1. **The correct answer is (C).** If $x = 0$, then $2x < 8$ because $2(0) < 8$. None of the other pairs result in a true statement.

2. **The correct answer is (C).** Substitute n for the blank space.

$$7(3 \times n) + 4 = 2104$$
$$7(3n) + 4 = 2104$$
$$21n + 4 = 2104$$
$$21n = 2100$$
$$n = 100, \text{ or } 10^2$$

3. **The correct answer is (A).** Since 1% = 0.01, one half of one percent is written 0.005. Refer to the percentage review section for help if necessary.

4. **The correct answer is (C).** A scalene triangle has no equal sides.

5. **The correct answer is (C).** There are 1,000 millimeters in a meter.

6. **The correct answer is (D).** Choice (A) is also a common denominator, but it is not the least common denominator.

7. **The correct answer is (A).** The area of a triangle is found by using $A = \frac{1}{2}bh$.

$$A = \frac{1}{2} \bullet 14 \bullet 20$$
$$= 140 \text{ sq. in.}$$

8. **The correct answer is (B).** $(4 \times 10^3) + 6 = 4,006$

$(2 \times 10^3) + (3 \times 10) + 8 = 2,038$

The difference is 1,968.

9. **The correct answer is (A).** The set of factors for 24 is:

$\{1, 2, 3, 4, 6, 8, 12, 24\}$

The set of factors for 30 is:

$\{1, 2, 3, 5, 6, 10, 15, 30\}$

The set of common factors is:

$\{1, 2, 3, 6\}$

10. **The correct answer is (A).** The intersection of the two line segments is the place they overlap. Note that they overlap in the interval marked $\overline{BC}$.

11. **The correct answer is (A).** One third of the board will be driven into the ground, leaving 4 feet exposed. The exposed part of the board has 5 faces: two faces 4 feet long by 4 inches wide; two faces 4 feet long by 2 inches wide; and one face (the end) 2 inches by 4 inches. Because the answer choices are in units of square feet, we will calculate in square feet:

$$2 \bullet 4 \bullet \frac{1}{3} = \frac{8}{3} \text{ or } 2\frac{2}{3} \text{ sq. ft.}$$
$$2 \bullet 4 \bullet \frac{1}{6} = \frac{8}{6} \text{ or } 1\frac{1}{3} \text{ sq. ft.}$$
$$1 \bullet \frac{1}{3} \bullet \frac{1}{6} = \frac{1}{18} \text{ sq. ft.}$$

The sum is $4\frac{1}{18}$ sq. ft. of board remaining above ground.

12. **The correct answer is (D).** The rate of the first runner is $\frac{M}{H}$ miles per hour. The rate of the second is $\frac{N}{L}$ miles per hour. The second runner is faster, so the difference in their rates is written $\frac{N}{L} - \frac{M}{H}$.

13. **The correct answer is (C).** Mary's age now $= x$. Her sister's age now $= x - 3$. In five years her sister's age will be $x - 3 + 5 = x + 2$.

14. **The correct answer is (C).** The area of a square $= s^2$.

The area of this square $= 2^2 = 4$

The area of a circle $= \pi \cdot r^2$

$$\left(r = \frac{1}{2}d\right)(\pi = 3.14)$$

The area of this circle =

$\pi \cdot 1^2 = \pi\,1 = \pi$

The difference between the area of this square and the area of this circle is approximately $4 - 3.14 = 0.86$.

15. **The correct answer is (C).** Area of a square $= s^2$.

$49 = 7^2$

one side $= 7$ inches

$P = 4s$

$P = 4 \times 7'' = 28$ inches

16. **The correct answer is (C).** One half hour $= 30$ minutes.

Amount $=$ Rate $(G) \times$ Time (30 minutes)

17. **The correct answer is (C).** One car went 20 mph for $\frac{1}{2}$ hour $= 10$ miles. The other car went 36 mph for $\frac{1}{2}$ hour $= 18$ miles.

Since they went in opposite directions, add the two distances to find the total number of miles apart. $10 + 18 = 28$.

18. **The correct answer is (B).**

$$\left[5a(4t)\right]^3 = \left[-10(12)\right]^3$$
$$= (-120)^3$$
$$= \text{negative answer}$$
$$\left[4a(5s)\right]^2 = \left[-8(5)\right]^2$$
$$= (-40)^2$$
$$= \text{positive answer}$$

A positive product is greater than a negative one.

19. **The correct answer is (D).** Since x could be any non-zero value from 4 to -3, the values of the fractions are impossible to determine.

20. **The correct answer is (A).** $a < b \therefore b > a$ (given).

$\therefore KR > KT$ (in a triangle the greater side lies opposite the greater angle)

21. **The correct answer is (A).**

$$\frac{2}{3} + \frac{3}{7} = \frac{14}{21} + \frac{9}{21} \quad \bigg| \quad \frac{16}{21} - \frac{3}{7} = \frac{16}{21} - \frac{9}{21}$$
$$= \frac{23}{21} \qquad\qquad\qquad = \frac{7}{21}$$

22. **The correct answer is (C).**

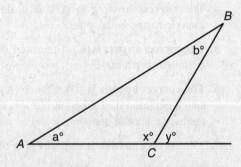

$y = a + b$ (an exterior angle of a triangle is equal to the sum of the two interior remote angles)

23. **The correct answer is (D).** There is not enough information, as y could equal 1, which would make both quantities equal; or y could be greater than 1, which would make y^3 greater than y^2. If y were a negative integer, then y^2 would be greater than y^3.

24. The correct answer is (B).

$$(8+6) \div [3 - 7(2)]$$
$$= (14) \div (-11) = \frac{14}{-11}$$
$$(6+8) \div [2 - 7(3)]$$
$$= (14) \div (-19) = \frac{14}{-19}$$

25. The correct answer is (C).

$$\frac{3}{4} \times \frac{9}{9} = \frac{3}{4} \qquad \frac{9}{9} \times \frac{3}{4} = \frac{3}{4}$$

26. The correct answer is (B).

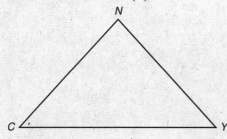

$NC = NY$ (given)

$\angle C = \angle Y$ (angles opposite equal sides are equal)

$\angle N > \angle C$ (given)

$\angle N > \angle Y$ (substitution)

$CY > NC$ (the greater side lies opposite the greater angle)

27. The correct answer is (C).

$$\frac{1}{\sqrt{9}} = \frac{1}{3}$$

28. The correct answer is (C).

$$5\left(\frac{2}{2}\right) = \frac{5}{1} \cdot \frac{2}{3} = \frac{10}{3} \qquad \left(\frac{5}{3}\right)2 = \frac{5}{3} \cdot \frac{2}{1} = \frac{10}{3}$$

29. The correct answer is (C). A triangle inscribed in a parallelogram is equal in area to one half the parallelogram. Therefore, the area of $\triangle DEC$ equals the combined areas of $\triangle ADE$ and $\triangle EBC$.

30. The correct answer is (A).

$$x^3 + x^2 - x + 1$$
$$= (-1)^3 + (-1)^2 - (-1) + 1$$
$$= -1 + 1 + 1 + 1$$
$$= 2$$
$$x^3 - x^2 + x - 1$$
$$= (-1)^3 - (-1)^2 + (-1) - 1$$
$$= -1 - 1 - 1 - 1$$
$$= -4$$
$$\therefore \text{ Column A} > \text{Column B}$$

31. The correct answer is (C).

$$e^3 = 27 \qquad 6e^2 = 54$$
$$e = 3 \qquad e^2 = 9$$
$$e = 3 \qquad e = 3$$
$$\therefore \text{ Column A} = \text{Column B}$$

32. The correct answer is (A).

$$\frac{\frac{1}{2}+\frac{1}{3}}{\frac{2}{3}} = \frac{\frac{3+2}{6}}{\frac{2}{3}} = \frac{\frac{5}{6}}{\frac{2}{3}} = \frac{5}{6} \times \frac{3}{2} = \frac{15}{12} = \frac{5}{4}$$

$$\frac{\frac{2}{3}}{\frac{1}{2}+\frac{1}{3}} = \frac{\frac{2}{3}}{\frac{3+2}{6}} = \frac{\frac{2}{3}}{\frac{5}{6}} = \frac{2}{3} \times \frac{6}{5} = \frac{12}{15} = \frac{4}{5}$$

$$\frac{5}{4} > \frac{4}{5} \therefore \text{ Column A} > \text{Column B}$$

33. The correct answer is (D). We cannot determine the areas of the circles unless the value of x is known.

34. The correct answer is (A).

$$\begin{pmatrix} \text{Area of} \\ \text{shaded} \\ \text{portion} \end{pmatrix} = \begin{pmatrix} \text{Area of} \\ \text{larger} \\ \text{circle} \end{pmatrix} = \begin{pmatrix} \text{Area of} \\ \text{smaller} \\ \text{circle} \end{pmatrix}$$

$$= \pi(10^2) - \pi(7^2)$$

$$= 100\pi - 49\pi$$

$$= 51\pi$$

$$\begin{pmatrix} \text{Area of} \\ \text{smaller} \\ \text{circle} \end{pmatrix} = \pi r^2$$

$$= \pi(7^2)$$

$$= 49\pi$$

$$51\pi > 49\pi$$

$$\therefore \text{ Column A} > \text{Column B}$$

35. The correct answer is (D). A number smaller than 0 is a negative number, so a is a negative number. A negative number squared becomes a positive number. Without knowing absolute values of a and b there is insufficient information to determine the relationship.

Section 3: Reading Comprehension

1. C	9. C	17. C	25. B	33. B
2. B	10. A	18. A	26. B	34. A
3. D	11. A	19. C	27. A	35. C
4. C	12. C	20. D	28. D	36. A
5. B	13. D	21. D	29. D	37. A
6. D	14. A	22. B	30. A	38. C
7. D	15. B	23. D	31. D	39. C
8. A	16. B	24. A	32. C	40. D

1. The correct answer is (C). The selection graphically details the movement of a snake. While much of the description is in terms of legs and feet, the point of the selection is to fully describe the means of locomotion.

2. The correct answer is (B). The second sentence of the second paragraph makes this statement. The remainder of the paragraph expands on the theme.

3. The correct answer is (D). This word appears in line 13. Read carefully and you can figure out the meaning from the context.

Terrain means *earth,* with reference to its topographical features.

4. The correct answer is (C). The detail in this selection indicates that the author knows a good deal about snakes.

5. The correct answer is (B). The last sentence of the first paragraph tells us that rope is absolutely vital for docking.

6. The correct answer is (D). The second sentence serves by way of definition.

7. The correct answer is (D). In lines 12–13, we learn that the ship is secured by nine-inch or ten-inch mooring lines. Since rope is measured by circumference rather than by diameter (lines 26–27), choice (D) is the correct answer.

8. The correct answer is (A). Check back and eliminate. Sisal does not come from the Philippines.

9. The correct answer is (C). Since State Department clerks took charge of getting the Constitution and Declaration of Independence out of Washington before the British burned the city, these important documents must have been housed in the State Department offices.

10. The correct answer is (A). See the first sentence of the last paragraph.

11. The correct answer is (A). The last sentence enumerates the disasters protected against.

12. The correct answer is (C). The documents were removed in 1814 to protect them from the War of 1812; in 1941, they were removed for protection from possible damage in World War II.

13. The correct answer is (D). Great blank spaces on a population map indicate very small population.

14. The correct answer is (A). (See lines 8–11.) You may eat the vegetables at a winter dinner, but the farm produces only the vegetables; it does not cook the dinner.

15. The correct answer is (B). In lines 12–14 we learn that broadcloth is made from silky cotton grown in Egypt.

16. The correct answer is (B). The third paragraph makes the statement that desert civilizations have made important cultural contributions. The last paragraph tells what these contributions are.

17. The correct answer is (C). See lines 26–31.

18. The correct answer is (A). The name of the town is *Ekalaka,* but they call it "Skeleton Flats."

19. The correct answer is (C). The answer to this main-idea question should be clear. The article is about the various fossil finds.

20. The correct answer is (D). In lines 8–10, we are given the definition: ". . . paleontologists, scientists who use fossils to study prehistoric life forms." Walter Peck's hobby was geology, and in the course of pursuing his hobby he made the first find, but he was not a paleontologist.

21. The correct answer is (D). The third paragraph discusses the people of Ekalaka in terms of their enthusiasm for digging and fossil discovery.

22. The correct answer is (B). See the last sentence.

23. The correct answer is (D). The selection describes the properties of zirconium in its various forms.

24. The correct answer is (A). Consider the use of the word *docile* as applied to solid zirconium, in contrast to the use of the word *violent* as applied to powdered zirconium.

25. The correct answer is (B). An emphasis of the selection is that increasing uses are being found for zirconium.

26. The correct answer is (B). The first paragraph makes this point.

27. The correct answer is (A). In both the second and third paragraphs, zirconium is described as a metal.

28. The correct answer is (D). If zirconium is too dangerous to be used in ammunition, it is most certainly too dangerous to be used in fireworks.

29. The correct answer is (D). The selection is about the beginning of Hudson ferryboat service.

30. The correct answer is (A). See lines 5–8.

answers practice test 8

31. The correct answer is (D). The next-to-last sentence discusses Fulton's invention of floating docks for the ferryboats.

32. The correct answer is (C). 1812 was in the nineteenth century.

33. The correct answer is (B). In the context of the paragraph, *shock* must refer to the *impact* of the boat running into the dock.

34. The correct answer is (A). The first paragraph describes the original trail as a path. The road is also described as an east-west route. It presented travelers with surprisingly few obstacles.

35. The correct answer is (C). The frontier outpost, Ithaca, was at the western end of the highway.

36. The correct answer is (A). See line 10.

37. The correct answer is (A). Guides are not mentioned in the selection.

38. The correct answer is (C). We are told that five positions for botanists have been created. The implication is that these are *new* positions.

39. The correct answer is (C). See lines 15-19. The Department says that listing and delisting are equally important.

40. The correct answer is (D). This is a difficult question. You can instantly eliminate choices (A) and (B), but choice (C) appears possible. If you reread the selection carefully a few more times, you will realize that past concepts of success are not really spelled out. Therefore, choice (D) would seem the most likely correct answer. The writer is anticipating a criticism and answering it in advance.

Section 4: Mathematics Achievement

1. D	10. A	19. A	28. C	37. D
2. A	11. A	20. C	29. D	38. B
3. C	12. D	21. C	30. A	39. C
4. A	13. A	22. A	31. B	40. D
5. D	14. A	23. B	32. C	41. D
6. B	15. C	24. D	33. A	42. B
7. C	16. A	25. C	34. D	43. C
8. A	17. D	26. C	35. B	44. D
9. B	18. C	27. D	36. A	45. D

1. The correct answer is (D).

Area = length × width

Area of square = 8 × 8 = 64 sq. in.

Area of rectangle = (8 + 4)(8 − 2)

= 12 × 6 = 72 sq. in.

72 − 64 = 8 sq. in.

2. The correct answer is (A).

$r = 35 - (9)(-n)$

$r = 35 - (9)(-2)$

$r = 35 - (-18)$

$r = 35 + 18 = 53$

To subtract signed numbers, change the sign of the subtrahend and proceed as in algebraic addition.

3. The correct answer is (C). First perform the operation within the parentheses. To cube a number, multiply it by itself, two times.

$(3 + 4)^3 = (7)^3 = 7 \times 7 \times 7 = 343$

4. The correct answer is (A). Copper and aluminum in the ratio of 10:1 means 10 parts copper to 1 part aluminum.

Let x = weight of aluminum

Then $10x$ = weight of copper

$10x + x = 77$

$11x = 77$

$x = 7$

5. The correct answer is (D).

Volume $= L \times W \times H$

Volume of carton $= 2' \times 3' \times 4'$
$= 24$ cubic feet

Volume of one box $= 2" \times 3" \times 4"$
$= 24$ cubic inches

1 cubic foot $= 12" \times 12" \times 12"$
$= 1,728$ cubic inches

$\dfrac{1,728 \times \overset{1}{24}}{\underset{1}{24}} = 1,728$ boxes will fit in the carton

6. The correct answer is (B). $\dfrac{3}{5}$ of 200 =

120 columns by machine @ 40 columns per hour = 3 hours

$200 - 120 = 80$ columns without machine @ 20 columns per hour = 4 hours

3 hours + 4 hours = 7 hours to complete the job

7. The correct answer is (C). His total income is equal to 7% of his sales plus $150; 7% of his sales is $945 \times 0.07 = $66.15.

$66.15 + $150 = $216.15

8. The correct answer is (A).

If $x^2 + 5 = 41$

$x^2 = 41 - 5$

$x^2 = 36$

$x = \pm 6$

9. The correct answer is (B). Perimeter = $2l + 2w$

If the two long sides are together, the perimeter will be:

$5 + 3 + 3 + 5 + 3 + 3 = 22$

If the two short sides are together, the perimeter will be:

$3 + 5 + 5 + 3 + 5 + 5 = 26$.

$26 - 22 = 4$ feet shorter

10. The correct answer is (A). 5 hours

30 minutes $= 5\dfrac{1}{2}$ hours

$1,000$ miles $\div 5\dfrac{1}{2}$ hours =

$1,000 \div \dfrac{11}{2} = 1,000 \times \dfrac{2}{11} = 181\dfrac{9}{11}$ mph

11. The correct answer is (A). 500 dozen @ $0.40 per dozen = purchase of two years ago

75% of 500 dozen = 375 dozen pencils purchased this year

20% of $0.40 = $0.08 increase in cost per dozen

$375 \times $0.48 = $180 spent on pencils this year

12. The correct answer is (D). A child's ticket costs x dollars. Each adult ticket costs twice as much, or $2x$ dollars. $2(2x) = 2$ adult tickets; $3x = 3$ children's tickets. Write a simple equation, and solve for x.

$2(2x) + 3x = $49

$4x + 3x = $49

$7x = $49

$x = $7

$7 is the cost of a child's ticket; $14 is the cost of an adult's ticket.

13. The correct answer is (A).

$$\frac{x}{2} + 36 = 37.25$$
$$\frac{x}{2} = 37.25 - 36$$
$$\frac{x}{2} = 1.25$$
$$x = 2.50$$

14. The correct answer is (A). One person raised 35% of $690.

$690 × 0.35 = $241.50

The remainder raised by the others was
$690 − 241.50 = $448.50

15. The correct answer is (C). For the length, 29 feet would be represented by 29 units of $\frac{1}{4}$", resulting in $\frac{29}{4}$, or $7\frac{1}{4}$ inches. For the width, 23 feet would be represented by 23 units of $\frac{1}{4}$" resulting in $\frac{23}{4}$, or $5\frac{3}{4}$ inches.

16. The correct answer is (A).

Area = length × width
= 176 ft. × 79 ft.
= 13,904 sq. ft.

17. The correct answer is (D).

$$63 ÷ \frac{1}{9} = 63 × \frac{9}{1} = 567$$

This is a good answer to estimate. By dividing a number by $\frac{1}{9}$, you are, in effect, multiplying it by 9. Only one of the suggested answers is close.

18. The correct answer is (C). The problem asks, "What number is $13.23 18% of ?"

$13.23 ÷ 0.18 = $73.50.

19. The correct answer is (A). Each fast worker is equivalent to two slow workers; therefore, the three men are the equivalent of five slow workers. The whole job, then, requires 5 × 56 = 280 minutes for one slow worker. It also requires half that time, or

140 minutes, for one fast worker, and half as much again, or 70 minutes, for two fast workers.

20. The correct answer is (C). Subtract from the total population of 18,000 the 756 children and the 2,244 married people. 18,000 − 756 − 2,244 = 15,000 single men and women. Because there are $1\frac{1}{2}$ times as many men as women, we know that 60% of the 15,000 single people are men, and 40% are women. 60% of 15,000 = 9,000.

21. The correct answer is (C). No calculations are needed here. Note that a 20-mile trip at 60 mph (which is 1 mile per minute), would take 20 minutes. Since the vehicle is traveling half as fast (30 mph), the 20-mile trip should take twice as long, or 40 minutes.

22. The correct answer is (A).

$$2x^2 + 3 = 21$$
$$2x^2 = 21 - 3$$
$$2x^2 = 18$$
$$x^2 = 9$$
$$x = ±3$$

You should have been able to predict that x would be a small number, since, according to the equation, twice its square is smaller than 21.

23. The correct answer is (B). The area of a circle is A = πr^2; the radius equals $\frac{1}{2}$ the diameter. $r = 3$, and $\pi ≈ \frac{22}{7}$, or 3.14.

A = πr^2
A = $\pi(3)^2$
A = 9π
A = 9(3.14) = 28.26 sq. in.

24. The correct answer is (D). The scale is $\frac{1}{8}$" = 25 miles. In $3\frac{7}{8}$" there are thirty-one $\frac{1}{8}$" units. The distance is 31 • 25 = 775 miles.

25. The correct answer is (C). The amount the house was insured for is 80% of $83,000, or $66,400. The insurance is calculated at 45¢ per hundred, or $4.50 per thousand of value. Since there are 66.4 thousands of value, 66.4 × $4.50 per thousand equals the yearly premium of $298.80.

26. The correct answer is (C). The size of the job can be thought of this way: 18 clerks working for 26 days do 18 × 26 or 468 clerk-days of work. To do 468 clerk-days of work in only 12 days would require 468 ÷ 12 = 39 clerks.

27. The correct answer is (D). The digits in the answers are all alike, so you do not need to calculate. Move the decimal point of the divisor two places to the right; do the same for the dividend. Then approximate.

28. The correct answer is (C). Solve this problem as you would any mixture-value problem. The numbers of cars sold are all related to the number of those sold for $4200. Call the number of $4200 cars sold x. Then, the number of $5400 cars sold is $3x$, and the number of $4800 cars is $2x$.

The value of $4200 cars sold is $4200 • x.

The value of $4800 cars sold is $4800 • $2x$.

The value of $5400 cars sold is $5400 • $3x$.

The sum of these values equals the total sales.

($4200 • x) + ($4800 • $2x$) + (5400 • $3x$) = $360,000

$4200x$ + $9600x$ + $16,200x$ = $360,000

$30,000x$ = $360,000

x = $360,000 ÷ $30,000

x =12

Since x = 12 of the $4200 cars, $3x$,or 36, of the $5400 model were sold.

29. The correct answer is (D). There is not enough information to answer this problem. We must know how many attended the game to determine how many paid full price.

30. The correct answer is (A). You must borrow one day's worth of hours and one hour's worth of minutes and rewrite the problem as:

```
  6 days 26 hr. 80 min.
− 4 days  9 hr. 31 min.
  2 days 17 hr. 49 min.
```

31. The correct answer is (B). The formula for the area of a triangle is $A = \frac{1}{2}bh$. Plug in the numbers:

$$A = \frac{1}{2} \bullet 12 \bullet 14$$
$$A = 84 \text{ sq. ft.}$$

32. The correct answer is (C). This is a tricky question. It doesn't ask for 150% of 72, but rather to increase 72 by 150%. Since 150% of 72 = 108, we add 72 and 108 for the correct answer, 180.

33. The correct answer is (A). Choice (B) is read, "Four times the square of a certain number, minus 6, equals 2." Choice (C) is read, "Four times the square of a number, divided by 3, minus 6, equals 2." Choice (D) is read, "One fourth a given number, divided by 3, minus 6, equals 2."

34. The correct answer is (D). Write down both equations and add them together.

```
14x − 2y = 32
+ x + 2y = 13
      5x = 45
       x = 3
```

35. The correct answer is (B). An ordinary die has six sides, each having a different number of dots. The chance of any face coming up is the same: $\frac{1}{6}$.

36. The correct answer is (A). First, pick the two longest times, then compare them. 1,440 minutes and 25 hours are obviously the longest periods. 25 hours contains 1,500 minutes.

37. The correct answer is (D). The cars are traveling toward each other, so the distance between them is being reduced at 60 + 50 or 110 miles per hour. At a rate of 110 mph, 550 miles will be covered in 5 hours. If both cars left at 1 p.m., they should meet at 6 p.m.

38. The correct answer is (B). Choice (A) is 4930; choice (C) is 483; choice (D) is 133.

39. The correct answer is (C). If 10 men earn $5400 in 12 days, each man earns $540 in 12 days, or $45 per day. Therefore, 6 men working for 15 days at $45 per day will earn $4050.

40. The correct answer is (D). The map distance is $4\frac{1}{2}$", or $\frac{9}{2}$" or $\frac{36}{8}$". Each $\frac{3}{8}$" = 5 miles, and we know there are twelve $\frac{3}{8}$" units in $\frac{36}{8}$". Therefore, the twelve $\frac{3}{8}$" units correspond to 60 miles in actuality.

41. The correct answer is (D). The area of a circle is found by $A = \pi r^2$. The radius is half the diameter. To find the diameter when the area is known, divide the area by π to find the square of the radius.

$78.5 \div 3.14 = 25$

Since the square of the radius is 25, we know the radius is 5, and the diameter is twice the radius, or 10 inches.

42. The correct answer is (B). If $a = 6$, $ab + 4 = 52$ becomes $6b + 4 = 52$.

If $6b + 4 = 52$

$$6b = 52 - 4$$
$$6b = 48$$
$$b = 8$$

43. The correct answer is (C). If $\frac{2}{3}$ of the jar is filled in 1 minute, then $\frac{1}{3}$ of the jar is filled in $\frac{1}{2}$ minute. Since the jar is $\frac{2}{3}$ full, $\frac{1}{3}$ remains to be filled. The jar will be full in another $\frac{1}{2}$ minute.

44. The correct answer is (D). First convert to a 24-hour clock.

3:30 p.m. = 15:30 o'clock

Then borrow one hour to make subtraction easier.

$$15:30 = 14:90$$
$$-8:50 = -8:50$$
$$= 6:40 = 6 \text{ hours } 40 \text{ minutes}$$

45. The correct answer is (D). Assign arbitrary values to solve this problem:

A square 10 ft. × 10 ft. = 100 sq. ft.

A rectangle 9 ft. × 11 ft. = 99 sq. ft.

$100 - 99 = 1$; $\frac{1}{100} = 1\%$

Section 5: Essay

Example of a well-written essay.

If I could spend an afternoon with any author, I would have a wonderful conversation with Jules Verne. I think of Jules Verne as the father of science fiction. We would talk about his books and why they make such good reading. I would tell him how much of his fiction has become fact. Then we would probably talk about recent science fiction and about the latest scientific and technological advances. Perhaps we would predict future developments.

The first book I would mention is my favorite, *Twenty Thousand Leagues Under the Sea*. I would ask Mr. Verne how he thought up the book and would tell him how much I admire his works and how I respect his imagination. Then I would tell him about submarines and submarine warfare and would describe all the deep sea explorations that I know about. It is hard to predict a conversation in advance, but *Around the World in Eighty Days* would certainly be a good next topic, and we might well consume the remainder of the afternoon with discussion of modern travel and of all the countries and cultures that can be visited today.

No conversation with Jules Verne could conclude without mention of modern science fiction and of how predictive it might be. I wonder what Jules Verne would think of *Star Trek*. Finally I would tell him about space exploration, moon landings, satellites, and all the exciting space work that is unfolding.

The prospect of a conversation with Jules Verne is very appealing. Even though I know it cannot happen, I am thinking of more and more things I would like to discuss with him. What a stimulating afternoon it would be.

SCORE YOURSELF

Scores on the ISEE are determined by comparing each student's results against all other students in his or her grade level who took that particular test. A scaled score is then calculated. You can use the following calculations to determine how well you did on this practice test, but keep in mind that when you take the actual test, your score might vary.

Test	Raw Score ÷ No. Questions	× 100 =	%
Synonyms	÷ 20	× 100 =	%
Sentence Completions	÷ 20	× 100 =	%
Total Verbal Ability	÷ 40	× 100 =	%
Multiple-Choice Quantitative	÷ 17	× 100 =	%
Quantitative Comparisons	÷ 18	× 100 =	%
Total Quantitative Ability	÷ 35	× 100 =	%
Reading Comprehension	÷ 40	× 100 =	%
Mathematics Achievement	÷ 45	× 100 =	%

High percentage scores should make you feel very good about yourself, but low percentages do not mean that you are a failure.

Remember:

- Scores are not reported as percentages. A low percentage may translate to a respectable scaled score.

- The same test is given to students in grades 8 through 12. Unless you have finished high school, you have not been taught everything on the test. You are not expected to know what you have not been taught.

- You will be compared only to students in your own grade.

Use your scores to plan further study if you have time.